LET'S GO PUBLICATIONS

TRAVEL GUIDES

Alaska & the Pacific Northwest 2003
Australia 2003
Austria & Switzerland 2003
Britain & Ireland 2003
California 2003
Central America 8th edition
Chile 1st edition **NEW TITLE**
China 4th edition
Costa Rica 1st edition **NEW TITLE**
Eastern Europe 2003
Egypt 2nd edition
Europe 2003
France 2003
Germany 2003
Greece 2003
Hawaii 2003 **NEW TITLE**
India & Nepal 7th edition
Ireland 2003
Israel 4th edition
Italy 2003
Mexico 19th edition
Middle East 4th edition
New Zealand 6th edition
Peru, Ecuador & Bolivia 3rd edition
South Africa 5th edition
Southeast Asia 8th edition
Southwest USA 2003
Spain & Portugal 2003
Thailand 1st edition **NEW TITLE**
Turkey 5th edition
USA 2003
Western Europe 2003

CITY GUIDES

Amsterdam 2003
Barcelona 2003
Boston 2003
London 2003
New York City 2003
Paris 2003
Rome 2003
San Francisco 2003
Washington, D.C. 2003

MAP GUIDES

Amsterdam
Berlin
Boston
Chicago
Dublin
Florence
Hong Kong
London
Los Angeles
Madrid
New Orleans
New York City
Paris
Prague
Rome
San Francisco
Seattle
Sydney
Venice
Washington, D.C.

LET'S GO

THAILAND

LAUREN EVE BONNER EDITOR
EMMA NOTHMANN EDITOR
KATE GREER ASSOCIATE EDITOR
NINA JACOBI ASSOCIATE EDITOR
JAY PENDSE ASSOCIATE EDITOR

RESEARCHER-WRITERS
ANTHONY BARKER
NICK GROSSMAN
TOMOHIRO HAMAKAWA
BASIL LEE

YAW D.K. OSSEO-ASARE MAP
AMÉLIE CHERLIN MANAG
CHRIS CLAYTON
ᴇW YORK

ST. MARTIN'S

HELPING LET'S GO If you want to share your discoveries, suggestions, or corrections, please drop us a line. We read every piece of correspondence, whether a postcard, a 10-page email, or a coconut. Please note that mail received after May 2003 may be too late for the 2004 book, but will be kept for future editions. **Address mail to:**

> **Let's Go: Thailand**
> **67 Mount Auburn Street**
> **Cambridge, MA 02138**
> **USA**

Visit Let's Go at **http://www.letsgo.com,** or send email to:

> **feedback@letsgo.com**
> **Subject: "Let's Go: Thailand"**

In addition to the invaluable travel advice our readers share with us, many are kind enough to offer their services as researchers or editors. Unfortunately, our charter enables us to employ only currently enrolled Harvard students.

Maps by David Lindroth copyright © 2003 by St. Martin's Press.

Distributed outside the USA and Canada by Macmillan.

ISBN: 0-312-30596-6

First edition
10 9 8 7 6 5 4 3 2 1

Let's Go: Thailand is written by Let's Go Publications, 67 Mount Auburn Street, Cambridge, MA 02138, USA.

WHO WE ARE

A NEW LET'S GO

With a sleeker look and innovative new content, we have revamped the entire series to reflect more than ever the needs and interests of the independent traveler. Here are just some of the improvements you will notice when traveling with the new *Let's Go*.

MORE PRICE OPTIONS

Still the best resource for budget travelers, *Let's Go* recognizes that everyone needs the occassional indulgence. Our "Big Splurges" indicate establishments that are actually worth those extra pennies (pulas, pesos, or pounds), and price-level symbols (❶ ❷ ❸ ❹ ❺) allow you to quickly determine whether an accommodation or restaurant will break the bank. We may have diversified, but we'll never lose our budget focus—"Hidden Deals" reveal the best-kept travel secrets.

BEYOND THE TOURIST EXPERIENCE

Our Alternatives to Tourism chapter offers ideas on immersing yourself in a new community through study, work, or volunteering.

AN INSIDER'S PERSPECTIVE

As always, every item is written and researched by our on-site writers. This year we have highlighted more viewpoints to help you gain an even more thorough understanding of the places you are visiting.

IN RECENT NEWS. *Let's Go* correspondents around the globe report back on current regional issues that may affect you as a traveler.

CONTRIBUTING WRITERS. Respected scholars and former *Let's Go* writers discuss topics on society and culture, going into greater depth than the usual guidebook summary.

THE LOCAL STORY. From the Parisian monk toting a cell phone to the Russian *babushka* confronting capitalism, *Let's Go* shares its revealing conversations with local personalities—a unique glimpse of what matters to real people.

FROM THE ROAD. Always helpful and sometimes downright hilarious, our researchers share useful insights on the typical (and atypical) travel experience.

SLIMMER SIZE

Don't be fooled by our new, smaller size. *Let's Go* is still packed with invaluable travel advice, but now it's easier to carry with a more compact design.

FORTY-THREE YEARS OF WISDOM

For over four decades *Let's Go* has provided the most up-to-date information on the hippest cafes, the most pristine beaches, and the best routes from border to border. It all started in 1960 when a few well-traveled students at Harvard University handed out a 20-page mimeographed pamphlet of their tips on budget travel to passengers on student charter flights to Europe. From humble beginnings, *Let's Go* has grown to cover six continents and *Let's Go: Europe* still reigns as the world's best-selling travel guide. This year we've beefed up our coverage of Latin America with *Let's Go: Costa Rica* and *Let's Go: Chile;* on the other side of the globe, we've added *Let's Go: Thailand* and *Let's Go: Hawaii.* Our new guides bring the total number of titles to 61, each infused with the spirit of adventure that travelers around the world have come to count on.

CONTENTS

MAPS

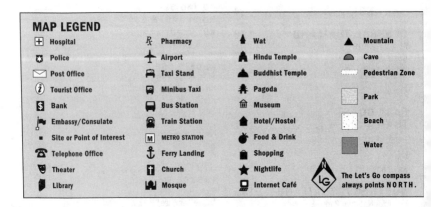

MAP LEGEND

⊞ Hospital	℞ Pharmacy	♠ Wat	▲ Mountain
⊠ Police	✈ Airport	⛩ Hindu Temple	◠ Cave
✉ Post Office	🚕 Taxi Stand	▲ Buddhist Temple	⋯ Pedestrian Zone
ⓘ Tourist Office	🚐 Minibus Taxi	🌲 Pagoda	Park
$ Bank	🚌 Bus Station	🏛 Museum	
⚑ Embassy/Consulate	🚆 Train Station	🏠 Hotel/Hostel	Beach
■ Site or Point of Interest	M METRO STATION	🍎 Food & Drink	
☎ Telephone Office	⚓ Ferry Landing	▮ Shopping	Water
⚑ Theater	🏢 Church	★ Nightlife	The Let's Go compass always points NORTH.
📕 Library	🕌 Mosque	💻 Internet Café	

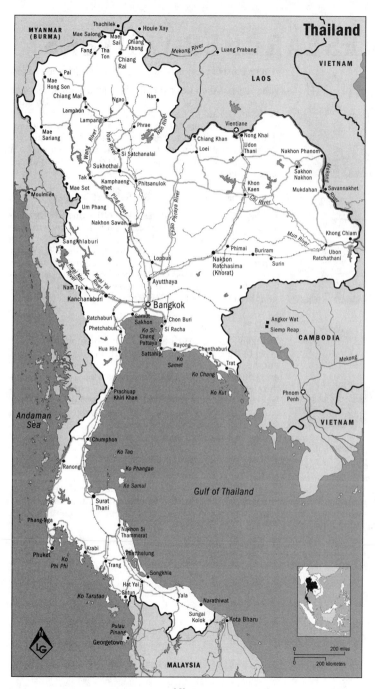

IX

RESEARCHER-WRITERS

Anthony Barker   *Central and Northern*

Volunteering at clinics along the Myanmar border, learning how to prepare Thai food with some of the country's top chefs, and spending his months talking, dancing, and eating with locals, Anthony left no stone unturned in Thailand. His charming humility disguises travel experiences from all over the world and extensive cultural knowledge. One of our most meticulous and devoted RWs, Anthony plans to attend medical school in 2003.

Tomohiro Hamakawa   *Bangkok, East Coast, and Northern*

The heartthrob of the Southeast Asia office and RW Extraordinaire, Tomo left for Southeast Asia and never stopped impressing (or charming) the bookteam. Though his route was long and his travel arduous, his compassion for oppressed peoples and devotion to publicizing forgotten causes were always fervent. He covered Myanmar and Thailand with appropriate graciousness and delight. *Let's Go* submitted his name for TIME Magazine's person of the year.

Basil Lee   *Bangkok, Central, East Coast, and Northeast*

Swinging through Northeast Thailand, Basil wasn't thrown off to find a gray shaft of wiggling terror (a leech) burrowing into his flesh. His rigorous route had him seeing and doing everything from cruising down a stream on a tube to racing through Bangkok faster than a tuk-tuk. Despite his particular predilection for clean bathrooms, he did Thailand the backpacker way with New York style. Basil is currently a student at Harvard School of Design.

Nick Grossman   *Central and Southern*

No one had more fun on his route than Nick Grossman. A master of negotiation and international man of mystery, Nick was always flexible and helpful in every way he could be throughout the writing of this book. He and his travel companion, Andrea, were indispensable resources and researchers for many, many, many months. Nick is now working in Bangkok for the monthly nightlife magazine *The Bangkok Metro*.

CONTRIBUTING WRITERS

Matthew Firestone was a Researcher-Writer for *Let's Go: Britain and Ireland 2002*. While in Thailand, he spent some time living in a Buddhist monastery. He is currently in sub-Saharan Africa researching the dietary practices of hunter-gatherer populations inhabiting the Kalahari.

Derek Glanz was the editor of *Let's Go: Spain & Portugal including Morocco 1998*. He is now a freelance journalist who recently began pursuing postgraduate studies in international relations. He has been published in *The Associated Press* and *The Miami Herald* (via AP), and served as a guest TV analyst on Colombia's *TeleCartagena*.

Ted Osius edited the first editions of *Let's Go: Greece 1983* and *Let's Go: Israel and Egypt 1983*. He edited and contributed to the Europe and Italy Let's Go guides from 1980 to 1984. Since 1989, he has served in the US Department of State as a political and consular officer in Manila, Philippines; a political and administrative officer at the US embassy to the Vatican; and an executive assistant to then-Permanent Representative to the United Nations Madeline Albright. In 1997, he opened the US Consulate General in Ho Chi Minh City, becoming the first American political officer in Saigon in 23 years. From 1998 to 2001, he served as Senior Advisor on International Affairs to Vice President Al Gore. He is now a Regional Environmental Affairs Officer in Southeast Asia, based in Thailand, for the US embassy. Ted is also the author of *The U.S.-Japan Security Alliance: Why It Matters and How To Strengthen It* (CSIS/Praeger, 2002).

Brett Renfrew is currently living and working in Bangkok as a teacher, as well as a corporate writer. He also runs a project to import used computers for use in rural schools all over Thailand.

Graeme Wood was the editor of *Let's Go: Southeast Asia 2001* and a Researcher-Writer for *Let's Go: South Africa 2002* and *Let's Go: Eastern Europe 2003*. He lived in Khlong Toei, the dock district of Bangkok, where he worked for the Human Development Foundation in orphanages and hospices.

ACKNOWLEDGMENTS

LET'S GO

THAILAND THANKS. Thailand for being such a kickass country. DK for being great and making the book pretty. Amelie for everything, Alex for love, Megha for laughs, Anne & Brian for walking softly and carrying a big stick, Matt for funniness, Michelle for sincerity, Adam & Adam, Production for being helpful. Jasmine Sola, Bagel Friday, and, most importantly, The Scooter.

LAUREN. The team, my parents, Gonga, Nana & PopPop, the Winthrop family for 50 Line & kindness, Laura, Fern & Lily for lovin and fun-lovin, Ana for sanity & ideas, Steve for losing monopoly & being cool, Zoolander, the makers of Tangueray, Campo for giving me that donut that one day.

EMMA. My family for everything, Dusty for daily dosages of sanity, Billy for Beijing, the couch for being comfy, Blaz for letting me steal his music, the cool Toscanini's people for giving me free coffee.

KATE. Carrie & Jenny—your names in print! woohoo! (Mum and Dad, you guys too), Eric for lending me your headphones, Blockbuster for that Super US$25 Lord of the Rings deal.

NINA. My incredible bookteam for late nights and letting me steal post-its. Mom & Dad for love. Anna for phone calls. Brenda for excellent typing & coffee breaks. Blockmates for LA & being awesome. Noah for dinner haikus. Two pods down for musical inspiration.

JAY. The team; Oz; my roommates; Anna for *Postkarden*; a ▨ Crew that isn't; my family.

DK. SEAS pod for being so fun and so on-point, Tomo for being the man, M + P for loving the world; and, of course, the requisite shout-out to all of P-ville.

Editors
Lauren Eve Bonner, Emma Nothmann
Associate Editors
Kate Greer, Nina Jacobi, Jay Pendse
Managing Editor
Amélie Cherlin
Map Editor
Yaw D.K. Osseo-Asare

Publishing Director
Matthew Gibson
Editor-in-Chief
Brian R. Walsh
Production Manager
C. Winslow Clayton
Cartography Manager
Julie Stephens
Design Manager
Amy Cain
Editorial Managers
Christopher Blazejewski,
Abigail Burger, D. Cody Dydek,
Harriett Green, Angela Mi Young Hur,
Marla Kaplan, Celeste Ng
Financial Manager
Noah Askin
Marketing & Publicity Managers
Michelle Bowman, Adam M. Grant
New Media Managers
Jesse Tov, Kevin Yip
Online Manager
Amélie Cherlin
Personnel Managers
Alex Leichtman, Owen Robinson
Production Associates
Caleb Epps, David Muehlke
Network Administrators
Steven Aponte, Eduardo Montoya
Design Associate
Juice Fong
Financial Assistant
Suzanne Siu
Office Coordinators
Alex Ewing, Adam Kline,
Efrat Kussell

Director of Advertising Sales
Erik Patton
Senior Advertising Associates
Patrick Donovan, Barbara Eghan,
Fernanda Winthrop
Advertising Artwork Editor
Leif Holtzman
Cover Photo Research
Laura Wyss

President
Bradley J. Olson
General Manager
Robert B. Rombauer
Assistant General Manager
Anne E. Chisholm

HOW TO USE THIS BOOK

Thailand is an aesthetic heaven; from golden Buddhas to turquoise waters, the visual landscape will thrill you. *Let's Go* lists 1000-year-old temples and friendly people who will help you along the way, but the adventure is yours to find. Relish in the uncertainty of life on the road. Slide your finger over the "Sights" section as you cruise from wat to wat. Swat mosquitoes with this book on the beach. Let these pages and your instinct be your guides. Trust no other.

ORGANIZATION OF THIS BOOK

INTRODUCTORY MATERIAL. The first chapter, **Discover Thailand,** provides an overview of travel in the region. The **suggested itineraries** give an idea of the places you shouldn't miss and how long it takes to see them. **Essentials** outlines practical information, like bureaucratic formalities, health and safety concerns, and transport information, that you'll need both before you leave and once you're there. The **Life & Times** section will give you a picture of Thai history, culture, politics, and life.

COVERAGE. Each chapter covers a region, Bangkok to Southern Thailand, alphabetically. Two special sections are **Alternatives to Tourism,** which lists opportunities to study, work, and volunteer in Thailand, and **Sidetrips,** which has coverage of Angkor Wat, Vientiane, and Penang. The **black tabs** in the margins—and knowing that "S" comes after "N"—will help you to navigate the chapters quickly and easily.

APPENDIX. The appendix has useful **conversions** and **phone codes,** a **phrasebook** of handy phrases, and a **climate** chart.

RANKING ESTABLISHMENTS. In each section, we rank establishments, starting with our favorites. Our absolute favorites are so denoted by *Let's Go*'s highest honor, the *Let's Go* thumbs-up (🌑). With each accommodation and food listing, you'll find an icon indicating a price range, as follows:

SYMBOL:	❶	❷	❸	❹	❺
ACCOMM.	Under US$3 Under 120฿	US$3-4.50 120-180฿	US$4.50-9 180-360฿	US$9-14 360-560฿	Over US$14 Over 560฿
FOOD	Under US$0.75 Under 30฿	US$0.75-2 30-80฿	US$2-4 80-160฿	US$4-6 160-240฿	Over US$6 Over 240฿

GRAYBOXES AND IKONBOXES. Grayboxes and **sidebars** provide cultural insights but, once in a while, are simply expressions of our bizarre sense of humor. In any case, they're usually amusing, so enjoy. **Whiteboxes,** on the other hand, provide important practical information, such as warnings (**M**), helpful hints and resources (🔊), and border crossing information (🚌).

OUR QUIRKS. Thailand has more islands (kos) than grains of sands on its beaches. To aid your island hopping, **View from Above** boxes summarize the highlights of major islands.

A NOTE TO OUR READERS The information for this book was gathered by *Let's Go* researchers from May through August of 2002. Each listing is based on one researcher's opinion, formed during his or her visit at a particular time. Those traveling at other times may have different experiences since prices, dates, hours, and conditions are always subject to change. You are urged to check the facts presented in this book beforehand to avoid inconvenience and surprises.

DISCOVER THAILAND

Requiring no advertising, Thailand is a trip through a sensual paradise. Your travel agent will never be able to exaggerate the wonders and beauty of this Southeast Asian country—you will inevitably be astounded. Among the easiest travel destinations in Asia, Thailand is filled with aesthetic charms from the heaven-on-earth beaches to the glittering golden *chedis* to the prowling tigers in dense tropical jungles. Explore the ancient cities of Central Thailand, where the ruins of once-great kingdoms now lie in silent majesty, testament to a glorious past. Dive into the world's bluest waters and search for a different kind of wildlife than the backpackers you encounter on shore. Meditate amid saffron-cloaked Buddhist monks in temples adorned with mother-of-pearl inlay and frescoes older than the Magna Carta. Throughout Thailand, mouth-watering cuisine will be your sustenance, delightfully warm people will be your companions, and a smile will be your currency. After all, they don't call it "Amazing Thailand" for nothing.

FACTS AND FIGURES

Official Name: Kingdom of Thailand.

Government: Constitutional monarchy.

Capital: Bangkok.

Land Area: 513,000 sq. km.

Geography: Borders Malaysia, Myanmar, Laos, and Cambodia. Chao Praya River flows through the fertile central plain. Northern Thailand and the Burmese border to the west are mountainous.

Climate: Dry (high season) Nov.-Mar., rainy (low season) Apr.-Oct.

Major Cities: Chiang Mai, Khon Khaen, Nakhon Ratchasima, Ubon Ratchathani.

Population: 60,700,000.

Language: Thai.

Religions: Theravada Buddhism (95%); Muslim, Christian, Hindu (5%).

Average Income Per Capita: US$2000.

WHEN TO GO

Thailand has rainy and dry seasons, which roughly correspond to low and high tourism seasons. During the low season, sights are less crowded, fewer services are offered, and prices are reduced. Some beaches and islands close down and fewer trekking opportunities are available.

The rainy (low) season spans May to September in the north and runs later in the year the farther south you travel. The dry (high) season is roughly the other 6-7 months of the year. Closer to the equator, the hotter the weather, the less the variation among seasons. Thailand is hot and humid; temperatures fluctuate around 27°C (80°F) year-round everywhere except the extreme uplands of the mainland, where night-time temperatures can drop dramatically (see **Average Temperatures,** p. 415). For a rough conversion from °C to °F, multiply by two and add 30. (For a temperature chart, see **Temperature Conversions,** p. 415.)

DISCOVER

WHAT TO DO

Thailand has enough wats, beaches, jungles, museums, and markets to keep you fascinated or, better yet, peaceful, for the rest of your earthly days. But peaceful-ness can be overrated, especially when there are sharks to swim with, handicrafts to shop for, religions to learn about, cultures to understand, species to save, and nirvanas to reach. The editors of *Let's Go Thailand 2003* challenge you to do it all. Because in Thailand, you can.

BACKPACKER BONANZA

If you're looking for a backpacker scene, Thailand is the undisputed mecca. With the proliferation of charming guest house communities and the Southeast Asian gateway city of Bangkok, it's no surprise that tourists under thirty are everywhere. You may run into your best friend from primary school buying spring rolls on **Khao San Road** (p. 104), and you'll definitely meet people who have crazy stories about near-death experiences with dysentery or malaria, a wild tiger, Burmese border guards, and the token hyped-up narcotic of the week. Most of these stories are true. **Kanchanaburi** (p. 134) is the best place for these story-telling sessions. **Ko Samet** (p. 166), on the east coast, is the spot for low-key chilling, swimming, and snorkeling. **Chiang Mai** (p. 238), the largest city in Northern Thailand, has cultural and commercial attractions that also suit the *farang* crowd. The scene in the southern kos is even more relaxed and can be an ideal break from green curry three times a day. **Ko Samui** (p. 341) was discov-ered in the 1970s and has been a backpacker haven since. And what backpacker trip would be complete without a **Full Moon party** (see **Appendix** for **lunar calen-dar,** p. 415) on **Ko Phangan** (p. 335)? Enjoy the spirit of the culture and bond over banana pancakes, but make sure you leave time to get stories of your own.

GLEAMING TEMPLES

Chiang Mai has over 300 wats, including its most famous, **Wat Phra That Doi Suthep** (p. 250), whose golden *chedi* glows for miles. Bangkok is no light-weight when it comes to wats, however, boasting **Wat Phra Kaew** (Temple of the Emerald Buddha, p. 113), which is perhaps Bangkok's best. **Ayutthaya**'s (p. 132) collection of wats are among the oldest, but most were ruined when the Burmese sacked it in 1767. Brightly colored **Wat Thawet** (p. 307) in Sukhothai has a maze of Buddhist sculptures. Also in Sukhothai, **Wat Mahathat** (p. 308) has a lotus-shaped *chedi*, characteristic of the era when Sukhothai was the capital of the Thai empire. In Khorat, **Wat Sala Loi**'s (p. 194) inner sanctuary is shaped like a Chinese ship, symbolizing the passage of the devoted students to nirvana. **Wat Khaek** (p. 219) in Nong Khai was designed according to Bud-dhist cosmology by a Lao monk. Among the millions of guest houses and drunken *farang* in Southern Thailand is **Wat Borom That Chaiya** (p. 352) in Chaiya. Besides being an anomaly in terms of location, it is also rare as a Mahayana Buddhist wat, not a Theravada one, like most in the country. **Wat Suwannakuha** (p. 355) is composed of several attached caves near Phang-Nga. Nearby, **Wat Tham Sua** has Buddha's footprints, a Tiger Cave, and a working monastery with monks and nuns.

SNORKELER'S DELIGHT

And scuba diver's too! As the largest diving-training center in Southeast Asia, **Ko Tao,** with over 20 dive spots, is the first stop on a scuba tour (with over 20 dive spots). Leopard sharks and rock "swim-throughs" are just the beginning. Snorkelers will love the island's **Ao Leuk** and **Ao Thian Bay** (p. 333) or the off-beach snorkeling in **Ao Ta-Note.** A daytrip from Ko Tao to **Ko Nang Yuan** (p. 335) also has great snorkeling. Gurus hail **Hat Karon** and **Hat Kata** beaches on **Phuket** (p. 361) as homes to some of the world's best marine life, particularly around the Similan and Racha islands. Near Trang, **Ko Tarutao National Marine Park** (p. 382) is an archipelago of 51 islands that is nothing short of an aquatic enthusiast's visual paradise. Off **Ko Samui,** the **Ang Thong Marine National Park** (p. 348) is made up of 40 limestone islands which offer phenomenal snorkeling and diving, particularly at **Ko Sam Sao (Tripod Island)** and **Hat Chan Charat (Moonlight Beach).** The **Outer Islands of Ko Chang** on the East Coast, **Ko Rang** and **Ko Wai** (p. 182), are almost completely coral, spotted with scary sharks.

TASTE THAILAND

Forget main courses, the fruit in Thailand is among the strangest and most delicious in the world. Though the indigenous durian has been banned in public places for its pungent, onion-like smell, the pineapples are fantastic, especially at the day market in **Nan** (p. 290). The fruit in **Chanthaburi** (p. 171) is amazing, but *Let's Go* does not recommend taking seeds home with you—customs will surely nail you, even if you are doing your native nation a favor. For a real meal, **Si Racha** (p. 161) in East Coast Thailand is a culinary heaven. **Sukhothai** (p. 304) markets have yummy *nam rik noom,* a chili paste dip. Fried scorpions and ants are protein-packed snacks; buy them from vendors in **Bangkok** (p. 109). **Udon Thani** (p. 228) has Isaan specialties, as well as spectacular ice cream and seafood, but the real treasures— live eels and turtles—are found at the market. Try some flaming morning glory vine in **Loei** (p. 224). Way down south on the Malaysian border, **Sungai Kolok** (p. 383) stirs up the local specialty of *kang tai pla*—spicy curry with fermented fish kidney. Southern Thailand has sweet delicacies too, like crepes with shredded coconut in **Hat Yai** (p. 377). **Phuket** (p. 355) is famous for Chinese crepes and *kanohm jin Phuket* (breakfast noodles in spicy curry). It's never too early for curry in Thailand.

MEDICATE, EDUCATE, OR MEDITATE

There are countless opportunities to medicate and educate yourself and others, not to mention the welcoming monasteries with teachers who will guide you to spiritual healing. The **Population and Community Development Association (PDA)** in **Chiang Rai** (p. 272) is a major organization that accepts volunteers who are willing to help with rural development and AIDS education/outreach. PDA is one of many, many organizations in need of volunteers. Opportunities abound for travelers interested in teaching English or almost any special skill. For more specific information about volunteering at community development organizations, NGOs, clinics, animal refuges and preserves, see **Alternatives to Tourism** (p. 84). **Lampang Medical Plants Conservation Center** (p. 725) does botanical research and also has a spa for all your physical self-healing needs. **Wat Pa Nanachat Beung Wai,** a forest monastery outside **Ubon Ratchathani,** invites serious students of Buddhism to stay there with monks (p. 203). Meditation retreats at **Wat Suan Mokkha Phalaram** in **Chaiya** (p. 785) are terrific for the travel-weary.

TRIBAL TRIBULATIONS

Ethnic tribes and villages predominate in the north, as they were mostly settled by Burmese refugees (particularly Mon and Karen) who crossed the nearby Myanmar border. Over 99.5% of all refugees in Thailand are Burmese. In **Sangkhlaburi** (p. 144), a **Mon** village of ethnic Burmese refugees is connected to a Thai village by a wooden bridge, with the halfway point distinguishing the territories. **Pha Ma Lo** is home to an affluent White Karen community. The **Red Karen** state is just across the border from **Mae Hong Son** (p. 260). And the much publicized **Long-Necked Karen** village with "giraffe women" is nearby. Mae Hong Son also accommodates the **KMT** camps and **Shan, Lisu, Hmong,** and **Lahu** hill tribes. The **Hmong villages** in **Chiang Khong** (p. 287) are accessible only by bike during the dry season. **Nan National Museum** in **Nan** (p. 290) displays a thorough history of Thai hill tribes. **Village Weaver Handicrafts** in **Nong Khai** (p. 216) has silk products made by Isaan women. If you're just interested in the tribal handicrafts, not the tribes, you're ignorant, but you can go right to the night market in **Chiang Rai** (p. 272).

ELEVATED ELEPHANTS

The most revered animal in Thailand, elephants hold a special place in the heart of every Thai citizen. White elephants have even greater significance, symbolizing royalty and prosperity. Celebrate these majestic beasts during the **Elephant Roundup,** a two-day festival in **Surin** (p. 200) at the end of November. The **Karen Elephant Camp** outside **Chiang Rai** (p. 272) rescues the jungle creatures and rehabilitates them. To help out with the bathing and feeding, see **Alternatives to Tourism** (p. 90). Just outside **Lampang** (p. 294), the **Thai Elephant Conservation Center** trains elephants to do manual labor. The masters operate under the belief that the only reason elephants have survived as long as they have is that they are useful as creatures of burden. Their mission is to make them useful once again, despite the technology that forced them into unemployment. The masters work with the elephants one-on-one from the time they are three until they reach age 61, when the elephants retire from obligations. If the real ones are overwhelming, **Wat Ban No Muang** has a 50m three-headed elephant statue in **Ubon Ratchathani** (p. 203).

BUDDHAS

Get your sitting, reclining, walking, roadside, crystal, golden, bronze, soapstone and emerald Buddhas here! **Bangkok** has the famous **Emerald Buddha.** Glass paintings and wooden Burmese dolls adorn the inside of **Wat Chong Klang** in **Mae Hong Son** (p. 260). **Wat Tha Ton** in **Tha Ton** (p. 270) has life-size Chinese, Hindu and Buddhist figures. The **golden, dragon-headed Buddha,** also in Tha Ton, is not to be missed. In Thai history, it is not uncommon for a bolt of lightning, a wat-sacking, or an accident to destroy a Buddha, only to reveal a more beautiful, valuable Buddha underneath. Most recently, in 1955, an 800-year old stucco Buddha was dropped, breaking the stucco shell around a stunning, 5½-ton gold Buddha in **Wat Traimit** in Bangkok (p. 94).

WATERFALLS

It may take three days, but the trek to **Pa La-u Falls** (p. 156), with its eleven tiers of cascades, is worth it. Its rival might be **Nam Tok Krathing** in **Khao Khitchakut National Park** (p. 173), where you can swim in six of the thirteen tiers of falls. After coming up from a shallow dive into the the thirteenth, you emerge from the water into a swarm of hundreds of golden butterflies. And, of course, the trail up to it is marked by a sitting Buddha. The jungle pool at **Than Mayom Falls** (p. 181) was the royals' pick at the turn of the 20th century. Deserted and soothing, the **Pha Phung** upper waterfalls in **Tak** (p. 310) are stunning. The **Buddha Cave Waterfall** has thousands of Buddha images outside **Mukdahan** (p. 210). Swim in the second tier of the **Than Thip Falls** in **Sangkhom** (p. 220) and hike the 11km to **Namnang Waterfall** in **Ko Samui** (p. 341). Famous for waterfalls, the **Than Sadet Historical Park** on **Ko Phangan** (p. 335) has giant cascades with tiny pools. Or you could be like the Little Prince and chase sunsets instead—Thailand's are certainly spectacular.

DISCOVER

◪ LET'S GO PICKS: THAILAND

BEST PLACE TO MAKE A WISH: The wats in **Chiang Mai** (p. 246) are the most sacred of all Thai Buddhist sights, but the Crystal Buddha (protected by a moat) may bring you the best luck. It has survived 2000 years, after all.

BEST PLACE TO HAVE A WISH COME TRUE: With a level for each stage of enlightment, **Wat Phu Thawk,** atop a mountain outside **Nong Khai** (p. 216), is the place for making dreams happen.

BEST RIDE: Go horseback riding in **Mae Salong** (p. 278) or try the hide of an older and wiser jungle native—go elephant riding at the Karen elephant camp in **Chiang Rai.**

BEST SPA: The natural hot springs off the Mae Yen River in **Pai** (p. 266) soothe you before your traditional Thai massage.

BEST FIGHT: Muay Thai kickboxing matches all over the country never end without blood and gore.

BEST PLACE TO SNAG JEWELS: 50-60% of the world's sapphires and rubies travel down Si Chan Rd. in **Chanthaburi** (p. 171) on the way to counters near you.

BEST TIME WARP: If the American G.I. bar in **Khorat** (p. 188) doesn't make you ready for war, nothing will.

BEST WAY TO SEE STARS: During a night dive, algae phosphorescence glows with every motion you make in the waters off the Southern coast, especially **Ko Tao** (p. 329).

BEST BUDDHAS: The "thousand Buddhas" tucked into caves in **Phetchaburi** (p. 148) almost beat the Emerald Buddha in **Bangkok** (p. 94).

SUGGESTED ITINERARIES

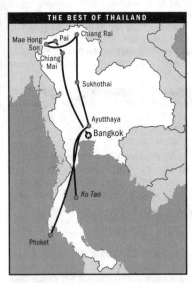

THE BEST OF THAILAND

Mae Hong Son · Pai · Chiang Rai · Chiang Mai · Sukhothai · Ayutthaya · Bangkok · Ko Tao · Phuket

FROM PAGODAS TO PATPONG: THE BEST OF THAILAND (6 WEEKS)

Begin where all good trips do, in bustling **Bangkok** (p. 94). Head north, reaching the hills of **Chiang Mai** (p. 238), where the best trekking and aesthetic treats in the region await you. To find it, look for the city's golden *chedi*—it will beckon from miles away. The infamous **Golden Triangle** of Chiang Mai, **Pai** (p. 266), and **Mae Hong Son** (p. 260) bring together the best of indigenous Thai culture, amazing mountain views, and a respite from the sizzling Southeast Asian summer, not to mention the intrigue of the narcotics trade. Having conquered the triangle, move onto the gentler **Chiang Rai** (p. 272) for more insights into northern culture. Venture to the west for exposure to Burmese refugee camps and hill tribe villages along the **Myanmar border.** Shoot south via the ancient capitals of **Sukhothai** (p. 304), whose ruins will remind you of the long history of Thailand, and **Ayutthaya** (p. 128), with its concentrated collection of wat ruins. End your trip with

a relaxing jaunt on the beaches of the ko of your choice, but if you want more than just relaxation, **Phuket** (p. 355) and **Ko Tao** are the best destinations for aquatic activities.

THE CULTURAL CONNECTION (4 WEEKS)

Fly into **Chiang Mai** (p. 238) and spend your first days at the **Chiang Mai Thai Cookery** (p. 254) in their renowned cooking class. Check out the *chedis* and then go to **Mae Hong Son** (p. 260) for the tribal villages and forest monasteries. Head to **Nan** for a **homestay** (p. 85) to live and work with a local hill tribe family. Visit the **Thai Payap Project**, which sells hill tribe handicrafts to fund community development programs in the area. On your way east, stop at **Nong Khai** and the **Phu Phra Bat** (p. 216) to see the prehistoric paintings. For Southeast Asia's most significant archaelogical site, travel to **Ban Chiang** in **Udon Thani** (p. 232), a UNESCO World Heritage site. Next, it's onto Wat

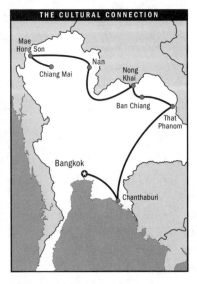

THE CULTURAL CONNECTION

Mae Hong Son · Nan · Chiang Mai · Nong Khai · Ban Chiang · That Phanom · Bangkok · Chanthaburi

That Phanom in **That Phanom** (p. 211) for the most sacred structure in Isaan culture. Then see the east coast: go to **Wat Khao Sukim** in **Chanthaburi** (p. 171), a Thai and Chinese center of Buddhist meditation with more mother-of-pearl than the Pacific Ocean. Finish up in **Bangkok** (p. 94), with the requisite tour of museums and wats.

cases the intermingling of Chinese and Western influences in Thailand. Check out **Mae Sot** (p. 311), farther north, where you'll run into more armed border police and fair trade coffeehouses than local refugees. Much farther north, finish the tour at the **Golden Triangle,** whose drug trade is the source of major political controversy.

POLITICAL PILGRIMAGE (3 WEEKS)

After seeing the palaces and parliament buildings in **Bangkok** (p. 94), travel east to **Kanchanaburi** (p. 134). The notorious River Kwai Bridge, "Death Railway Bridge," was built here by Japan's Allied POWs and workers. Take **Route 323** up to **Sangkhlaburi** (p. 144), stopping at the historical sights and park along the way. Once in Sangkhlaburi, visit Burmese Karen and Mon refugee camps. If you have more time, perfect the trip with a hands-on political experience—teach English to refugees, or get involved with a local community development program. Continue on to **Phetchaburi**'s (p. 148) historical park and national museum, which show-

BEACH BABY: ISLAND-HOPPING (3 WEEKS)

Begin your trip on **Ko Samet** (p. 166) with your back to the jungle, your feet sinking into a tiny crescent of sand, and your eyes focused on the vibrant sunset. Off the main island is **Ko Thalu,** one of the only places in Thailand for skindiving. For even more excitement, check out the colony of fruit bats nearby. From there, head to the peninsula where **Ko Phangan** (p. 335) awaits you with its über-exciting Full Moon party. Then a quick ride will bring you to **Ko Tao** (p. 329), one of the best diving and snorkeling sites in the world. Head farther south to **Trang** (p. 373) for wild orchid-covered coves and cave spelunking at **Hat Yong Ling.** Nearby **Ko Ngai**

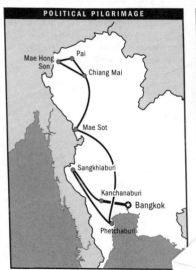

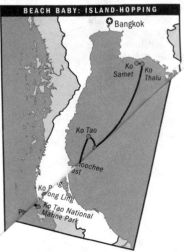

is a sweet dive spot with pristine beaches. The **Ko Tarutao National Marine Park** (p. 382) has 51 islands' worth of scuba diving excellence. Then it's off to **Ko Phi Phi Ley** (p. 367) for the hot springs and endangered species in **Khao Nawe Choochee Lowland Forest.** Stop at **Phuket** (p. 355) for one last dose of beach and aquatic sports before going to **Ko Panyi** (p. 355) to see the three-centuries-old **Muslim fishing village.**

SPIRITUAL PICK-ME-UPS (AS LONG AS YOUR HEART DESIRES)

Start the rejuvenation journey with a traditional Thai massage by Mr. Noi in **Bangkok** (p. 94). Then head far south to **Surat Thani** for a meditation retreat at **Wat Suan Mokkha Phalaram** (p. 348) to center your thoughts and focus your energy. After this spiritual renewal, hop on a boat for **Ko Phangan** (p. 335). Skip the full moon party in favor of a healthier option: **The Sanctuary.** Remarkably secluded for the crowded island, the spa specializes in yoga and ten-day fasts. Then treat yourself to one more of Thailand's best massages in **Trat** (p. 174) on the east coast. Complete your revitalization with a trip to the revolutionary **Udon Sunshine Fragrant Orchid Farm,** where the plants are bred to have healing powers of all kinds. It's been said that flowers from this **Udon Thani** (p. 228) gem help people with mental illnesses, and AIDS patients have sworn by its soothing

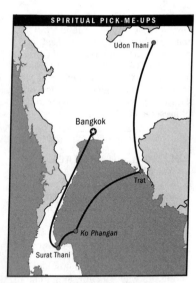

SPIRITUAL PICK-ME-UPS

effects. Sing to the plants, and watch them dance. Drink the tea and improve your complexion or cure stomach ailments. And if that doesn't work, the orchids are just plain beautiful.

THE WHOLE SHEBANG (YOUR NATURAL LIFE)

Seeing and doing everything in Thailand will undoubtedly take you the rest of your natural life, but it will be worth it. Explore all the wats and jungles and volunteer at every possible opportunity. Take this book with you.

LIFE AND TIMES

The only people of Southeast Asia never to have been colonized, the Thai have a proud and independent history that infuses the spirit of Thai society even today, in spite of the hordes of tourists who tramp through the country's beaches, temples, and jungles. A period of economic depression has made living very cheap for foreigners, even as the Thai economy slowly begins the road to recovery. While fifteen years ago, a million people descended on the "Land of Smiles" every year, today that number has risen to 8½ million, and catering to tourists has become the country's lifeblood. There are sights to suit every taste: beachgoers head to the picturesque islands off the eastern and southern coasts, while more adventurous travelers trek through hill tribe homelands in the mountainous north. Others explore the ancient cities of Central Thailand, where the ruins of once-great kingdoms now lie in silent majesty, a testament to a glorious past. Throughout Thailand, mouth-watering cuisine and gracious people will be your companions, and a smile will be your currency. For travelers new to Southeast Asia, there is no better place to start than *Amazing Thailand*.

■ HIGHLIGHTS OF THAILAND

BEACHES. Idyllic **Ko Samet** (p. 166) and **Ko Chang** (p. 177) off the east coast are cheap and mellow. Down south, **Ko Samui** (p. 341), **Ko Phangan** (p. 335), and **Ko Tao** (p. 329) offer a more raucous brand of sun-and-fun with a broader slate of aquatic activities. **Krabi**'s (p. 368) seaside cliffs offer world-class climbing.

HIKING AND TREKKING. Northern Thailand (p. 238) offers the greatest range of affordable treks. Less-touristed **Mae Hong Son** (p. 260) and **Sangkhlaburi** (p. 144) have activities ranging from elephant excursions to river rafting.

HANGING OUT. Towns along the Mekong, including **That Phanom** (p. 211) and **Nong Khai** (p. 216), are unparalleled spots to unwind and take in stunning natural settings. Nothing tops **Kanchanaburi** (p. 134) for top-notch accommodations and tasty victuals. Itsy-bitsy **Pai** (p. 266), nestled in the northern highlands, has much to explore.

CULTURAL HERITAGE. The temples and palaces of **Bangkok** (p. 94), the ancient capitals of **Sukhothai** (p. 304) and **Ayutthaya** (p. 128), and the Angkorian ruins of the **Phimai** (p. 196) are engrossing and accessible. **Chiang Mai** (p. 238) is not to be missed for its stunning architectural legacy and religious significance.

NIGHTLIFE. Bangkok (p. 94), **Chiang Mai** (p. 238), **Ko Phangan** (p. 335), **Ko Samui** (p. 341), and **Khon Kaen** (p. 233) rock on when the rest of the kingdom goes to bed.

LAND

With nearly every topological feature short of a frozen steppe, Thailand is a geography teacher's dream and a cartographer's nightmare. Kos (islands) off the coast of the "elephant trunk" peninsula have sparked intrigue and attracted tourists with claims of paradise. Best known for their white beaches, tranquil islands, coral reefs, caves, shimmering turquoise waters, and gushing waterfalls, the kos uphold their promise. The range of terrain extends from seashore to mountain peak: Doi Inthanon in the north is Thailand's highest peak (2576m). Farther north, the Moon River flows into the "Emerald Triangle" where Laos, Cambodia, and Thailand converge in the lush jungle, leaving the rice terraces around Chang Mai behind. The

Parts of the Thai borders with Laos and Cambodia are still indefinite.

12.5% of the Thai population is under the poverty line.

Since 1980, over 100 cases have been reported of women attempting or succeeding in amputating men's penises.

The average life expectancy in Thailand is 69.

The Thai language has 44 consonants and 32 vowels.

A study conducted in the 1970s found that Americans were best able to pronounce Thai sentences after consuming one ounce of alcohol.

In Thai, *mun* is a special third-person singular to use about backpackers that roughly translates to "it."

In order to change your surname in Thailand, you must make a reservation with the government for one of the 2545 surnames that have been created by monks at nine temples and blessed by the Supreme Patriarch.

Thais don't step on their doorsteps; it is believed that a spirit lives in the threshold of every home.

Khorat Plateau in the east holds dense jungle, mostly inside Khao Yai National Park. Despite seasonal monsoons, the dry climate often results in regional draughts.

PEOPLE

DEMOGRAPHICS

Use of the word "Thai" began in the 20th century as a political and geographical designation referring to all citizens of Thailand. "Tai," however, refers to the ethnic Tai-Kadai people, who speak Tai-based languages, live mostly in China, Laos, and Myanmar (where they are known as the Shan), and account for 75% of the population of Thailand. At 12% of the population, the **Chinese** are Thailand's largest minority. Homeland starvation and poverty are the leading causes behind the high Chinese immigration rate over the past decades. Hill tribe groups, including the **Karen, Hmong, Yao, Lahu, Akha,** and **Lisu,** are concentrated in the north, while the country's one million Muslims are concentrated mainly in the south.

Ever tolerant, Thais have interwoven elements of all ethnicities into the national culture, in part due to the proliferation of intermarriage. There are virtually no ethnic clashes with Muslim or Chinese groups and little racial violence. After all, Thai culture is itself considered a fusion of two giants: Indian and Chinese. The conflicts that do occur are usually between the urban and the rural or the wealthy and the poor.

LANGUAGE

Like the people themselves, the Thai language has evolved with influences and adaptations from English, Chinese, and Sanskrit (to name only a few) while still retaining the characteristic five tones, monosyllabic words, and ancient alphabet. King Ramkhamhaeng of Sukhothai created the first **Thai alphabet** in 1283 as a combination of Sanskrit syntax and Khmer characters, and this alphabet has survived almost entirely intact to this day. This standardized language has lent the Thais a sense of cultural identity and national unity. **Grammar** is delightfully simple: there are no suffixes, genders, articles, declensions, or plurals in spoken Thai. Like English, it is written from left to right; it lacks capital letters and punctuation, however. The national language has four major **dialects** that have developed geographically: Central, Northern (Tak), Northeastern, and Southern. See the Appendix (p. 413) for specific phrases. Aside from regional dialects, Thai also employs different vocabulary and syntax depending on the relative social status of the speaker to his audience. The most distinctive of these is the royal language, **rachasap.** Below *rachasap* are: the **ecclesiastical language,** the **polite vernacular** used most commonly on a daily basis, and finally the spicy **slang** used only between close friends. The Thai language readily lends itself to adaptation in terms of vocabulary. Somewhat like German, Thai combines existing words to create new meanings. For example, the word "ice" in Thai, *nam khaeng*, literally translates to "solid water." Western concepts and scientific and technological terms are somewhat more difficult to create by combining existing Thai words, however. To remedy the situation, the **Royal Institute** convenes a committee of linguists to concoct new vocabulary words by delving into Pali and Sanskrit.

RELIGION

Although the Thai Constitution requires the reigning monarch to be Buddhist, it does not name Theravada Buddhism as the state religion and guarantees complete freedom of religion for its citizens. Speech that insults Buddhism is strictly prohibited, however. New religions are officially recognized if they have more than 5000 followers, can demonstrate a unique theology, and are not politically active. However, since 1984, the government has not recognized any new faiths, including the Church of Jesus Christ of Latter Day Saints. Since 1999, government-issued National Identity Cards include a religious designation in response to those who wanted an easier means of identifying individuals requiring a Muslim burial.

THERAVADA BUDDHISM. The religion of 95% of the Thai people, Theravada Buddhism informs both their faith and their lifestyle. The Thai outlook is better understood in light of the **Four Noble Truths of Buddhism:** there is suffering; the source of suffering is desire; there is a cessation to suffering; and that cessation is achieved through an adherence to the **Eightfold Path,** which is a path of virtue, mental cultivation, and wisdom. Anti-materialism, forgiveness, and a vigorous spirit that has mastered tranquility are all characteristics of this highly scriptural religion and of the Thais themselves. The **Spirit of Free Enquiry** is central to Buddhism: the Buddha encouraged his followers to investigate His Teaching for themselves instead of adhering to it blindly. This teaching inspires a high degree of tolerance for difference—racial, religious, ethnic, or sexual—and teaches kindness and compassion in the hope that individuals can live in harmony with the people, creatures, and natural environment around them. Monks are a common sight in Thailand; their saffron robes, shaved heads, and gentle manner serve as a reminder of a search for inner peace that is the mainstay of Theravada Buddhism. It is an accepted **male rite of passage** to serve temporarily (usually about three months) in the monkhood. The goal of this religious service is increased maturity and spirituality in everyday life. Only below the monarchy in social hierarchy, monks are discussed and addressed in language that denotes the great respect awarded them.

MAHAYANA BUDDHISM. Buddhism evolved over time into two schools, Theravada ("tradition of the elderly") and Mahayana ("the big vessel"). The latter believes that it is impossible for individuals to achieve their own **nirvana.** Rather, they can only approach this enlightened state. According to Mahayana

To disseminate information about religions other than Buddhism, you must get permission from the government's Religion Department.

Buddhist monks wear their robes differently during the morning alms procession than they do for the rest of the day.

Temples double as sanctuaries for stray dogs and cats.

There are over 650 Chinese and Vietnamese Mahayana Buddhist shrines and temples in Thailand.

Thai primary and secondary school students are required by law to take 80 hours of religious training per school-year in both Buddhism and Islam.

The world's largest mass cremation took place in 1997 in Bangkok, when the remains of over 21,000 people who had been killed in road accidents or other fatal incidents and left unclaimed for ten years were incinerated.

In 1955, the 800-year-old Golden Buddha, once covered in stucco, was dropped while being moved, revealing 5½ tons of gold.

Thailand has over 2000 mosques, about 200 of which are in Bangkok alone.

Buddhists are forbidden from cracking eggs; local shop keepers get around this proscription by keeping a stash of "accidentally" cracked eggs on hand.

Buddhist monks are not allowed to touch, to be touched by, or to receive anything directly from a woman.

According to the Vinya, or Buddhist Monastic Rule, an animal cannot become a monk.

It was not until 2002 that the first woman was ordained as a monk in Thailand.

It was not until 1816 that the Catholic Church declared inquisitional torture to no longer be a valid practice.

Thailand has a special "religious visa" for missionaries.

Buddhism, nirvana will only come when all of humankind is ready for salvation. This belief leads Mahayana Buddhists to work to relieve universal suffering. Many scholars believe that during the **Nanchao Kingdom,** Mahayana Buddhism was the predominant religion in Thailand. Although today it is more popular in other parts of Southeast Asia, Mahayana Buddhism is still practiced in Thailand mainly by ethnic Chinese and Vietnamese immigrants. There is a particularly large ethnic Chinese community in Phuket that practices a combination of Mahayana Buddhism and Taoism. Recent differences of opinion (see **Scriptural Debates,** p. 23) have led to the disclosure that a prominent wat previously thought to espouse Theravada Buddhism was adhering to the Nirvana-as-Heaven theory, which is found only in Mahayana Buddhism.

ISLAM. Thailand's largest religious minority, Muslims account for approximately 4% of the population. They live mostly in Southern Thailand, close to the Malaysian border, and many Thai Muslims are originally of **Malay** descent. In fact, in the south, there are more mosques than wats. Thailand accommodates Islamic law in Muslim communities in matrimonial and educational spheres. Although Islamic law necessitates a lifestyle significantly different from that of Theravada Buddhists or nihilist backpackers, Muslims are well assimilated into Thai culture. In Chiang Mai, the Tourism Authority of Thailand (TAT) has recently granted 47 establishments a certificate of **halal** (Muslim kosher) quality in an effort to market the area to a growing number of Indonesian, Russian, and Chinese Muslim tourists. But in the aftermath of the **September 11, 2001** attacks on the United States, the Thai government has become more wary of possible separatist movements in Southern Thailand.

CHRISTIANITY. Christianity was introduced by western missionaries in the 16th and 17th centuries. Thailand's Christian population is proportionally the smallest of any Asian nation though it is certainly not for lack of trying. The religion suffered a setback when foreigners were expelled from Siam in 1688 (see **The Ayutthaya Kingdom,** p. 16). When they were eventually allowed back into the kingdom, King Rama IV is reported to have remarked to a missionary friend, "What you teach us to do is admirable, but what you teach us to believe is foolish." Christianity's first Thai converts were actually of Chinese origin. A few of the hill tribes were converted to Catholicism, but more recent centralized efforts by the Thai government to bring them into the Buddhist fold have eroded Christianity's popularity.

HINDUISM. Although it has been diluted over the centuries, Thai culture is infused with Hinduism from early contact between the Thai and Khmer. This influence is particularly apparent in early art and architecture (see **History: Architecture,** p. 29). Only a small percentage of modern Thai are Hindu—mostly immigrants from India—and the majority of them live in Bangkok, where there are four main Hindu temples. There are also separate Hindu schools where, in addition to the regular curriculum, Hindi and Sanskrit are also taught.

SIKHISM. Like Hindus, Thailand's Sikhs are concentrated mainly in Bangkok. They are heavily involved in the community and operate free schools for poor children and support the sick and the aged. They are divided into two sects, which worship at different temples.

ANIMISM. Predating both Hinduism and Theravada Buddhism, animism formed the first layer of Thai religion, later incorporating Theravada Buddhism. One example can be found in the ubiquitous Thai spirit houses (see **Wai Not,** p. 26). Today, most animists are found among the northern hill tribes or the **Chao Lay** of the Andaman Sea (see **Surviving "Survivor,"** p. 23).

FLORA & FAUNA

Thailand's diverse topology and unique geographical location yield a wealth of plant and animals species. This great variety means that the country makes it onto every international "best list": best scuba diving, best bird-watching, best trekking. Even the world's best veterinarians travel to Thailand to care for the country's endangered wildlife in one of the many sanctuaries and nature preserves.

PLANTS

FLOWERS WITH POWERS. The white or pink **lotus,** seen floating on a pond or depicted in Buddhist art, is a sacred symbol of fertility, purity, peace, and compassion. It gained religious significance when one blossom grew from each of the young Buddha's first seven footsteps. A hot commodity in the Western hemisphere and the national flower of Thailand, **orchids**—over 1000 species—grow everywhere in Thailand. Though the flowers are still on the endangered species list, the orchid industry is a major source of income for Thais. Typically a flower associated with Christian winters in the West, the scarlet **pointsettia** is quite popular in Thailand, especially in Chiang Mai province. Interestingly, it is also more common during the winter months because its bright, cheerful blooms, though poisonous, help to compensate for the fewer hours of daylight. Common roots and berries are also picked for traditional Thai remedies, and used for inspiration, creativity, and medicine.

RICE AND EVERYTHING NICE. Thailand's most important crop is not significant simply because it is a staple of local cuisine but because of its **religious symbolism.** Rice is celebrated as a representation of nature's beneficence in providing sustenance. Early every morning, people, mostly in smaller villages, leave offerings of rice for the Buddhist monks who collect donations of food and basic daily necessities, collectively known as **binderbaht.** These offerings are particularly significant during Harvest Festivals (timing varies by region). During these festivals, it is customary to celebrate all the earth's flora and fauna as well as man's labor, which brings the flora and fauna into the home.

The Mekong River is home to the *pla beuk,* the world's largest freshwater fish, measuring up to 3m and weighing 300kg.

In 1884, the British Consul-General of Bangkok introduced the Siamese cat to Britain.

More people die every year from bee stings than from shark attacks.

Thais often present a bride with a pair of Blue Korats (a kind of cat) as a symbol of future marital bliss.

The closest known relatives of the elephant are the dugong, manatee, hyrax, and aardvark.

Elephants are the only mammals that can't jump.

Thailand is home to over 400 varieties of figs and 250 species of coral.

Having cultivated rice for over 700 years, Thailand is today the world's largest exporter of rice.

The coconut is actually classified neither as a fruit, nut, or vegetable, but as a drupe.

LIFE AND TIMES

LIFE AND TIMES

The grounds of the Thai royal palace are home to a milk farm; much of the milk is made into an inexpensive baby formula that is sold locally.

Killing sea turtles and stealing their eggs is illegal and punishable by up to four years in jail and/or a fine of 40,000฿.

Thailand's *Cryptotora thamicola* is the most specialized fish in the world; it has no eyes, no pigment, breathes through its skin, and can climb walls with a pair of lateral extended fins.

An elephant's trunk is made up of around 100,000 different muscles.

The Thai Red Cross owns and operates a snake farm in order to extract venom and make anti-venom serum.

90% of all Thai animals are insects.

Originally crippled by an anti-personnel mine, Thailand's famous logging elephant, Motola, received an artificial foot from a US company that makes prosthetic devices.

TREES. It is believed that Buddha attained enlightenment in the shade of the **Boddhi tree.** Those grown from a cutting of the original tree in India are the most precious, but all Boddhi trees command respect. Long-reaching branches, an irregularly shaped trunk, and heart-shaped leaves are its species' most noticeable characteristics. Buddha also sat in the shade of the **Rose Apple** tree, meditating on man's earthly sufferings. Its enormous branches (13m) protected Buddha thousands of years ago; they now do the same for Thais. The **Chomphu Phukha** tree in Nan's Doi Phuka National Park (see p. 293), is extremely rare, though it isn't the only one in the world as locals claim. When it blooms in February, it becomes a regional attraction.

WILDLIFE

MAKING HEADLINES. Unlike many other cultures, the Thai take their animals very seriously to the point of personification. The Buddhist influence has encouraged the Thai to regard animals in the same way they would regard other human beings. Almost daily, special interest articles appear in the well-respected *Bangkok Post* about various animals whose names, personalities, and salient characteristics are well known. Rare animal sightings, the transfer of an animal from one zoo to another, or even an everyday event at a zoo makes national headlines. One recent saga involved a celebrity orangutan named **Mike,** who was the star of the Lop Buri Zoo. Having contracted herpes from a contaminated piece of food fed to him by a visitor at the zoo, Mike was admitted to Chulalongkorn Animal Hospital and fed intravenously for two weeks. He died of pneumonia soon afterward at age 17. Fans had been following Mike even before he married his first mate, **Zuzu** from Taiwan, in 1996. The wedding was celebrated by a festival in Lop Buri complete with a parade, ceremony, and international media coverage. Fans also celebrated his second marriage to **Mali,** an orangutan from Southern Thailand. He was laid to rest with a hero's funeral attended by 500 people who threw roses on his coffin as Buddhist monks chanted in the background. His actual body will be kept in storage until a decision is reached about whether to bury him or preserve his body for public viewing in a mausoleum, and a statue will be erected in his memory. Eager to help, Taiwan has offered to send another male orangutan to Lop Buri to "replace" Mike. This new orangutan will be paired with his second mate, Mali, because according to Thai custom, Zuzu must mourn Mike's death for a suitable amount of time before she is allowed to mate again.

ELEPHANTS. Culturally and historically, elephants are the good luck charms of Thailand. They are on the national currency, the national flag, and are the symbol of the monarchy. Thailand is even geographically shaped like an elephant's head and trunk. Used for centuries as the main means of transportation in Thailand and as battle animals, today they are drugged to be docile as they pose for cheesy photographs with drunk tourists, or are overworked and underfed by illegal loggers.

White elephants are considered particularly lucky, as they once only belonged to kings. Today, when a white elephant is found, it immediately becomes the property of the reigning monarch. Despite the efforts to save these precious beasts, their numbers have diminished by almost 40% in the past ten years.

ENDANGERED ANIMALS. The **Asiatic Black Bear** and the **Malaysian Sun Bear,** the world's smallest bear, are two species native to Thailand, but poaching has put both on the endangered species list. A popular pet in Southeast Asia, the Sun Bear's skin is so loose that when it's grabbed by an attacker, it is able to turn around completely and counter-attack. Though it is illegal, both species are poached for their skins, and older bears are killed for medicinal purposes. The recipes for many traditional remedies include the gallbladder and bile of these bears in cures for inflammation, fevers, and liver disease. Herbal alternatives to these recipes exist, but the products containing actual animal parts are far more popular. Tourists, mostly from Korea, also visit Thailand with the express purpose of eating bear-paw soup, which appears on Thai menus for over US$1000 per bowl. Discovered only in 1974, **Kitti's Hog-Nosed Bat** is also on the endangered species list. In an attempt to protect its native animals, Thailand has set aside 13% of its land for natural preserves. Collectors soon eliminated Kitti's Bat from Sai Yok, the national park created specifically for it; but the effects of these natural preserves have yet to be seen on the Asiatic Black Bear and Malaysian Sun Bear populations.

HISTORY

PREHISTORY

IMPORTANT DATES		
4000 BC Farmers settle in Khorat Plateau.	**AD 651** First kingdom of Thai tribes formed.	**7-12th Centuries** Tai-Kadai tribes found kingdoms.

Scholars disagree about the origins of the Thai people. Some argue that their ancestors originated in Mongolia or Northern China and were driven south to Yunnan, where the tribes coalesced and established the kingdom of Nanchao in AD 651. Other theorists trace the origins to Northeast Thailand. Recently discovered human remains in Ban Chiang (see p. 232) in the Khorat Plateau suggest that farmers settled there around 4000 BC before leaving for Nanchao two centuries later. In the next four centuries, various tribes of the Tai-Kadai moved south into northern Myanmar, Thailand, and Laos, establishing minor kingdoms and city states.

THE SUKHOTHAI PERIOD (1238-1350)

IMPORTANT DATES		
1238 Kingdom of Sukhothai founded by King Si Inthrathit.	**1275** King Ramkhamhaeng ascends the throne.	**1283** Thai alphabet established by King Ramkhamhaeng.

Taking advantage of the weakening Khmer and Srivijaya, two Thai chieftans, **Khun Bang Klang Thao** and **Khun Pha Muang,** rebelled and moved north. In 1238, **King Inthrathit** (formerly Khun Bang Klang Thao) founded the kingdom of **Sukhothai,** considered by most to be the first true Thai polity. Sukhothai, meaning "Dawn of Happiness," reached its zenith in power and size (incorporating present-day Laos, Thailand, Singapore, Malaysia, and much of Myanmar) in 1275, when **King Ramkhamhaeng the Great** ascended the throne. Modern Thai ideals of the benevolent monarch and his place in society originate in the Sukhothai period. His rule marked the first unification of Thais under a single monarch, and Ramkhamhaeng worked tirelessly to better the condition of his people, abolishing slavery and codifying laws. He also invited Ceylonese monks to come to Sukhothai to purify the kingdom's Buddhism; as a result, the Ceylonese school of Theravada Buddhism was established as the national religion. The Thai historical imagination has been most inspired by Sukhothai as a utopian golden age, which, to a certain degree, it was; it has often been conveniently overlooked, however, that Thai states such as **Lanna** and **Phayao,** in the northern part of modern Thailand, also flourished contemporaneously. A famous inscription from this period reads, "In the water there are fish, in the fields there is rice. Whoever wants to trade in elephants, so trades... Whoever wants to trade in silver and gold, so trades. The faces of the citizens are happy." It's no wonder everyone was smiling; King Ramkhamhaeng levied no taxes and made himself available to his citizens, building a bell in front of his palace so that at any time, his subjects could ring it, confident that he would arbitrate justly. In 1283, the king introduced the Thai **alphabet** as a symbol of the nation's cultural and political independence. Except for a few later changes, mostly in the late 17th century under **King Narai,** King Ramkhamhaeng's script remains intact today.

THE AYUTTHAYA KINGDOM (1351-1767)

IMPORTANT DATES

1350 Kingdom of Ayutthaya founded.	**13-16th Centuries** Ayutthaya grows in stature and number of temples.	**1511** Portuguese embassy established in Ayutthaya.	**1605-1662** Spanish, Dutch, English, Danish, and French arrive.	**1688** Foreigners plot, lie, and steal; get expelled from the kingdom.

In 1350, **King U Thong** (later called King Ramathibodi I) established the magnificent island-city of **Ayutthaya,** which served as the capital for the next four centuries. Ayutthaya incorporated many Khmer court customs such as the idea of an absolute monarch into its traditions. By this time, Thai cultural and national identity had gelled, and the kingdom of Ayutthaya merely consolidated and expanded the existing kingdom of Sukhothai. With its capital in modern Thailand's central plains region, Ayutthaya was safe from external invasions during the rainy season, which was marked by massive flooding. Relatively impregnable, Ayutthaya turned inward and developed a complex system of administration, the forerunner of the modern Thai bureaucracy. To compliment this administrative structure, Thai society began to develop internal hierarchies that persist to this day. The lowest rung on the social ladder was **phrai,** commoners and slaves; above them were **khunnang,** or nobles. At the top were **chao,** the princes. Ever classless, the **monks** remained the one social group that could bridge these divisions. The rise of Ayutthaya also coincided with the inevitable arrival of the first Europeans; a dispute over the Melaka territory brought the **Portuguese** into the picture. They established an embassy in Ayutthaya in 1511. The Portuguese were followed by a veritable stampede of curious foreign visitors beginning with the **Spanish,** followed by the **Dutch, English** and **Danish,** and concluding with the **French** in 1662. Under **King Narai,** Ayutthaya reached its peak of power and influence, boasting a population far greater than that of London. But in 1688 while the king was seriously ill, his chief minister, a Greek named **Constantine Phaulkon,** was accused of conspiring to replace the king with a puppet-king loyal to France. He had successfully kept the Dutch and English at bay but permitted the French to station over 500 troops throughout Ayutthaya. That year, King Narai cut off relations with the French and expelled virtually all foreigners from Ayutthaya for 150 years. The degree to which this incident has become a part of the Thai national psyche is clear from the modern word for "foreigner," *farang,* a derivative of the word for "French."

THE FALL OF AYUTTHAYA (1767-82)

LIFE AND TIMES

IMPORTANT DATES

1767 Burmese annex, sack, and burn Ayutthaya.

1767-83 General Taksin reclaims Thai kingdom, believing himself to be the Buddha.

1782 King Rama I comes to power.

After a two-year siege, Burmese forces stormed Ayutthaya in 1767. They burned it to the ground, destroying culturally and religiously significant manuscripts, paintings, and sculptures. The Burmese also killed the king of Ayutthaya, slaughtering tens of thousands along the way. Only 10,000 out of over one million original inhabitants survived, including **General Phraya Taksin** and a few hundred of his followers. The Thai have never forgiven the Burmese or forgotten what they did to the glorious kingdom of Ayutthaya, and much of the modern conflict between the two countries is a result of this historical hangnail. Regrouping on the east coast, Taksin led an army of several thousand men to expel the Burmese and gain sweet revenge. Within 15 years, the Thais had successfully recaptured Chiang Mai, Cambodia, and parts of Laos. Taksin ruled from his new capital at **Thonburi,** just across the river from Bangkok. Soon after he won the war, however, King Taksin began to suffer from the unfortunate misconception that he was a **reincarnation of the Buddha.** He also made the inopportune decision to proclaim this publicly. Needless to say, his declaration was poorly received in court. In their counter-declaration, the other royals and generals decided that not only was Taksin definitely not a reincarnation of the Buddha, but he was insane to think so. He was executed in royal fashion: thrown into a velvet sack (so as not to spill any royal blood) and then beaten to death with a sandalwood club. Commander-in-chief **Thong Duang** was recalled from his campaign in Cambodia and crowned **King Rama I** in 1782, founding the **Chakri dynasty.**

THE EARLY BANGKOK PERIOD (1782-1868)

IMPORTANT DATES

1785 Bangkok becomes the capital; King Rama I builds Grand Palace.

1851 King Rama IV ascends the throne.

1855 King signs treaty with British, imports Western technology.

When Thonburi became too vulnerable to the Burmese, Rama I moved the capital across the Chao Phraya River to **Bangkok.** There he built his most lasting legacy, the Grand Palace and Royal Chapel (Temple of the Emerald Buddha), and unified the kingdom's many fiefdoms. He ordered an editorial overhaul of the **Tripitaka,** the Buddhist scriptures, by a learned council. He also codified and edited Thai law into the *Kotmai Tra Samdung* (Three Seals Code), which set economic, political, and military rules and was the major achievement of his reign. It was also during this period that Chiang Mai was added to the Thai kingdom. The reign of King Mongkut, or **King Rama IV,** was one of the most significant transitional periods of modern Thailand. Unfairly portrayed as a flippant and frivolous monarch in Margaret Landon's *Anna and the King of Siam,* Mongkut was actually a serious man, having spent the reign of his half-brother, **King Rama III,** in the monkhood, traveling extensively throughout the kingdom and accumulating experiences that would later prove invaluable. Seeking to strengthen Siam and silence his Western critics, Rama IV negotiated a foreign trade treaty with the British in 1885—reversing 150 years of virtual isolation. Intellectually stimulated by the cultures and ideas brought to Siam by western missionaries, he studied English and French and imported western technologies and organizational techniques.

COLONIALISM AVERTED (1868-1932)

IMPORTANT DATES

1868-1910 King Rama V attains god-like status.	**1893** French ships enter Bangkok.	**1897** Rama V is the first Thai monarch to travel to Europe.	**1907** First statue of a Thai king (Rama V) erected.	**1909** Siam gives up claims to peninsular Malaysia.

Malaria cut short Mongkut's rule, however, and the government fell into the able hands of his teenage son, **Prince Chulalongkorn,** who was crowned **King Rama V.** His 42 years of rule were marked by the abolition of slavery, reforms in the Thai justice, education, and public welfare systems and a courageous foreign policy in an era of aggressive European colonialism. In 1893, after prolonged tension between **France** and Siam in the northeast, two French gunboats shelled Siamese defenses at the mouth of the Chao Phraya River and sailed into Bangkok. Thanks to the swift diplomatic action of Foreign Minister **Prince Devawongse,** war between the two countries was narrowly averted. A subsequent treaty with the French established Siam as a regional **buffer state,** guaranteeing its independence. In return, Siam ceded much of the territory that is modern Laos and Cambodia to the French and what is now peninsular Malaysia to the British. By his death in 1910, Rama V had become the most revered Thai monarch in modern history and the last Thai royal to be revered as a god. **King Vajiravudh** was the next in line for the throne in 1910. The pride and popularity the Thais accorded royalty during Rama V's reign were all but destroyed during **Rama VI's** 15-year term. Having graduated from Oxford with a degree in literature, King Vajiravudh wrote "The Jews of the East," a work about the issue of overseas Chinese in Thailand, which had not yet been addressed by the government. Though his intellectual capacity was undeniable, his financial finesse was dubious. His massive expenditures on everything from art to the **Wild Tiger Corps,** a specialized private paramilitary group he started, incurred a tremendous debt that damaged the Thai economy long after his reign. His Wild Tiger Corps initiative, in addition to doubling the military budget, embittered the regular Thai army. In 1913, he introduced the concept of surnames, coining hundreds of them himself.

THE RISE OF THE MILITARY (1932-1942)

IMPORTANT DATES

1932 Absolute monarchy abolished; People's Party comes to power in a bloodless coup.	**1933** Dr. Pridi Banomyong advocates socialist economic plan.	**1935** King Rama VII goes into voluntary exile in England.	**1941** Tokyo Convention: France returns Indochinese territory to Thailand.	**1941** Outbreak of the War of Greater East Asia.

During the Great Depression, the Thai treasury nearly went bankrupt from the millions of baht poured into public works projects. Prominent academics and intellectuals demanded a civil constitution. In June 1932, government workers and the military launched a bloodless coup. Proclaiming themselves the **People's Party,** the revolutionaries, led by **Major Luang Phibunsongkhram** (commonly known as **Phibun**) and Dr. Pridi Banomyong, moved quickly to occupy high government posts. Dr. Pridi Banomyang agitated for a socialist economic plan that would nationalize land and labor. More conservative leaders in the Thai government were horrified by his proposal and forced him into exile. During this period, the Thai **military,** the pet project of King Rama VI, became increasingly influential. Unable to satisfy the demands of his people, **King Rama VII** abdicated in 1935 and went into a voluntary exile in England, where he died six years later. In his place, the ten-year-old

Ananda Mahidol (later **King Rama VIII**), who was studying abroad in Switzerland at the time, was placed on the throne. As the country experimented with **constitutions** granting varying degrees of democracy, the pendulum of Thai political power swung back and forth between the military and the civilian bureaucratic elite. In 1940, Phibun requested that France return the territories that it had taken just a few decades earlier. The French were reluctant, to say the least. The resulting military skirmishes only ended with the arbitration by the occupying **Japanese.** The 1941 **Tokyo Convention** returned much of French Indochina to Thai control. Unfortunately, later that year, the **War of Greater East Asia** merged with World War II, and Thailand joined up with the Japanese forces against the Allies.

THE WORLD WAR II ERA (1942-1971)

IMPORTANT DATES

1942 Thai Field Marshal declares war on Allies; ambassador refuses to honor declaration.	**1946** Thailand joins UN after explaining their WWII behavior to the US.	**1957** Military *coup d'état* during general elections; Field Marshal Sarit Thanarat takes over.	**1964** First US military personnel stationed in Thailand.	**1967** Association of Southeast Asian Nations (ASEAN) founded.

Field Marshal **Phibul Songkhram** declared war on the Allies in 1942. Thai Ambassador to the US, **Seni Pramoj,** reluctantly went to deliver the declaration to American Secretary of State Hull; the Ambassador said he was obligated to deliver something that he didn't want to deliver. Hull's innovative suggestion was that he not deliver it. Seni Pramoj concurred, and many now understand the events to mean that Thailand remained neutral during WWII. Thailand later had to explain this incident to the US by claiming that the declaration of war was invalid since it ran contrary to the will of the Thai people. After this brush with disastrous foreign policy, the Thai Ambassador organized the people against Field Marshal Phibul Songkhram, who ultimately resigned only to come to power again after the death of King Rama VIII. In 1946, after his brother was found shot dead in his bed, **King Rama IX** began his reign. Thailand continued to develop economically through the late 1940s and early 50s and adopted increasingly democratic practices, although corruption persisted in the government. The country also became more actively involved in international affairs, joining the **United Nations** in 1946 and even sending troops on a UN mission to Korea in 1950. In 1957, the military staged a *coup d'état* during the general elections, and Field Marshal **Sarit Thanarat** took over. The new government re-established full military control while purging the police force of corruption, executing drug dealers, and suppressing Communist propaganda. By the time Thanarat died in 1963, Thailand had become a staunch US ally in Southeast Asia. Under his successor, **Thanom Kittikachorn,** US forces were permitted to build air bases in Thailand to support the war in Vietnam.

MILITARY REPRESSION (1971-1975)

IMPORTANT DATES

1973 Students hold pro-democracy demonstrations.	**1975** Height of agitation for government reforms.	**1976** Government quells demonstrations, resulting in the October Massacre.

By late 1971, Thailand had reverted to full military rule. However, the nation's patience with new constitutions, coups, and regime changes was wearing thin. In June 1973, students from three universities converged on Bangkok's **Democracy Monument** and held demonstrations in the streets, calling for a democratic government. Although many students were killed, the people were elated with their new-found power. In response, Field Marshal Thanom resigned in favor of **Professor Sanya Dharmasakti.** Radicals left the cities to join Communist guerrilla forces, leftist activists were emboldened, and by mid-1975 agitation for reform had reached a fever pitch. On October 6, 1976, the government responded, sending troops, accompanied by violent rightist gangs, into **Thammasat University** to quell demonstrations. More than 300 protestors were shot, clubbed to death, and hanged in what was called the **October Massacre.** Subsequently, troops arrested 1700 more protestors, and the remainder left the city to regroup. Even today, the events of 1971-1976 are taboo and rarely taught in Thai schools.

TOWARD DEMOCRACY (1977-1992)

IMPORTANT DATES

1988 First elected, non-military Prime Minister since 1977.	**1991** Army launches bloodless coup, dissolves legislature, abolishes Constitution.	**1992** Troops kill hundreds of protestors on Suchinda's orders.

The October Massacre was curtailed by the intervention of the king. Though he has no legal authority, he commands great respect and loyalty among the people, and his intervention shamed the Prime Minister and other high-ranking officials into voluntary exile. The new **interim government** drafted a new, democratic **constitution** that provided universal suffrage for all Thai citizens over 20 and greater freedom of speech and religion. But democracy was short-lived; the military reclaimed power, citing an increased number of demonstrations (which many believed were staged) as a resurgence of socialist and Communist tendencies nurtured by democratic lassitude. A stand-off between students and police at Thammasat University, Thailand's hotbed of political activism, exploded into another bloody assault. Scores of people were killed, and the military once again took control of the government. In 1988, after 16 coups in 40 years, public dissatisfaction and shrinking support for the military culminated in general elections and the end of military rule. Early in 1991, the army launched a successful bloodless coup under **General Suchinda Kraprayoon** who abolished the constitution, dissolved the legislature, and curtailed general freedoms. Accusations that the army influenced the framing of the new constitution to institutionalize its rule spurred thousands to protest in May 1992. Under Prime Minister Suchinda's orders, the military killed hundreds of people, many of whom were strategically located in front of the Democracy Monument and Western TV cameras. Horrified, King Bhumibol forced Suchinda out of office and appointed **Panyarachun** as transitional prime minister.

END OF MILITARY RULE (1992-1998)

IMPORTANT DATES

1992-96 Economic prosperity slows down.	**1996** Stock market crashes.	**1997** Asian Financial Crisis.

Panyarachun fired the top four military officers in August 1992, kicking off a new era in Thai politics that was marked by an effort to separate the government and the military. The following regimes, however, faced charges of corruption and mismanagement, and the resulting political instability damaged Thailand's previously spectacular 8-10% annual growth rates. In 1996, Thailand had a 7.4% inflation rate—the highest in five years—0% export growth, and a drop of 30% in stock market prices. Then **Prime Minister Banharn Silpa-archa** was harshly criticized for meddling in economic affairs and was held responsible for the nation's dire economic situation. Tougher times were still to come. In July 1997, heavy external debts, financial deregulation, and an unsustainable fixed exchange rate culminated in the collapse of the Thai baht in what became known as the **Asian**

Financial Crisis. From 1985 to 1995, Thailand had maintained the highest growth rate in the world—a whopping 9% annually. But in 1997, the baht hit the lowest point in history: 56 baht to the US dollar. Economists discovered the hard way that the national economic infrastructure, riddled with corruption and hidden debt, was too weak to absorb the shock and rebound. Waves of **currency devaluations,** accompanied by economic and political havoc, spread across Southeast Asia. The **International Monetary Fund (IMF)** initiated a US$17.2 billion emergency international rescue package for Thailand in August 1997. In spite of (or perhaps as a result of?) IMF intervention, the baht's value fell 40%, over 350 factories shut down, and Thailand's stock market hit a nine-year low. The Thai still blame the IMF's shaky financial advice for the ensuing economic devastation.

THAILAND TODAY

IMPORTANT DATES		
1999 Thailand's economy begins recovery.	**2000** "Amazing Thailand" launched by TAT.	**2000** Bangkok Sky Rail opened.

With positive growth rates since 1999, Thailand seems to be well on its way to economic recovery, aided by the unprecedented popularity enjoyed by the government of **Prime Minister Chuan Leekpai.** The Tourism Authority of Thailand (TAT) inaugurated the ambitious **Amazing Thailand** campaign to boost the economy, and by February 2000, officials declared the worst of the economic crisis to be over.

KING BHUMIBOL ADULYADEJ (RAMA IX)

King Rama IX was born in December 1927 in Cambridge, Massachusetts while his parents were studying medical-related fields at Harvard University and Simmons College. After his father's death, the King's family moved to Switzerland. Ascending the throne when he was only 18, the young king's actual coronation was postponed by four years so he could finish his education. As the longest-reigning monarch in the world, he's revered for his dedication to the underprivileged, his role in resolving government conflicts, and his commitment to the peace and unity of his country. He may have no direct legal power, but his word commands tremendous loyalty and respect. As king, he has three rights: to encourage, to warn, and to be consulted. Since 1974, he has become particularly active in **reforestation projects** in order to preserve Thailand's flora and fauna. Heavily influenced by his parents's medical careers, King Bhumibol also places a great deal of emphasis on **health care.** While he's not busy governing the kingdom, the king devotes himself to a variety of hobbies. He is a world-class **yachtsman** as well as a famous **composer** with 43 jazz and blues compositions to his name.

HOOKED ON THAILAND

According to the United States Central Intelligence Agency, Thailand is considered a **drug money-laundering center.** And, despite the low percentage of Thailand's narcotics production in comparison to its Southeast Asian neighbors, the backpacker mythology about drug abuse in Thailand, particularly in the South and the Northeast, has resulted in a nation-wide crackdown. Recently, a man was shot dead outside of Pai as he was trying to smuggle **amphetamines** into Chiang Mai along a nearby river; the key concept is "zero tolerance." But backpackers in Thailand don't seem to understand this; the erroneous mythology has its origins in the northeastern treks of the 1970s. Guides, who usually came from Central Thailand and had little or no knowledge of the hill tribes' customs, told foreigners that **opium** was an integral part of hill tribe culture used to welcome guests and to ease the aches of manual labor. Later anthropological study revealed that most hill tribes viewed opium as a privilege reserved for elderly men. But gradually, the villagers realized the financial advantages of catering to foreign tourists, selling opium and **heroin.** Unfortunately, the new local dealers began experimenting with the drugs themselves, and soon most of the money they made selling the drugs to foreigners was spent on their own addictions. In many northeastern villages today, as much as 80% of the population is addicted to either opium or heroin. With the rapid spread of **AIDS/HIV** through intravenous drug use, these poppy derivatives are causing Bangkok quite a headache. In dramatic gestures timed to coincide with the **UN International Narcotics Day,** Thailand and Myanmar incinerated well over US$1 billion worth of illicit drugs in order to combat their image as the nexus of the international drug trade. Now, however, much of the energy formerly devoted to poppy cultivation has turned to the production of **methamphetamines** (locally known as *ya ba*), which are much less easily detected by authorities. Backpacker tales of full moon acid parties on Ko Phangan have become the stuff of legends, inspiring many travelers to venture south in search of the perfect tropical high. Full moon parties don't just draw tourists, however; the police are also out in full force (see **Sex, Drugs, and Lunar Cycles,** p. 339). Despite the medical and social dangers, one Thai Senator has spoken out in favor of the **legalization** of methamphetamines as a political move to undermine the United Wa State Army (see **Thai-Burmese Relations,** p. 24), believed by Bangkok to be the source of most regional poppy products.

AIDS

A thriving sex and intravenous drug industry drove the **Acquired Immune Deficiency Syndrome (AIDS)** to epidemic status in parts of Thailand during the late 1990s. By the end of 1999, 66,000 people had died of HIV/AIDS in Thailand. Medical researchers warned that the country's AIDS-related deaths would total approximately 286,000 by the beginning of the new millennium, and many feared that the disease was spreading to new sectors of Thai society. Today, these trends are slowly reversing. The effects of **safe-sex practices** such as condom use, first advocated in the early 1990s by **Senator Mechai Viravaidya** (justly dubbed "Mr. Condom"), are now becoming apparent in HIV/AIDS statistics. The use of condoms in commercial sex is up from 14% to 95%, and protective measures have resulted in a 90% decrease in the rate of Sexually Transmitted Diseases (STDs). Traditionally, AIDS prevention efforts have focused on **prostitutes** and those intimately involved in the skin trade. Illegal immigrants to Thailand make up a large percentage of workers in the sex industry, and they have little to no access to federally funded HIV/AIDS prevention and treatment programs. But **drug users** are now seen as the main obstacle in Thailand's path to victory over HIV because the proportion of new infections in this category has grown steadily. Recent budget cuts have also severely hampered the efforts of **AIDS awareness programs.** Thailand introduced an inexpensive **AIDS cocktail** during the summer of 2002 designed to consolidate patients' medications. The generic Thai form of the drug created by three Western pharmaceutical companies will cut patients' medical bills in half, making the retroviral medicine accessible to more people.

GRASSROOTS ACTIVISM IN LAMPHUN

Widening gaps between urban and rural populations plague the nation as a whole, but land controversies between landless farmers and wealthier investors flare up regularly in the northern province of **Lamphun.** Land ownership in Thailand is concentrated in the hands of 10% of the population, leaving 1.5 million farming households out in the cold. The latest outbreak of tensions occurred in April 2002 when activists and landless farmers occupied private land that was not being used. An official investigation revealed that the authenticity of the land deeds for the private property was indeed debatable, but the **corrupt officials** who were responsible for the shady dealings went unpunished. Northern farmers also complain that they are fighting an uphill battle against the prejudices of people from Bangkok and other large cities. Many small communities had formed in protected forested areas even before laws in Bangkok prohibited it. And although officials claim that villagers have been aware of their possible **eviction** from these areas since 1994, these communities are still protesting what they perceive as an unfair policy. The agitation of these farmers has spurred plans to test a **model land reform program** in Lamphun that could later serve as a blueprint for nation-wide restructuring. Academics say that this plan should begin with a blanket amnesty for Lamphun farmers who have knowingly or unknowingly violated land laws. Moreover, officials should enforce the 1954 **Land Act,** which would confiscate the deeds to land that has been unused for ten years or has been obtained through illegal channels.

SURVIVING "SURVIVOR"

For centuries, **Ko Tarutao** and the surrounding islands of the Andaman Sea near the Thai-Malaysian border have been home to the **Chao Lay,** or Sea Gypsies, who have managed to maintain their own distinct language, nomadic life style, and animist religion (see **Animism,** p. 13). Recovering from the lawless days of World War II when it was a famed pirate hide-out, Tarutao and the 51 surrounding islands became Thailand's first national marine park in 1974. The park is home to approximately 25% of the world's species of fish, and three species of endangered species of migratory sea turtles breed on the island annually. In the local language, Tarutao means "old," "mysterious," or "primitive." Perhaps it was this mystique that drew executives at the American CBS television network to the island when they were searching for a site for the fifth season of the reality TV show **"Survivor,"** to be shot during the summer of 2002. However, controversies arose during filming about **extra-territorial rights** that the Thai government was creating in their preferred treatment of the Americans over the Thai **fishermen** who use the abundant marine life in the area as the source of their livelihood. The provincial governor requested that the "Survivor" production team allow local fishermen seeking shelter from the torrential monsoon rains that drench the area from May to October to dock their boats on the island. However, fishermen still reported being chased away from the sheltered bays during the monsoon rains by the production company's patrol boats; they were also forbidden from fishing within 2km of Tarutao for fear they will disrupt filming. **Suthichai Viriyakosol,** chief of the marine park, agreed that locals had to be kept away; the **Law Society of Thailand,** however, insisted that CBS's alleged actions constituted human rights violations. The National Film board denied that fishermen were prevented from landing on the island.

SCRIPTURAL DEBATES

In a nation that takes its Buddhist scriptural differences as seriously as Brazil takes its soccer, the most recent controversy is not unusual. For the past few years Thailand has been embroiled in a dispute involving the country's most prominent and well-respected monk, **Phra Dhammapitaka,** who has accused **Wat Dhammakhaya** of polluting Theravada Buddhist scripture with elements of Mahayana Buddhism to serve its own purposes. Comparing the *Tripitaka* text to a nation's constitution, Phra Dhammapitaka worries that if it isn't cleared up, this misconception could rot the roots of Thai Buddhism. The argument centers on the question of whether the state of nirvana possesses *atta*, self, or *anatta*, non-self. While Wat Dhammakhaya, claims that there is no scriptural evidence that nirvana is *atta*, Phra Dhammapitaka maintains that the Buddha's teaching specifically describes nirvana as a state free of defilement and therefore of *anatta*. The majority of international Buddhism experts agree with Phra Dhammapitaka's interpretation. Another point cited by Phra Dhammapitaka is Dhammakhaya's teaching that heaven can be achieved solely through their methods of meditation and donations. In late 2000, **Phra Dhammachayo,** the abbot of Wat Dhammakhaya was removed from his post on charges of sexual misconduct and embezzlement. The Dhammapitaka-Dhammakhaya debate subsequently led to the drafting of a law, known as the **Sangha bill,** that many perceive as potentially infringing on fundamental freedoms of speech, granting some senior monks virtual immunity from the press and bypassing standard slander defence proceedings. Additionally, the ambiguous wording of this bill would make it difficult for the media to challenge monks on sexual misconduct allegations and the increasing commercialization of Buddhism, a hot topic in Thailand today. Recent religious betrayals include a monk who had a penchant for hitting the town after evening prayers and indulging in the extravagances of Thai nightlife. Another monk repeatedly impersonated a womanizing police officer; he was eventually caught on videotape. The question of the Sangha bill has initiated a power play between rival clerical factions, each claiming to represent the majority opinion.

THAI-BURMESE RELATIONS

Since the Burmese sacked the Thai capital of Ayutthaya in 1767 (see **The Fall of Ayutthaya,** p. 17), Thai-Burmese relations have been off and on—at best. Most Thai view the Burmese with suspicion and antipathy. Thai and Burmese officials both claim that relations are also complicated by a lack of "mutual understanding." On the Thai side, Bangkok's Chulalongkorn University recently instituted a masters program in Southeast Asian studies in order to remedy this problem. The issue of illicit drugs has only added to the Thai-Burmese bout of "he said, she said." The Thais have blamed the **Wa,** a Burmese ethnic group, for the steady flow of **amphetamines** into Thailand; the Burmese counter with accusations that the **Shan** rebel army, supported by the Thai military, is equally involved in the regional drug trade.

The most recent controversy between the two neighbors erupted in May 2002 when officials in Yangon accused the Thai military of firing shells over the border during a routine Thai military exercise. Myanmar claimed that Thailand's action supported ethnic Shan rebels and closed all border checkpoints with Thailand indefinitely. Many Burmese soccer fans and gamblers were resentful because the upset in border relations meant that Burmese television stations were unable to broadcast live coverage of the 2002 World Cup. Both Thailand and Myanmar have played the **nationalism** card in this controversy. *Bang Rachan,* a Thai story about a village's brave stand against Burmese military aggression, is a book with dramatic and cinematic adaptations that seems to resurface whenever the Thai government needs to bolster nationalism with an anti-Burmese tint. Similarly, the Burmese military junta uses nationalism to consolidate its political power and legitimacy, requiring citizens to fly the flag and stepping up anti-Thai rhetoric. A Burmese journalist has wryly commented that the Burmese military junta's recent domestic xenophobic slant is the result of a failed attempt to unify its people. **Ma Ta Win,** a Burmese writer, published articles in the state-sponsored newspaper *New Light of Myanmar* that were interpreted in Bangkok as defamation of their Thai Monarchy. Given the Thai reverence for the Monarchy, it is not surprising that Ma Ta Win is now *persona non grata* in Thailand. Moreover, the Thai government has demanded an official apology from Myanmar. In order to prevent the further deterioration of relations, the Thai government has forbidden army radio programs and senior military officers from commenting on Thai-Burmese issues.

The Burmese military has teamed up with the United Wa State Army, led by reclusive druglord **Wei Hsieo-kang,** to wage a military offensive against the Shan. In late June 2002, they decided to attack the Shan from the rear to recapture the outpost at Kaw Muang, crossing the Thai border in the process. Disgruntled Thai troops fired warning shots and informed Yangon that under no circumstances could Myanmar wage war on its enemies from Thai territory again.

In early July, Yangon withdrew its troops from the region without giving any specified explanation. Some believe their withdrawal was due to surprise at the heavy casualties suffered. The government suppressed exact casualty statistics, however, newspapers have been forbidden from publishing the obituaries of soldiers killed, and mourning families have been advised against performing traditional funerals. Some note that border conflicts give Burmese generals a convenient excuse to ignore the "problem" of talks with opposition leader, **Aung San Suu Kyi,** who was released from house arrest in May 2002. A plot by the **Ne Win** family to overthrow the government in early 2002 has left the Yangon junta feeling vulnerable and paranoid, fearing that the army may have divided loyalties. Even those outside of government circles, however, are not oblivious to **General Than Shwe**'s tactic of using the border skirmishes to unify the army.

But Thailand cannot turn a blind eye to internal Burmese affairs. Military offensives launched against tribal groups in the border area have flooded Thailand with **refugees.** At the end of 2001, Thailand was hosting 227,000 refugees in camps that stretch the length of the Thai-Burmese border from Ratchaburi to Mae Hong Son; only about 700 of these asylum seekers were not from Myanmar. Hidden deep in the jungle away from the usual backpacker routes, most refugee camps have a culture of their own, running on Burmese time (half an hour earlier than Thailand) and using Burmese dialects rather than Thai as their *lingua franca.* Nearly 20% of the refugees in the camps were tortured before fleeing Myanmar. Recently, 11 ethnic Shan women (the youngest was 12 years old) escaped into Thailand to break the silence surrounding the Burmese army's systematic rape of minority women. The collaborating reports of two NGOs, the **Shan Human Rights Foundation** and the **Shan Women's Action Network,** are finally being taken seriously after strong statements by the US State Department that drew international attention to the situation. For information on the Karen refugees, visit www.karen.org.

CULTURE

CUSTOMS & ETIQUETTE

THE THREE SPIRITS

The Thai attitude toward life rests on three major concepts. The first, *jai yen,* explains the Thai aversion to any sort of confrontation, especially in public. Most Thais avoid raising their voices or displaying any visible irritation, instead embracing the idea of *mai pen rai,* literally translated as "it can't be helped, so why bother?" This verbal equivalent of a shrug is ideally complemented by the last of the three Thai spirits, *sanuk,* which literally means "fun." Thais believe that everything in life should have a little bit of *sanuk,* or else everything degenerates into mere drudgery. Join in the national water fight in April (see **Festivals,** p. 38) for a healthy helping of *sanuk* in action.

HEADS UP

According to an ancient Hindu belief (now incorporated into Buddhism as well), the head is the most sacred part of the body, and, by extension, the feet are the most unclean. A pat on the head in Thailand is neither playful nor cute—it's simply disrespectful. Similarly, don't stretch your feet out toward an image of the Buddha in a temple or toward another person sitting across from you, especially if he or she is older. Shoes, even more unclean than feet, are unwelcome in temples and most private homes.

WAI NOT?

To show respect, put palms together at chest level, pointing your fingers away from you, and gently bow your head. This is called a *wai*. The degree to which your waist bends as you perform a *wai* is determined by your social status relative to the other person. Older people receive lower—and therefore more respectful—*wais*. You should never perform a *wai* to a child; you will only embarrass yourself and make everyone around you uncomfortable. Inanimate objects that should receive a *wai* include **spirit houses,** miniature temples blessed by Brahman priests that house the spiritual guardians of the land on which the house resides.

TABOOS

The tourism industry has so successfully marketed Thailand for its tolerance that many travelers mistakenly think that the Thai take a generally laissez-faire attitude. This is simply not the case. Don't ever speak disparagingly of the Monarchy, and avoid dropping, defacing, or even stepping on currency or stamps, which carry the king's portrait. When near a portrait of King Bhumibol or any past Thai king, never raise your head above the head in the portrait. Be especially careful in restaurants and public buses, which are often plastered with royal portraits. In short, don't mess with the man whose name means "Strength of the Land, Incomparable Power." The Thai speak in a special language of higher respect when referring to the **Monarchy.** Always remove your **shoes** when entering a home or temple even though your Thai hosts may profess to accept your *farang* ways, assuring you it's okay to keep them on. Thais appreciate foreigners who make an effort. Ladies, keep your **clothes** to your elbows and knees so as not to be mistaken for a Patpong serveuse, and never touch a monk or give him anything directly. Similarly, **public displays of affection** between lovers are frowned upon. Affectionate same-sex caresses or hugs are commonplace and rarely have sexual overtones. Despite its liberal tolerance of different cultures, Thailand does imprison foreigners for actions considered sacrilegious.

STAND AND DELIVER

Remember your national anthem? The Thais certainly remember theirs. Visitors to Thailand are struck by how citizens respond so patriotically to their national anthem and the national flag. Whether they're in the bus or train station, on the street or in the market, all Thai people stop what they're doing when they hear the anthem (and they do, indeed, hear it often). In some smaller cities, traffic comes to a screeching halt. Thailand's national flag is raised each morning at 8am and lowered at 6pm. If you don't stand still, old ladies will stare with disapproval, children will laugh and point, and your karma value will take a serious nose-dive, greatly increasing your chances of being reborn as, say, a termite. So, to be termite-free in the next life, respect Thailand's national custom—be still and stand up when the anthem is played before movies and public events.

THE FLAG

Historians believe that the first Thai national flag was flown in 1680 when a French diplomatic ship sailed into the Chao Phraya River. They presume that the flag was flown earlier, but there's no documentation to prove its existence. At the time it was a rectangular red flag, but in 1816 Singapore declared that Siamese ships needed a more distinctive flag for trading purposes. Coincidentally, King Rama II had just purchased his third white elephant, the sacred Thai symbol of royalty. So, to the middle of the flag he logically added a white elephant, with its trunk facing the flag post. Ninety-nine years later, however, King Rama IV saw the flag being flown upside down in a rural village in the North. He promptly eliminated the elephant from the flag and redesigned it entirely before he had returned home to his palace. With European patterns as his template, he created the new flag to have five horizontal stripes: red, white, blue, white, red. Being both horizontally and vertically symmetrical, the flag could never be flown upside down. The modern flag, which is raised every morning at 8am and taken down every evening at 6pm and accompanied by the national anthem (see **Stand and Deliver,** above), was officially declared as such on September 28, 1917.

FOOD

FRUIT

As if to top the wildlife and scenery, Thailand's fruit is colorful, exotic, and occasionally dangerous. The most controversial fruit at the market is the **durian.** Its smell is so potent that the fruit has been banned from public places. For centuries, people have either loved or hated the taste—see for yourself. A large fruit from an enormous tree, durians are considered dangerous to pick due to their weight and hard shells. Custard-like, they are high in protein, minerals, and fats, making excellent milk shakes and ice cream. Roughly the size of an orange, **mangosteens** are dark red (purple if past ripe) and are innately repellent to insects. The **jackfruit** originated in India but frequents the Thai marketplace—its pointy shell is quite memorable. It is the largest edible tree-grown fruit. **Breadfruit** has a dual identity: fruit when ripe, vegetable when mature. It usually just tastes like a potato, though. The most popular fruit in China, the **lychee** has been cultivated for over a millennium. Until 1950, it was only available as a nut, with the fruit dried inside the shell; now the juicy, delicate fruit can be eaten by biting through the squash ball-sized shell. Don't eat the seed, it's toxic. The **longan** is Thailand's greatest fruit export. In 2002, the Thai Commerce Ministry launched a campaign to boost its fruit exports, and in August 2002, they sent 100 tons of longans to Bangladesh and other nations at a lowered price.

LIFE AND TIMES

The average speed of a car in Bangkok during rush hour traffic is under 4km/hr.

Modern-day Thailand was known as Siam until 1939 when it changed its name to *Prathet Thai* (Land of the Free).

The white stripe on the Thai flag symbolizes the country's adherence to Buddhism; the wide blue center represents the monarchy, and the red stripes stand for the lifeblood of the Thai people themselves.

You should never bring a white rose to a funeral in Thailand because it is believed that it will only make the spirit more sad than it already is.

Bangkok Airways has a 99% rate of punctuality.

If you fit the Thai definition of "hippie," posted at all border checkpoints, chances are you will be stopped. The definition includes people with open-toed shoes, tie-dyed clothing, and men with long hair.

It is illegal to use or take a picture of the king without official permission; if you take a picture as he passes, you will go to jail.

As the first to bring chillis to Thailand, Portuguese merchants revolutionized Thai cuisine; chillis are not indigenous.

In Thailand, "Mc" has become synonymous with "hamburger," so Thais will order a "Mc" instead of a burger regardless of whether or not they're in a McDonald's.

Dunkin' Donuts opened its 1000th international store in 1995 in Thailand.

When eating in groups in Thailand, it's impolite to get up while others are still eating.

Mangosteens always have a scar at one end; this scar is the remnant of a flower. Counting the number of remnant flower parts in the scar will tell you how many segments of fruit are inside.

In Thailand, a traditional remedy for people who suffer from bad breath is to chew on oversized guava peels.

COCONUTS

Close on the heels of the tomato fruit-or-vegetable debate is the coconut fruit-or-nut dispute. Actually, the coconut is all three: fruit, vegetable, and nut—and technically classified as a drupe! The hard, green, oval fruit is 300-450mm long and has a thick husk around its *copra* (nut), which is the coconut you know and love. And the young coconut palm is a vegetable. According to an Indonesian proverb, the coconut has more uses than there are days in a year. Vegetable oil, milk, alcohol, sugar, rope, and porcupine wood are among its products. First documented in Sanskrit and then introduced to Europe in the 6th century, the coconut was finally named by the Portuguese in the 15th century. Its rapid spread throughout the tropics was achieved naturally; a combination of the proximity of palm trees to the ocean and the buoyancy of the fruit facilitated the coconut's quick multiplication.

HERBS

One of the most familiar Thai ingredients—**chili**—was actually not incorporated into the cuisine until Portuguese missionaries brought it over from South America in the 17th century. **Lemon grass,** the integral ingredient in most curries, is native to Thailand and actually looks like long grass. Thais also use relatives galanga and ginger for flavoring. Shallots, cumin, and tumeric are common ingredients. All these herbs have several **therapeutic properties,** including stomachic, respiratory, cardiac, antimicrobial and diuretic benefits.

TRADITIONAL DISHES

Though internationally considered distinct, Thai food today is actually a collection of influences and spices from Asia, India, South America, and Europe. The Chinese brought the technique of frying to Southeast Asia. While taking ideas from India, Thais replace spices with herbs and curries.

It is a sea-based cuisine, with most of its indigenous ingredients (fish, vegetables, and herbs) taken directly from Thailand's rivers and oceans. A **traditional Thai meal** focuses on a harmony of spices, tastes, and textures. It always includes a fish plate, a vegetable dish, a curry with condiments, and a soup. **Sticky rice,** a special breed of the grain, is everywhere and eaten with everything, even desserts. Backpackers will inevitably eat their weight in **phat thai** by the time they leave Thailand. Pan-fried noodles, garlic, bean sprouts, peanuts, eggs, dried red chili, and shallots are the defining ingredients in this über-common dish. Fried and veggie-stuffed **spring rolls,** or *po pia thot,* are similarly ubiquitous. **Green curry,** made of lemon grass, cilantro, coriander root, garlic, jalapeño peppers, and galanga, is mixed with meat or fish for another common meal.

THE ARTS

HISTORY

ARCHITECTURE. Classical Thai architecture focused primarily on **religious structures**. Greatly influenced by the Khmer of central and eastern Thailand during the Sukhothai period, Thai Buddhist architects managed successfully to fuse external influences with indigenous ideals and existing styles to create structures that mirrored the paradoxical Thai way of life—flamboyant yet tranquil. Structures built during that period often sport ornate gold leaf, mother-of-pearl inlay, and porcelain tiles. They consist principally of carved stone and are bound by vegetable glue. Buddhist **monasteries** are the finest examples of Thai architecture. The **bot,** or main chapel, is a tall, oblong building with a three-level, steeply sloped, layered roof that houses the principal Buddha image and serves as the site of most ceremonies. The highest corners of the *bot* end in sharp points called **chofa,** which represent swans, the carriers of Brahma. Similar to the *bot,* the **wiharn** holds fewer Buddha images and functions primarily as a place for meetings, meditation, and sermons. The **sala** is an open, gazebo-like structure for meditation and preaching. Above some monastic compounds looms a tapering, spire-like tower, called a **phra chedi.** Derived from the Indian **stupa,** the *chedi* houses the possessions and cremated remains of high priests, members of royalty, and the Buddha. While the most spectacular example of classical Thai Buddhist architecture is Bangkok's **Wat Phra Kaew** (see p. 113), **Wat Benchamabophit** (see p. 116), in Bangkok's Dusit district, is widely considered the most impressive example of modern Thai Buddhist architecture. By the end of the 20th century, increased contact with Europeans and North Americans led to the steady decline of traditional Thai architecture. Thai architects began turning to Western greats such as **Frank Lloyd Wright** and **Miles Van Der Rohe** for inspiration. The late 20th century saw a revolution in architectural materials and style that emphasized the Western concepts of industrialism and functionalism.

DANCE AND DRAMA. In their classical forms, Thai dance and drama are inseparable. The three main types of dramatic media in Thai culture are **khon, lakhon,** and **likay.** The first two forms are generally patronized by the elite, but *likay* is favored in the countryside among poorer Thais, making it the most popular of the three. *Khon,* or masked dance drama, is based on Indian temple dances and rituals; its various stories come exclusively from the Indian epic, the *Ramayana,* known in Thai as the **Ramakien,** which recounts the triumph of good over evil. The plot follows the adventures of the hero, **Phra Ram,** on his quest to recover his consort, **Nang Sida,** who was abducted by wicked **King Thotsakand of Longa.** Over the centuries, this Indian tale has been adapted to Thai culture, with certain portions expanded and others reduced or dropped completely. During the Ayutthaya period, only men performed *khon* drama; women didn't

All statues in the image of the Buddha are "leased" from their makers because they are considered too sacred to be assigned any material value and can therefore never be bought or sold.

Bangkok boasts nearly 400 temples.

The avenue from Bangkok's Grand Palace to the new Dusit Palace was modeled after the Parisian Champs Elysées.

Wat Phra Kaew has more carvings and ornamentation per square centimeter than any other comparable structure in the world.

The architect of Bangkok's Wat Benchamabophit was one of King Rama V's brothers; he was dissatisfied with the blueprints and wanted to forget about the whole thing. The king saw the plans, however, and ordered them carried out.

When you burn incense, always light three or more sticks.

A complete performance of the Ramakien (with 311 characters) would take over 720 hours (one month).

appear on stage until the mid-19th century because the movements were considered too strenuous for the female frame. With the exception of the leading male and female characters, all actors wear elaborate masks. As in Greek drama, verses are recited by a chorus that sits next to a small band known as a **piphat.** *Khon* is performed with a great deal of stylized action; the movements are suggested by motifs in the music. The *lakhon* form of drama is less structured and stylized than *khon*. Masks are reserved for monkeys, demons, and other non-human, non-celestial creatures. Like *khon*, *lakhon* is derived from the *Ramakien* but also adds stories from Thai folk tales and Buddhist *Jatakas*. **Lakhon chatri** is a simple play performed at shrines for the benefit of gods. **Lakhon nai,** with a traditionally all-female cast, dramatizes romantic stories and focuses on graceful movements. **Lakhon nok,** once performed only by men, is characterized by quick movements, fast-paced music, and risqué humor. In contrast to *khon* and *lakhon*, the *likay* style is bawdy and humorous with loud, sharp music, lyrics sprinkled with sexual innuendos, improvisation, pantomime, and social satire. It's often performed at festivals, combining local and court stories to create a workable plot.

LITERATURE. The most enduring work of Thai literature is the *Ramakien*, the Thai version of the Indian epic, the *Ramayana*. Early versions of this lengthy document were lost when Ayutthaya was sacked in 1767; by far the most famous of the three surviving versions was written in 1798 by **King Rama I.** This version, written in conjunction with several courtiers who were close to the king, incorporates uniquely Thai and Buddhist attributes and portrays the rites, traditions, and customs of the Ayutthaya state. Given early Thai literature's focus on religion, **Sunthon Phu** (1786-1855) revolutionized the tradition with his portrayal of the emotions and adventures of common people in a common language that all classes could understand. His 30,000-line poem, **Phra Aphaimani,** is arguably Thailand's most famous literary work. It details the physical and emotional journey that an exiled prince must complete before he can return victorious to his kingdom. Modern Thai literature, impelled both by foreign influences and by changing perceptions of the individual's place in society, has picked up on this trend of addressing personal and social problems.

MUSIC. In all, there are over 50 types of Thai musical instruments, including local variations. Uniquely Thai musical instruments have onomatopoetic names such as **krong, chap, ching, krap,** and **pia.** Simpler instruments were combined to create more complex sounds. Still more instruments were developed as Thai music assimilated elements of the Indian, Mon, and Khmer traditions. The oldest surviving Thai songs are from the Sukhothai period. In the Ayutthaya period, music was an official part of court life. Territorial expansion brought instruments and musical styles from neighboring regions such as Myanmar, Malaysia, and Java. During this period, rules defining musical forms were introduced. Songs were composed in a form called **phleng ruang,** a suite of melodies. Three orchestral types of music, appropriate to different occasions, further order Thai musical form: **piphat** is used at ceremonies and in the theater; **kruang sai** is used in performance at village festivals; and **mahori** often accompanies vocalists. Contemporary Thai music takes many forms. Regional folk music, less studied than classical music, is common. One of the most popular styles is **luk thung,** country music, which has developed into upbeat electronic versions. **Western pop music** was introduced to Thailand in the 1950s, and many modern groups fuse it with traditional Thai music, creating a unique sound. An internationally recognized **jazz** aficionado, **His Majesty King Bhumibol Adulyadej** is an accomplished saxophone player with many compositions to his name, one of which was featured in a 1950s Broadway show. He also has his own **palace jazz band.** Instead of using a five-note scale like many other Asian countries, Thai music works on a **seven-note scale.** The music composed in this unique system was passed down orally, but many today fear that the institutional memory of traditional Thai music may soon run out. Therefore, many modern Thai musicians are working to invent a system by which traditional Thai music can be translated into western musical notation and thus recorded for future generations.

PAINTING. Like classical architecture and literature, most traditional Thai painting was restricted to religious subjects or was designed for temples, palace interiors, or manuscript illustrations. Rarely the centerpiece of an artistic statement, classical Thai **mural paintings** were meant to complement and enhance the beauty of religious or royal objects they surrounded as well as to inspire faith and meditation in their beholders. The two main mural painting techniques are **tempera** and **fresco.** While the former technique demands that the wall contain no salt, the fresco style, borrowed from Chinese paintings, requires that the paint be applied while the wall itself is still wet. The western artistic concept of perspective was not emphasized; instead, the two-dimensional figures were large or small based on their social importance. Landscapes were usually cursorily painted only to serve as a background for the detailed action in the foreground. This action most often depicted scenes from the Buddha's life or Buddhist *Jataka* stories. Paintings were originally colored using five main pigments: scarlet lake, yellow ochre, ultramarine blue, pipe-clay white, and pot-black. The introduction of Chinese pigments during the Bangkok period enriched the genre's palette; it was not until the mid-19th century, however, that chemical pigments and a western sense of perspective were introduced. Most of the traditional Thai mural paintings that are still in good condition today are from the Ayutthaya, Thonburi, and Bangkok periods. The murals at Bangkok's **Wat Suthat** (see p. 115) and Chiang Mai's **Wat Phra Singh** (see p. 251) are widely considered the finest extant examples of this traditional style of Thai painting. Recently, a greater number of Thai artists are being trained in the western style, and their works have blended the two traditions.

During the Ayutthaya period, the royal court institutionalized arts in order to educate new artisans in the rigid methods—so as to avoid creative variations. The new school was called *Krom Chang Sip Mu,* which means the Organization of the Ten Crafts.

There are roughly 50 different kinds of Thai instruments.

In 1964, King Bhumibol Adulyadej was the first Asian composer to receive honorary membership to the famous Institute of Music and Arts of the City of Vienna.

About 100 years ago, *pinn pia* performances were banned following a fight in which the long neck of the instrument was used to strike and kill somebody.

Each step in the Thai musical scale is slightly under a Western semitone and three-quarters.

There is only one English-language radio station in Chiang Mai; other stations play Western music but are DJed in Thai.

LIFE AND TIMES

In the earliest murals and paintings, all pigments were made from roots, herbs, and berries.

80% of Thai carvings and drawings is done in *kanok,* meaning gold, which is a style noted for its simplicity and elegance.

Popular art was originally a rural art form—it depicted the harvest and life cycles.

There are three schools in Thailand to teach elephants how to paint.

One of the world's largest murals is in the Temple of the Emerald Buddha in Bangkok; it depicts tales from the *Ramakien.*

During the reign of King Rama III, Bangkok's Wat Arun was being decorated with porcelain mosaics, but the artisans ran out of porcelain. The king asked his subjects to contribute porcelain plates and bowls from their own households.

Though the Khmer artistic traditions were initially very influential in Thai sculpture, post-18th-century Khmer sculpture relied on the Thai arts for inspiration instead.

SCULPTURE. Ancient Thai sculpture focused primarily on Buddha images, choosing to emphasize the spirituality of the image over the figure's anatomical details. Who needs muscles or bone structure anyway? The giant seated Buddha at Sukhothai's **Wat Si Chum** (see p. 308) is a prominent example of the artistic achievement of the Sukhothai period. Indeed, the art of casting images of the Buddha was considered the pinnacle of Thai artistic achievement. Innovation and artistic originality were not valued as they were in the West; instead, rigid artistic rules ensured that a relatively uniform tradition was passed down from generation to generation. Thus, the tradition of Thai sculpture r\emained fairly constant until recently. Widely considered the father of the modern Thai art academy, **Corrade Feroze,** an Italian who became a Thai citizen in 1944 (and changed his name to Silpa Bursary), founded the Fine Arts School, which subsequently became Silpakorn University. Several of his students went on to become nationally recognized artists, many of whom subscribe to modern artistic philosophies and borrow from industrial materials or modern technology in order to create their works of art. A recent trend in modern Thai art has been to convert ordinary, everyday objects into works of art.

WEAVING. Even before it became a cottage industry, weaving was an important part of rural life-cycle rituals. A woman spent much time and energy handweaving the material for her wedding dress; and, for the most important day in a man's life, when he entered the monkhood, his mother similarly prepared his saffron robes for him. The female head of the household would also hand-weave all the shrouds to be used at the funerals of each family member. For centuries, village women in the northeast bred silkworms and worked at hand looms to produce bolts and bolts of traditional Thai silk. However, cheaper fabrics imported from China and Japan devastated the industry in the second half of the 19th century. Jump-started by the famous American expatriate **Jim Thompson** (see **The Mystery of Jim Thompson,** p. 114) after World War II, the silk industry soon became symbolic of Thailand on the international market. Today, the company founded by Thompson at **Park Thong Chain** (see p. 195) is still the largest hand-weaving facility in the world. Each region has its own special style and technique; the most famous Thai silk, however, is still woven in the northeast. The **mud-mee** style of silk weaving, characterized by geometrical and zoomorphic designs, is particularly popular. Favored by Her Majesty Queen Sirikit, *mut-mee* requires the most time and skill and is therefore predominantly used at joyous formal occasions such as weddings.

REGIONAL VARIATIONS

ARCHITECTURE. The Khmer were responsible for much of the architectural influences in **Northeastern** Thai architecture. In fact, the first northeastern stone wat complexes, called **prasats,** were built by the Khmer. A distinctive feature of the *prasat* is the central staircase, ornamented with stone *nagas* (serpents), that lead to a main sanctuary area decorated with carvings of scenes from Hindu mythology. A central stone tower, known as a **prang**, often housed images of the Buddha. This synthesis of religious influences adds a distinctive flavor to the artistic traditions of the region. Two of the best regional examples of Khmer architecture in the northeast are **Prasat Hin Phimai** (see p. 196) and **Hin Khao Phanom Rung** (see p. 197).

DANCE. The traditional dance of **Southern** Thailand has been more heavily influenced by dances from India and Sri Lanka than other Thai dances. It is accompanied by an ensemble of a *pi* (oboe), *glong tuk* and a pair of *thap* or *thon* (drums), *krap* (bamboo castanets), and a *mong* (gong). The dancers' movements mimic those of local birds and animals. Another popular southern dance, called the **lakorn chatri**, is performed at the beginning of *wai khru* ceremonies to honor the gods. The costumes for this dance are elaborately decorated with beads. The traditional regional dance of **Northeastern** Thailand is the **soeng**. More earthy and sensual than most other Thai dances, northeastern dances are firmly entrenched in the agrarian tradition and celebrate the festivals and rituals associated with the harvest. Thailand's most popular folk dance, **ram wang**, originated in **Central** and **Eastern** Thailand during World War II, when western ballroom dancing was replacing traditional folk dances. Fearing cultural assimilation, then Premier Phibunsongkhram introduced *ram wang* as a compromise of sorts. Today, it is the standard Thai dance and is still taught in primary and secondary schools. The traditional **Northern** dance is the **kon**, by far more graceful than many other regional dances. It is also more formal, performed primarily at official gatherings.

DRAMA. The earliest Thai dramas are believed to be **nang talung** (shadow plays). Today, performances are rare except for in **Southern** Thailand. The plays depict scenes from other popular dramas but use puppets made from the hides of water buffalo that are then held against back-lit screens. The story line is chanted. In the 19th century, **Northern** folk dances were adapted to the stage after **Phra Ratchachaya Dararatsami**, a princess from Chiang Mai, returned to the north after seeing a popular dance-drama in Bangkok. Ever since, dance and drama have been inseparable in the northern tradition.

MUSIC. Southern Thailand has its own local musical instruments, including the percussion instrument, **tapon.** Folk songs such as **pleng na** (performed during Thai New Year celebrations, ordinations, house-warmings, weddings, and funerals) and **pleng bok** (literally "herald song," sung by groups of singers who make rounds at dusk to bring news to the villagers in the local dialect) rely heavily on improvisation. The music of **Northeastern** Thailand is upbeat and exhilarating with lively rhythms and colorful melodies. A well-known folk style from the northeast, **mo lam** is fast-paced and features a male and a female vocalist who sing as if courting one another, accompanied by a *khaen*. The **pleng khorat,** particularly famous in Nakhon Ratchasima province, involves a series of musical exchanges between groups of female

Made in Thailand for centuries, lacquerware is Thai pottery made completely from natural products: bamboo baskets, burned rice paddy husks, clay, and black lacquer from a tree native to the northern provinces.

On Thai silk, an imprint with Jim Thompson's name is a marker of quality and prestige.

Based on a variety of factors, the World Meteorological Organization declared Bangkok the "world's hottest city."

Buddhist temples are designed to represent the five elements: fire, earth, air, water, and wisdom.

There is an odd number of steps in every staircase in Thailand.

The Thais call their religion *Lanka-vamsa* ("Sinhalese lineage") because of the Sri Lankan influence on Thai Buddhism.

The "Sukhothai Dance" has been reconstructed from images in stone reliefs found at archaeological sites in Sukhothai.

There are over 100 masks for demonic characters in *khon* drama; they are divided into 14 categories to avoid confusion.

Some of the costumes for *khon* drama are so tight that they are actually sewn onto performers just before they go on stage.

King Rama VI classified legitimate theater as two distinct types: either *khon* or *lakhon*. He conspicuously omitted *likay*.

After a *khon* drama mask has been made, it must undergo a special ceremony to "open its eyes" called the *Beuk Phra Netra.*

A total of 143 senior artists have been honored with the title "National Artist of Thailand."

During the late 80s and early 90s, a man named Lam Morrison was considered the most accomplished guitarist ever in Thailand.

The first hip-hop festival in Thailand was held on November 21, 2001 in Bangkok.

In 2002, the annual Asia-Europe Puppet Festival was held in Bangkok's Thailand Cultural Centre.

and male performers without accompaniment. Common in Buriram and Surin, **kan truem** is the native music of the High Khmer, and both the words and music to this song are Khmer in origin. Perhaps not surprisingly, the main instrument is the *kan truem* drum. Another instrument common in northeastern Thai music is the deep **hai song,** an earthen jar with elastic stretched over the opening. This instrument is usually reserved for female players. The centrality of rice cultivation to the lifestyle of the **Central** Thai is evident in their music; one of the most famous regional songs, **rong khak,** celebrates the seasonal rituals of rice cultivation. Most common folk songs include witty repartees between male and female performers, accompanied only by **ching** (small cymbals) or **klong** (drum) to keep time. Accompanying folk songs, **Northern** musical groups form an ensemble called **salaw saw serng** after their three instruments: **salaw, pisaw,** and **serng.** Both the *salaw* and the *serng* are stringed instruments, while the *pisaw* is a woodwind. Another common instrument is the stringed **pinn pia,** a result of the regional Lanna influence. *Pinn pia's* elegant, subdued sound and the difficulty of becoming proficient in its technique makes those who master the instrument highly regarded in the community.

SCULPTURE. Lying closer to maritime trading routes, **Southern** Thailand developed unique styles of sculpture based on contact with Indian and Khmer culture. Images of Hindu gods add a layer of complexity to the Thai religious landscape. Khmer artistic traditions have exerted the greatest influence over the sculpture of the **Northeast.** In Thailand, Khmer art is referred to as the **Lop Buri style,** which produced stone and bronze sculptures mainly of Hindu gods, Bodhisattvas, or Tantric Buddhist deities. Images of the Buddha often included him seated on a coil of the famous seven-headed *naga,* Muchalinda. Also significant are the distinctive Khmer **lintels** of northeastern temples. They feature detailed carvings of Hindu stories and exhibit the skill and craftsmanship of the artists.

CURRENT SCENE

DRAMA. On the cutting edge of modern drama is Swiss expatriate, **Manuel Lutgenhorst** (mlutg@yahoo.com; www.geocities.com/Broadway/Stage/212), the redesigner of New York's Studio54 and designer, director, and writer of many Broadway productions. In an effort to revitalize it and make it relevant to modern society, he recently converted Bertolt Brecht's "The Good Person of Szechwan" into the traditional Thai dramatic style, *likay.* In Thai, the title is **"Kon Dee Muang Nuea"** ("The Good Person of the North"). In classic *likay* fashion, the performance includes improvisational bantering about topics of local interest such as a recent explosion, the prostitution industry, and bureaucratic corruption.

LITERATURE. Former Prime Minister **M.R. Kukrit Pramoj** wrote prolifically. Among his most notable works are **Si Phandin,** describing the court life between the reigns of King Rama V and Rama VII, and **Phai Daeng,** about the conflict between Communism and Buddhism. **Seni Saowaphong,** or Sakdichai Bamrung-phong, often writes about class exploitation and the widening gulf between the rural and the urban. Along similar lines, the protagonist of the late **Suwanee Sukhontha**'s most famous novel, **Khao Chu Kan,** is a young doctor with a promising career lined up in a big city who leaves to work in a rural area where the peasants have little access to modern medicine. **Krisna Asokesin,** on the other hand, writes almost exclusively on more personal issues such as love and family life. All the authors mentioned above have been awarded National Artist status in Thailand or Southeast Asian literary awards, indicating both the accessibility of their styles and the popularity of their subjects.

FILM. While cinemas are common in large cities, about 2000 mobile film units travel from village to village in rural areas of Thailand, offering open-air screenings for large numbers of people. Most of the movies shown, however, are either of the Chinese *kung-fu* or Hollywood variety. Thai films are less popular. Focusing less on deep probes of the Thai cultural psyche than on pure, unadulterated entertainment, Thai films have traditionally been low-budget productions that pack a sensationalist punch. But 2001 seems to have been a turning point for the industry, and Thai movies are beginning to gain recognition on the international film circuit. Co-directed by the **Pang brothers** from Hong Kong, **"Bangkok Dangerous"** is a dramatic thriller to a frenetic techno beat—a change for Thai audiences, who usually favor upbeat comedies. Many film critics have enthusiastically noted the release of director **Nonzee Nimibutr**'s third film, **"Jan Dara"** (2001, Buddy Films), as possibly indicating a new stage of maturity for the Thai film industry. Based on a novel by journalist **Pramoon Un-hathoop** (who writes under the pen name of Utsana Pkleungtham), the movie only passed Thailand's **film censorship board** after repeated screenings. 70% of the board members are police, with only 30% from the actual film industry; however, many filmmakers and directors believe that it's only a matter of time before this number is split evenly. "Jan Dara" ran into trouble with this official body because of the prevalence of sexual themes throughout: the protagonist is caught in a web of Oedipal lusts and primal urges. **Prince Chatreechalerm Yukol**'s much anticipated film, **"Suriyothai"** details the life of a young princess as a 16th-century battle for the throne of Thailand rages above her head. Lasting over three hours, "Suriyothai" is well beyond the attention span of most Western audiences; **Francis Ford Coppola** is chairing the editing committee for the international version. **Yuthlert Sippapak**'s debut film, **"Killer Tattoo,"** takes place in an ambiguous post-IMF future and thinly conceals an anticolonialist ideology—rare for Thai cinema given that Thailand has no colonial experience—underneath a slapstick surface. In the wake of **The Beach,** the blockbuster starring **Leonardo DiCaprio,** foreign films are increasingly being shot in Thailand. The most recent is **Beyond Borders,** a love story starring **Angelina Jolie** and **Clive Owen.** (The movie is actually supposed to be set in Cambodia.) "Beyond Borders" employed 300 Thai technical crew members and a fur-

Manuel Lutgenhorst was the winner of the 13th Asian Games Opening and Closing Ceremony concept.

Like the Thai art of *likay,* Brecht's theory that the actor should be both the character and the actor allows the actor to play freely with the script and its ideas.

A modern Thai painter named Pornchai has started using coffee as his medium of choice in order to give his works a weathered appearance.

Since 1994, "The Simpsons" have been aired every Saturday at 9pm; in 2001, UBC moved it to 8:40pm. It is repeated twice on Sunday and then again on the following Thursday. It has always been subtitled and never dubbed.

The movie "Suriyothai" set records for the Thai film industry: longest shooting time ever, highest budget (400 million baht), and highest grossing movie (110 million baht in three days).

Buffalo horns are the symbol of the pop group Carabao, after the wild buffaloes that are so integral to Thai culture.

More than 200 foreign films were shot in Thailand between 1995 and 1998.

About two million tourists visit James Bond Island, known as Ko Ping Kan, annually.

Though about Thailand, "Brokedown Palace" was filmed in the Philippines because the National Film Board turned down the script.

Carabao was the first Thai band to perform a large outdoor concert.

In 2002, Thailand threatened to cut off relations with the US because an advertisement for a Philadelphia club portrayed the king as an urban, hip-hop guru complete with buzz-cut lines in his hair, bleached highlights, and rhinestone glasses.

The Vengaboys song, "Boom Boom Boom Boom," received increased airtime in Bangkok clubs after the March 3, 2001 explosion of Thai Airlines flight 114, slated to take the Prime Minister to Chiang Mai.

ther 700 locals as extras in the refugee camp scenes. The Thai government has actively promoted the shooting of foreign films in Thailand because it boosts state revenue, but all scripts still have to be approved. Also, the potential environmental damage from the shooting of large commercial films and Western television shows has recently become a very real concern both of the government and of local NGOs.

MUSIC. In the 1960s, Thai pop met folk to create the genre of **protest songs,** which focused primarily on criticizing the US military presence in Thailand. The Thai student band **Caravan** filled the musical vacuum of the 70s with pro-democracy songs that fused Western and Thai styles. Caravan inspired other bands to take up causes. The most famous rock band in modern Thailand, **Carabao,** also sings about social issues such as the AIDS crisis. However, many Thai disagree with their political message and won't attend Carabao concerts for fear of associating themselves with the band's bad-boy image. In the late 1980s, there was a movement to promote ethnic Thai pop music led by Grammy Entertainment Company, a local record label.

SPORTS & RECREATION

MUAY THAI (THAI BOXING)

Muay Thai was developed to keep Thai soldiers battle-ready during the 15th and 16th centuries and also to supplement their swords and pikes in close-range combat. The first boxer to win historic recognition was **Nai Khanom Tom.** Captured by the Burmese, he won his freedom after dispatching a dozen Burmese soldiers in a boxing challenge. When word of his amazing feat reached Thailand, King Naresuan and his generals made Muay Thai a mandatory component of Thai military training. The discipline's roots lie in the Buddhist philosophy of **Tantrasect.** Muay Thai reached the peak of its popularity in the first decade of the 18th century during the reign of Phra Chau Sua, when the nation was at peace. Today these fights, full of ritual, music, and blood, are put on display. Every blow imaginable is legal, with the exception of head-butting. Fighters exchange blows for five three-minute rounds; the winner either knocks out his victim or takes the bout by points (most bouts are decided in the latter manner). Fights are packed with screaming fans, most of whom have money riding on the outcome. While many provinces have venues, most of the best fighting occurs in **Bangkok's Ratchadamnoen** and **Lumpini Boxing Stadiums** (see **Muay Thai (Thai Boxing),** p. 120).

TRADITIONAL PASTIMES

Every year during the hot season, a strong southerly wind lifts handmade **kites** high over Bangkok. Often shaped to represent animals, they are sometimes flown in games of aerial tag. Kite-fighting is even patronized by the king.

Crowds watch and bet on the ill-tempered **Siamese fighting fish.** When let loose in a tank with another, these fish battle to the death in a flurry of fins and scales. The fish are so aggressive that they will often kill themselves trying to attack fish in neighboring jars or tanks. These fish have been raised in households since the Sukhothai period and breeders are constantly developing new varieties that accentuate different qualities of the fish. Their international popularity is a great source of pride for Thais. **Cockfighting** is also popular in the countryside.

HILL TRIBES AND TREKKING

The safest bet when searching for tour guides is to use companies that meet **Tourism Authority of Thailand (TAT)** and **Northern Thailand Jungle Club** (see **Welcome to the Jungle,** p. 253) regulations. Ask around when picking a company and talk to fellow travelers; reputable operations make reports from former customers available. Treks affiliated with guest houses are generally safer than the packages arranged by independent organizations. TAT publishes a list of trekking agencies, indicating those that use licensed guides (who have studied at the Tribal Research Institute in Chiang Mai). Trekking companies, guides, and customers are required by TAT regulations to be registered with the tourist police. Most companies provide insurance, food, accommodations, transportation, and extra supplies like small backpacks. Bring water with you. Go in a group of eight or fewer people, as smaller groups are less disruptive to village culture. The best way to learn about hill tribe culture is to hire a personal guide (500฿ per day). Make sure your guide speaks both English and the languages of the villages on your itinerary.

HEALTH AND SECURITY. Bring a first-aid kit, sunscreen, a hat, mosquito repellent, a water bottle, and long pants. Baby wipes and anti-bacterial cream are also a good idea. Some regions contain malarial mosquitoes; be sure to get the proper medications before you go (see **Insect-Borne Diseases,** p. 54). Before embarking on a trek, try to find a safe place to leave valuables in your absence. TAT recommends that trekkers utilize a bank safety deposit box; there have been numerous reports of credit cards being lifted from guest house "security" boxes. **Bandits** have been known to raid trekking groups. Should this occur, hand over your belongings to the bandits to avoid physical harm. **TAT discourages independent trekking.**

TREKKING ETIQUETTE. Hill tribe societies are being rapidly integrated into Thai society. Their unique, centuries-old cultures are ever changing, and there's no question that tourism speeds up the process. **Always ask before taking photographs.** Some individuals or even whole villages may object even if your guide says it's okay. Ask permission from the specific people you want to photograph. Smile and give a ▨"thumbs-up" sign. Respect people, space, and things, particularly hill tribe beliefs, and be careful about what you touch. For example, the gate at the entrance to Akha villages marks the point past which spirits may not enter; don't touch this. Use the old hiking maxim: see as it is, leave as it was.

A 1358 royal edict banned kites from the royal palace and surrounding areas because the Thai royal families were spending so much time flying kites that they were neglecting affairs of state.

There are 78 kite-fighting rules in Thailand.

Thailand has plans to build a golf course in a heavily mined border area near Laos and Cambodia: nine holes will be in Thailand, nine in Laos, and nine in Cambodia.

Muay Thai (Thai boxing) is the largest spectator "ring sport" in the world; wrestling does not exist in Thailand.

Cockfighting has been going on for over a millennium.

The best fighting cocks are half-jungle fowl.

To show their support for International Narcotics Day, Thailand and Myanmar incinerated 3000kg of opium, 240kg of pure heroin powder, and 40 million speed derivatives.

WHEN TO GO. Of Northern Thailand's three distinct seasons, the cool season (Oct.-Feb.) is the best time for trekking. The vegetation is most lush, and temperatures are usually in the mid-20s (°C) by day, falling to near freezing at night. In the rainy season (July-Sept.), paths are muddy, and raging rivers make rafting fun but dangerous. In the hot season (Mar.-May), the land is parched and the air is dry.

HOLIDAYS & FESTIVALS (2003)

The Thai, Buddhist, and international holidays listed below are current as of the book's publishing date. Many of the religious days, whose dates are not determined by a lunar cycle, will be given a date by the Royal Family or religious VIPs at the beginning of 2003. The listed dates are subject to change. Make sure to check with the Tourism Authority of Thailand before planning to attend one of the festivals or holiday celebrations. Also, note that on national holidays, all banks and most establishments are closed.

DATE	NAME & LOCATION	DESCRIPTION
Jan. 1	New Year's Day	International celebration of the passing year.
Jan. 17-19	Bosang Umbrella Festival, Chiang Mai	Vivacious celebration of Bosang's famous umbrellas with fairs, crafts, and contests.
Feb. 1-2	Flower Festival, Chiang Mai	Thailand's tropical answer to the Rose Parade.
Early Feb.	Phra Nakhon Khiri Fair, Phetchaburi	Local cultural performances, art shows, and contests.
Feb. 4-7	Chinese New Year	Celebrated by nearly all of Thailand, as most Thais have Chinese blood.
Feb.	Dragon & Lion Parade, Nakhon Sawan	Golden Dragon, lion, and ancient deity parade with bands and the Chinese community.
Feb. 16	Makha Bucha	Full moon of third lunar month. Commemoration of the 1250 disciples of Buddha coming to hear him preach. Public holiday.
Mar.-Apr.	Poi Sang Long, Mae Hong Son	Stunning Shan tribal celebration.
Apr. 6	Chakri Day	National holiday to commemorate the first king of the present dynasty to ascend to the throne.
Apr. 13-16	Songkran, Thai New Year	Best in Chiang Mai, the holiday is known for water: washing with scented water and throwing water at everyone.
Apr.	Pattaya Festival, Phuket	Delicious food, floral floats, and fireworks.
May 1	Labour Day	Banks, factories, and offices closed.
May 6	Coronation Day	National holiday.
May	Royal Ploughing Ceremony, Bangkok	Official beginning of rice-planting outside the Royal Palace, with re-enactments of ancient Brahman rituals. Government holiday.
May	Bangfai Rocket Festival, Northeast Thailand	Celebration for a plentiful upcoming rain season for rice-planting. Beautiful homemade rockets launched.
May 16	Wisakha Puja	*Full moon of sixth lunar month.* Birth, enlightenment, and death of Buddha. Holiest holiday, celebrated at every temple with candlelight processions.
May-June	Wai Kru Day	Usually a Thursday, specific date varies from school to school. A day for students to honor their teachers for their important role in children's lives.
June	Phi Ta Khon, Loei	People dress as spirits and carry Buddha images while monks read the story of the visit of his incarnation.

DATE	NAME & LOCATION	DESCRIPTION
July 6	Khao Pansa Day: Buddhist Lent begins. Candle Festival, Ubon Ratchathani	Townspeople celebrate the monks' Buddhist Rains Retreat by walking up to the temple with ornate, huge candles. A time of giving up indulgences, the first day is commemorated with particular attention by students.
Aug.	Rambutan Fair, Surat Thani	Anniversary of the first rambutan tree planted in Surat Thani is commemorated with fruit floats and performing monkeys.
Aug.	Cake Festival	Chamber of Commerce holiday for Southern Thailand's yummy pastries.
Aug. 12	The Queen's Birthday, Mother's Day	Best celebration is in Bangkok, as the city is draped in lights. Thais celebrate their queen's birthday by honoring their own mothers.
Sept. 7-8	Boat Races, Phichit	Annual regatta down the Nan River.
Sept.	Barbecue Festival	Chamber of Commerce holiday for Thai food.
Oct. 5-14	Vegetarian Festival, Phuket	Chinese festival enjoyed since the 1800s with parades, rituals, and of course only vegetarian food to honor two emperor gods.
Oct. 18-21	Wax Castle & Boat Racing Festival, Sakhon Nakhon	Procession of beeswax carvings of Buddhist temples to mark the end of the Buddhist Rains Retreat, trailed by boat races.
Oct.	Buffalo Races, Chonburi	Water buffaloes stop work and race each other and farmers.
Oct.	Nakhon Phanom Boat Procession	Evening ritual in which thousands of exquisitely carved boats with candles atop them are placed on the Mekong.
Oct. 23	Chulalongkorn Day	King Rama V died on this day. National holiday.
Nov. 16-17	Elephant Roundup, Surin	Celebration of the majestic beasts, with 100 of them performing, some even in medieval costume.
Nov.	Hill Tribe Festival, Chiang Rai	Cultural performances and handicrafts.
Nov. 23- Dec. 5	River Kwai Bridge Week, Kanchanaburi	Remembrance of the site, with historical and archaeological exhibitions; rides on vintage trains available.
Nov. 9-12	Loi Krathong & Candle Festival	Best in Sukhothai, where it originated, with fireworks, folk dancing, banana-leaf river floats. Also good in Chiang Mai.
Dec.	Trooping of the Colors, Bangkok	In the Royal Plaza, the elite Royal Guards, dressed in bright colors, renew their allegiance to the Royal Family.
Dec. 5	His Majesty's birthday, Father's Day	Thais celebrate their king's birthday by honoring their own fathers.
Dec. 10	Constitution Day	Thai military pays homage to the constitutional statue in Bangkok, but no festivities ensue. National holiday.
Dec. 12-18	World Heritage Site Celebration, Ayutthaya	Celebration of the past with exhibitions and traditional performances.
Dec. 25	Christmas	Not a public holiday, but celebrated by schoolchildren.

ADDITIONAL RESOURCES

GENERAL HISTORY

The Chastening: Inside the Financial Crisis That Rocked the Global Financial System and Humbled the IMF, by Paul Blustein (2002). A cogent description of the Asian Financial Crisis of 1997.

Southeast Asia: An Introductory History, by Milton Osborne (1995). A basic survey of Southeast Asian history, revised and updated many times.

Thailand's Durable Premier: Phibun through Three Decades 1932-1957, by Kobkua Suwannathat-Pian (1996). A biography of Thailand's most controversial and influential political leader, Field Marshal Phibunsongkhram.

Thailand's Struggle for Democracy: The Life and Times of M.R. Seni Pramoj, by David Van Praagh (1996). A dramatic documentation of the turbulent history of Thai politics.

The Lands of Charm and Cruelty: Travels in Southeast Asia, by Stan Sesser (1994). A collection of essays originally published in the *New Yorker*.

Modern Thailand: A Volume in the Comparative Societies Series, by Robert Slagter and Harold Kerbo (1999). An educational review of contemporary Thai institutions and social change.

Thailand: A Short History, by David Wyatt (1982). The best one-volume history of Thailand. Available in Thailand.

CULTURE

Night Market: Sexual Cultures and the Thai Economic Miracle, by Ryan Bishop and Lillian Robinson (1998). Explores the trade-off between the lives of young Thai women who are lured into the prostitution industry and the country's economic recovery.

When Elephants Paint: The Quest of Two Russian Artists to Save the Elephants of Thailand, by Dave Eggers, Vitaly Komar, and Alexander Melamid (2000). From the author of *A Heartbreaking Work of Staggering Genius* and two Russian artists, this book tells the artists' story of their comedic pop art of elephants, with the profits, which are bigger than the elephants, going to Thai elephant sanctuaries.

Endangered Relations: Negotiating Sex and AIDS in Thailand, by Chris Lyttleton (2000). Describes the intersection of Thai conceptions of sexuality and public health measures to reverse the nation's infamous AIDS/HIV trend.

Genders and Sexualities in Modern Thailand, ed. by Peter Jackson and Nerida Cook (2000). A compilation of essays interpreting the roles and patterns of gender in Thailand since the 1800s.

Peoples of the Golden Triangle: Six Tribes in Thailand, by Paul and Elaine Lewis (1998). A historiography of local hill tribes in Northern Thailand, with personal vignettes.

FICTION AND NON-FICTION

Singing to the Dead: A Missioner's Life Among Refugees from Burma, by Victoria Armour-Hilleman (2002). The journal of a Catholic missionary working with displaced Mon refugees at an illegal camp in Thailand.

4,000 Days: My Life and Survival in a Bangkok Prison, by Warren Fellows (1998). The true story of an Australian who was caught for trafficking heroin and spent 12 years suffering cruelty in a Thai jail.

The Beach, by Alex Garland (1997). A page-turner narcotics adventure about backpackers in search of paradise. A perfect beach read.

Ban Vinai, by Lynellyn Long (1992). First-person narrative based on the author's ethnographic research in Ban Vinai, one of many Thai camps sheltering Laotian and Cambodian refugees in the 1970s.

The Poison River, by Steve Raymond and Mal Karmon (1994). A true story of an American businessman wrongly accused of operating a lucrative international business in sex tourism in Thailand and imprisoned for two years.

Monsoon Country, by Pira Sudham (1981). Personal documentary of the evolution and even revolution Thai culture and politics endured 1954-1980. Sudham was nominated for the **Nobel Prize** for this work.

The Force of Karma, by Pira Sudham (2001). The sequel to Monsoon Country is more politically controversial and socially provocative, depicting Thai massacres of 1973, 1976 and 1992.

A Fortune-Teller Told Me: Earthbound Travels in the Far East, by Tiziano Terzani (2001). A journalist's land trek through Southeast Asia, focussing on myths, religions, and fortune-tellers.

Siam: Or the Woman Who Shot a Man, by Lily Tuck (2000). A novel highlighting cross-cultural misunderstandings in marriage and daily life and an obsession with a lost American entrepreneur.

FILM

The Bridge On the River Kwai, directed by David Lean, starring Alec Guinness and William Holden (1957). A WWII epic based on a true story about Allied POWs forced by the Japanese to build a bridge connecting Thailand to Burma. The film garnered 7 Academy Awards, including Best Picture.

The Beach, directed by Danny Boyle, starring Leonardo DiCaprio (2000). The movie of the Alex Garland book described above.

The Iron Ladies, directed by Thongkongtoon (2001). Hysterical comedy about a Thai volleyball team, composed of men with varying sexualities, winning the national championship. Second-highest grossing film in Thailand exposes local homophobia.

The Man with the Golden Gun (1974). A classic 007 flick in the Roger Moore era, featuring what is now dubbed "James Bond island."

Mysterious Object at Noon, conceived and directed by Weerasethakul (2001). Documentary written by Thai villagers with a science fiction element.

TRAVEL BOOKS

Dream of a Thousand Lives: A Sojourn in Thailand, by Karen Connelly (2001). A young Western woman's experience working and studying on a small Thai farm.

Travelers' Tales: Thailand, ed. by James O'Reilly and Larry Habegger (1993). A wide-ranging collection of stories about Thailand, Thai culture, and traveling in Thailand. Read about meditating in a Thai forest, unfortunate brushes with rotting fruit, and what it means to be from Ko Samui.

Travels in the Skin Trade: Tourism and the Sex Industry, by Jeremy Seabrook (2001). In-depth look at the relationship between tourism, Western media, and the people of the sex industry.

Thailand: The Golden Kingdom, by William Warren and Luca Tettoni (1999). Photograph-filled travel companion book that details Thai art, history, and culture.

ON THE WEB

Tourism Authority of Thailand (www.tat.or.th). Official website of TAT is possibly the best launching pad for information on visiting Thailand.

Thailand Youth Hostel Association (www.tyha.org). The name says it all: solid budget accommodations.

Thailand.com (www.thailand.com/travel/). Great resources on everything from nightlife to accommodations.

ESSENTIALS

SO YOU WANT TO GO TO THAILAND

Passports (p. 43): Required of all travelers. Must be valid for at least 6 months after intended period of stay.

Visas (p. 44): Visas are required of all travelers staying more than 30 days.

Inoculations (p. 52): Visitors who have been in Africa or South America must have a certificate of vaccination against yellow fever. *Let's Go* lists other specifically recommended inoculations.

Work Permits (p. 44): Required of all foreigners planning to work in Thailand.

Driving Permits (p. 76): International Driving Permits required for car rental, if you dare rent a car.

EMBASSIES AND CONSULATES

THAI CONSULAR SERVICES ABROAD

Australia: Embassy, 111 Empire CTT, Yarralumla, Canberra, ACT 2600 (☎06 273 1149 or 273 2939); www.geocities.com/CapitolHill/7789). **Consulate General,** 2nd fl., 75-77 Pitt St., Sydney NSW 2000 (☎02 9241 2542 or 9241 2543). **Consulates,** 5th fl., Silverton Place, 101 Wickham Terrace, Brisbane QLD 4000 (☎07 3832 1999); 6th fl., 277 Flinders Lane, Melbourne VIC 3000 (☎03 9650 1714); 1st fl., 72 Flinders Street, Adelaide SA 5000 (☎08 232 7474); 135 Victoria Ave., Dalkeith WA 6009 (☎09 386 8092).

Canada: Embassy, 180 Island Park Dr., Ottawa, ON K1Y 0A2 (☎613-722-4444; www.magma.ca/~thaiott/mainpage.htm). **Consulate,** 1040 Burrard St., Vancouver, BC V6Z 2R9 (☎604-687-1143; www.thaicongenvancouver.org).

New Zealand: Embassy, 2 Cook St., P.O. Box 17-226, Karori, Wellington 6005 (☎04 476 8618 or 476 8619). **Consulate-General,** Level 22, Phillips Fox Tower, 209 Queen St., P.O. Box 160, Auckland (☎09 300 3890).

South Africa: Embassy, 840 Church St., Eastwood, Arcadia, Pretoria 0083 (☎012 342 5406 or 342 4516).

UK: Embassy, 29-30 Queen's Gate, London SW7 5JB (☎020 7589 2944; www.thai-inuk.com/h_emuk.html).

US: Embassy, 1024 Wisconsin Ave. NW #401, Washington, D.C. 20007 (☎202-944-3600; www.thaiembdc.org). **Consulates,** 351 E 52nd St., New York, NY 10022 (☎212-754-1770 or 754-2536); 700 N Rush St., Chicago, IL 60611 (☎312-664-3129); 611 N. Larchmont Blvd., 2nd fl., Los Angeles, CA 90004 (☎323-962-9574 or 962-9575; www.thai-la.net); 1024 Wisconsin Ave. NW suite 101, Washington, D.C. 20007 (☎202-944-3608).

CONSULAR SERVICES IN THAILAND

Australian Embassy: 37 South Sathorn Rd., Bangkok 10120 (☎02 287 26 80). Open M-F 8am-5pm. **Consulate:** 165 Sirimungkrajarn Rd., Suthep Sub-District, Chiang Mai 50200 (☎053 221 083). Open M-F 9am-5pm.

Canadian Embassy: 990 Rama IV Rd., Abdulrahim Place, 15th fl., Bangkok 10500 (☎02 636 05 40). Open M-F 8am-noon. **Consulate:** 151 Moo 3 Super Highway, Tambon Tahsala, Chiang Mai 50000 (☎053 850 147 or 242 292).

Irish Embassy: 205 United Flour Mill Bldg., 11th fl., Ratchawong Rd., Bangkok (☎02 223 08 76). Open M-F 9am-noon and 1:30-4pm.

New Zealand Embassy: M Thai Tower, 14th fl., All Seasons Place, 87 Wireless Rd., Lumpini, Bangkok 10330 (☎02 254 25 30). Open M-F 7:30am-noon and 1-4pm.

South African Embassy: Park Palace, 6th fl., 231 Soi Sarasin, Ratchadamri Rd., Bangkok (☎02 253 84 73). Open M-Th 7:45am-4:30pm, F 7:45am-3:15pm.

UK Embassy: Wireless Rd., Bangkok (☎02 305 83 33). Open M-Th 7:45am-noon and 12:45-4:30pm, F 7:45am-1:15pm. **Consulate:** Unit 201, Airport Business Park, 90 Mahidol Rd. (☎053 203 408). Open M-Th 8am-noon and 1-4:30pm, F 8am-1pm.

US Embassy: 120-122 Wireless Rd., Bangkok 10300 (☎02 205 40 00). Consular services M-F 7am-noon and 1-4pm. **Consulate:** 387 Wichayanond Rd., Chiang Mai 50300 (☎053 252 629). American citizen services open M and W 1-3:30pm.

TOURIST SERVICES

Thailand Tourism Board: www.tourismthailand.org. 75 Pitt St., 2nd fl., Sydney 2000 (☎02 9247 7549); 49 Albemarle St., London W1S 4JR (☎44 207 499 7679); 611 North Larchmont Blvd., 1st fl., Los Angeles, CA 90004 (☎323-461-9814).

Tourism Authority of Thailand: www.tat.or.th. Locations all over Australia, Europe, and North America. Webpage is regularly updated for dates of festivals and recent news.

DOCUMENTS & FORMALITIES

PASSPORTS

REQUIREMENTS. You need a valid passport to enter Thailand and to return to your home country. Thailand, like most Southeast Asian countries, requires that your passport be valid for six months beyond your anticipated departure date.

PHOTOCOPIES. Be sure to photocopy the page of your passport with your photo, as well as your visas, traveler's check serial numbers, and any other important documents. Carry one set of copies in a safe place, apart from the originals, and leave another with someone at home. Consulates also recommend that you carry an expired passport or an official copy of your birth certificate separate from other documents. These additional documents can cut through a lot of bureaucracy in the event that you need to replace an important travel document.

LOST PASSPORTS. If you lose your passport, immediately notify the local police and the nearest embassy or consulate of your home government. To expedite its replacement, you will need to know all information previously recorded in it and show identification and proof of citizenship. In some cases, a replacement may take weeks to process and may only be valid for a limited time. Any visas stamped in your old passport will be irretrievably lost. In an emergency, ask for immediate temporary traveling papers that will permit you to re-enter your home country.

As of April 8, 2002, US embassies and consulates are no longer permitted to issue American passports abroad. Applying for a passport in a foreign consulate will now take longer, because it needs to be printed in the US. In the case of "emergency travel"—lost or stolen passports that need to be replaced—consulates are only authorized to issue temporary passports, which cannot be extended. More detailed info regarding lost or stolen passports is available at www.usembassy.it/cons/acs/passport-lost.htm.

NEW PASSPORTS. All applications for new passports or renewals should be filed several weeks or months in advance of your planned departure date. Most passport offices offer emergency passport services for a hefty extra charge.

VISAS, INVITATIONS, & WORK PERMITS

VISAS. American, Australian, British, Canadian, European, New Zealand, and South African citizens can stay for 30 days without a visa. For longer stays, Thai consulates abroad issue 60-day tourist visas, or travelers can apply for extensions in Thailand. If you wish to sojourn in nearby countries, obtain a re-entry permit at an immigration office before departure. Check entrance requirements at the nearest embassy for up-to-the-minute information before departure. US citizens can take advantage of the **Center for International Business and Travel** (☎800-925-2428), which secures visas for travel to almost all countries for a variable service charge.

If you have a 60-day visa and you go to Myanmar, Cambodia, Malaysia, or Laos for a daytrip, you will lose your visa and will need to reapply. To avoid having to get a new visa when you hop across the border for a day, make photocopies of your passport (usually 5฿). Then proceed directly to Thai border control, at whichever border point you are hoping to cross, with your two photocopies of your passport. Surrender your passport to the Thai authorities, who will stamp the photocopies. Take your newly stamped photocopies and the border crossing fee to the border control authorities of the country you are entering. They will stamp your photocopies and keep one of them. All stamps are on the copies, so when you return to Thailand, you get your unmarked passport back. Foreign authorities will keep one photocopy, Thai authorities the other. Either way, when you surrender your passport photocopies to the Burmese (for example), they will give you a very thin piece of paper—that piece of paper is your passport. Hold on to it if you ever want to see home again.

SPECIAL VISAS. Thailand issues 90-day visas for business, education, medical treatment, and even settlement after retirement. Applications for business and education visas require letters of sponsorship or invitation from businesses, organizations, or universities in Thailand. Extensions are granted within Thailand with support from the business or institution. Contact the embassy for specific details. For more information and ideas for how to use a work/study permit, see **Alternatives to Tourism,** p. 84.

IDENTIFICATION

When you travel, always carry two or more forms of identification on your person, including one photo ID. A passport and driver's license or birth certificate is usually adequate. Never carry all your forms of ID together; split them up in case of theft or loss. It is useful to bring extra passport-size photos (2" x 2") to affix to the visas and IDs you may acquire or in case you need replacements.

STUDENT AND TEACHER IDENTIFICATION. The **International Student Identity Card (ISIC)** (AUS$15 or US$20) is accepted in Thailand for discounts on some sights and other services, like car rentals, cinemas, and upscale restaurants. Check out the ISIC discount database (www.istcnet.org/DiscountDatabase) for more information. Cardholders have access to a 24hr. emergency helpline for medical, legal, and financial emergencies. US cardholders are also eligible for insurance benefits (see **Insurance,** p. 57). Applicants must be degree-seeking students of a secondary or post-secondary school and be at least 12 years old. The **International Teacher Identity Card (ITIC)** offers the same insurance coverage and limited discounts. For more info, contact the **International Student Travel Confederation (ISTC),** Herengracht 479, 1017 BS Amsterdam, Netherlands (☎31 20 421 28 00; fax 421 28 10; istcinfo@istc.org; www.istc.org).

YOUTH IDENTIFICATION. The International Student Travel Confederation issues a discount card to travelers who are 25 years old or under but not students. This one-year **International Youth Travel Card** (**IYTC**; formerly the **GO 25 Card**) offers many of the same benefits as the ISIC and is sold in the same places (US$20).

CUSTOMS

Upon entering you must declare certain items from abroad and pay a duty on the value of those articles if they exceed the allowance established by that country's customs service. Note that goods and gifts purchased at **duty-free** shops abroad are not exempt from duty or sales tax at your point of return and thus must be declared as well. Travelers may bring one still camera with ten rolls of film, or one video camera with three tapes. These restrictions are meant to ensure the film/equipment is for personal use only and are flexible. The total amount of currency taken out should not exceed the amount taken in (max. US$10,000). No authentic Buddha or Bodhisattva images, or fragments thereof, may be exported without permission from the Bangkok National Museum (☎(02) 224 1333) and the Department of Fine Arts; you must prove you are a practicing Buddhist or are using them for cultural or academic purposes. Such certification often takes three to five days to process; make sure you leave enough time to complete the process or your purchases cannot leave the country with you. These rules do not apply to souvenirs. For art purchased in the country, keep receipts for customs. There is a 500฿ airport tax on departure.

Additionally, the Thai government has harsh penalties for **drug possession and trafficking,** which are often considered synonymous. The import of **firearms, weapons,** and **pornography** is prohibited. Travelers should note that though Thailand's regulations are among the most stable, customs requirements do vary.

MONEY

CURRENCY & EXCHANGE

The Thai **baht** (**฿**) comes in denominations of 20, 50, 100, 500, 1000; coins come in 1, 5, 10฿, and 25 and 50 satang. Thailand has a **10% VAT** (value-added tax) on most items, including hotel rooms and food; it's usually already included in stated prices. Menus, tariff sheets, etc., specify if VAT is not included in the listed price. Check the currency converter on the *Let's Go* homepage (www.letsgo.com/thumb) or a major newspaper for the latest rates (*Bangkok Post,* www.bangkokpost.com).

THAI BAHT (฿)		
AUS$1 = 24.09฿	10฿ = AUS$0.42
CDN$1 = 27.52฿	10฿ = CDN$0.36
NZ$1 = 20.87฿	10฿ = NZ$0.48
ZAR1 = 4.19฿	10฿ = ZAR2.38
US$1 = 42.32฿	10฿ = US$0.23
UK£1 = 62.20฿	10฿ = UK£0.16
EUR€1 = 40.01฿	10฿ = EUR€0.25

As a general rule, it's cheaper to convert money at your destination. Bring enough currency to last for the first 72 hours of a trip—banks might be closed when you arrive. Travelers from the US can get foreign currency from the comfort of home: **International Currency Express** (☎888-278-6628) delivers currency or traveler's checks overnight (US$15) or second-day (US$12) at competitive exchange rates. Banks generally have the best rates outside the black market. A good rule of thumb is to go only to banks that have at most a 5% margin between their buy and sell prices. Since you lose money with each transaction, **convert in large sums** (unless the currency is depreciating rapidly), **but no more than you'll need.** Freelancers on the black market often offer excellent rates, but you run the risk of being swindled or arrested.

Smart travelers will carry **US dollars** even if it isn't their national currency, as many establishments in Thailand prefer transactions to be in US dollars. For small transactions, on the other hand, put your dollars away and use local currency. Throwing dollars around for preferential treatment is offensive, and it attracts thieves. If you use traveler's checks or bills, carry some in small denominations (US$50 or less), especially for times when you are forced to exchange money at disadvantageous rates.

TRAVELER'S CHECKS

Traveler's checks (**American Express** and **Visa** are the most recognized) are one of the safest and least troublesome means of carrying funds. Several agencies and banks sell them for a small commission.

While traveling, keep check receipts and a record of which checks you've cashed separate from the checks themselves. Keep a copy of check numbers and leave a copy with someone at home. Never countersign checks until you're ready to cash them, and always bring your passport with you to cash them. When purchasing checks, ask about toll-free refund hotlines and the location of refund centers in the event that your checks are lost or stolen.

Most establishments in well-traveled areas accept traveler's checks, especially banks and hotels. They are less widely accepted in smaller towns and rural areas. Check individual city and town listings for more information.

American Express: In Australia, call ☎800 251 902; in New Zealand ☎0800 441 068; in the UK ☎0800 521 313; in the US and Canada ☎800-221-7282. Elsewhere US collect ☎+1 801-964-6665; www.aexp.com. Traveler's checks are available for a small fee (1-4%) at AmEx offices and banks, commission-free at AAA offices. *Cheques for Two* can be signed by either of 2 people traveling together.

Travelex/Thomas Cook: In the US and Canada call ☎800-287-7362; in the UK call ☎0800 62 21 01; elsewhere call UK collect ☎+44 1733 31 89 50. Checks available in baht (2% commission). Thomas Cook offices cash checks commission-free.

Visa: In the US call ☎800-227-6811; in the UK ☎0800 89 50 78; elsewhere UK collect ☎+44 20 79 37 80 91. Call for the location of their nearest office.

CREDIT CARDS

Where they are accepted, credit cards often offer superior exchange rates—up to 5% better than the retail rate used by banks and other currency exchange establishments. **MasterCard** and **Visa** are the most welcomed; **American Express** cards work at some ATMs, AmEx offices, and major airports. However, budget travelers will find that few of the establishments they frequent will accept credit cards; you will probably have to reserve your credit card only for financial emergencies.

THE ART OF THE DEAL In Southeast Asia, bargaining is more than a pricing system. It is an art form, a crucial part of everyday social interactions, the lifeblood of every market, a riveting, exciting, and skillful mind game, and, if your attitude is right, a great deal of fun. The concept of "saving face," deeply embedded in many Asian cultures, is fundamental to an understanding of bargaining. So put your cut-throat attitude aside; this game of skill is built on a foundation of mutual respect and cheeky smiles of understanding.

1. Always approach with a smile, it'll start things off on the right foot.

2. As a rule, visible interest should be inversely proportional to actual desire; covetous eyes are the cat's meow to sellers and the kiss of death to buyers. But don't confuse a calm manner of carefully calculated semi-disinterest with a look of disdain.

3. Know when to bargain. In most cases, it's clear when it's appropriate to pull out your guns. When in doubt, smile and ask tactfully whether discounts or given, or say, "Oh! Is that the best we can do?" Never bargain for prepared food.

4. Openly bargaining with several sellers simultaneously is unacceptable and usually yields higher prices. Thus, it's always best to pull one person aside and settle in private.

5. To start bargaining without an intention to buy is a major *faux pas*. Agreeing on a price and declining it is the lowest of the low.

6. Cut-throat bargaining to a rock-bottom price often results in the seller's losing face. It's also worth considering that an hour of work in most Western nations yields enough money to feed a family for a week in many parts of Southeast Asia.

Credit cards are also useful for **cash advances,** which allow you to withdraw local currency from associated banks and ATMs throughout Thailand instantly. However, transaction fees for all credit card advances (up to US$10 per advance, plus 2-3% extra on foreign transactions after conversion) tend to make credit cards a more costly way of withdrawing cash than ATMs or traveler's checks. Be sure to check with your credit card company before you leave home in order to get a numerical **Personal Identification Number (PIN)** so that you are eligible for an advance.

CASH CARDS (ATMS)

Cash cards are an increasingly popular way to get money in Thailand. ATMs are common in Bangkok, Chiang Mai, and Phuket. The two major international money networks are **Cirrus** (☎800-424-7787) and **PLUS** (☎800-843-7587). To locate ATMs around the world, call the above numbers, or consult http://usa.visa.com/personal/atm_locator/plus_atm.html or www.mastercard.com/cardholderservices/atm. ATMs get the same wholesale exchange rate as credit cards, but there is often a limit on the amount you can withdraw per day (around US$500), and computer networks sometimes fail. There is typically also a surcharge of US$1-5 per withdrawal. Have your home bank issue you a four-digit PIN, the only variety accepted at some Thai ATMs. Be sure to memorize your PIN code in numeric form, since machines abroad often don't have letters on their keys.

Visa TravelMoney is a system that allows you to access money from any Visa ATM. Deposit money before you travel (plus a small administration fee), and you can withdraw up to that sum. The cards give you the same favorable exchange rate for withdrawals as a regular Visa. Check with your local bank to see if it issues Travel-Money cards (☎877-394-2247; www.usa.visa.com/personal/cards/visa_travel_money.html). **Road Cash** (☎877-762-3227; www.roadcash.com) issues cards in the US with a minimum US$300 deposit.

GETTING MONEY FROM HOME

AMERICAN EXPRESS. AmEx has ATMs throughout Thailand, mostly in major cities. Cardholders can withdraw cash from their checking accounts at any of AmEx's major offices and many representative offices (up to US$1000 every 21 days; no service charge, no interest). To enroll in Express Cash, call ☎800-227-4669 in the US. The AmEx international travel assistance number is ☎800-732-1991; call from Thailand for the nearest AmEx ATM. For other inquiries, in the US, the Caribbean, and Canada, call ☎800-678-0745; the international direct number is ☎336-393-1111.

WESTERN UNION. Travelers from the US, Canada, and the UK can wire money abroad through Western Union's international money transfer services. In the US, call ☎800-325-6000; in Canada, ☎800-235-0000; in the UK, ☎0800 833 833. Money can be wired online via www.westernunion.com. The rates for sending cash are generally US$10-11 cheaper than with a credit card, and the money is usually available at the location you're sending it to within an hour.

FEDERAL EXPRESS. Some people choose to send money abroad in cash via FedEx to avoid transmission fees and taxes. In the US and Canada, call ☎800-463-3339; in the UK, ☎0800 123 800; in Ireland, ☎800-535-800; in Australia, ☎13 26 10; in New Zealand, ☎0800 733 339; in South Africa, ☎021 551 7610. FedEx is reliable, but note that this method is illegal and somewhat risky. Also, it may take anywhere from a few days to several weeks for the package to reach you in Thailand, depending on where it was sent from and where it is going.

US STATE DEPARTMENT (US CITIZENS ONLY). In dire emergencies, the US State Department will forward money to the nearest consular office, which will then disburse it for a US$15 fee. Contact the Overseas Citizens Service, Consular Affairs, Room 4811, US Department of State, Washington, D.C. 20520 (☎202-647-5225; nights, Sundays, and holidays ☎647-4000; http://travel.state.gov).

COSTS

The cost of your trip will vary considerably, depending on where you go, how you travel, and where you stay. The single biggest cost of your trip will probably be your round-trip **airfare** (see **Getting to Thailand: By Plane,** p. 69). Traveling in Thailand can be done on a rather small budget, spending as little as US$5 per day in some parts of the country. Before you go, spend some time calculating a reasonable per-day **budget** that will meet your needs. Always keep emergency reserve funds (at least US$200) when planning how much money you'll need.

STAYING ON A BUDGET. The traveler's cost of living is very low in Thailand, relative to most Western countries. This is particularly true because of the Asian Financial Crisis. The difference between the cheapest option and the midrange options is often only a few dollars in Thailand, giving the budget traveler the option of an occasional night of luxury. Travelers looking to spend more than one night in comfort also have that option, especially in the more populated areas and beach resorts. At the moment, package tours are on the rise. Often, they offer more efficient ways to travel while still being affordable but, for many travelers, packaged trails can feel limiting. In any case, travel in Thailand will certainly not drain your savings.

TIPS FOR SAVING MONEY. Some simpler ways include searching out opportunities for free entertainment, buying food in supermarkets rather than eating out, splitting accommodation, food, and travel costs whenever possible with other trustworthy fellow travelers. Do your **laundry** in the sink (unless you're explicitly prohibited from doing so). That said, don't go overboard with your budget obsession. Though staying within your budget is important, don't do so at the expense of your health or a great travel experience.

TIPPING & BRIBERY

Tipping is not customary but much appreciated. However, a general rule is that the more Western the establishment, the more likely a tip is expected. If an establishment includes a service charge in the bill, tipping is not necessary. In restaurants that don't levy service charges, a 15% gratuity is appropriate. Still, most people will welcome the extra baht, as the average yearly income for some regions of Thailand is as low as US$150. Foreigners should expect to pay higher entrance fees at some places, including beaches, museums, and monuments.

While corruption is rife in Thailand, as a general rule, officials are unwilling to accept bribes from foreigners, and it is unwise to initiate an under-the-table transaction. If an official demands a fee or fine that you feel may be illegal, proceed with caution. Paying the bribe might be preferable to the alternative, but keep in mind that it is also illegal. If you politely ask for a receipt, or to speak with the official's superior, you might be able to defuse the situation. As a last resort, threatening to contact your embassy may also be effective.

SAFETY & SECURITY

PERSONAL SAFETY

EXPLORING. Be careful about leaving yourself vulnerable to thieves. As pickpockets know, tourists carry a lot of cash and are not as street savvy as locals. You can reduce your risk of getting robbed or hurt by **keeping a low profile:** the loudmouthed, camera-toting gawker looks more witless than a quietly thoughtful—but friendly—traveler. Respecting local customs (in many cases, dressing more conservatively) may placate would-be hecklers. Be open-minded and courteous; a smile goes a long way. If you show genuine interest in the local language and practices, the locals are more likely to watch your back when a mugger starts trailing you. If you are traveling by yourself, be sure someone at home knows your itinerary, and never admit that you're traveling alone.

Carry yourself with confidence and familiarize yourself with your surroundings before setting out; if you must check a map while exploring, duck into a shop. When walking at night, stick to busy, well-lit streets. Avoid dark alleyways; do not cross through parks, parking lots, or other large, deserted areas. Look for children playing, women walking in the open, and other signs of an active community. If you feel uncomfortable, leave as quickly and directly as you can, but don't allow fear of the unknown to turn you into a hermit. Careful, persistent exploration will build confidence and make your stay more rewarding.

GETTING AROUND. Renting a **motorbike** is one of the cheapest and most convenient ways to explore Thailand, but you should understand the risks involved before you hop on—motor vehicle crashes are a leading cause of injury among travelers. Wear a helmet and drive with care to reduce the chance of serious injury. If you are driving a **car,** learn local driving signals and wear a seatbelt. Officially, Thais drive on the left side of the road, but most drive on both at once.

Observing local traffic patterns and studying maps before you hit the road will help prevent accidents. Children under 40 lbs. should ride only in a specially designed carseat, available for a small fee from most car rental agencies. If you plan on spending a lot of time on the road, you may want to bring spare parts. If your car breaks down, wait for the police to assist you. For long drives in desolate areas, invest in a cellular phone. Be sure to park your vehicle in a garage or well-traveled area, and use a steering wheel locking device in larger cities. **Sleeping in your car** is one of the most dangerous (and often illegal) ways to get your rest. Not for the weak-hearted, the roads of Thailand are an adventure in themselves.

SELF DEFENSE. There is no sure-fire way to avoid all the threatening situations you might encounter when you travel, but a good self-defense course will help you react effectively to aggression. **Impact, Prepare, and Model Mugging** can refer you to local self-defense courses in the US (☎800-345-5425). Visit their web site at www.impactsafety.org for a list of nearby chapters. Workshops (2-3hr.) start at US$50; full courses run US$350-500. Women and men are welcome. If you find yourself in danger, remember that the best strategy is usually to run and scream "help" or "fire" in the local language. In Southeast Asia, especially, attracting attention to yourself in public can help deter any immediate threat to your safety.

TRAVEL ADVISORIES The following government offices provide travel information and advisories by telephone, by fax, or via the web:

Australian Department of Foreign Affairs and Trade: ☎ 1300 555 135; faxback service 02 6261 1299; www.dfat.gov.au.

Canadian Department of Foreign Affairs and International Trade (DFAIT): In Canada and the US call ☎800-267-6788, elsewhere call ☎+1 613-944-6788; www.dfait-maeci.gc.ca. Call for their free booklet, *Bon Voyage...But.*

New Zealand Ministry of Foreign Affairs: ☎04 494 8500; fax 494 8506; www.mft.govt.nz/trav.html.

United Kingdom Foreign and Commonwealth Office: ☎020 7008 0232; fax 7008 0155; www.fco.gov.uk.

US Department of State: ☎202-647-5225; faxback service 202-647-3000; http://travel.state.gov. For *A Safe Trip Abroad,* call ☎202-512-1800.

POLITICS AND TERRORISM. Travelers should always check travel advisories and world news before departure. The box on travel advisories (see above) lists offices to contact and webpages to visit to get the most updated travel warnings and information. It is always helpful—and sometimes essential—to be aware of the political situation in the region; using current, proper titles for government officials and organizations is a must.

Recently, Northern Thailand and its border with Myanmar have been prone to violence due to the **Burmese ethnic conflict.** Check the news and your embassy for the latest before going to those areas (see **Thai-Burmese Relations,** p. 24). Thailand has a good safety record. Nevertheless, scams abound: taxi and tuk-tuk drivers, guest house operators, and fellow travelers have all been known to attempt various con-games and thievery. On buses and trains and in the airport, be careful when accepting food or drink from strangers; travelers have been drugged and robbed. Most likely their friendliness is genuine, but exercise common sense. Crime committed against foreigners is usually petty thievery; violence is rare. Most Thai cities have separate tourist police forces. **All narcotic drugs in Thailand are illegal,** despite what your guest house owner may tell you. Penalties for drug-related crimes can be very stiff—up to life in prison.

FINANCIAL SECURITY

PROTECTING YOUR VALUABLES. There are a few steps you can take to minimize the financial risk associated with traveling: First, **bring as little with you as possible.** Second, don't forget to label your luggage both inside and out. Third, buy a few combination **padlocks** to secure your belongings in hostel or train station lockers or in your pack; even twist-ties or dental floss will slow down pickpockets. Fourth, **carry as little cash as possible** and never count your money in public. Don't put a wallet with money in your backpack or back pocket. Instead, keep your traveler's checks and ATM/credit cards in a **money belt** along with your passport and ID cards. Watch out for moped riders who snatch purses and backpacks by cutting the straps. Finally, **keep a small cash reserve separate from your primary stash.** This should be about US$50 sewn into or stored in the depths of your pack, along with your traveler's check numbers and important photocopies. Be sure to photocopy both the visa page and the identification page of your passport. Leave another copy at home.

CON ARTISTS & PICKPOCKETS. Con artists abound in all large cities. They often work in groups; children are among the most effective. Beware of tricks designed to distract you while someone snatches your bag. **Don't ever let your passport and your bags out of your sight.** In city crowds and especially on public transportation, **pickpockets** are impressively deft. Be aware of your surroundings and look sure of yourself. Confidence is the greatest anti-theft device you can have.

ACCOMMODATIONS & TRANSPORTATION. Never leave your belongings unattended; crime occurs in the safest-looking guest house or hotel. If you feel unsafe, look for places with a curfew or a night attendant. Most guest houses don't have lockers, and even if they do, your valuables are not entirely secure. Bring a **padlock** and chain or cord with you to secure your belongings to your bed.

Be particularly careful on **buses** and **trains;** horror stories abound about determined thieves who wait for travelers to fall asleep. Carry your backpack in front of you where you can see it. Thieves thrive on trains; professionals wait for tourists to fall asleep and then carry off their bags. When traveling with others, sleep in alternate shifts. If you are alone, use good judgement in selecting a train compartment: never stay in an empty one, and use a lock to secure your pack to the luggage rack. Try to sleep on top bunks with your luggage stored above you or in bed with you, and keep important documents and other valuables on your person.

DRUGS & ALCOHOL

Drugs are easily accessible in Thailand and, especially in some rural communities, drug use may seem to be common and public. Despite the glamor surrounding the Thai drug scene, narcotics are illegal and travelers do get caught. Buying or selling *any* type of drug may lead to a stiff prison sentence. A meek "I didn't know it was illegal" will not suffice; if you break the law, your home embassies will visit you in jail and bring you candy, but they **cannot and will not do anything else** to help.

There is no established minimum drinking age in Thailand. You can drink yourself silly at the age of 10, but *Let's Go* does not recommend it. Whenever you do drink, make sure you take extra personal safety precautions.

HEALTH

Common sense is the simplest prescription for good health while you travel. The heat of Thailand, combined with foreign foods and water that may cause diarrhea, make dehydration a major concern. Drink plenty of fluids to prevent dehydration and constipation; a supply of salt-tablets and anti-diarrheal medicine might prove useful. Sturdy, broken-in shoes and clean socks will keep your feet happy.

BEFORE YOU GO

Preparation can help minimize the likelihood of contracting a disease and maximize the chances of receiving effective health care in the event of an emergency. In your **passport**, list any allergies or medical conditions and write the names of any people you wish to be contacted in case of a medical emergency. Matching a prescription to a foreign equivalent is not always easy or possible, so carry up-to-date, legible prescriptions or a statement from your doctor with the medication's trade name, manufacturer, chemical name, and dosage. To be cautious, bring any medication you think you might need with you. Bangkok will have most over the counter medications that you will need; stock up here before you travel out. Keep all medication with you in your carry-on luggage. For tips on packing a basic **first-aid kit,** see p. 58.

IMMUNIZATIONS & PRECAUTIONS

Travelers over two years old should make sure that the following vaccines are up to date: MMR (for measles, mumps, and rubella); DTaP or Td (for diptheria, tetanus, and pertussis); OPV (for polio); HbCV (for haemophilus influenza B); and HBV (for hepatitis B). See **Inoculation Requirements & Recommendations,** below, for a list of inoculations you might need. For recommendations on immunizations and prophylaxis, consult the CDC (see below) and check with a doctor for guidance. **Malaria** is prevalent in most of Thailand; the CDC also provides information about malaria risk by region. Strains resistant to certain prophylactics are common, so ask your doctor to recommend the best preventative drug for your region of travel. While **yellow fever** is only endemic to parts of South America and sub-Saharan Africa, Thailand may deny entrance to travelers arriving from these zones without a certificate of vaccination.

INOCULATION REQUIREMENTS & RECOMMENDATIONS

The inoculations needed for travel in Thailand vary with the length of your trip and the activities you plan to pursue. Visit your doctor at least 4-6 weeks prior to your departure to allow time for the shots to take effect. Be sure to keep your inoculation records with you as you travel–you may be required to show them to border officials.

Diptheria and tetanus, measles, and polio: booster doses recommended as needed.

Typhoid: strongly recommended.

Hepatitis A or immune globulin (IG): recommended.

Hepatitis B: if traveling for 6 months or more, or if exposure to blood, needle-sharing, or sexual contact is likely. Important for health care workers and those who might seek medical treatment abroad.

Japanese Encephalitis: only if you will be in rural areas for 4 weeks or more, or if there are known outbreaks in the regions you plan to visit; elevated risk usually from May to October.

Rabies: if you might be exposed to animals while you travel.

Yellow Fever: if you are traveling from South America or sub-Saharan Africa or other infected areas, a certificate of vaccination may be required for entry into Thailand. There is no risk in Thailand.

USEFUL ORGANIZATIONS & PUBLICATIONS

The US **Centers for Disease Control and Prevention** (**CDC**; ☎877-FYI-TRIP; toll-free fax 888-232-3299; www.cdc.gov/travel) maintains an international travelers' hotline and an informative web site. The CDC's comprehensive booklet *Health Information for International Travel*, an annual rundown of disease, immunization, and general health advice, is free online or US$25 via the Public Health Foundation (☎877-252-1200).

The **United States State Department** (http://travel.state.gov) compiles consular information sheets on health, entry requirements, and other issues for most countries of the world. Government agencies of other countries offer similar services (see the listings in the box on **Travel Advisories**, p. 50). For quick information on health and other travel warnings, call the **Overseas Citizens Services** (☎202-647-5225 or the toll-free hotline ☎888-401-4747), or contact a passport agency, embassy, or consulate in Thailand. For information on medical evacuation services and travel insurance firms, see the US government's web site at http://travel.state.gov/medical.html or the **British Foreign and Commonwealth Office** (www.fco.gov.uk).

For detailed information on travel health, including a Thailand-specific overview of diseases, try the **International Travel Health Guide,** by Stuart Rose, MD (US$19.95; www.travmed.com). For general health info, contact the **American Red Cross** (☎800-564-1234; www.redcross.org).

MEDICAL ASSISTANCE ON THE ROAD

Hospitals in Thailand vary from region to region, but generally larger, centralized cities like Bangkok and Chiang Mai have high-quality facilities. Thailand's healthcare system is balanced between public and private institutions. The public system often has limited technical support and is overcrowded and bureaucratic. Public hospitals tend be more crowded and less expensive than private hospitals, which are more likely to have English-speaking doctors, language interpreters, foreign insurance claim assistance, international emergency medical evacuation access, and embassy liaison services. Travelers should note, however, that though private healthcare is better, it is somewhat inefficient. For the most trusted medical care, go to Bangkok.

General practitioners and dentists are readily available; most medical staff at large medical institutions speak English. Thai medical services are always availble: walk-in services are common during the daytime; many hospitals offer 24hr. emergency room service. Emergency hotlines are only useful if you speak Thai. If you need an injection, be sure to watch the doctor or nurse unwrap a new syringe.

If you are concerned about obtaining medical assistance while traveling, you may wish to employ special support services. The *MedPass* from **GlobalCare, Inc.,** 6875 Shiloh Rd. East, Alpharetta, GA, 30005-8372, USA (☎800-860-1111; fax 678-341-1800; www.globalems.com), provides 24hr. international medical assistance, support, and medical evacuation resources. The **International Association for Medical Assistance to Travelers** (**IAMAT**; US ☎716-754-4883, Canada ☎416-652-0137; www.iamat.org) has free membership, lists English-speaking doctors worldwide, and offers detailed info on immunization requirements and sanitation. **International Security Overseas** (**ISOS**; worldwide headquarters: 331 N Bridge Rd., #17-00 Odeon Towers, Singapore 188720; www.internationalsos.com) provides medical services, travel insurance, and around-the-clock emergency assistance services. ISOS offers medical insurance for both short-term and long-term travel; couples and families can purchase cheaper packages. Call ☎800-523-8930 for more information or to enroll in a plan.

Those with medical conditions (such as diabetes, allergies to antibiotics, epilepsy, or heart conditions) may want to obtain a **Medic Alert** membership (first year US$35, annually thereafter US$20), which includes a stainless steel ID tag bracelet, among other benefits, including a 24hr. collect-call number. Contact the **Medic Alert Foundation,** 2323 Colorado Ave., Turlock, CA 95382, USA (☎888-633-4298; outside US ☎209-668-3333; www.medicalert.org). Diabetics can call the **American Diabetes Association** for a copy of their booklet, *The Diabetes Travel Guide* ($14.95, $12.95 for members; ☎800-342-2383).

HENNA TATTOOS A synthetic dye (PPD) found in some forms of henna tattooing can cause severe blisters and permanent scarring. Ask the henna artist to tell you everything that is in their paste before proceeding with the tattoo. Even natural oils and herbs—clove oil, eucalyptus oil, or walnut powder—that other artists use in natural henna paste can be irritating to the skin. If you have sensitive skin, patch test the henna first, or ask the artist for a simple mix of henna powder and lemon juice.

ONCE IN THAILAND

ENVIRONMENTAL HAZARDS

Heat exhaustion, characterized by **dehydration** and **salt deficiency,** can lead to fatigue, headaches, and wooziness. Prevent it by drinking plenty of fluids, eating salty foods, and avoiding dehydrating beverages (e.g. alcohol and caffeinated beverages). Adding salt or lemon juice to water also helps.

Sunburn: If you are planning to spend time on the beach or in the sun, bring sunscreen along. If you get burned, drink more fluids than usual and apply an aloe-based lotion.

INSECT-BORNE DISEASES

Many diseases are transmitted by insects—mainly mosquitoes. Be careful in wet or forested areas, especially while hiking and camping; wear long pants and long sleeves, tuck your pants into your socks, and sleep under a mosquito net. While traveling in the kos and rural areas, you should be particularly careful. Use insect repellents such as DEET; consider soaking or spraying your gear with permethrin (licensed in the US for use on clothing), but be aware that permethrin can cause an allergic reaction. Natural repellents include vitamin B-12 and garlic pills. Sleeping with a mosquito net is a good way to prevent being bitten at night. To stop the itch after being bitten, try Calamine lotion or topical cortisones like Cortaid, or take a bath with a half-cup of baking soda or oatmeal.

Malaria: Transmitted by *Anopheles* mosquitoes that bite at night. The incubation period varies from 6-8 days to several months. Symptoms include fever, chills, aches, and fatigue, followed by high fever and sweating, sometimes with vomiting and diarrhea. See a doctor for any flu-like sickness that occurs after travel in an a risk area. To reduce the risk of contracting malaria, use mosquito repellent, particularly during the evenings and in forested areas, and take oral prophylactics such as **mefloquine** (sold under the name Lariam) or **doxycycline** (ask your doctor for a prescription). Be aware that these drugs can have serious side effects, including slowed heart rate and nightmares.

Dengue Fever: An "urban viral infection" transmitted by *Aedes* mosquitoes, which bite during the day rather than at night. Dengue has flu-like symptoms and is often indicated by a rash 3-4 days after the onset of fever. Symptoms for the first 2-4 days include chills, high fever, headaches, swollen lymph nodes, muscle aches, and, in some instances, a pink rash on the face. If you experience these symptoms, see a doctor immediately, drink plenty of liquids, and take fever-reducing medication such as acetaminophen (Tylenol). **Never take aspirin to treat dengue fever.**

Japanese Encephalitis: Most prevalent during the rainy season in rural areas. Symptoms include delirium, chills, headache, fever, vomiting, and muscle fatigue. Go to a hospital as soon as any symptoms appear. According to the CDC, there is little chance of being infected if proper precautions are taken: use mosquito repellents containing DEET and sleep under mosquito nets.

Other insect-borne diseases: Filariasis is a roundworm infestation transmitted by mosquitoes. Infection causes enlargement of extremities and has no vaccine. The **plague** is still a risk as well; early symptoms include fever, nausea, sore throat, and swollen lymph nodes. A vaccine is available for the plague; both diseases can be treated.

FOOD- & WATER-BORNE DISEASES

Thailand's **tap water** is not potable. It is not even safe for brushing teeth. Prevention is the best cure: be sure that your food is properly cooked and the water you drink is clean. Never drink unbottled water that you have not treated yourself. Buy bottled water, or purify your own water by bringing it to a rolling boil or treating it with **iodine tablets;** note however that some parasites such as *giardia* have exteriors that resist iodine treatment, so boiling is more reliable. Alternatively, using a high-quality **water filter** in addition to iodine treatment will prove more effective than iodine alone. Peel fruits and veggies; avoid ice cubes and anything washed in tap water, like salad. Most Western establishments, or Thai establishments that cater to tourists, serve water and ice that has been purified—it will usually say so on the menu, but it never hurts to ask. Watch out for food from markets or street vendors that may have been cooked in unhygienic conditions. Other culprits are raw shellfish, unpasteurized milk, and sauces containing raw eggs. Always wash your hands before eating, or bring a quick-drying purifying liquid hand cleaner. It may seem like a hassle, but your bowels will thank you.

Traveler's Diarrhea: A rite of passage for travelers, caused by bacteria in untreated water or uncooked foods. Symptoms include nausea, bloating, and urgency. Try quick-energy, non-sugary foods with protein and carbohydrates to keep your strength up. Over-the-counter anti-diarrheals (e.g. Imodium) should be used in moderation for temporary relief. Drink sweetened liquids, uncaffeinated soft drinks, or salted crackers to avoid dehydration. If you develop a fever or your symptoms don't go away after 4-5 days, consult a doctor. Consult a doctor immediately for treatment of diarrhea in children.

Cholera: An intestinal disease caused by a bacteria found in contaminated food. Symptoms include diarrhea, dehydration, vomiting, and muscle cramps. See a doctor immediately; if left untreated, it may be deadly. Rehydration and antibiotic treatment are crucial if you contract cholera. The 50% effective vaccine can have serious side effects.

Dysentery: Symptoms include bloody diarrhea (sometimes mixed with mucus), fever, and abdominal pain and tenderness. **Bacillary dysentery** generally only lasts a week, but is highly contagious. **Amoebic dysentery,** which develops more slowly, is a more serious disease and may cause long-term damage if left untreated. A stool test can determine which kind you have; seek medical help immediately. Dysentery can be treated with the drugs norfloxacin or ciprofloxacin (commonly known as Cipro). Consider obtaining a prescription before you leave home.

Hepatitis A: A viral infection of the liver acquired primarily through contaminated water. Symptoms include fatigue, fever, loss of appetite, nausea, dark urine, jaundice, vomiting, aches and pains, and light stools. Ask your doctor about the vaccine (Havrix or Vaqta) or an injection of immune globulin (IG; formerly called gamma globulin).

Parasites: Microbes, tapeworms, etc., that hide in unsafe water and food. **Giardiasis,** for example, is acquired by drinking untreated water from streams or lakes. Symptoms include swollen glands or lymph nodes, fever, rashes or itchiness, and digestive problems. Boil water, wear shoes, and eat only cooked food.

Schistosomiasis: A parasitic disease caused when the larvae of flatworm penetrate unbroken skin. Symptoms include an itchy localized rash, followed in 4-6 weeks by fever, fatigue, painful urination, diarrhea, loss of appetite, and night sweats. To avoid it, try not to swim in fresh water. If exposed to untreated water, rub the area vigorously with a towel and apply rubbing alcohol.

Typhoid Fever: Caused by the salmonella bacteria; common in villages and rural areas. While mostly transmitted through contaminated food and water, it may also be acquired by direct contact with another person. Early symptoms include fever, headaches, fatigue, loss of appetite, constipation, and sometimes a rash on the abdomen or chest. Antibiotics can treat typhoid, but a vaccination (70-90% effective) is recommended.

OTHER INFECTIOUS DISEASES

Hepatitis B: A viral infection of the liver transmitted via bodily fluids or needle-sharing. Symptoms may not surface until years after infection. A 3-shot vaccination sequence is recommended for health-care workers, sexually-active travelers, and anyone planning to seek medical treatment abroad; it must begin 6 months before traveling.

Hepatitis C: Like Hepatitis B, but the mode of transmission differs. IV drug users, those with occupational exposure to blood, hemodialysis patients, and recipients of blood transfusions are at the highest risk, but it can also spread through sexual contact or sharing items like razors and toothbrushes that may have traces of blood on them.

Rabies: Transmitted through the saliva of infected animals; fatal if untreated. By the time symptoms (thirst and muscle spasms) appear, the disease is in its terminal stage. If you are bitten, wash the wound thoroughly, seek immediate medical care, and try to have the animal located. A rabies vaccine, which consists of 3 shots given over a 21-day period, is available but is only semi-effective.

AIDS, HIV, & STDS

Travelers seeking pleasure in the quasi-legal bars, massage parlors, and brothels of Patpong and similar red-light districts stand a good chance of bringing back unwanted viral souvenirs of their trip. The best advice is to follow all precautions concerning any sexual encounter—use a condom with spermicide, and avoid sex with strangers or with people who engage in high-risk behavior (such as IV drug use or promiscuity or unprotected sex). Many prostitutes do not know that they are infected, and even if they do, they probably won't tell their clients. Though protected commercial sex has risen to 95%, there's still that 5% (see **AIDS**, p. 22). Condoms aren't always easy to find when traveling; and even if you do find them, Western brands tend to be more reliable, so bring a supply with you. *Never* share intravenous drug, tattooing, or other needles. For detailed information on AIDS, call the **US Centers for Disease Control**'s 24hr. hotline at ☎800-342-2437, or contact the **Joint United Nations Programme on HIV/AIDS (UNAIDS)**, 20 Ave. Appia, CH-1211 Geneva 27, Switzerland (☎ +41 22 791 3666).

Sexually transmitted diseases (STDs) such as gonorrhea, chlamydia, genital warts, syphilis, and herpes are easier to catch than HIV and can be just as deadly. **Hepatitis** B and C can also be transmitted sexually (see above). Though condoms may protect you from some STDs, oral or even tactile contact can lead to transmission. If you think you may have contracted an STD, see a doctor immediately.

WOMEN'S HEALTH

Women traveling in unsanitary conditions are vulnerable to **urinary tract** and **bladder infections,** common and severely uncomfortable bacterial conditions that cause a burning sensation and painful, frequent urination. Over-the-counter medications can sometimes alleviate symptoms, but if they persist, do not hesitate to see a doctor. Thailand's hot and humid climate also makes women especially susceptible to **vaginal yeast infections.** Wearing loosely fitting trousers or a skirt and cotton underwear will help, as will over-the-counter remedies like Monistat or Gynelotrimin. Bring supplies from home if you are prone to infection, as they may be difficult to obtain on the road. In a pinch, some travelers use natural or readily available alternatives such as a plain yogurt and lemon juice douche.

Since **tampons, pads** and reliable **contraceptive devices** are sometimes hard to find, bring supplies from home. Most toiletries can be found in Western establishments like UK's Boots on Khaosan Rd. and malls on Silom Rd. in Bangkok. Women using birth control pills should bring enough to allow for possible loss or extended stays. Also bring a prescription, since forms of the pill vary considerably. However, if you need contraceptive services, contact the Planned Parenthood Association of Thailand in Bangkok (☎2 941 2338; ppat@samart.co.th; www.ipp.org; 8 Soi Vibhavadi-Ransit Rd., Ladyao, Chatuchak, Bangkok 10900). English is the primary language spoken at the branch.

INSURANCE

Travel insurance generally covers four basic areas: medical/health problems, property loss, trip cancellation/interruption, and emergency evacuation. Although your regular insurance policies might extend to travel-related accidents, consider purchasing travel insurance if the cost of potential trip cancellation/interruption or emergency medical evacuation is greater than you can absorb. Prices for travel insurance purchased separately generally run about US$50 per week for full coverage, while trip cancellation/interruption may be purchased separately at a rate of about US$5.50 per US$100 of coverage.

Medical insurance (especially university policies) often covers costs incurred abroad; check with your provider. **US Medicare** does not cover foreign travel. **Canadians** are protected by their home province's health insurance plan for up to 90 days after leaving the country; check with the provincial Ministry of Health or Health Plan Headquarters for details. **Homeowners' insurance** (or your family's coverage) often covers theft during travel and loss of travel documents (passport, plane ticket, railpass, etc.) up to US$500.

ISIC and **ITIC** (see p. 44) provide basic insurance benefits, including US$100 per day of in-hospital treatment for up to 60 days, US$3000 of accident-related medical reimbursement, and US$25,000 for emergency medical transport. Cardholders have access to a toll-free 24hr. helpline (run by the insurance provider **TravelGuard**) for medical, legal, and financial emergencies overseas (US and Canada ☎877-370-4742, elsewhere call US collect ☎+1 715-345-0505). **American Express** (US ☎800-528-4800) grants most cardholders automatic car rental insurance (collision and theft, but not liability) and ground travel accident coverage of US$100,000 on flight purchases made with the card.

INSURANCE PROVIDERS. Council and **STA** (see p. 70) offer a range of plans that can supplement your basic coverage. Other private insurance providers in the US and Canada include: **Access America** (☎800-284-8300; www.accessamerica.com); **Berkely Group/Carefree Travel Insurance** (☎800-323-3149; www.berkely.com); **Globalcare Travel Insurance** (☎800-821-2488; www.globalcare-cocco.com); and **Travel Assistance International** (☎800-821-2828; www.travelassistance.com). Providers in the **UK** include **Columbus Direct** (☎020 7375 0011; www.columbusdirect.net). In **Australia,** try **AFTA** (☎02 9375 4955).

PACKING

PACK LIGHTLY. To appreciate the virtue of traveling light, pack your bag with what you think are only the bare essentials, strap it on, and imagine walking uphill for three hours on hot asphalt. Now take out about half of what you packed so you don't rue the day that you packed that hairdryer "just in case," or, for that matter, the unnecessary handle end of your toothbrush. Don't forget that you can purchase all necessary items in Thailand for a fraction of the cost.

LUGGAGE. For travel in Thailand, a sturdy **frame backpack** is unbeatable. Toting a **suitcase** or **trunk** is all right if you plan to explore from just one or two cities but a very bad idea if you're going to be moving at all. Regardless, a **daypack** (a small backpack or courier bag) is a must. Locks on the packs are a good initial deterrent, but shouldn't replace common sense. Plastic bags will keep things dry and sorted. If you use a brightly-colored fanny pack, you will get robbed.

CLOTHING. The clothes you bring should be sturdy, light, comfortable, and quick-drying. Local custom usually demands conservative dress that covers your arms and legs. Try to bring only two outfits, one to wash and one to wear. Clothing is very inexpensive, so pack light and buy what you need on the road. **Flip-flops** or waterproof sandals are must-haves for grubby hostel showers. Essentials that you should bring with you include a good **rain jacket** (Gore-Tex® is both waterproof and breathable), underwear, and sturdy boots.

SLEEPSACK. Some hostels require that you either provide your own linen or rent sheets from them. Save cash by making your own sleepsack: fold a full-size sheet in half the long way, then sew it closed along the long side and one of the short sides. If you plan to camp, a sleeping bag is a good idea. Either way, you'll want something between you and the bed in most hostels in Thailand.

CONVERTERS AND ADAPTERS. Electricity in Thailand is 220 volts AC, enough to fry a 110V appliance. **Americans** and **Canadians** should pick up an **adapter** and a **converter** (US$20) at a hardware store. **New Zealanders, South Africans,** and **Australians** will also need adapters, but not converters.

TOILETRIES. Toiletries are readily available and cheap in Thailand. To be safe, stock up in larger cities before going to rural areas. Contact lenses may be expensive, so bring enough pairs for your entire trip. Bring your glasses and a copy of your prescription in case you need emergency replacements.

FIRST-AID KIT. For a basic first-aid kit, pack: bandages, pain reliever, antibiotic cream, a thermometer, a Swiss Army knife, tweezers, moleskin (for blisters), decongestant, motion-sickness remedy, diarrhea or nausea medication (Pepto Bismol or Imodium), an antihistamine, sunscreen, insect repellent, burn ointment, and a syringe for emergencies (get an explanatory letter from your doctor).

FILM. Less serious photographers may want to bring a **disposable camera** or two rather than an expensive permanent one. Despite disclaimers, airport security X-rays *can* fog film, so buy a lead-lined pouch at a camera store or ask security to hand-inspect it. Always pack film in your carry-on luggage, since higher-intensity X-rays are used on checked luggage.

OTHER USEFUL ITEMS. For safety purposes, you should bring a **money belt** and small **padlock**. Basic **outdoors equipment** (plastic water bottle, compass, waterproof matches, pocketknife, sunglasses, sunscreen, hat) may also prove useful. **Quick repairs** of torn garments can be done on the road with a needle and thread; also consider bringing electrical tape for patching tears. If you want to do laundry by hand, bring detergent, a small rubber ball to stop up the sink, and string for a makeshift clothes line. Other things you're liable to forget: an umbrella, an alarm clock, safety pins, rubber bands, a flashlight, earplugs, and garbage bags.

IMPORTANT DOCUMENTS. Don't forget your passport, traveler's checks, ATM and/or credit cards, and adequate IDs.

ACCOMMODATIONS

Choosing accommodations in Thailand can sometimes be a gamble, as electricity, running water, and air-conditioning have not yet reached many rural areas. Finding inexpensive accommodations, however, never proves to be a problem. Hotels and guest houses, many with Internet facilities and small cafes, line the streets of major cities and towns. For a few dollars, facilities can vary from a shared room with several beds to a single room with a private bath and fan. Modern and more expensive hotels can be found in highly touristed areas, allowing for a cooler and more comfortable stay.

While you should make reservations at the more expensive lodgings, finding a hotel on a day's notice is not difficult. It is not uncommon, and most often expected, to ask to see rooms before committing to a hotel; this also allows room for bargaining. Some hotels and guest houses require that you leave your passport with them during your stay. If you feel uncomfortable about doing this, some places will allow you to leave your customs slip from immigration.

ESSENTIALS

ECOLOGICALLY RESPONSIBLE TOURISM

Traveling through Thailand takes visitors into ecologically sensitive areas. Avoid buying natural souvenirs such as teeth, hides, coral, butterflies, or turtle shells. Products made of animals often come at the expense of endangered species. Women may consider buying feminine hygiene products with minimal packaging. Choose glass soda bottles over marginally recyclable plastic equivalents and reuse plastic bags. Bucket showers and squat toilets are more water-efficient than their Western counterparts. To be even more water-friendly, carry a water bottle or canteen. While tap water is unsafe, purifying tablets or iodine drops save buying countless plastic water bottles.

CAMPING & THE OUTDOORS

An excellent general resource for travelers planning on camping or spending time in the outdoors is the **Great Outdoor Recreation Pages** (www.gorp.com).

USEFUL PUBLICATIONS & RESOURCES

A variety of publishing companies offer hiking guidebooks to meet the educational needs of novices or experts. For information about camping, hiking, and biking, write or call the publishers listed below to receive a free catalog. **Sierra Club Books,** 85 Second St., 2nd fl., San Francisco, CA 94105, USA (☎ 415-977-5500; www.sierraclub.org/books), publishes general resource books on hiking, camping, and women traveling in the outdoors.

NATIONAL PARKS

Thailand's national parks are among its secret treasures. From the deep dark jungle to the sun-soaked depths of the ocean, thousands of acres of land are preserved as refuges for endangered species of wildlife and for *farang* who need a break from each other. Tourists may be uncommon in these parts, but they may also be endangered if they're not careful. The beautiful habitats have precious sights to uncover; travelers should be sure to be careful while enjoying them.

WILDERNESS SAFETY

THE GREAT OUTDOORS. Stay warm, stay dry, and stay hydrated. The vast majority of life-threatening wilderness situations can be avoided by following this simple advice. Prepare yourself for an emergency, however, by always packing raingear, a hat and mittens, a first-aid kit, a reflector, a whistle, high energy food, and extra water for any hike. Dress in wool or warm layers of synthetic materials designed for the outdoors; never rely on cotton for warmth, as it is useless when wet.

Check **weather forecasts** and pay attention to the skies when hiking, since weather patterns can change suddenly. Whenever possible, let someone know when and where you are going hiking, either a friend, your hostel, a park ranger, or a local hiking organization. Do not attempt a hike beyond your ability—you may be endangering your life. See **Health,** p. 51, for information about outdoor ailments and basic medical concerns.

WILDLIFE. If you are hiking in an area which might be frequented by **bears,** which is most of northern and northeastern Thailand, ask local rangers for information on bear behavior before entering any park or wilderness area and obey posted warnings. No matter how irresistibly cute a bear appears, don't be fooled—they're powerful and unpredictable animals that are not intimidated by humans. If you're close enough for a bear to see you, you're too close. If you see a bear at a distance, calmly walk (don't run) in the other direction. If it seems interested, back away slowly while speaking to the bear in firm, low tones, and head in the opposite direction or toward a settled area. If you are attacked by a bear, get in a fetal position to protect yourself, put your arms over the back of your neck, and play dead. In all situations, remain calm, as loud noises and sudden movements can trigger an attack. Don't leave food or other scented items (trash, toiletries, the clothes that you cooked in) near your tent. **Bear-bagging,** hanging edibles and other good-smelling objects from a tree out of reach of hungry paws, is the best way to keep your toothpaste from becoming a condiment. Bears are also attracted to any **perfume,** as are bugs, so cologne, scented soap, deodorant, and hairspray should stay at home.

Look out for unwanted critters at all times. Shake out your shoes before putting them on, sleep with a mosquito net, and always wear bug repellent (especially with DEET). Leeches are suave and quiet predators—buy leech guards and cover every inch of flesh. If you are bitten by any creature of the wild, get medical help immediately. For more information, consult *How to Stay Alive in the Woods,* by Bradford Angier (Macmillan Press, US$8).

CAMPING AND HIKING EQUIPMENT

WHAT TO BUY...

Good camping equipment is both sturdy and light. Camping equipment is generally more expensive in Australia, New Zealand, and the UK than in North America. While weather in Thailand is generally quite hot, temperatures can drop significantly at night, particularly in the north. See the **Appendix** (p. 415) for more information on climate and average temperatures.

Sleeping Bag: Most sleeping bags are rated by season ("summer" means 30-40°F at night; "four-season" or "winter" often means below 0°F). They are made either of **down** (warmer and lighter, but more expensive, and miserable when wet) or of **synthetic** material (heavier, more durable, and warmer when wet). Prices range US$80-210 for a summer synthetic to US$250-300 for a good down winter bag. **Sleeping bag pads** include foam pads (US$10-20), air mattresses (US$15-50), and Therm-A-Rest self-inflating pads (US$45-80). Bring a **stuff sack** to store your bag and keep it dry.

Tent: The best tents are free-standing (with their own frames and suspension systems), set up quickly, and only require staking in high winds. Low-profile dome tents are the best all-around. Good 2-person tents start at US$90, 4-person at US$300. Seal the seams of your tent with waterproofer, and make sure it has a rain fly. Other tent accessories include a **battery-operated lantern,** a **plastic groundcloth,** and a **nylon tarp.**

Backpack: Internal-frame packs mold better to your back, keep a lower center of gravity, and flex adequately to allow you to hike difficult trails. **External-frame packs** are more comfortable for long hikes over even terrain, as they keep weight higher and distribute it more evenly. Make sure your pack has a strong, padded hip-belt to transfer weight to your legs. Any serious backpacking requires a pack of at least 4000 in^3 (16,000cm^3), plus 500 in^3 for sleeping bags in internal-frame packs. Sturdy backpacks cost anywhere from US$125 to US$420—this is one area in which it doesn't pay to economize. Fill up any pack with something heavy and walk around the store with it to get a sense of how it distributes weight before buying it. Either buy a **waterproof backpack cover,** or store all of your belongings in plastic bags inside your pack.

Boots: Be sure to wear hiking boots with good **ankle support.** They should fit snugly and comfortably over 1-2 pairs of wool socks and thin liner socks. Break in boots over several weeks first in order to spare yourself painful and debilitating blisters.

Other Necessities: Synthetic layers, like those made of polypropylene, and a **pile jacket** will keep you warm even when wet. A **"space blanket"** will help you to retain your body heat and doubles as a groundcloth (US$5-15). Plastic **water bottles** are virtually shatter- and leak-proof. Bring **water-purification tablets** for when you can't boil water (you should already have these for backpacking in Thailand).

...AND WHERE TO BUY IT

The mail-order/online companies listed below offer lower prices than many retail stores, but a visit to a local camping or outdoors store will give you a good sense of the look and weight of certain items.

Campmor, 28 Parkway, P.O. Box 700, Upper Saddle River, NJ 07458, USA (US ☎888-226-7667; elsewhere US ☎+1 201-825-8300; www.campmor.com).

Discount Camping, 880 Main North Rd., Pooraka, South Australia 5095, Australia (☎08 8262 3399; fax 8260 6240; www.discountcamping.com.au).

Eastern Mountain Sports (EMS), 1 Vose Farm Rd., Peterborough, NH 03458, USA (☎888-463-6367 or 603-924-7231; www.shopems.com).

L.L. Bean, Freeport, ME 04033, USA (US and Canada ☎800-441-5713; UK ☎0800 891 297; elsewhere, call US ☎+1 207-552-3028; www.llbean.com).

Mountain Designs, 51 Bishop St., Kelvin Grove, Queensland 4059, Australia (☎07 3856 2344; fax 3856 0366; info@mountaindesigns.com; www.mountaindesigns.com).

Recreational Equipment, Inc. (REI), Sumner, WA 98352, USA (☎800-426-4840 or 253-891-2500; www.rei.com).

YHA Adventure Shop, 14 Southampton St., Covent Garden, London, WC2E 7HA, UK (☎020 7836 8541; www.yhaadventure.com). The main branch of one of Britain's largest outdoor equipment suppliers.

ORGANIZED ADVENTURE TRIPS

Organized adventure tours offer another way of exploring the wild. Activities include hiking, biking, skiing, canoeing, kayaking, rafting, climbing, photo safaris, and archaeological digs. Tourism bureaus can often suggest parks, trails, and outfitters; other good sources for info are stores and organizations that specialize in camping and outdoor equipment like REI and EMS (see **And Where to Buy It,** above). **Specialty Travel Index,** 305 San Anselmo Ave., #313, San Anselmo, CA 94960, USA (☎800-442-4922 or 415-459-4900; fax 415-459-9474; info@specialtytravel.com; www.specialtytravel.com), offers tours worldwide.

WATER SPORTS

SCUBA CERTIFICATION

Most scuba agencies require that you have a **Professional Association of Diving Instructors (PADI)** certification in order to dive with them. The **Open Water Diving** course is the beginner course. The "performance-based" progress means that it will last as long as it takes for you to be good enough. However, most courses consist of a knowledge section, a skill training section (usually in shallow water) and four training dives. There is a 183m nonstop swimming requirement or 300m nonstop snorkel and a 10min. treading water or floating session. **Ko Tao** is the largest diving training center in Southeast Asia. In addition to having some of the best snorkeling and diving in the world, it also has a plethora of scuba agencies, which is the island's primary source of income (for specific scuba agency listings, see **Ko Tao,** p. 335). To get your certification before your trip, see the listings of PADI certification sites in Australia, Canada, South Africa, the United States, and Europe, at the PADI web site: www.padi.com.

ENVIRONMENTALLY RESPONSIBLE TOURISM The idea behind responsible tourism is to leave no trace of human presence behind. A camp-stove is a safer (and more efficient) way to cook than using vegetation, but if you must make a fire, keep it small and use only dead branches or brush rather than cutting vegetation. Make sure your campsite is at least 150 ft. (50m) from water supplies or bodies of water. If there are no toilet facilities, bury human waste (but not paper) at least four inches (10cm) deep and above the high-water line, and 150 ft. or more from any water supplies and campsites. Always pack your trash in a plastic bag and carry it with you until you reach the next trash receptacle. For more information on these issues, contact one of the organizations listed below.

Earthwatch, 3 Clock Tower Place #100, Box 75, Maynard, MA 01754, USA (☎800-776-0188 or 978-461-0081; info@earthwatch.org; www.earthwatch.org).

International Ecotourism Society, 28 Pine St., Burlington, VT 05402, USA (☎802-651-9818; fax 802-651-9819; ecomail@ecotourism.org; www.ecotourism.org).

National Audubon Society, Nature Odysseys, 700 Broadway, New York, NY 10003, USA (☎212-979-3000; fax 212-979-3188; webmaster@audubon.org; www.audubon.org).

Tourism Concern, Stapleton House, 277-281 Holloway Rd., London N7 8HN, UK (☎020 7753 3330; fax 020 7753 3331; info@tourismconcern.org.uk; www.tourismconcern.org.uk).

ESSENTIALS

SNORKELING

Unlike scuba diving, snorkeling requires no training—anyone can grab a mask and snorkel and start swimming. Since excellent snorkeling can be found in only 1m deep water, popping your head above water is always an option. However, the breathing technique is an adjustment, so practice by the shore before heading for deeper waters. Travelers can also take classes at scuba centers—nearly every center caters to both activities.

HEALTH RESTRICTIONS

While PADI only mandates average health for certification, a prudent traveler will check with his or her doctor before signing up for a scuba course. Travelers with respiratory and heart ailments should be particularly careful with both diving and snorkeling. Contact lens wearers should not have a problem using them with a scuba or snorkeling mask, but prescription masks are also available.

SAFETY

Before you go out adventuring, check with local agencies and fellow backpackers about water conditions, currents, geological features of the area, and current weather conditions. A strong current or an unexpected underwater boulder can be extremely dangerous. Always check your equipment in shallow water before using it, and always swim with a buddy.

Arguably the coolest part of getting your certification (besides being able to scuba dive) is buying the gear for your aquatic adventures. When you buy your gear, make sure that the retailer is both reliable and reputable. There are many discount stores offering top quality merchandise, but before you skimp, keep in mind that the oxygen meter needs to be precise when you're 20m under the sea.

CORAL PRESERVATION

Learn about the marine life in the waters you hope to explore. This will not only improve the quality and enjoyment of the excursion, but it will give you an idea of which species are particularly delicate and prone to destruction. Never stand or kneel near coral. Simply touching it can kill it. Try not to disturb the environment; passive observation will provide better sights anyway.

KEEPING IN TOUCH

BY MAIL

SENDING MAIL HOME FROM THAILAND

Airmail letters under 1 oz. between North America and Thailand cost US$1. Envelopes should be marked "air mail" or "*par avion*" to avoid having letters sent by sea. Sea or **"surface mail"** is an option—by far the cheapest and slowest. It takes 1-3 months to cross the Atlantic and 2-4 to cross the Pacific—appropriate for sending large items you won't need to see for a while. When ordering books and materials from abroad, always include one or two **International Reply Coupons (IRCs)**—a way of providing the postage to cover delivery. IRCs should be available from your local post office (US$1.05).

SENDING MAIL TO THAILAND

Mail in Thailand is quite reliable. Mark envelopes "air mail" or "*par avion*" or your letter or postcard will never arrive. Expect standard mail to take 2-3 weeks to reach major cities and longer to get to rural areas. **Federal Express** (Australia ☎ 13 26 10; Canada and US ☎800-247-4747; New Zealand ☎0800 73 33 39; UK ☎0800 12 38 00) handles express mail services from most home countries to all Southeast Asian countries.

RECEIVING MAIL IN THAILAND

There are several ways to arrange pick-up of letters sent to you by friends and relatives while you are abroad.

General Delivery: Mail can be sent through **Poste Restante** (the international phrase for General Delivery to almost any town with a post office), usually for no surcharge. Address *Poste Restante* letters to the recipient, with the last name underlined and in capital letters: "Dael NORWOOD, Poste Restante, Bangkok, Thailand." The mail will go to a desk in the central post office, unless you specify a post office by street address or postal code. As a rule, it is best to use the largest post office in the area, as mail may be sent there regardless of what is written on the envelope. When picking up mail, bring a photo ID, preferably a passport. If the clerks insist that there is nothing for you, have them check under your first name as well. *Let's Go* lists post offices in the **Practical Information** section for each city and most towns.

American Express: If you contact them in advance, AmEx's travel offices throughout the world will act as a free mail service (the **Client Letter Service**) for cardholders, holding mail for up to 30 days and forwarding it upon request. Address the letter in the same way shown above. Some offices will offer these services to non-cardholders, but you must call ahead to make sure. Check the **Practical Information** section of the cities you plan to visit; *Let's Go* lists AmEx office locations for most large cities. A complete list is available free from AmEx (US ☎800-528-4800).

BY TELEPHONE

CALLING HOME FROM THAILAND

A **calling card** is probably your cheapest bet. Calls are billed collect or to your account. You can frequently call collect without even possessing a company's calling card just by calling their access number and following the instructions. To obtain a calling card from your national telecommunications service before leaving home, contact the appropriate company listed below (using the numbers in the first column).

COMPANY	TO OBTAIN A CARD, DIAL:
AT&T (US)	☎800-361-4470
British Telecom Direct	☎800 34 51 44
Canada Direct	☎800-668-6878
Ireland Direct	☎800 40 00 00
MCI (US)	☎800-444-3333
New Zealand Direct	☎0800 00 00 00
Sprint (US)	☎800-877-4646
Telkom South Africa	☎10 219
Telstra Australia	☎13 22 00

To call home with a calling card, contact the operator for your service provider in Thailand by dialing the appropriate toll-free access number (listed on the inside back cover of this book). International calling booths abound; for a small fee, some may let you receive a call as well if you ask nicely. Many hostels also have International Direct Dial (IDD) facilities.

PLACING INTERNATIONAL CALLS To call Thailand from home or to call home from Thailand, dial:

1. The **international dialing prefix.** To dial out of **Australia,** dial ☎0011; **Canada** or the **US,** ☎011; the **Republic of Ireland, New Zealand,** or the **UK,** ☎00; **South Africa,** ☎09; **Thailand,** ☎001.
2. The **country code** of the country you want to call. To call **Australia,** dial ☎61; **Canada** or the **US,** ☎1; the **Republic of Ireland,** ☎353; **New Zealand,** ☎64; **South Africa,** ☎27; the **UK,** ☎44; **Thailand,** ☎66.
3. The **city/area code.** *Let's Go* lists the city/area codes for cities and towns in Thailand in a chart (see **Calling within Thailand,** below) and opposite the city or town name in its listing, next to a ☎. If the first digit is a zero (e.g. 020 for London), omit the zero when calling from abroad (e.g. dial 20 from Canada to reach London).
4. The **local number.**

CALLING WITHIN THAILAND

Prepaid phone cards (available at many guest houses, shops, and restaurants), which carry a certain amount of phone time depending on the card's denomination, usually save time and money in the long run. Just insert them into the phone and proceed with your call. Other prepaid phone cards come with a Personal Identification Number (PIN) and a toll-free access number. Call the access number and follow the directions on the phone to make both international and domestic calls.

Purchase them in advance from major telephone companies in your country, and check to make sure that service from the company will be available in the region where you'll be traveling. Phone rates typically tend to be highest in the morning, lower in the evening, and lowest on Sunday and late at night.

CITY/TOWN	DIALING PREFIX	CITY/TOWN	DIALING PREFIX
Ayutthaya	☎035	Mae Sariang	☎053
Bangkok	☎02	Mae Sot	☎055
Buriram	☎044	Mukdahan	☎042
Chanthaburi	☎031	Nakhon Phanom	☎042
Chiang Khan	☎042	Nakhon Ratchasima	☎044
Chiang Khong	☎053	Nan	☎054
Chiang Mai	☎053	Nong Khai	☎042
Chiang Rai	☎053	Pai	☎053
Chong Saen	☎053	Pak Chong	☎044
Chumphon	☎077	Phang-Nga	☎076
Hat Phra Nang	☎075	Phetchaburi	☎032
Hat Rai Lay	☎075	Phitsanulok	☎055
Hat Yai	☎074	Phuket	☎076
Hua Hin	☎032	Phuket Town	☎076
Kanchanaburi	☎034	Sakhon Nakhon	☎042
Khon Kaen	☎043	Sangkhlaburi	☎034
Ko Chang	☎01	Satun	☎074
Ko Phangan	☎077	Si Racha	☎038
Ko Phi Phi Don	☎075	Sukhothai	☎055
Ko Samet	☎01	Surat Thani	☎077
Ko Si Chang	☎038	Surin	☎044
Ko Tao	☎077	Tak	☎055
Krabi	☎075	That Phanom	☎042
Lampang	☎054	Trang	☎075
Loei	☎042	Trat	☎039
Mae Hong Son	☎053	Ubon Ratchathani	☎045
Mai Sai	☎053	Udon Thani	☎042
Mae Salong	☎053	Um Phang	☎055

TELEPHONE CARDS

Let's Go has recently partnered with **ekit.com** to provide a calling card that offers a number of services, including email and voice messaging. Before purchasing any calling card, always be sure to compare rates with other cards, and to make sure it serves your needs (a local phone card is generally better for local calls, for instance). For more information, visit www.letsgo.ekit.com.

BY EMAIL AND BY INTERNET

Internet cafes are everywhere in Thailand, even in some of the smallest towns. Many guest houses have Internet access. You can also log on for free at a public library. *Let's Go* lists Internet access locations in the **Practical Information** sections of most cities and towns. Often Internet access is listed as **CATNET**, an access network. It's usually difficult to forge a remote link with your home server from Thailand, so take advantage of free web-based email accounts (e.g. www.hotmail.com and www.yahoo.com).

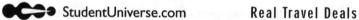

GETTING TO THAILAND

BY PLANE

A little effort can save you a bundle. If your plans are flexible enough to deal with the restrictions, courier fares are the cheapest. Tickets from consolidators and standby seating are also good deals, but last-minute specials, airfare wars, and charter flights often beat them. The key is to hunt around, be patient, be flexible, and ask persistently about discounts. Students, seniors, and those under 26 should never pay full price for a ticket.

Thailand has four major **international airports:** Bangkok (p. 94), Chiang Mai (p. 239), Phuket (p. 356), and Hat Yai (p. 377). Numerous international airlines, including **Thai Airways** (☎ 02 535 5173; www.thaiair.com), **Bangkok Airways** (☎ 02 229 3456; www.bangkokair.com), and **PB Airways** (☎ 02 261 0220) fly to these destinations. Thai Airways has a near-monopoly within the country, with extensive domestic connections. **Bangkok Airways'** most popular destinations from Bangkok include Ko Samui and Phuket.

Southeast Asia regional package tickets (offered by **Cathay Pacific Airlines;** www.cathaypacific.com), and round-the-world (RTW) flights are pricier but reasonable alternatives. Patching one-way flights together is the least economical way to travel.

DETAILS AND TIPS

Timing: Airfare to Thailand peaks on holidays and between May and September. The cheapest times to travel are October and April. Midweek (M-Th morning) round-trip flights run US$40-50 cheaper than weekend flights, which are generally more crowded and less likely to permit frequent-flier upgrades. Traveling with an "open return" ticket can be pricier.

Route: Round-trip flights are cheapest; "open-jaw" (arriving in and departing from different cities, e.g. New York-Chiang Mai, Bangkok-New York) tickets tend to be pricier. Instead, purchase a round-trip ticket to Bangkok and then a one-way flight to Chiang Mai upon arrival. That way you can purchase another one-way ticket from another city to Bangkok, which is very cheap. Flying into regional hubs is usually cheaper. Regional transportation is easier to handle while in Southeast Asia, and domestic flights can usually be purchased just hours or days in advance.

Round-the-World (RTW): If Thailand is only one stop on a more extensive globe-hop, consider a RTW ticket. Tickets usually include at least 5 stops and are valid for about a year; prices range US$1200-5000. Try **Northwest Airlines/KLM** (US ☎ 800-447-4747; www.nwa.com) or **Star Alliance,** a consortium of 13 airlines including United Airlines (US ☎ 800-241-6522; www.star-alliance.com).

Boarding: Confirm international flights by phone within 72hr. of departure. Most airlines require that passengers arrive at the airport 3hr. before departure. One carry-on item and 2 checked bags is the norm for non-courier flights.

BUDGET AND STUDENT TRAVEL AGENCIES

While knowledgeable agents can make your life easy and help you save, they may not spend the time to find you the lowest possible fare—they get paid on commission. Students and those under 26 holding **ISIC** and **IYTC cards** (see p. 44) qualify for discounts from student travel agencies. Most flights are on major airlines, but in peak season some may sell seats on less reliable chartered aircraft.

Council Travel (www.counciltravel.com). Countless US offices, including branches in Atlanta, Boston, Chicago, L.A., New York, San Francisco, Seattle, and Washington D.C. Check the web site or call ☎800-2-COUNCIL (226-8624) for the office nearest you.

STA Travel, 7890 S. Hardy Dr., Ste. 110, Tempe, AZ 85284, USA (24hr. reservations and info ☎800-781-4040; fax 480-592-0876; www.statravel.com). A student and youth travel organization with over 250 offices worldwide (check web site for a listing of all offices), including **US offices** in Boston, Chicago, L.A., New York, San Francisco, Seattle, and Washington, D.C. Ticket booking, travel insurance, railpasses, and more. In the UK, walk-in office in Macadam Bldg., Surrey St., **London** WC2R 2LE (☎207 379 4856). In New Zealand, 229 Queen St., **Auckland** (toll free ☎0800 100 677). In Australia, Forrest Hill Chase Shopping Ctr., 270 Canterbury Rd., **Melbourne** Vic 3131 (☎03 9878 9766), or 366 Lygon St., **Carlton** Vic 3053 (☎03 9349 4344).

Travel CUTS (Canadian Universities Travel Services Limited), 187 College St., **Toronto,** ON M5T 1P7 (☎416-979-2406; fax 979-8167; www.travelcuts.com). 60 offices across Canada. Also in the UK, 295-A Regent St., **London** W1R 7YA (☎0207 255 1944 or 255 2082).

COMMERCIAL AIRLINES

The commercial airlines' lowest regular offer is the **APEX** (Advance Purchase Excursion) fare, which provides confirmed reservations and allows "open-jaw" tickets. Generally, reservations must be made seven to 21 days ahead of departure, with a seven- to 14-day minimum-stay and up to 90-day maximum-stay restrictions. These fares carry hefty cancellation and change penalties (fees rise in summer). Book peak season APEX fares early; by May you will have a hard time getting your desired departure date. Use **Microsoft Expedia** (http://msn.expedia.com) or **Travelocity** (www.travelocity.com) to get an idea of the lowest published fares, then use the resources outlined here to beat those fares. Low-season fares should be appreciably cheaper than high-season fares (June to Sept.).

AIR COURIER FLIGHTS

Light packers should consider courier flights. Couriers help transport cargo on international flights by using their checked luggage space for freight. Generally, couriers must travel with carry-ons only and deal with complex flight restrictions. Most flights are round-trip only with short fixed-length stays (usually one week) and a limit of one ticket per issue. Most of these flights operate only out of major North American gateway cities. Generally, you must be over 21 (in some cases 18). Groups such as the **Air Courier Association** (☎800-282-1202; www.aircourier.org) and the **International Association of Air Travel Couriers,** P.O. Box 980, Keystone Heights, FL 32656 (☎352-475-1584; www.courier.org) provide lists of opportunities and courier brokers worldwide for an annual fee. For more information, consult *Air Courier Bargains* by Kelly Monaghan (The Intrepid Traveler, US$15) or the *Courier Air Travel Handbook* by Mark Field (Perpetual Press, US$13).

CHARTER FLIGHTS

Charters are flights that a tour operator contracts with an airline to fly extra loads of passengers during peak season. Charter flights fly less frequently than major airlines, make refunds particularly difficult, and are almost always fully booked well before their departure. Schedules and itineraries may also change or be canceled at the last moment (as late as 48 hours before the trip and without a full refund), and check-in, boarding, and baggage claim are often much slower. But they are usually cheaper than commercial flights.

Discount clubs and fare brokers offer members savings on last-minute charter and tour deals. Study contracts closely; you don't want to end up with an unwanted overnight layover. Pay with a credit card if you can and consider traveler's insurance against trip interruption.

TICKET CONSOLIDATORS

Ticket consolidators or "bucket shops" buy unsold tickets in bulk from commercial airlines and sell them individually at discounted rates. Look in the travel section of any major newspaper, where many ticket consolidators place tiny ads. Call quickly, as availability is typically extremely limited. Not all bucket shops are reliable, so insist on a receipt that gives full details of restrictions, refunds, and tickets. Pay by credit card (in spite of the 2-5% fee) so you can stop the payment if you never receive your tickets. For more info, see www.travel-library.com/air-travel/consolidators.html, or pick up Kelly Monaghan's *Air Travel's Bargain Basement* (The Intrepid Traveler, US$8).

TRAVELING FROM THE US AND CANADA. Travel Avenue (☎800-333-3335; www.travelavenue.com) rebates commercial fares from the US (5% for over US$550) and will search for cheap flights from anywhere for a fee. Other consolidators worth trying are **Interworld Travel** (☎800-468-3796 or 305-443-4929; www.interworldtravel.com); **Cheap Tickets** (☎800-652-4327; www.cheaptickets.com); **Travac** (☎800-872-8800; www.travac.com); **Internet Travel Network** (www.itn.com); **Travel Information Services** (www.tiss.com); and **TravelHUB** (www.travelhub.com). These are just suggestions to get you started; *Let's Go* does not endorse any of these agencies. Be cautious, and research companies before you hand over your credit card number.

TRAVELING FROM THE UK, AUSTRALIA, AND NEW ZEALAND. In London, the **Air Travel Advisory Bureau** (☎020 7636 5000; www.atab.co.uk) can provide names of reliable consolidators and discount flight specialists. In Australia and New Zealand, look for consolidator ads in the travel section of the *Sydney Morning Herald* and other papers.

> **FLIGHT PLANNING ON THE INTERNET** The web has great travel bargains—it's fast, it's convenient, and you can spend as long as you like exploring options without driving your travel agent insane. The Air Traveler's Handbook provides tips on finding cheap fares (www.cs.cmu.edu/afs/cs.cmu.edu/user/mkant/Public/Travel/airfare.html). Travelhub (www.travelhub.com) is a directory of travel agents that includes a searchable database of fares from over 500 consolidators. Other sites do the legwork and compile the deals for you—try www.bestfares.com, www.onetravel.com, and www.travelzoo.com. ■ **StudentUniverse** (www.studentuniverse.com), **STA** (www.sta-travel.com), and Orbitz.com provide quotes on student tickets, while **Expedia** (http://msn.expedia.com) and **Travelocity** (www.travelocity.com) offer full travel services. **Priceline** (www.priceline.com) allows you to specify a price, and obligates you to buy any ticket that meets or beats it; be prepared for odd routes. **Skyauction** (www.skyauction.com) lets you bid on both last-minute and advance-purchase tickets.

SPECIALTY CONSOLIDATORS. A limited number of travel agencies deal in unconventional arrangements of flights. Circle Pacific and Circle Asia tickets provide one-way flights to, from, and around Southeast Asia, especially Thailand. These tickets are best for extended trips; most have flexible dates, and are valid up to

ESSENTIALS

one year from the commencement of travel. For itineraries more complicated than a simple round-trip, RTW and other unconventional tickets are often a better deal. Try **Air Treks** (☎877-350-0612 or 415-912-5600; www.airtreks.com) or **Ticket Planet** (☎800-799-8888; www.ticketplanet.com), and leave plenty of time (at least a month) to book and confirm tickets.

FURTHER READING

The Worldwide Guide to Cheap Airfare, Michael McColl. Insider Publications (US$15). Out of print, check local library.

Discount Airfares: The Insider's Guide, George Hobart. Priceless Publications (US$18).

Air Traveler's Handbook, a detailed, comprehensive guide to consumer travel (www.cs.cmu.edu/afs/cs/user/mkant/Public/Travel/airfare.html).

FROM SOUTHEAST ASIA

BY PLANE

Flights between countries in Southeast Asia are inexpensive. Find the best deals on tickets in Bangkok, Singapore, Hong Kong, Kuala Lumpur, and Penang. Popular airlines include Malaysia Airlines, Singapore Airlines, Thai International, Cathay Pacific, and KLM Airlines. Booking tickets should be relatively worry-free, but travel agents can scam you. Be sure to make sure your deal is legitimate before you buy. *Let's Go* lists reliable tourist offices and travel offices in the **Practical Information** section of large cities. In general, use common sense—don't trust agents vending tickets in coffee bars. To be sure, always reconfirm with the airlines after receiving your ticket.

 AIRCRAFT SAFETY The airlines of developing world nations do not always meet safety standards. The *Official Airline Guide* (www.oag.com) and many travel agencies can tell you the type and age of aircraft on a particular route. This can be especially useful in Southeast Asia, where less reliable equipment is often used for internal or short flights. The **International Airline Passengers Association** (US ☎800-821-4272, UK ☎020 8681 6555) provides region-specific safety information. The **Federal Aviation Administration** (www.faa.gov) reviews the airline authorities for countries whose airlines enter the US. **US State Department** travel advisories (☎202-647-5225; http://travel.state.gov/travel_warnings.html) sometimes involve foreign carriers, especially when terrorist bombings or hijackings may be a threat.

BY BUS

Bus travel between Southeast Asian countries can be arranged. Thailand can be reached by bus from Cambodia, Laos, Malaysia, and Myanmar. A/C buses are usually very comfortable and reliable, but others offer sparse leg room and bumpy rides. Inquire about purchasing tickets, as some buses require reservations in advance, whereas others sell tickets upon departure and don't leave the station until completely full. Check visa availability before taking a bus ride; visas may not always be available at the border and must be acquired in advance in other towns. Most tourist cafes can help you with information and reservations.

BY BOAT

Boat trips from Malaysia to Thailand are possible, particularly from one point on the Malay peninsula to another. There's a ferry from Pulau Langkawi in Malaysia to Satun, though boats are not the best way to travel in Southeast Asia. They're generally slow and unreliable.

BORDER CROSSINGS

Overland border crossing points represent legal points of transit between Southeast Asian countries. Check local news agencies and embassies to confirm which border crossing points are open. Though Thailand's border crossing regulations remain stable, those of its neighboring countries do not. The result is unpredictable closings of crossing points, particularly with Malaysia and Myanmar.

BORDER CROSSINGS

CAMBODIA. Travelers can access Cambodia from **Aranyaprathet** (p. 182) to **Poipet**, or via a **Trat-Sihanoukville** boat (p. 177).

LAOS. Numerous land crossings exist across the Mekong River: **Chiang Khong** to **Houie Xay** (p. 289); **Nong Khai** to **Vientiane** (p. 221); **Nakhon Phanom** to **Tha Kaek** (p. 216); **Mukdahan** to **Savannakhet** (p. 211); **Ubon Ratchathani** to **Pakse** (p. 208).

MALAYSIA. The border is traversed from **Satun** to **Kuala Perlis** (p. 381); **Padang Besar** to **Kangar; Sadao** to **Alor Setar** (this is currently closed); **Betong** to **Keroh;** or **Sungai Kolok** to **Kota Bharu** (p. 384).

MYANMAR. Foreigners may enter Myanmar by land at: **Mae Sai** (p. 284), **Mae Sot** (p. 314), and the **Three Pagoda Pass** (p. 148). These border crossing points close the most frequently and unexpectedly, so check at the local embassy first.

GETTING AROUND THAILAND

LOCAL TRANSPORTATION

Thailand has every type of vehicle imaginable. From buses to taxis, tuk-tuk to *songthaew*, if it moves on land and has wheels, you'll find detailed information in the **Local Transportation** section of each city. Here's a glimpse of Thailand's most common mechanical marvels:

LOCAL VEHICLES	
River Taxi	Long, sometimes ornate boats that criss-cross the water.
Skytrain	Monorail-type train launched on December 5, 1999 to celebrate the king's 72nd birthday.
Songthaew	Three wheeler pickup with two rows of seats—more room but less spunk than a tuk-tuk.
Tuk-tuk	An opinionated and noisy three wheeler pickup that spitters and sputters on every road in Thailand.

BY CAR

RENTING

You can generally make reservations before you leave by calling major international offices in your home country. However, occasionally the price and availability information they give doesn't jive with what the local offices in your country will tell you. Try checking with both numbers to make sure you get the best price and accurate information. Local desk numbers are included in town listings; for home-country numbers, call your toll-free directory. Budget and AVIS both rent cars all over Thailand, below is a listing of only their primary locations.

Generally, the minimum age to rent a car is 21 in Thailand. Rentals start around 1500฿ for a compact car. Higher-end hotels will arrange a **"self-service"** (rental) car for you. Rental agencies, particularly Western ones like AVIS and Budget, are fairly safe, although a safe car won't protect you from bad road conditions and other drivers. Budget and AVIS both rent cars all over Thailand, below is a listing of only their primary locations.

AVIS (www.avis.com) has a location at the **Bangkok international airport** (☎66 2 55 4052; open daily 7am-midnight), on the first floor of Meeting Hall. Other locations in **Bangkok:** 2/12 Wireless Rd., Bangkok 10330 (☎66 2 255 5300; open daily 8am-6pm.); Le Meridien President Hotel, 971 Plonchit Rd., Bangkok 10330 (☎66 2 253 0444; open daily 8am-6pm.); Grand Erawan Hotel, 494 Rajdamri Rd., Bangkok (☎66 2 254 1234; open daily 7am-midnight). At the **Chiang Mai international airport:** 60/27 Chiang Mai Airport, Chiang Mai 50200 (☎66 053 201 798; open daily 8am-9pm). In **Chiang Mai:** Royal Princess Chiang Mai Hotel, 122 Changklan Rd., Chiang Mai (☎66 053 281 0336; open daily 8am-8pm).

Budget Rental (US and Canada international reservations ☎800-467-9337; www.budget.com) has three main locations in **Bangkok:** Tesco Lotus Rama 4, 3300 Rama 4, Kwang Klongton, Bangkok 10230; 19/23 Royal City Avenue, New Phetchaburi Rd., Bangkok 10320; 335/16 Donmuang Railway Station, Viphavadee Rungsit Rd., Bangkok 10320. In **Chiang Mai:** Tambon Haiya 201/2 Mahidol Rd., Tumbon Suthep Muang, Chiang Mai 50100.

DRIVING PERMITS

Car rental in Thailand is not only rare, it's unreliable. If you do choose to rent a car, an **International Driver's Permit (IDP)** is almost always asked for, though documentation requirements vary. Apply for an IDP at your home country's Automobile Association. Thailand can also grant IDPs if you take the road test, but unless you speak fluent Thai, get it at home. Remember that if you are driving a conventional vehicle on an unpaved road, you are almost never covered by insurance; ask about this at the rental agency.

DRIVING PRECAUTIONS When traveling in the summer or in the desert, bring substantial amounts of water (a suggested 5 liters of **water** per person per day) for drinking and for the radiator. For long drives to unpopulated areas, register with the police before beginning the trek, and again upon arrival at the destination. Check with the local automobile club for details. When traveling for long distances, make sure tires are in good repair and have enough air, and get good maps. A **compass** and a **car manual** can also be very useful. You should always carry a **spare tire** and **jack, jumper cables, extra oil, flares, a torch (flashlight),** and **heavy blankets** (in case your car breaks down at night or in the winter). If you don't know how to **change a tire,** learn before heading out, especially if you're planning on traveling in deserted areas. Blowouts on dirt roads are exceedingly common. If you do have a breakdown, **stay with your car;** if you wander off, there's less likelihood trackers will find you.

CAR INSURANCE

Most credit cards cover standard insurance. If you rent, lease, or borrow a car, you will need a **green card,** or **International Insurance Certificate,** to certify that you have liability insurance and that it applies abroad. Green cards can be obtained at car rental agencies, car dealers (for those leasing cars), some travel agents, and some border crossings. Rental agencies may require you to purchase theft insurance in countries that they consider to have a high risk of auto theft.

BY MOPED & BICYCLE

Almost every kind of personal vehicle short of a pogo stick can be rented in Thailand. Mopeds, bicycles, and motorcycles are the most common. Safety varies from town to town and establishment to establishment. These methods of transportation are often quite convenient, so to ensure safety, always rent a helmet. If possible, ask other travelers in the area what their experience has been with local rental agencies before renting.

BY THUMB

Let's Go strongly urges you to consider the risks before you choose to hitchhike. Though the Thai people are kind and generous, hitchhiking is never a safe option. Pay the extra baht, and take something official.

SPECIFIC CONCERNS

WOMEN TRAVELERS

Women inevitably face some additional safety concerns, but it's easy to be adventurous without taking undue risks. If you are on your own, consider staying in hostels which offer single rooms that lock from the inside or in religious organizations with rooms for women only. Communal showers in some hotels are safer than others, but check them first. Stick to centrally located accommodations and avoid solitary late-night treks.

Always carry extra money for a phone call, bus, or taxi. **Hitchiking** is never safe for lone women or even for two women traveling together. Choose train compartments occupied by women or couples; ask the conductor to put together a women-only compartment if there isn't one. Look as if you know where you're going (even when you don't) and consider approaching older women or couples for directions if you're lost or feeling uncomfortable.

Generally, the less you look like a tourist, the better off you'll be. Dress conservatively, especially in rural areas. Wear shirts with sleeves and pants/skirt that fall below the knee; the more coverage the better. Trying to fit in can be effective, but dressing to the style of an obviously different culture may cause you to be ill at ease and a conspicuous target. Wearing a **wedding band** may help prevent unwanted overtures. Some travelers report that carrying pictures of a "husband" or "children" is extremely useful to document marital status. Even a mention of a husband waiting back at the hotel may be enough to discount your potentially vulnerable, unattached appearance. If someone asks you how long you've been in the country, **always lie** and say 3-4 weeks.

Your best answer to verbal harassment is no answer at all; feigning deafness, sitting motionless, and staring straight ahead at nothing will do a world of good that reactions usually don't achieve. The extremely persistent can sometimes be dissuaded by a firm, loud, and very public "Go away" in the appropriate language. Learn how to say "help" in Thai (see **Inside back cover**). In Thailand, making a public display is the most effective way of getting a heckler off your back. If you feel threatened, **shout** your heart out—help will instantly be on the way.

Don't hesitate to seek out a police officer or a passerby if you are being harassed. Memorize each city's emergency numbers (listed in the **Practical Information** sections). For tourist police in Bangkok, the number is always ☎ 1155. Carry a **whistle** or an airhorn on your keychain, and don't hesitate to use it in an emergency. An **IMPACT Model Mugging** self-defense course will not only prepare you for a potential attack, but will also raise your awareness of your surroundings (see **Self Defense,** p. 50). See **Women's Health** (p. 56) for specific health concerns.

For general information, contact the **National Organization for Women (NOW),** 733 15th St. NW, Fl. 2, Washington, D.C. 20005, USA (☎202-628-8669; www.now.org), which has branches across the US.

FURTHER READING

A Journey of One's Own: Uncommon Advice for the Independent Woman Traveler, Thalia Zepatos. Eighth Mountain Press (US$17).

Adventures in Good Company: The Complete Guide to Women's Tours and Outdoor Trips, Thalia Zepatos. Eighth Mountain Press (US$7).

Active Women Vacation Guide, Evelyn Kaye. Blue Panda Publications (US$18).

Gutsy Women: More Travel Tips & Wisdom for the Road, Marybeth Bond. Traveler's Tales (US$13).

TRAVELING ALONE

There are many benefits to traveling alone, including independence and greater interaction with locals. However, any solo traveler is more vulnerable to harassment and street theft. Lone travelers need to be well-organized and look confident at all times. Try not to stand out as a tourist and be especially careful in deserted or very crowded areas. If questioned, never admit that you are traveling alone and lie about how long you've been in the country—always say you've been there at least for 3-4 weeks. Maintain regular contact with someone at home who knows your itinerary. For more tips, pick up *Traveling Solo* by Eleanor Berman (Globe Pequot Press, US$17) or subscribe to **Connecting: Solo Travel Network,** 689 Park Road, Unit 6, Gibsons, BC V0N 1V7, Canada (☎604-886-9099; www.cstn.org; membership US$25-35). Alternatively, several services link solo travelers with companions who have similar travel habits and interests; for a bi-monthly newsletter for single travelers seeking a travel partner (subscription US$48), contact the **Travel Companion Exchange,** P.O. Box 833, Amityville, NY 11701, USA (☎631-454-0880 or 800-392-1256; www.whytravelalone.com). **American International Homestays,** P.O. Box 1754, Nederland, CO 80466, USA (☎800-876-2048), has a listing of lodgings with English-speaking host families in Thailand.

MINORITY TRAVELERS

People in Thailand are largely tolerant and accepting of minority travelers. However, travelers of African descent have reported stray incidents of harassment, though there have been no reports of violence. To be safe, travelers of African descent are advised not to travel alone in rural areas.

OLDER TRAVELERS

Travel in Thailand has the potential to be particularly taxing for senior citizens, despite it being the most developed nation in Southeast Asia. However, there may be some extra benefits to age, including greater respect from the people you encounter. The books *No Problem! Worldwise Tips for Mature Adventurers* by Janice Kenyon (Orca Book Publishers, US$16) and *Unbelievably Good Deals and Great Adventures That You Absolutely Can't Get Unless You're Over 50* by Joan Rattner Heilman (McGraw-Hill, US$15) are both excellent resources. A few agencies for senior group travel are:

ElderTreks, 597 Markham St., Toronto, ON M6G 2L7, Canada (☎800-741-7956; elder-treks@eldertreks.com; www.eldertreks.com). In addition to Thailand, tours are also offered in Cambodia, Indonesia, Laos, Malaysian Borneo, Myanmar, and Vietnam.

Elderhostel, 11 Ave. de Lafayette, Boston, MA 02111, USA (☎877-426-8026; www.elderhostel.org). Programs at colleges, universities, and other learning centers in Thailand and other countries in Southeast Asia. Programs last 1-4 weeks. Must be 55 or over (spouse can be of any age).

The Mature Traveler, 2224 Beaumont St., Ste. D, Sacramento, CA 95815, USA (☎800-460-6676). Deals, discounts, and travel packages for the 50+ traveler. Subscription $30.

BISEXUAL, GAY & LESBIAN TRAVELERS

The spirit of Buddhist tolerance and non-confrontation make Thailand largely accepting, if not actively supportive, of same-sex relationships. There are no legal restrictions against homosexuality, and little social stigma is attached to it. The boundary between homosexual and heterosexual, which is so concrete in the West, is much more fluid in Thailand. Homosociality (camaraderie between members of the same sex, particularly between men) is much more common than Western travelers may be accustomed to; hand-holding between two men cannot be interpreted according to typical "Western" norms. Many Westerners even describe the country as a "gay paradise."

In fact, most Thais are horrified at the idea of gay-bashing and would regard it unthinkable to spurn a child simply because he is gay. Due largely to familial structures that stress carrying on the family lineage, however, most lesbians and gays feel pressured to stay closeted. The absence of blatant discrimination based on sexual orientation in Thai society takes away any impetus for the gay community to mobilize itself. It comes as no surprise, then, that informal social networks predominate over political organizations. However, most Thais believe that sexuality is a private matter and should be treated with discretion, regardless of one's sexuality. **Public displays of affection are not acceptable under any circumstance.**

Although active gay communities exist in **Bangkok,** the Thai government still has a rather unfavorable outlook toward homosexuality (even if laws banning homosexuality no longer exist) and rural communities may be much less accepting. Many Thais feel that the preponderance of male *farang* who frequent the "no money, no honey" scenes centered in Pattaya and Bangkok misrepresent the gay lifestyle. The stigma of the sex trade is such that many gay travelers find it difficult to integrate themselves into local communities. However, a booming gay nightlife—much of it divorced from the sex industry—remains quite accessible to foreigners. Thai tourism officials have seen the financial benefits of tolerating gay bars and establishments. Lesbian communities, often inaccessible to outsiders, remain largely underground, their nightlife comparatively subdued.

There is no gay or lesbian movement in Thailand like those in many Western nations, partly due to a lack of overt homosexual repression. However, this description masks more complex social issues. On the one hand, many educated, upper-class Thais have absorbed homophobic prejudices from Westerners. On the other hand, many Thai homosexuals who have had contact with Western gay movements have returned to Thailand to spearhead domestic awareness campaigns. Thus, cross-cultural exchange between Thailand and the West has been a double-edged sword. Also, Thai health officials are beginning to connect homosexuality with the skin industry in their crusade against HIV/AIDS so more attention is likely to be focused on the gay community in the future.

Let's Go lists resources for gay and lesbian travelers in the **Practical Information** sections of certain cities. Listed below are contact organizations, mail-order bookstores, and publishers that offer materials addressing specific concerns.

Utopia, 116/1 Soi 23, Sukhumvit Rd. (☎02 259 9619; www.utopia-asia.com), is Bangkok's best resource for gay and lesbian listings and support groups, with a cafe and gallery to boot. Their web site includes detailed information on clubs, events, and accommodations.

Dreaded Ned's (www.dreadedned.com) has detailed info on gay venues throughout Thailand.

Out and About (www.outandabout.com) offers a bi-weekly newsletter addressing travel concerns.

International Gay and Lesbian Travel Association, 4331 N Federal Hwy. #304, Fort Lauderdale, FL 33308, USA (☎954-776-2626 or 800-448-8550; www.iglta.com). An organization of over 1350 companies serving gay and lesbian travelers worldwide.

Gay's the Word, 66 Marchmont St., London WC1N 1AB, UK (☎44 20 7278 7654; www.gaystheword.co.uk). The largest gay and lesbian bookshop in the UK, with both fiction and non-fiction titles. Mail-order service available.

Giovanni's Room, 1145 Pine St., Philadelphia, PA 19107, USA (☎215 923 2960; www.queerbooks.com). An international lesbian/feminist and gay bookstore with mail-order service (carries many of the publications listed below).

International Lesbian and Gay Association (ILGA), 81 rue Marché-au-Charbon, B-1000 Brussels, Belgium (☎+32 2 502 2471; www.ilga.org). Provides political information, such as homosexuality laws of individual countries.

FURTHER READING

Utopia-Asia (www.utopia-asia.com): the best and most comprehensive resource for the gay or lesbian traveler in Southeast Asia.

Spartacus: International Gay Guide 2002/2003. Bruno Gmunder Verlag (US$33).

Ferrari Guides' Gay Travel A to Z, Ferrari Guides' Men's Travel in Your Pocket, and *Ferrari Guides' Inn Places.* Ferrari Publications (US$16-20).

The Gay Vacation Guide: The Best Trips and How to Plan Them, by Mark Chesnut. Citadel Press (US$15).

TRAVELERS WITH DISABILITIES

Thailand is ill-equipped to accommodate disabled travelers. Thailand has a history of not accepting people with disabilities. Often people with physical disabilities have been thought to have been immoral in past lives and to be bearers of bad luck. Further, it is also a cultural belief that a person's physical disabilities are emblematic of other mental and emotional disabilities. While these attitudes still persist in Thailand, they are changing, though slowly. The 1997 Constitution and 1998 Declaration on the Rights of Thai People with Disabilities have reflected the government's attempts to give the issue national attention as well as to facilitate the participation of people with disabilities in society. In 2001, Thailand received the Franklin D. Roosevelt International Disability Award for its progress toward fulfilling the goals set out by the United Nations World Programme of Action Concerning Disabled Persons. Thai people with disabilities rarely come out in public. Despite this, bold travelers will find many people eager to aid them.

Those with disabilities should inform airlines and hotels of their disabilities when they are making arrangements for travel; some time may be needed to prepare special accommodations. Call ahead to restaurants, museums, and other facilities to find out if they are handicapped-accessible. Hospitals cannot be relied upon to replace broken braces or prostheses; orthopedic materials, even in

Bangkok, Jakarta, and Manila, are often faulty at best. All public transportation is completely inaccessible. Rural areas have no sidewalks, and larger cities are packed with curbs and steps.

USEFUL ORGANIZATIONS

Mobility International USA (MIUSA), P.O. Box 10767, Eugene, OR 97440, USA (☎541-343-1284 voice and TDD; www.miusa.org). Sells *A World of Options: A Guide to International Educational Exchange, Community Service, and Travel for Persons with Disabilities* (US$35).

Moss Rehab Hospital Travel Information Service (☎215-456-9900; staff@mossresourcenet.org; www.mossresourcenet.org). An information resource center on travel-related concerns for those with disabilities.

Society for Accessible Travel & Hospitality (SATH), 347 5th Ave., #610, New York, NY 10016, USA (☎212-447-7284; www.sath.org). An advocacy group that publishes free online travel information and the travel magazine *OPEN WORLD* (US$13, free for members). Annual membership US$45, students and seniors US$30.

TOUR AGENCIES

Directions Unlimited, 123 Green Ln., Bedford Hills, NY 10507, USA (☎800-533-5343). Books individual and group vacations for the physically disabled; not an info service.

TRAVELERS WITH CHILDREN

Travel in Thailand with young children can prove a hassle. Except in Bangkok, hygienic environments and proper medical facilities are scarce. The combination of heat, mosquitoes, and dirty water might prove too much for a young child. That said, it is possible to bring children along as long as you take extra precautions and remain especially alert to potential dangers. Family vacations often require that you slow your pace and always require that you plan ahead. When deciding where to stay, call ahead to inquire about an establishment's ability to meet the special needs of young children. **Be sure that your child carries some sort of ID** in case of an emergency or if he gets lost. Arrange a reunion spot in case of separation when sightseeing. International fares are usually discounted 25% for children ages two to eleven. Finding a private place for **breast feeding** is often a probem while traveling. For more information, consult one of the following books:

Adventuring with Children: An Inspirational Guide to World Travel and the Outdoors, Nan Jeffrey. Avalon House Publishing (US$15).

Backpacking with Babies and Small Children, Goldie Silverman. Wilderness Press (US$7).

How to take Great Trips with Your Kids, Sanford Portnoy, Linda Ziedrich, and Joan Portnoy. Harvard Common Press (US$7).

Have Kid, Will Travel: 101 Survival Strategies for Vacationing With Babies and Young Children, Claire and Lucille Tristram. Andrews McMeel Publishing (US$13).

Trouble Free Travel with Children, Vicki Lansky. Book Peddlers (US$3).

DIETARY CONCERNS

Although Thai food often contains meat or uses meat bases, **vegetarian** dishes abound. For more information about vegetarian travel, contact the **North American Vegetarian Society,** P.O. Box 72, Dolgeville, NY 13329, USA (☎518-568-7970; www.navs-online.org), which publishes *Vegetarian Asia* ($10).

While **kosher** meals are practically nonexistent, the 5% Muslim presence in Thailand makes **halal** food an integral part of the national cuisine (especially in the Malay-speaking regions). If you are strict in your observance, consider preparing your own food on the road. For more information, visit your local bookstore, health food store, or library, and consult *The Vegetarian Traveler: Where to Stay If You're Vegetarian, Vegan, Environmentally Sensitive*, by Jed and Susan Civic (Larson Publications, US$16).

ESSENTIALS

ADDITIONAL RESOURCES

Let's Go's brief historical and cultural sketches are no substitute for more in-depth reading and research. As a rule, the more background knowledge you can acquire before you leave, the more you will appreciate all Thailand has to offer. Moreover, Thais are always pleased to meet foreigners who have made the effort to learn something about their heritage.

TRAVEL PUBLISHERS & BOOKSTORES

Hippocrene Books, Inc., 171 Madison Ave., New York, NY 10016, USA (☎212-685-4371; orders ☎718-454-2366; www.netcom.com/~hippocre). Free catalog. Publishes foreign language dictionaries and language learning guides.

Hunter Publishing, 470 W. Broadway, 2nd fl., South Boston, MA 02127, USA (☎617-269-0700; www.hunterpublishing.com). Has an extensive catalog of travel guides and diving and adventure travel books.

Rand McNally, 8255 N. Central Park, Skokie, IL 60076, USA (☎847-329-8100; www.randmcnally.com), publishes road atlases.

Adventurous Traveler Bookstore, P.O. Box 2221, Williston, VT 05495, USA (☎800-282-3963 or 802-860-6776; www.adventuroustraveler.com).

Travel Books & Language Center, Inc., 4437 Wisconsin Ave. NW, Washington, D.C. 20016, USA (☎800-220-2665 or 202-237-1322; www.bookweb.org/bookstore/travel-bks). Over 60,000 titles from around the world.

WORLD WIDE WEB

There is a wealth of information on Thailand available on the World Wide Web. Recently many regional newspapers, including the *Bangkok Post*, have launched on-line editions. Listed here are some budget travel sites to start off your surfing; other relevant web sites are listed throughout the book. Because web site turnover is high, use search engines (such as www.google.com and www.yahoo.com) to strike out on your own.

WWW.LETSGO.COM Our newly designed web site now features the full online content of all of our guides. In addition, trial versions of all nine City Guides are available for download on Palm OS™ PDAs. Our web site also contains our newsletter, links for photos and streaming video, online ordering of our titles, info about our books, and a travel forum buzzing with stories and tips.

THE ART OF BUDGET TRAVEL

How to See the World: www.artoftravel.com. A compendium of great travel tips, from cheap flights to self defense to interacting with local culture.

GET CARD.

TRAVEL HARD.

There's only one way to max out your travel experience and make the most of your time on the road: The International Student Identity Card.

 Packed with travel discounts, benefits and services, this card will keep your travel days and your wallet full. Get it before you hit it!

Visit **ISICUS.com** to get the full story on the benefits of carrying the ISIC.

Call or visit STA Travel online to find the nearest issuing office and purchase your card today:
www.statravel.com   (800) 777-0112

90 minutes, wash & dry (one sock missing)
5 minutes to book online (Detroit to Mom's)

Save money & time on student and faculty
travel at **StudentUniverse.com**

 StudentUniverse.com   Real Travel Dea

Rec. Travel Library: www.travel-library.com. A fantastic set of links for general information and personal travelogues.

Lycos: http://travel.lycos.com. General introductions to cities and regions throughout Southeast Asia, accompanied by links to applicable histories, news, and local tourism sites.

INFORMATION ON THAILAND

CIA World Factbook: www.odci.gov/cia/publications/factbook/index.html. Tons of vital statistics on Thailand's geography, government, economy, and people.

Bangkok Post: www.bangkokpost.com. Major daily newspaper is printed in English on the web site.

Chiang Mai News: www.chiangmainews.com. A northern newspaper with a different perspective.

CNN: http://asia.cnn.com. News service gives constant updates on Thailand in the Southeast Asia section.

MyTravelGuide: www.mytravelguide.com. Country overviews, with everything from history to transportation to live web cam coverage of Thailand.

Geographia: www.geographia.com. Highlights, culture, and people of Thailand.

Atevo Travel: www.atevo.com/guides/destinations. Detailed introductions, travel tips, and suggested itineraries

Business Day: www.bday.net. Thai newspaper focuses on Thai business and financial issues.

World Travel Guide: www.travel-guides.com/navigate/world.asp. Helpful practical info.

TravelPage: www.travelpage.com. Links to official tourist office sites in Thailand.

PlanetRider: www.planetrider.com. A subjective list of links to the "best" web sites covering the culture and tourist attractions.

Time-Asia Now: www.time.com/time/asia. The international version of the popular *Time Magazine*. Covers current events, cultural information, and technology news throughout Asia.

Cornell University Southeast Asia Program: www.einaudi.cornell.edu/southeastasia. Has links to hundreds of Thailand-related sites.

Australia National University: http://coombs.anu.edu.au/WWWVL-AsianStudies.html. Maintains a fantastic "virtual library" of Asia-related materials.

ESSENTIALS

ALTERNATIVES TO TOURISM

Traveling from place to place around the world is a memorable experience. But if you are looking for a more rewarding and complete way to see the world, you may want to consider Alternatives to Tourism. Working, volunteering, or studying for an extended period of time can be a better way to understand life in Thailand. This chapter outlines some of the different ways to get to know a new place, whether you want to pay your way through, or just get the personal satisfaction that comes from studying and volunteering. In most cases, you will feel that you partook in a more meaningful and educational experience—something that the average budget traveler often misses out on.

Though the beaches are soothing, the wats breath-taking, the guest house scenes entertaining, almost nothing beats working side-by-side with some of the friendliest people on earth, in a country with perhaps the richest culture in history.

VISA INFORMATION

To volunteer, study, or work for less than 30 days, American, Australian, Canadian, European, New Zealand and South African citizens do not need a visa. However, if you plan to stay past the 30-day free ride, you can get a tourist visa for 60 days. If you've set up a job or volunteer placement before arriving in Thailand, you may be eligible for a 90-day business visa, which covers work in medical and educational fields.

If you are among the truly devoted or hard-working and you wish to stay in Thailand for the long-term, you must apply to a Thai embassy for an extension. Extensions are granted from within the country if you already have a 90-day visa; if you don't, you must leave Thailand and apply for an extension at a Thai embassy. In either circumstance, the Thai government will require a letter from your academic institution, volunteer project, hospital, NGO, or place of work indicating their need for your assistance. It generally does not take more than two weeks to process the extension, whose length is dependent on your request and the length of the program or project. Extensions are largely given on a case-by-case basis, so contact the Thai embassy before your visa runs out and before you leave the country for the most up-to-date procedures. When you leave Thailand to apply, keep in mind that if you go to another country in Southeast Asia which is politically hostile to Thailand (i.e. Myanmar) your application may take longer to process.

STUDYING ABROAD

Study abroad programs range from basic language and culture courses to college-level classes, often for credit. In order to choose a program that best fits your needs, you will want to find out what kind of students participate in the program and what sort of accommodations are provided. In programs that have large groups of students who speak the same language, there is a trade-off. You may feel more comfortable in the community, but you will not have the same opportunity to practice a foreign language or to befriend other international students. For accommodations, dorm life provides a better opportunity to mingle with fellow students, but there is less of a chance to experience the local scene. If you live with a family, there is a potential to build lifelong friendships with natives and to experience day-to-day life in more depth, but conditions can vary greatly from family to family.

Those relatively fluent in Thai may find it cheaper to enroll directly in a university abroad, although getting college credit may be more difficult. Some American schools still require students to pay them for credits they obtain elsewhere. Most university-level study-abroad programs are meant as language and culture enrichment opportunities, and therefore are conducted in Thai. Still, many programs do offer classes in English and beginner- and lower-level language courses. A good resource for finding programs that cater to your particular interests is www.studyabroad.com, which has links to various semester abroad programs based on a variety of criteria, including desired location and focus of study. The following is a list of organizations that can help place students in university programs abroad, or have their own branch in Thailand.

AMERICAN PROGRAMS

AFS, 310 SW 4 Ave., Ste. 630, Portland, OR 97204-2608, USA (☎800-237-4636; fax 503-248-4076; info@afs.org; www.afs.org). Runs study abroad and community service programs for both students and educators. Volunteers live with host families in Indonesia, Malaysia, Thailand, and dozens of other countries around the globe. Programs last from several months to a year; cost varies widely with program type and duration.

Council on International Educational Exchange (CIEE), Council ISP, 633 3rd Ave. 20th fl., New York, NY 10017, USA (☎888-268-6245 or 800-407-8839; www.ciee.org/study). Sponsors study abroad programs in Thailand.

International Association for the Exchange of Students for Technical Experience (IAESTE), 10400 Little Patuxent Pkwy. Suite 250, Columbia, MD 21044-3519, USA (☎410-997-2200; www.aipt.org). 8- to 12-week programs in Thailand for college students who have completed 2 years of technical study. US$25 application fee.

ITTA, 3600 S. 60th Ave, Shelby, MI 49455, USA (☎231-861-0481). Thai massage classes and travel throughout Thailand. US$1800 includes airfare and accommodations.

Lexia International, 25 South Main St., Hanover, NH 03755, USA (☎800-775-3942 or 603-643-9898; www.lexiaintl.org). Students live at Payap University in Chiang Mai and choose a field research project in Thai culture.

Pacific Challenge, P.O. Box 3151, Eugene, OR 97401, USA (☎541-343-4124; hq@pacificchallenge.org; www.pacificchallenge.org). Experiential adventure travel program in Cambodia, Laos, Thailand, and Vietnam. US$4700 includes round-trip international flight, internal travel, program activities, accommodations, and visas.

School for International Training, College Semester Abroad, Admissions, Kipling Rd., P.O. Box 676, Brattleboro, VT 05302, USA (☎800-336-1616 or 802-257-7751; www.sit.edu). Semester- and year-long programs in Thailand run US$10,600-13,700. Also runs the **Experiment in International Living** (☎800-345-2929; fax 802-258-3428; www.usexperiment.org), 3- to 5-week summer programs that offer high-school students cross-cultural homestays, community service, ecological adventure, and language training in Thailand. Programs cost US$1900-5000.

Where There Be Dragons (☎800-982-9203; info@wheretherebedragons.com). Runs youth summer programs and short adult trips to Cambodia, Laos, Thailand, and Vietnam. Youth programs range from US$5950 to US$6150. Adult programs range from US$3550 to US$4500. Fee includes food, accommodations, and internal travel.

PROGRAMS IN THAILAND

English and Computer College, see **Teaching English,** p. 89

The Chiang Mai Cooking School, 44 Ratchamanka Rd., Chiang Mai. Run out of The Wok (see **Chiang Mai: Food,** p. 248), this school was established in 1993 and is the most widely known in all of Thailand. As a general rule at most cooking schools in Chiang Mai, one day will teach you the basics of curry, while a two-day course is enough to cover basic Thai dishes. Depending on your interest, check whether a market tour is included, and whether you can choose the dishes you learn. A free recipe book should be standard. One-day courses cost 700-900฿. The Chiang Mai Cooking School provides a comprehensive course: 1-day 900฿, 2-day 1800฿, 3-day 2600฿, 4-day 3400฿, 5-day 4200฿. (See also **Chiang Mai: Courses and Forums,** p. 254.)

Chiang Mai Thai Cookery, 1-3 Moon Muang Road, Chiang Mai 50200 (☎66 53 206 388; www.thaicookeryschool.com), offers courses for up to 5 days in Thai cooking and fruit tasting (5days, $100).

Lanna Boxing Camp (www.lannamuaythai.com) in Chiang Mai will teach you to box like Nong Toom, the infamous cross-dressing kickboxing superstar (see p. 119). Train for a day 250฿; for longer training periods, price varies.

Mama Nit at Baan Nit, 1 Chaiyaphum Rd. Soi 2, Chiang Mai (☎01 366 8289). Mama Nit learned her unique blend of deep tissue and nerve therapy massage from her Chinese grandfather when she was 13. Ever since, she has been able to help those with nagging back pain and piercing nerve twinges. Those taking the 10-day to one-month massage courses follow Mama's technique with translation from aides. A 1hr. massage is 150฿, but if you want to have it with Mama Nit, it'll cost you 200฿. Courses run: 2-day 1000฿; 10-day 3800฿; 15-day 5800฿; one-month 9500฿. Open M-Sa roughly 9:30am-5pm. (See also **Chiang Mai: Courses and Forums,** p. 254.)

The Old Medicine Hospital, 238/8 Wuolai Rd., Chiang Mai (☎275 085), the soi is opposite and slightly south of the Chiang Mai Cultural Center. The hospital garners praise for its relaxing massages. Ten-day course starting on the first and middle Monday of each month (4000฿). Students receive a certificate for Thai Massage, overseen by Thailand's Ministry of Education. Herbal sauna 60฿; 1½hr. massage 150฿, with A/C 200฿. Open daily 8:30am-4:30pm. (See also **Chiang Mai, Courses and Forums,** p. 254.)

Thai Kitchen Cookery Center, on Chiang Moi Kao Soi 3, Chiang Mai, next to the Eagle Guest House (☎233 966). It's run by Tim and his wife Malee. If you sign up for the course, with 3 different menus each day (800฿), you will be cooking and chopping all day—you truly do everything with a fun staff. Their sister establishment, Thai Chocolate, has 4 menus each day, which do not change. Courses run 9am-5pm, and they will pick you up from your guest house.

Thai Language Courses, in Chiang Mai are offered at **Payap University** (☎304 805, ext. 247) and at **AUA,** on Ratchadamnoen Rd., 100m west of Tha Pae Gate opposite the AUA library. Offers 60hr. courses. Classes meet M-F for 2hr. per day, 3500฿; tutoring 250฿ per hr. (See also **Chiang Mai: Courses and Forums,** p. 254.)

Vandee's Cooking Courses, at Peter and Vandee's Guest House in Pai, are known to be absolutely fabulous. For a 1-day course, it's 400฿. A 5-day course, 1200฿, will grant you a certificate at the end. Prices include recipe book. Start time for lunch 11:30am, dinner 6:30pm.

Voravihara Insight Meditation Center (☎826 869), housed in Wat Pratat Sri Chom Thong, 60km from Chiang Mai in the town of Chom Thong. In the back right-hand corner of the wat. After the turn-off to Doi Inthanon, the wat is the first one on the left. First-timers are requested to put aside at least 26 days for the course which covers Samatha Bhavana, the repetition of a mantra, and Vipassana Bhavana, freedom from your body. After the course, 10-day retreats are advised to solidify the teachings. All students report daily to their Thai, Canadian, or Swedish instructor, and are expected to obey the 8 precepts—for many the most difficult precept is limiting themselves to two meals per day taken before noon. Accommodations are provided for the duration of the course and the price of the "donation" is up to you. If you're up for the challenge of this course, reservations are essential. (See also **Chiang Mai: Courses and Forums,** p. 254.)

Wat Pa Nanachat Beung Wai and **Wat Nong Pa Pong,** in Ubon Ratchathani, are forest monasteries that let you stay if you're interested in meditation and Buddhism. Both wats are places for serious study and learning with one of the most renowned monks in the region. Not for dabblers. (See also **Forest Monasteries,** p. 207.)

Wat Ram Poeng (☎278 620), in the foothills of Doi Suthep, 1.5km from Wat U-Mong. From Wat U-Mong's entrance turn right and take the first right. Offers 26-day Vipassana Meditation Courses and 10-day retreats at its Northern Insight Meditation Center. Donations for either course, both of which include room and board, are appreciated but not solicited. (See also **Chiang Mai: Courses and Forums,** p. 254.)

Wat Suan Mokkha Phalaram (Suan Mok), a working monastery, offers 12-day meditation retreats. In that time, the resident monks urge restraint in all its attendees, discouraging vices like cigarette smoking and mosquito slapping. The 1200฿ fee covers food, accommodations, and expenses for the retreat. Retreats start on the last day of each month and run to the 11th day of the following month. It's not possible or necessary to reserve a spot; you need only show up a few days before the end the month.

HOMESTAYS

Center for Cultural Interchange, 17 North Second Ave., St. Charles, IL 60174, USA (☎888-227-6231 or 630-377-2272; www.cci-exchange.org), offers 2-14 weeks family homestays for $250, including room and board, for the purposes of cultural exchange.

Thai Payap Project (☎772 520) sells hill tribe handicrafts but also sets up homestays with 15 different local hill tribes to live and work with a family. All proceeds help the hill tribes in the area around Nan in Northern Thailand. (See also **Nan,** p. 293.)

SPAS & HERBAL MEDICINE

Lampang Medical Plants Conservation Center (☎350 787), in Lampang, has herbal everything for self-healing. Massages, body scrubs, and vapor baths are available, too. They have remedies for every ailment and ache. (See also **Lampang: Sights,** p. 297.)

The Sanctuary, on Ko Phangan, although a backpacker place, is still quiet, secluded, and impeccably clean. Free evening meditations. Many are happy to pay 60฿ for a dorm bed and splurge on yoga classes (150฿) and oil massages (400฿). Singles and doubles with bath 200-1000฿. (See also **Ko Phangan: Sights,** p. 341.)

Tamarind Springs (☎77 424 436; www.tamarindretreat.com), on Ko Samui, offers alternative medicine and outstanding spa facilities, including a hot spring pool amid ancient boulders.

Garden Beach Resort Pattaya (☎38 411 940 or 2 673 9015), on the eastern coast near Chonburi, has spa facilities in a tropical setting.

Tropical Herbal Spa (☎75 637 940), on Ao Nang Beach in Krabi. All-natural ingredients, many of them local, are used to soothe and relax your muscles and mind.

Sawasdee Spa (☎75 637 072), on Ao Nang Beach in Krabi. This resort spa has less of a backpacker feel and includes Thai philosophies of well-being in the treatments.

WORKING

There are two main schools of thought. Some travelers want long-term jobs that allow them to get to know another part of the world in depth (e.g. teaching English, working in the tourist industry). Other travelers seek out short-term jobs to finance their travel. They usually seek employment in the service sector or in agriculture, working for a few weeks at a time to finance the next leg of their journey. This section discusses both short-term and long-term opportunities for working in Thailand. Make sure you understand Thailand's **visa requirements** for working abroad. See the box on p. 84 for more information.

It's easiest to find a job once in Thailand. Look at listings on lampposts, guest house bulletin boards, signs in windows, and ads or listings in newspapers. Don't be afraid to ask, either. Establishments, particularly in the tourism industry, are always looking for native English-speakers to accommodate their customers.

LONG-TERM WORK

If you're planning on spending a substantial amount of time (more than three months) working in Thailand, search for a job well in advance. International placement agencies are often the easiest way to find employment abroad, especially for teaching English. **Internships,** usually for college students, are a good way to segue into working abroad, although they are often unpaid or poorly paid (many say the experience, however, is well worth it). Be wary of advertisements or companies that claim the ability to get you a job abroad for a fee—often times the same listings are available online or in newspapers, or even out of date. It's best, if going through an organization, to use one that's somewhat reputable. Some good ones include:

Archaeological Institute of America, 656 Beacon St., Boston, MA 02215, USA (☎617-353-6550; www.archaeological.org). The *Archaeological Fieldwork Opportunities Bulletin* ($15.95) lists field sites in Southeast Asia, most notably in Thailand. Buy the books from Oxbow/David Brown Book Co. online at www.oxbowbooks.com (☎800-791-9354).

World-wide Opportunities on Organic Farms, P.O. Box 2675, Lewes BN7 1RB, England, UK (www.wwoof.org). Provides connections between volunteers and organic farms in Cambodia, Laos, Malaysia, the Philippines, Singapore, and Thailand. A minimal WWOOF membership fee is required in order to participate.

TEACHING ENGLISH

Teaching jobs abroad are rarely well paid, although some elite private American schools can pay somewhat competitive salaries. Volunteering as a teacher in lieu of getting paid is also a popular option, and even in those cases, teachers often get some sort of a daily stipend to help with living expenses. Salaries at schools, even private schools, may seem low, but Thailand's low cost of living makes it much more profitable. In almost all cases, you must have at least a bachelor's degree to be a full-fledged teacher, although oftentimes college undergraduates can get summer positions teaching or tutoring.

Many schools require teachers to have a Teaching English as a Foreign Language (TEFL) certificate. Not having one does not necessarily exclude you from finding a teaching job, but certified teachers often find higher paying jobs. Native English speakers working in private schools are most often hired for English-immersion classrooms where no Thai is spoken. Those volunteering or teaching in public, poorer schools, are more likely to be working in both English and Thai. Placement agencies or university fellowship programs are the best resources for finding teaching jobs in Thailand. The alternative is to make contacts directly with schools or just to try your luck once you get there. If you're going to try the latter, the best time of the year is several weeks before the start of the school year. The organizations listed below are extremely helpful in placing teachers in Thailand. However, do not stop here. There is tremendous demand for English teachers in Thailand and it's always possible to find work as an English teacher. Not all places will be able to provide work permits; the "visa run" is a common phenomenon among permanent visitors. The **Australia Center** (p. 244) is a good source of information and provides a leaflet on working in Chiang Mai. (☎810 552. 75/1 Moo 14, Suthep Rd., on a soi after the turn-off to Wat U-Mong.) If these resources are not right for your plans, keep looking or simply show up—many travelers have been hired on-site.

Burma Volunteer Programme, see **Volunteering,** p. 90.

Camping and English offers free room and board to travelers who will teach English to kids throughout the Northeast region. Contact San-Seri (volynthai@yahoo.com) for more information.

Cross Cultural Solutions, see **Volunteering,** p. 90.

Fulbright English Teaching Assistantship, U.S. Student Programs Division, Institute of International Education, 809 United Nations Plaza, New York, NY 10017-3580, USA (☎212-984-5330; www.iie.org). Competitive program sends college graduates to teach in Thailand.

English and Computer College, 430/17-24 Chula 64, Siam Square, Patumwan, Bangkok 10330 (☎66 2 253 3312, in the US ☎425-930-5421, in the UK ☎0870 161 1256; jobs@ac.th; www.eccthai.com). Constantly recruiting teachers for schools all over Thailand, from the most rural to the most urban. Also offers courses in teaching certification, with a guaranteed job placement after completion of the course.

Global Service Corps, see **Volunteering,** p. 91.

International Schools Services (ISS), 15 Roszel Rd., Box 5910, Princeton, NJ 08543-5910, USA (☎609-452-0990; fax 609-452-2690; www.iss.edu). Hires teachers for more than 200 overseas schools including Thailand. Candidates should have experience with teaching or international affairs, 2-year commitment expected.

Involvement Volunteers Association Inc., P.O. Box 218, Port Melbourne, Victoria 3207, Australia (☎03 9646 9392; ivworldwide@volunteering.org.au). Volunteer at the Sunrise Organic Farm and the Computer School and help fulfill the goal of self-sufficiency for this community of orphaned Cambodian children. Police Records Clearance and a minimum of six weeks commitment are required. Single placement fee of US$140.

Office of Overseas Schools, US Department of State, Room H328, SA-1, Washington, DC 20522, USA (☎202-261-8200; www.state.gov/www/about_state/schools/). Keeps a comprehensive list of schools abroad and agencies that arrange placement for Americans to teach abroad, including schools in Cambodia, Indonesia, Laos, Malaysia, Myanmar, the Philippines, Singapore, Thailand, and Vietnam.

Tum (☎471 918; tumthai76@hotmail.com), at the Old Phimai Guest House in Phimai, can hook you up with a teaching position or a short-term work opportunity in Phimai. He can arrange the position, with compensation to be negotiated. (See also Phimai, p. 196.)

Teaching & Projects Abroad, see **Volunteering,** p. 93.

Danny, at the Punnee Cafe in Kanchanaburi (p. 136), can talk to you about the possibility of working at the local private Catholic school teaching English. 1-month, 3-month, and 1-year commitments. Teachers receive room and board plus stipend. You can also contact the school directly (☎09 889 0050, ask for Orawan).

SHORT-TERM WORK

Traveling for long periods of time can get expensive; therefore, many travelers try their hand at odd jobs for a few weeks at a time to make some extra cash to carry them through another month or two of touring around. A popular option is to work several hours a day at a hostel in exchange for free or discounted room and/or board. Most often, these short-term jobs are found by word of mouth, or simply by talking to the owner of a hostel or restaurant. Many places, especially due to the high turnover in the tourism industry, are always eager for help, even if only temporary. *Let's Go* tries to list temporary jobs like these whenever possible; check the practical information sections in larger cities. Also, long-term or teaching positions may need short-term workers, so ask about the possibility at other listed establishments.

VOLUNTEERING

Volunteering can be one of the most fulfilling experiences you can have in life, especially if you combine it with the wonder of travel in a foreign land. Many volunteer services charge you a fee to participate in the program and to do work. These fees can be surprisingly hefty (although they frequently cover airfare and most, if not all, living expenses). Try to do research on a program before committing—talk to people who have previously participated and find out exactly what you're getting into, as living and working conditions can vary greatly. Different programs are geared toward different ages and levels of experience, so make sure that you are not taking on too much or too little. The more informed you are and the more realistic your expectations, the more enjoyable the program will be.

Most people choose to go through a parent organization that takes care of logistical details, and frequently provides a group environment and support system. There are two main types of organizations—religious (often Catholic) and non-sectarian—although there are rarely restrictions on participation for either.

ACDI/VOCA, 50 F St. NW, Suite 1075, Washington, DC 20001, USA (☎800-929-8622 or 202-383-4961; fax 202-626-8726; volunteer@acdivoca.org; www.acdivoca.org). Volunteer opportunities in Thailand for professionals, lasting from two weeks to three months. Volunteers provide short-term technical assistance in banking, business and cooperative planning, and agricultural production. All expenses paid.

Burma Volunteer Programme (maesotel@loxinfo.co.th; www.geocities.com/maesotesl) needs volunteers to teach English, organize women's welfare centers, work on activism and publicity, and run organizations for human rights and education. Positions are available in towns along the Myanmar border—Kanchanaburi, Sangkhlaburi, Mae Sot, and Mae Hong Son. Burmese refugees of all ethnicities need basic education in order to establish citizenship anywhere and to have access to medical and national protection. Room and board may be provided.

Childlife is a program in Mae Sai which works with 63 children (a number that constantly increases) who are orphaned, have AIDS, or are homeless. All the children are Akkha, a minority discriminated against in both Myanmar and Thailand. They are in need of volunteers—no experience necessary. The contact is a German phone number, but the web site is in English and the coordinators speak English (☎0163 650 8758; kinderleben_ev@yahoo.de; www.kinderleben.org).

Cross Cultural Solutions, 47 Potter Avenue, New Rochelle, NY 10801, USA (☎800-380-4777; www.crossculturalsolutions.org). Offers a wide variety of programs (3-20 weeks) focusing on HIV/AIDS education and outreach, teaching English, and working at community centers ($2000-5000).

CUSO, 500-2255 Carling Ave., Ottawa, Ontario, Canada, K2B 1A6 (☎888-434-2876 (in Canada) or 613-829-7445; fax 613-829-7446; cuso.secretariat@cuso.ca; www.cuso.org). Two-year volunteer opportunities for Canadian citizens in Thailand. CUSO volunteers work in human rights, legal advocacy, and development. Airfare, housing, and a stipend provided.

Doctors Without Borders, 6 E. 39th St., 8th fl., New York, NY 10016, USA (☎212-679-6800; doctors@newyork.msf.org; www.doctorswithoutborders.org). Provides emergency aid to victims of armed conflict, epidemics, and natural and man-made disasters in Thailand. Requirements for medical positions are at least two years professional experience.

Earthwatch, 3 Clocktower Pl. Suite 100, Box 75, Maynard, MA 01754, USA (☎800-776-0188 or 978-461-0081; www.earthwatch.org). Arranges 1- to 3-week programs in Thailand to promote conservation of natural resources. Fees vary based on program location and duration, costs average $1700 plus airfare.

Ecovolunteer, Meijersweg 29, 7553 AX Hengelo, Netherlands (☎31 74 250 8250; info@ecovolunteer.org; www.ecovolunteer.org). Volunteer opportunities with wildlife in Thailand. See web site for more information.

Foundation to Encourage the Potential of Disabled Persons, 195/197 Ban Tanawan, Moo 8, Tambon Sanpheeseu, Amphur Muang, Chiang Mai 50300 (☎053 852 172; assist@loxinfo.co.th; www.infothai.com/disabled). The only center of its kind in Chiang Mai, the foundation teaches disabled persons a variety of skills and welcomes volunteers.

GAP Activity Projects (GAP) Limited, GAP House, 44 Queen's Road, Reading, Berkshire RG1 4BB, UK (☎0118 957 6631; www.gap.org.uk). Organizes voluntary work placements for 18- and 19-year-olds in a "transition year" after secondary education. Programs are 5-6 months and costs vary from US$2600 to 4000. Financial aid is available. Programs are designed for British and Irish citizens but applicants of other nationalities may be accepted.

Global Routes, 1814 7th St., Berkeley, CA, USA (☎510-848-4800; www.globalroutes.org). Has high school programs focused on construction and college teaching internships throughout the world; both involve homestays. Programs cost around US$4000 plus airfare.

Global Service Corps, 300 Broadway #28, San Francisco, CA 94133, USA (☎415-788-3666; www.globalservicecorps.org). Programs and internships in education, health care, and environment (can be specialized) for 3-10 weeks ($2000+).

Greenway, P.O. Box 21, Hat Yai Airport, Hat Yai, Songkhla, Thailand 90115 (☎0 7447 3506; fax 0 7447 3508; camps@greenwaythailand.org; www.greenwaythailand.org; www.greenwaybizland.com). Volunteer your help to indigenous communities throughout the country, including a hill tribe in Northern Thailand (see p. 278). Applications must be completed in your home country.

Habitat for Humanity International, 121 Habitat St., Americus, GA 31709, USA (☎229-924-6935, ext. 2251 or 2252; www.habitat.org). Offers international opportunities in Indonesia, Malaysia, Singapore, Thailand, Vietnam, and the Philippines to live with and build houses in a host community. Costs average US$2000-3800.

Human Development Foundation (www.fatherjoe.org) is devoted to a grassroots development of Bangkok's poorest neighborhood, Khlong Toei. The founder, Father Maier, constantly needs donations and volunteers for his schools, HIV/AIDS and drug prevention programs, legal aid projects, and infirmaries. (See also **Bangkok's Mother Theresa,** p. 126.)

International Conservation Holidays, 36 St. Mary's St., Wallingford, Oxfordshire OX10 0EU, UK (☎01491 821600; www.btcv.org/international). They offer conservation ecology trips throughout Thailand and Southeast Asia.

ALTERNATIVES TO TOURISM

International Executive Service Corps, 333 Ludlow St., PO Box 10005, Stamford, CT 06904-2005, USA (☎203-967-6000; fax 203-324-2531; iesc@iesc.org; www.iesc.org). Sends professionals to Indonesia, the Philippines, and Thailand. Volunteers serve as consultants to businesses, government organizations, and non-profits. Assignments last from 2 weeks to 3 months; IESC can also arrange longer-term work. Major expenses paid; spouse's expenses covered if project lasts for at least a month.

Maryknoll Mission, P.O. Box 307, Maryknoll, NY 10545, USA (☎914-762-6364; mmaf@mkl-mmaf.org; www.maryknoll.org). Become a Maryknoll Missioner and work to build Christian communities in Thailand.

Operation Smile, 6435 Tidewater Dr., Norfolk, VA 23509, USA (☎757-321-7645; dmaynard@operationsmile.org; www.operationsmile.org). Provides reconstructive surgery and related health care, and training and education to health care professionals in Cambodia, the Philippines, Thailand, and Vietnam.

Peace Corps, Peace Corps Headquarters, 1111 20th St. NW, Washington, DC 20526, USA (☎800-424-8580; www.peacecorps.gov). Opportunities in 70 developing nations including Thailand and the Philippines. Volunteers must be US citizens ages 18+ willing to make a 2-year, 3-month commitment. A bachelor's degree is usually required.

Population and Community Development Association, 8 Sukhumvit, Soi 12, Bangkok, 10110 (☎66 2 229 4611; www.sli.unimelb.edu.au/pda). Has programs specializing in everything from environmental research and rehabilitation to family planning and AIDS education. Volunteers are especially welcome on health-related projects in Chiang Rai (see p. 278).

Project Trust, 12 East Passage, Long Lane, London EC1A 7LP, UK (☎44 020 7796 1170/1/3; fax 44 020 7796 1172; alex@projecttrust.org.uk; www.projecttrust.org.uk). Run by GAP Activity Projects Limited, Project Trust sends volunteers to 24 countries each year for 12 months to live, work, and travel in a foreign country. Though Project Trust is UK-based, applicants of other nationalities may be accepted. Participants are normally between 17 and 19 years old, and must fundraise as much as £4000 to fund their trips. Different projects are offered in Malaysia, Thailand, and Vietnam—almost all are exclusively educational.

The Rejoice Urban Development seeks to bring badly needed medical welfare resources to those suffering directly and indirectly from AIDS. One of only a handful of NGOs working directly with the HIV-infected community, **Rejoice** has implemented both a formula milk program and educational scholarships for orphaned children, in addition to their medical services. Qualified nurses, doctors, social workers, and medical students, as well as those who can serve in administrative or technical positions, are welcome to volunteer for stints of 2 weeks to 2 months. Volunteers are expected to cover their own room and board. Donations are welcome, or visit their office to buy handicrafts made by people affected by AIDS. Contact the founder, Gareth, for more information (☎806 227; www.rejoicecharity.com).

Relief for Oppressed People Everywhere (ROPE), 12 Church St., Rickmansworth, Hertfordshire, WD3 1BS, UK (☎44 019 2377 1821; fax 019 2377 5117; rope@rope.org.uk; www.rope.org.uk/default.html). A volunteer charity that helps the poor in 85 countries, including Cambodia, Indonesia, Laos, the Philippines, Thailand, and Vietnam, with direct aid, food, education, medical help, heating, housing, and clothing. Those helped include widows, orphans, refugees, the sick, the unemployed, and the homeless.

Service Civil International Voluntary Service (SCI-IVS), 5474 Walnut Level Rd., Crozet VA 22932, USA (☎/fax 206-350-6585; www.sci-ivs.org). Arranges placement in workcamps in Thailand for those 21+. A special application form and previous workcamp experience is required for those applying to work in Southeast Asia. Registration fee US$125.

Teaching & Projects Abroad, Gerrard House, Rustington, West Sussex BN16 1AW, UK (☎44 0 1903 859911; www.teaching-abroad.co.uk). Projects include care/community action and teaching English. Programs can be combined with projects in other countries (US$2000 for 3 months).

United Nations Volunteers, Postfach 260 111, D-53153 Bonn, Germany (☎228 815 2000; www.unv.org). Assignments vary in length and are located throughout several Southeast Asian countries. Inquire for information about specific projects' language and skill requirements. Minimum monthly stipend provided.

Voluntary Service Overseas, VSO Canada, 151 Slater St., Suite 806, Ottawa, Ontario KIP 5H3, Canada (☎613-234-1364; fax 613-234-1444; inquiry@vsocan.com; www.vso-canada.org). Opportunities to work in Indonesia, Laos, the Philippines, Thailand, and Vietnam on a wide range of projects. Most volunteer positions last two years, though some shorter-term placements are available. VSO covers expenses; stipend provided.

Volunteers for Peace, 1034 Tiffany Rd., Belmont, VT 05730, USA (☎802-259-2759; www.vfp.org). Arranges placement in work camps in Cambodia, Indonesia, Thailand, the Philippines, and Vietnam. Membership required for registration. Annual International *Workcamp Directory* US$20. Programs average US$200-500 for 2-3 weeks.

Youth International, 1121 Downing St., #2, Denver, CO 80218, USA (☎303-839-5877; director@youthinternational.org; www.youthinternational.org). A community service and experiential learning program in Thailand and Vietnam. Each program's fees are US$7500 and cover all expenses including airfare.

FOR FURTHER READING ON ALTERNATIVES TO TOURISM

Alternatives to the Peace Corps: A directory of third world and U.S. Volunteer Opportunities, by Joan Powell. Food First Books, 2000 (US$10).

How to Live Your Dream of Volunteering Oversees, by Collins, DeZerega, and Heckscher. Penguin Books, 2002 (US$17).

International Directory of Voluntary Work, by Whetter and Pybus. Peterson's Guides and Vacation Work, 2000 (US$16).

International Jobs, by Kocher and Segal. Perseus Books, 1999 (US$18).

Overseas Summer Jobs 2002, by Collier and Woodworth. Peterson's Guides and Vacation Work, 2002 (US$18).

Work Abroad: The Complete Guide to Finding a Job Overseas, by Hubbs, Griffith, and Nolting. Transitions Abroad Publishing, 2000 ($16).

Work Your Way Around the World, by Susan Griffith. Worldview Publishing Services, 2001 (US$18).

BANGKOK

☎ 02

THAILAND PRICE ICONS					
SYMBOL:	❶	❷	❸	❹	❺
ACCOMM.	Under US$3 Under 120฿	US$3-4.50 120-180฿	US$4.50-9 180-360฿	US$9-14 360-560฿	Over US$14 Over 560฿
FOOD	Under US$0.75 Under 30฿	US$0.75-2 30-80฿	US$2-4 80-160฿	US$4-6 160-240฿	Over US$6 Over 240฿

BANGKOK

After a day or two in the city, most travelers are amazed that Bangkok still remains standing at each sunset. Armadas of BMWs and Mercedes meet at intersections littered with infuriating traffic as legions of people battle for territory on the city sidewalks and ooze from every bus. Bangkok wasn't fashioned by city planners; it was hewn from unsuspecting rice paddies by the double-edged sword of Thailand's growing economy. To the western eye, the city resembles home more than ever: Nintendo has taken children permanently away from their mothers, 7-Elevens abound on every corner, and modern medicine, education, and technology are taken for granted.

Bangkok is perhaps the only city to see history buffs drool over the National Museum's treasures while steps away travel-weary backpackers reach their modern mecca on frenetic, narcotic Khaosan Road. Southeast Asia's best DJs blast the latest hits next to the pinnacles of royal Buddhism and ancient architecture in the Grand Palace. The Emerald Buddha poses contemplatively for praying worshipers as Muay Thai kickboxers fight it out in front of screaming fans. Chefs bargain for meat at the sunrise floating markets just hours after the "meat market" in the Patpong red-light district closes down. A businessman cruises by on a cell phone and passes a parade of orange-robed, smiling Buddhist monks. It is a city of constant surprises—no one knows the same Bangkok.

⚔ INTERCITY TRANSPORTATION

BY PLANE

Most flights to Thailand arrive at **Don Muang International Airport,** 171 Vibhavadi-Ransot Rd. (the main northern highway), 25km from the city center. The airport includes the **International Terminal 1** (departure info ☎535 1254, arrival info ☎535 1310), **International Terminal 2** (departure info ☎535 1386, arrival info ☎535 1301), and **Domestic Passenger Travel** (departure info ☎535 11 92, arrival info ☎535 1253). The **24hr. post office,** in the departure hall of International Terminal 1, has **international phones, EMS,** and **stamps.** Each terminal has **left baggage service** (70฿ per bag per day, each additional day over 3 months 140฿). Departure tax is 500฿ international, 30฿ domestic. The prices below are based on a round-trip fare.

DESTINATION	PRICE	DESTINATION	PRICE
Chiang Mai	4550฿	Phnom Penh	8000฿
Hanoi	10,500฿	Phuket	5450฿
Ho Chi Minh City	10,000฿	Singapore	6300฿
Hong Kong	7000฿	Udon Thani	3600฿
Jakarta	12,500฿	Ubon Ratchathani	3800฿

94

DESTINATION	PRICE	DESTINATION	PRICE
Kuala Lumpur	9200฿	Vientiane	8000฿
Manila	13,000฿	Yangon	7000฿

As you exit customs, take one of the waiting metered taxis (250-400฿ depending on traffic) or the useful and comfortable A/C airport buses (AB), which run four routes into the city center (every 30min. 4:30am-12:30am, 100฿). To get to the infamous Khaosan Rd., take AB2.

ROUTE #	STOPS
AB1: DON MUANG-SILOM	Don Muang Tollway, Dindaeng Rd., Pratunam, Ratchadamri Rd., Lumpini Park, Silom Rd., Charoen Krung Rd., Silom Rd.
AB2: DON MUANG-SANAM LUANG	Don Muang Tollway, Dindaeng Rd., Rachavithi Rd., Victory Monument, Phyathai Rd., Phetchaburi Rd., Larn Luang Rd., Tanao Rd., Phrasumen Rd., Chakrapong Rd., Banglamphu (Khaosan Rd.), Democracy Monument, Ratchadamnoen Klang Rd., Sanam Luang.
AB3: DON MUANG-THONGLOR	Don Muang Tollway, Dindaeng Expressway, Sukhumvit Rd., Asok, Eastern Bus Terminal (Ekamai), New Phetchaburi Rd., Thonglor Rd.
AB4: DON MUANG-HUALAMPHONG	Don Muang Tollway, Dindaeng Expressway, Ploenchit Rd., Siam Square, Phayathai Rd., Mahboonkrong, Rama IV Rd., Wongwien 2, Hualamphong Railway Station.

The cheap way to get from the airport to the city is to cross the bridge to the Don Muang Train Station and catch one of the many **trains** heading inbound to Hualamphong Railway Station (5-10฿) and then take a **city bus.** Night service is infrequent.

Suffocating **public buses** are available on the highway just outside the exit for 3.50-16฿ (regular #3, 24, 52; A/C #4, 10, 29), though other modes of transport are more reliable. A list of fares and schedules can be found at the **Tourist Authority of Thailand (TAT)** in the arrivals area of Terminal 1. (Open **24hr.**)

BY TRAIN

Second only to elephant transport in style and peanut-holding capacity, train travel is cheap, efficient, and safe. Five train lines, traveling the north, northeast (two lines), east, and south, start and end at **Hualamphong Railway Station** (☎220 4334, 24hr. info ☎1690), on Rama IV Rd. in the center of the metropolis. *Klong* (canal) and river ferries, coupled with public buses (see **By Bus,** p. 100), provide the easiest transportation to the station from the city. Metered taxis or tuk-tuks at the side entrance of the station are the best ways into town from the station. Otherwise, walk down Rama IV Rd. to a bus stop from which A/C bus #1 and regular buses #25 and 40 go to Siam Square. Walk down Sukhumvit Rd. for regular bus #53 to Banglamphu (Khaosan Rd. area), which continues to Thewet.

Daily ticket booking is left of the main entrance; advanced booking is to the right. The lower information counter has train schedules. **Upper-class** seats have bathrooms and A/C; **lower-class** seats put you right in the middle of many friendly Thai people. **Sleeper berths** are popular, so buy tickets eight to ten days before departure. In order of increasing speed, price, and service, the trains are: normal *(rot thamada),* fast *(rot reaw),* express *(rot duan),* and special *(rot pheeset).*

THE PRICE IS RIGHT! Prices listed are base fares for specific classes (3rd; 2nd; 2nd A/C; 1st). Add 40฿ for fast trains, 60฿ for express trains, and 80฿ for specials. Sleeper cars cost 100-500฿, depending on class. Duration listed is for fast trains; add 2-3hr. per 10 hours for normal trains.

Left of the main entrance is a **police booth** (☎ 225 0300, ext. 5295). A **luggage storage center** is at Platform 12. (10฿ per day. Open daily 4am-10pm.) An **information booth** sits near the right-hand ticket counter. **24hr. ATMs** cluster near the main entrance. A **post office** is outside the entrance. (Open M-F 7am-7pm, Sa 8am-4pm.)

DESTINATION	DURATION	FREQUENCY/TIME	PRICE
CHIANG MAI LINE			
Ayutthaya	2hr.	21 per day 5:45am-11:25pm	no sleeper; 15฿, 35฿
Chiang Mai	10-14hr.	7 per day 6:40am-10pm	121฿, 281฿, 381฿, 593฿
Don Muang Intl. Airport	1hr.	25 per day 5:45am-11:25pm	5฿
Lampang	9hr.	8 per day 6:40am-10pm	118฿, 273฿, 373฿, 575฿
Lopburi	3hr.	8 per day 7:45am-10pm	no sleeper; 28฿, 64฿
Phitsanulok	7hr.	11 per day 6:40am-11:10pm	69฿, 159฿, 324฿
NONG KHAI LINE			
Nong Khai	13hr.	daily 6:15am, 7, 8:30pm	103฿, 238฿, 338฿, 497฿
PADANG BESAR LINE			
Hat Yai	17hr.	5 per day 12:25-10:50pm	149฿, 345฿, 445฿, 734฿
Hua Hin	4hr.	12 per day 12:25-10:50pm	no sleeper; 44฿, 102฿
Surat Thani	10hr.	10 per day 12:25-10:50pm	107฿, 248฿, 348฿, 519฿
UBON RATCHATHANI LINE			
Surin	11hr.	10 per day 5:45am-11:25pm	73฿, 169฿, 269฿, 346฿
Ubon Ratchathani	13hr.	7 per day 5:45am-11:25pm	95฿, 221฿, 321฿, 460฿

WHEELS ON THE BUS

Government buses depart from four terminals. The **Eastern Bus Terminal** (**E;** ☎ 391 2504) is on Sukhumvit Rd., accessible via the Skytrain's Ekamai Station or by local A/C bus #1, 8, 11, or 13, or regular bus #2, 23, 25, 38, 71, 72, or 98. The **Northern** (**N;** ☎ 936 2852), **Central** (**C;** ☎ 936 1972), and **Northeastern** (**NE;** ☎ 936 36 60) **Bus Terminals** are in a new building west of Chatachak Park. Take the Skytrain's Sukhumvit Line to Mo Chit and a motorcycle taxi (5min., 30฿) from there to the terminals. The **Southern Bus Terminal** (**S;** ☎ 435 1199) is on Boromat Chonnani (Pinklao-Nakhonchaisi) Rd. across the river in Thonburi. Tickets for government and **private buses** can be bought at the Southern Bus Terminal. To get here, take A/C bus #3 or 11 from the Democracy Monument, or regular bus #30 from Sanam Luang. Although private companies can be cheaper and more convenient, and sometimes offer more modern accommodations, they have higher scam and accident rates.

DESTINATION	DURATION	TERMINAL, FREQUENCY	PRICE
Ayutthaya	1½hr.	C, every 20min. 5:40am-7:20pm	41฿, 52฿
Banpae for Ko Samet	3½hr.	E, every hr. 7am-5pm	A/C only; 124฿
Chanthaburi	4hr.	E, every 30min. 4:30am-midnight	82-103฿, 115-148฿
Chiang Mai	10hr.	N, 32 per day	205฿, 290฿, 369฿, 570฿

DESTINATION	DURATION	TERMINAL, FREQUENCY	PRICE
Chiang Rai	11-13hr.	N, 32 per day	229฿, 241฿, 321฿, 337฿, 412฿, 640฿
Hat Yai	14hr.	S, 14 per day	535฿, 830฿
Khon Kaen	7½hr.	NE, 27 per day	202฿, 259฿, 400฿
Krabi	12hr.	S, 6 per day	459-486฿, 710฿
Mae Hong Son	14hr.	N, 3 per day	292฿, 509฿
Nong Khai	7½-10hr.	NE, 5 per day	454฿, 705฿
Pattaya	2½hr.	E, every 30min. 6am-10:30pm	50฿, 70฿, 90฿
Phang-Nga	13hr.	S, 5 per day	326฿, 403฿, 419฿, 625฿
Phuket	14hr.	S, 12 per day	441฿, 685฿
Si Racha	2hr.	E, every 20-40min. 5:45am-7pm	39฿, 55฿, 70฿
Sukothai	7hr.	N, 16 per day	128฿, 230฿
Surat Thani	10hr.	S, 8 per day	142฿
Surin	6-8hr.	NE, approx. every hr. 6am-midnight	131฿, 225฿, 355฿
Trat	5hr.	E, every 1½hr. 7am-11:30pm	120฿, 147-176฿, 190฿
Ubon Ratchathani	5hr.	NE, 27 per day	297฿, 382฿

◢ ORIENTATION

Beyond the cliff-top shelters of **Khaosan Rd.** and other backpacker districts lies a bastion of unclaimed sights and experiences. The north-south **Chao Phraya River** is a worthy landmark and launch site. To the river's east rests the heart of the city: **Banglamphu** (home to Khaosan Rd.) is immediately north of **Ratchadamnoen/Ko Rattanakosin,** home of Sanam Luang Park, Wat Phra Kaew, and the Royal Palace. Farther north is **Thewet/Dusit,** a backpacker area and the location of the Dusit Zoo and the former royal mansions. Heading southeast along the river leads to **China-town,** the Indian district **Pahurat,** and the **Hualamphong Railway Station.** Farther south is the wealthy **Silom** financial district and its less upstanding bedfellow, the **Patpong** red-light district. East of the Hualamphong Railway Station are **Siam Square**'s shopping mall and the World Trade Center. Rama I Rd. slices through, connecting Wat Phra Kaew (on its western end) with Bangkok's eastern edge and the **Sukhumvit Rd.** area, where Thais and foreigners party until the wee hours. The *Bangkok Tourist Map* (40฿) or Nancy Chandler's *Map of Bangkok* (150฿) will make all of this clearer than we ever could. Our own guide to the neighborhoods, however, might offer a different kind of help:

KNOW THY NEIGHBOR BEFORE LOVING HIM...	
Wat Center: Ratchadamoen	**Expat Zoo:** Sukhumvit
No Wat in Sight: Patpong	**Real Zoo:** Dusit
Backpacker's Ghetto: Banglamphu	**Curry Heaven:** Pahurat
Chinatown: Chinatown	**Shopaholics Anonymous:** Siam Square

ADDRESSES. Buildings are often numbered twice in Bangkok—the first number represents the building's lot, and the second number signifies where on the lot it is. For example, 127/8-10 Sukhumvit Rd. signifies that the building is on lot 127 and occupies numbers 8-10. Minor roads that split off a main thoroughfare are called sois (alleys), although they can often be sizable roads.

B A N G K O K

BANGKOK

A B C

1

Charan Sanitwong Rd.
Samsen Rd.
Nakhon Chai Si Rd.
Rama V Rd.
Krung Thon Bridge
Sukhothai Rd.

Chao Phraya River
THEWET
Tha Thewet
Ratchasima Rd.
DUSIT
Ratchawithi Rd.
Luk Kuang Rd.
Rama V Rd.
Si Ayutthaya Rd.
Sawankhalok Rd.

2

TO SOUTHERN BUS TERMINAL (1km)
New Arun Amarin Rd.
Samsen Rd.
Krung Kasem Rd.
Prachathipok Rd.
Ratchadamnoen Nok Rd.
Phisanulok Rd.
Royal Turf Club

SEE KHAOSAN ROAD AREA MAP, P. 105
Tha Phra Athit
Phra Athit Rd.
Chakrabongse Rd.
Tha Banglamphu
Phra Sumen Rd.
Ratchadamnoen Nok Rd.
Soi Kasem 2
Phra Pinklao Bridge
Tha Thonburi
BANGLAMPHU
Khaosan Rd.
TAT
Nakhon Sawan Rd.
Soi Kasem 1

3

Thonburi Railway Station
Ratchadamnoen Klang Rd.
Larn Luang Rd.
Rama I Rd.
Phaya Thai Rd.
THONBURI
Na Phra That Rd.
Sanam Luang
Ratchadamnoen Nai Rd.
RATCHADAMNOEN
Klong Taxi Pier
Mahachai Rd.
Bamrung Muang Rd.
Tha Chang
Na Phra Lan Rd.
Sanam Chai Rd.
Ratchini Rd.
Atsadang Rd.
Tanao Rd.
Dinso Rd.
Boriphat Rd.
Worachak Rd.
Sua Pa Rd.
Luang Rd.
Krung Kasem Rd.
Luk Luang Rd.
Rong Muang Rd.
Banthat Thong Rd.
Rama I Rd.
NATIONAL STADIUM
Phayathai Rd.

GRAND PALACE & TEMPLE.

4

Itsaraphap Rd.
Tha Tien
Maharat Rd.
Pahurat Rd.
Charoen Krung Rd.
Yaowarat Rd.
Ti Thong Rd.
Tri Phet Rd.
Chakraphet Rd.
Ratchawong Rd.
Song Sawat Rd.
Naret Chai Rd.
Hualamphong Railway Station
Memorial Bridge
Tha Ratchawong
CHINATOWN
Song Wat Rd.
Khao Lam Rd.

5

Pratchathipok Rd.
Somdet Chao Phraya Rd.
Chao Phraya River
Lat Ya Rd.
Intharaphithak Rd.
Tha Si Phraya
GPO
Si Phraya Rd.
Naret Rd.
Sap Rd.
Patpong
Charoen Rat Rd.
Surawong Rd.
SILOM & PATPONG
Canada
Mahesak Rd.
Pan Rd.
CHONG NONSI

6

Taksin Rd.
King Thonburi Rd.
Tha Oriental
Tha Sathon
Charoen Krung (New) Rd.
Taksin Bridge
SAPHAN TAKSIN
Silom Rd.
Pramuan Rd.
Surasak Rd.
Myanmar
SURASAK

AQ *

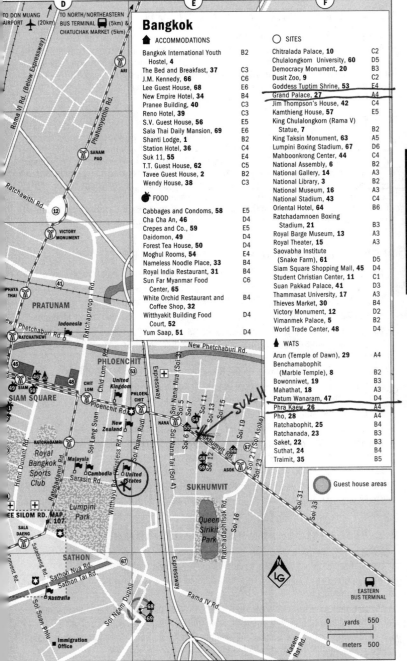

Bangkok

🏠 ACCOMMODATIONS

Bangkok International Youth Hostel, 4	B2
The Bed and Breakfast, 37	C3
J.M. Kennedy, 66	C6
Lee Guest House, 68	E6
New Empire Hotel, 34	B4
Pranee Building, 40	C3
Reno Hotel, 39	C3
S.V. Guest House, 56	E5
Sala Thai Daily Mansion, 69	E6
Shanti Lodge, 1	B2
Station Hotel, 36	C4
Suk 11, 55	E4
T.T. Guest House, 62	C5
Tavee Guest House, 2	B2
Wendy House, 38	C3

🍎 FOOD

Cabbages and Condoms, 58	E5
Cha Cha An, 46	D4
Crepes and Co., 59	E5
Daidomon, 49	D4
Forest Tea House, 50	D4
Moghul Rooms, 54	E4
Nameless Noodle Place, 33	B4
Royal India Restaurant, 31	B4
Sun Far Myanmar Food Center, 65	C6
White Orchid Restaurant and Coffee Shop, 32	B4
Witthyakit Building Food Court, 52	D4
Yum Saap, 51	D4

◯ SITES

Chitralada Palace, 10	C2
Chulalongkorn University, 60	D5
Democracy Monument, 20	B3
Dusit Zoo, 9	C2
Goddess Tuptim Shrine, 53	E4
Grand Palace, 27	A4
Jim Thompson's House, 42	C4
Kamthieng House, 57	E5
King Chulalongkorn (Rama V) Statue, 7	B2
King Taksin Monument, 63	A5
Lumpini Boxing Stadium, 67	D6
Mahboonkrong Center, 44	C4
National Assembly, 6	B2
National Gallery, 14	A3
National Library, 3	B2
National Museum, 16	A3
National Stadium, 43	C4
Oriental Hotel, 64	B6
Ratchadamnoen Boxing Stadium, 21	B3
Royal Barge Museum, 13	A3
Royal Theater, 15	A3
Saovabha Institute (Snake Farm), 61	D5
Siam Square Shopping Mall, 45	D4
Student Christian Center, 11	C1
Suan Pakkad Palace, 41	D3
Thammasat University, 17	A3
Thieves Market, 30	B4
Victory Monument, 12	D2
Vimanmek Palace, 5	B2
World Trade Center, 48	D4

🔺 WATS

Arun (Temple of Dawn), 29	A4
Benchamabophit (Marble Temple), 8	B2
Bowonniwet, 19	B3
Mahathat, 18	A3
Patum Wanaram, 47	D4
Phra Kaew, 26	A4
Pho, 28	A4
Ratchabophit, 25	B4
Ratchanada, 23	B3
Saket, 22	B3
Suthat, 24	B4
Traimit, 35	B5

Guest house areas

▐ LOCAL TRANSPORTATION

Maneuvering through Bangkok traffic is enough to bring out the Hyde in any Jekyll. Traffic has decreased recently, but getting from north to south is still frustrating. Taking canal boats and river taxis means less time sweating on buses and breathing exhaust. Travelers hoping to maneuver through Bangkok by public transportation will love the **Bangkok Tourist Map** (40฿), which has bus, water taxi, and Skytrain routes as well as information on sights.

BY BUS

The shiny, happy bus system, run by the Bangkok Metropolitan Transit Authority (BMTA), is extensive and cheap. Red-and-cream buses have no A/C (3.50฿); blue-and-white and yellow-and-white buses both have A/C (8-16฿). Pea-green **minibuses** (3.50฿) supposedly run the same routes as the buses but tend to stray easily. **Microbuses** cover long distances and stop only at designated places (5am-10pm, 30฿). Paying a higher price guarantees a seat and fewer stops. Buses run 5am-midnight or later. Make sure you get on the right type of bus, not just the right route number. This is a sample listing; there are many, many buses so for more options pick up a free **bus map** at any TAT office.

REGULAR BUSES WITH NO A/C (RED-AND-CREAM)

#1: Wat Pho—Yaowarat Rd. (Chinatown)—General Post Office—Oriental Hotel

15: Banglamphu (Phra Athit Rd., Phrasumen Rd.)—Sanam Luang—Democracy Monument—Wat Saket—Siam Sq.—Ratchadamri Rd.—Lumpini Park—Silom Rd.

18 and 28: Vimarnmek Teak Museum—Dusit Zoo—Chitralada Palace—Victory Monument

25: Wat Phra Kaew—Wat Pho—Charoen Krung Rd.—Rama IV Rd. (near Hualamphong Railway Station)—Phayathai Rd.—Mahboonkrong Center—Siam Sq.—World Trade Center—Ploenchit Rd.—Sukhumvit Rd. to outer Bangkok

48: Sanam Chai Rd.—Bamrung Muang Rd.—Siam Sq.—along Sukhumvit Rd.

59: Don Muang International Airport—Victory Monument—Phahonyothin Rd.—Phetchaburi Rd.—Larnluang Rd.—Democracy Monument—Sanam Luang

70: Democracy Monument—TAT—Boxing Stadium—Dusit Zoo

72: Ratchaprarop Rd.—Si Ayutthaya Rd.—Marble Temple—Samsen Rd.—Thewet

74: Rama IV Rd. (outside Soi Ngam Duphli)—Lumpini Park—Ratchadamri Rd.—World Trade Center—Pratunam-Ratchaprarop Rd.—Victory Monument

115: Silom Rd.—Rama IV Rd.—along Rama IV Rd. until Sukhumvit Rd.

116: Sathorn Nua Rd.—along Rama IV Rd. (passes Soi Ngam Duphli)—Sathorn Tai Rd.

204: Victory Monument—Ratchaprarop Rd.—World Trade Center—Siam Sq.—Bamrung Muang Rd.

A/C BUSES (BLUE-AND-WHITE, YELLOW-AND-WHITE)

#1: Wat Pho—Charoen Krung Rd.—Rama IV Rd. (near Hualamphong Railway Station)—Phayathai Rd. (Mahboonkrong Center)—Siam Sq.—along Sukhumvit Rd.

8: Sanam Luang—Bamrung Muang Rd.—Rama I Rd.—Ploenchit Rd.—Sukhumvit Rd. to outer Bangkok

10: National Assembly (Ratchavithi Rd.)—Dusit Zoo—Chitralada Palace—Victory Monument—Phahonyothin Rd.—Don Muang International Airport

11: Khaosan Rd.—Phra Sumen Rd.—Democracy Monument (Ratchadamnoen Klang Rd.)—Phetchaburi Rd.—World Trade Center—Sukhumvit Rd.

BY TAXI

Your lungs will thank you for using Bangkok's extensive taxi system. Simple and cost-efficient, taxis are under-utilized by most travelers. Single women find taxis much safer than tuk-tuks or motorcycles.

BY TUK-TUK

Tuk-tuks scour the city and slither through the traffic that brings taxis to a halt. Negotiation is key: drivers may charge you twice they would a local. Skillful negotiators can get prices 30% cheaper than taxi fares.

 TOURIST SCAMMING Tuk-tuk drivers are often con artists and have been known to harass women travelers. Drivers have also been known to drive off with passenger luggage, push the skin industry, deliver passengers to expensive restaurants, or tell travelers that sights are closed and take them to jewelry and tailor shops instead. To entice *farang,* they offer tours of the city for low rates (10-20฿ per hr.), but all you'll get is a sales pitch and inflated prices. Beware of these words: *free, sexy, massage, jewelry, tailor shop, go-go* (unless of course you really want to go to a masseur, jeweler, tailor, or prostitute). Tuk-tuks aren't all bad—just be firm and make it clear that you want to go to your intended destination and nowhere else.

BY MOTORCYCLE TAXI

Motorcycle taxi drivers loiter on street corners in brightly colored vests. Though faster in traffic and 10-25% cheaper than tuk-tuks, motorcycle taxis only carry a single passenger, can be dangerous for long journeys, and require calm nerves. Travelers should insist on a helmet, as police will fine non-wearers.

BY BOAT

Chao Phraya River Express ferries (6am-6pm, 3-25฿) are the best way to travel along the river and provide easy access to the Skytrain. Buy tickets at the booth at the pier or from the ticket collector on board. Specify your stop, as boats will stop only if passengers are waiting at the pier. Disembark quickly.

The main stops, from north to south, are **Thewet** (for the National Library and Dusit guest houses), **Phra Athit** (for Khaosan Rd./Banglamphu), **Thonburi Railway Pier** (for Thonburi Railway Station and Royal Barges), **Chang** (for Wat Phra Kaew and Royal Palace), **Tien** (for Wat Pho), **Ratchawong** (for Chinatown and Hualumphong Railway Station), **Si Phraya** (for GPO), **Oriental** (for the Oriental Hotel and Silom), and **Sathorn** (for the Skytrain to Silom). Small brown, box-like ferries with bench seats, easily confused with river taxis, shuttle across the river to every major stop. A small sign identifies each *tha* (pier).

Klongs are small canals that zig-zag through the city's interior. Thonburi, west of Chao Praya, has an extensive network, and Bangkok proper has two useful lines. **Klong Saen Saep** links Democracy Monument near Banglamphu with the area around Siam Sq. and the World Trade Center (10min., 6-15฿). Another route links **Klong Banglamphu** and **Klong Phadung Krung Kasem**. From Tha Banglamphu, at the Chakraphong and Phrasumen Rd. intersection, you can reach Hualumphong Railway Station (15min., 6am-6pm, 6฿). Boats run every 45min. during off-peak hours and weekends and every 30min. during rush hour.

Longtail boat rentals are available at almost every pier for tourist destinations on the river and *klangs*—agree on a price before setting off. Usual rates are 400฿ for the first hour, 300฿ each additional hour.

BY SKYTRAIN

The **Skytrain (Bangkok Mass Transit System, BTS)** is an A/C delight. Incredibly useful for navigating Siam Sq., Silom, and Sukhumvit, the train has two lines that meet at Siam Sq. The **Sukhumvit Line** runs from Mo Chit next to Chatuchak Market, past the Victory Monument to Siam Sq., through Sukhumvit Rd., and terminates at On Nut, beyond the Eastern Bus Terminal. The **Silom Line** runs from the National Stadium, past Siam Sq. and Lumpini Park, and along part of Silom Rd. before terminating at Taksin Bridge. All stations have useful **maps. Fares** are based on distance (10-40฿), and ticket purchase is automated. Trip passes (10-, 15-, 30-ride) are the most cost-effective for students; flaunt that ISIC card (160-360฿, adults 500-540฿). Insert the card at the turnstile to enter the station; **hold onto it and insert it at the turnstile at your destination to leave the station.** The Skytrain operates daily 6am-midnight.

BY CAR

Travelers should avoid cars, as driving in Bangkok can be dangerous. An International Driver's Permit (see p. 76) and major credit card are required. Rental agencies include **Avis,** 2/12 Witthayu Rd. (☎255 53 00). Renting a small sedan costs 1000-1500฿ per day and insurance costs 250฿.

⁊ PRACTICAL INFORMATION

TOURIST AND FINANCIAL SERVICES

Tourist Office: TAT, 4 Ratchadamnoen Nok Rd. (☎282 1672), 500m down on the right from the 8-way intersection east of the Democracy Monument. Very helpful staff doles out **free maps** and advice in English, French, Japanese, bad Italian, and worse German. Open daily 8:30am-4:30pm.

Immigration Office: 507 Soi Suan Phlu (☎287 3101), off Sathorn Tai Rd. 30-day transit visas extended for 10 days; 60-day tourist visas extended for 30 days (500฿). Open M-F 8:30am-4:30pm.

Embassies and Consulates: Australia, 37 Sathorn Tai Rd. (☎287 2680). Open M-F 8am-5pm. **Cambodia,** 185 Ratchadamri Rd. (☎254 6630). Consular services around the corner off Sarasin Rd. on first soi on left. 30-day visa; 2-day processing (1000฿). Open M-F 9-11am and 1:30-4pm. **Canada,** Abdulrahim Bldg., 15th fl., 990 Rama IV Rd. (☎636 0541). Open M-Th 7:30am-4pm, F 7:30am-1pm. **China,** 57 Ratchadaphisek Rd. (☎245 7043). Open M-F 9-11:30am and 2:30-5pm. **Indonesia,** 600 New Phetchaburi Rd. (☎252 3135). Take regular bus #2 or 11; or A/C bus #5, 11, or 12. Open M-F 8:30am-noon and 1-4pm. **Ireland,** 205 United Flour Mill Bldg., 11th fl., Ratchawong Rd. (☎223 0876). Open M-F 9am-noon and 1:30-4pm. **Laos,** 502/1-3 Soi Ramkhamhaeng 39 (☎539 3642). Visa 300฿; 2-day processing. Open M-F 8am-noon and 1-4pm. **Malaysia,** 33-35 Sathorn Tai Rd. (☎679 2190). Open M-F 8:30am-noon and 1-4pm. **Myanmar,** 132 Sathorn Nua Rd. (☎233 2237). Consular services on Pan Rd., off Sathorn Nua Rd., 1½ blocks from the Skytrain Surasak Station. 30-day visa 800฿ (inquire at embassy for up-to-date status of land crossings); 24hr. processing. Open M-F 8:30am-noon and 2-4:30pm. **New Zealand,** 93 Witthayu Rd. (☎254 2530). Open M-F 7:30am-noon and 1-4pm. **Singapore,** 129 Sathorn Tai Rd. (☎286 2253). Open M-F 8:30am-noon and 1-4:30pm. **South Africa,** Park Palace, 6th fl., 231 Soi Sarasin, Ratchadamri Rd. (☎253 8473). Open M-Th 7:45am-4:30pm, F 7:45am-3:15pm. **UK,** Witthayu Rd. (☎305 8333). Open M-Th 7:45am-noon and 12:45-4:30pm, F 7:45am-1:15pm. **US,** 120-122 Witthayu Rd. (☎205 4000). Consular services M-F 7am-noon and 1-4pm. **Vietnam,** 83/1 Witthayu Rd. (☎251 5836). Visa 2050฿; 2- to 3-day processing. Open M-F 8:30-11:30am and 1:30-4:30pm.

Currency Exchange: 24hr. ATMs abound. Those with "ATM" spelled in blue dots or with a purple hand holding an ATM card accept AmEx/Cirrus/MC/V. You can't throw a stone in Bangkok without hitting a bank, particularly in **Silom.**

American Express: IBM Building, 388 Phahonyothin Rd. (☎273 0033). Open M-F 8:30am-5pm. **Branch** at Sea Tours Co. Ltd, 8th fl., 128 Phayathai Plaza Bldg. (☎216 5783), on Phayathai Rd. between Phetchaburi and Si Ayutthaya Rd., next to Phayathai Skytrain station. Mail held for up to 60 days; no packages. Passport and AmEx card, check, or travel receipt needed for pickup. Open M-F 8:30am-noon and 1-5pm, Sa 8:30am-noon.

LOCAL SERVICES

Luggage Storage: The **airport's** the most reliable but a bit pricey (70฿ per day). Open 24hr. Also available at **Hualamphong Railway Station** for 10฿ per day. Open daily 4am-10pm. Guest houses may also offer this service, but proceed at your own risk.

English-Language Bookstores: Aporia Books, 131 Tanao Rd. (☎629 2129), opposite the end of Khaosan Rd. One of the best bookshops in Bangkok with new and used books for sale, trade, or rent. Open daily 9am-8:30pm. **D.K. Books** offers similar merchandise. Branch on Sukhumvit Soi 8 (☎252 62 61). Open daily 9am-8pm. **Asia Books,** in the Discovery Center, Siam Sq. and Sukhumvit Rd., has an extensive collection of English books.

Local Publications: *The Bangkok Post* is an English daily, sold everywhere (20฿). Monthly ▧ *Metro* (www.bkkmetro.com) divulges the trendiest nightlife secrets (100฿).

Gay and Lesbian Resources: Anjaree (☎477 1776). Lesbian organization with monthly newsletter. *Metro* (see above) has extensive gay nightlife listings.

EMERGENCY AND COMMUNICATIONS

Emergency: ☎191. **Tourist Police:** ☎1155. **Ambulance:** ☎252 2171.

Tourist Police: Tourist-specific grievances and complaints handled. Most useful office next to TAT, 4 Ratchadamnoen Nok Rd. (☎282 8129). All other stations will refer you here. **Branches** at 2911 Unico House Bldg., Soi Lang Suan (☎652 1721), off Ploenchit Rd. in Siam Sq., and at the corner of Khaosan and Chakraphonh Rd. English spoken. **24hr. booths** opposite Dusit Thani Hotel in Lumpini Park (☎221 6206) and at Don Muang International Airport (☎535 1641).

Pharmacies: Fortune Pharmacy (Banglamphu), in front of Khaosan Palace Hotel on Khaosan Rd. Open daily 8am-midnight. **Siam Drug** (Silom/Financial), at the cul-de-sac of Patpong 2 Rd. Open M-Sa 10am-3am, Su 3pm-3am. Many pharmacies cluster on **Sukhumvit Rd.** between Soi Nana and Soi II. Most open daily 8am-late.

Medical Services: Bamrungrad Hospital, 33 Sukhumvit Rd. Soi 3 (☎253 0250). **Open 24hr. Chulalongkorn Hospital,** 1873 Rama IV Rd. (☎252 8181). Ambulance service. The best and largest public hospital is **Siriraj Hospital** (Thonburi), 2 Pran Nok Rd. (☎411 0241). Take regular bus #19 from Sanam Luang. 24hr. ambulance. Cheapest vaccinations at **Red Cross Society's Queen Saovabha Institute** on Rama IV Rd.

Telephones: Make domestic calls at "cardphone" booths (5฿ per 3min.) and international calls at yellow "international cardphone" booths. Upper right metal button connects directly to an AT&T operator. Most post offices (see below) have **international phone** services. The **Public Telecommunication Service Center** next to GPO offers fax and telex. **Open 24hr.**

Internet Access: Try **Khaosan Rd.** and other backpacker areas. Average 40-60฿ per hr.

Post Offices: GPO (☎233 10 50), in Communications Authority of Thailand building on Charoen Krung Rd. near Soi 32. *Poste Restante.* Mail held for 2 months. Pick-up fee

(1฿ per item, 2฿ for parcels). Open M-F 8:30am-4:30pm, Sa-Su 9am-noon. **Banglamphu Office**, on Khaosan Rd.; turn left onto Bowon Niwet Rd. and walk to small square at bend in road. Open M-F 8:30am-5:30pm, Sa 9am-noon. **Overseas Telephone Office** on 2nd fl. of **Silom/Financial Office**, 113/6-7 Suriwongse Center Rd. From Silom Rd., head up Patpong Rd. to Surawong Rd. and turn left; it's a few lanes down to the left. Open M-F 8:30am-4:30pm, Sa 9am-noon. **Sukhumvit Rd. Office,** 118-122 Sukhumvit Rd. (☎251 79 72), between Soi 4 (Nana Tai) and Landmark Plaza. International calls 8am-10pm. Another at Soi 23, Sukhumvit Rd. (☎258 41 97), on the right. EMS and international calls. Open M-F 8:30am-5:30pm, Sa 9am-noon. **Postal code:** 10500; 10501 for *Poste Restante.*

ACCOMMODATIONS

Accommodations in Bangkok are as varied as the spectrum of exotic fruits lining its streets. Options range from the dirt-cheap flophouses to five-star hotels and every cookie-cutter guest house in between. Always check prices and rooms first to discern differences in quality between lodgings.

BANGLAMPHU AND KO RATTANAKOSIN

Within walking distance of Wat Phra Kaew, Wat Pho, the Grand Palace, and the National Museum, this hub of royal Buddhism and ancient architecture functions as a kind of decompression chamber for international travelers and budget backpackers as they enter Thailand. The heart of the fanfare is just to the north along **Khaosan Rd.,** a dubious backpacker mecca of cheap accommodations, free-flowing *Chang* beer, and fake designer clothing. Tourist services abound, but rooms are often cramped, noisy, and full—reserve ahead by phone. About as un-Thai an experience as Diesel shirts and Hollywood movies, "Khaosan" is laden with drunken *farang,* who haggle with Thais for overpriced goods and swap travel stories over banana pancakes.

GETTING TO BANGLAMPHU Chao Phraya River Express stop: Banglamphu Pier. Buses: Airport Bus AB2, regular bus #15, A/C bus #11.

New Siam Guest House, 21 Soi Chana Songkram (☎282 4554). On the small soi that connects the wat to the river. Though a few banana pancakes pricier than the competition, this recently renovated guest house has a comfortable feel that's worth the extra baht. Very popular and the sheets have maps of Thailand on them. Singles 200฿; doubles 245-320฿, with bath 395-450฿, with bath and A/C 550฿. ❸

ANTIDISESTABLISHMENTARIANISM, TAKE THAT!
"Bangkok," the capital city's Western name, is rarely heard in Thailand. Instead, Thais prefer "Krung Thep," or "City of Angels." But Krung Thep is an abbreviation: with over 167 letters and a place in the *Guinness Book of World Records,* the city's name is an orthographer's nightmare; in fact, it is so long that a song was written to make it easier for schoolchildren to memorize. Try saying *this* five times fast:

กรุงเทพมหานครอมรรัตนโกสินทร์มหินทรายอยุธยามหาดิลกภพนพพระรัตนราชธานีบุรีรมย์อุดมราชนิเวศน์มหาสถานอมรพิมานอวตารสถิตย์สักกะฐันติยะวิษณุกรรมประสิทธิ์

(Krungthep Maha Nakhon Amon Ratanakosin Mahinthra Ayutthaya Maha Dilok Phopnop Praratana Ratchathani Burirom Udom Ratchaniwet Maha Sathan Amon Phiman Awatan Sathit Sakkakhantiya Wisanukam Prasit.)

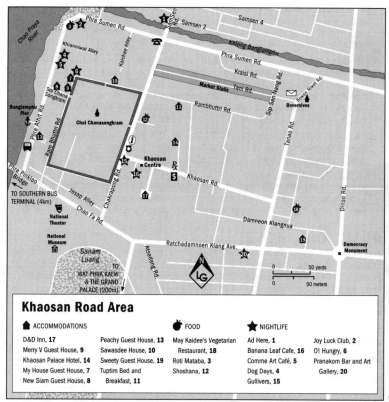

BANGKOK

Khaosan Road Area

🏠 ACCOMMODATIONS

D&D Inn, **17**
Merry V Guest House, **9**
Khaosan Palace Hotel, **14**
My House Guest House, **7**
New Siam Guest House, **8**
Peachy Guest House, **13**
Sawasdee House, **10**
Sweety Guest House, **16**
Tuptim Bed and Breakfast, **11**

🍎 FOOD

May Kaidee's Vegetarian Restaurant, **18**
Roti Mataba, **3**
Shoshana, **12**

⭐ NIGHTLIFE

Ad Here, **1**
Banana Leaf Cafe, **16**
Comme Art Café, **5**
Dog Days, **4**
Gullivers, **15**
Joy Luck Club, **2**
O! Hungry, **6**
Pranakorn Bar and Art Gallery, **20**

My House Guest House, 37 Soi Chana Songkram (☎282 9263). From Khaosan Rd., go toward the river and across the temple grounds; it's 50m to the right. My House features a popular sitting area and proximity to cafes and bars, but still maintains a relatively quiet atmosphere and clean rooms. Singles 120฿, with bath 160฿; doubles 200฿, with bath 300฿, with bath and A/C 500฿. ❷

Peachy Guest House, 10 Phra Athit Rd. (☎281 6471). Plastic-covered pink couches give it a bootleg grandma's house feel. Serene garden, Internet cafe (1฿ for 2min.), and bar are bonuses to a clean and well-run guest house. 4-bed dorms 80฿; singles with shared bath 100฿; doubles 160฿, with A/C 200฿, with A/C and shower 250฿, with shower, toilet, and A/C 350฿. ❶

Tuptim Bed and Breakfast, 82 Rambhuttri Rd. (☎629 1535). From Khaosan Rd. walk to Chakrapong Rd., turn right, and right again onto Rambhuttri Rd.; it's about halfway down on the right. Bright clean rooms, smiling staff, and filling breakfasts (included) make this a fantastic bargain. A new wing with courtyard and restaurant. Singles 250฿, with A/C 499฿; doubles with A/C 550฿; new wing rooms 650฿. ❸

Merry V. Guest House, 33-35 Soi Chana Songkram (☎282 9267). Walk through the cafe of lazy-eyed backpackers and a typical guest house with typically cramped, cheap rooms awaits. Typical of most accommodations in the area. That it's not on Khaosan Rd. makes it worthwhile. Singles with fan and shared bath 120฿; doubles 180฿. ❷

Sweety Guest House, 49 Ratchadamnoen Rd. (☎280 2191). Walk away from the river to the end of Khaosan Rd., cross Bowon Nivet Rd., and go 100m down the soi to the right. The cheapest stay in town. Singles 80-100฿; doubles 140-160฿, with bath 200฿, with A/C 350฿. ❶

Sawasdee House, 147 Soi Rambhuttri (☎281 8138). From Khaosan Rd., cross Chakrapong Rd. and walk down the soi along the right side of the temple wall; it's halfway down on the right. A socialite's dream, it's practically a backpacker convention. Beautiful restaurant and loads of traditional decor. Rooms are well kept but often full—plan ahead. Singles with fan 180฿, with balcony 250฿; twins 350฿, with A/C and bath 550฿; doubles 350฿, with A/C and bath 550฿. ❸

D & D Inn, 68-70 Khaosan Rd. (☎629 05 26). This beast of upmarket guest houses gives a Khaoson address and a spic-and-span, impersonal room. Ask to stay in the new section. Very popular, book ahead by phone. Singles 450฿; doubles 600฿. ❹

Khaosan Palace Hotel, 139 Khaosan Rd. (☎282 05 78), walk down the alley beneath the large green neon sign. For party animals willing to pay for comfort, the Palace is an oasis in the heart of the action. Rooms include private bath and towels. Singles with bath 280฿, with A/C, hot shower, and TV 400฿; doubles 350-580฿; triples 730฿. ❸

DUSIT AND THEWET

Just a quiet bus ride, boat jaunt, or walk from the sights of Ko Rattanakosin and Banglamphu, the guest houses behind the National Library on Thewet are some of Bangkok's best-kept secrets. Catering to those who wish to escape Khaosan Rd.'s frenetic atmosphere while retaining its affordability and accessibility, the area is quiet with little nightlife. Guest houses that line the end of Si Ayutthaya Rd. are pervaded by a laid-back tropical ease. Some taxi and tuk-tuk drivers don't even know it exists; be sure to tell them to go to Thewet, behind the National Library.

> **GETTING TO DUSIT** Chao Phraya River Express stop: Thewet. Regular buses #16, 23, 30, 32, 33, and 72. A/C bus #5. One bus from each soi stops near Thewet, check local listings for more complete schedules.

  Shanti Lodge, 37 Si Ayutthaya, Soi 16 (☎281 2497). Billed as "The Oasis of Bangkok," Shanti has some of the best accommodations in the city. Artsy explorer decor hangs from the walls and with smoking and shoes prohibited inside, the place feels like paradise. Impeccably clean rooms, sparkling shared baths and the vegetarian restaurant make it a spectacular guest house. Dorms 100฿; doubles 250-280฿, with shower 400-500฿, with A/C and shower 600฿. ❶

Tavee Guest House, 83 Si Ayutthaya, Soi 14 (☎280 1447). Large common spaces with fish tanks, well-decorated rooms, and a family atmosphere. All rooms with clean shared bath. Dorms 90฿; singles 140-250฿; doubles 350฿, with A/C 450฿. ❶

Original Sawutdee Guest House, 71 Si Ayutthaya (☎281 0757). Similar to Shanti and Tavee but less character and cheaper. All rooms with fans and clean, shared baths. Dorms 60฿; singles 200฿; doubles 250฿; family rooms available. ❶

Bangkok International Youth Hostel (HI), 25/2 Phitsanulok Rd. (☎281 0361), 300m from the Samsen Rd. intersection. Head south a short block from Si Ayutthaya Rd. and turn left on Phitsanulok Rd.; it's 500m on the left. Great, spacious dorm rooms. Sex-segregated. Good restaurant. Lockout. No smoking or alcohol. Great community atmosphere. Very, very friendly. No reservations. HI members only; non-members can buy a year-long membership on the spot for 300฿ or 50฿ per night. Dorm-style rooms 70฿, with A/C 120฿; singles with A/C and shared bath 280฿; doubles with fan 250฿, with A/C and shared bath 350฿. ❶

CHINATOWN, PAHURAT, AND HUALAMPHONG

A little more gritty than those in other neighborhoods, Chinatown accommodations line **Yaowarat Rd., Pahurat Rd., Chakraphet Rd.,** and **Rong Muang Rd.** Travelers staying here are either evading *farang* hordes or jumping on and off early-morning trains. Chinatown offers few budget rooms that are clean and safe. Some are rip-offs, others welcome only Asians, and many are brothels.

>
> **GETTING TO CHINATOWN, PAHURAT, AND HULAMPHONG**
> Chao Phraya River Express stop: Ratchawong. Regular buses #1, 4, 25, and 73. A/C bus #1. Boat taxi is easy and enjoyable.

T.T. Guest House, 516-518 Soi Sawang, Si Phraya Rd. (☎236 2946). Exit Hualamphong Railway Station, take a left on enormous Rama IV Rd., turn right on Mahanakhon Rd., and take the 1st left; it's at the end of the soi. Popular in high season (reserve ahead), this family-run home has clean rooms and a friendly atmosphere. Strict midnight lockout. Dorms 100฿; singles 200฿; doubles 250฿. ❶

New Empire Hotel, 572 Yaowarat Rd. (☎234 6990), opposite the Bank of Ayudhya near the intersection with Charoen Krung Rd. and Wat Traimit. Bright, clean rooms are packed into this behemoth of an impersonal hotel. Clean, some newly tiled, baths. Singles 580-650฿; doubles 593฿; triples 750฿; deluxe rooms 650฿. ❺

Station Hotel (☎214 2794), opposite the Hualamphong Railway Station. Entrance is down the small soi. Good location for those with a train to catch, but there's not much special here. Singles 250฿; decent doubles 250฿, with A/C 400฿. ❸

SILOM ROAD

Although towering skyscrapers dominate **Silom Rd.,** the surrounding area is home to diverse neighborhoods. On **Pan Rd.,** a Burmese community lives between the Burmese Embassy and the Hindu temple. The world-famous **Patpong** red-light district explores the raunchier side of Bangkok, while the wealthy trot in and out of the Oriental Hotel. Most budget establishments are 2km from Silom Rd. along **Soi Ngam Duphli** and **Soi Si Bamphen,** off Rama IV Rd., a bus or tuk-tuk ride away.

>
> **GETTING TO SILOM RD** Chao Phraya River Express: Oriental. Skytrain: Sarang Daeng. Regular buses #15, 76, 77, 115. A/C buses #2, 4, 5, 15.

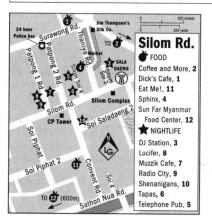

Silom Rd.

❶ FOOD
Coffee and More, 2
Dick's Cafe, 1
Eat Me!, 11
Sphinx, 4
Sun Far Myanmar Food Center, 12
★ NIGHTLIFE
DJ Station, 3
Lucifer, 8
Muzzik Cafe, 7
Radio City, 9
Shenanigans, 10
Tapas, 6
Telephone Pub, 5

Sala Thai Daily Mansion, 15 Soi Sapankoo (☎287 1436). From Rama IV Rd., walk up Soi Ngam Duphli and turn left onto Soi Si Bamphen; take the 1st soi to the left and then turn right. Quiet during low season and happenin' during high season, Sala Thai features sizable rooms with shared bath, a sitting area with cable TV, and a rooftop garden. Singles 200-300฿; doubles 300-400฿. ❸

J.M. Kennedy, 93 Pan Rd., Silom (☎635 2385), opposite the Myanma Airlines office. Walk down Silom Rd. toward the river, turn left at the Indian temple or take Skytrain to Surasak Station and walk 1½ blocks away from the

BANGKOK

river and turn left onto Pan Rd. Owner Michael dishes out Burmese and Indian food (curries with rice 30-60฿; open daily 6am-9pm) and advice on Thailand and Myanmar in 15 languages. Breakfast included. Basic but clean rooms with TV. Renovation scheduled for completion Oct. 2002. Singles 100฿; doubles 250฿, with A/C and bath 350฿.

Lee Guest House 3, 13 Soi Sapankoo (☎679 7045), and **Lee Mansion 4,** 9 Soi Sapankoo (☎286 78 74), next to Sala Thai, offer clean, fan-cooled rooms at reasonable prices. Small rooms 160฿; large rooms 200฿, with bath 200฿, with A/C 350฿.

SIAM SQUARE

In the shadow of Bangkok's ritziest malls, **Soi Kasem San 1** lies off Rama I Rd., opposite the National Stadium. Quieter than Khaosan and almost tout-free, Siam Sq. claims a loyal following of travelers. Prices run high, but accommodations are a good deal for those willing to splurge a little. Proximity to the Skytrain makes much of Bangkok's nightlife and the Eastern Bus Terminal easily accessible.

> **GETTING TO SIAM SQUARE** Skytrain: Siam Sq. Regular buses #15, 25, and 204. A/C bus #1.

The Bed and Breakfast, 36/42-43 Soi Kasem San 1 (☎215 3004). Fairly clean rooms and steel frame beds. A/C, phone, hot shower, and included breakfast make it a heavenly respite from the city. Reserve ahead Nov.-Feb. Singles 380฿; doubles 480-550฿; triples 650฿. ●

Pranee Building, 931/12 Soi Kasem San 1 (☎216 3181). A/C double rooms are like the old Mercedes outside the guest house: old and worn, but a hint of their past glory remains. The fan-cooled rooms make this the place if you're willing to pay extra for location but not luxury. Doubles 400฿, with hot-water bath 450฿; triples 500฿. ●

Reno Hotel, 40 Soi Kasem 1 (☎215 0026). If the rooms were as nice as the lobby, this place would be a goldmine. The higher price buys you a dresser, desk, mirror, A/C, and private bath, but not much more quality. Internet, pool, cafe, and A/C blasted lobby. Doubles 780฿, with TV 890฿. ●

Wendy House, 36/2 Soi Kasem 1 (☎612 3487). This popular guest house is clean and simple. Convenience sets it apart from its Kasem cousins. Laundry 50฿ per kg. Internet 65฿ per hr. Singles 350฿; doubles 400-450฿. Long-term stays offered: weekly doubles 2500฿, monthly 9000฿. ●

SUKHUMVIT ROAD

Beneath the Skytrain, Sukhumvit Rd. is a strip of expensive pasta places, upscale chain restaurants, and massage-touting tuk-tuk drivers. Both sides of the soi are filled with Bangkok's trendiest bars and cabana-style drinking nooks. Accommodations are pricier.

> **GETTING TO SUKHUMVIT RD** Skytrain: Nana or Asok. Regular buses #25, 38, 72, 115. A/C buses #1, 8, 11, 13.

Suk 11, 1/33 Soi 11, Sukhumvit Rd. (☎253 5927; www.suk11.com), 10m down soi on the left. A truly beautiful enclave in the heart of Bangkok's nightlife, Suk 11 is a gem with a fun vibe. A re-created labyrinth of wooden soi, reminiscent of 1800s Thailand, weaves you up to the glistening clean rooms and newly tiled shared baths. All rooms (and even dorms) have A/C and are worth every baht. Dorms 250฿; singles 450฿, with bath 500฿; doubles 550฿/600฿. ●

S.V. Guest House, 19/35-36 Soi 19, Sukhumvit Rd. (☎253 35 56), near Asok Station. Good prices, great location (close, but not too close, to the action), and quiet, furnished rooms. Reserve in high season. Singles 250฿, with A/C 300฿; doubles with A/C 350฿, with bath 400฿. ❸

◘ FOOD

Thai cuisine is world-renowned, but no one is more obsessed with and proud of Thai food than the Thais themselves. Thus, they become visibly excited by travelers who venture out from the Thai-Western fare of *farang*-friendly restaurants to eat food like they usually do—right on the street. While most guest houses connect to overpriced Thai and Western cafes, the most authentic, best tasting, and cheapest Thai victuals are served from carts and no-name restaurants lining back alleys. Lose your fears and find your senses.

SWEET STREET EATS

With the overwhelming abundance of sidewalk vendors, indoor and outdoor markets, and restaurants in Thailand, it's easy to understand the popular saying, "Half of Thailand is cooking, and the other half is eating." Streetside vendors, who pay for their little spot of concrete, are not only fast and cheap, but often provide fresher, not to mention better eats than what you'll find at twice the price in your guest house.

The communication difficulties, piles of raw pork (*moo*) and chicken (*kai*), and simple novelty of eating meals from a street vendor might make some travelers hesitate, but there is often less risk of getting ill from stalls on the street than from restaurants, which carry ten times the quantity of food in order to serve a larger menu. Language difficulties are easily overcome. Vendors usually specialize in just a few dishes (and sometimes only one), and by taking note of the ingredients or simply by watching, you can order with the confidence that you'll receive something you'll enjoy.

Specialties that you'll frequently find on the street (meats optional):

Phat thai: the national dish, it is made of pan-fried rice noodles with bean sprouts, peanuts, lime, bean curd, scallion, dried red chili, egg, and the meat of your choice.
Phat ka-phrao: a meat with chilis and basil, usually on rice.
Phat kee mow: stir-fried vegetables with chilis and a meat (this is a spicy one).
Phat see lew: wide noodles with oyster sauce, vegetables, and a meat.

Many street vendors know a little English; just don't let them assume you want something dull or generic. Vendors are very courteous about cutting down on spice, and if you want spicy, you'll most likely have to ask for it. Satay grills (with squid, pork, and every part of the chicken) and soup stalls (almost without exception delicious) are also extremely common.

BANGLAMPHU AND KO RATTANAKOSIN

For good food stalls, stroll down **Soi Rambhuttri, Krai Si Rd.** (in the evening), or **Phra Chan Rd.** (during the day) opposite **Thammasat University.** The university's **cafeteria** has good street grub at cheap prices. On weekends, hawkers hang out in the area around **Sanam Luang. Khaosan Rd.** bursts with overpriced Thai and Western cuisine. One or two blocks north on **Tani Rd.** and at **Wat Chai Chanasongkram,** food stalls fry noodles and rice dishes all day and into the night.

May Kaidee's Vegetarian Restaurant (☎ 282 5702). Walk to Bowon Niwet Rd. at the end of Khaosan Rd. Take a right, a quick left, and left again down the first soi; it's 50m down. An expat favorite. Sit on a street-side stool and suck on sweet Thai specialties: black sticky rice with coconut milk and fruit (30฿), Isaan vegetarian stir-fry (35฿). Open daily 9am-11pm. ❷

Shoshana, on Chakrapong Rd. Facing the temple at the end of Khaosan Rd., turn right and right again at the first alley. This guest house restaurant specializes in delicious Israeli and Middle Eastern cuisine such as falafel (50฿), shawarma (60฿), and salads. Plenty of vegetarian options. Open daily 11am-11pm. ❷

Roti Mataba, at the bend in Phra Athit Rd. where it becomes Phra Sumen Rd. This roadside corner is home to some of the best Muslim Thai food in the area; curry-stuffed *roti* (36฿) or beef *mataba* (25฿) are sure to satisfy. Abundant breakfast *roti* options (8-20฿). Open Tu-Su 7am-10pm. ❶

DUSIT AND THEWET

The pavement opposite the guest houses on **Si Ayutthaya Rd.** bustles with food stalls, as does the market at the end of the road by Thewet pier. With just about every Thai rice, noodle, and curry dish available at rock-bottom prices (30-40฿), these stalls are the best dining option for visitors in this area. Unfortunately, there are very few restaurants.

Si Amnouai, on Si Ayutthaya Rd., at the corner with Samsen Rd., opposite the National Library. No English sign. Si Amnouai serves the same rice and noodle dishes as the stalls outside at the same prices—only indoors. Open daily 5am-late. ❷

Bangkok Youth Hostel Cafe, 25/2 Phitsanulok Rd. Mostly Thai clientele despite international flags. Menu features noodles, curries, and a few Western treats (60-130฿). Live music some nights 8-11pm. Open M-F 9am-1am, Sa-Su 10am-1am. ❸

CHINATOWN, PAHURAT, AND HUALAMPHONG

The center of **Yaowarat Rd.** is a treasure of outdoor dining, and the sois that branch off it overflow with culinary delights prepared right on the street. Roasted chestnuts like none other and translucent, succulent lychees abound by the kilo. Excellent Indian restaurants are plentiful near **Chakraphet Rd.** where it meets **Pahurat Rd.** This area requires more adventurous tastes: sharkfin soups and abalone dishes are specialties.

Royal India Restaurant, 392/1 Chakraphet Rd. (☎ 221 6566), near the river; look for the sign on the left as you come from Yaowarat Rd. Delicious food. Menu features Indian dishes of all flavors and tastes (vegetarian included) at 50-100฿. The *thali*, curry, masala, and *naan* sampler (125-165฿) saves you from making a difficult choice. Open daily 10am-10pm. ❸

White Orchid Restaurant and Coffee Shop, 409-421 Yaowarat Rd., in the White Orchid Hotel. Famed dim sum (30฿ per dish, buy 5 get 1 free) and Friday night all-you-can-eat dinner buffet (160฿) are reliably delicious. Open 24hr. for late-night snacking. ❸

Nameless Noodle Place, on Yaowarat Rd., across from the White Orchid Hotel. Popular eatery serves up a mean noodle soup (30-50฿) and simple rice dishes. Stainless steel furniture and garage doors that open onto the street set it one notch higher than its food cart neighbors. Try rice with braised pork rump (30฿); wash it down with a cold chrysanthemum juice (10฿). ❷

SILOM ROAD

Silom Rd. brims with delicious, expensive restaurants, particularly near Silom Center. Small tourist cafes set up at night on **Surawong Rd.** opposite Patpong. Look for local fare along **Convent Rd.** and inside **Soi Ngam Duphli.** If all the go-go bars and fake Rolexes make you feel invincible, try the food cart opposite Dick's Cafe—it serves fried scorpions, grasshoppers, and other milky white grubs. For some power protein, try the worm salad.

▨ Eat Me!, 1/6 Piphat Soi 2 (☎238 0931), off Convent Rd. to the right. Creativity and food collide in this stylish, modern restaurant. Photography and sculpture downstairs, delicately prepared yet robust entrees upstairs (200-400฿). Live jazz Th-Sa 7-10pm goes nicely with shots of chocolate vodka. As luxurious as a Thai massage. Open daily 3pm-1am. AmEx/MC/V. ❺

Sphinx, 98-104 Soi 4 Silom Rd. (☎234 7249). This trendy, gay-friendly (though not exclusive) restaurant and bar serves set Thai meals (295฿) and Thai/Western dishes (80-150฿) by candlelight. The bar picks up around 11pm and doesn't let up until closing. Cocktails 125฿. Open daily 6pm-2am. AmEx/MC/V. ❹

Dick's Cafe, 894/7-8 Soi Pratoochai (☎637 0078). From Patpong cross Surawong Rd. and walk two sois to the right. This classy gay cafe and bar draws a *farang* male clientele of all ages. Well lit with wicker chairs, sofas, and modern art decor, it's perfect for lunch or late-night socializing. Thai/Western food 80-130฿. Beer from 70฿. Cocktails 140฿. ❸

Coffee and More, 990 Rama IV Rd. (☎636 1596). From Silom Rd., make a right onto Rama IV Rd., walk to the Abdulrahim Office Bldg. on your right. It's on the ground floor. One of the two places in Bangkok to offer free Internet (the other is the Coffee and More on Phraathit Rd.), and if that's not reason enough, the passion fruit sorbet (40฿) is worth the trip alone. Food generally 70฿. Coffees and smoothies 30-75฿. Open M-Sa 8am-9pm. ❷

Sun Far Myanmar Food Center, 107/1 Pan Rd. (☎266 8787). Look for the Hindu temple; it's on the left. Burmese curries and sides 30-50฿. Open daily 9am-8pm. ❷

SIAM SQUARE

Siam Square is bursting with culinary flavor. In the afternoon and evening, vendors grill up juicy meats in front of the **National Stadium** on Rama I Rd., at the mouth of **Soi Kasem 1,** and along the soi weaving through Siam Sq. Cafes punctuate the soi around the square while fast-food chains and Ramen shops pop up in the shopping centers. Sidewalk restaurants dot **Ratchaprarop Rd.** and **Soi Wattanasin** opposite the Indra Regent Hotel.

Yum Saap, 430/11-12 Siam Sq. Soi 10. Look for the yellow smiley face and the "Spicy Salad" sign. Numerous scrumptious Northeastern-style salads. Papaya salad with seafood 35฿. Open daily 10am-8pm. ❷

Cha Cha An, 484 Siam Sq. (☎252 5038), across from the Novotel Hotel in the parking lot at the end of Soi 6. As lively as a karaoke bar, but without discordant singing, Cha Cha An serves up steaming hot *yakitori* (50-200฿), finger foods, and well-portioned pieces of sushi (60-200฿). Open daily 11am-10:30pm. AmEx/MC/V. ❹

Forest Tea House, 400 Siam Sq. Soi 6 (☎251 2417), at the bottom of Siam Sq. Skytrain exit. As much nature as Siam Sq. can handle. Enjoy papaya salad, fried chicken, and sticky rice (80฿) in faux stone booths and jungle decor. Satisfying spicy meal and large pearl milk tea 140฿. Open daily 11am-11:30pm. ❸

THE INSIDER'S CITY

WHAT WATS?

Some of the awe-inspiring, famous wats in Bangkok conveniently crowd around the Grand Palace, making it possible to do a cultural-religious walking tour in an afternoon. Due to the wats' proximity to Khao San Rd., there is no excuse for backpackers staying in the area to miss out on this opportunity. From Khao San Rd., head across Sanam Luang, toward the Chao Phraya River.

1 See Thailand's cultural artifacts at its biggest museum, the **National Museum** right in the Grand Palace complex.

2 Once a house, now a learning center, **Wat Mahathat** is the place to be enlightened by beauty and religious significance.

3 Buddhas overflow the premises at **Wat Phra Kaew.**

4 It's the **Grand Palace.** What can we say? Just go.

5 **Wat Pho** is the mamma of temples in Thailand—biggest and oldest.

6 For beautiful ceramic and porcelain inlays, head across the river to **Wat Arun.**

Witthyakit Building Food Court. Walk through Soi 10 in Siam Sq., cross the street, and enter the basement of the tall building resembling a parking structure. Students and faculty from nearby Chulalongkorn University pack this food court for dozens of Thai dishes at 15฿ per plate. Open daily 6-11:15am and 12:45-6pm. ❶

Daidomon, 266/11-13 Siam Sq. Soi 3. Do away with "atmosphere," get down to business, and eat at this fast-food-esque all-you-can-eat Japanese buffet. Lunch 79฿. Dinner 99฿. Weekends 119฿ all day. Open daily 10:30am-10pm. ❸

SUKHUMVIT ROAD

Sukhumvit Rd. brims with expensive quality restaurants and tourist cafes for wealthier travelers. If you want to burn baht for a fancy meal and get your money's worth, this is where to do it. **Soi 3/1** specializes in Middle Eastern cuisine. The usual food stalls set up on many soi at lunchtime to sell Thai dishes for 20-40฿.

Cabbages & Condoms, 10 Sukhumvit Rd., Soi 12 (☎229 4611). The brainchild of Dr. Vichit, a family planning advocate, this restaurant, bar, and handicraft shop was established in 1986 to help support the Population and Community Development Association. Whether you eat the exceptional Thai food in the beautiful garden or A/C restaurant, it is guaranteed not to cause pregnancy. Basil and chili chicken 110฿. Most dishes 80-200฿. Reserve on weekends. Open daily 11am-10pm. AmEx/V. ❸

Crepes and Co., 18/1 Sukhumvit Rd., Soi 12 (☎653 3990), past Cabbages & Condoms. Every type of crepe imaginable: sweet, rich, Western, Thai—or design your own (80-250฿, most around 150฿). *Tapas* 80-120฿. Incredibly friendly and service-oriented staff. Open daily 9am-midnight. AmEx/MC/V. ❹

Moghul Room, 1/16 Sukhumvit Rd., Soi 11 (☎253 4465), down the short alley opposite "Sea Food Center." One of Bangkok's best Indian restaurants. Muslim and Indian curries. Vegetarian dishes 80-90฿. Excellent *dosas* 130-170฿. Open daily 11am-11pm. AmEx/MC/V. ❸

🔘 SIGHTS

BANGLAMPHU AND KO RATTANAKOSIN

Ko Rattanakosin requires at least an entire day to explore fully. Because this area is compact, a walking tour is the perfect way to see the sights.

Although extremely touristed, **Wat Phra Kaew** and the **Grand Palace** remain two of the most impressive sights in Bangkok. Chao Phraya River Express (Tha Chang) and buses (#1, 25, 47, 82; A/C #43, 44) stop near the compound. History and art lovers will be glued to the treasures in the nearby **National Museum.** A circuit of **monasteries** is also nearby.

WAT PHRA KAEW (TEMPLE OF THE EMERALD BUDDHA) AND THE GRAND PALACE. The Temple of the Emerald Buddha was initially the Royal Chapel of the Chakri Dynasty. Inside the main chapel building *(bot)* is the actual **Emerald Buddha,** Thailand's most sacred Buddha figure. The Emerald Buddha was discovered in 1434, when lightning shattered a *chedi* in Chiang Rai and an abbot found a stucco Buddha inside. He sloughed off all the stucco and found the glorious Emerald Buddha, made of precious jade, hidden underneath. The figure stayed in Lampang until 1468 before being carted off to Vientiane, Laos. General Chao Phraya Chakri captured Vientiane 214 years later and reclaimed the statue. In 1782, King Rama I ascended the throne, moved the capital to Bangkok, and built the Royal Chapel—Wat Phra Kaew—for the Buddha. Take a look at the frescoes that encircle the compound; the scenes are taken from the ancient Indian epic, *Ramayana.*

THE BUDDHA'S NEW CLOTHES Often described as the *Palladium* of Thailand, the Emerald Buddha is widely believed to have originated in India around 500 BE (BE is the Buddhist Era; to switch from BE to AD, subtract 243). However, no scriptures confirm its existence in India, or Ceylon (Sri Lanka), which was believed to be its next home. According to the mythical story of its creation, Indra ordered Vishnu (both Hindu deities) to obtain the most precious stone from Mount Velu for all to gaze upon with awe. Though it is a popular belief, there is little evidence of its validity. The only scripture that exists in Thailand about the early history of the Emerald Buddha was found in Chiang Mai. The *Chronicle of the Emerald Buddha*, as it is called, was written in Pali on palm leaves. It only documents the Buddha's movements since its sensational rediscovery in AD 1434 in Chiang Rai, which made the image a pilgrimage site. Wanting the sacred image closer to him, the King of Chiang Mai ordered the Buddha to be moved to Chiang Mai. As the story goes, the elephant sent to transport it refused to take the road to Chiang Mai and instead headed to Lampang. Two subsequent elephants carrying the Buddha did the same thing. Believing this to be an omen, monks and royalty alike insisted on keeping it in Lampang. After 22 years, King Tiloka installed it in Chiang Mai's Wat Chedi Luang (p. 251). When Laotian Prince Chaichettha ascended to the Thai throne (through marriage), he moved the Buddha image to Luang Prabang and then Vientiane (p. 403) in Laos, supposedly to keep it protected. It wasn't until AD 1782, during Thai King Taksin's conquest of Laos, that the Buddha image was returned to Thailand. With the shift of the capital from Ayutthaya to Bangkok, the Emerald Buddha was placed in magnificent Wat Phra Kaew on the grounds of the Grand Palace. There it has stood for the last 223 years as a representation of prosperity, stability, and power. Successive kings have sought this compact *muang* (66cm tall) to add strength to their reign. Traditionally, the king changes the robes of the Emerald Buddha every season. The Emerald Buddha has three robes. The summer and wet season golden garments were created by Rama I (1782). A subsequent cool season robe was added by Rama III (1824). The intricately detailed robes not currently being worn by the Emerald Buddha can be seen at the National Museum in the Grand Palace. The current practice of the ceremonial switching of the seasonal golden robes of the Emerald Buddha by the king highlights the religious-royal connection, as well as the sacred Buddha's important place in Thai culture.

IN RECENT NEWS

THE MYSTERY OF JIM THOMPSON

On Easter Sunday in 1967, Jim Thompson went for a walk and never returned. His disappearance remains unsolved. Neither credible evidence of foul play nor Thompson's body have ever turned up, leading to continued conjecture about what happened 35 years ago to the expat who single-handedly built Thailand's silk trade into a multi-million dollar industry.

Long before his disappearance gripped the public imagination, Thompson was famous, especially in Thailand. He fell in love with the country during World War II when he was training as a member of the Office of Strategic Services (OSS), the clandestine US wartime intelligence service that ultimately became the CIA. When the war ended two days before his scheduled mission, Thompson decided to stay for good.

Although he had no business experience, he was fascinated by the entrepreneurial possibilities of opening up Thailand to Western visitors. At the time, Thai silk was a cottage industry on the verge of extinction. Textile manufacturing had made the time-consuming traditional methods of hand-weaving almost obsolete. Thompson, who had a keen artistic eye (he was originally an architect), became fascinated with the fabric and founded the Thai Silk Company in 1948 using only a handful of local weavers to supply his small business. Although Thompson never learned more than a few words of Thai, through his sharp sense of design, uncanny business sense, and sheer

Next door to the Temple of the Emerald Buddha is the **Grand Palace,** accessible through a gate connecting the two compounds. Inside the gate, turn right and stroll down the path past royal buildings on the left. The first is **Amarinda Vinichai Hall,** which once held court ceremonies. Next, **Chakri Mahaprasad Hall,** the residence of King Chulalongkorn, is a hybrid of European and Thai design. Today, the reception areas and central throne hall are used for royal ceremonies and are off-limits to mere mortal backpackers. Farther on, **Dusit Hall** is a symmetrical Thai building with a mother-of-pearl throne.

The **Wat Phra Kaew Museum** is inside the Grand Palace (take a right after the gift shop). The first floor displays relics and parts from original buildings that have been replaced. The second floor contains hundreds of Buddhas and enamel and crystal wares. *(☎ 222 0094, ext. 40. Free tours in English at 10, 10:30, 11am, 1:30, 2pm. Headphone audio tours 100฿ for 2hr., with guidebook and map 200฿. Admission to Wat Phra Kaew and the Grand Palace includes admission to Vimanmek Palace in Dusit and the Royal Thai Decorations and Coins Pavilion. Polite dress required: full shoes, pants, and sleeves. Shirts, long pants, and shoes are available at the entrance. Complex open daily 8:30am-3:30pm. Museum open daily 9am-3:30pm. Entrance 500฿.)*

WAT PHO (THE TEMPLE OF THE RECLINING BUDDHA). Wat Pho is the oldest, largest, and most architecturally spectacular temple in Bangkok. Its grounds are divided by Soi Chetuphon: one side is home to the monastery, while the other contains temple buildings. Wat Pho was built in the 16th century during the Ayutthaya period and expanded by King Rama I. His grandson, King Rama III, built the *wiharn* that houses the Reclining Buddha, 46m in length and 15m in height. Wat Pho is also home to Thailand's first university, a monastery that taught medicine a century before Bangkok was founded. A world-famous **Thai massage school** (see **Traditional Thai Massage,** p. 119) is its latest achievement. *(From Wat Phra Kaew, walk around the block and take 3 left turns from entrance. ☎ 222 0933. Open daily 9am-5pm. 20฿.)*

WAT MAHATHAT. Also known as the Temple of the Great Relic, Wat Mahathat houses a large sitting Buddha and was home to King Rama I, who was an abbot before he took up military campaigning. Today, the temple is a famous center of Buddhist teaching and home to one of Thailand's two Buddhist colleges. The southern part of the complex offers English instruction in Buddhist meditation. *(Between Silpakorn University and Thammasat University on Na Phra That Rd., opposite Sanam Luang. Open daily 9am-5pm.)*

SANAM LUANG. Sanam Luang is the "national common" of Thailand. In the past, criminals were lined up and shot here. Although public executions have been discontinued, summer soccer matches and kite-fighting contests—in which the large "male" kites *(chula)* pursue the fleeing smaller "female" kites *(pukpao)*—have not. Renovation scheduled to finish by early 2003. *(On Na Phra That Rd.)*

NATIONAL MUSEUM. Southeast Asia's largest museum, it is the crown jewel of Thailand's national museum system. King Chulalongkorn (Rama V) founded the museum in 1874 with the opening of a public showroom inside the Grand Palace to exhibit collections from the reign of his father, King Rama IV. The galleries are poorly lit and aged, but a massive renovation promises to restore the museum to its past beauty by 2003. *(On Na Phra That Rd. past Thammasat University. ☎ 224 1333. Open W-Su 9am-4pm, tickets sold until 3:30pm. Free tours in English W-Th 9:30am. 40฿.)*

NATIONAL GALLERY. The National Gallery contains classical and contemporary Thai artwork and the National Film Archives (see **Film,** p. 35). Rooms upstairs display paintings of scenes from epics such as *Ramayana* and classical plays. *(On Chao Fa Rd. opposite the Phra Pinklao Bridge from the National Theater. ☎ 282 2639. Open W-Su 9am-4pm. 30฿.)*

DEMOCRACY MONUMENT. Commemorating Thailand's transition from absolute to constitutional monarchy in the Revolution of 1932, the monument is built on the site of the bloody demonstrations of May 1992, when students and citizens protested the dictatorial rule of General Suchinda Kraprayoon. *(At the intersection of Ratchadamnoen and Dinso Rd.)*

WAT SAKET. Notable for its Golden Mount (an artificial hill topped with a gilded pagoda) soaring 80m high, this popular mount was formerly the highest point in the city. Today, Wat Saket's spectacular 360° panoramic view and golden *chedi* reward those fit enough to make the trek to the top. *(On Worachak Rd. Open daily 7:30am-5:30pm. 10฿.)*

WAT SUTHAT. The wat is famous for housing the Sao Ching Cha (Giant Swing) and Thailand's largest cast-bronze Buddha. In the past, Sao Ching Cha was the scene of several of the more curious Brahmin rituals, including one in which a priest would swing on a rope to try to use his teeth to catch money suspended 25m high. Many priests lost their lives attempting this until a law passed during the reign of King Rama VII prohibited the ritual. The best part of the complex is the main *wiharn* compound, with marble floors, ornate statues, and impressive murals. *(On Tithong Rd. near the Giant Swing. Open daily 9am-5pm.)*

charm, he was able to expand his company into one of the country's most lucrative exporters. By exposing wealthy tourists to Thai silk, Thompson turned silk into a high-end fashion trend and was soon filling orders for Broadway shows.

But Thompson was not simply a successful businessman. He became perhaps the most popular foreigner in Bangkok, respected for his genuine passion for the preservation of Thai arts and culture. In 1962, he restored a teak house on a Bangkok *klong* in the traditional Thai architectural style.

The Cameron Highlands, an area of dense jungle where Thompson disappeared, provide the setting for a disappearance that remains shrouded in mystery. The facts of that day offer essentially no clues: as his friends napped, Thompson apparently left for a walk. Did he fall down a ravine in the jungle? Was he killed by aborigines or caught in one of their animal traps? Did he take his own life?

These common explanations were generally rejected after an exhaustive search failed to turn up a single shred of evidence, not to mention his body. The failure of the search only led to more speculation. Was Thompson, the former government agent, actually on a covert mission that went awry in the Malaysian bush? Was he kidnapped by Communist agents from neighboring Cambodia?

For years, private investigators turned up nothing, local seers and European psychics offered revelations, and newspapers continued to wonder, while Thailand waited for its adopted son to come home.

WAT BOWONNIWET. King Rama IV spent 27 years as chief abbot and King Bhumibol Adulyadej spent his time as a monk in this less-touristed temple. The wat is home to Thailand's second Buddhist college, Mahamakut University. Drop by to admire the chapel's gorgeous ornamental borders and Chinese-style statues or observe the Western monks who live here. Be polite and discreet. *(On the corner of Phra Sawn and Bowon Nivet Rd. in Banglamphu, near Khaosan Rd. Open daily 9am-5pm.)*

DUSIT AND THEWET

The sights of Dusit and Thewet are quieter then those in the heart of the city and make for a relaxing morning or afternoon of sightseeing.

VIMANMEK PALACE. Built of golden teak during the reign of King Chulalongkorn (Rama V), the palace is the largest teak mansion in the world. Held together with wooden pegs, the 72-room structure served as the king's favorite palace from 1902 to 1906. The palace displays many items from his reign. The museum in Aphisek Dusit Hall houses an impressive collection of silver jewelry, silk, and soapstone carvings. *(Entrance is on the left on U Thong Nai Rd. Bus #70 stops nearby. Open daily 9:30am-4pm, last admission 3pm. Thai dancing daily 10:30am, 2pm. 50฿, students 20฿, under 5 free, free with a Wat Phra Kaew and Grand Palace admission ticket. The palace can only be viewed on a tour. 45min. tours are given in English every 30min. Shorts and sleeveless shirts not allowed. Admission to the palace includes a visit to the museum. Open daily 10am-4pm.)*

DUSIT ZOO. Thailand's largest zoo was once part of the gardens of the Chitralada Palace. It now hosts a large collection of regional animals as well as some rare species, including white-handed gibbons and Komodo dragons. *(On the right on U Thong Nai Rd. Entrances also on Rama V and Ratchavithi Rd. Open daily 9am-6pm. 30฿, under 10 5฿.)*

WAT BENCHAMABOPHIT (MARBLE TEMPLE). The wat's symmetrical architecture and white Carrara marble walls were built in 1899 by King Chulalongkorn. The courtyard is lined with 52 bronze Buddhas that represent styles from different periods, while the garden contains sacred turtles given to the temple by worshipers. Early in the morning (6-7:30am), the monks line the streets to accept donations of food and incense. In February and May, the wat hosts Buddhist festivals and candlelight processions around the *bot. (On the right of Si Ayutthaya after the Ratchadamnoen Nok Rd. intersection. Take bus #72. Open daily 8am-5:30pm. 20฿.)*

OTHER SIGHTS. Past the Si Ayutthaya Rd. traffic light, Ratchadamnoen Nok Rd. opens into Suan Amphon, site of the revered **statue of King Chulalongkorn (Rama V)**. This beloved king, who ruled from 1868 to 1910, is remembered for abolishing slavery, modernizing Thai society (he introduced the first indoor bathroom, among other things), and fending off power-hungry British and French colonialists. On October 23, the anniversary of his death, patriotic citizens pay homage here.

Behind the statue, guarded by an iron fence and a well kept garden, stands the former **National Assembly** (Parliament Building). This domed building was commissioned by King Chulalongkorn in 1908 to replace his old residence. The new Royal Palace, called **Anantasamakhom,** was patterned after St. Peter's Basilica in Rome. Following the 1932 coup, the palace became the National Assembly building, but the Assembly has since been moved to Dusit. Past Wat Benchamabophit and Rama V Rd. on the left is **Chitralada Palace,** the official home of the Royal Family. The walled compound is protected by a moat and specially trained soldiers. The palace is closed to the public.

CHINATOWN, PAHURAT, AND HUALAMPHONG

Chinese immigrants first settled southeast of the royal center along the Chao Phraya River in the 18th century, just after construction of the Grand Palace evicted them from Bangkok's first Chinatown. Today, this area is called **Yaowarat** (after the road that runs through Chinatown) or **Sampeng.** The neighborhood's narrow sois and vibrant street life make it worth exploring on foot, especially at night, when the area comes alive. Near Yaowarat, in an area marked by Pahurat Rd., Chakraphet Rd., and countless alleys in between, lies **Pahurat District,** home of Bangkok's Indian population. Its markets are a great place to buy cheap clothing sold by Sikhs and Hindus.

■ **WAT TRAIMIT.** The only major temple in this area is home to the Giant Golden Buddha—a 3m, five-ton, gold Sukhothai-style statue. When the Burmese sacked Ayutthaya, residents saved the statue by covering it with stucco. Its identity remained secret until 1955, when the statue slipped from a moving crane as it was being transported to Wat Traimit. Cracks developed in the plaster, the stucco was removed, and the Golden Buddha was rediscovered. (*Main entrance on Yaowarat Rd. near the Charoen Krung Rd. intersection; a smaller entrance on Traimit Rd., accessible by bus #73. ☎ 225 9775. Open daily 9am-5pm. 20฿.*)

SILOM ROAD

LUMPINI PARK. Lumpini Park, the largest park in Bangkok, is an oasis in Bangkok's glass and steel. In the mornings, the Chinese practice *Tai Chi* while others rent paddle boats and cruise the park's lakes. During the day, locals and expats relax at nearby cafes along Ratchadamri Rd. (*The park is bordered by Ratchadamri, Rama IV, Sarasin, and Witthayu Rd. and is accessible from Silom by regular bus #15, 77, 115 or from Siam Sq. and Banglamphu by regular bus #15. Skytrain: Sala Daeng. Open daily 5:30am-7pm.*)

ORIENTAL HOTEL. Founded by two Danish sea captains, the Oriental is one of the world's most famous hotels. H.N. Andersen built the grand Italianate building in 1887, which still stands as the "Authors' Residence" wing of the hotel, and shelters some of its finest, most expensive rooms. (*48 Oriental Ave. along the Chao Phraya River. Chao Praya River Express: Tha Oriental.*)

SIAM SQUARE

Famed for its shopping malls, Siam Sq. also has some sights worth a look and is easily reached on the Skytrain.

■ **JIM THOMPSON'S HOUSE.** This elegant house was home to American Jim Thompson, who revitalized the Thai silk industry after World War II and later disappeared in 1967 during a trip to Malaysia. Actually a combination of six teak buildings, the house is home to one of Thailand's best collections of Ayutthaya- and Rattanakosin-period art. Admission includes a tour in English, during which guides discuss ingenious architectural oddities in Thai houses. (*Soi Kasem San 2, opposite the National Stadium. All Rama I Rd. buses access this site. Skytrain: National Stadium. ☎ 612 3744. Open daily 9am-4:30pm. Tours required; every 10min. 100฿, students 50฿.*)

CHULALONGKORN UNIVERSITY. Thailand's most prestigious academic institution is worth a visit. The buildings are an architectural representation of Thai classicism, and the bookstore contains a fine selection of English books. (*On the east and west sides of Phayathai Rd., south of Siam Sq. From MBK, cross Phayathai Rd. on the footbridge or take any bus heading south on Phayathai Rd. until you see the campus on the left.*)

SUAN PAKKAD PALACE. Suan Pakkad Palace's five traditional houses are set in an immaculate garden with plants from all over the world. In the back of the garden is the Lacquer Pavilion, filled with porcelain, Buddhas, and Ban Chiang pottery. (*352 Si Ayutthaya Rd. Take regular bus #54, 73, or 204 from Siam Sq. past the Indra Regent on Ratchaprarop Rd. Get off near the corner of Ratchaprarop and Si Ayutthaya Rd. and turn down Si Ayutthaya Rd.; it's on the left. Skytrain: Phayathai. ☎ 245 4934. Open M-Sa 9am-4pm. 150฿, students 30฿.*)

GODDESS TUPTIM SHRINE. One of Bangkok's more arousing sights, the shrine is famous for the large numbers of phallic objects around its spirit house, brought there by couples seeking an end to their infertility. *(Near the Hilton International Hotel on Witthayu Rd. at Phetchaburi Rd.)*

OTHER SIGHTS. Opposite Jim Thompson's House is the **National Stadium,** the most noticeable landmark on Rama I Rd. aside from the Mahboonkrong Shopping Complex and the Siam Sq. Shopping Center. The famous **Erawan Shrine,** built as a memorial to the workers who died in mysterious accidents during the construction of the Erawan Hotel, is farther along Rama I Rd., where it becomes Ploenchit Rd. Dancers hired by grateful worshipers often perform around the shrine.

SUKHUMVIT ROAD AREA

When Rama I/Ploenchit Blvd. crosses Witthaya Rd., it becomes Sukhumvit Rd., stretching southeast out of the city. The Sukhumvit Rd. area hosts trendy nightlife, upper-crust travelers, red-light districts, and great restaurants.

KAMTHIENG HOUSE. This ethnological museum is home to the Siam Society, a cultural society supported by the royals. The museum reconstructs daily life in 19th-century Thailand with exhibits on tools, utensils, and other objects. *(131 Soi 21 Asoke, on the left as you walk from Sukhumvit Rd. Near Asok Skytrain station. ☎ 661 6470.)*

THONBURI: WEST OF THE RIVER

■ **WAT ARUN (TEMPLE OF DAWN).** Named for Aruna, the Hindu god of dawn, this wat was built in the Ayutthaya period and embellished during the reigns of Kings Rama II and III into its present Khmer-style form. The distinctive 79m *prang* is inlaid with ceramic tiles and porcelain. The best view of the wat is from the Chao Phraya River's Bangkok side in the early morning or in the evening; the top of the *prang* affords beautiful views as well. *(In Thonburi, from Wat Pho, take a right from Chetupon Rd. onto Maharat Rd. and a left at Tani Wang Rd. This path goes to Tha Tien pier. From an adjacent pier, ferries make crossings to the wat for 1฿. ☎ 465 5640. Open daily 8:30am-5:30pm. 10฿.)*

ROYAL BARGE MUSEUM. The most impressive barge in the museum is the Suphannahongsa, a 46m vessel reserved for the king when he makes his annual offering of robes to the monks during the Kathin Ceremony. *(On Arun Amarin Rd., under the bridge over Klong Bangkok Noi. Take a river taxi to Bangkok Noi pier and walk upriver, over the canal, to the museum. ☎ 424 0004. Open daily 8:30am-4:30pm. 80฿.)*

▣ ENTERTAINMENT

NATIONAL THEATER

Dedicated in 1965, the National Theater, on Na Phra That Rd. past the national museum, has regular drama and dance shows. The performance program changes monthly but usually includes at least one *khon* or *lakhon* dance-drama performance and a concert by the Thai National Orchestra (see **Drama,** p. 33). Contact the theater for the month's schedule. *(☎ 224 1342. Open M-F 9am-3:30pm and 1hr. prior to performances. Tickets 30-80฿ for government-sponsored shows.)*

THAI CLASSICAL DANCE DINNERS

Missed the National Theater show? Don't worry, many restaurants offer Thai classical dance dinners with half a dozen traditional dances in an hour-long show. Shows usually include *khon* dances from the *Ramakien* (see **Dance,** p. 33). No shorts, sandals, or tank tops are allowed. Reserve at least a day in advance. At **Ruen Thep,** Silom Village, 286 Silom Rd., in the Narai Hotel, enjoy a dance dinner in a garden of turtle pools. Performances begin at 8pm and include seven dance styles that change monthly. (☎234 4581. Opens at 7pm; set Thai dinner at 7:30pm. Tickets 450฿. AmEx/MC/V.)

TRADITIONAL THAI MASSAGE

Quality among massage parlors varies tremendously, and many are fronts for prostitution. Pictures of women in the window are giveaways for the latter. Ask other backpackers about their favorite masseurs and safe places in addition to using the following listings.

At Wat Pho, **The Traditional Massage School** (see **Wat Pho,** p. 114) offers massages for 200฿ per hr. as well as a 10-day, 30hr. course for 6000฿. (☎221 2974. Open daily 8am-5pm.) ▧**Mr. Noi** is possibly the world's best masseur. (☎235 2148. 330฿ for 2hr. Open daily 9am-midnight.) **Winwan,** 45 Sukhumvit Rd., between Soi 1 and 3, offers excellent massages. (☎251 7467. 300฿ plus tip per 2hr. Open daily 10am-midnight.) **Marble House,** 37/18-19 Soi Surawong Plaza, one soi up Surawong Rd. from Patpong 2, has a capable, mostly Wat Pho-trained staff, including a cadre of blind masseurs, who are reputed to be the best in the business. A popular standby in the Banglamphu area is **Pian Massage Center and Beauty Salon,** 108/15 Soi Rambuttri, Khaosan Rd., down the tiny soi next to Nat Guest House on Khaosan Rd. (Massage 80฿ per 30min., 140฿ per hr.; 30hr. certification course 4000฿. Open daily 8am-midnight.).

LADY KILLER The words Muay Thai, the wildly exciting and dangerous sport of Thai kickboxing, conjure up images of a bloodbath. This is a sport in which competitors swing kicks and punches while wielding elbows with executed precision in a series of three to five three-minute rounds in order to knock out their opponent. You would think such a sport is no place for a drop-dead gorgeous woman, yet Nong Toom is tenaciously disproving assumptions, forcing her opponents to drop at her pedicured feet. When she burst onto the kickboxing scene at the age of 16, Nong Toom was a man. A *katoey* (transvestite), she fought as a man, but dressed as a woman. Known to wear fire-red lipstick and a bra in the ring, Nong Toom was anything but lady-like in her disposal of opponents. She amassed a 50-3 record with an impressive 18 of her 20 wins before the age of 16 coming from knockouts. As her celebrity grew, she assumed the name Prinaya Kiatbusaba, to honor her trainers at the Lanna Boxing Camp, in the foothills of Doi Suthep, Chiang Mai, where her parents were lychee farmers. At the beginning of one match, her opponent mockingly kissed her on the cheek. After Prinaya crushed him, she returned the kiss to the bewildered fighter.

In 1999, Prinaya underwent a sex change operation to be physically attuned to her inner gender. (Thailand does more sex change operations than any other nation in the world.) However, the operation officially ended her professional kickboxing career. Muay Thai regulations do not allow men to fight women. Having retired from one stage, she ascended another. Prinaya can still be found entertaining. In 2002, she was singing in Bangkok at the Icon Club on Silom Rd., Soi 4. She may still be there. Unsurprisingly, her incredible life, a story of beating adversity and discrimination, has been made into a movie. *A Beautiful Boxer* is scheduled for release at the end of 2002. For aspiring Thai kickboxers, the Lanna Boxing Camp will train you for a day (250฿) or longer (price depends on length of stay). See **Alternatives to Tourism,** p. 86, for more information on courses and location.

MUAY THAI (THAI BOXING)

One of the world's more brutal sports, Thai kickboxing is generally fought with opponents close together, protecting themselves against a kick to the head, which would entail not only a concussion but a sure knockout. For those who don't mind the actual fighting, the rituals and fervor that surround these matches are fascinating aspects of Thai culture (see **Muay Thai**, p. 36). Muay Thai occurs daily at one of two venues. On Mondays, Wednesdays, Thursdays, and Sundays, the action's at **Ratchadamnoen Boxing Stadium** (☎281 4205), on Ratchadamnoen Nok Rd. near the TAT office. Take regular bus #70 from Sanam Luang. On Tuesdays, Fridays, or Saturdays, head for **Lumpini Boxing Stadium** (☎251 4303), on Rama IV Rd. near Lumpini Park, which stages better fights—the top card's on Friday. Fights start around 6pm; the main fight begins around 7:30pm. Take regular bus #115 from Silom Rd. Prices vary depending on the venue and are cheaper at Ratchadamnoen (about 220-240฿, ringside 880฿+)l

SHOPPING

After a while in the Bangkok sun, the **Siam Sq.** and **Silom Rd.** areas begin to look like one big A/C shopping mall. Siam Sq. houses five immense shopping centers, four movie complexes, 200 restaurants, and a few discos. (Most open daily 10am-10pm.) The area is a hangout for many Bangkok teenagers and college students trickling in from Thailand's prestigious Chulalongkorn University.

The undisputed heavyweight of Bangkok's shopping centers is **Mahboonkrong Center (MBK)**, on the corner of Rama I and Phayathai Rd. in the Siam Sq. area. With seven floors of department stores, arcades, electronics, music stores, fast-food joints, and a cinema, MBK puts most Western shopping malls to shame. Connected to it by a skyway across Phayathai Rd. is the equally impressive **Siam Square Mall.** Spread over several soi are outdoor clothing and music stores, restaurants, two movie theaters, and a hotel. **Amarin Plaza,** at the intersection of Rama I and Ratchadamri Rd., and MBK's main competitor, the **Zen World Trade Center,** up Ratchadamri Rd. toward Phetchaburi Rd., have the same shops as MBK but are a little less busy.

■ MARKETS

Talat, street markets, all over the city are sources for knock-off designer watches, clothing (from Ralph Lauren to "Ralph Levis"), and pirated CDs and videos.

■ **CHATUCHAK MARKET.** This weekend market is a bargain-hunter's dream and a great example of market culture in Southeast Asia. The bustle is unmistakable and addictive as thousands of vendors sell everything from dalmatians to toucans, though the main focus is clothing and plants. Bring plenty of free time and patience to navigate the crowds, hone your wallet preservation skills, and bargain with relentless vendors—even the stingiest will be hard-pressed to go home empty-handed. *(Skytrain: Mo Chit. Open Sa-Su 7am-6pm.)*

BANGLAMPHU MARKET. This frenzied market branches onto Chakrapong, Krai Si, and Tani Rd., but the tourist-oriented section is along Khaosan Rd. A late-afternoon/early-evening affair, the market's offerings include food, souvenirs, leather products, and fake designer clothing. Everything is overpriced, but the feel of the market itself is priceless.

OTHER MARKETS. Thewet Market is on Krung Kasem Rd. along the Chao Phraya River. The selection is not as diverse, but it's the one-stop shopping center for food or garden landscaping. *(Chao Phraya River Express: Thewet.)* A sweet and brilliant sight is **Pakklong Market,** southwest of Pahurat District over Triphet Ave. Take a river taxi to Tha Rachini. A relaxing stroll through this wholesale flower market is worth the trip.

Opposite Chakraphet Rd., and east of the Pahurat Cloth Market is the **Sampaeng Lane Market.** This small alley continues for a few kilometers through the heart of Chinatown. If you need cutlery, jewelry, socks, monk's supplies, hats, or fishing equipment, this outstretched alley is the place to go. Extending northwest from the corner of Yaowarat and Chakrawat Rd. is the **Nakhon Kasea (Thieves Market),** best known for its machinery, ice cream makers, and ninja weaponry.

The **Pratunam Market** operates during the day along Ratchaprarop Rd., opposite the Indra Hotel. Clothes are the main event here, although there is also a wide selection of knick-knacks. In the **Silom** area, vendors set up along **Patpong Soi 1** after nightfall. This is *the* place to buy overpriced fake designer watches, clothing, or soap carvings or to take in the scene as Thais tout live "shows" to elderly couples and housewives.

▨ NIGHTLIFE

Bangkok's entertainment and nightlife need little introduction. The city's reputation as the epicenter of Southeast Asia's internationalism is rooted in its effortless mix of traditional art and culture with the hip, connected youth who want to get down and party until dawn. Like other global metropolises, Bangkok offers a wealth of activities from sophisticated bars to shady massage parlors, and dance shows to kickboxing—something to entertain and enlighten every type of traveler.

Silom is the center of after-dark amusement, although Sukhumvit, Siam Sq., and Khaosan Rd. are nothing to scoff at. Silom Sois 2 and 4 are centers for gay nightlife. Check out the free *Guide to Bangkok* (available at many bars and restaurants) or the *Metro* (100฿ at newsstands) for the latest in "cool." Places listed here are not associated with the skin trade (see **Red Light, Green Light,** p. 124).

BARS AND PUBS

▨ **Tapas,** 114/7 Silom, Soi 4 (☎632 7982). Resident DJs spin chill house nightly in this "room club" bar. Sink into a couch to soak up the sounds or get up and groove wherever there's space. Outdoor seating for fresh air and people-watching. No cover downstairs. 300฿ cover upstairs. Beer 120฿. Open daily 8pm-2am.

▨ **Q Bar,** 34 Sukhumvit, Soi 11 (☎252 3274). At the end of Soi 11 take a left. Posh. Dress well—you might meet someone special. Beer 160฿. Cocktails 200฿. Special parties F-Sa 400฿ cover, includes 2 free drinks. Open daily 8pm-2am.

Banana Leaf Cafe, 34/1 Khaosan Rd. (☎629 3343), 50m from Gullivers (see below). Psst—one of Bangkok's best new bars is on Khaosan Rd., and tourists haven't found it yet. Packed with Thais and just a few *farang*, this wood-furnished cafe is quiet and refreshing. Comprehensive Thai/Western menu 60-120฿. Drinks 60-140฿. Open daily 10am-2am. A dozen similar cafe/bars have recently opened along **Phra Athit Rd.** near the river. Many have live music. Most open daily 6pm-1am.

Joy Luck Club, 8 Phra Sumen Rd. (☎629 4128). Artsy + moody = atmosphere. Singha 60฿. Cocktails 100฿, 800฿ for Johnny Walker black label. Open daily 5pm-1am. This junction between Phra Sumen Rd. and Phra Athit Rd. is full of other very comfortable bars like **Dog Days** and **Comme Arts Cafe.** Open daily 11am-1am.

Ad Here, 13 Samsen Rd. (☎629 2897). Right before Samsen Rd. changes into Chakrapong Rd. at the Khlong Banglamphu. Old soul, jazz, and Beatles tunes belted out by a singer with a lovely Thai-English accent will soothe your fatigued muscles. Beer 60฿. Open daily 5pm-1am.

IN RECENT NEWS

WHAT'S LOVE GOT TO DO WITH IT?

While most travelers are wary of catching dengue fever, "dong" fever is the more conspicuous epidemic raging through Thailand. Not-so-pretty Western men coupled with young, beautiful Thai women is a frequent sight forcing travelers to, perhaps unexpectedly, confront the questions and issues surrounding the world's oldest trade.

Prostitution has existed in Thailand since Chinese sailors arrived and started taking "minor wives" centuries ago; today, scholars estimate that 150,000-200,000 women staff brothels and street corners all over the country, primarily servicing Thai locals. The industry centers in Bangkok, with Pattaya in the east and Phuket and Hat Yai in the south representing the largest satellites. To a lesser extent, conspicuous prostitution catering to tourists has infiltrated Ko Samui, Chiang Mai, and Hua Hin.

However, there is hardly an area of Thailand—save the blocks surrounding the king's palace—that isn't affected by the trade. Most tourists will hear first and most frequently about the skin carnivals of Patpong and Nana Plaza in Bangkok.

The majority of Thai prostitutes come from Thailand's poorer neighborhoods in Bangkok, the Northern provinces, and most especially the northeastern region of Isaan, Thailand's most impoverished area. Women also come from Cambodia, Myanmar, and Malaysia to work in the skin trade.

Saxophone Pub and Restaurant, 3/8 Phayathai Rd., away from Siam Sq., at the southeast corner of the Victory Monument. The city's best jazz club. Thai and Western food is delicious and expensive at 100฿ minimum per person. Beer from 120฿. Live jazz bands M-W, blues bands Th-Su.

O! Hungry, 45 Soi Chana Songkram (☎629 1412). Next to My House Guest House. It is not hard to find bars serving 40฿ Chang beer, but ones like O! Hungry, which show NEW Western movies (8pm showtime) for free and serve 45฿ banana pancakes, are harder to come by. Open daily 6am-1:30am.

Shenanigans, Sivadon Bldg., 1 Convent Rd. (☎266 7160). Just off Silom Rd. near Patpong. A classy Irish pub with a 100% *farang* clientele. A bit expensive but well worth it, especially during happy hour (4-7:30pm) when a Jameson and Coke costs 80฿ and a large Heineken is 90฿. Guinness on tap 320฿ per pint. Open daily 11am-2am.

Pranakorn Bar and Gallery, 58/2 Soi Ratchadamnoen Klang Tai. Three floors of art, tunes, and drink. Few *farangs*. Small Singha 60฿. Open daily 11am-2am.

Telephone Pub and Restaurant, 86-88 Silom Soi 4 (☎234 3279). All orientations welcome, but caters to a gay crowd, both Thai and foreign. Signature fixture of numbered telephones at tables provides fiber-optic flirting options. Serves beer and food indoors and out. Drinks 55-125฿. Western and Thai dishes 100-190฿. Open daily 6pm-2am.

Gullivers, 3 Khaosan Rd., at the corner of Chakrapong Rd. Look for the life-size tuk-tuk hanging over the door. One of the most popular bars on Khaosan Rd. Its specialties are Western food and beer in a dark tavern atmosphere. Pool tables and a bar that won't quit until sun-up. Expect to see hordes of drunk *farangs* flocking here on the prowl for the opposite sex. Beers 60-65฿ per bottle. Open daily 11am-2am.

Radio City and **Muzzik Café,** on the south end of Patpong 1 Rd. on opposite sides of the street. After 9pm these colorful and popular bars fill with *farang* seeking either refuge from the madness outside or the nightly live music. Skip the ping-pong shows elsewhere and check out the Elvis Presley (11pm) and Tom Jones (midnight) shows. Open daily 6pm-2am. Muzzik Café stays open until the wee hours and collects much of the drunken, post-go-go bar chaos. Open daily 6pm-5am.

Boh, Tha Tien pier, near Wat Pho. Enjoy the river view of the nearby temples at night, and get tipsy with Thammasat University students. Singha 70฿. Open daily 7pm-12am.

The Toby Jug Pub, 185 Silom Rd. A hole-in-the-wall next to Silom Complex. From the Dusit Thani, walk toward the river; it'll be on your left before Soi 1. Time passes a little slower in this cool, sedate hangout, which somehow mixes British appearance with Thai ambience. Kidney meat pie 160฿. Amstel and Carlsberg on tap 50฿. Open M-F 11am-11pm, Sa 3-11pm.

LIVE MUSIC

Bangkok's most rewarding nightlife centers on jazz establishments with live music and a classy Thai and foreign clientele. Off Ratchadamri Rd., **Soi Sarasin,** just north of Lumpini Rd., has restaurant/bars that play live music nightly. Bands generally start around 8pm, but things get cooking after 11pm. ■**Brown Sugar Jazz Pub and Restaurant,** 231/20 Sarasin Rd., opposite Lumpini Park, is regarded (along with Saxophone Pub, see above) as one of the best in the city, with jazz bands every night that draw well-dressed patrons. (☎250 1826. Food 90-360฿. Beer 120฿. Cocktails 150฿. Happy hour 4-9pm. Open daily 11am-1am, live music 9:45pm-1am.)

CLUBS

Given that Thailand is home to some of Southeast Asia's best DJs, it's no surprise that Bangkok has the largest selection of clubs in the region. Not all discotheques charge cover, but all feature pricey drinks.

Concept CM² (☎255 6888), as in "Siam Squared," in the basement of the Novotel Hotel on Soi 6, is as classy as it gets. The city's most recognized club, "Concept" features postmodern decor and talented bartenders. Dance to the beat of Thai and English techno or dine in the restaurant area where the silk menu comes in a bamboo tub. Beer 140฿. Dishes 150-300฿. No shorts or sandals. 18+. Cover 100฿. Officially open daily 7pm-2am, but the doors sometimes don't open until after 10pm.

DJ Station, on Silom Soi 2, was awarded the title of Best Gay Disco 2001 by *Metro.* With the no-nonsense metal decor, great house/techno, and the full range of openness, it's no wonder. It also features a nightly cabaret and hang-out room on the third floor. Cover F-Sa 200฿, includes 2 drinks; Su-Th 100฿, includes 1 drink. No shorts or sandals. 18+. Open daily 11pm-2:30am.

Lucifer, on Patpong 1 Rd., next to Radio City, is delightfully and elaborately designed to look like hell; the club surely takes in its share of devils from the street and bars below. Regardless, this venue still gets kicking around midnight with dance remixes and happy house. Drinks 120฿. No cover. Open daily 10pm-2am.

The Asian Financial Crisis forced more women into prostitution to feed their families. Many were sold by their own families to agents who often mislead parents to believe their daughters will work as servants. Some women work freelance as elite call-girls, some split earnings with their go-go bars, and an unfortunate few indentured prostitutes must work to pay off their "debt" to their brothel. Most work 1-2 years.

Though the rate of condom use in commercial sex is up to 95%, the prostitute's risk of HIV/AIDS is still extremely high (see **AIDS,** p. 22). Thai-Western marriages are not uncommon, but few marriages come out of a "working relationship." Rare is the Westerner who follows through on his promises of marrying the prostitute whom he visits.

Perhaps the most shocking aspect of the Thai skin trade is that it is not a matter of pressing debate among Thais or tourists in Thailand. Although a 1960 law prohibits the sex trade, it is blatantly unenforced, full of loopholes, and punishes prostitutes more harshly than pimps, club owners, and clients.

Thais, in general, assume an amused perspective on the whole subject. Ask the average Thai woman what she thinks of a man visiting a red-light district, and she'll most likely shrug her shoulders and say, "What else is a single man to do?"

RED LIGHT, GREEN LIGHT

Love it or loathe it, Bangkok's Red-Light District will not be denied. Thailand supports a massive sex industry, primarily for locals, but entrepreneurial Thais and expats have filled the niche for lonely male foreigners. Three locales—Patpong in Silom, and Nana and Soi Cowboy in Sukhumvit—are home to the densest concentration of these self-proclaimed "entertainment centers." The Sukhumvit area, in general, more prominently displays the skin industry in the higher number of go-go bars and white male-Thai female "couples" visible on the streets.

You can dabble to different degrees in the sex trade. Most innocent are regular bars staffed by Thai women, whose job is to provide company and suck on drinks purchased by male customers. On the next rung up (down?) the ladder are hostess bars, which are almost exclusively for Japanese tourists. Lines of well-dressed Japanese women wait street-side to be selected and escorted by the client into their karaoke bars for food, drinks, and singing. Third are go-go bars, which feature stages for topless and/or bottomless dancing, in addition to topless and bottomless girls for "company." Many of these go all the way, with back rooms where live trick shows or sex shows are put on throughout the night. Needless to say, additional "services" are purchased from these women (many or all of whom are heavily intoxicated with various substances) at any and all of these locations.

At first sight, Patpong appears to be yet another of Bangkok's numerous market/tourist attractions, with families and couples roaming between street stalls. But as the laminated "show lists" that street vendors hawk indicate, the goings-on are not as innocent as the crowds. Go-go bars—front rooms and back—host plenty of older single white men and groups of curious younger tourists (including a few women). "Boy go-gos" provide the gay equivalent on nearby sois (women are welcome in some, though all cater to men). Lesbian go-gos are elusive. Women are generally accepted at most go-gos on Patpong 1 and 2.

The Nana Entertainment Complex (Sukhumvit Soi 4) and Soi Cowboy (between Sukhumvit Sois 21 and 23) do not cater to tourist families (as Patpong does) but set about their missions more seriously. They have the same types of bars, but less wide-eyed *farang* and more business proceedings, with far fewer women or couples here.

Let's Go does not encourage the support of these industries. Nevertheless, these activities will continue with or without curious budget travelers. Those who wish to enter go-go bars for dancing or shows should be cautious. In Nana and Soi Cowboy, most of these establishments do not charge cover, and your bar tab (the only required charge, beers run 70-100฿) will be set in front of you at all times. If a woman sits with you, you will be expected to buy her drinks to consume at whatever rate she chooses. Be resolute or go to the manager if this is something you do not want. It is possible to sit and drink one beer by yourself for an hour if you so choose, although few people here do. Patpong is a different situation, and stories abound amongst travelers about those who enter these sex shows under the auspices of "no cover charge" only to be prohibited from exiting before paying thousands of baht. A few of the larger clubs really have free shows, but most don't, charging 200-300฿ for a ticket to a night's worth of shows. Lower priced (80-100฿) tickets are rumored to have similar consequences as the "no cover charge except 3000฿" bars. Regardless of where you go, the only way you can really be certain is, by seeking out the manager immediately upon entry and telling him what you expect of his club. He (managers are always male) is the only one who can guarantee a "free show" and will tell you if that is not the case. If there is any uncertainty, leave immediately, as you are expected to pay for any watching. Exercise caution, do not take pictures, and be discreet.

DAYTRIPS FROM BANGKOK

Travel agencies offer pricey daytrips to attractions outside Bangkok, but these sights can be seen more cheaply independently.

NONTHABURI

The best way to get to Wat Chalerm is by the Chao Phraya River Express ferry, which ends at the Nonthaburi Pier. From here, take another ferry to the west bank (1฿) and hire a motorcycle to Wat Chalerm (10฿). Open daily 9am-5pm.

Nonthaburi province straddles the Chao Phraya River 20km north of Bangkok. The town of Nonthaburi, on the east bank, is known for its fruit and earthenware. On the west bank of the river, in Amphoe Bangkluai, stands **Wat Chalerm Phra Kliad Wora Wihaan,** known to locals simply as Wat Chalerm. Chinese styles influence the statues around the grounds as well as the ceramics and flowering decorations. Set in a grove, the monastery grounds are as pleasant as the breezy boat ride.

SAMUT PRAKAN

Take A/C bus #11 from the World Trade Center; the Crocodile Farm is the last stop. To reach Muang Boran from the bus stop, backtrack to the corner at the Bank of Ayudhya. Along the side street, a row of songthaew go to Muang Boran for 3฿. Muang Boran: ☎ 323 9253. Open daily 8am-5pm. 50฿, children 25฿. Crocodile Farm: ☎ 703 84 91. Crocodile shows every hr. 9-11am and 1-4pm; additional shows on weekends and holidays at noon and 5pm. Open daily 8am-6pm. 300฿, students with ID 200฿.

The center of Thailand's leather industry, Samut Prakan is 30km south of Bangkok toward the Gulf of Thailand. The main reason to come to Samut Prakan, however, is to see two main attractions: Muang Boran and the Crocodile Farm. Muang Boran, the "Ancient City," is an open-air museum in the shape of Thailand that contains replicas of monuments and sights from around the kingdom. Highlights include the Ayutthaya-style **Saphet Prasat Palace,** the **Dusit Maha Prasat Palace,** and **Khao Phra Wihan,** which sit atop a hill affording a spectacular view. The Crocodile Farm houses the largest crocodile in captivity. At the "Crocodile Wrestling" show, trainers taunt the toothy behemoths. Other attractions include an aviary, snake pits, a dinosaur museum, and go-carts.

DAMNOEN SADUAK

Buses leave from Bangkok's southern bus terminal for Damnoen Saduak and drop off passengers in the thick of the action (every 20min. 6am-9pm; regular 30฿, with A/C 55฿). Upon arrival, visitors are approached by locals offering 1hr. boat tours for 300฿. The best time to visit is 8-10am. The market closes down at 11am weekdays, 2pm weekends. To return to Bangkok, take a yellow songthaew (5฿) into the center of Damnoen Saduak and wave down one of the buses as it turns around.

Only 109km from Bangkok, this **floating market,** though touristy, captures a quick snapshot of a transient canal economy. A boat tour (300฿ per hr.) is a must, but service and quality vary greatly. A ride through the actual market is included in any tour. Boats pass on either side filled with tourists or Thai women selling exotic fruits like champoo, a red or greenish fruit resembling a bell pepper which is said to have a cooling effect when eaten (30฿ per kg). Browse through the woodcarvings and cowboy hats, then head to the sugar farm and sample some palm flower juice or fresh-from-the-hive honey. Depicted in paintings, postcards, and picture books, the bustling scene has become the poster child for traditional Thai life. Some visitors may find the not-so-picture-perfect reality—murky waters, swarming flies, and spitting vendors—disappointing. Feeding the fish outside the Buddhist temple (5฿ per bag of food) is a popular show of respect for vegetarianism.

BANGKOK

BANGKOK'S MOTHER TERESA
Community Involvement: Bangkok's Dock District

In Bangkok, as in every port city, the toughest neighborhoods are down by the docks. Follow the stench of Bangkok's foulest *khlongs*, and you'll eventually get to Thailand's most wretched waterfront slum—Khlong Toei. A sprawling maze of alleys and shantytowns, the area packs huge numbers of families into tiny wooden houses, owning the land by squatters' rights only. Now and then, one of the houses catches fire and burns the whole neighborhood down.

Khlong Toei's residents are cheap muscle for the Thai Port Authority's loading centers. Not the brawny loading-dock type you might find in Newcastle or Miami, Khlong Toei's workers tend to be a little scrawny, sometimes because of malnutrition, sometimes because of AIDS. These Port Authority slums have long been Bangkok's poorest and most dangerous neighborhoods. One Indian traveler reports that it wasn't until his sixth journey to Bangkok (in the mid-1980s) that he mustered the nerve to venture late at night into a Khlong Toei bar. "I went out with a friend," he said. "I was too spooked to go alone." Within ten minutes of stepping into the bar, they saw one local start a brawl with another and pry out his eyeball with a hunting knife.

The days of knives-in-the-eye are over, mostly. But the Asian financial crisis of 1997 exacerbated the social problems. Jobs, even horrid menial labor of the port, disappeared. Shipyard workers wander jobless or underemployed (and most certainly underpaid); at night they drink too much Mekong Whiskey and beat their kids. The poorest families can afford little more than rice and salt for an evening meal.

And there is AIDS. Condom distribution has slowed the disease's spread, and starting in 1996 the Thai government began taking child prostitution plights seriously. But Khlong Toei is still rife with disease and child prostitution. Children, especially young girls (though young boys are far from unaffected), are driven into prostitution by poverty and inadequate schools. These prostitutes do not even have the limited security of a brothel, as some do in Patpong; they work the streets. Khlong Toei is Tijuana to Patpong's Las Vegas. Many of the rest of Khlong Toei's children are hooked on drugs. It is not uncommon to see a kid huffing glue out of a plastic sack, and virtually everyone out after midnight is hopped up on speed. Besides frying the children's brains, it causes periodic tragedies, like kids who leap off buildings thinking they can fly.

The man who treats the sick, tends to the unfortunate, and buries the dead is Father Joe Maier, an American priest who came to Thailand over 30 years ago to work with Thailand's impoverished families. Maier has lived in the heart of the slums from the beginning—"sleeping on the floor with cockroaches," he says. In 1972, he started the **Human Development Foundation,** a grassroots Thai charity. The organization's mission is to help Bangkok's poor help themselves. Maier speaks bluntly about his work: the skeletal men who come seeking palliative care as they waste away with AIDS; the kids in the group home who sneak out at night to turn tricks; the campaign for the Thai monarchy to condemn juvenile drug abuse explicitly.

Over the years, Maier's group has grown from a tiny network of schools to an empire of social services. HDF runs several preschools and teenage drug and sex prevention programs, ministers to chronically ill patients, and acts as an outpost of order, a community center of sorts, in an otherwise chaotic neighborhood. The newest project is a legal aid clinic, which ensures that children caught in the Thai legal system have lawyers to shepherd them through their punishment and rehabilitation. Maier still says the Catholic Mass weekly in fluent Thai; his parishioners are a small Christian minority that specializes in hog-slaughtering—a task whose karmic baggage Thailand's Buddhist majority passes off to others (although Thai Buddhists eat pork with gusto).

The prospects for speedy improvement are grim; every few hours there is an economic fiasco, a fire, a new epidemic, or a local disaster that sets everything back, seemingly to square one. The attitude at HDF is that hopeless battles are nobler than careful ones, and that time spent helping is never wasted. Treat the dying, even though they'll be dead in a week; teach the children, even if they will be back sniffing paint fumes before they learn their times-tables.

The Human Development Foundation (www.fatherjoe.org) needs volunteers and donations. For more information, see **Alternatives to Tourism,** p. 91.

Graeme Wood lived in Khlong Toei, where he worked for the Human Development Foundation. He primarily worked in orphanages and hospices. He was the editor of Let's Go: Southeast Asia 2001. *He was a Researcher-Writer for* Let's Go: Southern Africa 2002 *and* Let's Go: Eastern Europe 2003. *A long-time veteran of* Let's Go, *Graeme has been to 68 countries.*

CENTRAL
THAILAND

THAILAND PRICE ICONS					
SYMBOL:	❶	❷	❸	❹	❺
ACCOMM.	Under US$3 Under 120฿	US$3-4.50 120-180฿	US$4.50-9 180-360฿	US$9-14 360-560฿	Over US$14 Over 560฿
FOOD	Under US$0.75 Under 30฿	US$0.75-2 30-80฿	US$2-4 80-160฿	US$4-6 160-240฿	Over US$6 Over 240฿

Fertile Central Thailand, also known as the Chao Phraya River Basin, stretches from Hua Hin in the south to Nakhon Sawan in the north. The region's attractions include the awe-inspiring ruins of Ayutthaya and the lush landscapes fanning west of Bangkok around Kanchanaburi, as well as the banks of the River Kwai and the province's national parks. Southbound buses and trains wind through the beginnings of peninsular Thailand, a teaser for the sandy playgrounds farther south.

AYUTTHAYA   ☎035

Entering the city of Ayutthaya is like walking into a time warp. For four centuries the city was the capital of Siam, raising 33 kings, withstanding 23 invasions by Burmese troops, and extending its rule west to Bago in Myanmar and east to Angkor in Cambodia. In 1767, however, good times turned bad when Ayutthaya was sacked by the Burmese (successfully, this time), and the capital was moved to Bangkok, leaving the city a mere echo of its royal past. Tuk-tuks and motorcycles weave around the massive ruins that dot Ayutthaya, and pedestrians walk by former royal palaces without so much as batting an eye. Perhaps most impressively, traffic routinely comes to a standstill as elephants bearing camera-toting tourists head from ruin to ruin. Modern Ayutthaya is loud, busy, and impersonal but comfortable with its royal past and ruins, which blend into the cityscape.

▣ TRANSPORTATION

Trains: Ayutthaya Railway Station (☎ 241 54), on the mainland east of the island. Take the ferry from U Thong Rd. and walk up the street. Otherwise, it's a long walk across **Pridi Damrong Bridge** and up your first left, or a 30฿ tuk-tuk ride. Trains to: **Bangkok** (1½-2hr.; 21 per day; 15฿, rapid or express 20฿); **Chiang Mai** via **Phitsanulok**; 4 per day; 3rd-class 296฿, 2nd-class sleeper 586฿, 1st-class 1138฿); **Lopburi** (1½hr., 5 per day, 13฿); **Saraburi** (1hr., 10 per day, 9฿); **Udon Thani** (9hr.; 3 per day; 3rd-class 145฿, 2nd-class 306฿).

Buses: Ayutthaya has 2 bus stations.

Naresuan Rd. has a chaotic mess of buses that go to: **Bangkok** (#901; 1½hr.; every 30min. 6am-7pm; 20฿, with A/C 30฿); **Saraburi,** connecting to destinations in the northeast (#358; 2¼hr., every 30min. 6am-5pm, 27฿); **Suphanburi,** connecting with #411 to **Kanchanaburi** (#703; 1¾hr., every 30min. 6am-5pm, 17฿).

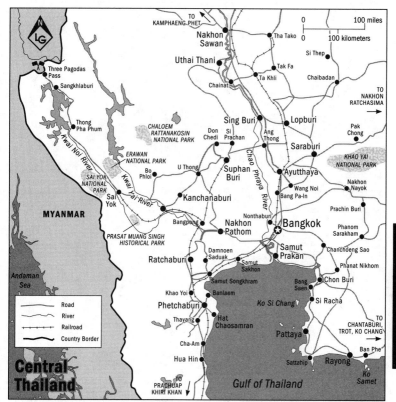

Central Thailand

Road
River
Railroad
Country Border

MYANMAR

Andaman Sea

Gulf of Thailand

Mainland bus terminal, 5km east of the island (50฿ by *tuk-tuk*) serves destinations farther away. Buses to: **Chiang Mai** (9½hr.; 9 per day; 2nd-class with A/C 283฿, VIP 570฿); **Phitsanulok** (5hr.; 9 per day; 85฿, 2nd-class with A/C 120฿, 1st-class with A/C 194฿, VIP 300฿); and **Sukhothai** (6½hr.; 6 per day; 2nd-class with A/C 146฿, 1st-class with A/C 230฿).

Ferries: Continuous ferries to the mainland (and the train station) leave from an alley off U Thong Rd. near the intersection with Horattanachai Rd. (2฿). **Long-tailed boats** and **cruisers** can be hired at the Chantharkasem Palace pier at the island's northeast tip for a 1hr. trip around the island (500฿, with two temple stops 600฿).

Local Transportation: Tuk-tuk/songthaew hybrids wheel around the island for 30-100฿. Rent by the hour (200฿) or for a full day (700-900฿). Most guest houses rent **bicycles** (50-60฿ per day).

🔷 🔷 ORIENTATION AND PRACTICAL INFORMATION

The Ayutthaya **city center** is an island at the intersection of the **Chao Phraya, Pa Sak,** and **Lopburi Rivers**. U Thong Rd. encircles the entire island. **Buses** from nearby cities stop next to the **Chao Phrom Market** at the corner of **Naresuan** and **Khlong Makham Rieng Rd.** in the island's northeastern corner. Buses from Northern Thailand arrive east of the island, 5km beyond the **Pridi Damrong Bridge.** Though wats are found all over the island, most tourist attractions cluster near the **Tourist Information Center (TAT)** on Si Sanphet Rd.

CENTRAL THAILAND

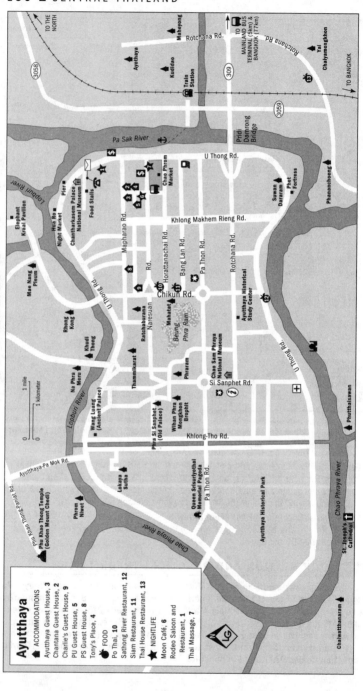

Ayutthaya

ACCOMMODATIONS
Ayutthaya Guest House, 3
Chantana Guest House, 2
Charlie's Guest House, 9
PU Guest House, 5
PS Guest House, 8
Tony's Place, 4

FOOD
Po Thai, 10
Sathong River Restaurant, 12
Siam Restaurant, 11
Thai House Restaurant, 13

NIGHTLIFE
Moon Café, 6
Rodeo Saloon and
Restaurant, 1
Thai Massage, 7

Tourist Offices: TAT (☎322 730), Si Sanphet Rd., a 5min. walk south of Wat Phra Si Sanphet. Carries timetables and large, handy maps. Open daily 9am-5pm.

Currency Exchange: Banks abound along the eastern stretch of Naresuan Rd. and the northeastern curve of U Thong Rd.; many have **24hr. ATMs. Bangkok Bank,** 20 U Thong Rd. (☎245 346/7), opposite the school near the GPO. Open M-F 8:30am-3:30pm.

Markets: Chao Phrom Market, at the corner of Naresuan and U Thong Rd. Open daily 7am-7pm. **Hua Ro Night Market,** farther north along U Thong Rd. from Chao Phrom. Open daily 4pm-2am.

Emergency: ☎191. **Tourist Police (Bangkok):** ☎1155. **Police:** ☎241 174.

Local Tourist Police: ☎242 352. Next to TAT on Si Sanphet Rd. Some English spoken. **Open 24hr.**

Medical Services: Phra Nakhon Si Ayutthaya Hospital, 46 U Thong Rd. (☎241 728), at the intersection of Si Sanphet and U Thong Rd. English spoken. **Open 24hr.** No credit cards.

Telephones: International Telephone Office, on the 2nd fl. of the GPO. Also a booth outside. Collect calls 33฿. Open daily 8am-8pm.

Internet Access: Available all over the city, especially north of the Chao Phrom Market. **9 To Nine Net,** on Bang Lan Rd. off U Thong Rd. 30฿ per hr. Open daily 9:30am-10pm. More convenient is the **nameless Internet place** next door to The Moon Cafe. 1฿ per 2min. Open daily 9am-midnight.

Post Offices: GPO, 123/11 U Thong Rd. (☎251 233), on the island's northeast corner. Open M-F 8:30am-4:30pm, Sa 9am-noon. **Postal code:** 13000.

ACCOMMODATIONS

Budget accommodations cluster in two distinct areas: off **Chikun Rd.**, across from Wat Ratburana, and north of **Naresuan Rd.**, near Chao Phrom. Market bus stop (these are generally cleaner and better picks). Room rates increase during festival season (Nov.-Dec.), and lodgings are harder to find. Most lodgings offer laundry service and bike rental.

PU Guest House, 20/1 Soi Thor Korsor (☎251 213). In the lane across and left of the bus terminal at Chao Phrom Market. Completely renovated, the rooms are sunny, large, and ultra-clean. All with private toilet and shower. Plush common room with TV and dining travelers. Motorcycle rental 250฿ per day. Singles 150฿, with bath 200฿; doubles 200฿, with bath 250฿, with A/C 450฿. ❷

Ayutthaya Guest House, 16/2 Naresuan Rd. (☎232 658), on the soi for PU Guest House, across from the bus station. Two main buildings; the satellite one has better rooms. Rooms are large and clean, and the tiled, shared baths are blessed with flushing Western toilets. Extremely popular and occasionally full. Dorms 70฿; singles 100-120฿; doubles 180฿, with shower and toilet 350฿. ❶

Tony's Place, 12/18 Naresuan Rd. (☎252 578), north of the bus stop across from Ayutthaya Guest House. Tony's features 12 clean rooms above a common garden. Baths, both shared and private, have Western toilets, but some are cleaner than others. The TV lounge, pool table, Internet access, outdoor drinking area, and occassional music stage round out the social atmosphere. Breakfast starts at 7am; bar open until midnight. Motorcycle rental 250฿ per day. Dorms 80-100฿; doubles 180฿, with bath 250฿. ❶

Chantana Guest House, 12/22 Naresuan Rd. (☎232 300), next to Tony's Place. Ayutthaya's newest guest house is quiet, simple, and clean. After a long day wat-hopping and sweating in the sun, the A/C rooms are a godsend. All rooms have Western toilets and shower. Worth the extra baht. Singles and doubles with large bed 250฿, with A/C and hot shower 450฿. ❸

PS (Phatsaporu) Guest House, 23/1 Tanon Pratuchai (☎242 394). Take a right off Chikun Rd., 1 block north of intersection between Chikun and Naresuan Rd. PS is down that soi on the left. Friendly, efficient owner. Rooms are large and fairly clean with wooden floors, but the shared bath is less than ideal. If full, ask to camp for free on the front lawn. Vegetarian food served. Singles 100฿; doubles 150฿, with A/C 300฿. ❶

Charlie's Guest House, on Chikun Rd. (☎232 807) opposite the entrance to Wat Ratburana. Large rooms overlooking the ruins. Seldom full, more of a last resort. Singles 160฿; doubles 200฿, with A/C 300฿. ❷

▢ FOOD

Food stalls ❶ serving 20฿ chicken and rice are interspersed between tables of plastic guns, dried fish, and piles of fruit at **Chao Phrom Market,** one block east of the local bus stop. More stalls line U Thong Rd., particularly on the eastern side of the island after the post office. For dinner, try the **night markets;** the **Hua Ro Night Market** is growing in popularity. With all the market stalls, make sure to choose a place that thoroughly heats the food or your stomach will pay the price later.

Sathong River Restaurant, 4 Mu 2 U Thong Rd. (☎241 449). A local crowd enjoys the cool breeze and views of the wat across the river while sipping Tom Yum, a hot and sour soup with prawns (120฿). A full meal will run about 200฿ per person if you share, which you should because the portions are huge. Open daily 10am-9:30pm. ❸

Thai House Restaurant (Ruenthai Maisuay Restaurant), 8/2 Mu 3 Klongsuanplu District, is down the road from Wat Yai Chai Mongkhon and around the bend on the left. On F and Sa nights, live traditional music (6-9pm) and tasty curry (80-120฿) spice up this sober steak house. Open daily 11am-10pm. ❸

Siam Restaurant (☎211 070), on Chikun Rd. between Horattanachai and Bang Lan Rd. serves a Thai/Vietnamese menu. The reasonably priced Vietnamese beef noodle soup (60฿) is filling, a welcome change from green curry (which they also serve, 100฿). Open daily 10am-11:30pm. MC/V. ❷

Po Thai, at the intersection of Chikun and Naresuan Rds. splendidly combines two Thai favorites—food and massage—to satiate both mouth and muscles.

▣ SIGHTS

Ayutthaya's crumbling ruins span several dozen kilometers; exploring all the ruins would take several days. The **Tourist Information Center** has free maps that locate and explain nearly every sight. A new exhibit on the second floor showcases the city on slick multi-media torch screens (closed W). Make the best of your time by renting a bicycle or motorcycle, available for rent at most guest houses. Otherwise, tuk-tuk drivers will take you to the sights and wait while you visit (200฿ per hr., around 700-900฿ per day). All temples and wats are open daily 8:30am-6pm.

▧ ANCIENT PALACE AND WAT PHRA SI SANPHET. If you visit only one ruin in Ayutthaya, this should be it. The area was the home of the ancient Royal Palace until 1448, when a monastery was built on the grounds. As a royal monastery, Wat Phra Si Sanphet hosted important rituals and ceremonies, but no monks. The site's three charred *chedis* that once held the remains of the king, his father, and his brother are now empty. *(30฿.)*

WIHAN PHRA MONGKHON BROPHIT. At 12.45m high and 9.5m wide, the 15th-century Buddha snuggled inside this wat is the largest bronze Buddha in Thailand. On display are photographs and blurbs explaining this restored Buddha's many "incarnations." *(Just south of Wat Phra Si Sanphet. Free.)*

WAT PHRARAM. Overshadowed by its more glamorous neighbors, the wat of Phraram was built in 1369 by King Ramesnan to commemorate the spot where his father and founder of the city, King U Thong, was cremated. Dozens of broken Buddha representations sit silently around the wat's landmark *prang* (corncob-shaped *chedi*). *(Across the street from Wihan Phra Mongkhon Brophit. 30฿.)*

WAT MAHATHAT. This impressive royal monastery was founded by King Borom-marachathirat in 1374 and restored several times, most recently in the 18th century. Excavations done in the 1950s uncovered relics of the Buddha hidden deep in a seven-layered reliquary in the *stupa*. With those finds safely stored at the Chao Sam Phraya National Museum, the wat's most precious attraction is a representation of the Buddha's face enshrouded in the roots of a tree. *(At the corner of Chikun Rd. and Naresuan Rd. Open daily 8am-6:30pm. 30฿.)*

WAT RATCHABURANA. Wat Mahathat's most impressive neighbor was built by King Chao Sam Phraya in 1424. Legend has it that the king's two oldest brothers coveted the throne and killed each other in a heated duel, allowing Chao Sam Phraya to ascend to the throne. To commemorate (or perhaps celebrate) his brothers' deaths, the king ordered the construction of Wat Ratchaburana over the site of their cremations. This wat is known for its wealth of gold artifacts and the mural paintings in its crypt. *(North of Wat Mahathat. 30฿.)*

WAT YAI CHAIYAMONGKHON. This fabulous wat was founded in 1357 by U Thong who had mastered meditation techniques. The sect grew tremendously, granting its head monk the title of the "Supreme Patriarch." The giant *chedi* was built by King Naresuan the Great to commemorate the 1592 victory over the Burmese. The wat's name, Chaiyamongkhon ("Auspicious Victory"), refers to this event. *(Southeast of the island on the mainland. At least 20min. by bicycle ride from the island or a 40฿ tuk-tuk ride. 20฿.)*

WAT PHANANCHOENG. The massive brick-and-mortar Buddha dates back to 1324, 26 years before Ayutthaya was founded. Legend has it that tears formed in its eyes when the city was sacked by the Burmese in 1767. *(West of Yai Chaiyamongkhon, about 2km farther down the road. Open daily 8am-4:30pm. 20฿.)*

AYUTTHAYA HISTORICAL STUDY CENTER. The modern building houses a US$8 million research institute funded by the Japanese government, featuring displays on the ancient city's political, economic, and social life. Touring the surprisingly small upstairs exhibition hall shouldn't take more than 45min. *(On Rotchana Rd., 2 blocks east of the Chao Sam Phraya National Museum. Open M-F 9am-4:30pm, Sa-Su 9am-5pm. 100฿, with student ID 50฿.)*

CHAO SAM PHRAYA NATIONAL MUSEUM. An old-school presentation complete with wood-and-glass display cases, dusty artifacts, and missing labels, the Chao Sam Phraya Museum has little to offer besides the splendid jewels taken from Wat Ratchaburana. *(On Rotchana Rd., near the intersection with Si Sanphet Rd. A 5min. walk from the Tourist Information Center. Open W-Su. 30฿.)*

OTHER SIGHTS. A short bike ride north of the train station brings you to the impressive **Wats Maheyong** and **Kudidao** and the smaller **Wat Ayothaya**. All three are devoid of tourists. *(Free.)* North of the island, the **Elephant Kraal Pavilion** was where the king would watch his elephant army train. Ayutthaya is also the site of one of the country's largest **Loi Krathong** festivals, which usually takes place in November on the day of the full moon. Thais gather around **Beung Phra Ram,** the large lake in the center of the island, to see fireworks, watch *likay* (Thai folk dance), and groove to live pop music. The *loi* (floating) of *krathong* (lotus-shaped paper boats

(side margin) **CENTRAL THAILAND**

with candles and incense) takes place at the **Chantharkasem Pier** opposite the Chantharkasem Palace Museum and post office. Legend has it that two people who launch their *krathong* together are destined to become lovers.

♪ ▒ ENTERTAINMENT AND NIGHTLIFE

From 7:30 to 9:30pm nightly, **Wat Phra Si Sanphet, Wat Mahatat, Wat Ratchaburana, Wat Phraram** (diagonally across from Wihan Phra Mongkhon Brophit), and **Wat Chiawatthanaram** (southwest of the island) are illuminated by floodlights. Although *Let's Go* doesn't recommend it, locals suggest sneaking into the ruins around that time to drink. Often, tuk-tuk drivers gather a group at 7pm outside the Ayutthaya Guest House for a tour of illuminated wats, though these may be illegal.

▒ **Moon Cafe** (☎232 501), off Naresuan Rd., opposite Ayutthaya Guest House. A diverse crowd of travelers, A/C and 400 jazz, blues and classic rock CDs make it the best pub in town. Exchange travel stories and sing along to the Beatles. Large Singha 100฿. Under same ownership as the **Sun,** next door, which shows free and surprisingly new movies while serving food and drink.

Rodeo Saloon and Restaurant, 79/81 U Thong Rd. (☎251 616). Coming from the Chao Phrom Market, it's on the left side of the street 200m before the GPO; look for the Jack Daniels sign. A Thai take on the Old American West (yippee-thai-yai-yay). Large Heineken 95฿. The band doesn't get jumping until 9 or 10pm. Open daily 6pm-1am.

Thai Massage (☎244 582), at the Chao Phrom Market bus station. From Naresuan Rd., it's the 2nd building on the right. Treat yourself to the "good taste" massage. 2hr. of traditional Thai bodywork 240฿. Open daily 10am-midnight.

KANCHANABURI ☎034

The Japanese invasion during WWII immortalized the otherwise less-than-noteworthy town of Kanchanaburi and its humble River Kwai. Backpackers now use the city—once of strategic importance linking the overland route between Singapore and Rangoon—as a base for exploring the surrounding waterfalls, caves, and jungles. They return in the evenings to swap travel stories at their lively backstreet guest houses, the idyllic riverside lodgings that they share with Thai tourists from Bangkok who are glad to escape to the fresh air.

▨ TRANSPORTATION

Trains: Kanchanaburi Train Station (☎511 285), on Saeng Chuto Rd. To **Namtok** via the **River Kwai Bridge** (2½hr.; 6:10, 10:50am, 4:30pm; 17฿) and Thonburi Station in **Bangkok** (3hr.; 7:25am, 2:50pm; 25฿). Call ☎561 052 for info on weekend trains to **Bangkok** and other destinations (2hr., Sa-Su 5pm, 28฿). Trains are convenient only for those wanting to ride across the River Kwai Bridge; head to the bus station for other destinations.

Buses: The **Kanchanaburi Bus Station** (☎511 182) is in Ban Noue Village. To: **Bangkok** (#81; 3½hr., every 15min. 4am-6:30pm, 48฿; 2nd-class with A/C, 2hr., every 20min. 3:50am-6:50pm, 62฿; 1st-class with A/C, 2hr., every 15min. 4am-7pm, 79฿) via **Nakhon Pakhon** (1½hr., 28-48฿); **Erawan National Park** (#8170; 1½hr., every 50min. 8am-5:20pm, 26฿); **Ratchaburi** with connections to **Cha Am, Hua Hin,** and **Phetchaburi** (#461; 2hr., every 15min. 5:10am-6:20pm, 36฿); **Sangkhlaburi** (#8203; 5hr.; 6, 8:40, 10:20am, noon; 84฿; VIP bus #8203; 4hr.; 9:30am, 1:30, 3:30pm; 151฿); **Suphanburi** (#411; 1½-2hr., every 20min. 5am-5:45pm, 35฿) with

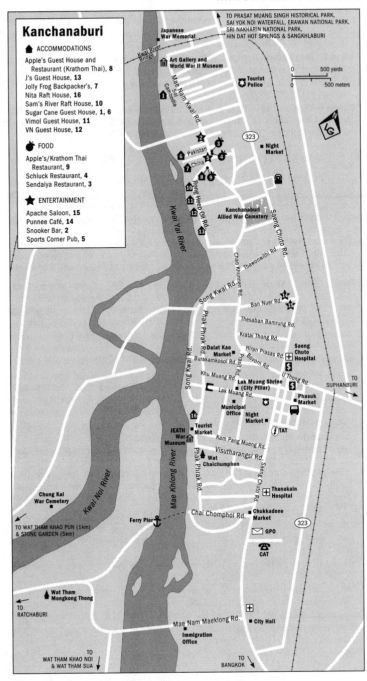

Kanchanaburi

⌂ ACCOMMODATIONS

Apple's Guest House and
  Restaurant (Krathom Thai), **8**
J's Guest House, **13**
Jolly Frog Backpacker's, **7**
Nita Raft House, **16**
Sam's River Raft House, **10**
Sugar Cane Guest House, **1, 6**
Vimol Guest House, **11**
VN Guest House, **12**

🍎 FOOD

Apple's/Krathom Thai
  Restaurant, **9**
Schluck Restaurant, **4**
Sendaiya Restaurant, **3**

★ ENTERTAINMENT

Apache Saloon, **15**
Punnee Café, **14**
Snooker Bar, **2**
Sports Corner Pub, **5**

Japanese
War Memorial

Art Gallery and
World War II Museum

TO PRASAT MUANG SINGH HISTORICAL PARK,
SAI YOK NOI WATERFALL, ERAWAN NATIONAL PARK,
SRI NAKHARIN NATIONAL PARK,
HIN DAT HOT SPRINGS & SANGKHLABURI

Kwai River Bridge

Tourist Police

0   500 yards
0   500 meters

Soi Cambodia

Mae Nam Kwai Rd.

323

Night Market

Pakistan

China

Pong Heep Oil Rd.

Kanchanaburi
Allied War Cemetery

Kwai Yai River

Saeng Chuto Rd.

Chao Khunmen Rd.

Thawonwithi Rd.

Song Kwai Rd.

Ban Nuer Rd.

Thesaban Bamrung Rd.

Phak Phrak Rd.

Kratai Thong Rd.

Dalat Kao
Market

Hiran Prasas Rd.

Saeng
Chuto
Hospital

Burakamkosol Rd.

Boyorn Rd.

Prasit Rd.

Song Kwai Rd.

Khu Muang Rd.

Lak Muang Shrine
(City Pillar)

U Thong Rd.

TO
SUPHANBURI

Lak Muang Rd.

Phasuk
Market

Municipal
Office

Night
Market

TAT

JEATH
War
Museum

Tourist
Market

Kam Pang Mueng Rd.

Visutharangsi Rd.

Wat
Chaichumphon

Phak Phrak Rd.

Thanakain
Hospital

Saeng Chuto Rd.

Mae Khlong River

Chung Kai
War Cemetery

Kwai Noi River

Chai Chomphol Rd.

Chukkadone
Market

323

Ferry Pier

GPO

CAT

TO WAT THAM KHAO PUN (1km)
& STONE GARDEN (5km)

Wat Tham
Mongkong Thong

TO
RATCHABURI

City Hall

Mae Nam Maeklong Rd.

Immigration
Office

TO
WAT THAM KHAO NOI
& WAT THAM SUA

TO
BANGKOK

CENTRAL THAILAND

connections to **Ayutthaya** and **Nakhon Sawan** (last connecting bus to these destinations leaves at 5pm). A/C **vans** to Sangkhlaburi depart from the corner of Lak Muang Rd. and Saeng Chuto Rd. (3hr.; 7:30, 11:30am, 4:30pm; 118฿).

Local Transportation: Orange **songthaew** run up and down Saeng Chuto Rd. including to the River Kwai Bridge (5-10฿). **Samlor** cost 10-20฿ from the railway station to TAT. Motorbike taxis to guest houses from bus station 30฿. A **ferry** crosses the river (5฿) at the end of Chai Chumphol Rd.

Rentals: Bicycles available from almost all guest houses for 20-50฿ per day. **Motorbikes** on Mae Nam Kwai Rd. with passport deposit. 200฿ for 24hr.; 150฿ for 9am-5pm. Cruising motorbikes 500฿ per day. Motorcross bikes are difficult to find.

■◼ ORIENTATION AND PRACTICAL INFORMATION

Kanchanaburi is 129km from Bangkok and stretches roughly 4km from northwest to southeast along the banks of the **Kwai River**, which flows parallel to **Saeng Chuto Rd.**, the city's main drag. North of town is the famous **Kwai River Bridge**; 2km south is the **train station** and the river-side **guest house area**, where *farang* congregate. Two kilometers farther south is **Ban Noue Village,** the city's main commercial area and home to the **bus station.** West of the bus station are the **city gate, day markets,** and **river wharf area.** Because Kanchanaburi is quite spread out, consider renting a bicycle to avoid the long, dusty walks between one part of town and the other.

Tourist Office: TAT (☎/fax 511 200), on Saeng Chuto Rd., a 5min. walk south of the bus station. Friendly English-speaking staff deal out glossy leaflets. Excellent regional map (20฿ donation). Bus/train schedules. Lenso phone. Open daily 8:30am-4:30pm.

Immigration Office: ☎513 325. On Mae Nam Maeklong Rd., 4km from TAT. Follow Saeng Chuto Rd. south away from Ban Noue Village and turn right at City Hall, 1km past the GPO. 1-month visa extension 500฿, 1-day processing. Bring 1 photo and 2 copies of passport including visa and departure card. Open M-F 8:30am-noon and 1-4:30pm.

Currency Exchange: Banks are common on the roads fanning out from the Kanchanaburi Bus Station. Several have **24hr. ATMs. Thai Farmers Bank** and **Thai Military Bank** are set one block from Saeng Chuto Rd. on Lak Muang Rd. heading toward the bus station. Open M-F 8:30am-3:30pm. The **Punnee Cafe** can exchange money after hours (see **Work Opportunity,** below).

Work Opportunity: Talk to Danny at the **Punnee Cafe,** 2/15 Ban Nuer Rd. (☎513 503), just off Saeng Chuto Rd., about the possibility of working at the local private Catholic school teaching English. 1-month, 3-month, and 1-year commitments. Teachers receive room and board plus stipend. You can also contact the school directly (☎09 889 0050, ask for Orawan). The cafe doubles as an **English-language used bookstore.**

PIG-HEADED SPIRITS When entering a Thai house, you are likely to see the *san phr pum* ("spirit house"), the dwelling of the household's guardian spirit. Ancient monuments, standard *san phr pum* are comprised of a house-shaped shrine, a figurine or tablet representing the guardian spirit, and figurines of followers, household servants, and pets. The shrines are raised to eye level and set on a pillar, and their location and construction are carefully facilitated by a specialist. Allowing the shrine to be overshadowed by the house at any time or facing it toward the house entrance would dishonor the guardian spirit and force it to withdraw its protection. The spirit must be appeased with offerings made during the annual April water festival. Offerings are placed in a banana-leaf container called a *bat phlee* and on a tray made of banana trunk. The spirits, it seems, are particularly fond of chicken and pig's head.

Markets: The **Dalat Kao Market,** bounded by Chao Khunnen and Burakamkosol Rd., offers fresh produce and meat. **Phasuk Market,** across from the bus station near Lak Muang Rd. in Ban Noue Village, sells clothing and accessories. Both open daily dawndusk. Closest **night market** to guest houses is the haphazard roadside affair just north of the train station on Saeng Chuto Rd. 10min. walk. Open daily 5-10pm.

Emergency: Police ☎ 191. **Tourist Police (Bangkok):** ☎ 1155.

Provincial Police Headquarters: ☎ 512 100 or ☎ 621 040. Opposite TAT. Some English spoken. **Open 24hr.**

Tourist Police: ☎ 512 795. 1.5km north of train station on Saeng Chuto Rd. on the right. Free **luggage storage.** English spoken. Open 24hr. Also 3 helpful **booths** at the foot of the Kwai River Bridge, on Song Kwai Rd. at Burakamkosol Rd., and on Mae Nam Kwai Rd. 50m past Apple's Guest House toward cemetery. Booths open daily 8:30am-6pm.

Medical Services: Saeng Chuto Hospital (☎ 621 129), 500m north of TAT on Saeng Chuto Rd. English spoken. 24hr. **pharmacy. Open 24hr.** MC/V.

Telephones: Kanchanaburi Telecommunications Office, on Saeng Chuto Rd., Soi 38. Turn left at the post office; the office is 200m on the right. International calls, phone cards, and CATNET **Internet** access. 1st min. 3฿, each subsequent min. 0.50฿. 24hr. HCD phone. Open daily 8:30am-10pm.

Internet: Available all over the city, especially on Saeng Chuto Rd. south of the bus station (10฿ per hr.). The best value near the guest houses is next to Snooker Bar on Mae Nam Kwai Rd. 10฿ for 30min. Open daily 9am-midnight.

Post Office: GPO (☎ 511 131), on Saeng Chuto Rd., 1km south of TAT on the left. *Poste Restante.* Open M-F 8:30am-4:30pm, Sa-Su 9am-noon. **Postal code:** 71000.

ACCOMMODATIONS

Most of Kanchanaburi's best budget accommodations sit along (or in) the River Kwai in the northern part of the city, a 10min. walk from the train station or a 25min. walk from the bus station. Guest houses on Rong Heep Oil Rd. are quieter, while the ones on Mae Nam Kwai Rd. are always flooded with *farang*. All establishments listed serve Thai and Western food and help arrange tours. A hot shower is not a necessity in Kanchanaburi's steamy heat—as a result it's an added extra or nonexistent at some establishments.

VN Guest House, 44 Rong Heep Oil Rd. (☎ 514 082). The friendly staff welcomes a crew of easygoing backpackers who congregate on the hotel's riverside veranda late into the night. The cheaper rooms take prime position on the pontoon or next to the river. Singles 50-60฿, with bath 100฿; doubles 150฿, with A/C 250-300฿. ❶

Jolly Frog Backpacker's, 28 Soi China, Mae Nam Kwai Rd. (☎ 514 579). Clean, attractive rooms overlook a resort-like courtyard as well as the river. Large and extremely popular, but if you've had enough of toe rings, tank tops, and tie-dye, keep moving. Nightly guest-picked movies. Singles 70฿; doubles 150฿, on raft portion 150฿, with bath 200฿, with A/C 290฿. ❶

J's Guest House, 32/4 Rong Heep Oil Rd. (☎ 620 307). Bargain accommodations for those traveling on the cheap. Rooms made of flimsy plywood are set over a still inlet from the river and come with mosquito netting and a hammock. The same family owns the more expensive **River Guest House** next door. Singles 50฿, with bath 100฿; doubles 80฿/120฿. ❶

Nita Raft House, 27/1 Pakpraek (☎ 514 521). An easy 10min. walk from the bus station (100m north of the JEATH museum). Proximity to Song Kwai Rd.'s touristy din means floating discos rock on right outside until 10pm. Clean but simple rooms all

THE LOCAL STORY

POWS

Few men left the POW camps spanning between Kanchanaburi and Thanbyuzayat (Three Pagoda Pass) without coming under the care of Edward "Weary" Dunlop. As one of the Senior Medical Officers in the region and known to the men as "King of the River," Weart inspired hope in what was a tortuous war. He was even dubbed "No. 1 Doctor" by the Japanese who heard of his miraculous surgical successes.

This soft-spoken gentleman towering at 6'4" worked tirelessly in work camps. Like his fellow POWs, he suffered from dysentery, tropical ulcers, and recurring malaria and cholera. With a tough rep from his days of playing rugby for Australia, he was just as driven to help his fellow POWs.

He was the Commanding Officer—an unprecedented appointment considering his non-combatant status. He regularly confronted Japanese Commanders about the appalling conditions of the camp. Weary ended these fiery exchanges by swearing he'd have them hanged at the end of the war.

In the wet season of 1943, Weary was instructed to force one-third of his patients to work, some 100 sick men. What came to be known as the "log sitting game" was Weary's solution. He instructed his sick patients to simply sit on the log irrespective of the Japanese orders to work and the subsequent beatings. The result was that more POWs were put in the hospital, less able to work. His rebellion boosted morale among the men and forced the Japanese to back down and let him keep as many patients in

set on a delightful, rambling connection of rafts. Singles 80฿; doubles 120฿, with Western toilet and shower 180฿. ❶

Sugar Cane Guest House in 2 locations. **22 Soi Pakistan ❷** (☎624 520), off Mae Nam Kwai Rd., marked turn-off one block north from turn-off to Jolly Frog Backpacker's. Solid bungalows around manicured riverfront garden with bath 150-250฿; upmarket raft house with A/C and hot shower 550฿. **7 Soi Cambodia ❸** (☎514 988), off Mae Nam Kwai Rd., 1km farther north toward the bridge, has more room to play in a quieter setting. Laundry 20฿ per kg. Similarly styled bamboo bungalows 200฿; huge concrete bungalow with TV 400฿.

Apple's Guest House and Restaurant (Krathom Thai), 52 Rong Heep Oil Rd. (☎512 017), at the juncture with Mae Nam Kwai Rd. The 15 rooms, clean and popular, surround a peaceful courtyard but lack the appealing river setting. Hospitable co-owner Apple leads an excellent full-day cooking course (750฿). Free pickup from the bus and train station. Singles 200฿; doubles 150฿. ❷

Vimol Guest House (formerly Rick's Lodge), 48/5 Rong Heep Oil Rd. (☎514 831). Pleasant river-view restaurant. One-seater speedboat 250฿ per hr. Fishing rod 50฿ per day. Unique bungalows with attic sleeping, fly-screen door ventilation, and bath 100฿. New, more expensive raft housing on the way (around 500฿ with A/C). ❶

Sam's River Raft House, 48/1 Rong Heep Oil Rd. (☎624 321). Clean, standard raft rooms include hot water and Western toilet. More exciting rustic bungalows across the street. Large TV room and sunning deck by the river. Bungalows with mosquito nets 80฿ for a single, 120฿ for a double; raft rooms 250฿, with A/C 350฿. ❶

🍴 FOOD

From May to July, be sure to try the *khanun* (jackfruit), a Thai delicacy. This and other tasty victuals can be found in cheap food stalls and open-air eateries that line the streets around the bus station. The **night market ❶**, north of the train station on Saeng Chuto Rd., is the most convenient spot for a nighttime snack for those staying in guest houses. Another **night market ❶**, north of TAT on Saeng Chuto Rd., is worth a stop. If market eating is not your style, head for **Song Kwai Rd.,** where dozens of indistinguishable restaurants cater almost exclusively to locals. Unfortunately, restaurants near the bridge and guest houses are overpriced. One exception is **Apple's/ Krathom Thai Restaurant ❷** (see **Accommodations,** above), which offers fabulous food (dishes 30-60฿). For a Thai-style Indian dish, try chicken massaman curry (65฿). All dishes can be substituted with tofu. **Schluck ❷**, on Mae Nam Kwai Rd., stands out from the rest, offering A/C dining comfort. The delicious chicken schnitzel baguette (45฿) is drenched in mayonnaise dressing. (Open daily 4pm-1am.) 50m toward the bridge from Schluck, opposite Woi's Travel, **Sendaiya Restaurant ❷** creates Japanese-inspired food eaten on comfy cushioned floors. (Miso soup 20฿; *gyoza* (dim sum) 60฿; *ton katsu* (fried chicken or pork) 80฿. Open daily 5pm-midnight.) The Western food at **Snooker Bar ❶** isn't always the greatest value, but the Thai dishes prove worthwhile. (Phat thai with chicken 25฿. Open daily 9am-2am.)

👁 SIGHTS

Today, World War II's Allies and their old opponents join forces, packing into A/C buses to see the graves of thousands of Allied soldiers and the Death Railway Bridge. Several excellent museums quickly dispel (or confirm) myths associated with the war, and all stand as testament to the strength of the POWs.

Kanchanaburi's attractions are spread over 6km. To take it all in over a couple of days, rent a bicycle or motorcycle—it's infinitely faster and easier than walking and cheaper than taking taxis.

▨ KWAI RIVER BRIDGE (DEATH RAILWAY BRIDGE).
Constructed from 1941 to 1942, the original Kwai River Bridge was the Japanese army's last attempt to complete the 415km Thai-Myanmar railway line (the "Death Railway") to be used in transporting war materials to military camps in Myanmar. To speed up the process, Japan used all the labor it could get, tapping its rich reserve of Allied POWs and Asian workers. Roughly 16,000 POWs and 96,000 Asians died building the bridge, which was subsequently destroyed by British air raids in 1945. During the war, engineers predicted that it would take five years to construct the bridge, but the Japanese forced POWs and local laborers to complete this vital section of the railway in 16 months, known today as the infamous "speedo" construction period. The bridge you see, although impressive, is a reconstruction built as a memorial to those who lost their lives. Kanchanaburi celebrates the **Kwai River Bridge Week** during the first week of December. Activities include archaeological and historical exhibitions, performances and musical events, and a spectacular light and sound show. *(3km northwest of the train station. Orange minibus #2 runs from the Focus Optic shop, 2 traffic lights from TAT (10min., 6am-7pm, 6฿). Approx. 2.5km walk north of guest houses on Mae Nam Kwai Rd.)*

the hospital as he wanted. The patients were given preferential treatment, which at the time meant protein-filled duck eggs.

When he came home to Australia after the war, he made sure the Thais who risked their lives to help the POWs were recognized. Boon Pong, a Thai trader who spearheaded an underground system of delivering the duck eggs via the Kwai River, was singled out for commendation.

Weary also came back from the war to become an internationally recognized surgeon, pioneering new techniques in thoracic cancer treatment. Ever devoted, he returned to Asia to train doctors in India, Vietnam, and Thailand. The Edward "Weary" Dunlop-Boon Pong Fellowship now exists to bring Thai nationals to Australia to study medicine at Melbourne University.

A companion of the Order of Australia, knighted in Britain by Her Majesty, given the Knight Grand Cross of the Most Noble Order of the Royal Crown of Thailand, made an order of the White Elephant, a fellow of the prestigious Royal College of Surgeions in London, and the recipient of honorary fellowships and doctorates, Weary died in 1993 just before turning 86. He wished that his ashes be returned to the Hellfire Pass with the following epitaph:

"When you go home,
tell them of us and say
We gave our tomorrow
For your today"

ART GALLERY AND WORLD WAR II MUSEUM. Luring bridge visitors with claims of extensive World War II exhibitions, the museum is actually a bizarre collection of odd, dusty exhibits. Everything from Thai stamps to dresses of former Miss Thailands are on display. Follow the "toilet" signs to the basement, where cobwebs hide life-sized portrayals of the bridge construction and automobiles/motorbikes used in the war. It's mildly interesting, but skip it if you're pressed for time. *(50m toward town from the bridge. Signs imply this is the JEATH museum; do not be confused, the JEATH museum is in town. ☎512 596. Open daily 8am-6pm. 30฿.)*

JEATH WAR MUSEUM. Established in 1977 by the chief abbot of Wat Chaichumphon (Wat Dai to locals) to honor victims of the Death Railway Bridge, JEATH (Japan, England, America/Australia, Thailand, and Holland) sits in a bamboo hut modeled after those used to house POWs. The collection of pictures, artifacts, and drawings is modest but nevertheless intriguing. The collection of newspaper articles posted on the walls highlights the accomplishments of famous POWs, and their efforts to raise awareness of wartime events. *(500m south of the town gate on Phak Phraek Rd. ☎515 203. Open daily 8:30am-4:30pm. 30฿.)*

KANCHANABURI ALLIED WAR CEMETERY. The cemetery is the final resting place of 7000 Allied POWs, mostly British and Dutch, who died working on the Death Railway Bridge. Western tour groups often seem to outnumber headstones. *(2km north of the bus station on Saeng Chuto Rd., a 5min. walk from the train station. Free.)*

CHUNG KAI WAR CEMETERY. Farther afield, Chung Kai holds the remains of 1700 Death Railway POWs in a setting more peaceful and pleasant than its larger counterpart in town, although the tranquility is broken by the ruckus from the party boats. The trip makes a nice escape from the congestion of Kanchanaburi City. *(4km across the bridge at Song Kwai Rd.'s northern end. Free.)*

STONE GARDEN. Grassed oases sit amongst barren rocks at Stone Garden, where the rock formations supposedly look like animals. This takes a bit of imagination. Stone Garden is ideal for a picnic but not much else. *(On the same road as Chung Kai War Cemetery and Wat Tham Kao Pun, but 5km farther than the cemetery and 4km farther than the wat.)*

WATS. Wat Chaichumphon (also called **Wat Dai**), next to JEATH, is the most frequented by townspeople. **Wat Tham Khao Pun**, 1km beyond Chung Kai War Cemetery, has a cave full of Buddhist shrines (5-20฿ donation suggested). Four kilometers across the river, Chinese-influenced **Wat Tham Mongkon Thong**, Cave Temple of the Golden Dragon, is renowned for its "floating nun," a young woman who can lie on water without sinking. (See **Floating Nun, Golden Dragon,** p. 142.) Early weekend mornings are the best time to catch her in action, or you can ask for her. Private shows are 200฿, or 10฿ per person with a minimum of 20 people to see her 10-15min. performance, which is not all that impressive if you know how to swim. The temple also features a small **museum** of Kanchanaburi's history. Behind the museum, dragon-shaped steps lead up the mountain and into a **limestone cave** that affords views of the surrounding mountains and valleys. Motorcycle taxis make the trip for 30฿; by motorbike, follow the road out over the bridge past immigration.

OTHER SIGHTS. Lak Muang Rd. is home to the **town gate** and the **city pillar shrine.** Drivers honk at the pillar to show respect to the spirit inside.

♫ ENTERTAINMENT

At night, most *farang* stick to bars and restaurants in the well-trodden area around the guest houses. The small but popular **Sports Corner Pub,** at the corner of

GO FISH On your walk toward the River Kwai Bridge, you may have noticed something rather fishy: the street signs. All streets in Kanchanaburi are marked not by typical, boring rectangles but by fish-shaped signs that colorfully point traffic to and fro. The fish guiding those near the bridge is the *pla yi sok* or Julien's golden-prized carp, a rapidly disappearing fish native only to Kanchanaburi Province. The names on the fish signs are significant too: all streets linking Mae Nam Kwai Rd. to Saeng Chunto Rd. from the bridge to the Allied War Cemetery bear the names of the over 20 countries whose citizens were POWs of the Japanese.

China Rd. and Mae Nam Kwai Rd., entertains Commonwealth folk with nightly showings of football, rugby, and cricket. (Open daily 9am-late.) Farther north on Mae Nam Kwai Rd. toward the bridge, **Snooker Bar** has three recent movie releases per night starting at 6pm. Staff are more than happy to let you sit and watch with just the purchase of a drink. (Large Singha 55฿. Open daily 9am-2am.) Though some report the atmosphere is inhospitable to *farang*, head to the **karaoke** and **live music bars** that line the east side of Song Kwai Rd. to experience a more authentic Thai night out. For dives that float, check out the tacky and charmingly mobile floating discos that launch from the west side of Song Kwai Rd. and merrily cruise down the river toward the bridge. You'll probably have to talk (or motion) your way onto these, as they're mainly for Thai tour groups.

The most popular bar in town is **Apache Saloon**, on the corner of Saeng Chuto and Ban Nuer Rd., but like the Wild West it can draw a rough crowd. (All food 55฿; large Heineken 75฿. Open daily 7pm-1am; band 7-9:30pm.) A *farang*-friendly option that's both terrestrial and away from guest houses is the **Punnee Cafe** (see **Work Opportunity**, p. 136), 2/15 Ban Nuer Rd., just off Saeng Chuto Rd. This English establishment features a used bookstore and full bar, along with the requisite fish and chips (150฿). Danny, the friendly proprietor, organizes treks with a slant toward the history of the railway and gives useful advice. (☎513 503. Treks 500฿ minimum for 4 people. Open daily 8am-midnight.)

▶ DAYTRIPS FROM KANCHANABURI

Kanchanaburi makes an ideal base for exploring the dozens of waterfalls, caves, and parks that stretch all the way to Sangkhlaburi and the Thai-Myanmar border.

Routes 3199 and 323 bisect the province at the northern end of Kanchanaburi and make good points of reference. The first, Rte. 3199, is a well-paved passage to the Erawan waterfalls. The second, Rte. 323, heads west to Sangkhlaburi and the Thai-Myanmar border (Three Pagoda Pass), passing Namtok, Hellfire Pass, the hot springs, and several more waterfalls. Independent travelers can take public transportation but may be limited to visiting only one or two attractions per day. Motorcycles are an efficient way to see the sites; however, novice riders would be safer using other means of transport. While the roads are generally excellent, the places of interest are separated by long stretches of highway driving. The scenic and paved 221km to Sangkhlaburi along route 323 (3-4hr. non-stop) has a steep final ascent that is tiring for both body and bike—make sure you're well rested and have the bike serviced before leaving. Pick up the excellent regional map from the TAT for any independent exploration (20฿ donation).

A very reasonable alternative for a few extra baht is to use a tour agency. Most guest houses guide or arrange tours for 150-1000฿, with a minimum of 3-5 people. **A.S. Mixed Travel** (☎512 017), at Apple's Guest House, and **B.T. Travel Center,** 44/3 Rong Heep Oil Rd. (☎624 630), 50m down the soi opposite VN Guest House, can pack in one-day sightseeing tours to Erawan Waterfall, Hellfire Pass, and the

Death Railway (650฿ at Mixed Travel, 580฿ at Travel Center). Adding bamboo rafting and elephant riding cuts one attraction and brings the price to 850฿/750฿. As always, ensure that your agency has a TAT license and that you know exactly what is included in the price (whether the tour includes national park entrance fees and English-speaking guide or just transportation). Mixed Travel's package includes only transport and national park entrance fees; Travel Center's includes English-speaking guide and transport.

ALONG ROUTE 3199

ERAWAN NATIONAL PARK. The foremost tourist destination near Kanchanaburi is **Erawan** ("Three-Headed Elephant") **Waterfall.** The spectacular seven-tiered waterfalls may not be the biggest cascades, but they're certainly the most accessible. It's best to arrive early to beat the maddening crowd of locals and *farang*. The first three levels are a 5-10min. walk from the trailhead. The 2.2km challenging trail to the top (45min.-1hr.) leads past enticing clear-water swimming holes and 50cm long fish, and it rewards the intrepid with more seclusion. But watch out—the trail at the seventh tier is slippery; sturdy shoes are recommended. Maps, photos, and a slide show are at the **Visitors Center,** next to where the bus from Kanchanaburi stops. **Accommodations ❶** range from camping (30฿ per person; 100฿ to rent a tent) to dorms (mattresses 10฿; dorm 30฿) and bungalows (4 beds and bath 250฿ per person or 800฿ per bungalow). The **National Park Headquarters,** opposite the **Visitors Center,** handles accommodation and emergencies. *(65km from Kanchanaburi. Take public bus #8170 (1½hr.; every 50min. 8am-5:20pm, last bus back at 4pm; 26฿). Open daily 8am-4:30pm. 200฿; motorcycle 20฿; cars 30฿.)*

　Phrathat Cave, also in the national park, 9km from Erawan Waterfall, has impressive stalagmites and stalactites undisturbed by *farang* due to their remote location. For 20฿, a guide at the park office will take you on an hour-long tour of the caves. *(From the market at Erawan Waterfall, turn left and follow the signs to Huay Mae Khamin Waterfall and Phrathat Cave. The journey is over a rough dirt road. It may be possible to charter transport from the market (300-400฿), but it's easier and cheaper if you have your own wheels. Open daily 8am-4pm, but arrive by 3pm to see the caves.)*

SRI NAKHARIN NATIONAL PARK. Sri Nakharin has more animals and fewer tourists than Erawan, but getting there demands considerable time, money, and effort. About 105km from Kanchanaburi, **Huay Mae Khamin Waterfalls'** nine tiers are best reached from **Erawan.** Only motorcross bikes and 4WD vehicles can traverse the 42km dirt road parallel to the reservoir that leads from Erawan (about 1½hr.). If you insist on taking your Honda Dream into this area, be advised that it may turn into your Nightmare; the first few kilometers of dirt

---

FLOATING NUN, GOLDEN DRAGON　For over 25

years, Wat Thum Mongkong Thong, Cave Temple of the Golden Dragon, was famous for its **"floating nun"**—a young woman who could lie on water without sinking. She was so famous that when she passed away in 1997, another woman (not actually a nun, but apparently pure enough) stepped in to fill her floating duties. The 15min. performance takes place in a miniature version of a greek amphitheater surrounding a green pool of water. The "nun," dressed in white, but without the requisite short hair, then floats in various meditation positions. Opinions on the performance vary from "Not impressive if you know how to... you know... swim" to "*You* try to float in the lotus position!" Best viewed with a tour in the mornings (20฿); otherwise it's 200฿ for a solo viewing.

track are a good indication of the roughness of the road. Service facilities are available along the way, so you won't run out of gas. A romantic alternative is to charter a boat (1-2hr., up to 10 people, 1000-1500฿) from **Tha (Pier) Kraden,** 13km northeast of the Sri Nakharin Dam, 5km past Mongatet Village. The pier is accessible over dirt road from Ban Kradan, but boat options may be limited. Continue the rough journey to Sisawat if this is the case. The National Park at Huay Mae Khamin has **accommodation ❶** options from camping (30฿ per person) to bungalows with fully serviced grounds and restaurant. *(Park open daily 8am-4:30pm. 200฿ per person, children 100฿, motorbike 20฿, car 30฿.)*

ALONG ROUTE 323

▧**HELLFIRE PASS.** In their quest to complete the Thai-Myanmar railway (the notorious "Death Railway"), the Japanese Imperial Army would not let a mere mountain stand in their way. Thousands of Allied POWs and oppressed Asian laborers worked for months, manually chipping away rock under grueling conditions to create the **Hellfire Pass,** so named for the ghostly campfire shadows that would dance on the mountain walls at night. Today, the pass is a trail leading down the former railway on a stunning 3km circuit around the area. The new adjoining **Hellfire Pass Memorial Museum** showcases pictures, articles, and personal stories of the POWs whose lives were sacrificed in the construction of the pass. When not busy shepherding tourist groups, the knowledgeable Aussie curators are eager to answer questions. *(Between Sai Yok Noi and Sai Yok Yai. Take bus #8203 from Kanchanaburi and tell the attendant where you want to get off (1½hr.; every 30min. 6am-6:30pm, last bus returns at about 4:45pm; 38฿). Open daily 9am-4pm. Suggested donation 30-100฿.)*

PRASAT MUANG SINGH HISTORICAL PARK. This walled "City of Lions" rests along the Kwai Noi River and contains 2000-year-old artifacts and skeletal remains. Prasat Muang Singh (Tower of the City of Lions) is believed once upon a time to have constituted the westernmost outpost of the Khmer empire. The Visitors Center, to the right of the main ruins, has a large park map. *(Trains (1¼hr.; leave Kanchanaburi 6:10, 10:50am, 4:35pm; return 6:20am, 1:50, 4:30pm; 10฿) come closer to the park than buses. Get off at Thakilen; from the train station, walk 1km to the main road, then 1km to the right. Bus #8203 stops 7km from the park; transportation for the final leg may be hard to find. Return buses are best caught before 4pm. ☎ 591 122. Open daily 8:30am-4:30pm. 40฿, motorcycle 20฿, car 30฿.)*

WAT LUANGTA-MAHABUA FOUNDATION. This foundation runs a tiger conservation project and wild animal rescue park. The grounds of the wat contain seven Indo-Chinese tigers, one leopard, water buffalo, deer, gibbon monkeys, and all types of farm animals. The best time to visit is in the late afternoon, when the tigers are brought out of their cages for feeding. If you arrive in the morning, the monks will gladly bring the tigers out for photo ops (suggested donation 20-40฿). The tigers are very tame, having been raised by the monks since birth. However, a few large scars on the shoulders of the monks suggest that they sometimes misbehave. *(The turn-off to Wat Luangta-Mahabua is 5km toward Sangkhlaburi from the turn-off on Rte. 323 to Muang Sing Historical Park; a large billboard on the right markes the 1.5km dirt road leading to the wat's imposing green gate entrance.)*

SAI YOK NOI WATERFALL. Although the "little" *(noi)* Sai Yok Falls are fairly large, they offer only food stalls and concrete paths instead of scenery or hiking trails. Tours stop here for quick photographs, and that's probably about enough. *(60km from Kanchanaburi. Bus #8203 to Sai Yok Noi runs every 30min. 6am-6:30pm, last return 5pm; the hour-long ride costs 25฿. The waterfall is free.)*

WANG BADANG CAVE. This is for spelunkers only, not casual tourists. There are no guided tours, so those who choose to come should bring their own flashlight or rent one from the Visitors Center (20฿) for the 1½hr. round-trip. *(Turn from Rte. 323, 100m south of Sai Yok Noi, then continue 2.5km on the dirt road. Free.)*

LAWA CAVE. The electrically lit 200m cavern is the region's largest. Unfortunately, the user-friendly features do not extend to getting there. Hire a longtail boat (45min. one-way, up to 10 people 800฿, it's a further 350m walk to caves from landing) from Pak Saeng Pier, 2km southwest of Sai Yok Noi. Boats can continue up the river to Sai Yok Yai Waterfall and National Park. Alternatively, complete the 30min. trip on motorbike. After crossing the bridge next to Pak Saeng Pier, turn right just past the 3km marker and follow the partially sealed road to the caves. *(Open daily 6am-6pm. National Park entrance fee 200฿, children 100฿.)*

SAI YOK YAI WATERFALL AND NATIONAL PARK. Celebrated in poetry and song, the Sai Yok Yai Waterfall dribbles unimpressively, except between July and September, when it gushes unimpressively. One of the world's smallest mammal species, the Kitti hog-nosed bats, lives in the park's Bat Cave, 2km from the visitors center and accessible by trails. You can pick up maps and leave gear at the Visitors Center. Accommodations include **camping ❶** (30฿) and **rooms ❹** for two to twelve over the river (500-1000฿). *(45min. by bus from Sai Yok Noi; take any bus or songthaew heading north (15฿). Bus #8203 goes from Kanchanaburi every 30min. 6am-6:30pm, last return 4:30pm (2hr., 38฿). You'll still need to walk 3km or take a motorcycle lift (10-15฿) to the Visitors Center. Open daily 6am-6pm. 200฿, children 100฿, motorcycle 20฿, car 30฿.)*

HIN DAT HOT SPRINGS. The two springs are rather dingy and small but nevertheless extremely popular with Thai tourists. One stays a constant 40°C, while the other fluctuates between 35 and 38°C. *(1km off Rte. 323. The pools have no English road signs, but their turn-off is 127km from Kanchanaburi and 15km before Thong Pha Phum. Bus #8203 goes from Kanchanaburi every 30min. 6am-6:30pm, last return bus 4pm; 2¾hr. trip, 54฿. Hot springs 5฿, private room 20฿.)*

SANGKHLABURI ☎034

Unlike its neighbor Kanchanaburi, Sangkhlaburi relies mostly on its natural beauty. The few man-made attractions in town pale in comparison to the fresh air, rugged mountains, and dense jungle that envelop it. Travelers are entranced by the relaxing views of Khao Laem Lake, the numerous jungle-trekking adventures, and the opportunity to mingle with the Karen and Mon migrants who now call this town home. Nearby, Three Pagoda Pass hosts a typical border market, which was not possible in 1989 when the border was closed due to fighting between Shan and Wa separatist troops. With the continued recent stability, travelers are beginning to trickle into the region. While the tiny city center offers little to visitors, its setting makes it a desirable destination.

⌨ TRANSPORTATION AND PRACTICAL INFORMATION. Public transportation from Sangkhlaburi only runs to **Kanchanaburi** (Bus #8203: 5hr; 6:45, 8:15, 10:15am, 1:15pm; 84฿; with A/C: 3½hr.; 8:45, 10:45am, 2:30pm; 150฿; A/C van: 3hr.; 6:30, 7:30, 9:30, 11:30am, 3:30pm; 118฿) and to the **Three Pagoda Pass** by *songthaew* (30min., every 40min. 6am-6pm, 30-35฿). A/C buses and minibuses from Kanchanaburi drop passengers at the **market** in the middle of town. Regular buses and *songthaew* arrive at the end of the street at the **bus station,** where **motorcycle taxis** congregate ready to take visitors to guest houses (10-20฿) or Wat Wang Wiwekaram (50฿). The Sangkhlaburi **city center** is laid out in simple grid fashion,

**Kanchanaburi
to Sangkhlaburi**

TO THREE PAGODA
PASS (15km)

Wat Wang
Wiwekaram

Mon Village

MYANMAR

Sangkhlaburi

0   10 miles

0   10 kilometers

Sukho

Da Chong Thong
Waterfall

Ban Thi Kaio

Khao Laem Dam

Ban Thi
Phu Ye

Thong
Phaphum

Ban Huai Haeng

Ban Thi Phu

Kup Luang
Waterfall

Saphan Lao
Waterfall

Hin Dat
Hot Springs

Daowadum

Huay Mae
Kharmin
Waterfall

Sri Nakharin
National Park

Sai Yok
Waterfall

Sai Yok ■
National Park

Hellfire Pass ■

Lawa

Sisawat

Prathat

Ban Kraden

Pak Saeng
Pier

Sai Yok Noi
Waterfall

Erawan
Waterfall

Wang
Badang

Namtok
Station

Erawan
National Park

Saiyok

Prasat Muang Singh
National Park

Tha Kilen
Station

Ban Kao

River Kwai
Bridge

Kanchanaburi

Thamuang

Thamaka

bordered at each end by the two turn-offs from the highway to Kanchanaburi. Arriving from Kanchanaburi, take the first turn-off to get to the **police** and **hospital,** the second to go to the bus station, **post office,** and **guest houses.** To get to the **wooden bridge** from the bus station, walk past the post office and turn right at the first paved intersection.

Currency exchange can be handled at **Siam Commercial Bank** opposite the marketplace. **No ATM.** (☎595 263. Open M-F 8:30am-3:30pm.) In case of emergency, contact the **police** (☎595 300) or the **hospital** (☎595 058). To get to either, with your back to the bus station, turn left at the post office; follow the road to its end, passing the immigration office ¾ of the way down, turn right and then take the first left. The police is 50m on your right opposite the hospital. (Limited English. Both open 24hr.) The **immigration office** handles visa extensions and the necessary permit to cross the Three Pagoda Pass into Phayathonzu, Myanmar. (☎595 335. 2 passport-sized photos, photocopies of the front page of your passport and Thai visa, and US$10 are required for permit. Return to immigration by 5pm to collect passport. Myanmar time is 30min. behind Thailand's. Open daily 8:30am-6pm.) **Internet** access is available opposite and left of the market on the road directly across from the motorcycle taxis. (30฿ per hr. Open daily 4-10pm.) The **post office,** 25m right of the regular bus stop, has an **international telephone booth** and CAT-NET **Internet** access. (☎595 115. Open M-F 8:30am-4:30pm, Sa 9am-noon.) **Postal code:** 71240.

■■ ACCOMMODATIONS AND FOOD. The **Burmese Inn** ❶, 52/3 Tambon Nong Loo, is 1km to the right from the bus station. Armin, Meo, and their young daughter Alissa make the clean but simple guest house feel like home. The open-air veranda offers stunning views of the bridge. Amateur astronomer Armin is a veritable walking tourist office and can arrange individually tailored two- and three-day jungle treks (1300-1750฿). Meo, a cooking enthusi-

CENTRAL THAILAND

THE LOCAL STORY

WEAVING WONDERS

Wandering through the streets of Sangkhlaburi, you're bound to stumble upon a beautiful store showcasing fine handcrafted hill tribe weavings. The store "Women for Weaving," run by the indomitable and affectionate Daisy Dwe with the help of her daughter provides the desperately poor Karen and Mon refugees with a valuable outlet for their skills.

"It didn't work for the first two years, but now we have eight weavers and eight setter," Daisy says with triumph in her voice. Her path to Sangkhlaburi is filled with tragedy and courage, perseverance and hope, but it has inextricably tied her to the plight of her fellow refugees.

"My father was an exiled Karen democratic leader. Frightened for our lives we followed him to Thailand...We were planning to apply for a visa to Australia." However, just then, her husband came down with malaria. She and her husband had established a health care service for similarly displaced people and he most likely got sick from one of his patients. Though he was not officially recognized by the Thai government, he was so valuable to his community, as one of the few doctors, that the Thai government airlifted him to Kanchanaburi for the best medical attention. Unfortunately, he still died.

Without a husband, Daisy felt Australia would not give her a visa. "There was no way [of going]. Australia only needs doctors, not women...he was looking after so many poor people and he left me with four children."

ast, runs a staggered two-day seven-dish cooking course for 500฿. (☎/fax 595 146. Motorbike rentals 200฿ per day. Singles with fan and mosquito net 80฿, with bath 120฿; doubles with fan, net, and bath 180฿; bungalow with bath 250฿; family bungalow with satellite TV 500฿.) **P. Guest House ❸**, 81/2 Tumbon Nong Loo, 300m beyond the turn-off to the Burmese Inn, is a fusion of a wooden ranch with a cobbled Swiss chalet. Worth the extra baht, the large rooms are immaculate and the shared baths boast some of the cleanest (and most aesthetically pleasing) squat toilets in Thailand. (☎595 061. Canoe 25฿ per hr. Motorcycle 200฿ per day. Bicycle 100฿ per day. Singles and doubles 200฿. Elephant riding, rafting, and one-night accommodation 850฿.)

Dining is primarily limited to guest houses. The **restaurant** at **P. Guest House ❷** can cater for large groups and has exquisite food, such as paneng curry (red curry with a hint of coconut milk and lime leaves; 55฿). It also has a foosball table and a lovely view of the lake. **Burmese Inn ❷** offers a more relaxed atmosphere. Around the market, several **open-air restaurants ❶** line up unidentifiable but tasty curries in pots during the day (20฿ per plate).

◙ SIGHTS. Most attractions in Sangkhlaburi are a ways from the town center. Arrange **trekking trips** through P. Guest House or the Burmese Inn (see **Accommodations,** above). You can also arrange trekking trips in Kanchanaburi where more options exist. Inquire at the Kanchanaburi TAT. Those looking to take it easy might consider a **boat trip** on beautiful **Lake Khao Laem,** which features a partially submerged wat from pre-dam Sangkhlaburi.

The **longest wooden bridge in Thailand,** the 400m bridge of the Reverend Auttamo, crosses the massive Lake Khao Laem and connects the city of Sangkhlaburi to **The Mon Village.** Although they don't possess Thai citizenship, the Mon people are not quite refugees as they live under the protection of the elderly Luang Phaw Utama, who watches over the temples and households in the area. Utama has plenty of money, thanks to the many Chinese and Thai who believe he has healing powers and flock to him bearing offerings. To get to his main temple, walk uphill straight from the bridge to the stop sign. Turn left, follow the winding road, and take a left at the next stop sign. The red-and-gold **Wat Wang Wiwekaram** sits at the end of the road, 4km from Sangkhlaburi opposite the **handicrafts market** and *chedi* (30min. walk from wooden bridge; 20฿ donation). The wooden bridge is open only to pedestrian traffic. If going by motorbike, head to the highway and turn left following the road over the commuter bridge. At the police box turn left (right heads to the village of Huay Malai) and take another left at the stop sign 25km down.

■ **DAYTRIPS FROM SANGKHLABURI.** The border crossing to **Phayathonzu** in Myanmar is marked by three stunted pagodas, hence the name **Three Pagoda Pass.** The small and sedate **market** displays numerous teak products and boasts some of the best prices for jade in Thailand. During World War II, the Death Railway crossed into Myanmar at this point, but after the war it proved not to be viable and has since been dismantled. A third allied war cemetery (two others are in Kanchanaburi, see **Sights,** p. 140) lies in Phayathonzu as testament to the railroad's existence. More recently, Shan and Wa troops fought for control of the royalties of the black market trade. Shortly after, the Burmese government, realizing the strategic importance of the pass, regained control of the region. It is possible to make a daytrip into Phayathonzu, but travelers are not permitted to go any farther. (See **immigration office** in Sangkhlaburi for details, p. 145. Border open daily 6am-6pm.) For the past decade the area has seen relative stability—check at guest houses for reports of border skirmishes.

Due to poaching, the elephants, tigers, tapirs, bears, gibbons, and peacocks that inhabit **Thung Yai Sanctuary Park,** Thailand's largest conservation area, have moved deep into the forest. Many visitors make the trip to see Karen villages. Most areas are accessible only by 4WD vehicles, even during the dry season. **Takian Thong Waterfall** in Thung Yai Sanctuary Park is an anomaly with fully paved access. The waterfalls, more accurately described as a river cascade, are a 20min. walk from the park office through dense jungle. Sign in at the park office before completing the trip. (Open daily 8am-6pm.) Talk to Armin at the Burmese Inn (see **Accommodations and Food,** above) about accessibility, road conditions, and possible jeep rental to other parts of the sanctuary (dry season 1000฿, more in the wet season).

Songthaew complete the 22km from Sangkhlaburi to Three Pagoda Pass from 6am to 6pm (30min., 30-35฿). The clearly marked turn-off to Thung Yai Sanctuary Park and Takian Thong Waterfall is 18km from Sangkhlaburi along the road to Three Pagoda Pass. From here, it's a lonely 8km, so having your own transport is necessary. The turn-off to Three Pagoda Pass from the highway is 3km from Sanghklaburi toward Kanchanaburi.

Daisy showed me a picture of he family. "If I'm not a strong woman, m children are in trouble. Never give up Women must be the same as men. She sent her children back to Burma to live with her sister so they could ge an education while she set up a gues house at the Three Pagoda Pass "Many, many people...Oh what fun we had!" she says. "I had a guide who dove in the pond, speared fish, and cooked it for my guests."

But when war broke out at the Three Pagoda Pass in 1989 between Karen and Mon groups, it was impossible to keep the business. "I've seen so many killed," she says, referring to women and children. "I'm trying to help all minorities since that time. It's a big job for one person."

After moving to Sangkhlaburi and being reunited with her children (who all attended university in Rangoon) Daisy used her English skills to become an interpreter. She worked with Aid workers at the refugee camps.

She then set up a weaving factor both to employ and benefit Burmese refugees. "So many people came to me. I am not a rich woman, but [have saved] a little money...now I'm working for my people—I don't do this for myself...I'm looking after people through my weaving."

Open every day, **Women for Weaving** (☎595 413) is a few blocks from the Burmese Inn, on the same road Daisy or her daughter will be delighted to answer your questions Souvenirs start at 30฿, pencil cases 50฿, strap shoulder bags 150฿.

—Anthony Barker

BORDER CROSSING: THREE PAGODA PASS About 24km from Sangkhlaburi, the **Three Pagoda Pass** is an anticlimax for those with visions of border intrigue. The border crossing from Three Pagoda Pass to **Phayathonzu, Myanmar,** is sporadically open to foreigners with several caveats: prior authorization from the immigration office in Sangkhlaburi is required; US$10 (450฿) will get you up to 2km into Myanmar, but only from 6am to 6pm; the Burmese military requires one passport picture. Just as the sign says, "Every foreigner welcome to Myanmar. No videocams are allowed." Recent tensions between Thailand and Myanmar have resulted in frequent closures of the border crossing. Be sure to check with the Thai embassy for the most current information. The area is also occassionally considered dangerous (see Thai-Burmese Relations, p. 24), so even more reason to get the latest update from the Thai embassy or your home nation's embassy, which keeps close tabs on the border situation. *Songthaew* leaving from Sangkhlaburi's bus station make the trip (30min., every 40min. 6am-6pm, 30-35฿). If you're making the trip for a rich, historical experience, you'll be disappointed. The diminutive Three Pagoda communicates little of the place's turbulent past. According to one story, as the Burma Wars came to an end in the mid-1700s, the King of Thailand laid down three stones (representing Siam, Burma, and peaceful unity) to mark the border between the two countries. Villages constructed three pagodas *(Chedi Sam Ong)* over the stones, and monks have used the middle shrine to pray for peace. To make the trip more worthwhile, consider backtracking to the **Sawan Bundarn Cave,** located on the way to the Three Pagoda Pass. From Three Pagoda, walk 2km back toward Sangkhlaburi and turn left. Follow the wide dirt road for 700m and turn right onto a smaller track for 500m. There a monk will lead you on a flashlight tour of the cave—for a donation, of course. (See **Myanmar, To Go or Not To Go?**, p. 312.)

PHETCHABURI ☎ 032

Tiny "Phetburi" is something of an oddity, but a worthwhile stop on the route south from Bangkok. With no beaches to draw masses of tourists, Phetchaburi still caters predominantly to locals. Visitors enjoy a small-town atmosphere unspoiled by commercialism. In addition, there are several outstanding cultural sights in town, including historic wats and a former royal palace, which overlooks the city from Khao Wang Hill. Halfway between Bangkok and the beach getaway of Hua Hin, Phetchaburi offers a cultural welcome to Southern Thailand.

▐ TRANSPORTATION

Trains: Phetchaburi Railway Station (☎425 211) is on the northern edge of town, a 15min. walk from the center. Head left from the station and, after 1km, take the second right on Damnernkasem Rd. To **Bangkok** (4hr., 11 per day 7:15am-10:30pm, 3rd-class 74฿) and **Hua Hin** (1hr., 13฿ plus 40-80฿ surcharge depending on the type of train) and other destinations in the south. Buses are more convenient.

Buses: There are three bus stations in town. **A/C buses** from **Bangkok** (2½hr., every 30min. 4am-8:30pm, 90฿) arrive at the intersection of Damnernkasem Rd. and Rot Fai, the road that leads to the train station. The **regular bus station,** on Phetkasem Hwy., on the eastern edge of town about 300m before the entrance to the Khao Wang cable car, has non-A/C buses to **Bangkok** (2½hr., every 20min. 5am-5pm, 70฿) and A/C buses to **Hua Hin** (1hr., frequent, 30-50฿). Finally, orange (non-A/C) buses to **Cha-am** (1hr., 20฿) and **Hua Hin** (1½hr., 30฿) depart frequently from Matayawong Rd., around the corner from Wat Kampaeng Laeng.

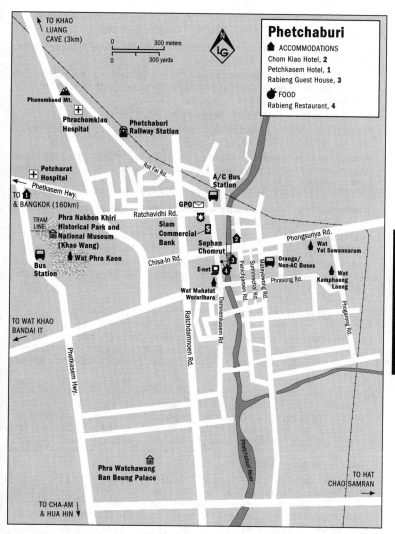

Phetchaburi

🏠 ACCOMMODATIONS
Chom Klao Hotel, **2**
Petchkasem Hotel, **1**
Rabieng Guest House, **3**

🍎 FOOD
Rabieng Restaurant, **4**

TO KHAO LUANG CAVE (3km)

Phanomkued Mt.

Phrachomklao Hospital

Phetchaburi Railway Station

Rot Fai Rd.

A/C Bus Station

Petcharat Hospital

Phetkasem Hwy.

TO & BANGKOK (160km)

TRAM LINE

Phra Nakhon Khiri Historical Park and National Museum (Khao Wang)

Wat Phra Kaeo

Bus Station

GPO

Ratchavidhi Rd.

Siam Commercial Bank

Saphan Chomrut

Chisa-In Rd.

E-net

Wat Mahatat Worariharn

Phongsuriya Rd.

Wat Yai Suwannaram

Orange/ Non-AC Buses

Phrasong Rd.

Wat Kamphaeng Laeng

Malayawong Rd.

Surinreechai Rd.

Panichjaroen Rd.

Ratchdamnoen Rd.

Damnernkasem Rd.

Phetkasem Hwy.

TO WAT KHAO BANDAI IT

Phetchaburi River

Phogaong Rd.

Phra Watchawang Ban Beung Palace

TO HAT CHAO SAMRAN

TO CHA-AM & HUA HIN

Local Transportation: Downtown can be traversed on foot. For longer distances, take **samlor** or **songthaew**. Bargain hard—any trip around town should be no more than 20฿, outside of town 30฿.

⚞ 🛈 ORIENTATION AND PRACTICAL INFORMATION

Phetchaburi is 160km south of Bangkok. **Damnernkasem Rd.** is the city's main drag and runs parallel to the murky brown waters of the slow **Phetchaburi River.** To the north, the road curves to the left, leading to the hospital and train station. To the south, it intersects with **Ratchavidhi Rd.,** heading westward to Khao Wang Hill, and **Phongsuriya Rd.,** leading eastward to several hotels, wats, and the **Saphan Chomrut**

(Chomrut Bridge) across the Phetchaburi River. Another main road is **Panichjaroen Rd.**, the first right after the bridge, with an all-purpose market.

Tourist Office: The closest tourist office is the regional **TAT office** in nearby Cha-am (☎471 005). Open daily 8:30am-4:30pm.

Currency Exchange: Siam Commercial Bank, 2 Damnernkasem Rd. (☎425 303). Halfway between the bridge and the Ratchavidhi Rd. intersection. **ATM.** Open M-F 8:30am-3:30pm.

Emergency: ☎191. **Tourist Police (Bangkok):** ☎1155.

Police: Phetchaburi Police Station (☎425 500), on Ratchavidhi Rd. close to the mountain and opposite the GPO. No English spoken.

Medical Services: Phrachomklao Hospital (☎401 125), 50m from the train station on the left. Some English spoken. No credit cards. **Open 24hr.** Farther away is the **Petcharat Hospital** (☎417 029), on Phetkasem Hwy. north of town, close to the Khao Wong cable car stop. No credit cards. **24hr.** emergency care.

Telephones: 2nd fl. of GPO. **Long-distance** and **international phone.** Fax. Open M-F 8:30am-6pm, Sa-Su 9am-5pm.

Internet Access: E-net, on Damnernkasem Rd., between Wat Mahathat and Rabieng Guest House. A/C and fast Internet connections. 30฿ per hr. Open daily 9:30am-11pm.

Post Office: GPO (☎425 146), at the intersection of Ratchavidhi and Damnernkasem Rd. *Poste Restante.* Open M-F 8:30am-4:30pm, Sa-Su 9am-noon. **Postal code:** 76000.

▶ ACCOMMODATIONS

Given Phetchaburi's small size and lack of tourism, there are a surprising number of high-quality budget options. Most accommodations cluster around **Chomrut Bridge,** a few minutes from the A/C bus station or a 15-20min. walk from the railway station.

Rabieng Guest House (☎425 707), snuggled at the foot of the Chomrut Bridge on the west bank, diagonally across from the Chom Klao Hotel. The young, friendly staff keeps this small guest house in tip-top shape. Tiny green rooms and street racket (bring earplugs) are concessions in return for laid-back atmosphere. You'll probably spend most of your time in the adjoining backpacker restaurant, which offers good food, good views, and good music. Clean shared baths. Request room 104 or 205 for the least street racket. Singles 120฿; doubles 240฿. ❷

Petchkasem Hotel, 86/1 Phetchkasem Rd. (☎425 581 or 410 973). a 20min. walk from the town center, behind Khao Wang Hill. *Samlor* should cost 20฿. A rather impersonal hotel with enormous rooms that suggest a previous life as an office building. All rooms have private bath. Clean and well-maintained. Singles 350฿; doubles 450฿. ❸

Chom Klao Hotel (☎425 398), on Chisa-in Rd., across the street and bridge from Rabieng Guest House. The large rooms are clean though they show their age with peeling paint and 70s furniture. Some come with balcony, private bath, and Western toilet. Shared baths have squat toilets. Singles 120฿, with bath 160฿; doubles 200-240฿. ❷

▶ FOOD

By far the best place to eat is the **Rabieng Restaurant ❷,** on the premises of the Rabieng Guest House (see above). The absurdly extensive, reasonably priced menu (30-70฿) offers everything under the Thai sun. From serpent heads to spicy banana blossom salads, here's the place to experiment. Fun mixes of eighties rock and a

PHETCH ME SOME FOOD

The "throw-together" technique in Thai cuisine is at its peak here. All ingredients are fresh, since the central region has access to the best products in the nation. Central Thailand benefits from all of Thailand's resources—great fish, fruit, grains, and vegetables.

Keep your eyes, ears, mind and mouth open for these options:

Kao niow dahm: black sticky rice pudding with sesame seeds, unsweetened coconut, strawberries, and mint leaves.

Breadfruit salad: boiled breadfruit with spring onions, lemon juice, parsley, sliced eggs, and red capiscum.

Gkai pad gkaprow: spicy basil chicken (chopped into tiny pieces, typical of Thai cooking), fried in peanut oil with holy basil, jalapeño peppers, lime leaves, white pepper, and garlic.

Tom kha kai: chicken coconut soup with galanga, lemon grass, black chili paste, green chili peppers, coriander, and sugar.

Stuffed lychees: cold, brandy-soaked lychees filled with cream cheese, pecans, and ginger served on lettuce. It should be eaten with salad or coffee.

view of the river complete the ambience. American-style breakfast is available for 70฿. (Open daily 8:30am-1am.) There are many **food vendors ❶** on Panichjaroen Rd., the first right after crossing the bridge past Rabieng. One of Phetchaburi's specialties is a delicious egg custard (35฿), enough for two.

SIGHTS

With the exception of Khao Wang and the Khao Luang Cave, all sights are an easy walk from the town center.

PHRA NAKHON KHIRI HISTORICAL PARK AND NATIONAL MUSEUM. In the 1850s, King Rama IV, tired of the heat and exhaustion of Central Thailand, looked south to build a new royal retreat. His search ended on the hilltops overlooking Phetchaburi, where in 1858, he built **Phra Nakhon Khiri** (or Khao Wang). An original mixture of Chinese and Western architecture, it spreads across the hill's three peaks. The westernmost peak houses the **royal residence,** a collection of halls and pavilions, where Rama IV and his son relaxed and entertained guests. The palace's original furnishings are still on display. **Phra That Chom Phet,** a 49m tall *chedi*, sits on the middle peak. On the eastern peak is **Wat Phra Kaew,** which Rama IV ordered to be constructed in the same style as the Temple of the Emerald Buddha in Bangkok's Grand Palace. The park is accessible by a cable car that runs up to the royal residence. Your other option is the steep but short footpath (whose trailhead is guarded by monkeys) from the end of Ratchavidhi Rd. In early February, the town celebrates the **Phra Nakhon Khiri Fair,** which features local art shows, cultural performances, and cart races. (*To reach the cable car, located on the opposite side of the hill town, take a samlor for 20฿ from the town center. Cable car runs 8:30am-5:15pm; round-trip 30฿, children 10฿. Museum open daily 9am-4pm. 40฿. Park open M-F 8:15am-5pm, Sa-Su 8:15am-5:15pm.*)

WAT YAI SUWANNARAM. This 17th-century religious compound features outstanding examples of art and architecture from the Ayutthaya period. Many of the structures are currently under renovation, but try asking one of the monks to open the two wooden buildings that contain well-preserved 18th-century murals. (*On Phongsuriya Rd., about a 10min. walk east from Chomrut Bridge.*)

RITES OF PASSAGE In Thailand, Laos, and Cambodia, over half the male Buddhist population spends a few months as monks during adolescence. The monastery stay is voluntary, but for many Buddhist boys, it is expected that for a few months before they marry, they will don saffron robes and leave their families and schools. Monks shave their heads, renounce sex and money, and spend their days in study and meditation, emerging to resume their old lives with renewed spiritual vigor.

WAT KAMPHAENG LAENG. The five very impressive laterite-block structures hold Buddha images that were originally part of a 12th-century Khmer Hindu shrine. Each of the five *prangs* is thought to be dedicated to one of the five major Hindu deities. In the Ayutthaya period, the temple was reconsecrated to Buddhism, and images of Buddha now replace the Hindu sculptures within two *prangs*. Currently, the temple is the residence of **Phra Khruu Yanwitmon,** Phetchaburi's most revered monk. *(Follow Phongsuriya Rd. past Wat Yai Suwannaram and turn right on Phogarong Rd., about 500m down. The wat will be on the right after about 500m. If the front gate is locked, turn right on the road just after the wat and enter at the gate on the right.)*

WAT MAHATHAT WORARIHARA. With its giant white *prang* dominating the Phetchaburi skyline, Wat Mahathat Worarihara is understandably one of the most popular religious sites in the area. The dozens of Buddha images that surround the main *prang* and the stuccos on the *prang* pedestals are what draws the crowds. The *bot* (main sanctuary) contains several gorgeous carvings. Ask a monk to access the cloisters (through a small door on the right of the *bot*) to see its endless line-up of peaceful Buddhas. *(On Damnernkasem Rd., about a 10min. walk south of its intersection with the bridge.)*

WAT KHAO BANDAI IT. A set of steps between two elephant statues leads to several caves, which, in terms of sheer Buddha quantity, are impressive. A flashlight will help illuminate the "Thousand Buddhas" tucked into the crevices. *(Take the road leading west from the highway opposite the hospital past Khao Wang. The entrance is on the right side of the road at the series of 3 ornate shelters. Go through the right archway and up the short road guarded by monkeys. Motorcycle taxis from town run 40฿.)*

KHAO LUANG CAVE. This underground religious cave, about 4km north of town, is a bizarre and mildly interesting mix of Buddhist imagery, ill-tempered monkeys, and tourist gimmickry. The cave is best seen between 11am and 2pm, when sunlight illuminates the golden Buddhas and the red-tiled floor. Local entrepreneurs offer flashlight tours of the darker recesses, but the good stuff's out in the open. *(The best way to get there is by taxi. Motorcycle taxis charge 40-50฿ from the town center, 100-150฿ round-trip)*

◪ DAYTRIPS FROM PHETCHABURI

KAENG KRACHAN NATIONAL PARK. Thailand's largest national park envelops 3000 sq. km of rain forest in the western half of Phetchaburi Province. Since the park's opening in 1981, four white elephants, long considered symbols of royal prestige and good fortune, have been captured here and presented to the king. The Phetchaburi and Phanburi Rivers entice rafters, and rangers lead three-day hikes in the high season for four people (200฿ per day, with food 352฿). Inquire at the visitor station near the park entrance. To reach the park's center and the waterfalls there, get to the park by 9:30am, as the 68km road becomes one-way in the wrong direction at 10am. Car rental is 1000฿, and though *Let's Go* doesn't recommend it, hitchhiking is the preferred method of transportation among many park visitors. The alternative, spending the night at Kaeng Krachan Lake near park headquarters, gets old quickly. Four-person **bungalows** ❶ are 100฿; **tents** ❶ can be pitched for 10-30฿. *(To get to the park, take a dark blue* songthaew *to Tha Yong (20฿). There, switch to a Koeng Krachan* songthaew *(20฿) to park headquarters.)*

CHAO SAMRAN BEACH. Quieter than some beaches to the south, Chao Samran gets crowded on weekends much like it did when the royal family basked here. *(Minibuses leave from the station on Matayawong Rd., and* songthaew *(10฿) run to the beach until 5pm.)*

HUA HIN ☎032

Long before Phuket and Pattaya were catapulted into jet-set stardom, Hua Hin ("Head Rock") catered to the Thai upper crust. Following the example of King Rama VII, who built his summer palace here in the 1920s, wealthy Thai families vacationed on this long stretch of clean sand, mingling with local fishermen and squid vendors. Today, affluent Europeans have replaced the Thais, and towering resorts have stolen the beachfront away from the fishermen. Still, there's something about this great dame of beach resorts that remains unchanged; the night market still bustles with activity, the seafood still tantalizes the palate, and the beach still satisfies even the most critical beachcomber. Hua Hin may look different, but the new faces and facades only complement its aging grace.

▐ TRANSPORTATION

Flights: Hua Hin Airport (☎522 305), on the north side of the city, is served by **Bangkok Airways.** Four flights per week (Su-M, W, F) to **Bangkok** (1hr., 7:20pm, 950฿) and **Ko Samui** (45min., 9:40am, 2080฿).

Trains: Railway Station (☎511 073), at the end of Damnernkasem Rd. A 10min. walk from the town center. Fares listed are for 3rd class on "ordinary" trains which only run a couple times per day. To: **Bangkok** (4hr., 15 per day, 54฿); **Chumphon** (4hr., 14 per day, 48฿); **Phetchaburi** (1hr., 12 per day, 34฿); **Surat Thani** (7hr., 10 per day, 73฿).

Buses: VIP bus station (☎511 654), 1st fl. of the Siripetchkasem Hotel on Srasong Rd. near Decharnuchit Rd. A/C buses to **Bangkok** (3½hr., every 40min. 3am-9pm, 120฿) via **Cha-am** (20min., 30฿). Buses heading south depart from the **regular bus station** (☎511 230), a dirt path roundabout at the end of Liab Tang Rodfai Rd., about 500m north of the railway station. To: **Bangkok** (4hr., 100฿); **Cha-am** (30min., 20฿); **Chumphon** (4hr., 4 per day, 120฿); **Phuket** (12hr., 6 per day 10am-11pm, 305-486฿); **Prachuap Khiri Khan** (1½hr., every hr. 6:30am-4pm, 50฿); **Surat Thani** (8hr.; 10am, 210฿; 11pm, 340฿).

Local Transportation: Motorcycle taxis and **samlor** go round-trip to **Khao Kai Las** and **Khao Takieb** (every 15min. 6am-7pm, 7฿). Green **songthaew** leave from the motorcycle shop at Decharnuchit Rd. and Srasong Rd. (every 15min. 6am-7pm, 7฿).

✈ 🛈 ORIENTATION AND PRACTICAL INFORMATION

Hua Hin is a stop for most southbound buses and trains. **Phetkasem Hwy.** and the train tracks run parallel to the beach. Perpendicular to the tracks, **Damnernkasem Rd.** leads from the train station to the beach and forms the southern boundary of the town proper. To the north and running parallel are **Decharnuchit Rd.** and **Chomsinthu Rd.** Most hotels, restaurants, and bars cluster around **Naresdamri Rd.,** which branches off Damnernkasem Rd. close to the beach. Free maps are available at the tourist office and several restaurants and bars.

Hua Hin

ACCOMMODATIONS

All Nations Guest House, **2**
Banpak Hua Hin Hotel, **9**
Fulay on the Sea, **4**
Memory Guest House, **5**
Pattana Guest House, **1**
Taxi Jack's, **7**
Willo's Guest House, **6**

FOOD

Hua Hin Brewery, **8**
Thai Restaurant, **3**

Tourist Office: Tourist Information Service Center, 114 Phetkasem Hwy. (☎532 433), on the ground floor of the municipal building, at the Damnernkasem Rd. intersection. Helpful maps. The free *Hua Hin Observer,* a monthly English journal available at the tourist office and select establishments, provides tourist information, listings, and amusing news articles. Open daily 8:30am-4:30pm.

Currency Exchange: Banks and **exchange booths** line Naresdamri Rd. by the Hilton Hotel. **Siam Commercial Bank** (☎532 420), next to the post office. Open M-F 8:30am-3:30pm; window open Sa-Su 1-7pm.

English-Language Bookstore: Bookazine, 166 Naresdamri Rd., opposite Sofitel Hotel. Great beach reads, books on Thai culture, newspapers, and even the classics. Open daily 9am-10pm.

Markets: The **night market,** on Donamuchit Rd. between Srasong Rd. and Phetkasem Hwy., has excellent Thai food. **Chatchai Market,** between Srasong Rd. and Phetkasem Hwy., is another great place to sample local street culture during the day.

Emergency: ☎191. **Tourist Police (Bangkok):** ☎1155.

Police: ☎511 027. On Damnernkasem Rd., 400m from the beach opposite the post office. No English spoken; go to the tourist police first. **Open 24hr.**

Local Tourist Police: ☎515 995. In the little white building on the left side of Dam-nernkasem Rd. just before the beach. English spoken. **Open 24hr.**

Medical Services: All services listed provide **24hr.** care. **San Pau Lo Hospital** (☎532 576), on Phetkasem Hwy., 400m south of the Tourist Center. Credit cards accepted. **Hua Hin Hospital** (☎520 371), 4km north of town on Phetkasem Hwy. A **Red Cross station,** next door to the municipal building, provides basic services.

Telephones: Next to the GPO. **International phone**/fax. Open daily 8am-midnight.

Internet Access: Cups & Comp, 104/1 Naeb-Khehars Rd., near corner with Decharnu-chit Rd. A great ethno-cybercafe with A/C. 1฿ per min. (minimum 20฿). Open daily 9:30am-midnight.

Post Office: GPO (☎511 063), opposite the police station on Damnernkasem Rd., as soon as you turn off Phetkasem Hwy. toward the beach. *Poste Restante.* Open M-F 8:30am-4:30pm, Sa-Su and holidays 9am-noon. **Postal code:** 77110.

ACCOMMODATIONS

Most budget hotels cluster around Naresdamri Rd. and on the alleys that branch off it. While prices are similar in all hotels, style varies, so shop around. Reservations are recommended during the high season.

Pattana Guest House, 52 Naresdamri Rd. (☎513 393). Look for the sign pointing down an alley off Naresdamri Rd. 10m to the left of the pier. Serenity abounds in this enchanting, traditional 200-year-old Thai home with clean rooms and teak furnishings. Good staff and relaxed clientele. No A/C. Cold water. Shared bath. Singles and doubles 350-400฿, with bath 550฿. ❸

Memory Guest House, 108 Naresdamri Rd. (☎511 816), on the ocean, about 25m to the right of the pier, on Naresdamri Rd. toward the beach. Extremely tidy and tastefully decorated. Memory is classier than other budget places in town. TVs 50฿. Rooms with fan 150฿; doubles 200-350฿, depending on size. Rooms with A/C 500฿, with fridge 600฿. ❷

Fulay On the Sea, 110/1 Naresdamri Rd. (☎513 145; fulayhuahin@hotmail.com), across from Memory. You've always wanted to sleep by the sea, so why not over it? Breaking waves, comfortable patios, friendly staff. Rooms are simple and clean. All have private baths. Great breakfast menu 30-70฿. Rooms 250-350฿, with A/C and TV 750-1500฿, depending on size of room. ❸

Willo's Guest House, 32 Selakam Rd. (☎511 708; willo850@yahoo.co.uk). Absolutely sparkling with wooden floors, Buddhist shrine, and very comfortable rooms all with bath (if you can grab one—there are only 3). Homey feel. Internet 2฿ per min. Call ahead for reservations. Rooms 300฿. ❸

All Nations Guest House, 10-10/1 Decharnuchit Rd. (☎512 747; cybercafehua-hin@hotmail.com), on the left about 100m from the beach. True to its name, All Nations draws backpackers from around the world, most of whom stay inebriated in the down-stairs reception-cum-bar. All Nations' saving grace is its balcony rooms overlooking the sea. Shared baths with hot water. Internet access available. Singles 150-250฿; doubles 250-450฿, with A/C and TV 600฿. ❷

Taxi Jack's, 23 Selakam Rd. (☎524 021), off Poolsuk Rd. near the Hilton Hotel. Small but clean rooms. Bar. Breakfast 50฿. Shared baths have hot water. Rooms 250฿. ❸

Banpak Hua-Hin Hotel, 5/1 Poolsuk Rd. (☎511 653), near the intersection with Soi Bintaban opposite the temple. Large and slightly impersonal, the 70s-style rooms are comfortable and have private baths. Watch Western men hit on Thai women from the seating area. Singles and doubles 250฿, with A/C 350฿, with A/C and TV 450฿. ❸

⬛ FOOD

Though Western-style restaurants are moving in, seafood reigns here, and for good reason. Every morning, Hua Hin's fishing fleet returns to the pier with a fresh catch. The lively ▨**night market** ❶ is the best place to sample authentic Thai seafood. (Dishes 10-50฿. Open daily 5pm-midnight.) **Chatchai Market** ❶ sets up during the day. Otherwise, head to Naresdamri Rd. opposite the Hilton Hotel, where pricier restaurants prepare dishes before your eyes. One that stands out is the imposing **Hua Hin Brewery** ❸, next to and part of the Hilton Hotel, 33 Naresdamri Rd. Delicious grilled filets of fresh fish with baked potato cost 150฿, and the seafood skewer goes for 180฿. (Open daily 5-10pm.) **Fulay on the Sea** (see above) has an extensive breakfast menu, including great pancakes and waffles. For cheap and excellent Thai food, head to the **restaurant** ❷ (sign in Thai only) at the corner of Decharnuchit Rd. and Poolsuk Rd. (Noodles, fried rice, and other dishes 50-100฿. Open daily 6am-9pm.)

◉ ♫ SIGHTS AND ENTERTAINMENT

Hua Hin's major attraction is the **Hua Hin Beach,** which rolls along for kilometers in either direction from town. While more scenic and finer beaches can be found farther south, Hua Hin's is clean with soft white sand. The fishing pier, at the base of Chomsinthu Rd., dominates one area of the beach; the prettier part of the beach begins just past the entrance to the Sofitel Hotel. Farther south, vendors wander the sand offering massages, food, and pony rides (100-400฿ for 30min.).

The **Sofitel Central Hotel,** 1.5km south of the pier, recreates a bygone era. Originally the Railway Hotel, it was built by Prince Purachatra, the former Director General of State Railways; it also had a brief stint in cinema as Phnom Penh's leading hotel in the film *The Killing Fields*. One of Southeast Asia's grandest five-star hotels (rooms start at 6000฿), Sofitel has beautiful grounds worthy of a stroll. Tourists on a budget can come for high tea (130฿) and meander through the topiary gardens.

If you head north past the Hilton Hotel and the pier, you can see **Klai Kang Won (Far From Worries) Palace**. A royal summer residence in the 1920s, the palace now houses the ailing king, and the grounds are closed to visitors.

The twin hills of **Khao Takieb** (Chopstick Hill) and **Khao Krailas,** 6km south of Hua Hin on Phetkasem Hwy., are accessible by motorbike or *songthaew* (7฿). Khao Takieb features a temple, hundreds of friendly monkeys (monkey grub sold on the spot for 120฿), and an excellent view of Hua Hin. Khao Kai Las has a small lighthouse and a decent view of Hua Hin. Pine tree-lined **Suan San Beach** is farther south and has unbeatable swimming. Charter a *songthaew* or tuk-tuk (150฿). Still farther south is **Khao Tao** (Turtle Hill).

Hua Hin's **nightlife** centers on pubs and beer gardens on **Soi Bintabaht,** which connects Poolsuk and Naresdamri Rd., and the go-go bars liberally sprinkled throughout the city. If you've had enough of the fat-Western-man-beautiful-Thai-woman combination, head to the bar of the **Hua Hin Brewery,** next to the Hilton Hotel, for loud live music. (Open daily 10am-2am.) **Thai Boxing Garden,** on Poolsuk Rd. between Damnernkasem and Decharnuchit Rd., has amateur and professional boxing matches nearly every weekend (9pm, 250฿).

⬛ DAYTRIPS FROM HUA HIN

TANAO SRI AND PA LA-U. The region between Hua Hin and the Burmese border has spectacular natural sights. The **Tanao Sri Range** forms the border and backdrop for the **Pa La-u Forest** in Kaeng Krachan National Park (see p. 152). Deep in the jungle, the twin waterfalls La-u Yai and La-u Noi merge to become **Pa La-u Falls**, an 11-tier cascade. While three days are required to reach the source, trekkers can explore the first few levels in a day's hike. Longer stays require a guide and camping equipment. During high season, the park rents **tents ❶** and **bungalows ❸**. It's best to come between November and April.

To get there, take a taxi from outside Chatchai Market in Hua Hin (up to 1200฿; it will wait for you). A more affordable but dangerous option is to rent a motorbike (200฿) in Hua Hin and travel the 63km alone. From Hua Hin, follow local Hwy. 3218 until it meets Hwy. 3219, then follow signs. The route is well paved up to the park entrance and the scenery is inspiring. Past the checkpoint, the road turns to dirt and can be treacherous. Walk the last few kilometers to the waterfall and trailhead. It's a short hike (30min.) to the first cascade and swimming hole. A **small eatery ❶** on the left-hand side of the road (look for a "Food & Beverages" sign) sells Thai staples (fried rice 20฿). Overnight trekkers should contact the **Sub-Forestry Office** one week in advance by writing to Kaeng Krachan National Park, Pa La Hua Hin, Prachuap Khiri Khan 77110. The office is past the checkpoint at the entrance.

Try spelunking in the three **caves** on the way to Pa La-u on Rte. 3219, 30km from Hua Hin near Nongphlab Village. At the main intersection in town, make a right onto Rte. 3301 and look for signs advertising the **Daow Lap Lae** and **Kailon** caves, which are simultaneously spectacular caves and the standard Buddha brigade.

KHAO SAM ROI YOD NATIONAL PARK. Stunning limestone hills (the "Three Hundred Peaks") rise from the surrounding sea and marshland. The park is 63km south of Hua Hin off Hwy. 4. Park **bungalows ❷** accommodate up to 20; reserve in advance (☎ 02 579 05 29). There are a couple of excellent **hikes** from the headquarters for daytrippers, as well as extensive **caves** and canals in the park for overnight visitors to explore. Insect repellent is a must for any visit. *(Take a southbound bus from Hua Hin, get off at Pranburi Market, and hire a taxi or songthaew to park headquarters. Park open M-F 8:30am-4:30pm.)*

PRACHUAP KHIRI KHAN ☎032

Flanked by lush rock formations jutting sharply out from its bay, Prachuap Khiri Khan is an unassuming fishing town. Along the pleasant waterfront promenade, fishing boats and seafood restaurants meet, and hip teenagers gather in small groups for an evening beer by the pier. Prachuap's easygoing attitude and mere handful of tourists mean that visitors will have the two outstanding sights to themselves: nearby caves which hide a pair of magnificent reclining Buddhas, and the hilltop wat, which overlooks the bay.

▐ TRANSPORTATION

Trains: The **railway station** (☎ 611 175), on the corner of Maharat Rd. and Kong Kiat Rd., has frequent trains to **Bangkok** via **Hua Hin,** but only the 5am and 10:10am trains are without surcharges. To: **Bangkok** (5hr., 56฿); **Chumphon** (3hr., 1:45pm, 34฿); **Hua Hin** (1½hr., 19฿); **Phetchaburi** (3½hr., 32฿); **Surat Thani** (5-6hr., 101฿). Buses are generally more convenient.

Buses: A/C buses to **Bangkok** (4-5hr., every 30min., 130฿) leave from Phitak Chat Rd., between Kong Kiat Rd. and Maitri Ngam Rd. Most Bangkok-bound buses stop at **Hua Hin.** The **regular bus station,** on Phitak Chat Rd., across from the Inthira Hotel (see below), runs buses to **Chumphon** (4-5hr., every hr., 100฿). For **Surat Thani,** catch a southbound bus from Bangkok on the highway 3km from Prachuap (taxi 30฿), or take a bus to Chumphon and transfer there.

FROM THE ROAD

EVOLUTIONARY *FARANG*

At the base of the Khao Chong Kra-ok hill was a statue of a monkey, sculpted to resemble a sitting Buddha and adorned with a monk's saffron shawl—it was our first hint that something was amiss. The effigy foreboded what we would find at the hilltop temple: monkeys reigned here, or at least had free reign.

Two monks, upright and clearly human, descending the steps, implied normality. But after passing through the open gate at the top, we were fixed by the glare of an overwrought mother monkey, surrounded by her sweet-faced young. She met my tentative step with two antagonistic movements: a direct turn toward us and one stride forward. I was now ready to scamper down the hill. My companion, Andrea, kept her wits. She remembered having read to avoid eye contact, so with downcast eyes we scurried past, feeling that roles were absurdly reversed. Nothing produces the feeling of being weak and hopelessly over-evolved more than being terrified by a smaller relative, supposedly only a few million years ago.

Tiles were ripped from the roof and lay broken on the ground as if hurled through the air in a moment of freneticism. Another monkey was perched like a lookout from the top of the *chedi*. We half expected to find a gang of them molesting a giant magnetic obelisk and approaching us on hind legs wielding clubs. With all the spectacular wats in Thailand, it was not surprising no one had mentioned this one. But the 360° panorama of the ocean, countryside, and town

Local Transportation: Downtown can be traversed on foot. For longer distances, look for tuk-tuks. Any trip around town should be no more than 20฿. Tuk-tuks to **Ao Manao** 20฿ one-way; to **Khao Khan Krad Cave** 30-40฿ per person one-way.

⬛ 🔢 ORIENTATION & PRACTICAL INFO

Prachuap Khiri Khan is extremely easy to navigate and can be traversed on foot in 15 minutes. Its streets roughly follow a grid layout. The waterfront, **Chai Thaleh,** runs north-south on the eastern edge of town. **Khao Chong Krajok,** Prachuap's impressive wat-topped mountain, rises on the northern edge of the waterfront. Between the railway tracks and the waterfront, and running parallel to them, are (from west to east) **Phitak Chat Rd., Sarachip Rd.,** and **Suseuk Rd.** Perpendicular to these is **Kong Kiat Rd.,** which runs across town from the **train station** in the west to the **pier** in the east. **Maitri Ngam Rd.,** south of Kong Kiat Rd., is home to the fruit and vegetable **market.**

Tourist Office: Tourist Information (☎611 591), on the waterfront next to the Thetsaban Bungalows (see below), gives out maps, and is mildly helpful. Open daily 8:30am-4:30pm.

Currency Exchange: Government Savings Bank, on Kong Kiat Rd., between Sarachip Rd. and Suseuk Rd., has a **24hr. ATM** outside. Open M-F 8:30am-3:30pm.

Emergency: ☎191. **Tourist Police (Bangkok):** ☎1155.

Police: ☎611 148. At the corner of Kong Kiat and Sarachip Rd.

Medical Services: Prachuap Hospital (☎602 060). From Kong Kiat Rd., it's 4 long blocks down Phitak Chat Rd., on the left.

Internet Access: VIP Shop, 48 Kong Kiat Rd. (☎611 180), a few steps from the train station on the left. 30฿ per hr. Open daily 8am-10pm. Also on the 2nd floor of the **post office.**

Post Office: GPO (☎611 035), on Suseuk Rd., at the intersection with Maitri Ngam by the market. Open M-F 8:30am-4:30pm, Sa-Su 9am-noon. **Telephones** and Internet on the 2nd floor. **Postal code:** 77000.

🏠 ACCOMMODATIONS

Although there are no exceptional backpacker accommodations, there is a small but sufficient selection of budget-friendly options.

Inthira Hotel (☎611 418), on Phitak Chat Rd. From the train station, go down Kong Kiat Rd. and take the first left, Smart, very clean rooms and friendly staff make Inthira marginally better than the rest of Prachuap's hotels. TVs 50฿. Rooms have private bath with cold water. Singles 150-180฿; doubles 200-250฿. ❷

Prachuap Suk Hotel, 69-71 Suseuk Rd. (☎611 019, mobile 01 3150 000). From the train station, go down Kong Kiat Rd., turn onto Suseuk Rd. and walk for 3 long blocks. It's past the the market on the left. A small, well-maintained hotel. Singles with fan 150฿; doubles with fan 180฿, with A/C 250฿. ❷

Yuttichai Hotel (☎611 055), a 2min. walk from the train station along Kong Kiat Rd., on the right. Similar in style and amenities to the other hotels. Simple breakfast available 20฿. Boiling pots of duck soup 20฿. Singles 180฿; doubles 240฿. ❸

Thetsaban Bungalows (☎611 010), on the waterfront at the northern end of the beach, just below the hill. With a new coat of paint and new plumbing in the bathrooms, the spacious, concrete bungalows might live up to their seaside location. Rooms 300฿, with A/C 500฿. ❸

🍴 FOOD

With fleets of fishing boats just off shore, it's not surprising that cheap seafood abounds in Prachuap Khiri Khan. On the waterfront, a 5min. walk south past the pier, is the ▨**Pub and Restaurant ❷**, which serves vegetarian options such as mixed vegetable coconut curry (70฿). With live music, great decor, and dim lighting, it's also a pleasant place to grab a drink in the evening. (Open daily 5pm-midnight.) **Phanphohcana ❸**, past the pier to the south, has an extensive menu in English and serves good seafood. (Dishes 70-120฿. American breakfast 70฿. Open daily 8am-10pm.) The extensive **fruit and vegetable market ❶** is on Maitri Ngam, close to the post office. For a wide selection of freshly brewed coffee, head to the surprisingly hip **Blue Mountain Cafe ❶**, on Sarachip Rd., just before the fruit and vegetable market. Green tea comes as a free "appetizer." Try the strong mountain coffee for 15฿. (Coffees 15-25฿; toasts and sandwiches 10-25฿. Open M-Sa 6:30am-5pm, Su 6:30am-noon.) Yuttichai Hotel's **restaurant ❶** serves good cheap eats (see above).

👁🚩 SIGHTS AND BEACHES

For a small town, Pratchuap Khiri Khan affords two remarkable sights that alone are worth the trip. What makes them even more exhilarating is their complete seclusion—you'll have them all to yourself.

possessed a magical height tha allowed us, between monkey encour ters, to spy a train crawling towar town like a centipede, watch dogs run circles on the beach, and most of all stop and realize that, for once in Thai land, we were alone.

Just before sunset, we set out for a cave about 5km from town. Again, we were alone. We clambered up to the cave and a group of Thais watched us intently as if we were headed to mee Kurtz. With our torch leading us through the pitch black, we came upon an 8m bronze reclining Buddha Lying propped on one elbow, his head in his hand, with a peaceful smile this Buddha was supremely mellow the pose reflective of the passing int nirvana. Continuing deeper into the cave, we made a startling new discov ery: another reclining Buddha, even larger than the first and flanked b about 30 Buddha images. Sitting on the cave floor, gazing at our own large shadows projected against the wall we felt enlightened. It was specia because the discovery was personal.

Thais have a popular saying the offer to tourists: "same-same but di ferent." It encapsulates the need to see more, to consume more visually to do it all. In Prachuap Khiri Khan we learned that purity now resides in the predictability of unspectacular places and interactions with locals. The secret now for travelers searching fo off-the-beaten-paths in Thailand is t favor those very sites that, for wha ever reason, are still not considered viable. The tourist must be unpredic able, spontaneously breaking from the pack, charting an independen course.

—Nick Grossman

KHAO CHONG KRAJOK (MIRROR TUNNEL MOUNTAIN). It's 421 steps to the golden *chedi* of this hilltop's **wat,** which offers a glorious 360° panorama of the surrounding bay and province. Its height allows for a lighthouse perspective of beachwalkers, approaching trains, and the general activity of the town. In addition, monkeys are given free reign of the hill and wat. Travelers should not approach or make contact with the monkeys. Visitors may also use the wat's vantage points to see the monkeys in fascinatingly close detail. *(On the northern tip of town overlooking the bay. The steps start on Sarachip Rd. Open 24hr. Free.)*

WAT KHAO THAM KHAN KRADAI AND CAVES. Overlooking the Ao Khan Kradai Bay are two impressive complexes of caves. A shiny, shell-paved set of steps leads to the first and smaller cave. On the hill to the left is the larger and superior complex, which holds two spectacular **reclining Buddhas.** The experience is heightened by the solitude and lack of light in the caves. *(8km north of town. Take a tuk-tuk. Bring a flashlight. Free.)*

AO MANAO (MANAO BEACH). The closest beach to town, Ao Manao lies on the grounds of a Thai airforce base. Unless you're desperate for a swim, it's not worth the trip. *(Sign-in and passport required at the entrance to the base. Take a tuk-tuk (20฿ one-way) from town.)*

EAST COAST THAILAND

THAILAND PRICE ICONS					
SYMBOL:	❶	❷	❸	❹	❺
ACCOMM.	Under US$3 Under 120฿	US$3-4.50 120-180฿	US$4.50-9 180-360฿	US$9-14 360-560฿	Over US$14 Over 560฿
FOOD	Under US$0.75 Under 30฿	US$0.75-2 30-80฿	US$2-4 80-160฿	US$4-6 160-240฿	Over US$6 Over 240฿

From Bangkok to Trat, the coastal highway travels the timeline of economic development. Shiny new refineries, power stations, and petrochemical plants dominate the coast from Si Racha to Rayong. East of Rayong up to the Cambodian border, Thailand's coast changes as construction sites and highway traffic thin, giving way to groves of durians and mangosteens that creep to the edge of the road. Off the coast of Trat, undeveloped Ko Chang and the Ko Chang National Marine Park await exploration by rainforest trekkers and beach-hunters. Farther west, Ko Samet offers convenience and beauty, while charming Ko Si Chang is overlooked by tourists. Perhaps most unfairly neglected, however, is the mainland east coast. Chanthaburi and Trat teem with mountains, jungles, waterfalls, and national parks, most of them completely untouched by backpackers.

SI RACHA ☎ 038

Thailand may be a culinary heaven, but few towns celebrate the taste buds like Si Racha does. The maritime heritage of this fishing-village-turned-bustling-town lives on in the restaurants and foodstalls whose blinking lights beckon visitors to sample Thailand's finest and most traditional seafood. Besides its culinary appeal, the town is home to one of Thailand's best zoos. If neither seafood nor caged animals strike your fancy, make sure to arrive with enough time to catch the ferry to Ko Si Chang; there is little other reason to dawdle in Si Racha.

▐ TRANSPORTATION

All transportation operates out of the de facto **bus stop**, the **Laemthong Department Store**, a 20min. walk from the city center. **Buses** to **Bangkok** (every 20-40min. 5am-6pm; 40฿, with A/C 55฿) and **Rayong** (every 20min. 5am-10pm; 40฿, with A/C 60฿) depart from **Sukhumvit Rd.**, next to the department store. Infrequent buses to other eastern destinations stop across from the department store's main entrance. To reach the **city center** and **ferry** to **Ko Si Chang**, take either a **tuk-tuk** or **motorcycle-taxi** (30฿) from the department store or walk a few blocks north on Sukhumvit Rd. and down service-laden **Surasak I Rd.**

East Coast Thailand

ORIENTATION AND PRACTICAL INFORMATION

Si Racha's main street, **Jermjompol Rd.**, intersects Surasak I Rd. at Soi 10 and runs parallel to the coast, the town's western border. It is bounded on the north by a small, white clock tower and the causeway to the small island Ko Loi, and to the south by a larger clock tower and the **market**.

Currency Exchange: Siam Commercial Bank, 98/9 Surasak I Rd. (☎311 313), halfway between Sukhumvit Rd. and Jermjompol Rd. Exchanges traveler's checks. Open daily 8:30am-3:30pm. **Bank of Ayudhya,** 50m from Jermjompol Rd., on Si Racha Nakon Rd. 3. Also has an **ATM**.

Emergency: ☎191. **Tourist Police (Bangkok):** ☎1155.

Police: Infrequently staffed **police booth** (☎311 111), at the corner of Jermjompol Rd. and Soi 10. Open daily "6am-9pm."

Medical Services: Phyathai General Hospital, 90 Si Racha Nakon Rd. (☎770 200 or 770 208). **Open 24hr.**

Internet Access: The 2nd fl. of the **Laemthong Department Store** has cheap Internet access (25-40฿). Open M-F 11am-9pm, Sa-Su 9am-9pm. **Internet East Co.,** 140 Si Racha Nakon Rd. 1, near Sri Racha Seafood Restaurant. Fast connections. 1฿ per min. Open daily 9am-9pm.

Post Office: ☎311 202. Past the park near the road to Ko Loi at the north end of Jermjompol Rd., a 10min. walk from the city center. **International phones.** Open M-F 8:30am-4:30pm, Sa-Su 9am-noon. **Postal code:** 20110.

ACCOMMODATIONS

Hotels near the bus stop at the Laemthong Department Store tend to be on the expensive side. Budget rooms hug the salty sea near the Ko Si Chang Ferry, a 20min. walk or 30฿ tuk-tuk ride from the bus stop.

Siri Watana (☎311 097), one block north of Soi 10, opposite Si Racha Nakon Rd. Literally on top of the ocean. Rooms are plain and generally clean in this 75-year-old guest house stretching out to sea. One of the better choices. Singles 200฿; doubles 300฿. ❸

Samchai Hotel (☎311 800), at the end of Jermjompol Rd. Soi 10, near Surasak I Rd. Large rooms by the sea. Baths, well—aren't that clean. Rooms with fan 260฿, with A/C and TV 380฿. ❸

Laemthong Hotel (322 886), just through the parking lot next to the department store—you can't miss the giant neon sign on the roof of this 20-story building. Drab apartment-style rooms are huge and well furnished. It's not the Ritz, but if you want a table and sink, it'll do. Singles or doubles 900฿. ❺

FOOD

Si Racha is famous for its **seafood,** often prepared with Si Racha sauce, a spicy red dressing. It appears as ซอสศรีราชา on Thai menus. The prime location for gorging on local cuisine is on **Si Racha Nakon Rd. 3** not long after it branches off Jermjompol Rd., one block north of Soi 10. This sizable section of road overflows with foodstalls, small restaurants, and larger open-air eateries, allowing diners to stroll through and take their pick. Sample fresh seafood in the **market ❶** by the clock tower at the south end of Jermjompol Rd.

Khor Kav Soy, 55 Si Racha Nakon Rd. (☎771 521). Make a right onto Si Racha Nakon Rd. from Jermjompol Rd. At the fork, head right, and it's 200m up on your right. Enjoy succulent steamed prawns with glass noodles (180฿) with karaoke and mood lighting. A Si Racha favorite. Most dishes 80-180฿. Open daily 4pm-1am. ❸

Hanamoto, 7 Si Racha Nakon Rd. Soi 8 (☎322 274). Si Racha's famous fresh seafood tastes great as sushi too. Lightly battered, fried-to-perfection shrimp tempura 160฿. Food generally 50-180฿. Large Singha beer 110฿. Open daily 5pm-midnight. ❸

Sri Racha Seafood Restaurant, 160-164 Si Racha Nakon Rd. Turn onto Si Racha Nakon Rd. 3 from Jermjompol Rd.; veer left at the first fork and right at the next. A decent restaurant surrounded by similar decent restaurants. Dishes 80-200฿. Open daily 9am-9pm. ❸

SIGHTS

Si Racha's main attraction is unquestionably the **Si Racha Tiger Zoo,** a rather gimmicky, amusement-park-style zoo 9km east of town. Take a tuk-tuk from anywhere in the city (25min., 100฿). The zoo's shows (in Thai only) are quite entertaining. Take your pick from elephant, crocodile, and tiger shows or the pig-racing extravaganza. The zoo displays, on the other hand, are disappointing, featuring mostly unhappy-looking caged animals. It's an unusual zoo and an interesting way to kill time waiting for the ferry. (☎296 556. Open daily 8am-6pm. Several shows per hr. 250฿, children 150฿.)

THE LOCAL STORY

MYSTIC MONARCHY

The fastest way to get punched in Thailand is to go to a bar and criticize King Bhumibol Adulyadej. On the throne for nearly 60 years, the Thai king holds the dearest place in the hearts of his people. Deference to him has kept anyone from seizing power and a decree from the throne has authority greater than law: if the king denounces drugs, the effect of his statement dwarfs that of anti-drug programs.

The Thai monarchy is a curious archaism, in existence for over 700 years. King Chulalongkorn (Rama V), who died in 1903, was the last king to be worshiped as a god. "Chula," the mustachioed gent whose picture is in nearly every public bus, is known for modernizing Thailand and keeping it independent during his 40-year reign.

Chulalongkorn's grandson, the present king (whose jug-eared, bespectacled mug is all over Thailand), was born in 1927 in Cambridge, Massachusetts, where his father was a student at Harvard Medical School. In 1946, his brother, 20-year-old King Ananda Mahidol, accidentally blew his own head off with a pistol in his bedroom. (Ananda was a gun fanatic, reportedly carrying a weapon at all times.) The three servants who were present were swiftly executed—raising suspicions about the specifics of the incident.

The present king accepted the crown from a distraught populace. In addition to a career as a jazz musician and composer—he played with Stan Getz and Benny Goodman—the king has been virtually everywhere in Thailand in efforts to connect with his peo-

Those with less time can head to the temples that sit on the mainland. From Jermjompol Rd., **Wat Radniyomtum** is several blocks down Surasak I Rd. on the right. Near the market, Surasak Suguan leads to **Wat Mahasiracha,** on the corner of Tesaban Rd. The town's most touristed temple is **Wat Ko Loi (Floating Island Temple),** reached via a pleasant walk to the causeway at the northern end of Jermjompol Rd. Release a pair of finches at the top (20฿), or see enormous **sea turtles** from the nearby moat. Maybe the best part though is just wandering around the base, where foodstalls and trinket shops create a lively atmosphere for the picnicking Thais who flock here on weekends. A shady park stretches along the waterfront on Jermjompol Rd. where you can test your athletic prowess on balancing beams and push-up logs. During the late afternoon, the park fills up with locals, and you can race the grown-ups around the track or see-saw with the kids.

KO SI CHANG   ☎038

Poor Ko Si Chang is all dressed up with no place to go. A tourist boom years back encouraged the residents of this 5000-person fishing village to spruce up their island with new bungalows and English signs and maps. But as the rest of Southeast Asia opened up, more and more visitors cut Ko Si Chang from their itineraries, heading to more spectacular Ko Samet and Ko Chang farther east. Accordingly, Ko Si Chang remains a pretty island with good tourist services, friendly locals, and hardly a trace of commercialism. Those seeking postcard-perfect scenes should keep heading east, but for a sandy respite from hot, dusty Bangkok, Ko Si Chang fits the bill.

▐ TRANSPORTATION. Ferries to **Ko Si Chang** depart from Si Racha's main pier at the end of Jermjompol Rd., Soi 14 (40min., every hr. 8am-6pm, 20฿). Boats returning to **Si Racha** leave from **Ta Lang Pier** or **Ta Bon Pier** depending on the tide; ask your guest house owner to verify which you should take (every hr. 6am-6pm, 20฿).

▓▐ ORIENTATION AND PRACTICAL INFORMATION. Assadang Rd. runs north along the water past the two piers, curves past the Chinese temple on the hill, and finally doubles back onto itself 4km later next to Tiew Pai Guest House. The road then runs south to **Hat Ta Wang** and **Hat Sai Kaew** beaches and branches off to **Hat Tampang,** the island's best beach. Take a right onto **Chakra Pong** Rd. up the hill, then follow the signs. *Samlor* go anywhere on the island for 20-50฿, but you can walk most places as well.

Thai Farmers Bank, 9-9½ Assadang Rd., between the piers, exchanges traveler's checks and has an **ATM.** (☎216 132. Open M-F 8:30am-3:30pm.) **Tiew Pai Guest House** rents **motorcycles** (170฿ for 12hr., 250฿ for 24hr.) and **pickup trucks** that seat up to 15 people (500฿). A man named Oo rents **mountain bikes;** look for the sign at the entrance of a small soi, 75m before Tiew Pai Guest House on the right as you come from the pier. (☎216 265. Mountain bikes 150฿.) In an **emergency,** dial ☎191 or call the **police** at ☎216 218. For **tourist police** in Bangkok, call ☎1155. The **post office,** in a white building at the north end of Assadang Rd., offers **Internet access** (3฿ for first min., 1฿ for every 2min. thereafter) and has **international** and collect calls for 30฿. (☎216 227. Open M-F 8:30am-4:30pm.) **Postal code:** 20120.

⛿⛿ ACCOMMODATIONS AND FOOD. Ko Si Chang's only budget-minded guest house is **Tiew Pai Guest House ❷,** south of Ta Lang Pier on Assadang Rd. Fortunately, it's cheap and well kept, and the owners are friendly. At night, a karaoke bar thumps to the latest Thai pop. (☎216 084. Singles with shared bath 150฿; doubles 250฿, with A/C and fridge 400฿; triples and family rooms 500-1000฿.) Pricier bungalows line the beach. The best of these is the **Sichang View Resort ❹,** opposite the Khao Khat Cliffs in the northwestern corner of the island, 2km from town, which offers comfortable rooms with TVs in one of the island's most beautiful settings. It's worth the extra baht. (☎216 210. Doubles with fan 500฿, with A/C 800฿, with hot water 900฿; add 200฿ to turn any room into a triple.) Conveniently located near the ferry, the **Sichang Palace Resort ❺** has clean rooms in a hotel atmosphere. From the ferry pier make your first right onto Assadang Rd., it's 40m up on the left. (☎216 276. Swimming pool in the back, restaurant in the front. Rooms facing the ocean 950฿, facing the pool 800฿.) **Camping ❶** is free on the beach; bring your own supplies.

Food vendors ❶ sell noodle and rice dishes along **Assadang Rd.** Try the tasty breakfast (60฿) and entrees from typical rice dishes (25-30฿) to fish 'n' fixin's (180-200฿) at Tiew Pai Guest House's **restaurant ❸.** (Open daily 7:30am-1am.) Munch on more rice dishes (40-50฿) and fresh fish (54-220฿) at the **Sichang View Resort ❸.** Their steamed fresh grouper in black bean sauce (54฿ per 100g) is simple and satisfying. (Open daily 7am-9:30pm.)

◙ SIGHTS. Although a quick tour of Ko Si Chang takes just a few hours by motorcycle or *samlor* (200-250฿), the island rewards more leisurely walks or even bike rides extended over a couple days. The

ple. He is also said to oversee man development projects personally.

For all its modernity, the Thai mon archy is shrouded in medieval courte sies and regulations. Speech concerning the monarchy is not free you can be locked in prison for 1! years with impunity. In 2002, Thai land revoked the visas of two journal ists for an article deemed overl' critical of the monarchy. In Philadel phia, a restaurant digitally added sun glasses and a punk hairdo to a photc of the king in an advertisement. The Thai government formally protested tc the United States, who said it was a private issue.

Even the Thai language is special ized for the Royal Family. The king refers to himself with an honorific "I" and people around him refer to them selves as "dust under His Majesty's feet." The standard ways of showing disrespect go triple for Thai royalty Dropping a 20-baht note on the ground is the equivalent of drop-kick ing the king; but if you do, quickly apologize to those around you. Tha theaters play the national anthem and show fawning photos of the king before a movie. Not standing up dur ing these ceremonies will bother fel low moviegoers. Expect to be cursec and slapped.

King Bhumibol, now 76, has mino health problems but continues to rule with broad public approval. His heir the Crown Prince Vajiralongkorn, is ir his mid-50s and on his third marriage (he dissolved the first, saying his wife played too much ping pong).

Graeme Wood was the editor o Let's Go: Southeast Asia 2001 and has worked in Thai orphanages and hospices.

town's main street, Assadang Rd., ends in a 163-step climb to a colorful **Chinese temple.** Four hundred steps farther up is an enshrined **Buddha footprint,** whose size makes it a good match for the **Yellow Buddha** on the island's west side. Beneath this 10m high statue are several caves accessible from the lower platform in front of the Buddha.

Toward the southern end of Assadang Rd., near the two eastern beaches, are the ruins of **King Rama V's summer palace.** An economic crisis halted the restoration of this royal residence, but you can still see pagodas, reservoirs, and European-influenced buildings. To get there, continue south on Assadang Rd. through the gate of the Marine Research Institute. Find **▊Hat Tampang,** Ko Si Chang's most swimmable beach, by taking the right branch of the road next to the gate and climbing over a steep hill. North of Hat Tampang, don't miss the **Khao Khat Cliffs,** where Rama V built a pavilion to enjoy the western horizon and compose poetry. The view from the king's seat is stunning. At the bottom, a path by the Sichang View Resort leads down to the cliffs, which are best visited at sunset.

KO SAMET   ☎ 01

Just four hours from Bangkok, Ko Samet is a popular vacation spot for Thais and foreigners alike. Over the last 20 years, beachside bungalows have slowly encroached on much of the shoreline, and loud *farang* pubs and Thai karaoke bars dominate the once still nights. Development aside, however, Ko Samet delivers, and a dip in its tranquil waters or a nap on its clean, white sand beaches will satisfy the traveler seeking good, old fashioned relaxation. Many travelers prefer Samet's low-key atmosphere to that of its rowdier and more developed island neighbors. Commercialism has not yet taken a strong hold on Samet's visitors or residents, so enjoy it while it lasts.

THE VIEW FROM ABOVE

The lowdown: Step 1 in your island hopping trip.
Beaches: At last count, 11.
Highlights: Snorkeling in Ao Kiu's coral reefs, hanging out at Ao Phai, and camping under the stars on Ao Thian (Candlelight Beach).

⊏ TRANSPORTATION

Ferries: Nuan Tip Pier and **Tarua Phe Pier** in the town of Ban Phe serve Ko Samet. Buses from Bangkok stop in front of Nuan Tip Pier, which offers service to Na Dan Pier in northern Ko Samet (40min., 20-person minimum, round-trip 100฿). To get to Nuan Tip Pier, walk through the market toward the ocean. Additional boats with a 7-passenger minimum are available during peak months to: **Ao Kiu/Ao Pakarang** (200฿); **Ao Phrao** (45min., 120฿); **Ao Wai** (50min., 200฿); **Ao Wong Duan** (45min., 120฿). If you arrive via *songthaew* from Rayong, you will be let off at Tarua Phe Pier, opposite the 7-Eleven, about 200m west of Nuan Tip Pier. Ferries here leave more regularly and go to **Ao Wong Duan** (9:30am, 1:30, 5pm; one-way 60฿) and **Na Dan Pier** (every hr. 8am-5:30pm, one-way 40฿) regardless of the number of passengers.

Buses: Ban Phe Bus Station (☎651 528), opposite Nuan Tip Pier on the mainland. Buses with A/C go to **Bangkok** (3½hr., 13 per day 4am-6:30pm, 124฿). If you're heading elsewhere, grab a *songthaew* to **Rayong** (every 15min. 6am-6pm, 20฿) and transfer to **Chanthaburi** (2½hr., every 50min. 5:50am-5:30pm, 55฿); **Khorat** (6hr.; every hr. 4:20am-9pm; 125฿, with A/C 225฿); **Nong Khai** (13hr.; 11 per day 7am-8:30pm; 241฿, with A/C 434฿); **Si Racha** (2hr., every 40min. 5:10am-6:30pm, 40฿); and other destinations. Many Ko Samet bungalows offer expensive but convenient direct service to Bangkok's **Khaosan Rd.** (around 220฿).

Local Transportation: Songthaew generally wait for 8-10 people before leaving. Going to more remote destinations may require you to charter the entire car—prices listed are per person, and to charter. From Na Dan Pier to: **Ao Kiu** (50฿, 400฿); **Ao Phai** (20฿, 150฿); **Ao Phrao** (30฿, 200฿); **Ao Thian** (40฿, 300฿); **Ao Tup Tim** (20฿, 150฿); **Ao Wai** (40฿, 400฿); **Ao Wong Duan** (30฿, 200฿); **Hat Sai Kaew** (10฿, 100฿). *Songthaew* returning to Na Dan Pier or offering taxi service wait at Ao Phai in front of Silver Sands Resort. The island is easily walkable once your pack is off. It's only a 500m stroll from Na Dan Pier to Hat Sai Kaew, and the walk from Ao Wong Duan to Ao Phai takes just 30min.

Rentals: Shops renting **motorbikes** cluster near Na Dan Pier and along the road to Hat Sai Kaew. 120฿ per hr., 500฿ per day with passport or 500฿ deposit. Open daily 7am-8pm.

◼◻ ORIENTATION AND PRACTICAL INFORMATION

With only two roads stretching through its 16km, Ko Samet is easily navigable. Boats disembark at **Na Dan Pier** on the island's northeast corner. A paved road runs south to the Park Service entrance booth, where you must pay a hefty **admission fee** to enter the island, technically a Thai national park (200฿, children under 10 100฿). Here, the path forks. Directly ahead is **Hat Sai Kaew;** the right-hand fork continues south, behind the bungalows of the eastern beaches: **Ao Cho, Ao Hin Klong, Ao Kiu, Ao Phai, Ao Nuan, Ao Thian, Ao Tup Tim, Ao Wai, Ao Wong Duan,** and **Hat Lung Dum.** To get to these beaches, bear left at the fork after Ao Phai. Head straight to go to Ko Samet's only west coast beach, **Ao Phrao.** Beach-side paths and jungle trails link all the beaches except Ao Phrao and Ao Kiu, making the island fairly walkable.

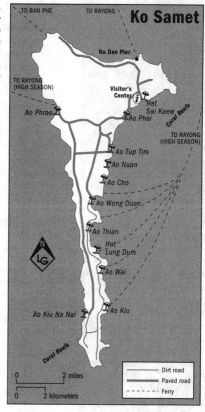

Tourist Office: The **Visitors Center,** next to the park entrance by Hat Sai Kaew, assists tourists and provides info on local wildlife. An English-speaking man named Thawil staffs the office and can be reached **24hr.** in case of emergency (☎01 663 5055). Open daily 8am-4pm.

Tours: Many of Ko Samet's larger guest houses offer air ticketing, domestic minibus service, and snorkeling tours.

Currency Exchange: Exchange as much money as you think you'll need at the banks in **Ban Phe,** west of the pier. Otherwise the **post office** at Naga Bungalows offers the most comparable rates for currency, traveler's checks, or cash advances.

EAST COAST

THE BIG SPLURGE

RIM VIMARN RESTAURANT

Ao Phrao is Ko Samet's black-tie beach, so it's no surprise that the Rim Vimarn Restaurant in the Vimarn Resort, at the northern end of the beach, is the island's swankiest place to dine. It's impossible to miss the steep thatched roof that soars above deep-bucket wicker chairs and teak tables. Well lit and romantic, it is the local VIP vantage point for enjoying golden sunsets and palm trees turning into black silhouettes against the night sky.

Both service and food are impeccable and exquisite, complementing the surrounding natural beauty. Start with an exotic cocktail decked out with fruit slices and a fresh orchid (190฿). Follow it with succulent stir-fried prawns and cashews (220฿).

Surprisingly, the restaurant prepares Western fare as well as it does traditional Thai (and everything in between). The duckling with peaches (580฿) is deep and tangy—a good choice to mix with ocean breezes and breaking waves. As the sun finally fades out of view and the sky and sea merge into one giant mass of darkness, dessert beckons—the giant half-pineapple filled with fresh fruit and ice cream (150฿) is tops.

Although the prices are sky high, so are the views and the quality of the food, more than assuaging the aching pain of your wallet. There is another branch of the restaurant at the other end of the beach with slightly lower prices. Reservations for both can be made through the Ao Phrao Resort. ☎ 01 906 5006. Open daily 7am-1pm. AmEx/MC/V.) ❺

English-Language Resources: Several accommodations, including Naga Bungalows and Sea-Breeze Bungalows at Ao Phai and Samet Ville Resort at Ao Wai, operate small English-language libraries.

Markets: Tasty food stalls surround the Nuan Tip Pier area. 30฿ per plate. Open daily 6am-8pm.

Emergency: ☎ 191. **Tourist Police (Bangkok):** ☎ 1155.

Police: ☎ 651 803. On the paved road between Na Dan and Hat Sai Kaew, by the Health Center. No English spoken. A **24hr. police box** is on the beach at Ao Wong Duan. **Mainland police** at Ban Phe (☎ 038 651 111). **Marine police** in Ban Phe (☎ 038 473 056).

Local Tourist Police: ☎ 038 651 669. On the mainland, a block east of the market at Nuan Tip Pier. English spoken. **Open 24hr.**

Medical Services: Health Center, halfway between Na Dan Pier and the park entry checkpoint. No telephone. Some English spoken. Open M-Sa 8:30am-4:30pm. In emergencies, phone the **hospital** in Rayong (☎ 038 611 104 or 038 614 708). Ko Samet's emergency services are inadequate.

Telephones: Pay phones are near the Visitors Center and the pier but work only for domestic calls. Most establishments offer **international telephone service** run through cellular phones, so service is expensive and faulty. Starts at 100฿ per min.

Internet Access: Access from Samet is like phone service—run on cellular phones and obnoxiously expensive. The **Naga Bungalows Post Office** has the cheapest rates (about 120฿ per 15min.).

Post Office: Naga Bungalows (☎ 353 25 75) operates a licensed makeshift **post office** next door to the hotel. Open M-F 8:10am-5pm, Sa 8:30am-1pm. **Postal code:** 21160.

■ ■ ACCOMMODATIONS AND FOOD

All of Ko Samet's beaches offer some bungalow-type accommodation. In general, **Ao Phai** and **Ao Cho** offer the cheapest accommodations, while **Hat Sai Kaew** and **Ao Phrao** cater to older travelers with fatter wallets. Hat Sai Kaew, Ao Phai, and **Ao Wong Duan** are the most heavily touristed beaches; **Ao Nuan** and **Ao Kiu** the most secluded. Establishments without generators have electricity from 6pm to 6am. Be prepared for major crowds on weekends and holidays; expect prices to jump then, too. **Camping** is available on all beaches, although your best bets are on secluded Ao Kiu, the rocks between Ao Phai and Ao Tup Tim, and the grassy knoll behind the Visitors Center near Hat Sai Kaew. Prices fluctuate between high and low season so call ahead for the most up-to-date figure. The following accommodations and food options are listed by beach.

AO PHRAO. Ko Samet's only western-facing beach is a smooth, white crescent of sand graced by sky-searing sunsets and the island's most luxurious accommodations and delectable fine dining. Well-spaced bungalows line this long stretch of beach punctuated with massage mats, ocean kayaks, and the island's only PADI certification course. With only three resorts, the beach is not crowded, and is perfect for a laid-back, romantic, do-nothing experience. But, if you're looking for a cheap place to stay, lively backpackers, and beach frisbee, you're better off staying on the east coast. Make a right when the road forks just after the last resort; a 25min. hilly walk later, you will arrive at the pearly gates of **Le Vimarn Cottages ❺**, the island's ultra-expensive, nothing-but-luxury, 6500฿ bungalows (discounted by 40% during low season). Next up is **Dome Bungalows ❺**, which offers clean and spacious bungalows at an almost-budget price. (☎038 651 377. Singles 1000฿, with A/C 1200฿; doubles 1200฿/1500฿.) If you can afford it, **Ao Prao Resort ❺**, at the southern end of the beach, mixes luxury with prices only slightly higher than Dome's. (Ao Prao Resorts also operates Le Vimarn Cottages. Make reservations through their Ban Phe office: ☎038 616 881. Singles and doubles start at 1875฿, including speed boat transfers to and from Ban Phe.)

AO NUAN. The best way to get to this beautiful, secluded spot is to ascend from the main road (take the next left after the turn-off for Ao Tup Tim) to a small hill overlooking the rocky beach below and then to descend upon the rustic hillside bungalows of **Nuan Bungalows ❸**. Waves crash onto the rocks that make up a tiny beach. Woven into the single hillside behind it are immaculate wooden huts with a mattress on the floor and a mosquito net hanging from the ceiling—this place is like no other on the island. And people don't seem to even know it exists. Perfect. (Singles 250฿; doubles 400-500฿. No telephone or reservations.)

AO KIU. With glistening white sand finer than anywhere else on the island, good swimming, and the possibility for coral reef snorkeling nearby, secluded Ao Kiu is Ko Samet's best beach. The security and seclusion come at a price, though; Ao Kiu is relatively hard to reach. A taxi from the pier will cost you a hefty 400฿, and from neighboring Ao Wai it's a 20-30min. walk along the back road. Once there, you can set up at the **Ao Kiu Coral Beach ❺**, which rules this remote roost. Bungalows are tiled, screened, and clean. Snorkeling gear rental runs 30฿ per hour. (☎01 218 6231, Ban Phe office ☎038 652 561. Rooms 600-800฿.)

HAT SAI KAEW. A 10min. walk from Na Dan Pier, Hat Sai Kaew caters mostly to package-tour travelers from Europe and Asia and is usually packed with sarong vendors, ferries, and overweight seniors bobbing in the water. Consequently, the beach, though good for swimming, is usually too crowded to enjoy. Budget accommodations are scarce. Your best bet is the rather glum **Ploy Thalay Resort ❹**, halfway up the beach. The exterior is worn, but the tiled rooms are tidy and come with private baths; the pillow seats that they put out are also great to enjoy the evening ocean rolling by. (☎01 451 1387. Doubles 500฿, with A/C and TV 800฿.) Farther south on the beach is the large **White Sands Resort ❹**, on the southern end of the beach, the only other hotel on Hat Sai Kaew approximating "budget." The dimly lit bungalows are clean but spartan. All come with TV and private bath. (☎038 644 000. Rooms 500฿, with A/C 1200฿.)

◢ **AO PHAI.** A 5min. walk from Hat Sai Kaew, Ao Phai is a backpacker haven—a more friendly and welcoming version of Bangkok's Khaosan Rd. Come here for quality, cheap lodging accompanied by a social atmosphere and great screenings of English-language flicks; don't come for romantic seclusion or quiet nights. Thankfully free of the litter and bobbing boats that sometimes plague Hat Sai Kaew and Ao Wong Duan, Ao Phai's waters are good for swimming, in spite of the crowds. Accommodations, while plentiful, fill up quickly. Try your best to arrive before 3 or 4pm. At the northern end is the cheapest of the accommodations, **Naga Bungalows ❷**, an old Ko Samet institution that still remains the most popular spot on the island. The plain bamboo bungalows sit on stilts. The **restaurant ❸** serves fresh bread, sundaes, tofu-veggie options, and more (30-250฿). Table tennis, a "Tosser's Hour" (10pm-midnight), and food available at all hours make Naga a lively nightspot. (☎01 353 2575. Huts 150฿, with fan 250฿, with A/C 700฿.) **Tok's Little Hut ❸**, south of Naga, is just as popular but slightly more upscale with wood-paneled bungalows with fans and baths. (☎038 218 1264. Bungalows 300-350฿, depending on distance from the beach.) The newer, more luxurious **Jep's ❺** features clean, bright rooms and bungalows with added luxuries like extra-large beds. Their **restaurant** is one of the best on the beach. (☎01 853 3121. Bungalows 600-800฿.) The hill-side bungalows at **Ao Phai Hut ❹** are relatively clean wooden huts. All have private baths. (☎01 353 2644. Singles 400฿; doubles 600฿, with A/C 800-1000฿.) **Sea-Breeze Bungalows ❹**, at the southern end of Ao Phai where the road branches off to Ao Phrao, has quiet bungalows with private baths and a book-exchange service (two of yours for one of theirs). (☎038 644 124. Fan bungalows 400฿; A/C rooms and bungalows 650฿.)

◢ **AO TUP TIM.** This small, crescent-shaped beach is an easy 5min. walk along the coast from Ao Phai. Although it's usually less crowded than Ao Phai, it's fairly congested compared to beaches farther south. **Tubtim Resort ❹**, on the southern end of the beach, offers the best deal on accommodations. The comfortable thatch bungalows all have private baths. (☎01 218 7750. Rooms 500฿, with A/C 1200฿.)

◢ **AO CHO.** Small Ao Cho is a quiet break from popular Ao Wong Duan next door, although it's far from being the most secluded or most beautiful beach on the island. Budget accommodations are limited to the bungalows at **Wonderland Resort ❷**. (☎01 438 8409. 150฿, with bath 200฿.)

◢ **AO WONG DUAN.** "Half Moon Bay" is a spacious beach filled with restaurants, bars, and tour operators. Traffic and congestion make it a noisy place to stay, and the constant roaring of jet skis and continuous ferry departures make it a less-than-ideal atmosphere for swimming or sunbathing. To get the most bang for your buck, try the red bungalows of **Samet Cabana ❹**, at the north end of the beach, which has rooms with two small beds and shared baths. (☎01 838 4853. Rooms 400฿, with bath 700฿.) **Sea Horse Bungalows ❸** has decent bungalows for a decent price. (☎01 945 9052. Bungalows with fan 200฿, with A/C and bath 500฿.)

◢ **AO THIAN (CANDLELIGHT BEACH) AND HAT LUNG DUM.** These beaches are separated by a a short stretch of rocks and are easily accessible from both Ao Wai and Ao Wong Duan. With cheap bungalows close to some of the island's best swimming and sunbathing, the Ao Thian area is a good choice for the slow-paced beach-lover. Stretching out across both beaches, **Lung Dum Hut ❸** is both remote and mellow, though quite busy. The well-priced bungalows have private baths. Ask about their special treehouse option (200฿, long weekends 600฿). In a pinch, they may let you borrow or rent a tent. (☎01 452 9472. Singles with toilet 400฿; doubles without toilet 800฿; tent 300฿.)

AO WAI. Clear water and clean, white sand make every second of the 25min. coastal hike from Ao Wong Duan to Ao Wai worth it. You'll have to charter a taxi from the pier (400฿), since few people venture so far south. The ride itself is a real off-road journey and almost makes the high fare worth it. Targeting package tourists, **Samet Ville Resort ❺** dominates the beach with pricey rooms. The **restaurant ❹** serves Thai dishes (40-300฿). Snorkeling gear rental is 100฿ per day. (☎01 949 5394. Restaurant open daily 7:30am-9pm. Rooms with fan 900฿, with A/C 1300฿.)

SIGHTS AND ENTERTAINMENT

With coral reefs and clear waters galore, it's no wonder that Ko Samet is popular for **snorkeling.** At Ao Phrao and Ao Kiu, reef communities are a 5min. swim from shore. Less-disturbed coral live in more remote reaches of the archipelago. Ko Thalu boasts excellent **skin-diving** and a colony of fruit bats. Many establishments offer snorkeling tours of Ko Samet and the surrounding islets. There are now several **scuba diving** operations on the island, so it pays to shop around. **Ao Prao Divers,** based in the lobby of the Ao Prao Resort on Ao Phrao, runs a PADI-certified scuba diving school year-round. The school makes daytrips around Ko Samet and to Ko Thalu from November to May. (☎038 616 883. Two dives 2500฿; 4- to 5-day certification courses 12,000฿; specialty and more extensive dives 10-13,000฿; 3-4hr. introductory courses 2500฿. Open daily 8am-4pm.)

A thirst for sightseeing can be satisfied at the 14m high **sitting Buddha** and the smaller Buddha images at his knees. A gate next to the **golden Buddha** abuts the road between Na Dan Pier and Hat Sai Kaew; follow the path to the statue.

Ko Samet remains free of Ko Phangan's drunken beachside debauchery, but it boasts a lively **nightlife** scene on Ao Phai. The bar at **Naga Bungalows,** which occasionally features a free dancing show, stays open until people go home, which is often as late as sunrise. Nearby **Silver Sands Resort** offers a beachside bar that becomes an impromptu disco when the crowds are large enough. The other beaches tend to quiet down when their restaurants close.

CHANTHABURI ☎039

Chanthaburi may be the "City of the Moon," but its attraction is grounded in the fertile earth. Between May and July, the city's fruit market bulges with mouthwatering produce, and the precious stones from nearby mines are traded in the famous gem district before being distributed around the world. These, in addition to the neighboring national parks, make Chanthaburi a worthwhile visit.

TRANSPORTATION. The **bus station** (☎311 299) on Saritidet Rd. sends buses to: **Aranyaprathet** (8hr.; 15 per day 3am-10pm; 80฿, with A/C 180฿); **Bangkok** (4hr., 27 per day, 115-148฿); **Khorat** (6hr.; every hr. 6am-10pm; 116฿, with A/C 209฿); **Mae Sot** via **Bangkok** (9am, 420฿); **Rayong** (2hr.; every 30min. 4:20am-6pm; 45฿, with A/C 55฿); **Trat** (1½hr., every hr. 6am-11:30pm, 30฿). **Taxis** go anywhere in town for 30฿.

ORIENTATION AND PRACTICAL INFORMATION. To get downtown from the bus station, head left onto **Saritidet Rd.** Saritidet Rd. ends at **Benchamarachuthis Rd.,** at the Kasemsarn 1 Hotel. The alley to the left of the hotel leads to **Sukhaphibal Rd.,** which runs parallel to Benchamarachuthis Rd. along the river where there are a few hotels. Heading right at the Kasemsarn 1 Hotel brings you to the commercial heart of town. Branching off Kasemsarn 1 to the right on **Si Rong Muan Rd.** leads to the **market.** The **gem district** is one block past Si Rong Muan Rd. on Kasemsarn 1; it is to the right down **Kwang Rd.** and left on **Si Chan Rd.** Si Chan Rd. eventually doubles back on itself.

FRESH AND FRUITY

Fruit doesn't get much better than in East Coast Thailand, particularly in Chanthaburi; fish doesn't either, for that matter. The combination of all fresh ingredients make every dish irresistible.

Some delicacies to indulge in:

Kao niow ma-muang: sweet and salty sticky rice cooked in a basket with mangos, jasmine, and bai dteuy leaves.

Stuffed jackfruit: the massive and pointy fruit is mashed, mixed with papaya, coconut, and honey.

Tom yum kung: hot and sour shrimp soup, this lemon grass, chili, and seafood combo is spicy and seems too hot for the weather, but is delicious.

Double-baked jackfruit biscuits: the recipe for these dunking breads is classically Thai—it originated in Italy, but was adapted to the Thai cuisine with local ingredients. It should be dipped in coffee or tea to bring out the almond flavor.

Thailand is known for its fish-eating tradition, so any seafood you have, either in East Coast Thailand or the rest of the nation, will almost undoubtedly be good. Thailand's geography—on the ocean, with inland freshwater lakes—translates into a wide range of menu options.

Bangkok Bank, on Benchamarachuthis Rd. next to the post office, has a **24hr. ATM** (Cirrus/MC/V). (☎311 495. Open daily M-F 8:30am-3:30pm.) The **24hr. police booth** is at the bus station (**emergency:** ☎191; **Bangkok tourist police:** ☎1155). The **hospital** is a short 20m walk to the left of the bus station on Saritidet Rd. (English spoken. Credit cards accepted. **Open 24hr.**) The **Chanthaburi Telecommunication Center** is next to the GPO on Thung Dondang Rd. near the Eastern Hotel, a 3km walk or a 30฿ taxi ride from town. (☎325 916. Open daily 7am-11pm.) **Internet access** is available all over, especially on **Tesaban 2 Rd.,** which intersects Saritidet Rd. at a traffic light halfway between the bus station and Kasemsarn 1 Hotel. Another option is the speedy 56k connection at **The Computer,** on Saritidet Rd., 40m past the bus station toward town. (☎301 140. 20฿ per hr. Open daily 8am-9pm.) The **Chantani Post Office,** more convenient than the large Chanthaburi GPO, is on Benchamarachuthis Rd. across from the Kasermsarn 1 Hotel. (☎311 013. Open M-F 8:30am-4:30pm, Sa-Su 9am-noon.) **Postal code:** 22000.

ACCOMMODATIONS AND FOOD. Accommodations of any sort are scarce in tourist-free Chanthaburi. The landmark **Kasemsarn 1 Hotel ❸,** 98 Benchamarachuthis Rd., at the intersection with Saritidet Rd., is clean and has large, comfortable rooms with desks and private baths. However, the luxury comes with traffic clamor and an impersonal atmosphere. (☎311 100. Rooms 200฿, with A/C 400฿.) The cheap and friendly **Chantra Hotel ❶,** 248 Sukhaphibal Rd., is quieter. Head down Soi Ratmaitri to the left of the Kasemsarn 1 Hotel. (☎312 310. Doubles 120฿, with bath 150฿.)

Take your grumbling stomach to Chanthaburi's immense **market ❶,** centered on the low-lying fountain one block west of Benchamarachuthis Rd. down Si Rong Muang Rd. After sundown, hordes of food vendors dole out curries and noodle dishes. By day, feast in one of the inexpensive surrounding restaurants. For a classier dining experience, head to the **seafood restaurant ❷** around the corner from the Chantra Hotel on the river. The views are almost as impressive as the extensive menu. (Dishes generally 60฿. Open daily 10am-midnight.) **Dream Restaurant ❷,** at 22/1 Saritidet Rd, is oddly shaped—one side is indoors and air-conditioned while the other side is an outdoor garden behind the Shell gas station. Be sure to try the Thai salads (50-80฿), fried rice or noodles (35-45฿), or their specialty: milky crab spring rolls (75฿), which are satisfyingly bready and creamy.

◙ SIGHTS. Chanthaburi's more spectacular sights are outside the city limits, but a few treasures within the town keep travelers entertained for a day or two. On weekends, shoppers head to **Si Chan Rd.,** the heart of Chanthaburi's **gem district.** Some 50-60% of the world's rubies and sapphires pass through Chanthaburi, most through this very street, on their way from Cambodia, Laos, and even Africa. The 19th-century **Cathedral of the Immaculate Conception,** across the footbridge near the southern end of Sukhaphibal Rd., was built without an architect by French soldiers, who occupied Chanthaburi from 1893 to 1905. Unfortunately, the doors to the magnificent cathedral are closed. On the southwest side of town, **Taksin Park** occupies many well-pruned acres. Chanthaburians come here to relax for an evening or admire the sculpture of the Burmese-bashing King Taksin in the middle of the park. (Open daily 5am-9pm.)

▨ NIGHTLIFE. Chanthaburi boasts a surprisingly dynamic nightlife scene. The enormous **Diamond Pub,** on the southwestern side of town, is its epicenter. Live bands belt out Thai pop while a beautiful young crowd schmoozes and looks on. It rocks all week, but it's packed Fridaysolm and Saturdays. Bottles of soda go for 30฿, and Singhas are 80฿. Grab a taxi from the city center for 30฿. (Open daily 8pm to anytime between 11pm and 2:30am.)

▣ DAYTRIPS FROM CHANTHABURI

KHAO KHITCHAKUT NATIONAL PARK

Songthaew depart from the corner of Prachaniyon Rd. and Benchamarachuthis Rd., opposite Bangkok Bank, south of the post office. The songthaew (20฿) will drop you off at the 1.5km access road marked by the number 2511 and a white fleur-de-lis. The 24hr. park headquarters (☎ 452 074) is beyond the entrance booth. Open daily 6am-6pm. 200฿.

Thirty kilometers north of town on Hwy. 3249 in Khao Khitchakut National Park, the **Chanthaburi River** churns down the 13 tiers of **Nam Tok Krathing** (Krathing Falls), the park's most popular attraction. A steep, rocky trail leads up from a Buddha at the mountain's base to the highest fall. Once you've bathed in cascades beneath enormous vines and golden butterflies, you'll understand why 2000 Thai tourists flock to the falls every weekend. Falls #7-13 are great for swimming; the butterflies swarm around #13. The climb is exhilarating and treacherous; come prepared with a swimsuit, good shoes, and lots of water.

A small **canteen ❶** stocks a few basic items and prepares simple rice dishes. (20-25฿. Open daily 6am-6pm.) **Food stalls ❶** set up on weekends and holidays. The **Visitors Center** has information in English. **Camp ❶** on your own (free), or rent a two-person **tent** (80฿). Lodging options are limited to **bungalows ❸** for five (200฿), eight (600฿), 12 (1000฿), or 14 people (1200฿). They're usually empty on weekdays, but for weekend stays, call the ranger station at least one week in advance.

NAM TOK PHLIU NATIONAL PARK

From Chanthaburi, yellow songthaew (30min., 30฿) leave from the north side of the market's roundabout and stop at the park gate. When leaving, take a taxi to the highway intersection (100-160฿) and wait for a passing songthaew. Open daily 6am-6pm. 200฿.

Welcoming over 80,000 visitors a year, Nam Tok Phliu is one of Chanthaburi's best-known parks, although it's hardly the most spectacular. A trail cuts through

FROM THE ROAD

DEAR ABBYTTHAYA

From ramen noodle soups to beans on bread and Bay Bell cheese rounds, learning to eat cheap on the road is a rite of passage for the backpacker. Throughout my own travels, I've consumed peanut butter and Chex mix and linguini with Heinz ketsup. When it comes to dining abroad, culinary sophistication is foregone in favor of museum admission and beer.

Travelers to Thailand are amazed by the scrumptious goodies that are as cheap as super-sizing your value meal back home. Add Thai hospitality, and you know why no one leaves.

Thais are adept at localizing foreign cuisines and finding substitutions for exotic ingredients. Unlike the stronger-spiced curries common to India, Thai curries emphasize intensity of the burn as opposed to duration. If you don't think your stomach can handle spicy food, simply smile at your waiter and politely say, *"Chan ahn pet mai dai."*

Due to the pervading influence of Theravada Buddhism, Thais shun large chunks of meat—animal cuts are usually finely shredded, laced with herbs and spices to subtly flavor a curry or soup. Instead, Thai cuisine tends to focus on the presentation of vegetables.

As a general rule, diners should order three dishes (in addition to their individual plates of steamed rice) and choose whatever they desire from the shared dishes to add to their own rice. Since grains are the cheapest part of the meal, a humble dinner guest will always eat a scoop of rice with every bite of the main dish. Be careful not to leave any rice on the table, as it is commonly believed that the grains will

the park linking the entrance to the park's namesake waterfalls, the **Phliu Falls,** where Thai schoolchildren gather to swim and catch fish in the nearby ponds. A 1km nature trail circles the falls and offers scenic views. The other falls, **Nam Tok Makok, Nam Tok Klong Nalai,** and **Nam Tok Nong,** offer more seclusion. The rest of the park's 184 sq. km of rainforest are bereft of trails. The **Park Headquarters** and **Visitors Center,** on the road leading to the Phliu Falls, has maps in English with directions to the falls as well as information on renting a **bungalow ❺** (800฿).

WAT KHAO SUKIM

Take a taxi (400฿ round-trip), or try to catch a songthaew for Na Ya-am at Chanthaburi's market, get off at Sathorn, and catch a songthaew to the temple. Songthaew rarely make the trip to the temple, so a taxi may be your only hope. Open daily 6:30am-5pm.

On a mountainside 20km outside Chanthaburi, Wat Khao Sukim is the pride of local Buddhists. Built as a center for meditation, the temple has drawn much attention from Thai and Chinese Buddhists, who have donated Buddhist statues and artwork to the temple. Though the temple is not spectacular, the display halls, crammed with everything from peach trees made of colored glass to furniture inlaid with mother-of-pearl, are overwhelming. Amid all these riches, life-like wax replicas of monks sit in meditation. The roof offers panoramas of mountains, a waterfall, and fruit groves, providing a glimpse of Chanthaburi's natural beauty for those who don't have time for its parks.

TRAT ☎ 039

Trat is the least developed of the eastern provinces. Most of its population subsists on fishing or growing fruit. Travelers who treat this frontier town as a transit point en route to Ko Chang and the surrounding islands are now joined by travelers en route to Cambodia via Hat Lek. For the adventurous backpacker, oft-overlooked Trat Province teems with jungles, waterfalls, temples, and beaches, few of them visited by *farang.* Its guest houses, markets, and plentiful transportation make Trat a worthy base.

▛ TRANSPORTATION

Trat is a frontier town. **A/C buses** from anywhere north or west of town stop on the east side of **Sukhumvit Rd.,** next to the cinema. Private bus companies offer A/C bus service to **Bangkok** (5hr., 157-221฿); their offices cluster around the market. **Buses** depart every 30min. 5:15am-2:30pm and once an hour until 5:30pm for **Chanthaburi** (1½hr., 22฿), where you can transfer to all other major destinations. Near the pharmacy and market, **minibuses** depart when full for **Chanthaburi** (1hr., 6am-6pm, 60฿). Blue **songthaew** heading to **Laem Ngop** (6am-6pm, 20฿) pull up one block south of the market, next to the pharmacy on Sukhumvit Rd. and leave when full. Blue **songthaew** going to **Klong Yai** (1½hr., every hr. 6am-6pm, 35฿) wait behind the market on Tat Mai Rd. Minibuses to **Klong Yai** (1½hr., every hr. 6am-6pm, 80฿) wait on Sukhumvit Rd. two blocks north of the market.

■🗗 ORIENTATION & PRACTICAL INFO

Trat is easy to navigate. The main road is **Sukhumvit Rd.**, which runs north toward Bangkok and south toward Laem Ngop. Sukhumvit Rd. has two traffic signals, at both its northern and southern ends. Most services, lie between or near them. At the northern traffic light, Sukhumvit intersects **Wiwattana Rd.**

Currency Exchange: Krung Thai Bank, 59 Sukhumvit Rd. (☎520 542), opposite the pharmacy and next to the Trat Department Store. Exchanges traveler's checks (13฿ per check). **24hr. ATM.** Open M-F 8:30am-3:30pm.

Emergency: ☎191. **Tourist Police (Bangkok):** ☎1155.

Police: ☎511 239. From Sukhumvit's northern traffic light, walk east on Wiwattana Rd.

Immigration Office: There is no immigration office in Trat. The nearest immigration office (☎597 261) is in Laem Ngop (see p. 177) grants **visa extensions** (10-30 days, 500฿).

Pharmacy: ☎512 312. South of the market, next to the *songthaew* bound for Laem Ngop. Open daily 7am-10pm.

Medical Services: Trat Hospital (☎511 040, 520 216, or 520 217, ext. 605) is on Sukhumvit Rd., just past the traffic light at the northern end.

Telephones: Telecommunications Office, 315 Chaimongkol Rd. (☎/fax 512 167). Marked by its radio tower and home to **international phones**/fax. Open daily 7am-10pm. There are also **international phones** in the lobby of the Trat Inn Hotel. Open daily 8am-midnight.

Internet Access: There is a small Internet cafe (☎532 119) in the lobby of the Trat Inn Hotel, at the corner of Sukhumvit Rd., at the southern traffic light. 20฿ for the first 10min., 1฿ per additional min.

Post Office: ☎511 175. On Wiwatanna Rd., east of the intersection with Sukhumvit Rd. *Poste Restante.* Open M-F 8:30am-4:30pm, Sa-Su 9am-noon. **Postal code:** 23000.

reappear as pockmarks on the face of your future spouse.

Thai food is customarily eaten with a fork and spoon. Since the spoon is traditionally the only utensil to go in your mouth, placing a fork in your mouth is considered highly offensive. Unlike in Western culture, it is a sign of disrespect to consume the entire contents of your plate, as this reflects your inability to be satiated by a meal and your host's failure to fully provide for his guests.

If there is one thing to know about Thai culinary etiquette, it is to never use your left hand to handle food at the table. Thais have a system of personal hygiene that involves a bucket, a spigot, and the left hand. Thus, Thais also maintain a strict division of right and left, and will always reach for dishes and eat with their right hand. Children are often instructed by their parents to sit on their left hand during mealtime.

Wherever you are when your Singha-haze kicks in, indulge in the salty goodness of fried insects. Cocoons and mealworms will pop and sizzle in your mouth and ooze with oily flavor. Although many travelers have likened fried scorpions to "warm, jelly-filled toenails," surely the experience is worthwhile, even if only to immortalize the moment with a photo.

So venture beyond the phat thai, banana pancakes, and melon Fanta. Just don't forget to pass that bowl of *tom yum kung* with your right hand. *Aroy mak.*

Matthew Firestone performs anthropological research and has lived in a Buddhist monastery in Thailand.

ACCOMMODATIONS

There are plenty of guest houses in Trat, and almost all of them are on **Thana Charoen Rd.** and **Lak Muang Rd.** To get there from the buses and *songthaew* stops, walk about 5min. south on Sukhumvit Rd., and take a left at the traffic light. This is Lak Muang Rd.; Thana Charoen Rd. is the next left after that.

Pop Guest House, 1/1-1/2 Thana Charoen Rd. (☎512 392). Bamboo bungalows are simple, clean, and bright. Attractive garden and friendly staff are added bonuses. Breakfast 25-50฿. Singles 60-80฿; doubles 100฿. ❶

Windy Guest House, 64 Thana Charoen Rd. (☎523 644). 25m from the Saritidet Rd. intersection, take a right down a small soi. Rickety, traditional, wooden Thai river house. Rooms are decent and well kept. Perks include plenty of travel info and a rowboat they let guests take on the river for free. Singles 80฿; doubles 100฿. ❶

Residang Guest House (☎530 103), near the end of Thana Charoen Rd. A real bargain, featuring enormous rooms with large windows that afford views of the river area, particularly on the third floor. Some rooms have balconies; all have shared baths. Singles 80฿; doubles 120฿. ❶

Foremost Guest House, 49 Thana Charoen Rd. (☎511 923). After a face-lift scheduled to be completed at the end of 2002, rooms should be nice and new. Singles 70฿; doubles 100฿; family rooms 200฿. ❶

N. P. Guest House (☎512 270), down the soi opposite Windy Guest House. Decent rooms. Owner speaks English well and has loads of info on traveling to Cambodia. He can also arrange tours and border crossings. Internet access 40฿ per hr. Singles 70฿; doubles 100฿; triples 150฿. ❶

FOOD AND NIGHTLIFE

There's no excuse for not eating in the **market ❶**. During the day, foodstalls set up on the first floor of the municipal market (elaborate soups with meat or fish 10-20฿). The **night market ❶** moves to the square two blocks north of the municipal market building behind the A/C bus terminal. (Open daily 7pm-midnight.) But if you must eat elsewhere, Trat has numerous cafes. A good choice is the **Sea House ❷**, at the southern traffic light on Sukhumvit Rd., which serves up a variety of drinks (large Singha 80฿) and Thai rice dishes (30-60฿) to the beat of hip Thai pop music. (Open daily 8am-1am.)

For a bit of nightlife, head to **Jean's Cafe,** next door to the Foremost Guest House. Jean's serves light food and all sorts of drinks. It also sports a great collection of music. (Small Singha 40฿; ginger tea 15฿. Open daily 7am-midnight.)

SIGHTS

Most attractions lie in the province, not in the town. The travel-weary can relax with a **traditional Thai massage;** look for the sign outside a house on Thana Charoen Rd., just a few meters from the intersection with Sukhumvit Rd. (2hr. massage 200฿. Open daily 8am-8pm.) This may be just enough to loosen your limbs for the 2.3km walk to **Wat Buppharam.** Walking south on Sukhumvit Rd., turn right down the little road before the Trat Department Store and follow it out of town to reach this mildly interesting wat on a little hill. The grounds contain buildings constructed in the traditional Thai wooden house style, including monks' picturesque wooden dwellings built on stilts in a little garden. During the day, you may catch the wat's monk school in session. The walk to the temple is level; another option is to rent a bicycle from Residang Guest House.

DAYTRIP FROM TRAT: LAEM NGOP

A sleepy village with a chaotic pier, Laem Ngop is the place to board ferries to **Ko Chang.** With Trat only a short *songthaew* ride away, there is no reason to dawdle here and certainly no reason to stay the night. The last **songthaew** to **Trat** (½hr., 20฿) leaves after the last boat arrives, usually around 6pm. The only other option is to take a **taxi** (150฿).

For **visa extensions** (10-30 days, 500฿) and official information on visiting **Cambodia,** head for the **immigration office** (☎597 261; open M-F 8:30-noon and 1-4:30pm), on the ground floor of a white building about a 15min. stroll up the road from Laem Ngop to Trat, about 300m beyond Thai Farmers Bank. **Thai Farmers Bank,** 500m from the pier on the Trat-Laem Ngop Rd., exchanges traveler's checks. (☎597 046. 13฿ per check. Open M-F 8:30am-3:30pm.) Laem Ngop's **hospital** (☎597 040), on Trat-Laem Ngop Rd., 2km from Laem Ngop toward Trat, sells **malaria** medication (150mg doxycycline pills 2฿), which is recommended for travelers en route to Ko Chang. The **TAT** office, 50m after the bank, has a friendly staff. (☎597 255. Open daily 8:30am-4:30pm.) For information on the national park, head to the **National Park Office.** From the pier, it's a 10min. walk down the first road on the left. (☎538 100. Open 24hr.)

> **BORDER CROSSING: KLONG YAI/SIHANOUKVILLE** To enter Cambodia, you must have a Cambodian visa. These have recently become available at the border on **Hat Lek** for 1000฿, but to be on the safe side, it is best to obtain your visa at the Cambodian embassy in **Bangkok** before leaving for Trat. The whole border-crossing process takes 9-13hr.; depending on the departure time of the boat to **Sihanoukville;** an overnight stay may be necessary. Either way, it pays to get an early start. To get from Trat to **Klong Yai,** take a blue *songthaew* from behind the market (1½hr., every hr. 6am-6pm, 35฿) or a mini-van from 2 blocks north of the market (1½hr., every hr. 6am-6pm, 80-100฿). At Klong Yai, take a taxi to the border town of **Ban Hat Lek** (30min., 20฿ per person). The border closes at 5pm, at which point a line begins to form. At 10pm, they will let the line cross the border to hit the casinos on the other side. Then the border officially closes until 6am the next morning. When you exit Thailand at the border, remember to obtain an exit stamp. After crossing the border, you can hire a taxi that crosses the newly finished bridge to **Ko Kong,** or take a small boat (10min., 100฿), where overnight accommodations can be found. A boat departs daily at 8am (sometimes earlier) for Sihanoukville (3½-4hr., 500-600฿). Stay the night in Sihanoukville or catch a bus to Phnom Penh (3½hr.; 10,000r).

EAST COAST

KO CHANG ☎01

Ko Chang is slowly going the way of its southern cousins. A steady stream of development with loads more on the way promises lots of tourists, piles of garbage, and resort commercialism. But, for the moment, Ko Chang is still a rough and rugged island bursting with rainforests, towering waterfalls, isolated beaches, and unexplored territory on its eastern coast. A new road that outlines the island is making it much easier to access even the most remote patches of sand and secluded fishing communities. During the low season, prices are often slashed by 40%, and the beaches are almost empty. There is frequent ferry service year-round, so any time is perfect for a visit to this easternmost paradise island.

THE VIEW FROM ABOVE

Gateway: Dan Mai Pier.
Beaches: Hat Kai Bae, Hat Khlong Phrao, Hat Sai Kaow.
Something fun: Snorkeling and chartering boats to the Ko Chang National Marine Park.

▣ TRANSPORTATION

To reach Ko Chang, take a bus to **Trat,** then a *songthaew* (every 30min. or when full 6am-6pm, 20฿) from the front of the municipal market on Sukhumvit Rd. to **Laem Ngop Pier,** and a ferry to the island. Basic one-way tourist tickets cost 50฿. The ferry lumbers to **Dan Mai Pier** on Ko Chang's northern end (1hr). From Ko Chang, pickup truck **taxis** run frequently to the west coast beaches: **Hat Khlong Phrao** (30min., 40฿); **Hat Kai Bae** (50min., 40฿); **Hat Sai Kaow** (15min., 30฿); and **Lonely Beach** (1¼hr., 70฿).

Ferries: Ferries between **Dan Mai Pier** and **Laem Ngop Pier** run frequently (every hr. 7am-6pm, 50฿). This is the most convenient way to get to the island, as minibuses and *songthaew* stop at this pier. However, two more piers, **Center Point** (10min. away by taxi) and **Ko Chang Ferry Pier** (20min. away by car) have faster service to the island (40min. from Center Point; 20min. from Ko Chang Ferry Pier). All ferries can accommodate vehicle crossings. To leave the island outside scheduled departure times, charter a **boat** from a fisherman (1000-1500฿). **Speedboats** to the mainland cost 1500฿ from Ban Rung Rang Bungalows (☎329 04 64) on Hat Sai Khaow, or 3500฿ from Sea View Resort (☎218 50 55) on Hat Kai Bae.

Local Transportation: Songthaew rule. A ride between beaches is 30-70฿. In theory, *songthaew* leave from Hat Kai Bae 1hr. before ferry departure, hit the other two beaches on the way up, and reach the pier just in time for departure.

Rentals: Resorts and petrol stalls across the road from Hat Sai Khaow rent **motorbikes,** ideal for exploring the east coast. 60฿ per hr.; 400-500฿ per day. Most guest houses rent as well. Contracts and insurance are uncommon.

Ko Chang

✦ ▨ ORIENTATION AND PRACTICAL INFORMATION

Ko Chang's interior is a trackless rainforest. There is a rudimentary road around part of the perimeter. From **Na Dan Pier** at the island's northeast end, the road goes south to the east coast, passes some waterfall trails, and ends at the village of **Sa**

Lak Pet. A right turn at the pier leads down past the west coast's three beaches: **Hat Sai Kaow, Hat Khlong Phrao, Hat Kai Bae,** and **Lonely Beach.**

Tourist Office: Ko Chang National Park Headquarters (☎09 251 9244) in Than Mayom, at the midpoint of the east coast, 20km from Hat Sai Khaow. Open daily 8:30am-4:30pm. There is also a national park office in Laem Ngop.

Currency Exchange: Most bungalow operations on Hat Sai Khaow, as well as Thor's Palace Restaurant, exchange traveler's checks for a 3% commission. **Ban Nuna** (☎01 821 4202), on Hat Sai Khao, doesn't charge a commission, but its rates are worse than on the mainland. Open daily 8am-10pm.

Emergency: ☎191. **Tourist Police (Bangkok):** ☎1155.

Medical Services: Hospitals in Trat handle emergencies. The island's six clinics are in Dan Mai, Khlong Son, Sa Lak Phet, Bang Bao, Jek Bae, and Hat Khlong Phrao. All are **open 24hr.** and have radios but no phones. **Malaria testing** is available at Hat Khlong Phrao and Dan Mai 8:30am-4:30pm. A **hospital** is planned for Dan Mai.

Telephones: Calls can be made at most bungalows on Hat Sai Khaow; at Magic Bungalows, K.P. Bungalows, and Chokdee Bungalows on Hat Khlong Phrao; and at Seaview Resort on Hat Kai Bae. International rates 100-150฿ per min.; 50-100฿ service charge for collect calls (some have a 10-20min. time limit).

Post Offices: Most bungalows mail letters and postcards. **Postal code:** 23000. (Ko Chang doesn't have its own postal code. Use Trat's, and write Ko Chang before it.)

🏠🍴 ACCOMMODATIONS AND FOOD

The northern end of the west coast is spiked with soaring cliffs, which soon level off to Ko Chang's celebrated beaches. Of the coast's three principal beaches, **Hat Sai Khaow (White Sand Beach)** is the closest to the pier and the most developed. More privacy can be had at **Hat Khlong Phrao** and **Hat Kai Bae,** 6km and 10km from Hat Sai Kaow, respectively. Farther south, **Lonely Beach,** of full-moon-party fame and the stuff of backpacker folklore, is the most laid-back and intoxicatingly sunny. The ultimate stretch of sand is a 15min. walk through the jungle from Hat Kai Bae's southernmost cove. During the low season, guest houses slash prices and are willing to negotiate. The following accommodation and food options are listed by beach.

⬛ HAT SAI KHAOW. This white-sand beach has a bad rap. True, the beach is thin and bungalows topple on top of one another, but it is a pleasant brand of commercialism. The far ends of the strip are more sparsely settled. Affordable rooms are at **K.C. Sand Beach Resort ❸,** at the north end. (☎01 833 1010. Bungalows in high season 250-1500฿; in low season 100-150฿.) **Cookie Bungalows ❺** (☎01 861 4227), 300m south, has similar bungalows (700-1500฿, depending on the view). At the southernmost point, **Phlamola Cliff Resort ❻** has bamboo huts overlooking the rocky point south of Hat Sai Khaow. (☎01 863 1305. Huts 700฿ high season, 300-400฿ low season; concrete rooms with A/C in the evening and private bath 1800฿/650฿.) The **Koh Chang Lagoon Resort ❺** is moving upscale, from bamboo bungalows to spacious but oddly colored rooms. All rooms include breakfast. (☎01 863 1530. Standard rooms 1600฿; deluxe rooms 1800฿.) The **White Elephant Restaurant ❷** serves the cheapest beer on the island. Walk 10min. south from Hat Sai Khaow, and it's on the right. (Large Chang 40฿; large Singha 50฿. Open daily 6am-2am.)

⬛ HAT KHLONG PHRAO. Although not the most remote, Hat Khlong Phrao is the most serene and sparsely settled of Ko Chang's three main beaches. Bunga-

NUTCRACKER Late-night muchies and nothing to eat? Let's Go can help. Crack a coconut to get all the essential fats, proteins, and vitamins you need until your next meal. You can use a screwdiver from your swiss army knife, or you can do it the way Thais have for hundreds of years:

Step 1: Get a cleaver or hammer.

Step 2: Use the cleaver to hit the ridge in the coconut until it splits. It will naturally split into two, nearly perfect, round halves.

Step 3: Hit the shell of the coconut lightly to separate the shell from the meat. You can also slip your swiss army knife into the edge between the meat and the shell and tap it until the gap widens and the meat pops out.

Step 4: Eat, be merry.

lows are widely spaced on wide expanses of sand, punctuated by creeks from the interior and rock outcroppings. Each establishment has its own entrance, and only a few connect to each other by beach walks. **K.P. Bungalows ❷,** toward the center of the beach, is the favorite. (☎01 863 7262. Rooms with one or two beds and shared baths 150-200฿, with fan 400-800฿; in low season 60-600฿.) **Magic Bungalows ❹** (☎01 861 4829) offers clean rooms with shower and fan (500฿) and with A/C (1200฿), motorbike rentals (60฿ per hr., 400฿ per day), and snorkeling trips to Ko Yauk (3hr., 200฿ per person). **Chokdee Bungalow ❹,** at the south end of the beach, has newly renovated bungalows with tidy toilets. (☎01 910 9152. Huts with shared toilet 500฿, with fan and ocean view 800฿; concrete bungalows with A/C 1500฿/1800฿. 3hr. snorkeling outing to Ko Yuak 150฿.)

◪ HAT KAI BAE. The most remote of the beaches, Hat Kai Bae nonetheless has a fun and lively backpacker environment. It also makes a good jumping-off point for exploring the island's south side. **Kai Bae/Comfortable Bungalows ❸** is south past graceful coconut groves. Bungalows with fans and baths (high season 200฿, low season 150฿) are maintained by Wee Wat, the young and hospitable owner. Motorcycles cost 60฿ for an hour (around 400฿ per day), but feel free to bargain. **Kaibae Hut ❸** is the last stop before more remote southern beaches. (☎01 862 8426. Bungalows with bath and mosquito nets 200฿, with fan 300฿/500฿.) Snorkeling tours to Ko Yuak (150฿) last half a day. The sand-floored **restaurant ❷** serves plenty of fried Thai food, from pineapples to squid, plus a wide array of cashew dishes. (Dishes 60-100฿. Breakfast 40฿. Open daily 7am-10pm.) Swankier **Kai Bae Beach Bungalows ❸** and its popular attached restaurant sprawl north of Kaibae Hut. (☎01 940 9420. Rooms with fan 200฿; with toilet in low season 500฿, high season 1500฿, with A/C in high season 2000฿.) **Siam Bay Resort ❸** is perched on a nice, quiet southern beach, but the grounds are not well kept, and the bungalows aren't much better. (☎01 859 5529. Bungalows with fan and shower 250฿; nicer rooms 400-1000฿. Upper end prices have A/C.) The **O₂ Bar ❷,** 15m south of Chang Park Resort, is cheery and shows Western movies in the evenings. (Breakfast 30-55฿. Most dishes 40-60฿. Open daily 11am-midnight.)

◪ LONELY BEACH. The new road connects this once secluded beach to the rest of the world, but it remains one of the most chilled-out, tailor-made backpacker hideouts in Thailand. Take the winding road past Siam Bay Resort. If you can avoid the careening motorbikes and lumbering trucks, you'll make the 25min. walk to the beach in one piece. The first bungalow on Lonely Beach is the **Treehouse Bungalow ❶,** at the far southern end of the beach—still cheap and very rustic. (Rooms 100-200฿.) Bungalows at the **Nature Beach Resort ❸** are of the simple bamboo variety and are very clean. (☎01 803 8933. Huts 200฿, with toilet 300฿; bigger rooms 400฿.) Across the road and up the hill is the **Jah Bar ❷.** Traditional Thai lounging pillows, hammocks, black lights, and moody music may make this place too chill for some, but for others it's a home away from home. "Orgy-porgy" monthly parties are rollicking good fun. (☎01 916 6129. Small Singha 50฿. Cocktails 100฿. Open daily 2pm-late.)

◪ **THE WEST COAST.** Popular **Mama's Very Famous Snorkel Trips** (☎09 831 1059) is just north of the road's end on Hat Kai Bae. A trip to Ko Yuak costs 150฿; special three-island trips leave at 9am (450฿). Fishing boats can be rented for 500฿ per hour. Ko Chang's snorkeling outings are designed for high-season crowds. During the low season, you'll have to wait for smooth seas and rustle up a group. If you do come to Ko Chang in high season, check out the **Seahorse Dive Shop** (☎01 219 3844), behind Kaibae Hut. The friendly Swiss instructor offers four-day PADI courses (10,500฿). Dives cost 1200-1500฿, including equipment and food. If you still hunger for physical and spiritual self-mastery, American Jerry Boxer has developed a unique and personal art, which he teaches at the **Wind Eagle School of Taiji,** on a platform beyond Kai Bae Beach Bungalows (lessons 60-75฿ per hr.).

◪ **THE EAST COAST.** The picturesque east coast is short on beaches but long on scenic beauty. Colonnades of rubber trees alternate with rambutan orchards, and several waterfalls are accessible by trails that begin along the shore. While the falls themselves are nothing to write home about, the opportunity to catch a glimpse of the island's rugged interior shouldn't be missed. The town of **Dan Mai** hides a path to **Khlong Nonsi Falls,** a 30min. walk inland. **Than Mayom,** 4km to the south, is home to the **National Park Headquarters** (☎039 521 122), with little to offer save a Visitor's Center, free public toilets, and showers. Nearby **Than Mayom Falls,** a favorite of King Rama V, still bears his initials. Clear mountain water gushes over a 7m high rock into a jungle pool (only in rainy season, July-Dec.). Rent a motorbike or take a *songthaew* to the pier and another down the east coast. Trails to the interior rise up just behind Hat Khlong Phrao; ask locals for details. On the west side of the peninsula, jutting out from the southeastern corner of the island, **Hat Sai Yao** awaits those who will settle only for the extremely remote. A **ferry** leaves Laem Ngop at 3pm, stopping at the beach on its way to **Ko Wai** (100฿); it leaves at 8am from Ko Wai to come back (in low season 3 per week). On the other side of the bay, **Sa Lak Phet** is Ko Chang's most lively fishing village, accessible by ferry (departs for Laem Ngop 6am, returns 1pm; 70฿). You can also charter boats to the Ko Chang National Marine Park.

▓ KO CHANG NATIONAL MARINE PARK

Forty-seven other islands besides Ko Chang make up the national park. Thirteen have accommodations, some of which cater only to package tourists; camping is free and legal anywhere. In the high season, many of these islands are easy to get to and have cheap lodgings. In the low season, most close up shop and head elsewhere. As the area becomes increasingly touristed, new operations pop up monthly. Food is available in island guest houses and is overpriced but tasty.

KO MAAK

A ferry leaves Ko Maak from Ao Nid pier at 8am and Laem Ngop at 3pm (in high season daily, in low season on even-numbered days; 2½hr.; 210฿). Boats go to Ko Kham twice in the morning and return around 4pm (15min., 50฿).

The most accessible of the outer islands, Ko Maak offers the same travel amenities as Ko Chang, but with more solitude and better beaches. The island itself is flat, with volcanic formations on the western tip that frame beaches on either side. In the low season, it is technically closed, but most guest houses will offer lodging and food to anyone who shows up. There is a **clinic** and a **police box** on the road heading into the island from the pier. Expensive bottled water, whiskey, and toilet paper are available at the store at the base of the pier. Just north, a casual **post office** can periodically patch through **international phone** calls at high rates. (Open daily 7am-8pm.) The complex also has a **minimart** and **bicycle** and **motorcycle rental.** Guest houses are easily accessible by trucks waiting by the pier. There are no official taxi services, so on arrival, pick a truck—each hotel and guest house usually sends one to meet every boat, free of charge. The west beach is very slender and parts have become very trashy, but it basks in the soft glow of splendid sunsets. The farthest south is **Lazy Days ❶**, with accommodations in a relaxed party atmosphere. (Bungalows and teepees with shared bath 100฿.) Just up the beach, **Aukao Resort ❶** has bungalows (with shared bath 100฿, with fan and bath 250฿).

On the north side, the beach is in a long bay with unobtrusive bungalows and calm, coral-strewn waters. At the west end, **Fantasia ❶** (open Oct.-May) has great (though fan-less) A-frame bungalows tucked back on the hill in the coconut grove, with mosquito nets, floor mattresses, and shared baths (100฿). Beachfront bungalows with private baths, beach chairs, and fans go for 250฿. Fantasia boasts the best collection of recorded music on the east coast. Up the beach, **Koh Mak Resort ❸** offers high-quality, spacious bungalows (300-600฿).

THE OUTER ISLANDS

To get to Ko Rang, charter a boat in Sa Lak Phet or check at Ko Chang bungalows for scuba or snorkeling tours. Sunsai Bungalows on Hat Sai Kaow runs daytrips to the islands of Ko Loi, Ko Ngam, Ko Gia, and Ko Rang during the high season. Trips leave at 8:30am and return at sunset (350฿). In high season, a ferry leaves for Ko Wai daily at 3pm from Laem Ngop, returning from Ko Wai at 8am the following morning (2hr., 120฿). A banana boat leaves year-round from the river in Trat (W, Sa 11am) for Ko Kud, returning the next morning (4½hr., 150฿). This boat often doesn't run in monsoons. In addition, a speedboat island-hopper service has started. Tickets cost 250฿. Check with guest houses on the islands in Trat.

The islands off Ko Chang's southern coast are famous for fishing, coral, rock formations, bird nests, and bat guano. You can scuba dive at **Ko Rang,** home to an abundance of coral, fish, and toothy sharks. **Ko Wai,** a less-remote version of Ko Rang, is surrounded by coral. The fishing is legendary. From Ko Maak, there is a ferry to **Ko Kham,** which features a cheap **guest house** (open Oct.-June) and more sun and solitude. There are also accommodations on far-flung **Ko Kud** (open Nov.-May). **Bungalows ❶** on the islands range from 100฿ to 300฿ and package tours run 2000฿ per night. Ask at guest houses in Trat.

ARANYAPRATHET

Aranyaprathet is the border town for the Cambodia-bound. A savvy traveler will arrive early enough to push straight on through without staying the night. The first train from Bangkok arrives early enough for those heading to Siem Reap to arrive the same day. Wide streets and impersonal hotels make friendly locals all Aranyaprathet has to offer.

▐ ▓ TRANSPORTATION AND PRACTICAL INFORMATION. In the center of town, **Mahadthai-Suwannasorn Rd.** and **Chaoprayabodin Rd.** intersect at a wee purple clock tower. The **railway station** sits nearby at the north end of **Suwannasorn Rd. Trains** arrive from **Bangkok** at 11:40am and 7:05pm; trains depart for Bangkok at

THAILAND IN THE MOVIES
With the explosion of Video CDs (VCDs) across backpacker districts everywhere, *Let's Go* rates four Southeast Asian blockbusters:

The Beach (1999)
Synopsis: One American and two French backpackers stumble out of Khaosan Rd. and into a hidden community of travelers in the Gulf of Thailand.

Pluses: Impressive cinematics, the stunning scenery of Ko Phi Phi, an accurate depiction of the backpacker scene, Virginie Ledoyen taking off her shirt, and Leonardo DiCaprio taking off his shirt.

Minuses: Leonardo DiCaprio taking off his shirt; the script; the plot; and damage to Ko Phi Phi during filming.

Score: ■

Return to Paradise (1997)
Synopsis: An American languishes in a Malaysian prison awaiting execution for trafficking hash unless two fellow travelers "return to paradise" and claim their share of the responsibility.

Pluses: Backpackers learn what happens if they get busted with a brick of hash.

Minuses: Backpackers learn what happens if they get busted with a brick of hash.

Score: ■ ■

Bridge On the River Kwai (1957)
Synopsis: A pre-Obi Wan Kenobi Alec Guinness foregoes tea and crumpets to maintain honor in the Burmese jungle, only to have an American private blow it all to hell.

Pluses: Spectacular jungle trekking scenes, British and Japanese working side-by-side, improving poor relations of the time.

Minuses: British officers, too proud to get their hands dirty, languish for days without food. American private leaves beach paradise in southern India to re-enter the jungle, only to be shot in the back and die in a river.

Score: ■ ■ ■

The Man with the Golden Gun (James Bond) (1974)
Synopsis: Taking time out from dueling the stylish assassin Scaramanga, the British superspy conquers Hong Kong, Bangkok, and the South China Sea (filming occurred near Phuket) before saving the world and winning the affection of his female co-spy.

Pluses: 007 lives out every backpacker's dream: in a time-efficient 109min., Bond steals a longtail boat, throws an elephant-obsessed boy into the river, masters the Bangkok canal system, and snubs an ignorant American tourist—all before escaping to Southern Thailand and getting the girl.

Minuses: Sub-nemesis Knick-Knack, for the senseless waste of vintage champagne as Bond gets the girl.

Score: ■ ■ ■ ■

EAST COAST

6:30am and 1:35pm (48฿). The bus station is on the west side of town: walk three blocks straight out and one block to the right to reach the clock tower. **Buses** run to **Bangkok** (every hr., A/C 144฿) and **Sa Gaeo** (every hr., 6am-6pm, 29฿). **Tuk-tuks** and **sambis** putter to hotels from the bus and train stations (20฿).

At the clock tower, the **general post office** has a **Lenso** phone card machine. (Phone cards 300฿ and 500฿. Open M-F 8:30am-4:30pm). For international calls, head to the **Telecommunications Office,** near the corner of Mahadthai and Raduthid Rd., 500m south of the clock tower. (Open M-F 8:30am-4:30pm.) The **pharmacy** is one block north of the Aran Garden I Hotel. (Open M-Sa 6:30am-7:30pm.)

ACCOMMODATIONS AND FOOD. Aranyaprathet has no guest houses and few accommodations of any sort. Many travelers stay at the **Aran Garden I Hotel ❷**. Walk 500m south from the clock tower to Raduthid Rd. and then 600m east to Chitsuwarn Rd.; it's on the corner. (Bicycles 40฿ per day. Singles 150฿; doubles 200฿.) Down Raduthid Rd. one block, **Aran Garden II ❸** has much nicer, quieter rooms. (Bicycles 10฿ per hr. Singles 230฿; doubles 300฿.) Another option, similar in value to the Aran Garden II but removed from the town's hubbub and equipped with a large pool table, is the **Great Hill Hotel ❸**, 1km north of the train station. (Singles with fan 250฿, with A/C 500฿; doubles 300฿/600฿.) In the low season, many travelers crash for free on the office floor of their Siem Reap-bound tour company, which might even provide breakfast. Restaurants are dismal; it's best to enjoy noodles or rice at a street stall near the Aran Garden Hotels.

SHOPPING. The border **market,** on Weruwan Rd., is colossal but caters mostly to Thais trying to look Western, sporting a dull mix of jeans, sunglasses, dresses, and other faux-Western items. (Open daily 6am-7pm.) Motorcycle rides to the market should cost 25-30฿; tuk-tuks run 40-50฿.

> **BORDER CROSSING: ARANYAPRATHET/POIPET** Travelers must obtain visas at the Cambodian embassy in Bangkok. In Aranyaprathet, touts materialize at the train and bus stations to offer trips to Siem Reap and Angkor Wat (for a trip to the temples at Angkor Wat, see **Sidetrips,** p. 388). They are helpful in navigating the chaotic bridge and boarding a public pick-up for the painful 7-8hr. ride ahead (in cab 350฿, in the back 200฿). Trucks leave from a station 500m on the Cambodian side on the left. Be sure to obtain an exit stamp from Thai immigration (open daily 7:30am-5:30pm) at the bridge. A tuk-tuk from anywhere in town to the bridge costs 60฿.

NORTHEAST THAILAND

THAILAND PRICE ICONS					
SYMBOL:	❶	❷	❸	❹	❺
ACCOMM.	Under US$3 Under 120฿	US$3-4.50 120-180฿	US$4.50-9 180-360฿	US$9-14 360-560฿	Over US$14 Over 560฿
FOOD	Under US$0.75 Under 30฿	US$0.75-2 30-80฿	US$2-4 80-160฿	US$4-6 160-240฿	Over US$6 Over 240฿

This plateau encompasses about one-third of Thailand's total landmass, and supports an equal proportion of the nation's population. Thais call it "Isaan," meaning prosperity and vastness. Ironically, largely agrarian Isaan is one of the country's poorest regions. The United States set up air force bases in Isaan's four largest cities during the Vietnam War, and these cities remain centers of transportation, commerce, and education. So close is the relationship with the Lao and Khmer across the Mekong River that the Isaan dialect carries striking similarities to Lao, and in some areas, Thai remains spoken as a second language. For skeptics who hold that any statement containing both "Thailand" and "off the beaten path" is oxymoronic, Isaan emerges as a buried treasure.

KHAO YAI NATIONAL PARK

For travelers hoping to rescue their lungs from the fumes of Bangkok, Khao Yai National Park offers salvation. Khao Yai was consecrated as Thailand's first (and perhaps best) national park in 1962. Only 160km from Bangkok, this dense jungle teems with macaques, gibbons, exotic birds, and insects. Wild elephants, tigers and bears also make their home in Khao Yai, though it's more likely you'll see monkeys climbing the watch towers than tigers slinking between the trees. While marveling at limber monkeys, beware of the even more limber leeches, especially after rainfall. The humbling 2100 square kilometers of tropical rainforest is flanked by a few luxurious but aging resorts. During weekdays and in the low season, they offer discounts as delightful as the wildlife. Khao Yai can only be reached via Pak Chong, an urban strip featuring little more than basic lodging and supplies.

PAK CHONG   ☎044

Approximately 1km long, Pak Chong extends on either side of the **Mitraphap (Friendship) Highway;** all its side streets are designated **Tesaban Rd.** followed by a number. The four major landmarks, starting from the side closest to Bangkok and heading toward Khorat, are the stoplight, the 7-Eleven store, the pedestrian overpass, and the Shell gas station.

Giant light-blue **songthaew** leave for **Khao Yai National Park** from the highway in front of the 7-Eleven on Tesaban 19 (every 20min. 6am-3pm, every 30min. 3pm-5pm; 20฿). The **train station** (☎311 534) lies at the end of Tesaban 15 from the overpass; it's the first right after the traffic signals, 400m down the road. Trains go to **Bangkok** via **Ayutthaya** (4½hr., 11 per day, from 36 to 262฿ with food and A/C) and **Khorat** (1hr., 6 per day, from 18฿). At the **first bus station,** beside the **Thai Farmers**

Northeast Thailand

LAOS

VIETNAM

Mekong River

Pak Chom

Vientiane

Beung Kan

Sangkhom

Phon Phisai

Nong Khai

Chiang Khan

Wanon Niwat

Tha Uthen

Thakhek

Loei

Udon Thani

Nakhon Phanom

PHU RUA NATIONAL PARK

Wang Saphung

Ban Chiang

Phang Khon

Si That

Sakhon Nakhon

LAOS

PHU KRADUNG NATIONAL PARK

Phu Kradung

Khon Kaen

That Phanom

Savannakhet

TO PHITSANULOK

NAM NAO NATIONAL PARK

Phu Wiang

Somdet

PHU PHA THEOP NATIONAL PARK

Mukdahan

Nong Rua

Kalasin

Loeng Nok Tha

Chanuman

Phetchabun

Maha Sarakham

Roi Et

Selaphum

Chaiyaphum

Muang Phon

Yasothon

Amnat Charoen

Chatturat

Prathai

Suwanaphum

Chi River

Ubon Ratchathani

Khong Chiam

Dan Khun Thot

Non Thai

Phimai

Muin River

Tha Tum

Si Saket

Phibun

Sikhiu

Buriram

Warin Chamrap

Det Udom

Pakxe

Pak Chong

Pak Thong Chai

Nakhon Ratchasima

Surin

Sikhoraphum

Khukhan

Buntharik

Chok Chai

Nang Rong

Prasa

KHAO YAI NATIONAL PARK

Prakhon Chai

Prasat Hin Phanom Rung Historical Park

Road

River

Railroad

Country Border

CAMBODIA

TO AYUTTHAYA

Preah Vihear

0   50 miles

0   50 kilometers

Bank just after Tesaban 19, you can catch buses en route from Bangkok to **Khorat** (1½ hr., every 20min. 5am-9pm, 46฿ A/C bus) and make connections to northern and northeastern destinations. An **A/C bus station** is between Tesaban 18 and the overpass, with service to **Bangkok** (3hr.; newer orange and red bus 74฿, blue bus 95฿). A **second A/C bus terminal** beneath the overpass has service to **Nakhon Sawan** via **Lopburi** (#121; 6:30, 8:20, 11:20am, 1:20pm) and **Sukhothai** via **Phitsanulok** and **Chang** (#572; 7:10, 9:20, 10:20, 11:20am). A **third A/C bus station** next to the Shell station serves **Roi Et** and **Chayaphurn**.

The **day market** starts near Tesaban 21 and extends one block uphill from the main road. It is stocked with flashlights, camping gear, and other useful items for Khao Yai treks. (Open daily 6am-4:30pm.) A **supermarket,** at the corner of Tesaban 16, sells similar wares. (Open daily 9am-10pm.) The **night market,** between Tesaban 17 and 19, is the place for dinner, with row upon row of food carts and young Thais on motorbikes. **Bank of Ayudhya** (☎311 411), centrally located between Tesaban 18 and the overpass, has an **ATM** (MC/Plus/V; open 24hr.), gives cash advances and cashes traveler's checks. (Open M-F 8:30am-3:30pm.) **Thai Military Bank** is located between Tesaban 19 and 21. (Open M-F 8:30am-4:30pm. 24hr. ATM accepts AmEx/ Cirrus/MC/PLUS/V.) The **post office** (☎311 736), on the corner of Tesaban 25, handles telegrams, faxes, and money and postal orders. (Open M-F 8:30am-4:30pm.) Directly across the strip, the **Communications Authority of Thailand** places **domestic**

and international phone calls. (☎311 787. Collect calls 30฿. Open M-F 8:30am-4:30pm.) Surf yourself silly at the brand-spankin'-new **Internet** between Tesaban 15 and 17. (20฿ per hr. Open daily 9am-11pm.) **Postal code:** 30130.

Guest houses are conveniently located near the bus stations. **Jungle Guest House ❶,** 63 Kongwaksin Rd., Soi 3, Tesaban 16 (☎313 836), is run by an amiable couple who organizes expeditions to the park. From the pedestrian overpass, head to the stoplight at Tesaban 17; take a left and, when the road forks, veer left onto Thanon Kong Vaccine Soi 1. A green and white sign announces the guest house, hiding 50m in on the right. (Dorms with fans, Western toilets, and small breakfast 70฿. Upgrades to unoccupied singles, with personal showers (normally 150฿) have been known to occur. Doubles 200฿, with bath 260฿, may be closed during low season.) **Phuphayon ❹,** 733 Mitraphap Highway (☎313 489), on the left before the Shell station, is clean and convenient, but low on the charm scale. All rooms have A/C and private bath. Deluxe rooms (650฿) are a bit cleaner than standard rooms (480฿). **Khao Yai Garden Lodge ❶,** is 7km out of Pak Chong on the way to the park,

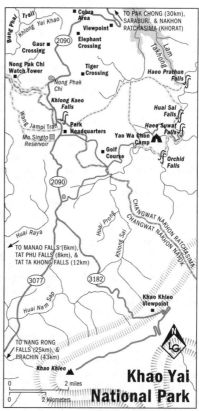

Khao Yai National Park

on the left side. A gorgeous garden weaves through a series of charming houses. A pool and calming waterfall are also on grounds. Quality of rooms varies from decent to spectacular. As always, ask to see the room first. (☎365 167. Singles with shared bath 100฿; doubles with bath 500฿; suite with marble bath 1800฿.)

MOST DANGEROUS COW IN THE EAST

The critically endangered kouprey (*Bos sauveli*), a wild forest-dwelling cow, has been spotted in Northeast Thailand. Males have frayed horns and a huge dewlap, stand 2m at the shoulder, and weigh up to 900kg. There are probably no more than 200 kouprey left in northern Cambodia, with a few spilling into northeastern Thailand, southern Laos, and northern Vietnam. Thanks to human warfare, the unlucky cow has been almost impossible to study. In the late 30s, a captive kouprey calf starved to death in a Paris zoo during German occupation. Since then, a handful of 50s field notes, one grainy 1967 photograph, and a few unverified sightings have comprised the best research in the kouprey's war-torn home turf; the official UN Conservation Plan states that kouprey data is "of a very sketchy nature." Beyond its mystery and rarity, the kouprey could be profitably interbred with domestic cattle to produce disease-resistant, tropics-adapted livestock.

Along the 30km stretch of road between Pak Chong and the park, more luxury resorts, such as **Juldi's ❺,** offer full bungalows on weekdays for 3600฿. Other bungalows in the area are as low as 650฿ per night ❺. It's a great choice for a group.

THE PARK

Park open daily 6am-midnight. 20฿, vehicle admission 50฿. Park Headquarters and Visitor Center open daily 8am-6pm. Trail map 2฿; guide 300-500฿.

Home to one of the last wild elephant herds and some of the world's few remaining wild tigers, the park has over 40km of hiking trails through rainforest and grasslands. Reptiles and insects both creepy and crawly scuttle through the vine-entangled jungle while hornbills, gibbons, and rhesus monkeys screech above in the canopy. The waterfalls alone are worth the trek. **Nong Pak Chi Watch Tower** is the spot to spot striped tigers. Visitors officially need "approval" for tower access, but regulation is rarely enforced. To avoid leeches, don't trek in sandals and steer clear of salty water. Leech-guards (70฿) are available at the souvenir shop near Park Headquarters. After stepping off the *songthaew* at the park entrance, it's another 12km to Park Headquarters and the Visitor Center. Though *Let's Go* does not recommend it, most travelers find that they have to hitchhike to headquarters.

If you are lucky and the phone is working that day, call ☎01 650 0164 to arrange a pickup at the entrance to go to headquarters. When night descends on the forest, there are two accommodation options. **Yao Wa Chon ❶,** 1km from headquarters, has outdoor hammocks. (Hard floor-space 20฿; blanket rental at headquarters 15฿; 12-person lodges 1200฿.) Alternatively, **Orchard Campsite ❶,** 10km from headquarters, offers tent space for 5฿ (tent rental 80฿). To ensure weekend lodging, call ahead to the **Royal Forest Department** in Bangkok (☎02 579 7221).

For a more convenient tour of the park, try **Jungle Adventure**—a 1½-day tour operated by the Jungle Guest House in Pak Chong. The tour, which incorporates Buddhist meditation caves, waterfall swims, elephant-trail treks, and a night safari, moves at a blistering pace and costs 950฿. Trips leave at 3pm and end the next evening. Alternatively, three different sized buses leave the souvenir shop near the cafeteria at 7pm and 8pm for rides around the park. (Cost is split between riders: bus that seats 10, 300฿; seats 20, 450฿; seats 40, 600฿.) A free guide can also be arranged.

NAKHON RATCHASIMA (KHORAT)   ☎044

Known locally as Khorat, the name of the plateau on which it rests, Nakhon Ratchasima straddles the main corridor to all other destinations in Isaan. Although it's one of Thailand's largest cities, the texture of urban life found here is worlds away from the manic snarls of Bangkok. Built during the Ayutthayan period and surrounded by a moat (the remains of which are still visible), Khorat enjoys close proximity to silk-weaving splendor in Pak Thong Chai, the pottery manufacturers of Dan Kwian, and the ruins of Phimai and Phanom Rung.

▐ TRANSPORTATION

Flights: Airport (☎680 086), 28km west of town. Catch a **Buriram** bus (10฿) at **Bus Terminal 2,** or a **shuttle bus** (70฿) with pickups at hotels. **Thai Airways** (☎257 211), at the corner of Suranaree and Buarong Rd. Open M-F 8:30am-4:30pm. Flies to **Bangkok** daily (8:30am, noon, 6pm; 660฿). Airport tax 30฿.

Trains: Nakhon Ratchasima Railway Station (☎242 044), on Mukkhamontri Rd. From the center of town, the station is 500m west on Mukkhamontri Rd., with an old boxcar out front. For a complete list of fares and departures, ask for an English timetable at the ticket booth. To **Bangkok** (5hr.; 11 per day; 3rd-class 58฿, 2nd-class 98฿, 1st-class 173฿).

Buses: Terminal 1 (☎ 262 899, for A/C ☎ 245 443), on Burin Lane. To: **Bangkok** (#21; 4hr., every 20min. 24hr., A/C with toilet 139฿); **Nakhon Sawan** (#572; 6hr.; every hr. 5am-11pm; A/C 95฿, A/C with toilet 113฿); **Pak Thong Chai** (#1303; 1½hr., every 30min. 5:30am-8:30pm, 12฿); and numerous stops within the province. **Terminal 2** (☎ 256 007), on Rte. 2 north of town beyond Takhong River; take a motorcycle or tuk-tuk (40-50฿). To: **Bangkok** (#21; 4hr., every 20min. 24hr., A/C 140฿); **Chiang Mai** (#635; 12hr.; 6 per day; 218฿, A/C 392฿); **Chiang Rai** (#651; 13hr., 4 per day, 464฿); **Nong Khai** (#22; 3½hr., every hr. 9am-3pm, 189฿) via **Khon Kaen** (2hr., 104฿) and **Udon Thani** (3hr., 162฿); **Phimai** (#1305; 1½hr., every 30min. 5am-10pm, 34฿); **Surin** (#274; 4hr., every 30min. 11:30am-4pm, 60฿); **Ubon Ratchathani** (#25; 4½hr., 6 per day 12:30-3pm, 220฿). The clearest way to find your bus is to inquire which platform it departs from. Purchase tickets on the bus.

Local Transportation: Samlor and **tuk-tuks** are omnipresent. From TAT to Thao Surana-ree memorial should cost no more than 60฿. City buses are just as convenient (5am-4pm; 5฿, A/C 7฿). Buses #1, 2, and 3 start on Mukkhamontri Rd. near TAT and all go into the center of town. They split where Mukkhamontri forks into Phoklang Rd. (#1), Suranaree Rd. (#2), and Jomsurangyard Rd. (#3). TAT city map has bus routes. **Songthaew** (5฿) run routes more frequently.

✦ 🛈 ORIENTATION AND PRACTICAL INFORMATION

Khorat is bordered between **Mittraphap Rd.**, which curves from southwest of town to run north of it, and the **Northeastern Railroad Line**, which runs south of town. It is bisected by **Ratchadamnoen Rd.** and **Chumphon Rd.**, two parallel streets separated by a park. In the middle of this divider, marking the center of the city, stands the dramatic **Thao Suranaree memorial**. The western half of Khorat is bounded to the south by **Mukkhamontri Rd.**, which forks into **Suranaree Rd., Phoklang Rd.**, and **Jom-surangyard Rd.** as it heads east toward the town center. These roads intersect Ratchadamnoen Rd. close to the memorial. A rectangular moat, a remnant of the city's old fortifications, circumscribes the city's east half. **Chomphon Rd.**, not to be confused with Chumphon Rd., begins behind Thao Suranaree Memorial and cuts east-west through the center of the old city.

Tourist Offices: TAT, 2102-2104 Mittraphap Rd. (☎ 213 666 or 213 030), on the west-ern edge of town, near the intersection with Mukkhamontri Rd.. Take bus #1, 2, or 3 heading west from the memorial; get off just before Mittraphap Rd. Cross the footbridge and it's beside Sima Thani Hotel. English spoken. Brochures and a useful map (all free). Staff has info on cultural events in Khorat and the status of the Cambodian border. Open daily 8:30am-4:30pm.

Tours: Supatha Tour, 138 Chainarong Rd. (☎ 242 758).

Currency Exchange: Bank of Ayudhya, 168 Chomphon Rd. (☎ 242 388). MC/V cash advances and traveler's check exchange M-F 8:30am-3:30pm. **24hr. ATM** (Cirrus/MC/PLUS/V). Other ATMs line Chomphon Rd.

Markets: Mae Kim Heng Market, between Suranaree and Phoklang Rd. about a block beyond the city gate, bustles 24hr. The **night bazaar** fills 2 blocks of Marat Rd. between Chomphon and Mahatthai Rds. Open daily 6-10pm. Both offer bargains on Pak Thong Chai's renowned silks and Dan Kwian's famous pottery.

Emergency: ☎ 191. **Tourist police (Bangkok):** ☎ 1155.

Local Tourist Police: ☎ 341 777. Beside the Thao Suranaree memorial.

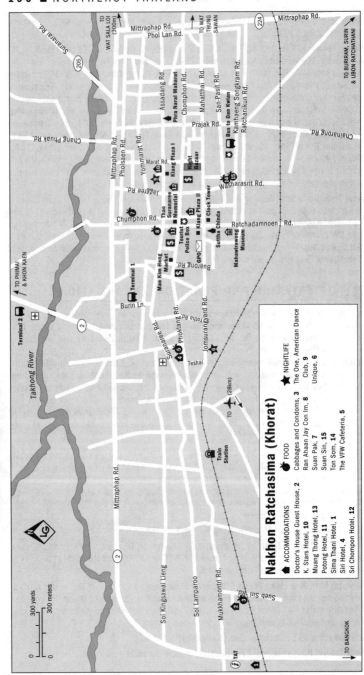

Nakhon Ratchasima (Khorat)

▲ ACCOMMODATIONS
Doctor's House Guest House, **2**
K. Stars Hotel, **10**
Muang Thong Hotel, **13**
Potong Hotel, **11**
Sima Thani Hotel, **1**
Siri Hotel, **4**
Sri Chompon Hotel, **12**

🍴 FOOD
Cabbages and Condoms, **3**
Ran Ahaan Jay Con lim, **8**
Suan Pak, **7**
Suan Sin, **15**
Ton Som, **14**
The VFW Cafeteria, **5**

★ NIGHTLIFE
The One, American Dance
  Club, **9**
Unique, **6**

Pharmacies: Amarin, 122 Chumphon Rd. (☎242 741), behind the memorial to the left. "Rx" on the glass doors. Adequate English. Open daily 8:30am-8:30pm. Also on the lower level of Klang Plaza II, on Jomsurangyard Rd. just off Ratchadamnoen Rd.

Medical Services: St. Mary's Hospital, 307 Mittraphap Rd./Rte. 2 (☎261 261), 50m south of Bus Terminal 2. Private hospital with excellent English-speaking staff. **Khorat Memorial Hospital,** 348 Suranaree Rd. (☎265 777). From the Thao Suranaree memorial, it's past the Sri Pattana Hotel on the right. Look for the new white building proclaiming "KMH." English spoken. Accepts Visa. **Open 24hr.**

Telephones: Communications Authority of Thailand (☎259 707), next to the post office. Overseas calls, fax, and telex. Open daily 10am-8pm.

Internet Access: Internet World (☎267 854), on the south side of Mittraphap Rd. near the corner of Ratchadamnoen Rd., halfway up the footbridge stairwell. 20฿ per hr. Open daily 10am-midnight. **CyNet Cafe,** 154/1 Manat Rd. (☎230 823). Following Chomphon Rd. from the statue's back, take the 2nd left. 40฿ per hr. Espresso 30฿. Open M-F 10am-9pm, Sa-Su 9am-9pm.

Post Office: 48 Jomsurangyard Rd. (☎256 670). Facing the memorial, go right on Ratchadamnoen Rd. until Jomsurangyard Rd. Turn right and pass Klang Plaza II; it's on the right. Open M-F 8:30am-4:30pm, Sa 9am-noon. **Postal code:** 30000.

⚑ ACCOMMODATIONS

Budget accommodations in Khorat are generally dingy and run-down. Cheap and good do not coincide here, so if you are sick of grimy squat toilets and have a few extra baht saved up, this is the place to splurge on nicer accommodations.

K. Stars Hotel, 191 Assadang Rd. (☎257 057). This centrally located hotel is in the thick of Khorat nightlife. All rooms are clean with A/C, shower, and Western toilets. Carpets are red red red. Singles 450฿; doubles 600฿. ❹

Doctor's Guest House, 75 Sueb Siri Rd. Soi 4 (☎255 846). On the western edge of the city near the TAT Office. The oldest and only real guest house in town. Strict 10pm lockout. Laundry service 5-15฿ per item. Small but clean rooms with fans 180฿. Distant location, but still the best place in its price range. ❸

Sima Thani Hotel (☎213 100), on Mittraphap Rd. Khorat's most luxurious hotel, miles above the rest. With a 1300฿ price tag, one night here could afford a week's stay elsewhere. Traditional Thai dancing, pool, gym, spa, cafe. Enjoy it well while it lasts. Deluxe rooms 1500฿. ❺

Muang Thong Hotel, 46 Chumphon Rd. (☎242 090). Look for the green wooden building. From the exterior it exudes an old world Asian charm. On the interior a real developing world experience awaits—only for the hardcore. Rooms 120฿, with A/C 350฿. ❷

Siri Hotel, 688-690 Phoklang Rd. (☎241 556), 200m down Phoklang Rd. after Mukkhamontri Rd. forks. Decent rooms, but pretty nasty baths. Singles with fan 120-140฿; doubles 180฿, with A/C 280฿; "special room" for two with TV, A/C, and fridge 380฿. ❷

Sri Chompon Hotel, 133 Chomphon Rd. (☎252 829), a short walk down Chompon Rd. from the memorial, on the left opposite the Buddhist paraphernalia shop. Rooms are reminiscent of the *Shawshank Redemption*. Singles with toilet and fan 160฿, with A/C 240฿; doubles 240-350฿. ❷

Potong Hotel, 658 Ratchadanoen Rd. (☎251 962), at the corner of Phoklang Rd. Popular, with a central (albeit raucous) location. Western toilets, but a last resort. Singles with fan 170฿, with TV and A/C 300฿; doubles with fan 220฿. ❷

CABBAGES & CONDOMS
The Story of Thailand's AIDS Fight

THE CONDOM KING. A man with more honorary degrees and awards than fingers and toes, Mechai Viravaidya is Thailand's knight in shining armor. The only thing he may have more of than accolades is causes. In 1974, he founded the Population and Community Development Association (PDA), which initially ran family planning programs in rural areas of Thailand. There are now 16 regional centers and branch offices throughout Thailand. The grassroots initiative Mechai envisioned has taken off. Recently, he's started programs aimed at teenagers, factory workers, and hill tribe villagers. The modern PDA is focused on the community as a whole, tending to every element of the larger picture. Mechai has been a senator, a cabinet member in the Prime Minister's administration, a visiting scholar at Harvard University, and a senior economist for the Southeast Asia region. In 1997, he was given the United Nations Population Award for outstanding contribution to population solutions and questions. He sits on the board of the Narcotics Control Foundation, is a trustee of the International Rice Research Institute, and is the Chairman of the Society for the Prevention of Cruelty to Animals. He is now a symbol for activism and, of course, safe sex.

THE EPIC FIGHT. Thailand's first AIDS case was discovered in 1984. In 1987, using techniques perfected during his family planning campaign of the 1970s, Mechai Viravaidya and his Population and Community Development Association launched an AIDS prevention campaign. By the late 1980s, one-third of Thailand's 200,000-400,000 injecting drug users had been infected with HIV. A thriving sex industry had facilitated the disease's rapid spread through the general population.

At an international AIDS conference in Montreal in 1989, Mechai used his keynote speech to sound the alarm about AIDS in Thailand. He called for a massive public education campaign. For the next two years, while the government dithered, he remained a focal point for anti-AIDS activism. PDA staff awarded t-shirts to the winners of condom-blowing contests. They opened the popular Cabbages & Condoms restaurants all over Thailand with condom-decor and appropriately named dishes. Captain Condom cruised the go-go bars in Patpong, Bangkok's red-light district, urging customers to practice safe sex. Mechai even crowned a queen in the Miss Condom beauty contest.

The epidemic in Thailand reached a crucial turning point in 1991, when Prime Minister Anand Panyarachun made AIDS prevention a national priority at the highest level. The Prime Minister chaired a National AIDS Committee, charging Mechai with waging the public education campaign he had called for in Montreal. The media, government, and non-government organizations (NGOs) promoted 100% condom use in commercial sex. The campaign reduced visits to prostitutes by half, raised condom usage, cut the cases of sexually transmitted diseases dramatically, and achieved significant reductions in HIV transmission.

In 1991, the number of new HIV infections was almost 150,000 annually. In 2000, that number was less than 30,000. With the Prime Minister in charge of AIDS prevention, all government ministries participated in the effort. Public education and the media led Thais to change unsafe behavior. The Ministry of Public Health's epidemiological surveillance system (used to track the progression of a communicable disease) proved a critical tool in generating public awareness and political commitment. Effective pilot projects helped ensure that policy led to the right outcome, and the NGO community played an important role in non-discrimination, respect for human rights, and a broad political dialogue on AIDS. All segments of society were involved: government officials, teachers, monks, prostitutes, and drug addicts.

With one million infected since the start of the pandemic, Thailand is still one of the world's hardest hit countries. Today, over 700,000 Thais live with HIV or AIDS—approximately 2% of Thai men and 1% of Thai women. Each year until at least 2006, over 50,000 Thais will die from AIDS-related causes. Ninety percent of them will be aged 20-44, the most productive sector of the workforce and, more importantly, the majority of parents of young children. Without heroes like the Condom King, however, the tragedy would be far worse.

For over a decade, the United States Armed Forces Research for Medical Science and the Atlanta-based Centers for Disease Control have collaborated with their colleagues in the Armed Forces in Thailand and the Ministry of Public Health, as well as the private sector, to fight HIV/AIDS. Their projects range from vaccine trials to studies of transmission from mother to child. International collaboration has been especially important since the 1997 Asian financial crisis, when Thailand cut its budget for HIV/AIDS by nearly 30%. HIV prevalence among injecting drug users is approaching 50%, demonstrating that the education campaign has yet to take hold in that population. Now, some Buddhist monasteries take in sick and dying AIDS sufferers who have run out of money and have nowhere else to go. The monumental task of prevention and care is far from complete and, unless efforts are sustained and new sources of infection addressed, the striking achievements in controlling the epidemic could be at risk.

Still, Thailand's response to the epidemic is one of the world's few examples of an effective national AIDS prevention program. Mechai Viravaidya's condom crusade has helped save millions of lives, both Thai and foreign. One man can make a difference.

The next international AIDS conference will be held in Bangkok in 2004.

The Population and Community Development Association (www.pda.or.th) is devoted not just to fighting the AIDS epidemic, but to community involvement and activism as well. To learn more, volunteer, make a donation, or attend an event, see **Alternatives to Tourism,** p. 90, for more information. Tom Agnes wrote a biography of Mechai, entitled *From Condoms to Cabbages.*

Ted Osius edited the first editions of Let's Go Greece 1993 *and* Let's Go Israel and Egypt 1983. *He edited and contributed to the Europe and Italy* Let's Go *guides from 1980 to 1984. Since 1989, he has served in the US Department of State as a political and consular officer in Manilla, Philippines; a political and administrative officer at the US embassy to the Vatican; and an executive assistant to then-Permanent Representative to the United Nations Madeline Albright. In 1997, he opened the US Consulate General in Ho Chi Minh City, becoming the first American political officer in Saigon in 23 years. From 1998 to 2001, he served as Senior Advisor on International Affairs to Vice President Al Gore. He is now a Regional Environmental Affairs Officer in Southeast Asia, based in Thailand, for the US embassy. Ted is also the author of* The U.S.-Japan Security Alliance: Why It Matters and How To Strengthen It *(CSIS/Praeger, 2002).*

FOOD

Mouth-watering cuisine is plentiful. The markets are fine places to sample regional specialties, such as *sai klog* (pork sausages; 5฿) and small, taco-shaped, coconut-stuffed pancakes (1฿). An alternative is the food court in the basement of the **Klang Plaza II** shopping center on Jomsurangyard Rd.

Ran Ahaan Jay Con Im, 191/2 Suranaree Rd., offers vegetarian entrees (10-20฿). Open daily 8am-midnight. ❶

Suan Sin, 163 Washarasrit Rd. Heading south on Chumphon Rd. behind Thao Suranaree shrine, take a left onto Mahatthai Rd. and then a right onto Washarasrit Rd. Open-air storefront. Isaan specialties like cow-tail soup, pig's neck noodles, and (drumroll please) bull penis salad. Dishes around 60฿. Open daily 9am-8pm. Next door is **Samram Lap,** which serves similiar food with outdoor seating at similar prices. ❷

Ton Som, 125-129 Washarsarit Rd. (☎252 275). From Chumphon Rd. take a left onto Mahatthai Rd. and a right onto Washarsarit Rd. Comfortable, A/C restaurant serving Thai and Western food, popular with tourists and locals. Spicy shrimp salad with lemongrass 85฿. Thai-topped pizza 110฿. Open daily 11am-11pm. AmEx/MC/V. ❸

Suan Pak (SPK), 154-158 Chumphon Rd., behind the shrine and to the left, past Dok Som. A sweet cafe serving sweet cakes and an extensive menu (13 pages) of Thai, Chinese, and Western food. Entrees 45-120฿. The crowd is Thai—always a good sign. Open daily 4pm-12:30am. ❸

Cabbages & Condoms (C&C Restaurant), 86/1 Sueb Siri Rd., just past Soi 4 and before the train tracks near Khorat Doctor's House. Serving the same food as its Bangkok sibling, though not quite as satisfying. C&C is a nutritious meal away from the lead-laden air of Khorat. Vegetarian options 55-65฿. "Chicken in herb leaf bikinis" 65฿. Open daily 10am-10pm. ❷

The VFW Cafeteria, adjacent to Siri Hotel on Phoklang Rd. A slice of displaced Americana straight from the silver screen, exemplifying the "bar-and-grill" G.I. hangout in every Vietnam War flick. Cheeseburger 30฿. Fries 10฿. Open daily 8am-9:30pm. ❷

SIGHTS

Khorat's handful of sights can be visited in a single afternoon. A good starting point is the **Thao Suranaree memorial.** Constructed in 1934, the memorial is a source of identity and inspiration for generations of Khorat citizens. **Wat Sala Loi** offers a

---

WAY TO GO, MRS. MO! Embodying the spirit of Khorat like no other symbol, the **Thao Suranaree Memorial** in the town center depicts the heroic Khun Ying Mo, wife of Khorat's deputy governor who, in 1826, rallied 300 women to defend the city from Lao invaders. A 19th-century equivalent to Judith of biblical lore, Thao Suranaree persuaded the women to seduce and then murder the Laotian soldiers, thus playing the key role in the defeat of Prince Anuwong of Vientiane. Locals reverently refer to her as "Yah Mo" (Grandmother Mo), wrap the shrine in ribbons, give offerings of bananas and coconuts, and burn incense. When prayers are answered, they sing thanks in the local Khorat dialect or hire young women to dance in her honor on a raised platform adjacent to the memorial marked "Khorat Song." An annual Thao Suranaree Fair (March 23-April 3) draws thousands to the bronze statue over the city moat between Ratchadamnoen and Chumphon Rd. The celebration entails a parade, folk songs and dances, and a beauty contest.

chance to set sail for new spiritual horizons. Look for its sign on Mittraphap Rd., at the old moat's northeast corner. Sala Loi's architecturally acclaimed inner sanctuary is shaped like a Chinese ship, which symbolizes the passage of the devoted to nirvana. Every Thai city has a sacred pillar from which distances are measured. Khorat's is enshrined at **Wat Phra Narai Maharat** on Prajak Rd., between Assadang and Chompon Rd. inside the city moat. This wat contains a sandstone image of the Hindu god Narayana as well as a *shiva linga* (phallus-shaped pillar). The **Mahawirawong Museum,** Khorat's branch of the National Museum, is on Ratchadamnoen Rd., two blocks toward the clock tower from the shrine. Its small collection contains artifacts from the Angkor and Ayutthaya periods. (☎242 958. Open daily 9am-noon and 1-4pm. 10฿.)

🎵 ENTERTAINMENT

The karaoke plague has reached epidemic proportions here. For temporary relief, the **Sima Thani Hotel,** next to TAT, holds outdoor performances of Isaan music and dance. (☎213 100. M-Sa 7-8pm. Free with *à la carte* dinner, about 250฿.) **Muay Thai** (Thai boxing) kicks off sporadically at Khorat's stadium; inquire at TAT. Khorat also has an array of movie theaters and discotheques.

The One, American Dance Club, 191 Assadang Rd. (☎248 944), next to K Stars Hotel. A full house of dance floors, live music, private karaoke rooms, and a cocktail lounge. Set the mood with some slow dancing (8-11pm), then get down to glittering disco (11pm-2am). 220฿ cover gets you 1 free drink. Karaoke rooms 1000฿ per night.

Unique, 1372 Jomsurangyard Rd. (☎258 540), 800m down the road from the post office, a half-block past Yotha Rd. on the left. Neon lights brag "Unique: It's Party Time." With an open-air terrace and a 10m waterfall, would-be dancers are often awe-struck, immobile water-watchers. When the novelty wears off, Unique is a hip dance destination. Cover 200฿, includes 1 drink. Open daily 9pm-2am.

🧭 DAYTRIPS FROM KHORAT

DAN KWIAN VILLAGE

From Khorat, follow Chomphon Rd. behind the Thao Suranaree memorial and turn right on Chainarong Rd. At the south gate, turn left onto Kamhaeng Songkhram Rd., and walk past the vendors. On the right, you should see a small blue-striped bus (#1307; every 30min., 5฿). Indicate destination to the driver. Disembark when the small road forks into three lanes lined with little shops. To return, wait on the left side of the road back to Khorat. When the bus comes, gesticulate wildly; with luck, it will stop (last one at 6pm).

Tiny Dan Kwian Village, 15km southeast of Khorat, has long been famous for its distinctive rust-colored pottery, cut with detailed geometric patterns. The work is beautiful but heavy and fragile.

PAK THONG CHAI

Take bus #1303 from Khorat's Bus Terminal 1 (every 30min. 8am-4pm, 15฿); show the driver the center's name in Thai.

Pak Thong Chai is a traditional silk-producing village 32km south of Khorat. Two factories, **Matchada** (☎441 684) and **Radtree** (☎441 284), can arrange tours through their facilities and allow visitors to observe the silk production cycle, from the raising of silkworms (fed on mulberry leaves) to the threading and weaving of garments. Both factories are open 9am-5pm and charge a reasonable fee for the tour. Call and arrange ahead of time as these tours are not a regular offering.

PHIMAI

Since the fall of Angkor in 1432, Phimai has been transformed from an important cultural center to an idyllic satellite of Khorat, 60km to the southeast. Roosters provide free wake-up calls at dawn in the shadow of Thailand's largest stone ruins, and the town's peaceful day lethargically unfolds where a great city once bustled. With only three points of attraction, all within walking distance of each other, Phimai is beautiful for its slow-going ease and relaxing vibe.

⊟ ⑦ TRANSPORTATION AND PRACTICAL INFORMATION. Buses to Phimai depart from Khorat's Bus Terminal 2 (#1305; Platform 41, 1½-2hr., every 30min. 5am-10pm, 34฿). They drop passengers at **New Phimai Town bus station,** in a tacky housing development outside of Phimai proper. Be sure to get out earlier at the **Phimai bus station,** at the south end of **Chomsudasapet Rd.** Bus #1305 leaves Phimai for **Khorat** (every 30min. 4am-6pm, 34฿). For those headed north to **Khon Kaen, Nong Khai,** or **Udon Thani,** get off at Talad Khae, 10km away from Phimai, and ask someone where to wait. Those moving onward to **Surin** may bypass Khorat and save considerable time by taking a *songthaew* from the New Phimai bus station to the train station at Hin Dat (30min., 8am, 20฿). From here, connect to a Surin-bound train (2hr., 3rd-class 22฿).

At the north end of **Chomsudasapet Rd.,** the temple is visible. Here, Chomsudasapet meets **Anantajinda Rd.,** which runs along the front of the park. Just around the corner to the left of this intersection is the **Thai Military Bank,** 222 Anantajinda Rd., which exchanges traveler's checks (☎471 334; open M-F 8:30am-3:30pm) and has an **ATM** (Cirrus/MC/V; open daily 6am-10pm). To the right of this intersection, Anantajinda Rd. passes a clock tower, which houses the **police pavilion** and the compact **night market. Tourist police** in Bangkok is always an option (☎1155). To reach the **post and telegraph office,** 123 Srikeaw Rd., go left on Anantajinda Rd. at the gate to the park. **Srikaew Rd.** is the first right; the post office is 150m down on the left. (Open M-F 8:30am-4:30pm, Sa-Su 9-11am.) **Postal code:** 30110.

⑦ ⓒ ACCOMMODATIONS AND FOOD. Phimai boasts two first-rate guest houses and an excellent restaurant, making overnight stays quite rewarding. **Old Phimai Guest House ❶,** 214 Mu 1 Chomsudasapet Rd., 2½ blocks down Chomsudasapet from the bus terminal down a small *soi* to the right (look for the sign), has palatial rooms in an airy wooden house overseen by an English-speaking family. (☎471 918. Dorms 80฿; singles 130฿, with A/C 300-350฿; doubles 160฿.) Right across the alley sits the **S&P New Phimai Guest House ❶,** 213 Mu 1 Chomsudasapet Rd. Their cosmopolitan graffiti and a crotchety iguana keep boredom at bay. (☎287 275. Huge singles 100฿; doubles 140฿.)

Baitely Restaurant ❸, 246/1 Chomsudasapet Rd., is a block before the soi leading to the guest houses. It doubles as an informal tourist info center and distributes free maps of Phimai. The menu features a variety of Thai dishes (30-150฿) but the specialty is *pad mee,* Phimai-style fried noodles (30฿). An English menu is available. (☎471 725. Open daily 7am-midnight.)

◙ SIGHTS. Phimai's main attraction is the stately Khmer ruins smack in the middle of town within the **Prasat Hin Phimai Historical Park.** At its zenith, the Angkor empire covered much of mainland Southeast Asia. Evidence of its power and wealth remain in the hundreds of temples that still dot the region. At one time, a laterite highway linked Phimai, along with nearby Muang Tham and Phanom Rung, with the empire's magnificent capital, Angkor Thom, 225km to the south. This white sandstone temple was built in a style similar to Angkor Wat in the late 11th century, probably during the reign of Suriyavarman I. The encircling walls of red sandstone and laterite were built over the next 150 years. Archaeologists went a bit overboard with their "restoration"—hence the abundance of cement and the incongruous plaster ceiling in the central sanctuary. On the right of the stone causeway with *naga* balustrades is a collection of faded sandstone lintels. Although the temple is dedicated to Buddhism, many of the lintels depict Hindu gods and myths or scenes from the epic *Ramayana*, evidence of the Hindu tradition that preceded the spread of Buddhism. (Open daily 7:30am-6pm. 40฿.)

Phimai National Museum is north of the park, 500m down the road that runs past the eastern perimeter of the temple complex, in a large white building with a red-tiled roof. The museum includes an extensive collection of Khmer and Dvaravati art, as well as interesting anthropological exhibits documenting the social, political, and economic history of the Isaan region. Those who miss the museum's opening hours can freely explore the pond in front and the outdoor displays of numerous lintels depicting Hindu gods. (☎471 167. Open daily 9am-4pm. 40฿.)

For a less cerebral diversion, **Sai Ngam,** the largest banyan tree in Thailand, stands on the banks of the Moon River 2km east of town. It's about a 10min. bike ride or 40฿ motorcycle jaunt from town. Facing the park, head to the right on Anantajinda Rd. past the clock tower: stick to the main road and follow the signs. Walking under Sai Ngam's thick green canopy is like entering a J.R.R. Tolkien-inspired netherworld. Wizened old men will read your palm for a few baht. At the center, a small pagoda houses the spirit of this 360-year-old miracle. Other attractions include a traditional Isaan house built on stilts, a flower garden, and a statue of **Sook Prasat Hin Phimai,** a famous boxer from Phimai.

PHANOM RUNG AND MUANG THAM

The ancient Khmer temples of Phanom Rung and Muang Tham are the tourist magnets of lower Isaan. Visit Muang Tham first, then explore Phanom Rung. While transportation is not too difficult, set out early to avoid getting stranded. From **Khorat** (Bus Terminal 2) or **Surin,** catch bus #274 or #98 and get off at **Ban Ta-Ko** (2hr., 37฿), which is clearly marked as the turn-off for Phanom Rung (16km) and Muang Tham, a farther 8km. If you're just going to Phanom Rung, you can catch a *songthaew* (around 30฿), but the return trip is more difficult to arrange, especially during the low season. Another option is to catch the Buriram-bound bus from **Aranyaprathet** (which starts in Chanthaburi) as early as possible. The bus passes through Ban Don Nang Nae, only 10km from Phanom Rung, before continuing to Ban Ta-Ko. If you're seeing both Phanom Rung and Muang Tham, **motorcycle** or **pickup** drivers will take you to the temples and wait while you tour the grounds (200-300฿). This latter option is recommended during the low season and on weekdays, when transportation is unpredictable. To return to Surin or Khorat, get back to Ban Ta-Ko before 5pm, as buses run less frequently after that.

Alternatively, book a full-day tour (380฿, 4-person minimum) to both temples at the **Old Phimai Guest House** in Phimai. Tours also visit **Prasat Hin Khau Praviharn,** a magnificent temple just across the Cambodian border (625฿, 4-person minimum).

MUANG THAM TEMPLE. Muang Tham, dating from the 10th century, is situated in a low valley 6km from Phanom Rung. Though fresh from an overhaul at the hands of the Thai Fine Arts Department, Muang Tham cannot match the splendor of Phanom Rung. Still, it provides a detailed picture of a Khmer temple in its present incarnation. *(Open daily 7:30am-6pm. 30฿.)*

PRASAT HIN KHAO PHANOM RUNG HISTORICAL PARK. This majestic temple, one of the largest surviving Khmer monuments, was built between the 10th and 13th centuries. Standing atop an extinct volcano 383m above sea level, the temple commands dramatic vistas of the surrounding plain, broken in the southeast by the Dongrek Mountains of Cambodia. Inside the complex, three terraced platforms lead up to the "white elephant hall," a partially reconstructed stone structure on the right. The 160m promenade lined with lotus-bud-shaped pillars leads to the main complex and its stairway. The stairs that follow lead to the main temple; at the top is a second bridge and the main gallery. Once you're through the hallway of the gallery, you'll be standing in daylight on the third bridge, facing a portico of the chamber leading to the main sanctuary. The lintel above this entrance, the **Phrai Narai Lintel,** depicts a Hindu creation myth featuring Lord Narayana, an *avatar* (incarnation) of Vishnu. It was stolen, resurfaced in the Art Institute of Chicago, and was returned in 1988. *(Open daily 6am-6pm. 40฿.)*

GREAT GRAINS

Northeastern Thailand's cuisine is marked by its lush landscape, yielding freshwater fish, fresh produce, and terrific grains. The region also offers taste-bud tantalizing Isaan food, which is a sensory overload in the best way. You'll find more flavorings here than on your mother's spice rack.

Gkaeng ped gkai: Asian eggplants are roasted and smoked over mesquite coals up to a full day before the rest of the dish—coconut milk, chopped chicken, palm sugar, sweet basil flowers, fish sauce, and red curry paste—is prepared and served.

Lahb: Isaan spicy minced meat salad served cool with chopped herbs and lemon juice.

Abiu tart: custard, milk, coconut, and abiu fruit mixed in a tart shell. Black persimmon pulp and whipped cream tops this cool dessert.

Tom yu: a clear soup made with shrimp and other seafoods, mushrooms, lemon grass, and ginger.

Sangkhaya fakthong: one of the most beautifully presented dishes in Thailand, this custard is served inside a pumpkin. Coconut cream custard is also cooked in the pumpkin.

Miang kam: this satisfying snack is a common street food, but it's also served as an appetizer. Zesty lime, ginger, and chilis are combined with shredded coconut, roasted peanuts, pickled garlic, cilantro, and dried shrimp. You scoop this mixture into a spinach leaf and then stuff it in your mouth. Wild pepper leaves can be substitued for spinach, but they're spicier and tougher.

Lychee pudding: with fresh lychees, local brandy, sponge cake, and whipped cream, it's hard to go wrong with this dessert.

Spicy salads are Northeastern specialties, but they are not for the faint of heart. Symptoms include cries of delight, sweat, runny nose, and a party in your mouth. Make sure to frequent the markets in Northeast Thailand—you'll be richly rewarded. If the actual food doesn't entice you, the spiced aromas and vivid colors will delight you.

BURIRAM
☎ 044

One of the most populated cities in Isaan, Buriram is a picture of suburban Thai life where the constant din of motorbike engines and uniformed students overshadow the decaying Khmer-era ruins of the province. It serves as a regional transportation hub for Northeastern Thailand. Surprisingly, Buriram sports an active nightlife of pumping dance clubs and on-the-prowl youth—a perfect ending to a day spent contemplating weathered lintels and darting dragonflies.

⌐ TRANSPORTATION

Trains: Buriram Railway Station (☎ 611 202), across from the clocktowers at the end of Romburi Rd. To: **Bangkok** (7hr., 10 per day, 2nd-class 265฿); **Khorat** (2½ hr.; 10 per day; 3rd-class 74฿, 2nd-class 165 ฿); **Ubon Ratchathani** (3hr.; 7 per day; 3rd-class 40฿, 2nd-class 160฿). Prices vary depending on train and service; call for more up-to-date fares.

Buses: (☎ 615 081). There are two terminals adjacent to each other on Bulamduan Rd. west of town. Only one station serves A/C buses. Ask which platform your bus leaves from and purchase tickets on the bus. To: **Bangkok** (5 per day, call ☎271 0101 or A/C ☎279 4484 for more information); **Khon Kaen** (1 per hr., 4:45am-4:15pm, 57฿); **Khorat** (every 20-40min.; 4:30am-6pm; 40฿, A/C 62฿); **Ubon Ratchathani** (every 30min. 1-5am, 7am, and 4pm, 100฿).

Local Transportation: Tuk-tuks congregate at the bus station and in the center of town around Romburi Rd. (40-60฿ around town). Motorbikes are the most convenient way to get around as they are more common than tuk-tuks (30-40฿ around town). There are no city buses in Buriram. Any transportation is hard to get at night or when it is raining.

◼ ⁊ ORIENTATION AND PRACTICAL INFORMATION

Most of the activity in Buriram hovers near the train station and **Romburi Rd.** The railway station and train tracks bound the city on the northern and western edges. An eye-shaped parcel of land ringed by a manmade canal to the east of Romburi Rd. contains the **post office** and **police station.** Two upscale hotels flank the city on the eastern and western edges off Jira Rd.

Tourist Offices: Much information available at the **TAT** in Khorat. The **Buriram Cultural Center** (☎ 620 195) can offer some assistance, although English is limited. Open daily 8:30am-4:30pm.

Currency Exchange: Thai Farmers Bank (☎611 036) on Romburi Rd. between Thaui and Phitak Rds. Open M-F 8:30am-3:30pm. **24hr. ATM** (Cirrus/MC/PLUS/V).

Markets: A bustling market runs the length of Phitak Rd. between Romburi Rd. and Sunthorn Thep Rd.

Emergency: ☎ 191. **Tourist police (Bangkok):** ☎1155.

Police: Buriram Police Station (☎615 234), on Jira Rd. 50m east of Romburi Rd.

Medical Services: Buriram Hospital (☎615 001), on Na Sathanee Rd. 5min. walk west of the railway station.

Internet Access: RCS Internet, on Thani Rd. 3 blocks west of Romburi Rd. 15฿ per hr.

Post Office: Buriram Post Office (☎611 142) on Lak Maung Rd. Head east on Jira Rd. past the police station, make a left onto Lak Muang Rd.; it's one block up. Open M-F 8:30am-4:30pm, Sa-Su 9am-noon. **Postal Code**: 31000.

⌐ ACCOMMODATIONS

There is a wide quality gap between Buriram's low-end digs and the more posh choices farther out of town. The more convenient—but also more grimy—options cluster around the railway station off Niwas Rd.

Thai Hotel, 38/1 Niwas Rd. (☎611 112), diagonally across from the train station. A few decent rooms close to the action. Singles 180฿, with A/C and hot water 320฿; doubles with A/C 360฿. ❸

Grand Hotel, 137 Niwas Rd. (☎611 089), at the end of Romburi Rd., take a left onto Niwas; it is 50m down on the left. The rooms aren't half bad, but definitely wear sandals into the shower. Singles with fan 210฿; doubles 250฿. ❸

Thepnakorn Hotel, 139 Jira Rd. (☎613 401), about 2km east of town. One of the two posh hotels in Buriram. Cafe and snooker bar on the premises. Singles/doubles 570฿; suites 700฿; VIP room 1320฿. ❺

Vongthong Hotel, 512/1 Jira Rd. (☎612 540), a convenient 5min. walk from the bus terminal. A real old-world charmer, this place is like an alpine lodge only tropical. Standard single/double rooms 540฿. Deluxe rooms are gigantic—like a cadillac, 800฿. ❹

🍴 FOOD

Buriram has an array of good restaurant choices. **Paladmuang Rd.,** between Thani and Niwas Rds., is loaded with open-air restaurants frequented by locals. The day market on **Phitak Rd.** behind the large pond is overflowing with mangostines (a deliciously fragrant fruit, 20฿ per kg) and fatty pork leg over rice (25฿).

Ok, My Milk (☎01 547 9138), on the left hand side of Paladmuang Rd. 70m south of Niwas Rd. A happy place to enjoy happy milk products. Get acquainted with the sweet and condensed. Iced milk drinks 15-20฿; ice cream 25-40฿; thick toasts with flavored jams 7-10฿. Open daily 7am-9pm. ❶

Porn Pen, 30/3 Romburi Rd. (☎611 553), between Thani Rd. and Niwas Rd. Very popular. Rice with Thai curry 35฿; baked river prawns and vermicelli caserole 150฿. Open daily 8am-10pm. ❸

Bamboo Beer Bar, 14/13 Romburi Rd. (☎625 577), on the corner of Romburi and Thani Rd. Soft bamboo furniture offsets the growing wall of beer cans in the back. Popular with the local expat community, this may be the only place in Isaan to flex your English muscles and to reconnect with Khaosan Rd. Western breakfast 85฿. Thai food 25-40฿. Most importantly, large Chang beer 50฿. ❷

🔭 🎭 SIGHTS AND ENTERTAINMENT

The most worthwhile sights are outside of Buriram proper. About 6km outside of town are the **Khao Kradung Park** and the **Kradong Reservoir.** Both are ideal picnic sites in the country, where bird-watching and observing spears of summer grass may occupy your time. However, within Buriram proper lies a raging dance club and nightlife scene living in a large parking lot on **Romburi Rd.** near the train station. **Speed Music Hall,** Romburi Rd., is a zany, two-floored outerspace extravaganza. Get cosmic before a live band and float amongst the glowing stars. (☎614 124. Small Singha or Heineken 70฿. No cover. Open daily 9pm-2am.) Next door is the **Cybork Discoteque,** and surrounded by snooker and other bars.

SURIN   ☎044

For one week each November, hordes of Thai and *farang* flood Surin to watch dancing, bejeweled, soccer-playing pachyderms on parade in the Surin Elephant roundup. The other 51 weeks of the year, Surin remains a rare stop on itineraries, as most travelers press on to the Mekong River. Their loss is your gain; this peaceful town, boasting one of the niftiest night markets around, is a jumping-off point for the many small Khmer ruins and traditional villages dotting the surrounding countryside. Only 50km from the Cambodian border, Surin reflects the province's unique mixture of Lao, Khmer, Thai, and indigenous Suay cultures.

▐ TRANSPORTATION

Trains: Surin Railway Station (☎511 295), beside the elephant statue on Thornsarn Rd. Trains to **Khorat** (3hr., 11-13 per day) and **Ubon Ratchathani** (3hr., 11 per day). Many of these trains continue to **Bangkok**. Prices vary according to the type of train and seat (Bangkok 73-229฿; Khorat or Ubon 32-114฿).

Buses: Surin Bus Terminal (☎511 756), on Chit Bam Rung Rd. From the traffic circle, go 1 block east past Mr. Donut, and then 2 blocks to the left; it's on the right. Buses to: **Bangkok** (10 per day 7:30am-9pm; fan 131฿, A/C 195฿, VIP 225฿); **Chiang Mai** (15hr.; 5 per day 2:45-6:50pm; fan 255฿, A/C 455฿, VIP 525฿); **Khorat** (3½hr.; about every 30min. 4am-6pm; fan 50฿, A/C 80฿); **Pattaya** (9hr.; 8 per day 8:20am-10:15pm; fan 125฿, A/C 230฿); and **Ubon Ratchathani** (4hr.; 9 per day 7:30am-9:30pm; fan 80฿, A/C 107฿).

Local Transportation: Samlor around town 20-25฿; **tuk-tuk** 30-40฿.

▐ ORIENTATION AND PRACTICAL INFORMATION

The provincial capital Surin is 452km from Bangkok and easily reached by bus or train from Bangkok, Khorat, or Ubon Ratchathani. Surin has no English street signs. The main street, **Thornsarn Rd.**, runs north-south. At its north end is the **train station,** which faces an elephant statue. Several blocks down Thornsarn Rd. from the train station is a **traffic circle.** To reach the traffic circle from the bus station, exit to the left, pass the soi with the sign for the Petchkason Hotel, and take the next right. Thornsarn Rd. is the first intersection. One block past the traffic circle on Thornsarn is the intersection with **Krung Sri Nai Rd.**, with **day** and **night markets,** the **post office** (on the right past the traffic circle), **banks,** and a **hotel.**

Tourist Offices: Brochure and map of Surin available at the **TAT** in Khorat. The **Surin City Hall** (☎516 075), on Lakmuang Rd., can also offer tourist info. Open M-F 8:30am-3:30pm. Mr. Pirom at Mr. Pirom's House (see **Accommodations,** below) is an invaluable English-speaking resource.

Currency Exchange: Bangkok Bank, 252 Thornsarn Rd. (☎512 013), just past the traffic circle on the right. **24hr. ATM** (AmEx/MC/PLUS/V). Open M-F 8:30am-3:30pm. Several other banks and ATMs also lie along Thornsarn Rd.

Markets: Day and **night markets** are in the same location along Krung Sri Nai Rd. From the train station walk 1 block past the traffic circle. The permanent market is on the right; the left side of the street comes to life at dusk.

Emergency: ☎191. **Tourist Police (Bangkok):** ☎1155.

Police: Surin Police Station (☎511 007), on Lakmuang Rd.

Pharmacy: Kayang Chelan Pesat, 294 Thornsarn Rd. (☎513 055). Near Krung Sri Nai Rd. Open daily 8:30am-9pm.

Medical Services: Ruam Paet, Tesaban 1 Rd. (☎513 192). In a tall building with a blue and white sign. Facing the train station at the traffic circle, turn right; it's after the 2nd stoplight on the right. English-speaking doctor.

Post Office/Telephones: Surin Post Office (☎511 009), on the corner of Thornsarn and Tesaban 1 Rd. at the traffic circle. **Phone** and **fax** available 7am-10pm. **International** pay phones (one on Thornsarn Rd., 1 block from train station) require phone cards—but phone cards aren't sold in Surin. Open M-F 8:30am-4:30pm, Sa-Su 9am-noon. **Postal code: 32000.**

ACCOMMODATIONS

Except for one superb guest house, accommodations are uninspiring. During the elephant roundup, rates can soar 50% and finding a room is nearly impossible.

Pirom's House, 242 Krung Sri Nai Rd. (☎515 140). From the traffic circle head away from the train station on Tanasan Rd. Make a right onto Krung Sri Nai Rd.; it is 2 blocks down when the road bends a sharp left. The teak wood house is rustic in the best sense. Gates lock at 11pm. Mr. Pirom offers several tours in his stylish green SUV (from 690฿ per day). All rooms have shared baths. Dorms 70฿; singles 100฿; doubles 150฿. ❶

Santhong Hotel (Nid Diew Hotel), 279-281 Thornsarn Rd. (☎512 009). From the train station, it's on the left just after the traffic circle, opposite Bangkok Bank. Singles 150฿, with A/C 320฿; doubles 250-390฿. ❷

New Hotel, 6-8 Thornsarn Rd. (☎511 322), outside the train station beside the mini-mart. It's convenient, but toilets are subpar. Singles 160฿; doubles 280฿; A/C rooms 380-500฿. ❷

FOOD

Surin has some of the best Isaan food around, especially at the market. On opposite sides of Krung Sri Nai Rd., at the intersection of Tesaban 3, the day and night markets stay open 24 hours.

Wai Wan Restaurant, 44-46 Sanitnikhomrat Rd. (☎511 614). From the train station, take the 2nd left onto Sanitnikhomrat Rd.; it's on the right. Yum yum tasty. *Khao nam phrik goong nam sand* (rice topped with shrimp in a red curry coconut milk sauce) 40฿. Open daily 8am-10pm. ❷

Patee Restaurant, 40-42 Thasaban 1 Rd. (☎511 682). From the traffic circle walk west toward the KFC sign; it's on the left behind the liquor store. A raucous hall of a restaurant. Most dishes 80-250฿, large seafood menu 120-180฿. Open daily noon-11pm. ❹

SIGHTS AND ENTERTAINMENT

Surin is a pleasant place to relax and enjoy Isaan life, but there's not much in the way of "official" sights unless you're there for the annual **Elephant Roundup,** which occurs in mid-November (check with the TAT in Khorat or with Mr. Pirom for exact dates). The stars of this two-day festival honoring the national animal are the 200 pachyderms who awe audiences with feats of strength and skill. Highlights include a battle reenactment and a staged "elephant hunt" exhibiting traditional Suay techniques. The finale features a soccer match played by the agile beasts.

For those whose idea of fun involves a good beat and a dance floor, **The Sparks Music Complex** is the place. From the traffic circle, head down Tesaban Rd. toward the Mr. Donut sign. Take a left at Sirirat Rd. (the 2nd stoplight) and proceed 300m—look up high for the red sign, next to the Thong Tarin Hotel. Sparks is packed on weekends when locals gather to get their groove on. (☎514 088. Open daily 9pm-2am. Cover 70฿.)

DAYTRIPS FROM SURIN

Anyone can visit the local **silk-weaving villages,** but the communication barrier, and sometimes wary villagers, make learning the entire silk-making process difficult for the average traveler. Luckily, Mr. Pirom can act as a go-between for travelers and locals (see **Pirom's House,** above); he knows the process and the people well.

His tours go to places like **Ban Ta Klang,** a Suay village featuring elephants that are trained and kept as pets, **Ban Khaosinarin,** a group of traditional silk-weaving villages, and numerous Khmer ruins and temples including **Prasat Srikhoraphum,** which are similar to the ruins of Muang Tham near Phimal.

To visit the villages solo, walk toward the train station on Thornsarn Rd. After the traffic circle, enter the second alley on the left. From here, trucks ferry visitors the 20km or so (approximately every hr. 7-9am). Return early to avoid a wait or an overnight stay in the village.

UBON RATCHATHANI ☎ 045

Ubon Ratchathani (simply "Ubon" to Thais), the trading and communications hub for the northeast corner of Thailand, attracts few travelers except during the Candle Festival in July. The festival features processions of beeswax-covered serpents, saints, and Buddhas—some candles are larger than the monks that carry them. Not far downstream, the Moon River flows into the "emerald triangle" where Laos, Cambodia, and Thailand converge in the lush jungle. The "Lotus City," with a fine museum and famed silk and cotton cloth, proves a worthy base from which to explore the many fine archaeological sites, national parks, and villages sprinkled along the Mekong River region to the east. Also, those interested in monastic Buddhism can visit many of the region's secluded forest monasteries.

▐ TRANSPORTATION

Flights: Ubon Ratchathani International Airport (☎263 916), on Thepyothi Rd. **Thai Airways,** 364 Chayangkun Rd. (☎313 340), 2km north of the river on the right. Open M-F 8am-4pm. Flights to **Bangkok** (3 per day, 2000฿).

Trains: Railway Station (☎321 276, advance ticketing ☎321 004), on Sathani Rd., Warin Chamrap District. Buses #2 and 6 run to the station from Upparat Rd. (5฿). Trains go to **Bangkok** (13-14hr.; 6:35, 6:55am, 1:25, 4:15, 4:50, 6:15, 7:40pm; seat with fan 95฿, seat with A/C 120-200฿, sleeper with fan 320-470฿, sleeper with A/C 450-700฿) via **Surin** (31-100฿) and **Khorat** (58-200฿).

Buses: Ubon has 2 main bus stations. At the far north end of town is the **Ubon Ratchathani bus station** (☎241 319); take bus #2, 3, or 11. To: **Mukdahan** (2hr.; 6:30, 7:30, 11:30am, 2, 3pm; fan 51฿, A/C 92฿) via **That Phanom** (45min.); 1st and 3rd buses continue to **Nakhon Phanom** (4hr.; fan 81฿, A/C 146฿); 2nd bus terminates in **Udon Thani** (6½hr.; fan 128฿, A/C 210฿). Buses leave from **Warin Chamrap station** south of the Moon River (take bus #1, 3, 6, or 7; 5฿) to **Phibun** (every 20min. 5am-7:40pm, 25฿) and **Surin** (every 30min. 7am-5pm, fan 43฿). From Phibun, *songthaew* run to **Chong Mek** and **Khong Chiam.**

Local Transportation: City buses run 5am-6pm (5฿). From Upparat Rd., buses #2 and 6 run to the train station and buses #2, 3, and 11 go to the Ubon bus station. **Tuk-tuks** and **samlor** roam the streets (up to 60฿ from the Moon River to Sahamit bus station).

✦ ▐ ORIENTATION AND PRACTICAL INFORMATION

Readily accessible by air, bus, or train, Ubon is the last stop on the northeastern branch of the national rail network. To go farther east or north, travelers must rely on the sometimes-daunting bus system. Ubon's main thoroughfare, **Upparat Rd.,** stretches north-south for 12km; at its north end it is called **Chayangkun Rd.** To the south, it crosses the **Moon River** into the **Warin Chamrap District,** where the train station is. Buses #1, 2, 3, and 6 go there from Ubon proper. North of the river, Upparat

Rd. passes the riverside **market** and, two blocks up, intersects **Khuanthani Rd.** The **hospital** and **museum** are here, and the **tourist office** is several blocks to the right.

Tourist Offices: TAT, 264/1 Khuanthani Rd. (☎ 243 770), away from the river on Upparat Rd. Turn right onto Khuanthani Rd. at the National Museum; it's on the left 2 blocks down. Free, useful maps and fluent English spoken. Open daily 8:30am-4:30pm.

Tours: Siri Ratana Tours (☎ 245 847), on Phalorangrit Rd. With your back to the river, turn right onto Phalorangrit Rd.; it's 1½ blocks down on the left. To: **Bangkok** (10hr.; 7:30am, 8pm; A/C 310฿) via **Surin** (2½hr., 100฿); **Buriram** (4hr., 120฿); **Nakhon Ratchasima** (6hr., 180฿); **Saraburi** (7hr., 310฿). **Sayan Tour,** opposite TAT. To: **Khon Kaen** (4hr., 116฿); **Roi Et** (2½hr., 74฿); **Udon Thani** (#268; 6hr.; 6:40, 8, 11am, 1pm; 162฿) via **Ban Pa Ao** (30min., 15฿). **Nakornchai Air Tour** (☎ 269 385), on Upparat Rd. 1km south of the Moon River. To: **Bangkok** (#98; 9hr.; 8:15, 9:30am and 5 between 7:30-9:30pm; A/C 393฿) via **Khorat** (6hr.; fan 110฿, A/C 200฿, VIP 300฿); **Chiang Mai** (#587; 13hr.; 6 per day 12:15-6pm; fan 300฿, A/C 540฿, VIP 600฿) via **Surin** (3hr.; fan 50฿, A/C 90฿, VIP 140฿); **Rayong** (#588; 10hr.; 6:30am and 5 between 3:30-7:30pm; fan 215฿, A/C 390฿, VIP 455฿) via **Pattaya** (9hr.; fan 200฿, A/C 355฿, VIP 415฿) and **Surin.**

Currency Exchange: Bangkok Bank, 13 Ratchabut Rd. (☎ 262 453). **24hr. ATM** (AmEx/MC/PLUS/V). Open M-F 8:30am-3:30pm. Banks line Upparat Rd.

Rentals: Thai Yont, 302-14 Khuanthani Rd. (☎ 241 242). Rentals should be returned on Upparat Rd. near Suriyat Rd. Reliable, well maintained and serviced. **Motorcycles** 200-300฿ per day. Open M-Sa 8am-5pm.

Markets: The **Riverside market** is an around-the-clock affair. As you cross the bridge into Ubon, the market is immediately to the right of Upparat Rd.

Emergency: Police ☎ 191. **Tourist Police (Bangkok):** ☎ 1155.

Local tourist Police: ☎ 244 941. At the corner of Suriyat and Thepyothi Rd., near the airport. English spoken. Call here before dialing the police.

Pharmacy: Chai Wit, 87 Promathep Rd. (☎ 254 077). From the TAT, walk 2 blocks toward the river. Chai Wit is 1 block to the left—look for the yellow and green sign across the street. Open M-F 7am-7:30pm, Sa 7am-noon.

Medical Services: Rom Klao, 123 Upparat Rd. (☎ 244 658), 2 blocks north on Upparat Rd. From the bridge, it's on the left before Khuanthani Rd. English spoken. **Open 24hr.**

Internet Access: The cheapest spot is on Nakhonbant Rd. 100m north of Phalorangrit (☎ 01 447 8612). Sign reads: "Internet." 20฿ per hr. Open daily 9am-midnight.

Post Offices/Telephones: GPO (☎ 260 465), on Phichitrangsan Rd. Walk east on Khuanthani Rd. past the TAT and turn left on Thepyothi Rd. It is 3 large blocks away from the river. *Poste Restante* behind the office. AmEx/MC/V. Open M-F 8:30am-4:30pm, Sa-Su 9am-noon. **Telephone** service available M-F 8:30am-4:30pm at a 2nd post office at 159-163 Phadaeng Rd. **Lenso** phone. Phone cards sold here. The Warin Chamrap branch office, on Tahaan Rd., has same hours and also offers **Internet** access (Internet cash cards 60฿ per hr.). **Postal code:** 34000.

ACCOMMODATIONS

River Moon House, 21 Si Saket 2 Rd., Warin Chamrap (☎ 286 093). From the train station, take the 2nd left after the iron horse display out front. Walk 200m until the road merges into Si Saket 2 Rd.; it's across the street, 10m to the right. Four teak houses sit back from the road. Pan, the owner, gives excellent travel advice. Monstrous breakfast 50฿. All rooms have shared baths. No A/C rooms. Singles 120฿; room with two double beds 150฿. ❷

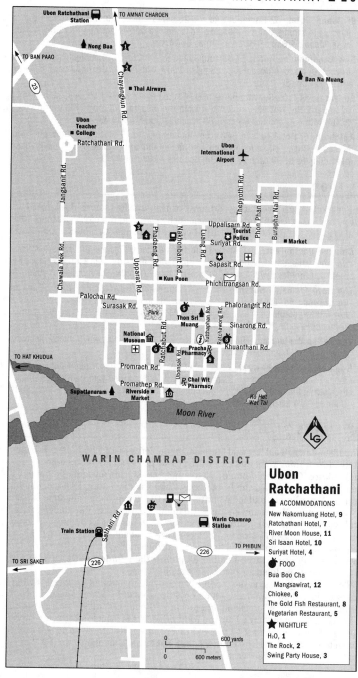

TO AMNAT CHAROEN

Ubon Ratchathani Station

Nong Bua

TO BAN PAAO

23

Chayangkun Rd.

Thai Airways

Ubon Teacher College
Ratchathani Rd.

Ban Na Muang

Jangsanit Rd.

Ubon International Airport

Chawala Nok Rd.

Phadaeng Rd.

Nakhonbant Rd.

Luang Rd.

Thepyothi Rd.

Phon Phan Rd.

Burapha Nai Rd.

Upparat Rd.

Uppalisarn Rd.
Tourist Police
Suriyat Rd.
Sapasit Rd.

Market

Kun Poon

Phichitrangsan Rd.

Palochai Rd.
Surasak Rd.

Park

Thon Sri Muang

Yutthaphan Rd.

Ratchawong Rd.

Phalorangrit Rd.

Sinarong Rd.

National Museum

Ratchabut Rd.

Pracha Pharmacy

Khuanthani Rd.

Promrach Rd.

Ubonsak Rd.

Chai Wit Pharmacy

Promathep Rd.
Riverside Market

Ko Hat Wat Tai

TO HAT KHUDUA

Supattanaram

Moon River

WARIN CHAMRAP DISTRICT

N
LG

Sathani Rd.

Warin Chamrap Station

Train Station

TO SRI SAKET

226

TO PHIBUN

226

0   600 yards
0   600 meters

NORTHEAST

Ubon Ratchathani

🏠 ACCOMMODATIONS

New Nakornluang Hotel, **9**
Ratchathani Hotel, **7**
River Moon House, **11**
Sri Isaan Hotel, **10**
Suriyat Hotel, **4**

🍎 FOOD

Bua Boo Cha
  Mangsawirat, **12**
Chiokee, **6**
The Gold Fish Restaurant, **8**
Vegetarian Restaurant, **5**

⭐ NIGHTLIFE

H₂O, **1**
The Rock, **2**
Swing Party House, **3**

Sri Isaan Hotel, 62 Ratchabut Rd. (☎261 011), near Moon River. Clean but small rooms are strung along a mosaic-tiled staircase and bright open-air atrium. Not the miser's choice. Singles 550฿; doubles 600฿. ❺

New Nakornhuang Hotel, 84-88 Yutthaphan Rd. (☎254 768), a block south of the TAT. Decent rooms for a decent price. Singles 160฿, with A/C 270฿; doubles with fan 240฿, with TV 270฿. ❷

Suriyat Hotel, 302 Suriyat Rd. (☎241 144), on the north end of town, 30m to the right of Upparat Rd. Not much to look at from the outside, but inside it's pristine. Singles 200฿, with A/C and hot water 400฿; doubles 350฿/450฿. ❸

Ratchathani Hotel (☎244 388), on Khuanthani Rd. 1 block over from the National Museum. Bright, clean rooms with tiled floors and comfortable sitting chairs—can't be beat. Singles 330฿, with A/C 500฿; doubles 450฿/650฿. ❸

🍴 FOOD

The **market ❷**, off Promathep Rd. east of Upparat Rd. serves duck salad, *kuay chap*, and other Isaan and Vietnamese dishes, around the clock. At night, **vendors ❶** also gather on Ratchabut Rd. off Khuanthani Rd. near the Ratchathani Hotel.

Chiokee Restaurant, 307 Khuanthani Rd. (☎254 017), diagonally across from the National Museum. Wooden screens open onto the street for a breezy meal. Serves breakfast, porridge with fish (40฿). Most dishes 30-120฿. Open daily 6am-6pm. ❷

The Gold Fish Restaurant, 142/1-2 Khuanthani Rd. (☎242 394), 50m east of Ratchawong Rd. On the upscale side, serving some nice fish dishes. Steamed *cheet* fish with vegetables in *isaan* sauce 120฿. Most dishes about 60-180฿. Thai menu only. Owner speaks English. ❸

Vegetarian Restaurant, 79/1 Nakhonbant Rd. Six-table joint with homemade creations. Soya milk 3฿. Meals 15-25฿. Open M-F 7am-2pm. ❶

Bua Boo Cha Mangsawirat, 11 Si Saket Rd., Warin Chamrap. Specializes in vegetarian food. From Warin Chamrap train station, walk straight and turn right onto Upparat Rd, then left at the next street; it's on the right. Glutinous rice balls stuffed with peanuts 5฿. Open M-Sa 6:30am-3pm. ❶

👁 SIGHTS

The **Ubon Ratchathani National Museum,** on the left side of Khuanthani Rd. immediately after turning right and east off Upparat Rd., documents the region's history and culture. Considered one of the country's best, this museum features a 1500-year-old bronze kettle drum from Khong Chiam, a 9th-century Dvaravati boundary stone, Khmer lintels, and local crafts. (☎255 071. Open W-Su 8am-4pm. 30฿.)

Wat Thon Sri Muang towers on Yutthaphon Rd. opposite the kindergarten. The wat, with interior wall paintings depicting life in ancient Ubon, is over 200 years old. The July **Candle Festival** takes place in the adjacent field. Those with access to wheels can check out **Wat Ban No Muang,** northeast of town, which features a modern-style, 50m tall, three-headed elephant. Pass underneath to view a giant *wihaan* being paddled away in a large sailing vessel.

Two relaxing spots on the Moon River provide diversions for locals. **Ko Hat Wat Tai** is an island surrounded by huts on stilts above the water. Locals order food from restaurants on the island and picnic in the huts. During the dry season, the island can be reached by a bamboo footbridge, but is inaccessible in the rainy season. To find it, walk east to the end of Promrach Rd., then turn right and walk down to the river bank (no entrance fee). **Hat Khudua,** similar to Ko Hat Wat Tai, is on the north bank 12km west of town.

♪ ♫ ENTERTAINMENT AND NIGHTLIFE

Ubon's nightlife is concentrated on Upparat Rd., a few kilometers north of the river. The **Nevada** multiplex, past the Ratchathani intersection on the right, shows the latest action flicks (60฿), but sadly they are all dubbed into Thai. Receive Isaan-style traditional massage at **Traditional Pharmacy,** 369-371 Sapasit Rd., near the corner of Pha Daeng Rd. (☎254 741. 100฿ per hr. Open daily 8am-6pm.)

Swing Party House, 140/1-2 Upparat Rd. (☎265 145), between Suriyat and Uppalisarn Rd., on the right from the river. Like black label whiskey: smooth and cool, the hottest bar in town. Live music nightly at 9:30pm. Large Singha 120฿. Open daily 7pm-1am.

The Rock (☎280 999), in the basement of the Nevada Hotel on the northern end of Chayangkun Rd. A sweaty, pumping discotheque at the base of Ubon's finest hotel. No cover. Large Singha 99฿. Open daily 9pm-2am.

H2O, 488/1 Chayangkun Rd. (☎280 315), 100m north of the Nevada Hotel. Housed in a glass and metal box, this chic pub is Ubon's epicenter of trendy. A popular restaurant is attached. Jug of Singha 140฿. Open daily 7pm-2am.

⌂ MARKETS

Ubon is famous for its silk and *khit*-patterned cotton cloth. Two stores sell clothing made from the area's handwoven cotton. **Maybe Cotton Hut,** 124 Sinarong Rd., is near Ratchawong Rd. (☎254 932. Open daily 7:30am-9pm.) **Peaceland,** 189 Thepyothi Rd., look left beneath the bougainvillea. (☎244 028. Open daily 10am-8pm.) **Kun Poon,** on Phadaeng Rd. between Sapasit and Phichitrangspan Rd., offers delicately woven silks. Prices are in the 2000฿ range. (Open daily 7:30am-7pm.)

Those looking for world-famous Isaan silk should try the **Women's Weaving Cooperative** in the village of **Ban Pa Ao,** 21km north of Ubon on Rte. 23. Ban Pa Ao is a 200-year-old village famous for its silk and bronze wares. Their traditional *mut-mee* silk is available in an array of colors and patterns. Prices begin at 650฿ per meter, and run into the thousands. Weavers perform demonstrations on request. The clothes, mostly women's blouses and skirts, sold in the showroom, start at 450฿. Any bus heading north from the Sayan Tour bus station passes Ban Pa Ao. (Open daily 8:30am-6:30pm.) Tell the ticket collector to drop you off there (20฿). From the main road, the cooperative is 3km east; motorcycle taxis can take you the rest of the way (20฿). To return to Ubon, flag down any bus heading south to the city, or catch a *songthaew* directly from the village (20฿).

For a more general selection of local handicrafts, try **Ban Phan Chat,** 158 Ratchabut Rd., which sells local silk, cotton, fish traps, rice containers, and bronze trinkets. Exit and turn right from the TAT office and then turn right again at the first intersection; it's on the immediate right. (☎243 433. Open M-Sa 9am-8pm.)

▶ DAYTRIPS FROM UBON RATCHATHANI

FOREST MONASTERIES

Wat Pa Nanachat Beung Wai is behind a rice field off the highway to Si Saket, near Beung Wai village. Catch a Si Saket-bound bus or songthaew from Warin Chamrap Station, and ask to get off at Wat Nanachat. Wat Nong Pa Pong temple is 10km south of Ubon and off the road to Katharalak (ask for directions at Pa Nanachat).

Northeast Thailand is known for its masters of meditation. Forest wats became the home of *dudtong* (serious and ascetic) monks who keep strict vows—limiting food to one meal a day, walking as their only means of transportation, and going

BORDER CROSSING: CHONG MEK/VANG TAO Travelers can enter Laos at the village of Chong Mek, 44km from Phibun. From the village of Vang Tao on the Lao side, it is a short ride to Pakse, an excellent springboard for exploring southern Laos. Other than the border crossing itself, there is little of interest for travelers here except on Sa and Su, when a lively market springs up on both sides of the border. From Ubon, take a bus from the Warin Chamrap station to **Phibun** (1hr., 5am-6pm, 20฿). At the Phibun market, locals can direct you to *songthaew* heading to **Chong Mek** (1¼hr., 7am-5pm, 20฿).

Travelers intending to enter Laos must first have a visa stamped with the name of the appropriate entry point (i.e. Vang Tao) from the Lao embassy in Bangkok, or from the Lao consulate in Khon Kaen. **Visas obtained in Nong Khai are not valid here.** Before crossing the border you must officially register your departure from Thailand at the **immigration office,** 30m. before the fence on the right. Once in Laos, present visas to immigration, just beyond the border on the right (entry tax 50฿). From Vang Tao, *songthaew* can drive you to **Pakse** (10฿).

barefoot. Ubon province has accessible monasteries. Visitors should wear proper dress and enter quietly, as silent meditation retreats are often in session.

Wat Pa Nanachat Beung Wai, a forest monastery with predominantly Western monks, is 12km west of Ubon on the way to Surin. Those studying meditation and Buddhism may want to visit; serious students can stay the night. It's a branch of the nearby **Wat Nong Pa Pong** temple, known principally for meditation teacher **Ajaan Chaa,** renowned for his clarity, insight, and discipline. Both wats have more than 20 acres of dense forest, providing a cool, pleasant place to spend a morning or afternoon. A major branch of the controversial **Santi Asok** sect resides 6km to the east of town; ask in town for details.

KHAO PHRA WIHAAN

Park open daily 8am-5pm. 100฿. During the week, the grounds are empty, and transportation requires some creativity. Whenever you go, start the 98km southern haul early to facilitate a smooth trip. Catch one of the buses to Katharalak, which leave from a lot in Warin Chamrap on Upparat Rd. near the minimart (2hr., every hr. 6am-7pm, 25฿). From Katharalak, tell locals where you want to go. On weekends they will put you on a bus directly to the site, but on weekdays they will direct you to another songthaew *that goes to the Poomsalon turn-off 10km north of the site (1hr., leave when full, 15฿). From there, some travelers ignore the greedy motorcycle taxis (200฿ round-trip) and try to hitch a ride from a few hundred meters south on the highway. Drivers and foreigners must cede their passports to police 3km from the park to guarantee return to Thailand.*

A kilometer over Thailand's contested southern border, one of Thailand's best monuments is actually in Cambodia. Basking in its own gravity-defying splendor, Khao Phra Wihaan is a temple/monument complex built by the Angkor kings. The complex rises 800m up a steep grade overlooking the Cambodian plains to the south; its principal chapel is on the peak of a great cliff 600m high.

A contemporary of Angkor Wat, it was built from the 10th to the 12th century by King Rajendravarman. Large steps lead past four pavilions and tourist markets. Although officially opened to the public in 1991, it was closed two years later because of violent hill skirmishes between the Khmer Rouge and the Cambodian government. In August 1998, it was reopened. Today, a ripped-up helicopter pays homage to the last government siege in 1998 that captured the mount. It lies near the first pavilion. As of April 2000, the region appears to have stabilized; however, don't stray from the well-trodden path. The area may still contain live landmines.

KHONG CHIAM

The tranquil hamlet of Khong Chiam is 60km east of Ubon, at the confluence of the Moon and Mekong Rivers. To local youths it's "Sticksville," but to the metropolis-weary traveler, it's a paradise where the pace of life echoes the somnolent flow of the river, and where children squeal and hide from *farang*.

 TRANSPORTATION. Take a bus from Ubon Ratchathani bus station to Phibun Mangsahan (platform #24, 1hr., every 30min. 5am-6pm, 28฿). From the Phibun market, take a *samlor* to the *songthaew* station on the Moon River (10฿ at most). *Songthaew* go to Khong Chiam at least once per hr. (45min., 25฿). A direct bus runs infrequently from Ubon (platform #26, 2hr., 50฿). It takes a similar route but doesn't require a bus change. If you get stuck in Phibun, **Hotel Phibun ❸** (☎441 201) has immaculate singles and doubles (with fan 200-250฿, with A/C 300-350฿). To get there, walk from the *songthaew* stop (with the market on the left) to the intersection, and take a right; it's ahead on the right.

 ORIENTATION AND PRACTICAL INFORMATION. Khong Chiam is shaped like a long acute triangle: its two main roads come together in a point as they jut out into the two rivers. **Klaewpradit Rd.** runs from the market and bus stop straight through the center of town, ending at a wat. Walking across the temple grounds leads to a pavilion with an excellent view of the Moon and Mekong Rivers, joining to become the "Two-Color" river, an effect created by the different levels of silt suspension in the water. In the dry season, this effect is not as stunning, but the low water level creates a dry mud moonscape from which travelers can almost touch Laos. The **post office** has an **overseas phone.** (☎351 016. Open M-F 8:30am-4:30pm, Sa-Su 9am-noon.) Khong Chiam's lone **bank** exchanges some currencies. (☎351 123. Open M-F 8:30am-3:30pm.) Both are on Klaewpradit Rd. **Rimkheng Rd.** runs along the Mekong River parallel to Klaewpradit Rd. Here, a stone tablet opposite the **police station** (☎351 023) identifies Khong Chiam as the easternmost point in Thailand. **Tourist police (Bangkok):** ☎1155. **Postal code:** 34220.

 ACCOMMODATIONS AND FOOD. Surprisingly, tiny little Khong Chiam is packed with comfortable guest houses. The **Mongkhon Guest House ❷**, 595 Klaewpradit Rd., 30m up from the bus station, has just been newly renovated with shiny new wood and impeccably clean rooms all with toilet and bath. (☎01 718 31 82. Singles 150฿, with A/C 300฿.) The **Apple Guest House ❷**, 267 Klaewpradit Rd., past the bank and opposite the post office, is less charming, but takes a close second place. Motorcycles are available for 150-200฿ per day. (☎351 160. Singles and doubles 150฿, with A/C 300฿.) The **Khong Chiam Hotel ❷**, 355 Pakumchai Rd., offers lackluster rooms in a green concrete building. Walking away from the bus station on Klaewpradit Rd., take a right at the sign for the hotel, before the Apple Guest House. (☎351 074. Rooms with bath 150฿, with A/C 300฿.) A few good **restaurants** line Rimkhong Rd. by the river—menus and prices are similar at all of them.

 SIGHTS. About 25km north of Khong Chiam is **Pha Taem National Park,** housing a 200m stretch of prehistoric rock paintings. There is little public transport, but you can get there easily with a map and rented wheels. Road signs along the way make the trip easier. During the high season, two or three *songthaew* may depart; inquire at Apple Guest House. Once at Pha Taem, it's a 500m walk to the paintings. **Tana Rapids National Park** is 3km south of Khong Chiam on the Moon River.

MUKDAHAN ☎ 042

Mukdahan Province was carved out of Ubon Ratchathani and Nakhon Phanom Provinces in 1982. A rich history of Thai and Lao influences is evident in the golden baguettes sold at the market and the annual boat races in October enjoyed from both sides of the river. The province's capital is easily traversed on foot and is a convenient border crossing with Savannakhet, Laos. The rest of the province is green with pristine landscapes and lush tropical forests.

▐ TRANSPORTATION. Buses: Main bus station, 33 Chayang Koolurd Rd. (☎630 486), 3km away on the side of the highway opposite the town. To walk into town, take a left out of the terminal and a right at Wiwitsurakan Rd., the first major intersection, 500m ahead. Follow this street as it merges and winds to the right. Make a left at Phitak Phanomket Rd. and walk 1km into the heart of town. Tuk-tuks to the river are 20-40฿. Buses run to: **Bangkok** (12hr.; 8, 8:30am, 4:30pm, and about every 30min. 6-7:30pm; fan 184-193฿, A/C 331-347฿, VIP 545฿) via **Khorat** (6hr.; fan 120฿, A/C 128-202฿). Prices depend on routing. However, there is regular service to: **Nakhon Phanom** (2½hr.; 7 per day 8:30am-5pm; fan 40฿, A/C 61฿); **That Phanom** (45min.; every 30min. 6am-6pm; fan 22฿, A/C 38฿); **Ubon Ratchatani** (2½hr.; every 30min. 6:30am-4:30pm; fan 51฿, A/C 92฿); and **Udon Thani** (4½hr.; 6 per day 9:30am-2pm; fan 82฿, A/C 148฿). With a Lao visa, you can take a **ferry** to **Savannakhet.** (Boats depart M-F 9am-3:30pm, Sa 9am-12:30pm 50฿.)

▐▌▐ ORIENTATION AND PRACTICAL INFORMATION. The town is laid out on a grid, with streets running roughly parallel (north-south) and perpendicular (east-west) to the Mekong, the town's east border. Along the river bank is **Samron Chaikhong Rd.,** site of the **Indochina Market,** the wat, and the pier. Parallel to Samron Chaikhong, heading from the river, are **Samut Sakdarak (Mukdahan-Domton) Rd.** and **Phitak Santirad Rd.** Perpendicular to these are **Song Nang Sathit Rd.,** which runs from the pier past the Huanum Hotel to the night market, and, one road south, **Phitak Phanomket Rd.,** where the **post office** is. The **bus terminal** is on the main highway (Rte. 212), **Chayang Koolurd Rd.,** 3km northwest.

Thai Farmers Bank, 191 Song Nang Sathit Rd., 2 blocks up the road from the pier and one block past Huanum Hotel, has a **24hr. ATM** (MC/V) and exchanges currency. (☎611 056. Open M-F 8:30am-3:30pm except holidays.) The **Indochina market** sets up every day at the waterfront. The **day market** is off Phitak Phanomket Rd., 500m west of the traffic circle, while the **night market** is 4 blocks from the river on Song Nang Sathit Rd. Some officers speak English at the **police station** (☎611 333) on Phitak Phanomket Rd., between the traffic circle and Song Nang Sathit Rd. **Huan Hong Osoth Pharmacy,** at 38 Samut Sakdarak Rd., opposite Huanum Hotel, has English-speakers. (☎612 002. Open daily 6am-8pm.) The **Mukdahan International Hospital** (☎611 379) is 1km south of downtown on Samut Sakdarak Rd., past Mukdahan Hotel. **Mukdahan Post Office,** 18 Phitak/Phanomket Rd., is at the traffic circle. (☎611 065. Open M-F 8:30am-4:30pm, Sa-Su 9am-noon.) The **Telekom office** (☎611 697) is downstairs. Yellow **Lenso** phones accept DC/MC/V and Access AT&T. (Open M-F 8:30am-4:30pm.) **Emergency:** ☎191. **Tourist police (Bangkok):** ☎1155. **Postal code:** 49000.

▐▐▐ ACCOMMODATIONS AND FOOD. Huanum Hotel ❷, 36 Samut Sakdarak Rd., is on the corner of Samut Sakdarak and Song Nang Sathit Rd., 1 block from the pier. It is a sprawling labyrinth of stairs and fairly clean rooms, but A/C rooms (with hot water and TV!) are cleanest. (☎611 137. Singles 120฿, with en suite bath 220฿, with A/C 280฿; doubles 270฿, with A/C 350฿.) Next to Pith Bakery, **Hong Kong Hotel ❷,** 161/1 Phithaksantirat Rd., opposite the police station, provides clean but worn rooms with firm beds and Western toilets. From the traffic circle facing the river, make a left; it's on the left. (☎611 143. 160฿, with A/C and TV 250฿.)

The **night market** ❶ along Song Nong Sathit Rd. is especially good. Clean and well-organized stalls serve up spicy *som tam* (papaya salad) and *larb sod* (a tangy and very spicy minced pork). *Pa piya* (Vietnamese spring rolls) come *sot* (fresh) or *thawt* (fried). Also, many French-Lao bakeries vend breads, eclairs, and more. Packed in single serving plastic bags, an entire meal is 20-30฿. **Foremost Restaurant** ❸ is on 74/1 Samut Sakdarak Rd. (☎612 251). From Huanum Hotel, walk 1 long block past the pharmacy; it's at the next intersection. It serves the obligatory noodle soup as well as a more substantial Thai and Western meal. (40-150฿. Open daily 7am-10pm.) The small **Mumsabai Restaurant** ❷ has good clean food. Walking toward the river on Song Nong Sathit Rd., it is on the right 1 block before the river. (☎633 616. Fried noodles with young kale and egg 30฿. Mixed vegetables in oyster sauce is 40฿. Decent vegetarian choices. Open daily 10am-10pm.) **Pith Bakery** ❷, 703 Phithaksantirat Rd., next to Hong Kong Hotel. Serving Western breakfasts and the only brownies this side of the Mekong. Owner speaks English and can offer good travel advice. (☎611 990. Open daily 8:30am-9pm.)

◙ **SIGHTS.** A larger-than-life golden Buddha contemplates the Mekong from **Wat Si Mongkan Tai**, on Samron Chaikhong Rd. **Chao Fa Mung Shrine,** far up Song Nang Sathit Rd., houses the city pillar. If you happen to arrive at the end of Buddhist Lent (in late fall), you'll catch boat races on the Mekong.

BORDER CROSSING: MUKDAHAN/SAVANNAKHET You **cannot** get a Lao visa in Mukdahan. Obtain one ahead of time in **Bangkok** (p. 102) or **Chiang Mai** (p. 244). From Mukdahan, you can take a **ferry** to Savannakhet. Boats depart M-F 9am-3:30pm, Sa 9am-12:30pm (50฿).

◪ **DAYTRIP FROM MUKDAHAN: PHU PHA THEOP NATIONAL PARK.**
Known for its rock formations and caves, **Phu Pha Theop National Park** (pronounced poo-PAH-tayp) also boasts prehistoric rock art, stunning landscapes, wildlife, and hiking trails. The collection of huge, oddly shaped rocks at the main entrance are the chief crowd-pleasers. The undersides of many overhanging rocks are decorated with now-faded prehistoric paintings. The rangers know the area well; one speaks English. Trail maps are available from the park office at the entrance.

The main 2km hike to the **Buddha Cave Waterfall** passes the rocks. Other short hikes pass through mountains and cliffs. The trails aren't always easy to follow; explore carefully. Signs in Thai direct trekkers; arrows pointing straight ahead lead to the waterfall. During the dry season, the falls shrink to a trickle. Rickety wooden stairs lead to the **Buddha Cave**, lined with thousands of Buddha images.

The park can be reached from Mukdahan by the orange buses and *songthaew* leaving town on the Mukdahan-Dontan Rd. (Rte. 2034) past Mukdahan Hotel on the right (2 per hr. 6am-6pm, leave when full, 10-15฿). Exit at Phu Pha Theop. Drop-off is on the main road next to a large "Mukdahan National Park" sign on the left. The entrance is a 15min. walk down a small paved road on the right. (Open daily 8am-6pm.)

THAT PHANOM   ☎042

That Phanom is a sleepy town overlooking the Mekong in south Nakhon Phanom Province. Wat That Phanom, the town's signature attraction, rises nearly 60m above ground, its Lao-style *chedi* glinting in the sun. The seamless syncretism of the architecture is mirrored by the food, with the ready availability of Lao and Vietnamese cuisine and the famed biweekly Lao waterfront market. Given That Phanom's pleasing aesthetics, backwater pace of life, and great guest houses, it is not surprising that many enchanted travelers linger here.

NORTHEAST

⚙🅿 TRANSPORTATION AND PRACTICAL INFORMATION. That Phanom, midway between Nakhon Phanom and Mukdahan, is easily reached from either town by bus or *songthaew* (20฿), which stop along **Chayangkun Rd.** (Hwy. 212) and at a small **bus station** (☎541 087) south of town. Buses leave for **Ubon Ratchathani** (3½hr.; 15 per day 7:10am-3:30pm; fan 76฿, A/C 119฿) via **Mukdahan** (1½hr.; fan 21฿, A/C 38฿) and **Udon Thani** (5hr.; 9 per day 10am-2:45pm; fan 81฿, A/C 119฿) via **Sakhon Nakhon** (1½hr.; fan 29฿, A/C 40฿). Several companies run to **Bangkok**, including **CTP Transport** (☎541 247), opposite the station (11hr.; 8am and frequently between 4:30-6pm; fan 218฿, A/C 311฿). **Thaisgoon Tour,** 158 Chayangkun Rd. (☎541 288), a block from the GPO toward the wat, has daily departures to **Bangkok** (11hr.; 8am and frequently between 5-7:30pm; fan 200฿, A/C 280฿, VIP 358฿) via **Khorat** (7hr.; fan 130฿, A/C 188฿, VIP 230฿). *Songthaew* to **Nakhon Phanom** (1½hr., every 10min., 20฿) leave from a stop 150m north of Thai Military Bank.

Wat That Phanom is on Chayangkun Rd. Diagonally across from the wat is **Siam Commercial Bank,** 359 Chayangkun Rd. (☎525 784. Open M-F 8:30am-3:30pm. Cirrus/MC/V **ATM.** Open 6am-11pm.) Past the bank and *songthaew* stop is the **GPO,** 322 Chayangkun Rd., which has **international phone** service. (☎541 169. Open M-F 8:30am-4:30pm, Sa-Su 9am-noon.) **That Phanom Hospital** (☎541 255) is 2km west on the highway. The **police station** (☎541 266) is in the north end of town on Phanom Phanarak Rd. **Emergency:** ☎191. **Tourist police (Bangkok):** ☎1155. **Postal code:** 48110.

🅿🅲 ACCOMMODATIONS AND FOOD. Travelers hail **Niyana Guest House ❶,** on 288 Mu 2, Rimkhong Rd., as the best in That Phanom. From the victory arch, head to the pier and turn left onto Rimkhong. Follow the river 800m; it's on a small soi to the left. Niyana serves food, offers short tours during the high season, gives Thai lessons, and rents out bicycles. (☎540 588. Dorms 60฿; singles 80฿; doubles 120฿; new bungalows facing the river 200฿, with A/C 300฿.) Another good option is **Tum Guest House ❶,** 110 Soi 14 Anvrakjaydee Rd., four soi down Rimkhong Rd. toward the town center from Niyana's. (Bike rental 40฿ per day; laundry 5-10฿ per item; overseas calling available. All rooms have shared bath and no A/C, 80฿.) **Rimkhong Bungalow ❸,** 103 Soi Prempoochanee, one soi north of Tum Guest House, is clean but pricey. (☎541 634. Singles 200฿, with A/C 400฿; doubles 300/500฿.) Accommodations fill up during the February festivals.

At **food stalls ❶** on Chayangkun Rd., 20฿ can buy savory roast chicken, sticky rice, or a bowl of Vietnamese *phở*. A **floating restaurant** bobs beside the pier and several terrestrial restaurants are on Phanom Phanarak Rd. A good **night market** sits near the 7-Eleven and dishes up tantalizing cuisine. (Open until around 9pm.)

🅶 SIGHTS. Wat That Phanom is the most sacred religious structure in Isaan. Legend has it that it was built to house one of the Buddha's clavicle bones, transported from India. Topped by a 110kg gold spire, the shrine has been restored seven times. Depending on who you ask, it's between 12 and 26 centuries old. The most recent reconstruction occurred in 1978, after heavy rains in 1975 collapsed the 57m *chedi.* The temple is circumscribed by a cloister housing dozens of golden Buddha images. At the beginning of February, thousands come to pay their respects during the annual 7-day **Phra That Phanom Homage Fair.**

About 15km northwest of That Phanom is the silk-weaving village of **Renu Nakhon.** Travelers can enjoy Isaan music and dance at the **Renu Nakhon Wat** on Saturdays during the winter; Niyana knows the performance times. To get there, take any Nakhon Phanom-bound *songthaew* to the Renu Nakhon junction 8km north of town; from there, hire a tuk-tuk. Check out the **Lao Market** near Niyana's Guest House on the far end of Rimkhong Rd. (M and Th 6am-7pm).

STUPA-STITIOUS That Phanom is a holy town, a *sathanee saksit*, blessed with a temple that radiates tremendous power. Just as the temple can grant everlasting happiness to those who worship there, so too can it bring tragedy to those who defile it. Residents here often point to 1975 as a remarkable year of misfortune. That year, the magnificent *chedi* collapsed following torrential rains. Some locals rushed to pillage "lucky" chunks from the fallen *stupa;* not long afterward, mysterious accidents and inexplicable illnesses befell the culprits and their families. Their abandoned houses stand forlornly to this day.

One late June night a few years ago, the townspeople witnessed another show of divine power. A young *songthaew* driver, unable to pay his rent, clambered up the scaffolding around Wat That Phanom, intending to swipe the three large diamonds embedded in the *chedi*. Unable to get back down, he was spotted in the floodlight's glare. Word spread through the sleeping town, and a crowd soon gathered on the street below, including the police. One officer, convinced that the thief was an illegal Lao immigrant, drew his pistol, and pulled the trigger—it didn't fire. He tried again—to no avail. Exasperated, he grabbed another gun, but it wouldn't shoot. Perhaps the divine one had taken pity on the would-be burglar and protected him. The hapless bandit was finally dragged down, and officers had to forcefully restrain irate townspeople intent on lynching him. Nothing, not even the most innocuous-looking pebble, can be taken beyond the wat's gates. If you inadvertently do so, return it immediately. If not, sleep light—and don't say we didn't warn you.

SAKHON NAKHON
☎ 042

Marking the entrance to Sakhon Nakhon is the city shrine, a giant bowl of golden Naga heads above a small pond, symbolizing the war with the Naga and his turning the city into water and forcing its relocation. The industrial cousin of rice paddies and thatched roofs, the city is a marketplace for all sorts of mechanical beasts of burden. Nonetheless, it is a pleasant stop between Nakhon Phanom and Udon Thani, home to the revered and sacred Buddhist shrine of Phra That Choeng Chum and the royal residence Phu Phan Raja Nivej.

TRANSPORTATION. Sakhon Nakhon Airport (☎ 713 919), 6km northwest of town, has flights to **Bangkok** (10am, 2140฿). **Thai Airways,** 332 Sookkasem Rd. (☎ 712 259), is near the Krung Thai Bank. (Open M-F 8am-5pm.) **Sakhon Nakhon Bus Terminal** (☎ 712 860), is at the southern end of Ratpattana Rd. From the post office, take a left onto Ratpattana Rd. and the terminal is about 1km down on the left. **Buses** run to **Bangkok** (8hr.; 7, 8, 9, 10am, 5, 6pm; fan 200฿, A/C 280฿, VIP 560฿); **Nakhon Phanom** (1½hr., 10 per day 8:30am-6:15pm, A/C 50฿); **Udon Thani** (2½hr., 10 per day 7am-5pm, A/C 80฿). **Tuk-tuks** are harder to find but **samlor** are everywhere and will take you around town (20-40฿).

ORIENTATION AND PRACTICAL INFORMATION. Sakhon Nakhon is 647km from Bangkok and 93km from the Mekong River. Most buses traveling from the northeastern edge of Thailand will siphon through the city on their way to Bangkok in the south or Udon Thani in the west. The provincial capital is host to Thailand's largest lake, **Nong Han,** which is teeming with liver flukes—freshwater parasites you don't want to mess with. East of the lake is **Ratpattana Rd.** with the bus station at its southern end. To the north, **Charoenmuang Rd.** runs east-west with the post office at its western end; a few guest houses line this street. **Sookkasem Rd.** connects these two roads and forms the eastern boundary making a truncated trapezoid, within which most of the city's activities cluster.

Krung Thai Bank, on Charoenmuang Rd. near the intersection with Sookkasem Rd., will change your money and give you money from the Cirrus/MC/V **24hr. ATM.** (☎ 733 004. Open M-F 8:30am-3:30pm.) A **day market** sets up on either side of Sookkasem Rd. east of the bus station. A small **night market** is located around the traffic circle where Charoenmuang and Jaiphasook Rd. intersect. The **Sakhon Nakhon Police Station** (☎ 716 409) is on Jaiphasook Rd. north of the traffic circle. **Sakhon Nakhon Hospital** (☎ 711 615) is on Charoenmuang Rd. east of the traffic circle. The **pharmacy** is on 1791/2 Sookkasem Rd. near the market. (☎ 732 678. Open daily 7am-9pm.) **T. A. Internet**, on Jaiphasook Rd. between Charoenmuang and Munkalai Rd., will connect you to the world wide web. (20฿ per hr. Open daily 9am-9pm.) **Sakhon Nakhon post office**, at the end of Charoenmuang Rd. when it intersects Ratpattana Rd., offers **international** calling and *Poste Restante.* (☎ 711 049. Open M-F 8:30am-4:30pm, Sa-Su 9am-noon.) **Emergency: ☎** 191. **Tourist Police (Bangkok): ☎** 1155. **Postal code:** 47000.

⛆ ☾ ACCOMMODATIONS AND FOOD. Accommodations in Sakhon Nakhon are fair and that's all. Hotels are generally located on Charoenmuang and Kumjaidpai Rd. in the center of town. The nicest hotel in town is **The Majestic Hotel (M.J.) ❹**, 399 Kumuang Rd., off Sookkasem Rd. near the market. Breakfast is included. Rooms start at 540฿ and quickly shoot to 840฿ for a superior room. (☎ 733 771). **Chareonsook Hotel ❷**, 635 Charoenmuang Rd., at the corner of Charoenmuang and Jaiphasook Rd., has clean and spacious rooms but baths are slightly less appealing. (☎ 716 116. Singles 150฿, with A/C 200฿; doubles 200฿/300฿.) A slight step down the ladder of quality from the Chareonsook Hotel, **Kusuma Hotel ❷** is on 316/1-2 Charoenmuang Rd., 2 blocks past the traffic circle toward the post office. (☎ 711 112. Singles 120฿, with A/C 250฿; doubles 300฿.)

There are two superb noodle and rice joints on Jaiphasook Rd. next to the Chareonsook Hotel. The first is **Clearwon ❶**, with blue plastic chairs, serving the most mouthwatering noodles with pork strips for 20฿. Open daily 8am-3:30pm, rice dishes served until 7pm. Right next door is **Chokun ❶**, with red plastic chairs and a similar menu. (Open daily 7am-3:30pm.) Outside Wat Phra That Choeng Chum on Charoenmuang Rd. are a few 50-gallon drums of red hot embers grilling up whole salted catfish (30฿). **Sweet Moo ❷**, 1658/5 Prempreda Rd. (☎ 09 843 1407), opposite the shopping complex, serves frothy milk shakes to cool the soul and dry the sweat. (Coldest lychee milk shake in all of Siam 10฿; most shakes 10-20฿. Open daily 10am-10pm.)

⛆ SIGHTS. Wat That Choeng Chum is Sakhon Nakhon's most sacred shrine. Located on Reuang Sawat Rd. at the intersection with Charoenmuang Rd., it houses a 24m gold and white Lao-style square Chedi. The annual **wax castle procession**, a collection of enough beeswax fashioned into miniature Buddhist temples and shrines to make any hive jealous, celebrates the end of Buddhist Lent and takes place at the wat (usually in mid-October). Behind the wat is **Nong Han Lake**, the largest lake in Thailand. Unfortunately, it's infested with liver flukes, freshwater parasites that infect fish and treat human skin as if it were an amusement park. **Don't swim in the lake, and don't eat undercooked fish, especially in Sakhon Nakhon.**

NAKHON PHANOM ☎ 042

Nakhon Phanom, the city of mountains, is named for the view of the jagged green mountains across the river in Laos. Indeed, the picturesque view dominates the city and sets the tone: an opalescent sheet of murky water, a thin coastline where Laos gently touches the river, a zig-zag of deep blue hazy green, and melancholy clouds drift in a clear blue expanse.

TRANSPORTATION. Nakhon Phanom Airport (☎513 264), 15km out of town, has flights to Bangkok (1:30pm, 2300฿). **Thai Airways,** 85 Nittayo Rd., is in the Bovon Travel office. (☎512 940. Open M-F 8am-5pm.) Airport shuttle from Thai office (70฿). The **Nakhon Phanom Bus Terminal** (☎511 037), on Piya Rd., is in the southwest corner of town. Buses go to **Bangkok** (12hr.; 4 per day 6:30-9am and 9 per day 3:45-9pm; fan 228฿, A/C 319฿, VIP 500฿); **Khon Kaen** (4hr.; 7 per day 7:30am-4pm; fan 90฿, A/C 173฿); **Mukdahan** (2½hr.; 7 per day 6-9:30am and 2pm; fan 40฿, A/C 50฿); **Nong Khai** (7hr.; fan 100฿, A/C 153฿); **Sakhon Nakhon** (1½hr., every hr. 7am-5pm, A/C 50฿); **That Phanom** (1½hr., every 20min. 7am-4pm, 25฿); and **Udon Thani** (9hr.; 10 per day 6am-2:50pm; fan 80฿, A/C 120฿). **Tuk-tuks** hang out near the night market on Apibanbuncha Rd. Getting around town costs about 20฿.

ORIENTATION AND PRACTICAL INFORMATION. The city is arranged on two main roads that run parallel to the river, and smaller roads perpendicular to the river connect the two. **Sunthon Wichit Rd.** is adjacent to the river and lined with a promenade to view the landscape for which the town is named—the mountains of Laos across the Mekong. The **TAT, police station,** and **post office** are on this road. The **Indochine market** is across from the **immigration office,** which is just south of the **clock tower** also on Sunthony Wichit Rd. Walking away from the river behind the clock tower is **Fuang Nakhon Rd.,** which turns into a night market around 6pm. At the end of Fuang Nakhon Rd. is **Piya Rd.,** where the **bus terminal** is located.

The local **TAT** is one block north of the post office at 184/1 Sunthon Wichit Rd., and is one of the more helpful TATs in the northeast. At least two people speak English well. (☎513 490. Open daily 8:30am-4:30pm.) The **Bangkok Bank,** on Srithep Rd. behind the Indochine market, exchanges currency and has an **ATM.** (☎511 209. Open M-F 8:30am-3:30pm.) The **Indochine market** sets up during the day on Sunthon Wichit Rd. across from the immigration office. A **night market** opens around 6pm on Fuang Nakhon Rd., 3 blocks behind the clock tower. On Sunthon Wichit Rd., one block north of the clock tower, is **Nakhon Phanom Police Station** (☎511 232). **Sawang Fhama,** 478/80 Apibanbuncha Rd., where it intersects with Fuang Nakhon Rd. is the best **pharmacy.** (☎511 141. Open daily 7am-7pm.) **Nakhon Phanom Hospital** (☎511 424), is on Aphibanbuncha Rd. a few blocks north of the library. Check email (15฿ per hr.) at **J Net,** on Sunthon Wichit Rd., across from the clock tower. (☎520 545. Open daily 9am-midnight.) **Nakhon Phanom Post Office,** on Sunthon Wichit Rd., next to the police station, has *Poste Restante.* (☎512 945. Open M-F 8:30am-4:30pm, Sa-Su 9am-noon.) **Overseas** calling is available at the **CAT** office on Salaklang Rd. 2 blocks north of the post office on the left. (Open M-F 8:30am-4:30pm.) **Emergency:** ☎191. **Tourist Police (Bangkok):** ☎1155. **Postal code:** 48000.

ACCOMMODATIONS AND FOOD. There isn't really a guest house scene in Nakhon Phanom. Generally, accommodations are mid-sized hotels showing signs of age. The hotel heavyweight of Nakhon Phanom—in terms of price and quality—is **Nakhon Phanom River View Hotel ❺,** 9 Nakhon Phanom-That Phanom Rd., about 2km south of town. Standard rooms 940฿; stay two nights and get the special rate of 800฿ per night on a deluxe room.) **Grand Hotel ❸,** 2210 Si Thep Rd. (☎511 526), is a few blocks south of the fork in the road. The A/C rooms are better kept than the fan rooms. (Singles 180฿, with A/C 330฿; doubles 230฿.) Behind the clock tower, at the **First Hotel ❷,** 16 Si Thep Rd., the rooms are fairly clean and the toilets are very squat. (☎511 253. Singles 160฿, with A/C 300฿.) The **River Inn ❷,** 137 Sunthon Wichit Rd., is diagonally across from the watch tower and has none-too-clean rooms. (☎511 305. Singles 150฿, with A/C 350฿.)

As in other towns along the Mekong, riverfront restaurants dominate Nakhon Phanom's culinary scene. A rare specialty are the giant catfish—often weighing

350kg or more, hauled out of the river only 35 times a year. A few open-air restaurants line Sunthon Wichit Rd. south of the immigration office. And you can always get a 20฿ bowl of noodles at the **night market** on Fuang Nakhon Rd. At the **Golden Giant Catfish Restaurant ❷**, 257-261 Sunthon Wichit Rd., on the riverside 2 blocks south of clock tower, the name says it all. Giant catfish soup is 60฿; most dishes are 60-120฿. (☎511 218. Open daily 7am-10pm.) **Rim Nam Restaurant ❸**, across from the clock tower on Sunthon Wichit Rd., is another good choice perched on the Mekong. If you've had enough fish try the *larb gai* (minced chicken, 80฿); it's light, spicy, and packs some real zing. They also have personal hot pots. (☎511 254. Open daily 10am-midnight. MC/V.)

 SIGHTS AND ENTERTAINMENT. **Wat Okatsribuaban** halves the river adjacent to the Indochine market. Venture through its gates and beyond its white walls to see two highly revered images of the Buddha. **Wat Srithep** is on the corner of Srithep and Phosri Rd. Relaxing evening strolls are always free and always satisfying along the **riverfront promenade.** And if all this wat-hunting and pleasure-strolling has worn you down, recharge with pumping MP3s and an ice-cold Heineken (small 50฿) at the **Y2K Pub,** 484 Sunthon Wichit Rd. As the sign says, "Let your happies be great in here." (☎521 335. Open daily 7pm-3am.)

> **BORDER CROSSING: NAKHON PHANOM/THA KHAEK** Travelers holding a Lao visa obtained in **Bangkok** or **Khon Kaen** (Nong Khai visas are invalid here) should seek an exit stamp from the **immigration office** just opposite the Indochine market on Sunthon Wichit Rd. (☎511 235. Open M-F 8:30am-4:30pm.) A **boat** behind the office shuttles passengers to Tha Khaek (8am-4pm, 50฿). The Lao entry tax vacillates, but currently stands at 70฿.

NONG KHAI ☎042

If Khao San Road is a noisy, spunky kid, then Nong Khai's riverfront is its calm, cool older brother. Nong Khai's streets are full of tourists passing through, and many who have never left. Drawn at first by the popular border crossing with Laos, travelers end up staying on to see one of Southeast Asia's best Buddhist temples—Sala Kaew Ku. The large influx of foreigners mixes with charming Nong Khai's Lao-French influence and ornate Buddhist temples to create one of Thailand's authentic tourist towns. Gazing at Laos from a river restaurant window, travelers are quickly caught by Nong Khai's dusty charm.

TRANSPORTATION

Trains: Nong Khai Railway Station (☎411 592), on Hwy. 212, 1.5km west of town. Tuk-tuk ride from Rimkhong Rd. 50฿. Trains to **Bangkok** via **Khon Kaen** and **Udon Thani** (Rapid: 10-13hr.; 8:15am, 7:30pm; 3rd-class 143฿, 2nd-class 278฿; express: 11hr.; 6:40pm; 3rd-class 163฿, 2nd-class 298฿) and **Khorat** (6hr., 1pm, 3rd-class 64฿). Booking office open daily 6:30-10:30am and noon-6pm.

Buses: Nong Khai Bus Terminal, on Prajak Rd. at the east end of town. To: **Bangkok** via **Khon Kaen, Khorat,** and **Udon Thani** (#23; 12hr.; every hr. 5:30am-8pm; 200฿, A/C 351฿, VIP 495฿); **Beung Kan** (#507; 3hr., every hr. 6-10:40am, 70฿); **Nakhon Phanom** (#224; 7hr., 5 per day 6:30-9:40am, 91฿); **Udon Thani** (#221; 1hr., every 30min. 5:30am-5:20pm, 21฿). Green buses go to **Loei** and **Pak Chom** (#507; 8hr., 5 per day 6am-10:40am, 84฿) via **Sangkhom** (2hr., 50฿) and **Si Chiang Mai** (1hr., 30฿), and **Rayong** (12hr.; 13 per day 6am-7:30pm; 211฿, with A/C 328฿). To get to **Chiang Khan,** switch buses at **Pak Chom.**

Local Transportation: For those who just want to walk, **tuk-tuks** are abundant to the point of distraction as drivers assume all *farang* are desperately in need of their services. 20฿ for short distances, never more than 60฿.

Rentals: Bicycle rental at Mekhong Guest House (30฿ per day) and Mut Mee Guest House (39-52฿ per day). **Motorcycle rental** (200฿ per day) at Nana Motor, 1160 Meechai Rd. (☎411 998), opposite Chayaporn Market. Open daily 7am-5pm.

✦ 🛈 ORIENTATION AND PRACTICAL INFORMATION

Nong Khai is a major border crossing to **Vientiane, Laos**—the **Friendship Bridge** joins the two countries. In the north, Nong Khai is bordered by the **Mekong River,** while **Hwy. 212** marks the town's southern boundary. Parallel to Hwy. 212, from south to north, are **Prajak Rd., Meechai Rd.,** and **Rimkhong Rd.** The **train station,** on Hwy. 212, 2.5km west of the town center, is a bit of a hike. Taking a right out of the **bus station** and stopping at the first intersection will leave you facing north on Prajak Rd. Guest houses are scattered to the northeast. Street numbers are haphazard; luckily, maps are available at all guest houses.

Currency Exchange: Bangkok Bank, 372 Soi Srisaket (☎412 675), in the ground floor office next to the ATM. Open M-F 8:30am-3:30pm. For currency exchange only—open Sa-Su 8:30am-5pm.

Markets: The **market,** along Rimkhong Rd. near the Mekong river, features a cornucopia of scented soaps, electronics, binoculars, disco balls, and, of course, massive grilled fish from China, Laos, Russia, Thailand, and Vietnam. Open daily 9am-5:30pm.

English-Language Bookstore: Hornbill Bookshop, 1121 Kaeworawat Rd. (☎460 272), on the right near Mut Mee Guest House. Buy, sell, or trade Thomas Pynchon, John Grisham, or Dalai Lama. Open daily 10am-7pm.

Emergency: ☎191. **Tourist Police (Bangkok):** ☎1155.

Police: ☎411 020. On Meechai Rd., facing the hospital.

Pharmacies: Tong Tong Pharmacy, 382/2 Meechai Rd. (☎411 690). Exit left from the post office; it's on the corner. Open daily 7:30am-9pm.

Medical Services: Nong Khai Hospital, 1158 Meechai Rd. (☎411 088), near City Hall and opposite the police station.

Internet Access: Cyberkids, 422 Prajak Rd., near the intersection with Haisok Rd. Best prices in town. 20฿ per hr. Open daily 8:30am-9pm. The cafe attached to the **Mekhong Guest House** costs a pricey 30฿ per hr. Open daily 9am-10pm.

Telephones: Lenso phones in the **GPO** and along Meechai Rd.

Post Office: GPO, 390 Meechai Rd. (☎411 521). **International phone.** *Poste Restante.* Open M-F 8:30am-4:30pm, Sa-Su 9am-noon. **Postal Code:** 43000.

🛏 ACCOMMODATIONS

▨ **Mut Mee Guest House,** 1111/4 Kaeworawat Rd., has riverside patio, scrumptious food, loads of information, and a steady stream of talkative travelers. Clean-as-a-whistle rooms and cute-as-a-button baths. Tai chi and yoga classes offered in high season or upon request. It's like a real holiday—enjoy. Dorms 80฿; singles 110฿; doubles 140฿, with private bath and hot water 360฿; triples 240-300฿. ❶

Sawasdee Guest House, 402 Meechai Rd. (☎412 502), 5 blocks east of post office, behind Wat Srikunmuang. This rickety wooden guest house has very clean rooms and real flavor. Glowing courtyard is the cream-filled center. Singles 100฿; doubles 140฿, with A/C and hot water 300฿. ❶

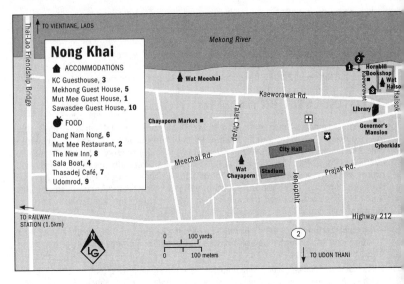

Nong Khai

🏠 **ACCOMMODATIONS**

KC Guesthouse, **3**
Mekhong Guest House, **5**
Mut Mee Guest House, **1**
Sawasdee Guest House, **10**

🍴 **FOOD**

Dang Nam Nong, **6**
Mut Mee Restaurant, **2**
The New Inn, **8**
Sala Boat, **4**
Thasadej Café, **7**
Udomrod, **9**

Mekhong Guest House, 519 Rimkhong Rd. (☎460 689), a few stores west of the immigration pier. Clean rooms upstairs, comfortable restaurant downstairs. Internet next door (30฿ per hr.). Dorms 80฿; singles 100-150฿; doubles 250฿. ❶

KC Guest House, 1018 Kaeworawat Rd. (☎09 842 8084), on the same soi that leads to Mut Mee Guest House. Basic rooms with character, almost in view of the river. Singles 100฿; doubles 150฿. ❶

🍴 FOOD

Although the anticipated tourism explosion has yet to hit with full force, eateries have already become bland and overpriced to accommodate the just-passing-through traveler. Good, inexpensive Thai food, however, can still be found. **Chayaporn Market** ❶ on the west side of town has loads of prepared eats available in clouds of chaos. More **food stalls** ❶, some offering fresh seafood, crowd the intersection of **Rimkhong** and **Haisok Rd.** Two blocks south where **Prajak Rd.** meets Haisok Rd., the smell of skewered meats wafts down the street.

Mut Mee Restaurant, 1111/4 Kaeworawat Rd. Great food matches great guest house. Thai, Western, and vegetarian menu. Most dishes 30-60฿. Open daily 8am-10pm. ❷

Udomrod, 423 Rimkhong Rd. (☎421 084), next to the immigration pier. Postcard-perfect views of the six bays of Laos and the Mekong. Standard menu of fish and Thai food. Most dishes 45-120฿; fresh fish 80-180฿. Open daily 8am-8pm. ❸

Dang Nam Nong, on Banterngit Rd., half a block north of the pharmacy. Serves one thing and serves it good: *nham nuang*, Vietnamese spring rolls you roll yourself. 50฿ per person or 155฿ for 4 buys you a platter of greens, mint, basil, meat, and fresh rice paper wrappers. Open daily 6am-7pm. ❷

Thasadej Café, 387/3 Banterngit Rd. (☎412 075). The antithesis to noodles and rice. Baguette with cheese 45฿; gyros 90฿. Rotating specials highlight various Western foods. Transforms into a crowded bar in the evening. English-speaking owner, Carsten, helps tourists with rides and train tickets. Open daily 8:30am-1am. ❸

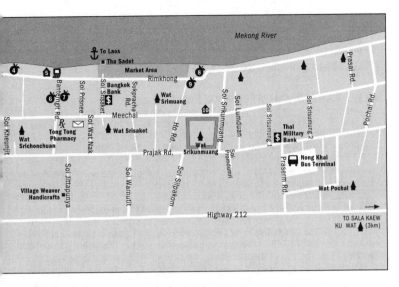

The New Inn, 429/2 Rimkhong Rd. (☎460 247), 20m east of the market. Open and comfortable, perfect for a cold drink along the river. Simple menu of noodles and fried rice (25-50฿). More a pub than a restaurant. Large beer 75฿; cocktails 80฿. Open daily 9am-midnight. ❶

Sala Boat, 527 Rimkhong Rd. Look for the Wall's Ice Cream sign, one block from Mekhong Guest House. Enjoy Thai food riverside or sit back in A/C comfort. Dishes 30-60฿. Open daily 10am-11pm. ❷

⚙ SIGHTS

▨ **SALA KAEW KU (WAT KHAEK).** A few kilometers east of Nong Khai on Hwy. 212, Sala Kaew Ku, also known as Wat Khaek, is one of Thailand's most bizarre temples. Towering concrete statues of Hindu and Buddhist figures represent various levels of Buddhist cosmology: the good and the evil, the mundane and the fantastic, the innocent and the freaky—all the brainchild of a Lao mystic, **Luang Poo Boun Leya Sourirat.** After building a park in Vientiane, Sourirat fled to Thailand when the Communists came to power in 1975. Most of the temple's gravity-defying figures are gods, goddesses, demons, and Buddhas found in the Indian pantheon of mythical deities. Enter the giant mouth in back to learn about *samsara*, the Buddhist belief in the endless cycle of rebirth and suffering. A circle shows the events of one life-cycle. (*15min. bike ride. Head east on Rte. 212, past "St. Paul Nong Khai School" on the right; Sala Kaew Ku is two turn-offs later. Grab a map if you want to take the more scenic river route. You can also arrange to have a tuk-tuk take you there and wait while you look around. The whole trip should cost 100-120฿ for the round-trip ride plus an hour wait. If you have trouble communicating, Carsten at the Thasadej Café (see Food, above) can arrange it for you. Open daily 8am-5pm. 10฿.*)

VILLAGE WEAVER HANDICRAFTS. Seekers of handwoven *mut-mee* fabrics can visit Village Weaver Handicrafts, off Prajak Rd. near the Honda dealership. This 19-year-old project promotes local industry and offers lucrative work to Isaan women who are at risk of turning to brothels for their livelihood. Seamstresses tailor outfits at warp speed and ship them everywhere in the world. (*1151 Soi Jittapunya. ☎411 236. Open daily 8am-5pm, weaving demos M-F.*)

▶️ DAYTRIPS FROM NONG KHAI

▥ PHU PHRA BAT HISTORICAL PARK

To have enough time to see the park and get back, catch a bus to Ban Phu (#294; 1½hr., 7:15am, 30฿) from the Nong Khai Bus Terminal. Take a left from the Ban Phu station and walk 100m over the bridge to where songthaew (15min., every 15min., 5฿) take you to the park. From here, hike 4km to park headquarters or grab a motorcycle taxi (50฿). Leave the park by 2pm, as the last bus back to Nong Khai leaves Ban Phu at 3pm.

Some 85km southwest of Nong Khai, not far from the dusty village of Ban Phu, the eerie wizardry of prehistoric hunters and gatherers lingers at Phu Phra Bat Historical Park. On 5.5 sq. km of forested mountains in the Phu Pan Range, the park boasts a fine collection of prehistoric cave paintings and rock shelters that date back to 1500 BC. Local lore intertwines these sites with the remains of various locations (see **The Things We Do for Love,** below). Over a dozen excavations lie scattered along a shady well-marked path. Buddhas abound in **Tham Phra (Cave of Buddha Images).** At the top of the mountain, the path yields an astounding vista of **Pha Sadet Cliff,** which has a perfect picnic area overlooking the Laotian mountains.

NEAR NONG KHAI

SANGKHOM

Drowsy Sangkhom is quiet and forlorn, but its geography has stunning vistas, waterfalls, and cliffs. The surrounding jungle is dotted with caves marked on maps available at Bouy Guest House. The impressive **Than Thip Falls** are a 30min. motorbike ride west of town. Bring your bathing suit—the second tier has a swimming hole. **Than Thong Falls** are east of Sangkhom. **Wat Hin Maak Peng** is a monastery set among boulders and bamboo groves.

The **Bouy Guest House ❶,** 60 M. 4 Sangkhom, offers romantic bungalows along the river. (☎441 065. Singles 80฿; doubles 100฿.) Mr. Toy, owner and chef of the guest house's **restaurant ❷,** prepares Thai and Lao specialties (jungle curry 40฿) and has tons of information—ask about boat trips. Just west is **TXK Guest House ❶,** formerly Mama's Guest House, which dispenses free papayas and bananas. (Bungalows 100฿.) TXK's **restaurant ❸** is famous for 100฿ Thai and Lao feasts. **River Huts Guest House ❶,** 80m to the right facing the river, has slow Internet access (2฿ per min.) and standard bungalows. (Singles 80฿; doubles 100฿; deluxe with bath, hot water, 2 fans 280฿.)

Sangkhom sits in the hills 95km west of Nong Khai. Buses go from Loei to **Sangkhom** (3½hr., every hr. 5:40-11:40am, 60฿) and **Nong Khai** (#507; 2hr., every hr. 6am-3pm, 38฿). The **police station** is 700m to the right of the guest houses facing the river. (☎441 080. **Open 24hr.**) The **post office,** 800m to the left, provides international phone service. (☎441 069. Open M-F 8:30am-4:30pm, Sa-Su 9am-noon.) **Postal code:** 4316 0.

WAT PHU THAWK AND BUENG KHAN

Although it's one of Northeast Thailand's most spectacular sights, **Wat Phu Thawk** remains untouristed. In the Isaan dialect, *phu thawk* means "single mountain." The shrine stands on a red sandstone outcropping rising from the Nong Khai plain with each of the wat's seven levels representing a stage of enlightenment.

THE THINGS WE DO FOR LOVE Although Phu Phra Bat Historical Park has attracted international attention for its 3500-year-old cave paintings, it's more renowned among locals for its connection to the legend of Nang Usa and Tao Baros.

Nang Usa was the only child of King Phaya Kong Phan of Phan. A slightly over-protective father, the king decided to have Nang Usa raised by a hermit in the seclusion of Phu Phra Bat where she remained without any social life whatsoever until the age of sixteen. One day, Prince Tao Baros stumbled upon her during a hunting excursion from his neighboring kingdom and they fell madly in love at first sight—perhaps because he was pretty much her only option at that point. When the king arrived the next day, Tao Baros asked him for Nang Usa's hand in marriage. The furious king realized he would lose his daughter's love if he killed Tao Baros and instead proposed a challenge: whoever could build the most beautiful temple between sundown and the rising of Venus would decide Nang Usa's fate; the loser would be beheaded.

The king requisitioned an entire village to help him, while Tao Baros was left with just one of his men. Tao Baros worked madly on his temple until he had an idea. He climbed a tree on a cliff and lit a fire above the king's temple site. The villagers believed this to be the morning star and left the temple unfinished, leaving Tao Baros free to complete his modest temple. The next morning the king was beheaded, and Tao Baros and Nang Usa were free to be together. But rumors that Nang Usa was untrustworthy and secretly overjoyed at the death of her father devastated her, and she made an irrevocable decision to return to her seclusion in Phu Phra Bat. Tao Baros died of a broken heart from the cruel irony of it all, while Nang Usa lived her life out as it began: without a social life.

BORDER CROSSING: NONG KHAI/VIENTIANE 15-day Lao tourist visas are issued on the **Friendship Bridge** for US$30 (3 passport photos required). 30-day visas are available from the Lao embassy in Bangkok (see p. 102) for 1100฿ (3-day processing). Ask Julian at Mut Mee Guest House for the latest info. A tuk-tuk from Nong Khai to the bridge should cost 30-50฿. A bus shuttles people across the bridge for 10฿; once there, expect to pay a 2000kip (10฿) entry tax. On the other side, public buses run the 25km to Vientiane (30฿), or you can take a taxi (150฿). For coverage of **Vientiane**, see p. 398.

Level five has a sanctuary built into the cliff. A skeleton encased in glass awaits your company at level six. On the opposite side of the mountain is a hermitage built on a pinnacle nestled under a boulder. Along the walkways are platforms and huts for meditation. Reaching the top involves climbing stairs into a maze of wooden platforms and staircases—don't look down. The view from the Isaan plains makes the sweaty ascent more than worth it, though climbing the stairs isn't recommended in windy weather.

The sheer isolation of Wat Phu Thawk makes tackling it in one day difficult. From the **Nong Khai Bus Terminal,** take bus #224 to **Bueng Khan** (2hr., every hr. 6am-3pm, 45฿). From the Bueng Khan bus stop (across from the ATMs), catch a bus to **Ban Similai** (#225; 40min., 17฿). From here, get to Phu Thawk on a motorcycle (30min., 40-50฿) or jump on a tuk-tuk (100฿). Bueng Khan, the largest town between Nakhon Phanom and Nong Khai along Hwy. 212, is the most sensible place for an overnight stay. Hwy. 212 becomes **Thaisamok Rd.,** home to a small bus stop, clock tower, and rotary near the center of town. To reach the guest houses, turn right onto **Maesongnang Rd.** (facing the rotary) and left onto **Prasatchai Rd.**

Two hotels are 100m down at the first intersection. **Santisuk Hotel ❷,** 21/2 Prasatchai Rd., is on the right. (☎491 114. Singles with TV and Thai-style bath 150฿; doubles 300฿). **Samanmit Hotel ❸,** 34/3 Prasatchai Rd., is directly across from Santisuk. (☎491 078. Doubles 300฿.)

CHIANG KHAN   ☎042

Tucked behind the Mekong River, north of Loei and west of Nong Khai, Chiang Khan is not to be missed. It offers the same stunning vistas and slow afternoons of other frontier towns, but the relative seclusion, few tourists, and spectacular guest houses make it a great rest spot. Its charm, punctuated by the meandering Mekong, has attracted investors, increasing land values tenfold with property near the Kaeng Khut Rapids fetching over two million baht per 3400 square meters. Life here, however, still remains relatively slow and isolated. With only a soothing atmosphere and a few sights to distract you, kick back, enjoy the cultural enrichment, and be rejuvenated.

⌷ TRANSPORTATION. Pak Chom and Loei serve as Chiang Khan's connection to the rest of the world. **Songthaew** leave from Chiang Khan Rd. for **Loei** (1hr., every 30min. 5:30am-5pm, 22฿) and **Pak Chom** (1hr., every 30-60min. 6am-4pm, 20฿). From Pak Chom, **buses** run to **Nong Khai** via **Sangkhom** (#507; 4½hr. total, 2hr. to Sangkhom; last bus noon). Buses to **Bangkok** leave from Soi 9, south of the market (6pm, 176฿; A/C 8am, 6:30pm; VIP 6:30pm, 490฿).

⊞ ⁊ ORIENTATION AND PRACTICAL INFORMATION. Resting on the muddy Mekong River, Chiang Khan is in northern **Loei Province,** 50km from the provincial capital. The two main roads, parallel to each other and the river, are **Chai Khong Rd.,** closer to the water, and **Chiang Khan Rd.,** the highway through town. **Sois 1-24** connect the two roads.

Services in Chiang Khan include: **immigration office,** past the hospital on the left (☎821 911; visa extensions 500฿; open M-F 8am-8pm); **police** (☎821 181; **tourist police (Bangkok):** ☎1155; **emergency:** ☎191), on a soi off Chiang Khan Rd. past the hospital; **Ruammith Osoth Pharmacy,** on Chiang Khan Rd. at Soi 9 (☎821 168; open daily 6am-9pm); **Chiang Khan Hospital** (☎821 101), on Chiang Khan Rd. past Soi 21; and **Chiang Khan Post and Telegraph Office,** near the immigration office (☎821 011; **international phone;** *Poste Restante;* open M-F 8:30am-4:30pm, Sa-Su 9am-noon). **Postal code:** 42110.

⌐☐ ACCOMMODATIONS AND FOOD. Chiang Khan is bursting with good guest houses. Unlike other backpacker havens where supply and demand are balanced, Chiang Khan's great guest houses far outnumber sweaty *farang*. ▨**Loogmai Guest House ❸**, 112 Chai Khong Rd., Soi 5, is modern and chic. White walls, abstract art, wood furniture, and concrete floors make this one of the best guest houses in Thailand. All rooms have a fan. (☎09 210 0447. Small rooms 250฿; large rooms 350฿; one room with has private bath 400฿.) **Chiang Khan Guest House ❷**, 282 Chai Khong Rd., has homey wooden rooms with shared Western baths. (☎821 691. Singles 150฿; doubles 200฿.) A wrap-around patio **restaurant ❷** serves good food (most dishes 30-60฿) and great views. **Rimkhong Guest House ❶**, 294 Chai Khong Rd., Soi 8, is a fragrant wooden guest house with squat toilets. English, French, and Thai spoken. (☎821 125. Dorms 60฿; singles 120฿; doubles 140-250฿.) **Friendship Guest House ❷** 300 Chai Khong Rd. (☎01 263 9068), has large, simple teak rooms. The pub downstairs is friendly. (Singles 150฿, doubles 200฿.) **Nongsam Guest House ❸**, about 1½km west of town on Chiang Khan Rd. offers truly secluded bungalows by the river—clean and with shared baths. Only those who are really looking for the get-away-from-it-all feel and are armed with strong mosquito repellent need apply. (☎821 457. All bungalows 300฿.) **Ton Khong Guest House ❷** is on 299/3 Chai Khong Rd., at Soi 10. Rooms are snug and spotless with shared western baths. (☎821 547. Singles 150฿; doubles 200฿.) The balcony **restaurant ❷** serves delectable Thai and Lao dishes (30-60฿).

Rabieng ❷, left of Ton Khong Guest House, churns out tasty Chinese food (50-80฿ per dish). (Open daily 9am-11pm.) **The Look Kosana ❶**, on Soi 9 near Chai Khong Rd. opposite Phoonsavad Hotel, serves phat thai (20฿) and morning glory vine in garlic bean sauce (50฿) to satisfy even the pickiest taste buds. (Open daily 6pm-midnight.) Chiang Khan does not have many restaurants, but the guest houses usually do a good job of satiating growling stomachs. **Rimkong Guest House ❷** and **Friendship Guest House ❷** also serve hot food and cold beers. Along the river by the **Kaeng Khut Khu Rapids** are a few **food stands ❶** serving a local specialty—*kung den*, tiny live shrimp that dance around your plate (around 40฿).

◪ SIGHTS. About 3km east of town, a turn-off leads left to **Kaeng Khut Khu Rapids**, where picturesque rock piles interrupt the Mekong's seaward schlep. Follow the sign to **Wat Thakhaek** and continue for 1km. A row of covered picnic areas are great for before receiving their bath at the temple. The second day is the transitional period into the New Year. Typically, sand is made into *chedis* outside temples in order to represent the sacred soil a lay person tramples upon during the year. The final day is the start of the New Year. In 2003, the year in Thailand will be 2546 (as in years after the death of Lord Buddha).

While every day has its associated customs, if you're just looking for some good old *sanuk* ("love of life" or "fun-loving"), you'll love the water fights of Songkran. If you can be in Thailand at the time, it's an unforgettable experience—like Holi in India.

Bangkok's parades are the most elaborate, while Chiang Mai appears to have been designed with Songkran in mind—the moat serves as a source of constant reloading for the patrolling pick-ups packed with would-be water assassins. But the villages are the place to be for a more traditionally Thai Songkran experience. Fortunately, Thailand has a lot of villages filled with water-lovin' friendly people who will share their festival with you.

If you're planning to be in any of the major cities and centers during Songrkan, book transport and accommodations early. As with every national holiday, a lack of vacancies and gross inflation of prices are the norm. Also keep in mind that all banks, museums, stores, and offices will be closed for those three days. And one last warning—don't wear anything white (it will be see-through in 10min.).

watching the rapids from February to May. Some guest houses and hotels provide boat transport to the rapids. *Songthaew* (10฿) and tuk-tuk (50฿ round-trip) make the trip from Chiang Khan Rd. On weekends, and occasionally during the week, vendors set up stalls selling local goods and cook up fresh fish and shrimp dishes.

LOEI
☎ 042

A big billboard on Hwy. 201 greets visitors to Loei with, "Welcome to Loei, Land of the Sea of Mountains and Coldest in All Siam." Grammar aside, the sign captures the essence of this seldom-visited but appealing province. It is the only base from which to venture into the misty mountain mornings of slate grey, in search of hermit caves and Thailand's version of the Napa Valley: the Chateau de Loei Vinyards. At the end of June, the three-day Phi Ta Khon Festival in Dan Sai features young costumed men, priapistic props, free food, libidinous rockets dancing through the streets, and recitations of Buddhist tales. It transforms the western district into a shamanistic orgy of brightly colored costumes, culminating in a final day of Buddhist sermon at the wat. Those who make the trip to Loei find a perfect place to unwind after a day exploring the countryside and national parks.

▛ TRANSPORTATION

Buses: All buses leave from the **main bus terminal** off Maliwan Rd. Green buses go to **Nong Khai** via **Pak Chom, Sangkhom,** and **Tha Bo** (#507; every hr. 5:40-10:40am, 84฿). If you're going straight to Nong Khai, take a bus to **Udon Thani** (platform #2; every 20min. 10am-5:30pm, 55฿) and then catch a bus to Nong Khai; it's at least 3hr. faster. Buses also run to: **Bangkok** (10-11hr.; 22 per day 7am-8:30pm; 188฿, A/C 320฿); **Chiang Mai** (9hr.; 11:15am, 8:30, 9:30pm; 165฿, A/C 231฿); **Chiang Rai** (11hr.; 6:30am, 10, 10:30pm; 1st-class 374฿). Chiang Mai and Chiang Rai buses travel via **Phitsanulok** (4hr.) and **Lampang** (7hr.). Many **long distance buses** may be full upon arrival; guarantee a seat by buying a ticket from the bus terminal counter. *Songthaew* go to **Chiang Khan** (1hr., every 30min. 5:30am-5:30pm, 20฿).

Local Transportation: The same as almost everywhere in Thailand: **samlor** and **tuk-tuk** 20-40฿. You can **rent motorbikes** (200฿ per day) at the **bike shop,** 20m north of the traffic circle at the intersection of Chum Saai and Sathon Chiang Khan Rd. Look for a row of motorbikes.

▚ ▐ ORIENTATION AND PRACTICAL INFORMATION

Loei town is a tangled mess of streets on Loei River's western bank. **Charoen Rat Rd.** runs the length of the river, beginning in the south at the **night market.** Moving north into town on Charoen Rat Rd., you'll see the **post office** and a white suspension footbridge, followed by **Chum Saai Rd.,** which becomes **Nok Kaew Rd.** three blocks down at a busy traffic circle. Continuing up Charoen Rat Rd., Thai Udom Hotel is at the intersection with **Oua Aree Rd.** Walk a block more to reach **Ruam Jai Rd.,** a major east-west thoroughfare.

Currency Exchange: Siam Commercial Bank, 3/8 Ruam Jai Rd. (☎813 020). Open M-F 8:30am-3:30pm. Cirrus/MC/V **ATM** open daily 6am-11pm. **Bangkok Bank,** at the intersection of Oua Aree and Charoen Rat Rd., has a **24hr. ATM** (AmEx/MC/PLUS/V).

Emergency: ☎191. **Tourist Police (Bangkok):** ☎1155.

Police: ☎811 254. On Pipat Mongkon Rd/Phipattanamongkhon Rd., the city's northern border.

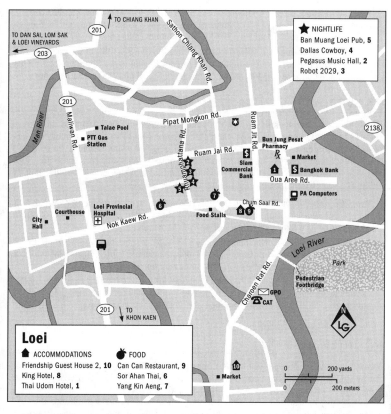

NIGHTLIFE
Ban Muang Loei Pub, **5**
Dallas Cowboy, **4**
Pegasus Music Hall, **2**
Robot 2029, **3**

Loei

ACCOMMODATIONS
Friendship Guest House 2, **10**
King Hotel, **8**
Thai Udom Hotel, **1**

FOOD
Can Can Restaurant, **9**
Sor Ahan Thai, **6**
Yang Kin Aeng, **7**

NORTHEAST

Pharmacy: Bun Jung Pesat Pharmacy, 83 Charoen Rat Rd. (☎830 634), on the corner of Ruam Jai Rd. Open daily 3am-9pm.

Medical Services: Loei Provincial Hospital (☎811 541), at the intersection of Maliwan Rd. (Hwy. 201), the town's western boundary, and Nok Kaew Rd., opposite provincial offices. Some English spoken. Cash only.

Internet Access: PA Computers (☎814 761), on Charoen Rat Rd. between Chum Saai and Oua Aree Rd. 20฿ per hr. Open daily 9am-midnight.

Telephones: International calls may be placed from the **CAT** office next door to the GPO.

Post Office: GPO (☎812 0222), on Charoen Rat Rd., between the footbridge and night market. Open M-F 8:30am-4:30pm, Sa-Su 9am-noon. **Postal code:** 42000.

ACCOMMODATIONS

King Hotel, 11/9-12 Chum Saai Rd. (☎811 701), has the cleanest rooms in town—decked out in tile, well furnished with phone, TV, A/C, and hot shower. There are 2 tinted window "massage" parlors next door. Singles 380฿; doubles 399-600฿; VIP room with fridge 1200฿. ❹

Thai Udom Hotel, 122/1 Charoen Rat Rd. (☎811 763), at Oua Aree Rd., has decent, clean rooms. Slightly worn down, they are furnished with a desk, phone, and TV. Singles 240฿, with A/C 350฿; doubles 320฿/500฿; VIP room 600฿. ❸

Friendship Guest House 2, 257/41 Charoen Rat Rd. (☎832 408), at the southern end of the road, across from the market. There's no English sign. Medium-sized rooms (150฿) in a concrete complex are tiled and clean. Sometimes it's full, so call ahead. ❷

⬛ FOOD

Some of the best places to eat are the **open-air restaurants** ❷ in front of the movie theater just off Oua Aree Rd., opposite Thai Farmers Bank, and at the main bus terminal. Pyromaniacs can order *pak boong fai daeng* (flaming morning glory vine). A couple of **food stalls** ❶ line Chum Saai Rd. where it turns into Nok Kaew Rd., just after the traffic circle. All of them serve fine noodle and rice dishes for about 30฿; the place next to the tire shop is the best.

Yang Kin Aeng, at the traffic circle at the intersection of Sathon Chiang Khan Rd. and Chum Saai Rd., has a 2-story patio and serves heaps of Thai classics. A local favorite even if it costs a few more baht. Open daily 5-11pm. ❸

Sor Ahan Thai, 32/106 Nok Kaew Rd. (☎813 436), 2 large blocks west of the traffic circle, away from the river. Garden restaurant has extensive Thai/English menu. Most dishes 40-100฿; tasty noodles with shrimp 40฿. Open daily 9am-midnight. ❷

Can Can Restaurant (☎815 180), on Chum Saai Rd., next to the King Hotel. Not exactly a budget restaurant, but its good food makes it one of the most popular restaurants in town. Most dishes 40-200฿; fresh fish and juicy steaks 120-200฿. Open daily 7am-11pm. ❸

⬛ ENTERTAINMENT

Discos and Western-style pubs line **Rhuamphattana Rd.** As you walk west on Nok Kaew Rd., toward the highway, Rhuamphattana Rd. will be the first right after the traffic circle. Halfway down on the left is **Ban Muang Loei Pub,** which has live country music in Thai (small beer 50฿). Directly across the street is the **Dallas Cowboy,** which is Ban Muang's twin. Continuing down the street, you'll see two Robocop statues on your right; a large, glowing millennium falcon past the gate marks the entrance to **Robot 2029.** Thai rock bands play nightly at 10:30pm in a neon-lit hall. Its rival, **Pegasus Music Hall,** is next door where house music thumps amid strobe lights until a band plays at 10:30pm.

⬛ MARKETS

Loei has two **day/night markets.** One is at the northern end of Charoen Rat Rd., opposite the 7-Eleven. The market has lots of silly things like plastic combs and space guns as well as grilled meats (flies no extra charge). The night market gets going around 6pm but closes between 9 and 10pm. The second market sets up at the southern end of Charoen Rat Rd. Six long rows under tin roofs deal almost exclusively with all the food under the Thai sky. (Open daily 10am-9pm.)

NEAR LOEI

The real attraction to Loei lies outside the provincial capital in the surrounding mountains. Transportation is somewhat difficult to arrange as there are no *songthaew* that travel that far out of the city, and distances are impractical for a tuk-tuk. However, a bus to Lom Sak runs along **Highway 203,** from which most of the sights are accessible. The first is a large **reservoir**—a local favorite during the high season. Rent a raft for a lazy afternoon of floating about; a small flag is provided which you can use to signal the boats filled with food to come serve you a bowl of noodles or a bag of fruit. To get there, keep an eye on the white mile markers on the right side of the highway. There is a turn-off leading right at the 14km mark—the numbers on the side face are 35 and 60. It's another 3.5km walk to the reservoir which is ringed by restaurants and raft rental places.

Further along Highway 203 on the left is the **Phu Luang Wildlife Sanctuary.** It is closed from June to December. Contact the Wildlife Conservation Dept. in Bangkok for more information (☎ 02 579 9446). Small nurseries cultivate a rainbow of flowers along the road culminating in a January flower show near the **Phu Rua National Park** opposite the PTT gas station. Finally, the **Chateau de Loei Vineyards** is about 20min. further on the left. Many resorts and bungalow operators line this road (see Phu Rua National Park, below), but they are often empty and sometimes closed in low season.

PHU RUA NATIONAL PARK

The majestic centerpiece of this park is a **1375m mountain.** Personal vehicles can travel to the top, where a large Buddha surveys the scene below. More low-key routes include a 2km trek to a **waterfall,** from which it's 5.5km to the peak. Pick up a map and consult park rangers before your trip.

To get to the park, catch bus #14 to **Lom Sak** via **Phu Rua** (1hr., every hr. 5am-5pm, 25฿); watch for the large English sign on the right. Snacks are available at the PTT gas station opposite the bus drop-off. Although *Let's Go* doesn't recommend hitchhiking, the easiest way to get to the park headquarters, 3.5km away, is to hike up the road and try to snag a lift (remember, the thumb points down). Otherwise, *songthaew* charge an outrageous 300฿. To return to **Loei,** wait for a bus in front of the gas station (last bus 6pm). Admission to the park is 200฿.

It is possible to complete the circuit in a day, but an overnight stay at the park is recommended. (Tents 50฿; lodging for 5-8 people 250-500฿.) Food is available daily during high season and until 6pm during low season. Large groups should contact the **National Parks Division** in Bangkok (☎ 02 561 4836). The **Song Pee Nong Bungalow ④** (☎ 899 399 or 899 258) is about 0.5km away from the park entrance on the right if you are heading toward Loei. It is a good alternative to camping in the park. Bungalows are simple and clean with decent shared western toilets. (Wooden bungalows 500฿; larger concrete bungalows 700฿.)

CHATEAU DE LOEI VINEYARDS

Thailand's only wine-producing vineyard is amazingly large by any standards. After a long process of securing permits to import foreign grape vines into Thailand and general skepticism, a thriving vineyard now stands in the middle of Loei's misty mountains. The wine itself is not for the connoisseur (nor really the avid novice) but a walk through the vineyards is pleasurable, and the ambling visitor may be surprised that so much land may be owned by one person. The rolling landscape offers views of marching rows of grapes, produce, a small reservoir, and a private runway.

To get there, take a **bus** bound for **Lom Sak** and get off when you see the sign in English marking the vineyard on the right, about 1hr. from the capital. The vineyard shop and restaurant are at the side of the road, selling fresh grapes, some local crafts, and, of course, bottles of wine. The actual vineyard is another kilometer down the road beneath the sign.

PHU KRADUNG NATIONAL PARK

The park's bell-shaped mountain inspired the name of this popular sanctuary (*kradung* means bell). Trails criss-cross the 60 sq. km plateau at the summit. The 9km hike from the mountain base to park headquarters is facilitated by bamboo stairways. Porters can tote your gear (10฿ per kg). Eager spirits can bid the Khon Kaen bus adieu at Nong Hin, the turn-off for **Ban Pha Ngarm,** a stone forest where limestone outcroppings form a natural labyrinth. Guides promise not to lose you for 100฿ per group. The 18km to Ban Pha Ngarm from the park entrance are traversed only by chartered *songthaew* (500฿). **Mountaintop lodging ❺** starts at 2000฿ per bungalow. The park is packed on weekends, and holidays, and in high season, but closes from June to September. For more information, contact the **National Park Division** of the Forestry Department in Bangkok (☎ 02 561 4292, ext. 724).

Buses to Khon Kaen (25฿) drop you off at the Amphoe Phu Kradung Administrative Office. From here, catch a minibus (15฿) to the National Park Office where trail #9 begins. Admission is 200฿.

NAM NAO NATIONAL PARK

Nam Nao, meaning "cold water," stretches for 1000 sq. km at the junction of Loei and Phetchabun provinces. An alluring park of sandstone hills and sandy plains make it ideal for hiking and comfortable for walking. During the ascent to the park's highest peak, **Phu Pha Chit** (1271m), a landscape of low shrubs and small yellow flowers rolls down the mountain. The park also has lush bamboo forests and the obligatory waterfall and cave pair. Lodging, tents, and bungalows are available through the **National Park Division** in Bangkok (☎ 02 561 4292, ext. 724). Call before your trip to arrange for lodging. **Resorts** line Hwy. 12 near the park, but these are more expensive choices. A daytrip to the park is possible but inadequate, especially if you are using public transportation. From Loei, catch a **bus** to **Lom Sak** (2½hr., runs regularly 6am-5pm, 58฿). At the Lom Sak bus terminal take a bus bound for **Khon Kaen** and get off at the turn-off for the park on the left. To return to Loei, backtrack the way you came. Plan your trip so that you stop at Nam Nao on the way to Khon Kaen—buses run to Khon Kaen directly fom the park.

UDON THANI   ☎ 042

Sheltering an almost six-digit population, Udon Thani is one the most prosperous cities in the northeast and the Isaan's chief agricultural, commercial, and transportation center. Udon Thani was the site of a US Air Force base during the Vietnam War, and the American presence can still be felt in its Western restaurants and expatriate community. The province also offers several worthwhile daytrips, most notably Ban Chiang's UNESCO World Heritage archaeological sites.

▐▀ TRANSPORTATION

Flights: Udon Thani Airport (☎ 246 567), on Udon Thani-Loei Hwy., 5km southwest of town. Limousine bus to Nong Khai (1hr., 100฿) after all flights from Bangkok. **Thai Airways,** 60 Makkhaeng Rd. (☎ 243 222). Open M-F 8-11:30am and 1-4:30pm. To **Bangkok** (8:40am, 1, 7:35pm; 1785฿).

Trains: Train station (☎ 222 061), at the east end of Prajaksinlapacom Rd. Booking office open daily 6am-8pm. To **Bangkok** (11hr.; 9:20am, 7:30, 8:30pm; 3rd-class 155฿, 2nd-class 279฿, A/C lower bed 599฿; 1st-class 1037฿) via **Khon Kaen** (3hr.); and **Nong Khai** (1hr.; 6:15, 7:45am, 5pm; 11฿).

Buses: Bus terminal #1, near Charoensri Shopping Center at the corner of Teekatahnanent and Prajaksinlapacom Rd. To: **Ban Chiang/Sakhon Nakhon** (#230; 3hr.; every

Udon Thani

🏠 ACCOMMODATIONS

Chai Porn Hotel, **2**
Chardensri Palace Hotel, **3**
Charoensri Grand Royal Hotel, **11**
Tang Porn Dhi Raska Hotel, **4**
Thailand Hotel, **10**

🍎 FOOD

Ban Isaan, **7**
Mr. T Restaurant, **5**
Mae Yha, **6**
Rabieng Pattani Restaurant, **1**
Steve's Bar and Restaurant, **8**

30min. 4am-7pm; 58฿, A/C 104฿); **Bangkok** (#407; 11hr., every 15min. 8:30am-11pm, 322฿) via **Khorat** (4½hr., 184฿); **Khon Kaen** (2½hr.; every 30min. 5am-6pm; 44฿, A/C 79฿); **Mukdahan** (5hr., 6 per day 5:45-11:30am, A/C 167฿); **Ubon Ratchathani** (#268; 6hr., 6 per day 7am-2pm, A/C 232฿). Northbound buses leave **bus terminal #2**, 2km northwest of town. To: **Ban Phu** (every 30min. 6am-5pm, 30฿); **Chiang Mai** (11hr.; 7:30am, 6, 8:30pm; 228฿, A/C 410฿); **Loei** (#220; 3½hr., every 20min. 4:20am-6:10pm, 55฿); **Nong Khai** (#221; 1hr., every 1½hr. 6am-7pm, 21฿).

Local Transportation: Songthaew #23 runs between bus terminals #1 and #2 (5฿). Plenty of **samlor** (20-30฿) and **tuk-tuk** (20-50฿) run around town.

✈ 🛈 ORIENTATION AND PRACTICAL INFORMATION

Udon Thani, 562km northeast of Bangkok, lies between Khon Kaen and Nong Khai along the railroad line and **Friendship Hwy.** Navigating the city requires a decent map, flexibility in interpreting street signs, and an eternal awareness of the landmark **Nong Prajak Reservoir,** a large park on the town's west side. **Prajaksinlapacom Rd., Posri Rd.,** and **Srisuk Rd.** run east-west through town from the reservoir. Each road sports a traffic circle where it intersects **Udondutsadee Rd.,** the major north-south thoroughfare. Away from the reservoir, Prajaksinlapacom Rd. ends at the **train station** near **bus terminal #2.** The **airport** and **bus terminal #2** are on the far side of the reservoir, west of the town center.

Tourist Office: TAT, 16/5 Mukkhamontri Rd (☎325 406), at the edge of the reservoir. Look for the back door on Tesa Rd. Not too helpful. Open daily 8:30am-4:30pm.

Currency Exchange: Bangkok Bank, 154 Prajaksinlapacom Rd. (☎221 505). Open M-F 8:30am-3:30pm; currency exchange open daily 8:30am-5pm. **24hr. ATM.**

Emergency: ☎191. **Tourist Police (Bangkok):** ☎1155.

Police: ☎328 515. At Srisuk and Naresuan Rd.

Pharmacies: Sunsak, 194 Posri Rd. (☎222 478). Very well stocked; carries gauzes and sports braces. Open daily 8am-9pm. Or try the pharmacy at **Aek Udon International Hospital** (see below). **Open 24hr.**

Medical Services: Aek Udon International Hospital, 555/5 Posri Rd. (☎341 555). One of the best hospitals in the Northeast. English-speaking doctors. Ask Peter Davison, Manager of International Services, for health advice. AmEx/MC/V.

Laundry Service: Patmoon Chai, 4/9 Pokanusom Rd. (☎244 053), 30m from Posri Rd. intersection. 15฿ per item except underwear and socks (10฿ per item). Open daily 6am-8pm.

Telephones: Communications Authority of Thailand, 108/2 Udondutsadee Rd. (☎222 805). North of the clock tower traffic circle before Wattananuvong Rd. **Lenso international** phone. Open daily 8am-10pm.

Internet Access: On virtually any street but Posri Rd. 15-60฿ per hr. **Click@Internet,** on Makkhaeng Rd., 40m from Posri Rd. intersection. 20฿ per hr.

Post Office: GPO (☎222 304), on Wattananuvong Rd. toward the reservoir. Open M-F 8:30am-4:30pm, Sa-Su 9am-noon. **Postal code:** 41000.

ACCOMMODATIONS

If you're looking for a nice room at a good price, you've come to the wrong town. A wide range of hotels does exist; if you have the baht, luxury is just around the corner.

Chardensri Palace Hotel, 60 Posri Rd. (☎242 611), at the corner with Pamphrao Rd. Best choice in the semi-budget range. Singles or doubles 300฿, with fridge and carpet 360฿, VIP 600฿. ❸

Charoensri Grand Royal Hotel, 277/1 Prajak Rd. (☎343 555), behind the Charoensri Shopping Complex. Nothing gritty or budget here. Udon's most luxurious hotel. Bar, garden, pool, gym. Singles or doubles 1100฿. Breakfast included. ❻

Chai Porn Hotel, 209-211 Makkhaeng Rd. (☎222 144), next to Mandarin Restaurant. Despite its name and outward appearance, Porn is not a house of ill repute. If you're into that stuff, though, congratulations, you're in the right country. Rooms are well worn and baths a bit stained (the innocuous kinds). Communal TV room. Tidy singles 150฿, with A/C 200฿; doubles 200฿/250฿. ❷

Tang Porn Dhi Raksa Hotel, 289 Makkhaeng Rd. (☎221 032). If Chai Porn Hotel were a glitzy, pay-per-view flick, this is a grainy home video. Private bath, shared toilets. Singles 140฿; doubles 200฿. ❷

Thailand Hotel, 4/1-6 Surakan Rd. (☎341 670), between Posri and Thahan Rd., a 10min. walk from the bus station. Decent rooms with peeling paint and vinyl furniture. Singles 200฿, with A/C 250฿; doubles with A/C 350฿. ❸

FOOD

Steve's Bar and Restaurant, 254/26 Prajak Rd. (☎244 523), about 30m east of the traffic light at Teekathananont Rd. A British affair—cricket on the telly, cold Carlsberg, and down-home pub food. Fish and chips 140฿; steaks 180-220฿. Open daily 10:30am-midnight. ❸

Mae Yha, 81 Ratcha Phat Sadu Rd., 4 blocks south of Posri Rd. Walking toward the reservoir from the fountain, take the 2nd left; it's on the 2nd block on the left. Colossal local superstar. A multi-story cafe bursting at the seams with a giant menu and yummy desserts. Nine-scoop sundae 95฿. Thai, Chinese, and Western food 40-150฿. Open daily 9:59am-10:59pm, sharp. ❸

Rabieng Pattani Restaurant, 53/1 Rim Nong Prachak. Walk toward the reservoir on Wattananuvong Rd. and make a right on Tesa Rd.; Rim Nong Prachak is 400m down on the left. Slightly out of the way, but well worth it. A local favorite with fabulous seafood 85-150฿. Open daily 8am-11pm. ❸

Mr. T Restaurant, 254/7 Posri Rd. (☎327 506), at Sisatra Rd. This restaurant/bar/coffeeshop has a mellow atmosphere and acoustic guitar in the evenings. Breakfast (lots of fruit) 80฿. Steaks 110฿. Open 24hr. ❸

Ban Isaan, 177 Adunyadet Rd. Sample all the regional specialties. Thai curries 30-40฿. Open daily 10am-7pm. ❷

Ngee Sun Superstore, 119-123 Posri Rd., between Makkhaeng and Pamphrao Rd. Offers supermarket selection and prices. Open daily 9am-9pm. ❶

◙ SIGHTS

About 2km northwest of town, the **◙Udon Sunshine Fragrant Orchid Farm** (☎242 475), 127 Nongsamrong Rd., is a botanical talent show. Mr. Pradit Kampermpoon devoted a decade of his life to developing the first scented orchid, aptly named "Miss Udon Sunshine." The next enclosure over, where *Desmodium gyrant* makes its home, is even more mind-boggling. These unremarkable-looking herbs perk up and shimmy to the vibes of music or human voice. Thanks to Mr. Kampermpoon's years spent cross-breeding, the plants respond almost instantaneously as opposed to their more lethargic wild counterparts. "Their performance can be helpful to unhappy people," claims Mr. Kampermpoon, crooning in a falsetto to the plants. Some AIDS patients swear by the plants' healing powers, and sufferers of mental illness show marked improvement through exposure. As if this miracle plant didn't do enough, its tea clears up skin and cures stomach ailments. Next on Mr. Kampermpoon's wish list is a plant that will sing background vocals for his upcoming album. Keep your ears peeled. The orchids thrive from September to April, while the dancing plants strut their stuff year-round. To find these living legends, take Posri Rd. past the reservoir and bear right on Phoniyom Rd. After the first stoplight, the farm is 100m ahead on the left. If you get lost, say the magic words "Udon Sunshine" to any passerby. (Open daily 6:30am-6pm. Admission 30฿, goes toward AIDS research.)

Nong Prajak Reservoir, in the northwest section of town, is sprinkled with benches, pavilions, and footbridges. Join mothers, children, and sweethearts to feed the catfish (bag of fish chow 10฿). For a full 360° view of Udon Thani Province from the northeast's only certified **heliport,** sidle into Aek Udon Hospital and ask for Peter Davison.

◙ NIGHTLIFE

Udon's nightlife is packed into a thumping section of **Teekathananont Rd.,** across from the Charoensri Grand Royal Hotel and Wattananuvong Rd. If you like loud techno and wandering elephants, this is the place to be. **Shaken** pumps out Eurohouse with Thai lyrics to a hip crowd. **Nasa's** larger dance floor rocks with hardcore techno. The **Underground** is dark and moody. About 200m past the discos, **Mr. Tong's** outdoor bar is a great place to finish the evening. The town's expats and the locals who love them swear by **Harry's Bar,** 19/4 Banliam Bypass. Heading past the reservoir on Srisuk Rd., take a left on Pracha Ruksa Rd. and a right on Suk Rd. Tuk-tuks from the town center cost 80฿. (At all listed establishments, beers cost 60-70฿ and mixed drinks cost 100-110฿. No cover. Open nightly until 1am.)

MARKETS

Thai Isaan Market, on Sai Uthit Rd. west of bus terminal #1, and **Rangsima Market,** across from bus terminal #2, are both uninspiring. The real deal is **Ban Huay Market** at the north end of Udon-Dutsadee Rd. A network of vendor-lined sois surrounds a huge, covered area with tons of delicious goodies. A number of Thai dishes are cooked on the spot and put into a bag for take-away. Not so delicious are the live turtles, eels, and mountain bikes.

DAYTRIPS FROM UDON THANI

BAN CHIANG

Orange and blue songthaew leave from Posri Rd. to Ban Chiang (#1371; 1½hr., every 30min., 20฿). Walking south on Sai Uthit Rd., passing the bus station on your left, make a right onto Posri Rd. You will see the songthaew on the right side of the road opposite the small supermarket. The turn-off for Ban Chiang is on the left—but if the driver drops you off here, take a tuk-tuk for the remaining 6km (40-50฿). To return to Udon walk straight out of the museum entrance, past the two souvenir shops on the corners of the road to the end. Make a left and then a right. There are many tuk-tuks at this small market which will take you to the highway (40฿). Cross the highway–there is a bus stop diagonally across on the left; any bus going in this direction will go back to Udon. If you are lucky a songthaew may leave from the museum entrance at noon and you can forgo the tuk-tuk ride.

Ban Chiang, 54km east of Udon Thani, is one of Southeast Asia's most significant archaeological discoveries and was recognized as a UNESCO World Heritage Site in 1992. The story of its discovery begins in 1966, when Stephen Young, a Harvard University archaeology student, tripped over a large root. Catching himself, he found the rim of a partially unearthed pot staring him in the face. Upon closer scrutiny, he found that the entire 5m by 15m area was littered with half-buried pots. By the time excavation began in the mid-1970s, many valuable artifacts had been sold to collectors in trading centers worldwide. Since then, archaeologists have learned about the people who lived here from 3600 to 1000 BC. The Ban Chiang people crafted cord-marked vessels and buried their deceased infants in jars. Over 100 skeletons and numerous bronze artifacts indicate that the civilization possessed knowledge of metallurgy much earlier than estimated, casting doubt on the theory that metallurgy came to Thailand from China.

The **village museum** documents the unearthing of Ban Chiang. The second-floor exhibits have comprehensive captions in English. (Open daily 9:30am-4:30pm. 30฿.) At the other end of the village, **Wat Phosi Nai** displays a well-preserved burial site with intact artifacts. Exit left from the museum; the **excavation site** is 600m down on the right.

ERAWAN CAVE

Erawan Cave is just off the Udon Thani-Loei Hwy. (Hwy. 210). Take a tuk-tuk along the highway until the cave becomes visible. From there, another tuk-tuk will transport you the additional 2km from the entrance to the cave.

The gaping crevice in the cliffs that shelter the large Buddha is clearly visible from the highway. A wat at the base of the cliff marks the end of the road. To the right, a huge flight of stairs ascends the mountain. Eventually the steps branch; take the flight to the left. You can start **spelunking** at the top. A path with a panoramic view of the nearby peaks runs through the mountain to the other side.

KHON KAEN   ☎043

Like other Isaan cities, Khon Kaen lacks a "big" tourist attraction. Nonetheless, its festive nightlife, open air markets, and efficient transportation system, give visitors the means to enjoy themselves. Khon Kaen University, Northeastern Thailand's largest university (7200 students), brings a vibrant young crowd to the evening scene. The city also serves as a base for rewarding daytrips to the rest of the province.

TRANSPORTATION

Flights: Khon Kaen Airport (☎346 305), 5km west of town off Maliwan Rd. **Thai Airways,** 9/9 Prachasamran Rd. (☎227 701), inside the Hotel Sofitel, flies to **Bangkok** (4 flights per day, 1500฿).

Trains: Khon Kaen Railway Station (☎221 112), where Ruen Rom Rd. ends at Darunsamran Rd. To: **Bangkok** (8hr.; 8:30, 11:20am, 9, 9:20, 10:40pm; 3rd-class 137฿, 2nd-class 289฿, A/C sleeper 559฿, 1st-class 948฿); **Khorat** (5hr., 5 per day, 38฿); **Nong Khai** (3hr.; 4, 5:30, 9:40am, 3:10pm; 35฿); **Udon Thani** (2hr., 7 per day, 25฿).

Buses: The **bus terminal** (☎237 472), on Pracha Samoson Rd., by the pedestrian overpass. Buses to: **Bangkok** (#20; 7hr., every 25min. 6:30am-9:30pm, 129฿); **Khorat** (3hr., every 30min. 5am-10am, 67฿); **Mukdahan** (4hr., every 30min. 8:10am-4:30pm, 72฿); **Ubon Ratchathani** (#282; every hr. 5:40-11:40am, 108฿); **Udon Thani** (#211 or #262; 2hr., every 20min. 7am-1pm, 3rd-class 44฿). **A/C bus terminal** (☎239 910), on Glang Muang Rd. A/C buses to: **Bangkok** (#20; 7hr., 25 per day, mornings and evenings, 302฿) via **Khorat** (3hr., 140฿); **Loei** (#319; 4hr.; 6:30, 11:30am, 4:30pm; 131฿); **Nong Khai** (#23; 3hr.; 4, 5:30am, 1, 3, 5pm; 110฿); **Ubon Ratchathani** (#268; 5hr., every 2hr. 9am-3pm, 169฿).

Local Transportation: Samlor 20-30฿. **Tuk-tuk** 20-50฿. **Songthaew** 5฿. TAT has a list of stops for all 20 *songthaew* routes. *Songthaew* #11 goes from Khon Kaen Railway Station to TAT. *Songthaew* #17 goes from TAT to the National Museum.

ORIENTATION AND PRACTICAL INFORMATION

Khon Kaen, 450km from Bangkok, is easily reached by plane, bus, or train. The main north-south thoroughfares, **Nah Muang Rd.** and **Glang Muang Rd.,** are lined with **hotels, restaurants,** and the **A/C bus terminal.** Farther south, the parallel Muangs cross **Sri Chant Rd.,** home to the best nightspots. Past Sri Chant Rd. on Glang Muang Rd. are the **post office, police station,** and **day market,** which ends at **Ruen Rom Rd.** A right turn onto Ruen Rom Rd. from Nah Muang Rd. or Glang Muang Rd. leads to the **train station.** The **regular bus terminal** and **TAT office** are on **Pracha Samoson Rd.**

Tourist Office: TAT, 15/5 Pracha Samoson Rd. (☎244 498). A brown and white building several blocks left from the regular bus terminal. Essential comprehensive maps and intracity transportation info. Open daily 8:30am-4:30pm.

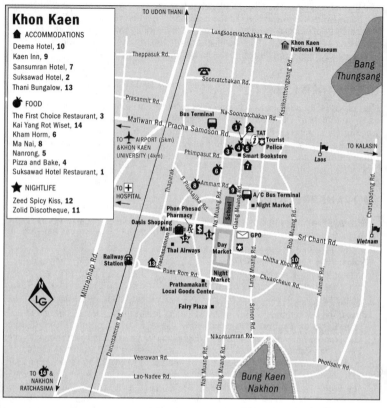

Khon Kaen

🏠 **ACCOMMODATIONS**

Deema Hotel, **10**
Kaen Inn, **9**
Sansumran Hotel, **7**
Suksawad Hotel, **2**
Thani Bungalow, **13**

🍴 **FOOD**

The First Choice Restaurant, **3**
Kai Yang Rot Wiset, **14**
Kham Horm, **6**
Ma Nai, **8**
Nanrong, **5**
Pizza and Bake, **4**
Suksawad Hotel Restaurant, **1**

⭐ **NIGHTLIFE**

Zeed Spicy Kiss, **12**
Zolid Discotheque, **11**

Consulates: Laos, 171 Pracha Samoson Rd. (☎242 856). 30-day visas US$30-35 available same day if you come early. Open M-F 9am-4pm. **Vietnam,** 65/6 Chatapadung Rd. (☎241 154). 15-day visas about US$40, 2-3 working days to process. Open M-F 8-11:30am and 1:30-4:30pm. Light-blue *songthaew* #10 runs to both consulates.

Currency Exchange: Banks and ATMs on Sri Chant Rd. **Bangkok Bank,** 254 Sri Chant Rd. (☎225 144), next to Charoen Thani Princess Hotel entrance. After-hours exchange during high season. Open M-F 8:30am-7pm, Sa-Su 9am-5pm. **24hr. ATM.**

Markets: Sizable **day market** hides behind storefronts along Nah Muang and Glang Muang Rd., stretching south to Ruen Rom Rd. Fruits, vegetables, and pig heads on sale. Popular items include *mut-mee* (see **Weaving,** p. 32) silks and triangular pillows. Open daily 5am-6pm. When other shops shut down, the **night market** gets going along Ruen Rom Rd. at the south end of the day market. Roadside eateries stretch into the horizon.

Bookstore: Smart Bookstore, 6/9-10 Glang Muang Rd. (☎334 122). Great collection of English books on Southeast Asia and Buddhism.

Emergency: ☎191. **Tourist Police (Bangkok):** ☎1155.

Local Tourist Police: 15/5 Pracha Samoson Rd. (☎236 937), left of TAT. **Open 24hr.**

Police: Khon Kaen Police Station (☎221 162), on Glang Muang Rd., between Chitha Khon and Sri Chant Rd.

Pharmacies: Phon Phesad (☎228 260), just off Sri Chant Rd. near the Bangkok Bank. Open daily 8am-midnight.

Medical Services: Khon Kaen-Ram Hospital, 193 Sri Chant Rd. (☎336 789), on the side of the tracks away from town. English-speaking doctors. **Open 24hr.**

Telephones: Khon Kaen Telecommunications Center, 294/1 Soonratchakan Rd. (☎245 371). The real building is behind the one that faces the street.

Internet Access: Several places on Glang Muang Rd. north of Ammart Rd. 15฿ per hr. It's impossible to beat schoolchildren to the computers Su 4-7pm.

Post Office: GPO, on Glang Muang Rd., just south of Sri Chant Rd. *Poste Restante* on ground floor. Open M-F 8:30am-4:30pm, Sa-Su 9am-noon. **CAT** next door open M-F 8:30am-4:30pm offering **international** calling and Internet service. **Postal code:** 40000.

🛏 ACCOMMODATIONS

Sansumran Hotel, 55-59 Glang Muang Rd. (☎239 611), between the giant plastic tusks, near Phimpasut Rd. Spacious rooms with baths and lots of those carved lions so popular in Isaan hotels. Khon Kaen's best value. Singles and doubles 150-250฿. ❷

Kaen Inn, 56 Glang Muang Rd. (☎245 420), at the intersection with Ammart Rd. Standard rooms are the best value–clean, comfortable, and perfectly located in the middle of town. Karaoke, restaurant, free airport transfers. Standard singles and doubles 500฿; deluxe 800฿. ❹

Suksawad Hotel, 2/2 Glang Muang Rd. (☎236 472), near Pracha Samoson Rd. English-speaking staff. The miser's choice in Khon Kaen. Small rooms 80฿, with toilet 100฿; double with toilet 160฿. ❶

Deema Hotel, 113 Chitha Khon Rd. (☎321 562). Very clean and comfortable, but it's a bit out of the way. Good value. Frequented by locals. Singles and doubles 200฿, with A/C 320฿. ❸

Thani Bungalow (☎221 428), at the intersection of Ruen Rom and Prachasamran Rd., next to the Nissan dealership. Bungalows are really large; and that's just about all it's got going for it. A/C bungalows have TV and hot water. Singles and doubles 250฿, with A/C 500฿. ❸

🍴 FOOD

Sidewalk **eateries** ❶ cluster on Phimpasut and Ammart Rd. Cheap Isaan meals like *sup nau mai* (shredded bamboo shoot salad) tempt hungry passersby at **night markets** on Lang Muang and Ruen Rom Rd.

Kham Horm Pub & Restaurant, 38 Nah Muang Rd. (☎243 252), between Phimpasut and Ammart Rd. The local heavyweight champ of restaurants. BBQ outdoors and live music in the evenings. Most dishes 40-120฿; stir-fried chicken with baby corn 60฿. Open daily 10am-2am. ❷

Nanrong, on Glang Muang Rd., near the intersection with Pracha Samoson Rd. Serves a simple menu and serves it well. Try the curry noodles with fresh herbs and sprouts (20฿); its subtle shock of coconut hits you like a Bangkok tuk-tuk. Open daily 8am-8pm. ❶

Pizza and Bake (☎258 883), on Glang Muang Rd. across from the Nanrong Hotel. Serving Vietnamese, Thai, and international food. *Nham nuang,* fresh spring rolls of pork meatballs, cucumbers, pineapple, banana, and fresh herbs you roll yourself are their specialty (99฿). Most dishes 50-100฿. Open daily 7:30am-11:30pm. ❷

NORTHEAST

Ma Nai (☎ 239 958), on Ammart Rd. 2 blocks west of Kaen Inn. From the outside it's a gentle pink European cottage—on the inside it's spicy Thai food all the way. Squid topped with chilis and garlic 150฿; curried seafood in coconut shell 80฿. Open daily 11:30am-10pm. ❸

The First Choice Restaurant, 18/8 Phimpasut Rd., at the corner of Nah Muang Rd. Powerful A/C. Numerous vegetarian choices. Set breakfast 70฿. Thai dishes 50-100฿. Steaks 150-300฿. Open daily 7am-11pm. ❸

Kai Yang Rot Wiset, 177 Mittraphap Rd. Take blue *songthaew* #10 toward Lotus Shopping Center (5฿); it's just beyond PTT gas station on the left. Buffet is easy on the linguistically challenged as well as the taste buds. Dishes 20฿. Open daily 7am-10pm. ❶

Suksawad Hotel Restaurant, 2/2 Glang Muang Rd. Even if you don't like the rooms, you might like the food on this small, outdoor patio. Affordable English/Thai menu. *Thao tom kung* (rice soup with shrimp) 20฿. ❶

👁 SIGHTS

The only noteworthy sight is the well-run **Khon Kaen National Museum,** at the Lung-soomratchakan and Kasikonthungsang Rd. intersection. Blue *songthaew* stop at the side entrance (5฿). The museum documents the history of central Northeast Thailand. The second floor has articles from the olden days (Lop Buri period) while the first floor is devoted to the really olden days (Ban Cihang period, etc.). Check with TAT for the temporary exhibit schedule. (☎ 246 170. Open W-Su 9am-4pm. 30฿.)

In the southeast corner of Khon Kaen is **Bung Kaen Nakhon,** a lakeside recreation center circumscribed by four wats and numerous food stalls. Every April it hosts the **Dok Khoon Siang Khaen Festival,** featuring Isaan music, floral processions, and dances. Check with TAT for specific dates. About 4km northwest of town, **Khon Kaen University** is the largest in northeastern Thailand. *Songthaew* #8 and 10 make the trip from town. If you're lucky, friendly students may give you a tour and show you their art work.

Prathamakant Local Goods Center, 79/2-3 Ruen Rom Rd., is 30m from the Nah Muang Rd. intersection. Those unable to visit Chonabot (see below) can enjoy silk handicrafts here. Lots of *mut-mee* silks, classy and funky shirts and skirts, wooden carvings, and instruments are for sale in air-conditioned comfort. Check out the small **museum** and huge wooden carving of village life in the back. (☎ 224 080. Open daily 9am-8:30pm.)

💶 🗂 NIGHTLIFE AND SHOPPING

The arcade near The First Choice Restaurant (see **Food,** above) is packed with karaoke bars, beer gardens, and pubs. Beware: many "karaoke bars" are laden with prostitutes, and travelers report being offered more than a just a beer. All the major hotels behind Sri Chant Road have some sort of nightlife, like the **Wow** discotheque at the Hotel Sofitel. Across the street is the Oasis Shopping Center, ageneric mall showing Hollywood movies (dubbed in Thai) and home to the fastest Internet connection in town, **KSC Internet** on the 2nd floor (20฿ per hr.). **Zolid Discotheque,** on the bottom floor of the Charoen Thani Princess Hotel, has three levels of dancing and huge screens showing music videos. (☎ 240 400. Small Singha 80฿. No cover. Open daily 9pm-2am.) Next to the Hotel Sofitel off Sri Chant Rd., the action is explosive at **Zeed Spicy Kiss,** where tiny tables meet rainbow lips. (☎ 227 455. Small Singha 69฿. Open daily 9pm-2am.)

🗺 DAYTRIPS FROM KHON KAEN

Although Khon Kaen Province has plenty of sights, the scant tourist facilities make exploring the area a healthy challenge.

CHONABOT

Catch a bus to Nakhon Sawan from Khon Kaen's regular bus terminal (1hr., every hr. until 1:30pm, 35฿) and ask to be let off at Chonabot. When you disembark on the highway, face the wagon-wheel fence and police station, walk right to the first intersection and turn left. The first silk factory is on the right before the post office. To return to Khon Kaen, walk down Phosi Sahat Rd. until it meets the highway. Wait in front of the police station for the last bus back to Khon Kaen at 5pm. Most factories open M-Sa 8am-5pm.

The town of Chonabot stocks hand-woven silk. Tour companies offer expensive trips, but it's best to go on your own. There are no formal showrooms, but owners will gladly display the wares that interest you. Prices vary depending on the thickness and weight of the material. *Mut-mee* silk runs 1000฿, and *sipuen* is 250฿.

PHUWIANG

Buses to Phuwiang leave daily from the regular bus terminal.

Those interested in ancient reptiles should swing by Phuwiang, home to the largest dinosaur fossils in the country. Fossils dug up from the nine quarries located in the area have added weight to the theory that Tyrannosaurus rex existed first in Asia Minor before crossing the Bering Channel to North America. Don't try to take any souvenirs from the sites, as tourist literature warns, "We must not backstop wrong doings such as taking away a dinosaur fossil to be developed into an amulet of portable Buddha image." Ask TAT to photocopy its single brochure for you.

BAN KOK SA-NGA

50km from Khon Kaen. From the regular bus station, take a bus to Kra Nuan (#501; every 30min., last return 6pm, 15฿) and ride a tuk-tuk to the village (30฿). Snake breeding center open to the public; 20฿.

Villagers in "King Cobra Village" have been taming deadly king cobras since 1951, using them as attention-getters for their herbal medicine businesses. Villagers stage "boxing" exhibitions: after tempting the snakes to strike, the masters skillfully sidestep death. Wear a cobra like a boa, if you dare.

NORTHEAST

NORTHERN THAILAND

SYMBOL:	❶	❷	❸	❹	❺
ACCOMM.	Under US$3 Under 120฿	US$3-4.50 120-180฿	US$4.50-9 180-360฿	US$9-14 360-560฿	Over US$14 Over 560฿
FOOD	Under US$0.75 Under 30฿	US$0.75-2 30-80฿	US$2-4 80-160฿	US$4-6 160-240฿	Over US$6 Over 240฿

Northern Thailand's mountains constitute the lowest crags of the Himalayan foothills. Its Salawin River flirts with Myanmar before flooding into the Bay of Bengal, and its northeastern border is none other than the mighty Mekong. Central **Chiang Mai,** formerly the capital of the prosperous Lanna Kingdom, serves as the first stop for many visitors. The magnificent historical ruins of **Sukhothai** break the journey from Bangkok. The hill-tribe haven of **Mae Hong Son** is to the west. Many just choose to savor a peaceful piece of **Pai,** accessible by the renowned loop. **Chiang Rai,** in the north, harbors poppy fields and the Golden Triangle. To the east, **Nan,** which borders Laos, is a good place for wat-lovers, as well as those seeking more off-the-beaten-path locales. Throughout the region, Chinese immigrants display pictures of the Thai Royal Family in shop windows, tribal minorities inhabit misty mountainsides, and refugee camps swell with Burmese escaping their military government—the dialect, cuisine, dance, and wat architecture of Northern Thailand owe much to this fusion of cultures.

CHIANG MAI   ☎ 053

Nothing more than mice scurrying down a hole convinced King Mengrai to establish the seat of his Lanna Kingdom in Chiang Mai in 1296—an inauspicious beginning for a city that has become Thailand's second-largest in both native population and tourist crowds. Thousands of *farang*, drawn by the promise of adventure and a cooler climate, clog the narrow streets of this ancient city. Some of them have long since surrendered to the charm, making the city home and giving strength to the small expatriate community. The beautiful "Rose of the North" bustles with a big-city gait around the protruding ruins, largely oblivious to their presence. The increased stampede of tourists heightens concerns that both hill-tribe culture and the natural environment are quickly eroding. Nonetheless, Chiang Mai seems to have retained its cultural autonomy. The distinctive dialect, Burmese-influenced art and architecture, and an abundance of sticky rice (a Northern specialty) prove that Chiang Mai residents are not about to surrender their heritage, and make Chiang Mai a necessary stop. The mice were on to something.

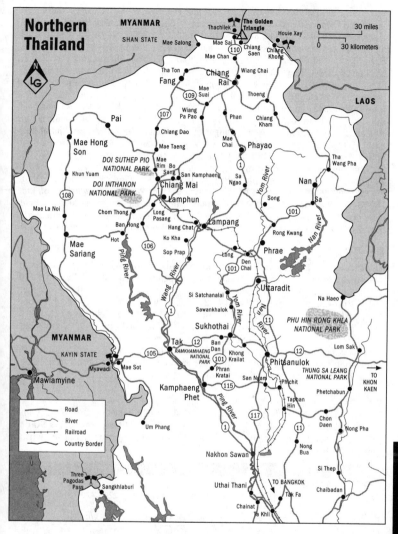

Northern Thailand

MYANMAR

SHAN STATE

Thachilek
The Golden Triangle
Houie Xay

Mae Salong
Mae Sai
Chiang Saen
Chiang Khong

110

Mae Chan

Tha Ton
Fang
Chiang Rai
Wiang Chai

109

Mae Suai
Thoeng

LAOS

Pai

107

Wiang Pa Pao
Phan
Chiang Kham

Chiang Dao

Mae Hong Son

Mae Taeng
Mae Chai
Phayao

DOI SUTHEP PIO NATIONAL PARK

Mae Rim
Bo Sang
San Kamphaeng

1

Tha Wang Pha

Khun Yuam

Chiang Mai

Sa Ngao

Nan

DOI INTHANON NATIONAL PARK

Lamphun

Song

Sa

108

Mae La Noi

Chom Thong

Long Pasang

101

Ban Hong

Hang Chat
Lampang

Rong Kwang

Nan River

Hot

Ko Kha

106

Mae Sariang

Sop Prap

Long
Den Chai

Phrae

101

Ping River

Wang River

Si Satchanalai

Uttaradit

Na Haeo

Sawankhalok

Yom River

1

PHU HIN RONG KHLA NATIONAL PARK

Sukhothai

Nan River

MYANMAR

KAYIN STATE

Tak

12

Ban Dan

RAMKHAMHAENG NATIONAL PARK

101

Khong Krailat

Lom Sak

Mawlamyine

Myawadi

Mae Sot

105

Phran Kratai

San Ngam

Phitsanulok

12

THUNG SA LEANG NATIONAL PARK

TO KHON KAEN

Pichit

Kamphaeng Phet

115

Tappan Hin

Phetchabun

Um Phang

117

Chon Daen
Nong Pha

Ping River

1

Nong Bua

Three Pagodas Pass

Sangkhlaburi

Nakhon Sawan

Si Thep

Uthai Thani

TO BANGKOK

Tak Fa

Chaibadan

Chainat

Ta Khli

Road
River
Railroad
Country Border

0 — 30 miles
0 — 30 kilometers

N

✈ INTERCITY TRANSPORTATION

The monthly *Guidelines*, available at travel agencies, guest houses, and hotels throughout the city, has comprehensive transportation schedules.

BY PLANE

Chiang Mai International Airport (☎ 922 100) sits on Sanambin (Airport) Rd., 3km southwest of the city center. From the airport, **taxis** (☎ 201 307; 100฿), tuk-tuks (50฿), and *songthaew* (15-20฿) can be picked up on the main road. **Thai Airways,**

240 Phra Pokklao Rd., has branches around the city (☎211 044; open daily 8am-5pm) and flies to: **Bangkok** (11 per day 7am-9:15pm, 2275฿); **Mae Hong Son** (10am, 1, 4pm; 870฿). **Air Andaman,** at the airport (☎022 299 555), can be booked through all travel agencies and flies to: **Chiang Rai** (7:30am, 5:25pm; 925฿); **Mae Sot** (M, W, F, Su 2pm; 1085฿); **Nan** (M, W, F, Su 11:30am; 1025฿); **Phitsanulok** (Tu, Th, Sa 11:30am; 1185฿). **Bangkok Airways,** at the airport (☎281 519), flies daily to: **Bangkok** (1 per day, 2170฿) via **Sukhothai** (940฿); **Jinghong** (Tu, Th, Sa 3:20pm; 4540฿); **Samui** (same flight as Bangkok; 4050฿); **Xian** (W, Su 4:20pm, F 5pm; 10,910฿). **Lao Aviation** flies to **Vientiane** (Th, Su 1:10pm; 3360฿). Their contact in Chiang Mai is **Chiang Mai BIS Travel,** 12/1 Loi Krap Rd. (☎206 738. Open daily 8:30am-6pm.) **Air Mandalay** flies to **Mandalay** (Th 4:50pm; 3200฿); **Yangon** (Su 2:35pm; 2895฿). Contact **Charal Business,** 123 Chiang Mai-Lamphun Rd. (☎252 054. Open M-F 8:30am-6pm, Sa 8am-5pm.) **Mandarin Airlines** (☎201 268), 2nd floor at the airport, flies to **Taipei** (W, Th, Su 12:55pm). **Silk Air,** at the Imperial Maeping Hotel, 153 Sri Donchai Rd. (☎276 459; open M-F 8:30am-5pm, Sa-Su 8:30am-1pm), flies to **Singapore** (Tu, Su 5:30pm, F 11:20am; 7000฿). A branch of STA Travel is **Trans World Travel Service Co., Ltd.,** 259/61 Tha Pae Rd. (☎272 416), which may offer cheaper student tickets than carriers do. You'll need a student card (200฿ with passport and proof of student status). All international flights are subject to a 500฿ departure tax (cash only).

BY TRAIN

The **Chiang Mai Railway Station,** 27 Charoen Muang Rd. (☎244 795), on the eastern outskirts of the city, is accessible by *songthaew* (10-20฿) and tuk-tuk (40-50฿). Trains run daily to **Bangkok** (11-14hr.; 7 per day 6:26am-8:40pm; 3rd-class 161฿, 2nd-class sleeper 421-561฿, 2nd-class with A/C 611-681฿, 1st-class sleeper 1193฿). Most Bangkok-bound trains also stop in **Lampang** (2hr.; 3rd-class 23฿, 2nd-class 53฿) and **Phitsanulok** (6-7hr.; 3rd-class 105฿, 2nd-class 190฿). Many options (including food service) are available for an extra charge. Reserve sleeper tickets well in advance; lower berths are pricier. Refunds: 80% 3 days before travel; 50% up to 1hr. after train departure; no refunds thereafter. (Ticket window open daily 6am-8pm.)

BY BUS

Tuk-tuks (30-50฿) and *songthaew* (10-20฿) shuttle between the old city and **Arcade Bus Station** (☎242 664), 3km to the northeast. **Chang Phuak Bus Station** (☎211 586), on Chang Phuak Rd., 1km north of the old city, runs buses within Chiang Mai Province.

DESTINATION, BUS#	DUR.	FREQUENCY/TIME	PRICE
ARCADE BUS STATION			
Bangkok, 18	10hr.	19 per day 6:30am-9pm	224฿, A/C II 314฿, A/C I 403฿, VIP 625฿
Chiang Rai, 166	3hr.	17 per day 6am-5:30pm	77฿, A/C 139฿
Chiang Khong, 671	6hr.	6:30, 8am, 12:30pm	121฿, A/C II 218฿, A/C I 169฿
Golden Triangle	4hr.	noon, 12:15pm	95฿, A/C 171฿
Khon Kaen, 633 or 175	12hr.	11 per day 5am-9pm	219-243฿, A/C II 307-437฿
Khorat, 635 (Ratchasima)	12hr.	10 per day 3:30am-8:30pm	243฿, A/C 340-510฿
Lampang, 152	2hr.	every 30min. 6am-4pm	29฿
Mae Hong Son, 170	8hr.	6:30, 8, 11am, 8, 9pm	143฿, A/C 257฿
via Mae Sariang	5hr.	1:30, 3pm (Mae Sariang only)	78฿, A/C 140฿
Mae Hong Son, 612	7hr.	7, 9, 10:30am, 12:30pm	105฿, A/C 147฿
via Pai	4hr.	4pm (Pai only)	60฿

DESTINATION, BUS#	DUR.	FREQUENCY/TIME	PRICE
Mae Sai, 619	4hr.	8 per day 6am-5pm	95฿, A/C 171฿
Mae Sot, 672	6hr.	11am, 1:10pm	134฿, A/C 241฿
Nan, 169 or 113	6hr.	15 per day 6:15am-10:30pm	117-128฿, A/C 164-230฿
Phitsanulok, 155, 132, or 623	6hr.	11 per day 6:30am-8pm	120-140฿, A/C 184-196฿
Rayong	17hr.	8 per day 5am-6:30pm	305฿, A/C 555-645฿
via Pattaya	16hr.		285฿, A/C 605฿
Sukhothai	5hr.	13 per day 5am-8pm	122฿, A/C 171฿
Ubon Ratchathani, 587	17	6 per day 12:15-6pm	325฿, A/C 590-685฿
CHANG PHUAK BUS STATION			
Chom Thong	1¼hr.	every 20min. 6:30am-6pm	23฿
Lamphun	1hr.	every 10min. 6:20am-6pm	12฿
Tha Ton	4hr.	6 per day 6am-3:30pm	70฿
via Fang	3½hr.	every 30min. 5:30am-5:30pm	60฿

ORIENTATION

Chiang Mai is 720km north of Bangkok. The primary area of interest is within the old city and the area to its east which stretches 1.5km to the **Ping River.** A square moat delineates the old city; within it, the east-west soi numbers increase as you go north. North-south **Phra Pokklao Rd.** and east-west **Ratchadamnoen Rd.** divide the square. **Moon Muang Rd.** follows the inside of the moat and intersects Ratchadamnoen Rd. at **Tha Pae Gate,** the center of backpacker activity. If Tha Pae Gate weren't closed to traffic, Ratchadamnoen Rd. would flow into **Tha Pae Rd.,** which runs east to the Ping River and **Nawarat Bridge.** Along the way, it intersects **Chang Klan Rd.,** home to the night bazaar, and **Charoen Prathet Rd.,** which flanks the Ping's west bank. TAT is on **Chiang Mai-Lamphun Rd.,** which hugs the Ping River's east bank. Driving in Chiang Mai has been likened to Formula One racing: complete with chicane work (U-turns to get to the other side) and countless pit stops (to catch your breath). The circuitous nature of the one-way roads, designed to make the traffic flow, is quite straightforward once you've mastered the pattern. Fortunately, there's no need, as walking is easy (15min. from Tha Pae Gate to the Night Bazaar) and tuk-tuk and *songthaew* flood the streets for longer trips.

Guest houses, TAT, and other tourist-geared establishments stock free copies of *Guidelines* and *What's on Chiang Mai,* which offer occasionally useful and often amusing practical information. Watch out for *Chiang Mai Newsletter,* the closest thing the expatriate community has to a local paper, with announcements, classifieds, and expatriate horror stories. Tough to find, it may be easiest to read it online at www.chiangmainews.com.

LOCAL TRANSPORTATION

Songthaew, Tuk-tuk, and Samlor: *Songthaew* 10฿ anywhere in the city, except for along special routes, to the airport or bus station, or at night. Don't pay more than 40฿. Already occupied *songthaew* are cheaper than empty ones. Tuk-tuks and *samlor* 20-30฿ within the old city, 40-60฿ for trips across the city, 400-500฿ per day. **Taxi** service (☎201 307) can also be arranged; to Doi Suthep 300฿.

Rentals: Bicycles 30-60฿ per day. Often require a passport photocopy, a 500฿ deposit, or both. **The Chiang Mai Disabled Center,** 133/1 Ratchaphakhinai Rd., rents mountain bikes (40฿ per day). Motorbike rental shops litter the Tha Pae Gate area; all require a deposit and photocopy of passport. Motorbike rental is typically 150฿ per day, 200฿ with insurance. Discounts for long-term rental. Check what the insurance covers—at

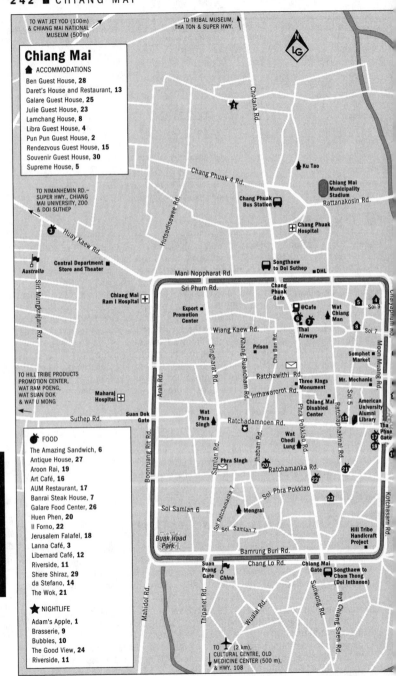

Chiang Mai

🏠 ACCOMMODATIONS

Ben Guest House, **28**
Daret's House and Restaurant, **13**
Galare Guest House, **25**
Julie Guest House, **23**
Lamchang House, **8**
Libra Guest House, **4**
Pun Pun Guest House, **2**
Rendezvous Guest House, **15**
Souvenir Guest House, **30**
Supreme House, **5**

🍴 FOOD

The Amazing Sandwich, **6**
Antique House, **27**
Aroon Rai, **19**
Art Café, **16**
AUM Restaurant, **17**
Banrai Steak House, **7**
Galare Food Center, **26**
Huen Phen, **20**
Il Forno, **22**
Jerusalem Falafel, **18**
Lanna Café, **3**
Libernard Café, **12**
Riverside, **11**
Shere Shiraz, **29**
da Stefano, **14**
The Wok, **21**

⭐ NIGHTLIFE

Adam's Apple, **1**
Brasserie, **9**
Bubbles, **10**
The Good View, **24**
Riverside, **11**

NORTHERN THAILAND

TO WAT JET YOD (100m) & CHIANG MAI NATIONAL MUSEUM (500m)

TO TRIBAL MUSEUM, THA TON & SUPER HWY.

TO NIMANHEMIN RD.– SUPER HWY., CHIANG MAI UNIVERSITY, ZOO & DOI SUTHEP

TO HILL TRIBE PRODUCTS PROMOTION CENTER, WAT RAM POENG, WAT SUAN DOK & WAT U MONG

TO ✈ (2 km), CULTURAL CENTRE, OLD MEDICINE CENTER (500 m), & HWY. 108

Chotana Rd.
Ku Tao
Chiang Mai Municipality Stadium
Chang Phuak 4 Rd.
Chang Phuak Bus Station
Rattanakosin Rd.
Chang Phuak Hospital
Hutsadisawee Rd.
Huay Kaew Rd.
Australia
Siri Mungkrajarn Rd.
Central Department Store and Theater
Mani Noppharat Rd.
Songthaew to Doi Suthep
DHL
Sri Phum Rd.
Chiang Mai Ram I Hospital
Chang Phuak Gate
@Cafe
Wat Chiang Man
Soi 9
Export Promotion Center
Thai Airways
Soi 7
Wiang Kaew Rd.
Khang Ruanchan Rd.
Cha Ban Rd.
Prison
Somphet Market
Moon Muang Rd.
Kotchasan Rd.
Ratchawithi Rd.
Three Kings Monument
Mr. Mechanic
Singharat Rd.
Arak Rd.
Inthawarorot Rd.
Chiang Mai Disabled Center
American University Alumni Library
Maharaj Hospital
Suan Dok Gate
Wat Phra Singh
Ratchadamnoen Rd.
Wat Chedi Lung
Pha Pokklao Rd.
Ratchaphakinai Rd.
Tha Phae Gate
Suthep Rd.
Boonruang Rit Rd.
Samlan Rd.
Jhaban Rd.
Phra Singh
Ratchamanka Rd.
Soi Ratchamanka 7
Soi Samlan 6
Soi Samlan 7
Mengrai
Buak Haad Park
Soi Phra Pokklao
Bamrung Buri Rd.
Suan Prang Gate
China
Chang Lo Rd.
Chiang Mai Gate
Songthaew to Chom Thong (Doi Inthanon)
Mahidol Rd.
Thipanet Rd.
Wualai Rd.
Suriwong Rd.
Rat Chiang Saen Rd.
Hill Tribe Handicraft Project

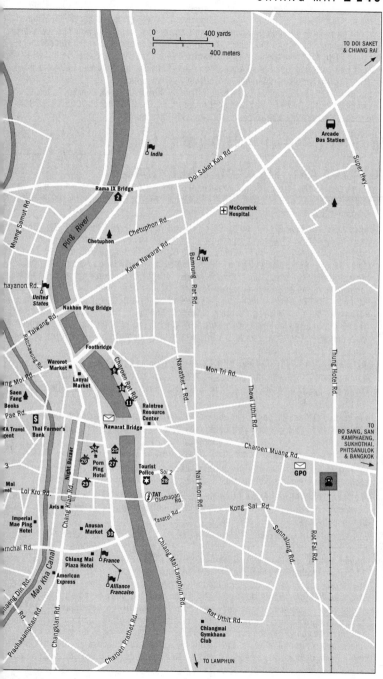

0   400 yards
0   400 meters

TO DOI SAKET
& CHIANG RAI

Super Hwy.

Arcade
Bus Station

India

Doi Saket Kao Rd.

Rama IX Bridge
2

McCormick
Hospital

Muang Samut Rd.

Ping River

Chetuphon Rd.

Chetuphon

Kaew Nawarat Rd.

Bamrung Rat Rd.

UK

Chayanon Rd.

United
States

Nakhon Ping Bridge

Taiwang Rd.

Ratchawong Rd.

Footbridge

Warorot
Market

Charoen Rat Rd.

Nawaket 1 Rd.

Mon Tri Rd.

Thung Hotel Rd.

ng Moi Rd.

Lanyai
Market

Saen
Fang
Books

9

10

Thewi Uthit Rd.

Pae Rd.

11

Raintree
Resource
Center

KA Travel
gent

Thai Farmer's
Bank

Nawarat Bridge

Charoen Muang Rd.

TO
BO SANG, SAN
KAMPHAENG,
SUKHOTHAI,
PHITSANULOK
& BANGKOK

3

24

25

GPO

Night Bazaar

26

Porn
Ping
Hotel

27

Mai
vel

29

Tourist
Police

Soi 2

28

Nai Phon Rd.

Loi Kro Rd.

TAT
Osathapan
Rd.

Avis

Tasatoi Rd.

Kong Sai Rd.

Rot Fai Rd.

Imperial
Mae Ping
Hotel

Chiang Klan Rd.

Anusan
Market

30

Sannaung Rd.

arnchai Rd.

Chiang Mai-Lamphun Rd.

Chiang Mai
Plaza Hotel

France

American
Express

Alliance
Francaise

hiang Din Rd.

Mae Kha Canal

Prachasamphan Rd.

Changklan Rd.

Charoen Prathet Rd.

Rat Uthit Rd.

Chiangmai
Gymkhana
Club

TO LAMPHUN

NORTHERN THAILAND

most places it will only partially cover damage to the motorcycle and not personal injury (unless you have a motorbike license). With similar pricing around Chiang Mai the quality of a shop's bikes and the service they provide in the event of a breakdown set them apart. High in both respects, **Mr. Mechanic,** 4 Moon Muang Rd. Soi 5 (☎214 708), also has comprehensive insurance. Motorbike 120฿; with insurance 170฿. As new 150฿/200฿. For bikes, full range of terrifyingly throaty options (125-200cc, 300-700฿ per day). Bicycle 30฿ per day; new bike with gears 60฿. **Avis,** Royal Princess Hotel, 112 Chang Klan Rd. (☎281 033), and at the airport (☎201 574). Toyota Corollas 1790฿ per day. Suzuki 4WD 1290฿ per day. Open daily 8am-5pm.

⑦ PRACTICAL INFORMATION

TOURIST AND FINANCIAL SERVICES

Tourist Office: TAT, 105/1 Chiang Mai-Lamphun Rd. (☎248 604), across from the next bridge 500m south of Nawarat Bridge. Chock-full of maps and brochures. Open daily 8:30am-4:30pm.

Consulates: Australia, 165 Siri Mungkrajaru Rd. (☎225 975). Open M-F 8am-5pm. **Canada** (☎850 147), several km southeast of the old city on Chiang Mai-Lampang Rd. Consular hours M-F 9am-noon. **China** (☎200 525), on Chang Lo Rd., at Suan Prung Gate. 30-day single entry visa 1100฿; multiple-day 1650฿. 4-day processing. Visa application M-F 9am-11:30am. **France** (☎281 466), on Charoen Prathet Rd., in the same building as Alliance Française. Open M-F 10am-noon. **India,** 344 Charoen Rat Rd. (☎243 066). 6-month tourist visa with multiple entries 2100฿ (Australian citizens); 3100฿ (US citizens). 4-day processing. Open M-F 9am-noon. **UK,** 198 Bamrung Rot Rd. (☎263 015). Open M-F 9-11:30am. **US,** 387 Witchayanon Rd. (☎252 629). Services for American citizens M and W 1-3:30pm. Office open M-F 8am-4pm. Duty officer (emergency only ☎01 881 1878).

Visa Services: Travel agents around town can organize visas for **Laos** (same price as it would cost in Bangkok; 4-day processing 750฿, 2-day wait 1050฿ for 15-day visa) and **Vietnam** (slightly more expensive than in Bangkok; 4-day processing, 2400฿ for a 1-month visa).

Immigration Office: 97 Sanambin (Airport) Rd. (☎277 510). **Visa extensions** 500฿; 1-day processing. Bring 2 passport photos, 2 copies of passport photo page, visa, and arrival/departure card. Open M-F 8:30am-noon and 1-4:30pm.

Currency Exchange: Banks line Tha Pae Rd. **Thai Farmers Bank,** 169-171 Tha Pae Rd. (☎270 151). Open M-F 8:30am-3:30pm. **24hr. ATM** (Cirrus/MC/PLUS/V). Currency exchange booths in the night bazaar on Chang Klan Rd. Open daily until 10pm.

American Express: Sea Tours Company, 2/3 Prachasamphan Rd. (☎271 441). The only AmEx affiliate in Northern Thailand. Will replace traveler's checks. Open M-F 8:30am-4:30pm, Sa 8:30-11:30am.

Work Opportunities: Australia Center, 75/1 Moo 14, Suthep Rd. (☎810 552), on a soi after the turn-off to Wat U-Mong, provides a leaflet on working in Chiang Mai as an English teacher. **Chiang Mai Disabled Center,** 133/1 Ratchaphakhinai Rd. (☎213 941; www.infothai.com/disabled). Volunteers who can teach English or are computer literate and can make a long-term commitment are always welcome. Those who can stay less than one month but would still like to volunteer may be able to help in an administrative capacity. Open daily 8am-8pm. **Rejoice Urban Development** (☎806 227; www.rejoicecharity.com). Take Suthep Rd. to Canal Rd., the next major intersection after the turn-off to the super-highway. Turn left; it's 7 bridges down on the right. One of only a handful of NGOs working directly with the HIV-infected community. Qualified nurses, doctors, social workers, and medical students, as well as those who can serve in administrative or technical positions, are welcome to volunteer for stints of 2 weeks to 2 months. Volunteers are expected to cover their own room and board. Contact the founder, Gareth, for more information. Open M-F 9am-5pm, Sa 9am-1pm.

LOCAL SERVICES

Luggage Storage: At the **train station** (☎245 363). 10฿ per day per piece for the first 5 days, 15฿ per additional day (20-day max.). Open daily 4:50am-8:45pm. At the **airport.** 30฿ per day (14-day max.). Open daily 6am-10pm. Most guest houses store luggage for free, although security can be dubious; never leave passport or credit cards in luggage.

English-Language Books: The best used bookstores, **Gecko Books** (☎874 066; open daily 10am-7pm) and **Backstreet Book** (☎871 413; open daily 9am-10pm) sit next to each other in heated rivalry on Chang Moi Kao Rd. at the Tha Pae Gate. The **American University Alumni (AUA;** ☎211 973) offers a library service with a large selection of English books and videos. One-day pass available if you just want to sit in A/C comfort and read the paper. Visitor membership 140฿ per month. Resident 400฿ per year. Open M-F 8:30am-6pm, Sa 9am-1pm. **Raintree Resource Center** (☎262 660), next to the police box east of Nawarat Bridge, also has a library but its service is geared to the expatriate community. **Movieline** is a recorded English announcement of what's playing around town (☎262 661). Open Tu-Sa 10am-noon, Su 4-4:45pm.

Markets: The **night bazaar,** a must-see of Chiang Mai, dominates Chang Klan Rd. 6pm-midnight, and is stocked with hill-tribe handicrafts, expensive furniture, and designer rip-offs. The southern end leads to sit-down food joints at Anusan Market where the English dishes on the menu may be up to double the price. Head north to the **nightly food stalls** at Warorot Market for a cheap and quick bite.

EMERGENCY AND COMMUNICATIONS

Emergency: ☎191. **Ambulance:** ☎1669. **Tourist Police (Bangkok):** ☎1155.

Police: ☎276 040, on Ratchadamnoen Rd. before Wat Phra Singh. **Open 24hr.**

Local Tourist Police: ☎248 130, on Chiang Mai-Lamphun Rd. 50m north of TAT. **Open 24hr.**

Pharmacy: Pharma Choice 2 (☎280 136), in Suriwong Plaza at Tha Pae Gate. Open daily 9am-7pm.

Medical Services: McCormick Hospital, 133 Kaew Nawarat Rd. (☎241 311), has ambulance service and a **24hr. pharmacy.** English-speaking doctors. MC/V. On the other side of town, the plush **Chiang Mai Ram I Hospital,** 9 Boonruang Rit Rd. (☎224 861), has the same services.

Telephones: Overseas calls at post offices. Internet cafes around town offer collect (30฿) and overseas calls. The cheapest overseas rates are on calls placed via the Internet. **HCD phones,** which connect you directly to your country's operator, can be found inside the GPO and Thai Airways buildings and outside TAT (not all carriers available).

HOLD THE STUFFING Thailand is a world leader in penis-reattachment surgery, but if you're considering penile surgical augmentation, make sure your doctor is reputable and has good taste. In October 1999, the Bangkok Post reported that unlicensed physicians had performed 100 penis-enlargement operations by injecting mixtures of olive oil, chalk, and other substances to provide bulk and springiness. According to the always reliable News of the Weird, one hospital official in Chiang Mai reported having seen bits of the Bangkok telephone directory stuffed into one unsuspecting penis.

NORTHERN THAILAND

Internet Access: Several Internet cafes line the northern half of **Ratchaphakhinai Rd.** 20฿ per hr. and around Tha Pae Gate 30฿ per hr. **The Chiang Mai Disabled Center,** 133/1 Ratchaphakhinai Rd., has Internet access. 20฿ per hr. Open daily 8am-8pm (Internet until approx. 10pm). **@Cafe,** 252/13 Phra Pokklao Rd., can download pictures from digital camera flashcards. 16-32 megabytes 50฿. Burn pictures onto a CD 50฿. Open daily 11am-midnight.

Post Offices: GPO (☎245 376), on Charoen Muang Rd., 150m toward the old city from the train station. *Poste Restante.* Open M-F 8:30am-4:30pm, Sa-Su 9am-noon. **Mae Ping Post Office** (☎252 037), on Charoen Prathet Rd., just north of Nawarat Bridge. Open M-F 8:30am-4:30pm, Sa 9am-noon. **Phra Singh Post Office** (☎814 062), on Samlan Rd., south of Wat Phra Singh. Open M-F 8:30am-4:30pm, Sa 9am-noon. All 3 provide **CATNET** Internet with PIN or card. GPO and Phra Singh have **international phone**/fax. **DHL Worldwide Express,** 160/1 Mani Noppharat Rd. (☎418 501), east of the Chang Phuak Gate. Open M-F 8:30am-6pm, Sa 8:30am-5pm. **Postal code:** 50000.

⛏ ACCOMMODATIONS

Guest house signs sprout from almost every soi entrance within a 1km radius of **Tha Pae Gate.** Reservations are recommended during festival periods, during which time certain guest houses will inflate their prices. The easiest way to choose an accommodation from the multitude of options is to pick a neighborhood. The area around Tha Pae Gate is in close proximity to everything, although the drone of traffic and bar tunes is unnerving. Heading north from Tha Pae Gate on Moon Muang Rd. (with the traffic) leads to Soi 7 and 9 in the Old City, which are packed with budget choices and blissfully quiet at night. Indeed, most places within the Old City offer refuge from the swirling traffic. The pace at the Ping River is frenetic, but it lures visitors with its bar scene and Night Bazaar. Unfortunately, it's difficult to find budget lodgings here, as upmarket hotels clog the area. Many guest houses make their money from treks. In the high season, if you don't sign up for your guest house's trek, you may be asked to sign out. Beware of louts who tell you that the guest house you're interested in is closed or full—all they want is a shady competitor's commission.

THA PAE GATE AREA

⛰ Libra Guest House, 28 Moon Muang Rd. Soi 9 (☎/fax 210 687), in the northeast corner of the old city. Complete with a new garden setting and renovated rooms, the popular family-run establishment just keeps getting better, delivering warm service with characteristic "friendly attitude." Consistently praised treks (3-day, 1600฿, max. 12 people). Cooking school 700฿ per day. Laundry service 25฿ per kg. Free pickup from bus, train station, or airport. Check-out 10am. Reservations recommended. Dorms 50฿; doubles with bath 100฿, with bath and hot water 150฿. ❶

Rendezvous Guest House, 3/1 Ratchadamnoen Rd. Soi 5 (☎213 763), 50m left off Ratchadamnoen Rd. Superb value with bath, TV, cable, and fan in every room. Laundry service 30฿ per kg. Safety deposit box. Rooms 280฿, with A/C 380฿. ❹

Lamchang House, 24 Moon Muang Rd. Soi 7 (☎210 586). Wooden house oozes charm in the middle of a concrete jungle. The handful of comfy bottom-floor bamboo thatch rooms are always full. All rooms with shared bath. Singles 90฿; doubles 160฿; private outdoor house sleeps three 300฿. ❶

Supreme House, 44/1 Moon Muang Rd. Soi 9 (☎222 480), 100m from Libra Guest House. Helpful owner. No hassle accommodation with flexible check-out time. 4000+ multi-language books, free for guest use. Singles with hot water 100฿, with A/C 200฿; doubles 150฿/250฿; triples and quads 200฿/300฿. ❶

Julie Guest House, 7/1 Soi 5 Phra Pokklao Rd., best reached by walking down Ratchaphakhinai Rd. following the signs. Aside from the cheap rooms, the attraction here is the unique rooftop setting decked with hammocks. Pool table, TV, and VCR. Dorm 50฿; singles 80-90฿; doubles with hot shower 130฿; triples with hot shower 180฿. ❶

Daret's House and Restaurant, 4/5 Chaiyaphum Rd. (☎235 440), opposite Tha Phae Gate's north end. A *farang* magnet. Central location and top-notch restaurant make up for a taciturn owner and unimpressive rooms. Small English bookstore. **International phone.** Internet 30฿ per hr. Check-out 10am. All rooms have bath. Singles 120฿; doubles and twins 140฿; with hot water 160฿. ❷

NEAR THE PING RIVER

Ben Guest House, 4/11 Chiang Mai-Lamphun Rd. Soi 2 (☎244 103). Down a soi adjacent to the tourist police. Large beds, hot showers, and fans. Nice garden and laundry service (40฿ per kg). Check-out 10am. Motorcycle rental 150฿, with insurance 200฿. Internet 30฿ per hr. All rooms 150฿. ❷

Pun Pun Guest House, 321 Charoen Rat Rd. (☎243 362), at Rama IX Bridge. The only budget accommodation by the river. Small restaurant/bar with cable TV and pool table (Carlsberg 30฿). Wooden bungalows by the river 150-175฿. Brick rooms with hot water and Western toilet 200-225฿. ❷

Souvenir Guest House, on Charoen Prathet Rd., at the intersection with Sri Donchai Rd. (☎818 786). Nicely set rooms on busy road. Gay-friendly establishment. Table tennis and weight room (2hr. 30฿). Best value rooms are A3 and A4 with shared bath and patio. Check-out noon. Singles 170฿, with bath 220฿, with A/C 370฿; doubles 200฿/260฿/410฿; twins 230฿/290฿/460฿. ❷

Galare Guest House, Charoen Prathet Rd. Soi 2 (☎818 887), last right turn before Nawarat Bridge. High-quality rooms set in manicured gardens on the riverfront. Prime location. Best rooms are downstairs. Singles with telephone and A/C 450฿; doubles with cable TV and fridge 860฿. ❹

◪ FOOD

Nowhere else in Thailand is there such a wide variety of restaurants as in Chiang Mai. Diners can alternate between the cheap and quick market scene and elaborate dining rooms. All options have one thing in common: great value. Thanks to the large expatriate community, you can find popular and authentic Western dishes around Tha Pae Gate. The culinary highlight of Chiang Mai, however, is Northern Thai food. Dishes are served with sticky rice; traditionally diners take a small ball of sticky rice in their right hand and then a morsel of the main dish. The curries, characterized by a lack of coconut milk, are generally spicier. The food connoisseur will love the *Chiang Mai Restaurant Guide Book* (40฿) put out by and available at the **Chiang Mai Restaurant Club,** 128/1 Rattanakosin Rd. (☎233 297; open M-F 10am-5pm), or at any of the member restaurants around town. Of the 54 places offering a 10% discount on Chef Recommendations, *Let's Go* lists the Chiang Mai Cultural Center, Huen Phen, The Good View, and Jerusalem Falafel.

MARKET FOOD. Somphet Market, on Moon Muang Rd. between Soi 6 and 7, serves banana pancakes (10-15฿), fried noodles (20-40฿), and *kuaytiaw lu chin pla* (fishball noodle soup, 20฿). It's open all day, but food stalls don't get going until after 7pm. **Anusan Market,** between Chang Klan and Charoen Prathet Rd., north of Sri Dornchai Rd., is an overpriced nocturnal snack zone. Dining is cheaper at the **Galare Food Court** in the middle of the night bazaar where a casual dinner is served with nightly entertainment. In the evening, the road that runs

NORTHERN THAILAND

> ### CHOWIN' DOWN IN CHIANG MAI
>
> **Yam prik yuak:** A yellow pepper salad with dried shrimp, cabbage, shredded onion, coriander, boiled egg, red pepper seeds, lemon, sugar, and fish sauce.
>
> **Gaeng oua:** A light red, northern curry served with river or pond fish. Cream is not normally added to northern curries but this dish is an exception.
>
> **Paad paak khome:** Fried green spinach with chopped or ground chicken, black mushrooms, bean curd, and oyster sauce.
>
> **Gaeng jued moo-sub gub khai:** Ground pork and egg soup.
>
> **Gaeng Buad Tua Dam:** Black beans, coconut cream, palm sugar, and salt.
>
> **Khao niaw mamuang:** A rich dessert of mangos and sticky rice.
>
> **Sticky or fried rice:** Need we say more? A staple with most dishes.
>
> **Sai oua:** Northern Thai pork sausage.
>
> **Num phrik:** Spicy chili paste blended with meats or seafood, served with sticky rice. Guaranteed to take your breath away.

between **Wararot Market** and **Lanyai Market** on the west bank of the Ping River north of Tha Pae Rd. is crammed with food stalls offering Chiang Mai's best Thai take-out. Freshly sliced fruit (10฿) is available at all the markets. The mango season (Mar.-May) brings ▓*khoa niaw mamuang* (mangos on sweet sticky rice), a simple Thai delicacy.

TRADITIONAL FOOD. For a serious culinary experience, try a *khantoke* dinner. At this formal meal, diners sit on the floor and use their hands to eat rice, two meat dishes, and two vegetable dishes from bowls placed on a *khantoke*, a low tray table. The **Old Chiang Mai Cultural Center,** 185/3 Wualai Rd. (☎275 097), 1.5km south of the old city, offers vegetarian and Muslim versions. State your preferences when calling ahead for the necessary reservation. The 3hr. affair, accompanied by traditional dancing, begins nightly at 7pm (270฿, transportation included).

THE OLD CITY—WITHIN THE MOAT

▓ **Huen Phen,** 112 Ratchamanka Rd., west of Phra Pokklao Rd. Northern Thai dining at its finest. Locals come here for the spicy *num phrik* (chili paste with meats, 35฿). *Farang* with soft palates may prefer the curries (50-60฿). Banana flower and pork rib curry 50฿. Banana in coconut milk 15฿. Portions are small, but have exquisite flavor—you'll be able to sample more. Try to go during dinner so you can sit in the cozy teak house. Open daily 8am-3pm and 5-10pm. ❷

The Wok, 44 Ratchamanka Rd., east of Ratchaphakhinai Rd. Owners run the Chiang Mai Thai Cookery School. Impeccable "special Northern style food" includes spicy Chiang Mai sausage (60฿) and Thai-style fishcakes (60฿). Chiang Mai curry 60฿; black sticky rice pudding 30฿; iced *panadanus* leaves drink 20฿. Open daily 11am-10pm. ❷

Banrai Steak House, Phra Pokklao Rd. Soi 13, around the corner from Thai Airways. This Chiang Mai institution lives up to its boast as "the best steak in town." Steak and chicken barbecued in Thai marinades served up with veggies and baked potato 99฿. Coconut shake 20฿; sandwich 50฿; fried rice 50฿. Open daily 3pm-midnight. ❸

The Amazing Sandwich, 252/3 Phra Pokklao Rd., next to Thai Airways. For those craving a yummy baguette. Choose toppings from an extensive selection. Sandwich 60฿; baguette 70฿; sub 85฿; salad platter 85฿. Open M-Sa 9am-8pm. ❸

Il Forno, 142 Phra Pokklao Rd., south of Ratchamanka Rd. intersection. Decorated in traditional Italian red, green, and white. Delivers fresh bread and pasta. Thin-crust pizza 110-150฿. Vegetable panini 45฿. Divine tiramisù 60฿. Open daily 9am-10:30pm. ❸

THA PAE GATE

Aroon Rai, 45 Kotchasarn Rd., south of Tha Pae Rd. and before Loi Kroa Rd. The multitude of *farang* and Thais who have dined under the splendor of portraits of His Majesty have left Aroon Rai looking well worn, and for good reason—the food is tasty and cheap. English menu highlights Northern specialties. Curries 40-50฿. Open daily 8:30am-10pm. ❷

da Stefano, 2/1-2 Chang Moi Kao Rd., off Tha Pae Rd. High quality Italian restaurant with reasonable prices considering the excellent service and elegant A/C dining room. All meals served with bread. Bruschetta 30฿. Gnocchi with asparagus pesto and ricotta cheese 120฿. Homemade pasta with eggplant, mushrooms, and tomato sauce 90฿; spaghetti bolognese 90฿; pizza margherita 110฿. Open daily 11am-11pm. ❸

AUM Restaurant, 65 Moon Muang Rd., just south of the Tha Pae Gate. Trendy vegetarian restaurant enhanced by convenient locale and second-hand bookstore. Cushioned seating area upstairs. All soups and stir-fries with Thai sauces 40-50฿. Vietnamese spring rolls with carrot sauce 40฿. Open daily 7am-2pm and 5-9pm. ❷

Art Cafe, 291 Tha Pae Rd., as central as you can get. The extensive menu reads well, but is suffering from an identity crisis—we'll just call it international. Caters to those hankering for Western cravings. Beef burritos 90฿. Crispy pizza 120-160฿. Real gelato 20฿ per scoop. Open daily 10am to 10 or 11pm. ❸

Jerusalem Falafel, 35/3 Moon Muang Rd., near AUM Restaurant. Incredible falafel pita with hummus, tahini, and fries 80฿. Feta salad 50฿. Open Sa-Th 9am-8pm. ❷

NEAR THE PING RIVER

▨ **Riverside,** 9-11 Charoen Rat Rd. From Nawarat Bridge, take a left on Charoen Rat Rd; it's the 1st building on the left. Phenomenal view from the "*farangda*" (veranda filled with *farang*) matched only by the food. Attentive staff serve beef salad with mint leaves (60฿). Open daily 10am-1:30am. ❷

Antique House, 71 Charoen Prathet Rd., before the turn-off to Porn Ping Tower Hotel on the opposite side of the road. Fancy the chair you're sitting on? Take it home—most of the decor in this serene, 131-year-old teak house is for sale. *Som tam* (papaya salad with seafood) 60฿. Dishes 40-150฿. Open daily 11am-midnight. ❸

Shere Shiraz, 23-25 Charoen Prathet Rd. Soi 6, off Chang Klan Rd. down the soi south of Porn Ping Tower Hotel. Delicious South Asian restaurant serves Middle Eastern and Thai food, too. Tandoori chicken 200฿. Chicken *tikka* 100฿. Naan 15฿. 10% service charge. Open daily 10am-11pm. ❸

COFFEEHOUSES

The hills of Northern Thailand have proved perfect for coffee plantations. The **Royal Project** and other NGOs have promoted this alternate cash crop to opium amongst the hill tribes; the fruits of their labor are ready to be tasted.

Libernard Cafe, 295-299 Chang Moi Rd., one block in from the moat. It's Sunday every morning as travelers and expatriates alike relax with a coffee in one hand and the paper in the other. Coffee is the highlight, but there are also impressive pancakes and breakfast options. Black coffee 30฿; latte 45฿; cappucino 45฿. Scrambled eggs, toast, bacon, and coffee 75฿. Whole wheat banana pancake with cappucino 80฿. Open daily 8am-5pm. ❷

Lanna Cafe, 81 Huay Kaew Rd., before Siri Mangkhlachian Rd. Originally established by a Japanese NGO to export coffee beans grown by 12 hill tribes to Japan, the cafe is the result of the expanding produce market. Feel virtuous even while indulging in the Ice Cafe Mocha Shake with whipped cream (40฿). Coconut cappucino 35฿. Roasted coffee beans 90฿ for 250g. Open daily 8am-6pm. ❷

⊙ SIGHTS

DOI SUTHEP AND ENVIRONS

Songthaew leave when full for **Wat Phra That Doi Suthep** from Chang Phuak Gate (6am-5pm, 30฿), and the **Chiang Mai Zoo** (6am-5pm, 30฿), continuing to **Bhubing Palace** (50฿) and **Doi Pui**, a Hmong village (80฿). Motorbikes are an option, but Huay Kaew Rd. is twisty, and the 4.5km dirt road to the Hmong village is rough. Watch for the **Kruba Scrivichai Shrine,** the monument to the left just before the road goes up the mountain. Kruba Scrivichai was a monk who inspired thousands of volunteers to build the road to Wat Phra That in 1934. Pausing to pay respect is supposed to ensure a safe journey up and down.

WAT PHRA THAT DOI SUTHEP. If you only have time to visit one of Chiang Mai's 300 wats, Wat Phra That Doi Suthep, one of Thailand's most sacred pilgrimage sights, should be it. *Phra that* refers to the Buddha's relics enshrined here, namely his *incus* (a teeny anvil-shaped bone in the middle ear). *Doi* is a Northern Thai word for mountain; and *suthep* is derived from the Pali *Sudevoy*, the name of the hermit who inhabited the area before the shrine was constructed. While the glint of the brilliant gold *chedi* is visible from the city's limits, the sweeping survey of the city from the temple's observation deck is sublime. Upon reaching the wat, voyeurs have the option of ascending either via covered cable-car (round-trip 20฿) or via the 297 steps through the market tourist traps.

DOI SUTHEP PIO NATIONAL PARK. A project started in 1987 by a Chiang Mai University professor has thus far collected 2062 species of plants in the park— more than in all of the UK. While the park's flora and fauna are regrettably being forced up the mountain as Chiang Mai proper expands, the park still offers much for wide-eyed wanderers. **Waterfalls** line Huay Kaew Rd. (Hwy. 1004), which leads up the mountain; keep an eye out for their turn-offs. The most impressive is **Namtok Monthatarn,** which lies 2km off Huay Kaew Rd. Standard national park entry fee of 200฿ applies. The **park headquarters** (☎295 117), 1km past Wat Phra That Doi Suthep, provides trail maps and accommodations. A nature trail leads from the park headquarters passing **Sai Yok Waterfall** (2km) and **Monthatarn Waterfall** (3km). Remember not to look at the waterfalls as you walk pass as you won't have to pay the park entry fee. After you reach Monthatarn Waterfall, follow the 2km access road to Huay Kaew Rd., where *songthaew* will shuttle you to Chiang Mai. **Camping ❶** costs 10฿ per night. Two-person (200฿) and five-person (500฿) tents, and two-person (200฿) and 10-person (2000฿) **cabins ❸** are available to rent. Reserve at least a week in advance.

OTHER SIGHTS. Bhubing Palace, 4km up the mountain from the wat, is the Royal Family's residence from roughly January to February. When they're not in residence, the palace and its lavish gardens are open to the public. *(Open daily 8:30am-4:30pm; tickets sold until 3:30pm; 50฿.)* **Doi Pui,** a Hmong Village 8km past the wat, suffers from tourist overcrowding. It is perhaps the only hill tribe village in which the women pair high heels with traditional apparel. Doi Pui's summit (1685m), 7km up the road from Bhubing Palace, makes for a nice hike. The road splits 2km after Bhubing Palace: to the left lies Doi Bhubing Hmong Village; to the right is Doi Pui's summit. The lush garden of the **Hill Tribes Village Museum,** 150m uphill from the parking lot for the village, contrasts sharply with the squalid village. The museum's main attraction is its collection of tiny pink opium flowers. *(Open whenever there are visitors. 10฿.)*

WITHIN THE MOAT

WAT CHIANG MAN. The oldest wat in the city, Chiang Man was built in 1296 by King Mengrai. With its low-sloping roofs and intricate facade, the temple is a classic example of Northern Thai design. The *wiharn* on the right contains two Buddha images: **Phra Setangamani (Crystal Buddha),** thought to have come from Lopburi 1800 years ago, and **Phra Sila (Stone Buddha),** imported from India some 2500 years ago. *(At the north end of Ratchaphakhinai Rd. Open daily 9am-5pm.)*

WAT CHEDI LUANG. Built by King Saen Suang Ma in 1401, the temple walls hold the spectacular remains of Chiang Mai's largest *chedi*, which once spiraled 86m toward the sky before being destroyed by an earthquake in 1545. The renovation of the *chedi* in 1995 proved to be extremely controversial. A *naga* staircase adorns the *wiharn*, which houses a **standing gold Buddha** and 32 *Jataka* story panels depicting scenes from the Buddha's life. Legend holds that Wat Chedi Luang was home to the Emerald Buddha during its stay in Chiang Mai. *(From Tha Pae Gate head west on Ratchadamnoen Rd. and turn left (south) onto Phra Pokklao Rd.; it's opposite the Yamaha music store.)*

WAT PHRA SINGH. This wat's chief attraction is the bronze **Phra Singh Buddha** in **Phra Wihan Lai Kam,** left of and somewhat behind the main *wiharn*. Experts aren't sure if this is the genuine Phra Singh Buddha, as there are identical statues in Bangkok and Nakhon Si Thammarat. The image is the focus of mid-April Songkran festivities when laymen bring sand to the wat to replace what has been dragged out by visitors during the year. Incense is lit and offerings are made to the Phra Singh Buddha, which is cleansed with holy water. *(On the western side of the old city.)*

OUTSIDE THE MOAT

WAT JED YOT. Inspired by the Mahabodhi Temple in Bodhgaya, India, King Tilokaraja built this shrine in 1455. In 1477, the Eighth World Buddhist Council met here to revise the *Tripitaka* scriptures of Theravada Buddhism. The two Bodhi trees are said to be descendants of the one Gautama sat under during his enlightenment. *(On the superhighway, 1km from the Huay Kaew Rd. intersection.)*

WAT U-MONG. Another remnant of King Mengrai's building spree, this peaceful forest temple has serene footpaths that lead through the trees. Several sculptures dot the grounds, none more disturbing than the emaciated image of "Our Lord Buddha before realizing that this wasn't the path to enlightenment." The sculpture is at the back of the confine before the pagoda representing the four noble truths (suffering, cause of suffering, path leading to cessation, cessation) and after the turn-off to the derelict farm. Tunnels leading into the hill at the site of the original wat are lined with niches housing Buddha figures. Other points of interest on the grounds are the **Herbal Medicine Garden,** a handicapped vocational training center, and the wat's **library** (open daily until 4pm). On Sundays from 3 to 6pm, enjoy a *dhamma*'s lecture in English. *(Off Suthep Rd., on the outskirts of town. Following Suthep out of town, the turn-off is marked by a faded green sign and is the 3rd left after the superhighway. It's 2km farther down the road.)*

WAT SUAN DOK. The "Temple of Flower Gardens" is also known as Wat Buppharam. King Ku Na constructed the shrine in 1383. The enormous Chiang Saen-style bronze building inside the *bot* dates from 1504. Inexpensive Buddhist amulets and literature are sold at nearly every *wiharn*. Originally, the grounds served as a pleasure garden for the first kings of Chiang Mai, but later became a cemetery for their graves. Today, Tai Chi is practiced in the gardens daily at 6:30am. Suan Dok hosts **monk chats** (M, W, F 5-7pm); follow the signs to the building in the back. *(On Suthep Rd., after the Hill Tribe Products Promotion Center.)*

CHIANG MAI NATIONAL MUSEUM. This museum features art and artifacts collected from Northern Thai royalty, commoners, and hill tribes. Chronological dioramas depict the rise and fall of the Lanna Kingdom ("Lanna," referring to the region of Northern Thailand, literally means "a million rice fields"). Lanna history is broken up into five periods: Muang Rai, Prosperous, Golden Age, Decadent (1525-1774, under the rule of Burma), and Revival (1782-1939, regained control from Burma). Lanna encompasses Phrae, Nan, Phayao, Mae Hong Son, Lamphun, Chaing Rai, and Chiang Mai. *(☎ 221 308. On the super-highway, 500m past Wat Jet Yod if coming from Huay Kaew Rd. Open daily 9am-4pm. 30฿.)*

TRIBAL MUSEUM. The polished exhibits, collected by the **Tribal Research Institute,** explore daily life, language derivation, gender roles, and costumes of various hill tribes in Northern Thailand. *(On Chotana Rd. in Ratchamangkhla Park, 4km north of Chang Phuak Gate. Follow the stadium turn-off to the left and turn right at the 1st sign for the park; the museum is in the middle of a lake. Tuk-tuk from Chang Phuak Gate 30-50฿. ☎ 210 872. Open daily 9am-4pm.)*

CHIANG MAI UNIVERSITY. Though architecturally uninspiring, the university's 725 park-like acres provide a pleasant break from the city's urban sprawl. The library is in the center of the grounds, just south of the central roundabout. *(6km northeast of the old city off Huay Kaew Rd.)*

CHIANG MAI ZOO. Everything from black bears to zebras are housed somewhere among the network of roads that are both confusing and exhausting to walk; pick up a map before heading into the civilized safari. No need to wait for feeding time—you can buy plates of hippo grub (5-10฿) to feed the animals yourself. In March 2002, the zoo announced plans to borrow two giant pandas from the Chinese government. The proposal was met with sharp criticism from environmentalists who believe that it's crazy to move the endangered species to a tropical climate. If the project moves forward, the pandas will arrive in mid-2003. *(☎ 221 179. On Huay Kaew Rd. at the base of Doi Suthep, after Chiang Mai University. Open daily 8am-6pm. Last ticket sold at 5pm. 30฿, children 5฿, bicycles 1฿, motorbikes 10฿, cars 30฿.)* Next door, the **Huay Kaew Arboretum**'s rare trees provide a shady respite, or an invigorating workout if you opt for the fitness track.

◪ TREKKING

Chiang Mai has over 200 companies itching to fulfill trekking prospects. Three-day/two-night treks (4-person min.) run 1500-1800฿ per person to the **Maeteang, Phrao, Sameong, Doi Inthanon,** or **Chiang Dao** areas. Extra days can be negotiated. These five are the only legal trekking areas around Chiang Mai. With 200 companies tromping through them, there is no such thing as a non-touristed area. This doesn't mean you'll have to elbow your way through mobs of tourists, but some villages see more tourists than they might care to. Many agencies will guarantee "private areas" to which they have exclusive access, but invariably there will be overlap. Maeteang, with its bucolic bamboo rafting, hosts the most trekkers; Chiang Dao gets the fewest because it runs along the sometimes dangerous Myanmar border. Chiang Mai's five areas encompass Akha, Lisu, Karen, Meo, Yao, and Padong villages. Pai has primarily Lisu and Karen villages; Mae Hong Son has almost exclusively Karen ones. During the low season, it's easier for solo travelers to join a trek in Chiang Mai. In Pai or Mae Hong Son, you might need to assemble your own group or you may end up paying more.

Some Chiang Mai-based companies also run treks to **Mae Hong Son** and **Pai.** If either of these locales tickles your fancy, it's better to hop on a bus and book from there, where a three-day trek will cost 1500-1800฿. Mae Hong Son and Pai see

WELCOME TO THE JUNGLE

As of summer 1999, only 39 out of 250 trekking companies met TAT and **Northern Thailand Jungle Club** regulations, which include: stipulations that guides have at least 10 years experience and speak both English and some hill-tribe dialects; that all costs (e.g. food, transportation, insurance, and elephants or bamboo rafts, if offered) be included in the stated price; that treks have no more than 12 participants; that the company employ men from the villages they visit as porters and charge the prices set by the Northern Thailand Jungle Club. Not every company with a Jungle Club Plaque is actually a member; many have been expelled for having three or more lawsuits brought against them. For updated information on legitimate outfits, contact the tourist police or Sangduen Chailert, the president of the Northern Thailand Jungle Club and manager of Gem Travel, 29 Charoen Prathet Rd. Soi 6 (☎272 855), which also runs treks. *Even with the stipulations set by the Northern Thailand Jungle Club and TAT, some feel that groups of 12 are far too large and have a negative impact on the hill tribes visited.*

fewer trekkers because Pai's rivers are too low to raft in the hot season and the rivers around Mae Hong Son may become too fast to navigate in the rainy season. Mae Hong Son abuts the troubled border with Myanmar.

In terms of specific outfits, treks run by **Libra Guest House** and **Eagle House,** 16 Chang Mai Gao Rd. Soi 3 (☎874 126), near Somphet market, opposite the old city, consistently receive rave reviews. **Chiang Mai Green Tour and Trekking,** 29/31 Chiang Mai-Lamphun Rd. (☎247 374), donates a portion of its proceeds to a conservation program and offers nature and bird-watching tours, as well as the more conventional "ethno-tourism" variety.

◪ ENTERTAINMENT AND SPORTS

The **Galare Food Center,** 89/2 Chang Klan Rd. (☎272 067), features traditional dancing exhibitions, cross-dressing cabaret shows, and Thai boxing on a rotating schedule between two stages. Galare I (sponsored by Chang Beer) has traditional dancing and music. Galare II alternates between a drag show and Thai boxing (cabaret 8-9pm; boxing 9-11:30pm). The **Bar Beer Center,** on Moon Muang Rd. at the Tha Pae Gate lets you watch the So Anucha Thai Boxing School Train from 4 to 7pm. Muay Thai boxing is held every night in the same arena at 10:30pm. The Central Department Store has a **Vista Movie Theater** on the fourth floor that shows newly-released movies (☎894 415; M-Th 70฿, F-Su 90฿). On the same floor there is both **Bully Bowling** (70-90฿ per game; shoe hire 30฿; open M-F 11am-1am, Sa-Su 10am-1am) and **Bully Ice Skating** (70฿; open M-F 11am-9pm, Sa-Su 10am-10pm). The Alliance Française hosts **French films** on Tu (4:30pm) and F (8pm); check guidelines for upcoming screenings (30฿). A **fitness track** can be found at Huay Kaew Arboretum before the Chiang Mai Zoo on Huay Kaew Rd. A better **fitness park** is on Nimonaha Min Rd. at the University Arts Museum. The track is set around a concrete moat (330m) with concrete logs and an archaic wooden bench press. (Open daily 5am-8pm.) **Buak Haad Park** in the southwestern corner of the Old City is a hidden oasis. (Open daily 5am-10pm.) Once you've worked up a sweat, cool off in one of the several hotel pools, which open up to public use for a price. Provided it's not still being renovated, the pool at Top North Hotel at Tha Pae Gate is a convenient option (50฿). **Golf** and **tennis** can be played at the **Chiengmai Gymkhana Club** (☎241 035; office open daily 9am-5pm), in the southeastern corner of town off the Chiang Mai-Lamphun Rd. The club was founded in 1898 by 14

English gentlemen who lived in Chiang Mai as teak traders, but whose true passions lay in racing, polo, and tennis. Today, club membership is 60% Thai. Nine holes on the monotonous golf course will cost 150-200฿. Caddies (80฿) are compulsory. (Golf club rental 300฿, driving range 25฿ for one bucket of balls. Tennis hard-courts 80฿ per hr., 40฿ extra per hr. for lighting. Open daily 6am-8pm.)

▣ COURSES AND FORUMS

Chiang Mai is the place to indulge in your favorite aspect of Thai culture. As the cultural heart of Thailand, Chiang Mai offers several types of courses. Most popular are the 1- to 5-day **cooking courses**. The standard in cooking schools is set by the **Chiang Mai Cooking School**. In addition to cooking classes, **massage classes** are also quite popular, and available at **The Old Medicine Hospital** and from **Mama Nit**. Meditation classes are offered at **Wat Ram Poeng**, or at the **Voravihara Insight Meditation Center**, which is housed in **Wat Pratat Sri Chom Thong**. Less intimate insight into Buddhism is available through **informal discussions** about the Buddhist faith held in the **Chinese Pavilion** at Wat U-Mong (Su 3pm) and **Monk Chat** at Wat Suan Dok (M, W, F 5-7pm). Wat Suan Dok also has free **Tai Chi sessions** (daily 6:30am). A forum on cultural aspects of Asia is the **Northern Thai Discussion Group** which meets the second Tuesday of each month (5:30pm) at the **Alliance Française.** Check the *Chiang Mai Newsletter* for upcoming speakers. The final step toward cultural immersion is taking a **language course** such as the ones offered at the **AUA** or **Payap University.** (For more detailed information on all courses, please see **Alternatives to Tourism: Studying Abroad**, p. 84)

▐ SHOPPING

Chiang Mai is handicraft central. **Tha Pae Rd.** is one of the best daytime hunting grounds, but avid consumerism takes off only after dark. The famed **Night Bazaar** on **Chang Klan Rd.** showcases a variety of antiques, silver jewelry, hill-tribe embroidery, Thai textiles, pottery, designer clothing knock-offs, and pirated DVDs. Haggle down the bloated tourist prices. Bangkok is still the home of tailored fashion, but options exist around the Night Bazaar.

Wararot Market is a multi-story undercover expanse encompassing food, textiles, and clothing. The higher up into the complex you go, the lower the prices. Next door in **Lanyai Market** on the river side, flower stalls are everywhere and spill out onto the road. Buy a *poung ma lai* (festive flower necklace, 5฿). Memorable Thai souvenirs include *morn sam laim* (triangular reclining pillow; approx. 200฿-1000฿ depending on quality). A popular choice is to have artists reproduce your photos in portrait-sized pieces on canvas. (Charcoal is the cheapest: one person approx. 1000฿; 2 people approx. 1500฿; 3 people approx. 2000฿.) Artists are primarily found in the center of the Night Bazaar near the Galare Food Center. There may be significant reductions in price with multiple photos, or if you're willing to wait longer for the reproduction.

The **Hill Tribe Handicraft Project,** 1 Moon Muang Rd., in a brick building at the southeastern corner of the old city, sells Karen, Lisu, Akha, Lahu, Yao, and Hmong village quilts, bags, pullovers, and sculptures. (☎274 877. Open M-F 9am-4:30pm.) The better-known **Hill Tribe Promotion Center,** 21/17 Suthep Rd., next to Wat Suan Dok, has a greater selection of traditional and innovative crafts. (☎277 743. Embroidered bag 280฿. Karen dress 650฿. Open daily 9am-5pm. MC/V.) Both government-run stores seek to shift tribal economies away from opium cultivation by providing alternate means of income. The **Export Promotion Center,** 29/19 Singharat Rd., opposite Cathay Pacific Airways, showcases high-quality Thai products for export. The Exhibition Hall has furniture on the first floor and decorative items such as ceramics and silks on the second floor. The manufacturer's business card is with each display, so if you like what you see among the hundreds of displays, it's possible to track it down. (☎216 350. Open M-F 8:30-noon and 1-4:30pm.)

NIGHTLIFE

Several wildly popular **bars** and **clubs** lie on the Ping's east bank, just north of Nawarat Bridge. The 30฿ tuk-tuk from Tha Pae Gate is well worth it. *Farang* pubs line **Moon Muang Rd.** Those immediately at Tha Pae Gate attract backpackers. Those to the south, on Loi Kro Rd. are sketchier. There are very few outright go-go bars in Chiang Mai; "karaoke" bars fill the void. The Night Bazaar hosts the most relaxed gay bars and attracts a mixed crowd. Other gay nightlife clusters in the sois west of Chang Phuak Bus Station, north of the old city.

Riverside, 9-11 Charoen Rat Rd. (☎243 239), has long been the most popular club. Two bands start rocking around 8pm, alternating between dual stages at either end of the club. Screwdriver 110฿. Large Singha 95฿. Corona 140฿. Pitcher of beer 300฿. Open daily 10am-1:30am.

Bubbles, 46-48 Charoen Prathet Rd. (☎270 099), in the Porn Ping Tower Hotel. Chiang Mai's premier disco. Mixed gay and straight crowd. Cover 100฿ includes 1 free drink, F-Sa and holidays 200฿ includes 2 free drinks. Open daily 9pm-2am.

Brasserie, 37 Charoen Rat Rd. (☎241 665). Croonin' tunes on an intimate stage start around 9:30pm. If you're lucky, the owner Took may take a turn himself. Whiskey and soda 90฿. Large Singha 90฿. Open daily 6pm-1:30am.

The Good View, 13 Charoen Rat Rd. (☎302 764), between Riverside and Brasserie. Music is like Riverside's—only louder. Great Japanese restaurant. Large Singha 120฿. Corona 150฿. Kamikaze 150฿. Open daily 6pm-1:45am.

Inter Bar, on Tha Pae Rd. near Art Cafe, always has a solid crowd even when other places are dead. Chill atmosphere and pool table. Music nightly 7:30pm-1am. Small Singha 60฿. Screwdriver 110฿. Open daily 2pm-2am.

Adam's Apple, on Wiang Bua Rd. The turn-off from Chofana Rd. is 300m past the Novotel. Indisputably the most popular gay venue in Chiang Mai with restaurant, bar, and karaoke downstairs, while go-go boys strut above. Raunchy cabaret (F-Sa 11pm). Singha 130฿.

DAYTRIPS FROM CHIANG MAI

LAMPHUN

Buses to Lamphun leave from the Chang Phuak Station in Chiang Mai and from just south of the footbridge near Wararot Market (1hr., every 10min. 6:20am-6pm, 12฿). Get off as the bus passes through the walled city; the Lamphun bus station is 1km outside of town. Electric blue songthaew leave from Chiang Mai-Lamphun Rd., south of TAT (every 20min. 5am-6pm, 15฿). Buses back to Chiang Mai depart from the front of the museum (every 30min. 6am-6pm).

Tiny Lamphun, 26km southeast of Chiang Mai, offers a handful of worthwhile sights. The town's most exciting event of the year is the **Lum-Yai Festival** in July or August, celebrating the *lum-yai* (longan) season. **Wat Phra That Haribhunchai** is considered one of the seven most sacred temples in Thailand. The wat, Lamphun's chief landmark, sits on Inthayongyot Rd. in the town center; it's the first temple on the left after you enter the walled city from Chiang Mai. Grassy grounds and little *wiharn* surround the *chedi*, crowned with a nine-tier gold umbrella. When coming from Inthayongyot Rd., you should enter from the back. There is a loosely enforced 20฿ entrance fee. A block away is the **Haribhunchai National Museum,** with a small collection of Buddhas, bells, and other bric-a-brac. With your back to the wat on Inthayongyot Rd., it's to the left. (☎511 186. Open W-Su 9am-4pm. 30฿.) With your back to Chiang Mai take a right directly after the museum onto Mukda Rd; when the road becomes Chamma Davi Rd. continue 2km to reach **Wat Chamma Davi.** The stepped-pyramid *chedi* once had a gold coating, but thieves broke it off, giving the temple its other name, Wat Ku Kat ("pagoda without top").

Wat Phra Phut Ta Bat Tak Pah, 20km south of Lamphun, has views that rival Doi Suthep's. Except for many discreet monks, you'll probably be the only one there. Before you reach the 472-step stairway, you'll pass some of the Buddha's footprints. Supposedly there is an imprint of the Buddha's robe on a cliff somewhere in the vicinity. Ask a monk for guidance—the print is hard to find. To get to the wat, board a light blue *songthaew* to Pasang (5฿) two blocks south of the museum, just off Inthayongyot Rd. on the left (electric blue *songthaew* to Chiang Mai also wait here). After everyone else gets off, the driver can take you the 9km to the wat for 15฿ more.

MAE SA VALLEY

Songthaew to Mae Rim, 17km from Chiang Mai, leave from Chotana Rd. north of Chang Phuak Gate. Alternatively, take a bus headed toward Fang. Once in the Mae Rim district, transportation can be arranged to all the sights. By car, head north out of Chiang Mai along Chang Phuak Rd. (Hwy. 107) and pass through the tiny town of Mae Rim. Right after the town, take the turn-off to the left onto Mae Rim-Somoeng Rd. (Hwy 1096).

A popular daytrip is an excursion to the **Mae Sa Valley.** The area's rural beauty barely compensates for the eclectic and very tourist-oriented attractions here. Numerous signs guide you to a plethora of sight-seeing opportunities. The main magnets are the elephant-training facilities—come here if you've never fraternized with or fed these wrinkly and surprisingly hairy creatures. The closest place, the **Mae Sa Elephant Training Center** (☎206 247), just 10km down the road (about 27km from Chiang Mai), is also the largest. The elephants and their riders put on a 40min. show daily at 9 and 9:40am (Nov.-Apr. there is a 1:30pm show as well). The anything-but-clumsy elephants demonstrate their strength and grace by handling teak logs, and reveal their balance by maneuvering their huge bodies into surprising positions (admission 80฿). There are also daily **elephant-back jungle tours** from 7am to 2:30pm (600฿ per hr.).

Much of the Mae Sa Valley is also part of Doi Suthep National Park. The most-beloved cascades in the park tumble down the 10-tier **Mae Sa Falls,** spread over 1.5km. Four kilometers before the Mae Sa Elephant Training Center, the entrance to the falls has a Visitors Center with maps of the area for further explorations. (National park entrance fee of 200฿ applies. Open daily 6am-6pm.)

Along Hwy. 1096 is a melange of sights including touristy shows displaying local poisonous **snakes.** Slightly more genuine are the **orchid farms** which feature "exotic hybrids." The adventurous and rich will head to **Jungle Bungy Jump** (☎298 442), where a plunge toward the pond starts at US$120.

BO SANG AND SAN KAMPHAENG

Located east of Chiang Mai on Route 1006, both Bo Sang and San Kamphaeng are extremely easy to reach. White songthaew at the market on the west bank of the Ping River make the 15-20min. trip regularly during the day (10฿).

Bo Sang and **San Kamphaeng** lay claim to Chiang Mai's "home industries," or "cottage industries." East 9km of Chiang Mai, **Bo Sang** is world-famous for its umbrella production. Hand-painted rain-repellers are made by stretching mulberry paper over bamboo frames. Silk and cotton parasols, sporting various bright floral, feral, and bucolic designs, are manufactured in Chiang Mai. The artisans laboring in the umbrella, lacquer ware, woodwork, glass, and silver factories are worth a look—prices, however, are lower in established stores near the Night Bazaar in Chiang Mai. **San Kamphaeng,** just 4km down the road from Bo Sang and 13km from Chiang Mai, is a village famous for cotton and silk weaving. One main road with workshops tucked out of sight is basically all there is to this town. Duck into a side street to catch a glimpse of production. Choose from a wide variety of plaids, brocades, stripes, and solid colors. Other handicrafts are available as well.

DOI INTHANON NATIONAL PARK

Buses from Chiang Mai leave from the Chang Phuak Station (1¼hr., every 20min. 6:30am-6pm, 23฿). Yellow songthaew leave from Chiang Mai Gate in the morning when full and cost 20฿. The turn-off to Hwy. 1009 and Doi Inthanon National Park lies before Chom Thong off Hwy. 108. From Chom Thong, songthaew head to the national park and glorious Mae Klang Waterfall, an 8km ride up to Hwy. 1009 to the turn-off. Songthaew cost 10-20฿ and leave when full—which may take a while—6am-5pm. All inquiries ☎311 608. Office open M-F 8:30am-4:30pm. Park and facilities open daily 6am-6pm. Park admission 200฿. Motorbikes 20฿; cars 50฿.

The 188km route from Chiang Mai to Mae Sariang along Hwy. 108 is ruggedly scenic. The drama picks up 58km away near **Chom Thong,** the point of access to Doi Inthanon National Park, home to one of Thailand's highest peaks. The Thanontongchai Range, capped by Doi Inthanon (2565m), is actually a distant part of the Himalaya Mountain Range. Doi Inthanon is just a baby however, in comparison to the mother of all mountains, Everest.

A trip to the **summit** of Doi Inthanon costs 70฿, but the wait is bound to be long, unless you want to charter the whole truck (500฿). A summit-bound *songthaew* may leave the Mae Klang Waterfall area every 2hr.; a motorbike hired in Chiang Mai can make the trip infinitely easier. The national park has some of the best tourist information of all the parks; pick up a map from either the vehicle checkpoint (500m after the turn-off to Mae Klang Waterfall), the Visitors Center (1km from the vehicle entrance on Hwy. 1009), or the park headquarters (at the 31km mark of Hwy. 1009). **Mae Klang Waterfall,** the park's largest waterfall, is the first stop for most visitors. It's possible to pay the national park entrance fee here, too. The 1km path above the falls leads to the Visitors Center. To get to a branch of the **Monk's College of Kamphaeng San** (Wittayalai Sung Kamphaeng San), based near Bangkok, cross the bridge just above the eating spots and take a left; after 1km there's a driveway entrance to the grounds. Its hill commands a view of the surrounding mountains amid lush gardens.

Just before the Visitors Center on Hwy. 1009, a 1km path leads to **Borichinda Cave.** Guided tours can be arranged at the Visitors Center, which also has information and exhibits on local animal life, notably the nocturnal pangolin.

Wachiratan Waterfall is the next stop at the 20.8km mark. At the 31km mark is the elegant **Siriphum Waterfall.** The lane leading to it winds through the park's **Royal Project,** where hill tribes are encouraged to supplant opium production with strawberry and flower cultivation. The road bids farewell at Doi Inthanon's summit (usually obscured by mist), 48km from Chom Thong.

The cool season (Oct.-Feb.) is the best time to visit. The average park temperature then is 12°C (50°F)—bring raingear and warm clothing, especially if you intend to hike. The park has **guest houses ❹** (500-2000฿), **camping ❶** (30฿), **tents ❶** (70฿), and a **restaurant** at park headquarters just past Siriphum Falls.

MAE SARIANG ☎053

Mae Sariang, a quiet retreat from the cities, is a base for adventurers. Trade of teak, rice, and heroin across the border with Myanmar has fueled a building boom, and the town has long prepared for an overflow of tourism from Mae Hong Son: information markers clutter every street corner. But neither the construction nor the as-yet-to-materialize tourist flood has managed to disrupt Mae Sariang's drowsiness. Charming countryside, the alluring border, and superb budget accommodations await those willing to leave the beaten path connecting Chiang Mai, Pai, and Mae Hong Son. Visiting Mae Sariang is a worthwhile way to complete the loop instead of merely backtracking.

TRANSPORTATION. The **bus terminal** (☎681 347) is on Mae Sariang Rd., 100m north of the traffic light, opposite the gas station. Buses run to **Chiang Mai** (4hr., 5 per day 7am-1am, 80฿; A/C 10:30am, 3pm, 1am, 140฿) and **Mae Hong Son** (4hr., 4 per day, 80฿; A/C 4 per day 10:30am, 3pm, 1am, 140฿). **Yan Yont Tours** (☎681 532) offers VIP buses from the gas station across the street to **Bangkok** (12hr.; 4, 7pm; 420฿). **Songthaew** head to **Mae Sot** (6hr., every hr. 7:30am-12:30pm, 150฿). **Motorcross-bike rental** is just south of the gas station (200-380฿ per day).

ORIENTATION AND PRACTICAL INFORMATION. Mae Sariang is bordered by the **Yuam River** to the west and **Hwy. 108** to the east. The main roads form an "H." **Langpanit Rd.** runs parallel to the river. **Mae Sariang Rd.** is one block east, parallel to Langpanit Rd. Perpendicular **Wiangmai Rd.** stretches from the river to the highway and intersects Mae Sariang Rd. at the traffic light in the town center. **Saripol Rd.,** site of the miniature morning **market,** connects Mae Sariang and Langpanit Rd. one block south of the traffic light. A second block south of the traffic light, **Waisuksa Rd.** heads west out of town to Mae Sam Laep.

Services in Mae Sariang include: **immigration office,** 200m north of the hospital on Hwy. 108, for visa extensions (☎681 339; open M-F 8:30am-4:30pm); **Thai Farmers Bank,** on Wiangmai Rd. west of Mae Sariang Rd., has an **ATM** (Cirrus/MC/PLUS/V) and **exchanges currency** (open M-F 8:30am-3:30pm); **police** (☎681 308), on Mae Sariang Rd. 150m south of the traffic light; **pharmacy,** on the corner of Sridpon and Langpanit Rd. (open daily 8am-9pm); **government hospital** (☎681 027; **emergency** ☎191), on Hwy. 108, 200m toward Mae Hong Son from the intersection with Wiangmai Rd.; **Internet access** on Wiangmai Rd. east of the traffic light (open daily 9am-10pm; 20฿ per hr.); and **post office,** 31 Wiangmai Rd., which has an **international phone/fax** but no IDD (☎681 356; open M-F 8:30am-4:30pm, Sa-Su 9am-noon). **Postal code:** 58110.

ACCOMMODATIONS AND FOOD. For a resplendent setting, try the **Riverside Guest House ❶,** 85 Langpanit Rd., 300m north of Wiangmai Rd. From the bus station, turn right onto Mae Sariang Rd., left at the first intersection, and left again on Langpanit Rd.; it's 100m down on the right. All rooms overlook the Yuam River. (☎681 188. Check-out 11:30am. Bicycles 50฿. Motorbike 200฿. Basic singles with bath 80-100฿; doubles 100-180฿.) The adjacent **Riverhouse ❹** and **Northwest Guesthouse ❶** (run by Riverhouse) have an excellent range of quality lodgings. Riverhouse has the best rooms in town, with a price tag to match. (☎621 201. Internet 40฿ per hr. Cable TV in lobby. Rooms with fan 400฿, with A/C 600฿.) Northwest sacrifices the view for exceptionally clean rooms and modern fixtures in a cozy saloon setting. (Singles with fan 100฿; doubles 200฿). **Mae Sariang Guest House ❶,** 11 Langpanit Rd., at Mongkolchai Rd., has dingy ground-floor rooms. (☎621 172. Dorms 50฿; singles with bath 80฿; doubles 100฿.)

Of all the open-air eateries along Wiangmai Rd., the popular **Renu Restaurant ❷,** 174/2 Wiangmai Rd., 50m toward the highway from the traffic light, probably has the best eats. (Most entrees 40-50฿. Cashew nut with some chicken thrown in for good measure 60฿. Open daily 6am-midnight.) The food is cheap and tasty at the

stands that set up on Mae Sariang Rd. around the bus station in the evening. Also, many guest houses have their own restaurants.

⬛ DAYTRIPS FROM MAE SARIANG. The country around town, dotted with hill-tribe villages, is perfect for walks or bike rides. The 6km to **Pha Ma Lo** is particularly scenic and isolated. This affluent White Karen village has a charming setting and a fine temple. On the other side of town, on the road to Mae Sot, the **Big Buddha** is an intriguing sight. Those curious enough to make the trip up the hill are rewarded with a magnificent panorama of Mae Sariang. Follow Wiangmai Rd. out of town. Just before the highway, turn right onto the road to Mae Sot. It's impossible to miss the 10m Buddha. Riverhouse (see **Accommodations and Food,** above) posts a map of suggested trails on the wall and has copies at reception. For a more tailored experience, Riverhouse can organize day or overnight trekking and rafting (4-person minimum, 1500฿ per day).

To explore **Mae Sam Laep,** 46km west of Mae Sariang, take a *songthaew,* which leaves Mae Sariang from just east of the bridge. From the center of town, walk south on Langpanit Rd. until it ends, turn right, and the bridge is 100m down. The first *songthaew* (1½hr., 50฿) leaves around 7am; others depart when full. The last comes back in the afternoon—ask your driver for a return time. If completing the journey by motorbike, you'll need a motorcross bike in the wet season—roads can be muddy and there are several creek crossings. Mae Sam Laep is across the river from Myanmar. (River boats depart by 9am, return 3pm; 100฿. Chartered vessels 750-850฿.)

Boats upstream pass **Salawin National Park;** it's possible to get off at the small beach. The path up the hillside leads to the ranger's headquarters—a friendly but uninformative stop. It's difficult to walk in the area without a guide, but the pleasant setting is reason enough to visit. It's possible to stay at Salawin National Park next to the headquarters in simple but pricey **lodgings ❹** with a stunning 🏔**view** of the Salawin River and the hill of Myanmar. (Doubles 400฿; lodge for 9 people 1200฿.) Alternatively, you can pitch **your own tent ❶** on the sand for 30฿ per person. Either way, bring extra blankets for warmth at night. The national park is serviced only in high-season. With any chartered boat to the national park, be sure to negotiate a visit, only 10min. farther upstream, to the hillside Karen village of **Ta Tar Fan,** which overlooks a Myanmar army camp.

Points downstream are arguably more scenic than those upstream. Check at guest houses in Mae Sariang to ensure the stability of the area before embarking on a trip. Border skirmishes still occur, and the Myanmar side is scattered with land mines, so don't venture there.

On the route to Mae Hong Son is the **Mae Surin Waterfall**—Thailand's tallest cascade. **Nam Tok Mae Surin National Park** lies 37km from **Khum Yuam,** halfway between Mae Sariang and Mae Hong Son. To get to the park, hop off when the Mae Sariang/Mae Hong Son bus stops in Khum Yuam. Catch a *songthaew* for the remaining distance in front of Ban Farang, 100m toward Mae Sariang from the bus stop, at the curve in the main road. This less-traveled route might set you back 500-700฿ for a private *songthaew* ride or leave you waiting for days.

Worth a quick look if you're waiting for the bus in Khum Yuam is the Japanese WWII Museum. It's not much more than a collection of artifacts (guns, uniforms, photos, etc.), but the English-language articles provide an insightful look at Japanese occupation in the area. (100m toward Mae Sariang from Ban Farang. Open daily 8:30am-noon and 1-4:30pm; 10฿.) If overnighting, **Ban Farang ❶** (see above) has suitable rooms for all budgets. (☎522 086. Open-air, clean, comfy dorms 50฿; room with cold shower 250฿; hot shower 350฿.)

MAE HONG SON

☎ **053**

Earlier this century, Mae Hong Son was used as a place of exile for criminals and corrupt officials. Though the city no longer serves this purpose, if recent reports of opium smuggling are correct, shady dealings persist in the area. Such sinister border activities, coupled with the most picturesque scenery in Northern Thailand, have piqued the curiosity of travelers—visitors now flock to the provincial capital. The best time to visit is during the Bua Tong Blossom Festival from November 1 to December 15, when the local wild sunflower turns the hillsides gold. The revenue from tourism can clearly be seen in the manicured gardens and modern infrastructure—the *songthaew* driver with the "Keep Mae Hong Son Small" sticker across his windshield must know he is fighting a losing battle.

▀ TRANSPORTATION

Flights: Mae Hong Son Airport (☎ 612 057), on Nivit Pisan Rd. Turn left at the hospital at the east end of Singhanat Bumrung Rd. To **Chiang Mai** (35min.; 12:45, 3:10, 5:30pm; 870฿). **Thai Airways,** 71 Singhanat Bumrung Rd. (☎ 612 220). Open M-F 8am-5pm. **Air Andaman** (☎ 620 451), with offices at the airport, flies to **Bangkok** (1¾hr., 4 per week, 2055฿).

Buses: 33/3 Khunlum Praphat Rd. (☎ 611 318). To: **Chiang Mai** (7½-8½hr.; 11 per day 6am-9pm; 105-145฿, with A/C 147-261฿) via **Mae Sariang** (4hr., 4 per day 6am-9pm, 78฿; 10:30am and 9pm, with A/C 140฿) or **Pai** (3½hr., 4 per day 7am-12:30pm, 53฿; 8am, with A/C 74฿); **Mae Sariang** (2pm) via **Khum Yuam** (2hr., 5 per day 6am-9pm, 35฿); **Pai** (4pm) via **Soppong** (2hr., 5 per day 7am-4pm, 33฿). **Yan Yont Tour** (☎ 611 514), south of town next to the Shell station, has an A/C bus to **Bangkok** (17hr., 3pm, 569฿).

Local Transportation: *Songthaew* leave for points north of Mae Hong Son from the day market on Punit Watana Rd. Motorcycle taxis and tuk-tuks wait at the bus station and airport (10-40฿).

Rentals: Numerous places around the traffic light rent **motorcycles. Highway,** 67/2 Khunlum Praphat Rd. (☎ 611 620), opposite Thai Farmers Bank, south of the lights, has "as new" motorcycles with good service facilities. 150฿ per day; passport or 500฿ and passport photocopy required for deposit. Open daily 8am-7pm. **TN tour,** 107/17 Khunlum Praphat Rd. (☎ 620 059), rents Suzuki 4WD.

✈ ? ORIENTATION AND PRACTICAL INFORMATION

Mae Hong Son is 348km from Chiang Mai via Mae Sariang (Hwy. 108, the southern route), and a meandering 274km via Pai (Hwy. 107 and 1095, the northern route). Buses stop on **Khunlum Praphat Rd.,** which is home to restaurants, trekking outfitters, and banks and runs north-south through the center of town. As you turn left out of the bus station and head south, the second intersection (with the traffic light) is **Singhanat Bumrung Rd.** Another block south, guest houses dot **Udom Chao Nithet Rd.,** which borders the lake glistening with reflections of wats and *chedis*.

Tourist Office: TAT (☎ 612 982), on Khunlum Praphat Rd., 200m south of traffic light, opposite post office. Eager staff hands out tourist brochures. Open M-F 8:30am-noon and 1-4:30pm; Nov.-Jan. open daily.

Immigration Office: 11 Khunlum Praphat Rd. (☎ 612 106), 1km north of the bus station. 10- or 30-day visa extensions depending on visa type. 2 photos and 2 copies of passport, departure card, and visa required. 500฿. Open daily 8:30am-4:30pm.

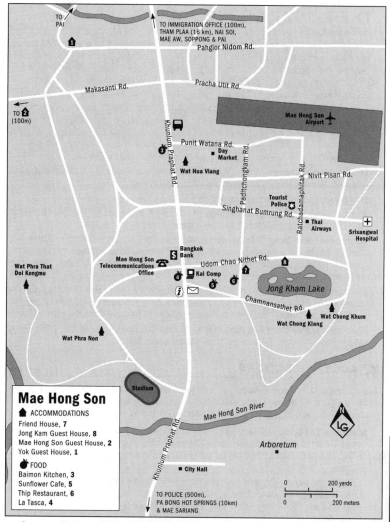

Mae Hong Son

▲ ACCOMMODATIONS
Friend House, **7**
Jong Kam Guest House, **8**
Mae Hong Son Guest House, **2**
Yok Guest House, **1**

🍴 FOOD
Baimon Kitchen, **3**
Sunflower Cafe, **5**
Thip Restaurant, **6**
La Tasca, **4**

Currency Exchange: Bangkok Bank, 68 Khunlum Praphat Rd. (☎611 275). Open M-F 8:30am-3:30pm. **24hr. ATM** (AmEx/MC/PLUS/V).

Bookstore: Saksarin, 88/5-6 Khunlum Praphat Rd. (☎612 124), next to La Tasca. Small selection of English travel and fiction books. Comprehensive map selection.

Markets: The **day market** is on Panit Watana Rd. next to Wat Hua Viang. Roadside stalls sell fruits and vegetables; the covered market sells mainly meat. Cookies mix with hill tribe bags and Jem (of the Holograms) umbrellas in the nearby sois. The overpriced **night market** (Chang Kham Bazaar) on Khunlum Praphat Rd. lacks selection.

Emergency: ☎191. **Ambulance:** ☎1669. **Tourist Police (Bangkok):** ☎1155.

THE PLIGHT OF THE PADONG

THE PLIGHT OF THE PADONG A favorite subject of Thailand's postcard photographers is the Padong tribe's "long-neck women" or "giraffe women." At the age of five, girls in this subset of the Karen hill tribe are fitted for their first heavy brass neck ring. By adulthood, the rings have compressed the woman's collarbone and ribcage so much that her neck appears stretched. Until recently, the bizarre custom had begun dying out, but when the Karen began to flee Myanmar (see **Thai-Burmese Relations**, p. 24), enterprising Thais seized the Padong as a potential gold mine. The Padong "villages" in Mae Hong Son Province (Nai Soi primary among them) are creations of these entrepreneurs. There is no "authentic" village life in Nai Soi—just a refugee-camp-turned-tourist-trap.

Police: ☎611 239. 1km south of the post office on the road to Mae Sariang.

Local Tourist Police: ☎611 812. At the corner of Rachadamphitak and Singhanat Bumrung Rd. Helpful. Maps. Open daily 9am-9pm. **24hr. emergency.**

Pharmacy: 37 Singhanat Bumrung Rd. (☎611 380). Open daily 7am-8pm.

Medical Services: Srisangwal Hospital (☎611 378), at the end of Singhanat Bamrung Rd. English-speaking doctors. **24hr. emergency care.**

Telephones: Mae Hong Son Telecommunications Office, 26 Udom Chao Nithet Rd. (☎611 711), just west of Khunlum Praphat Rd. **International phones** and fax (cash, collect, or HCD). **Lenso** phone at post office. CATNET Internet access. Open M-F 8:30am-4:30pm.

Internet Access: Cheapest (and slowest) is the CATNET Internet access at the Telecommunications Office (11฿ per hr.; buy 100฿ card). Several places congregate around the traffic light. **Kai Comp,** just north of the post office. 1฿ per min. Open daily 8am-11pm.

Post Offices: Mae Hong Son Post Office, 79 Khunlum Praphat Rd. (☎611 223). Open M-F 8:30am-4:30pm, Sa-Su 9am-noon. **Postal code:** 58000.

▎ ACCOMMODATIONS

Lakeside guest houses are central, but loud renditions of the Beer Chang jingle make for poor lullabies. Those venturing to Mae Hong Son from Pai may be disappointed with the budget options. With some effort, a nice place can still be found.

Mae Hong Son Guest House, 295 Mucksanti Rd. (☎612 510). Turn right out of the bus station and left on the 1st street; it's 500m away. Verdant garden and sleepy vibe. Doubles 150฿, with bath 300-350฿; private bungalows with bath 500฿. ❷

Friend House, 20 Paditchongkam Rd. (☎620 119). Turn left out of the bus station, 1st left after the traffic light, and then the 1st right; it's just off the intersection with Udom Chao Nithet Rd. Cleanest of the lakeside joints, but you might want to kill that rooster. Upstairs rooms have view of the lake. Laundry 30฿ per kg. Rooms 100฿, with shower 250฿. ❶

Yok Guest House, 14 Sirimongkol Rd. (☎611 532). Turn right out of the bus station, then take the 2nd left; it's down 300m on the right after the wat. Quiet residential surroundings set back from the main road. Free transport from airport and bus station. Clean rooms with fan, towels, and bath 200฿, with carpet 300฿, with A/C 400฿. ❸

Jong Kam Guest House, 7 Udom Chao Nithet Rd. north of the lake. Turn left from the bus station, and take the 1st left after the traffic light; it's 250m down on the right. Breakfast. Laundry 30฿ per kg. 3-day/2-night walking treks to Karen village 600฿ per day. Clean rooms in main building with very low ceiling fans 100฿. Only consider the 2 bungalows closest to the lake—otherwise you may have to contend with the vermin. Bungalows 100฿, with bath 150฿. ❶

FOOD

With increasing demand to satisfy more palates, Mae Hong Son's food options are diversifying. Most restaurants now offer Western specialties, but the best options are still the traditional Northern Thai dishes. **Baimon Kitchen ❶**, on Khunlum Praphat Rd., opposite and south of the bus station, has an English menu. Try their specialty, *khao soy*, a northern Thai coconut curry noodle dish, for 20฿. (Pineapple chicken 25฿. Lots of tofu dishes 10-40฿. Open daily 7am-11pm.) Stop by the **Sunflower Cafe ❶**, Soi 3 Khunlum Praphat Rd. near the lake, at 8am for oven-fresh bread and delicious breakfasts. To get there, face the post office, and follow the road's left fork 100m; it's on the left. The cafe also offers treks and information on the region. The comfy cushioned seating is a great place to put together a trekking group or to trade secrets with fellow travelers. (Cheesecake 25฿. Papaya shake 15฿. Open daily 7:30am-11:30pm.) The tranquil view from **Thip Restaurant ❷**, 23/11 Paditchongkam Rd., only serves to complement the food. (Crispy *hoi jou*, Chinese pork sausage, 60฿. Chicken with oyster sauce 30฿. Open daily 9am-10pm.) **La Tasca ❸**, 88/4 Khunlum Praphat Rd., opposite and north of the post office, has terrific (and caloric) meals. Homemade gnocchi and fettuccini start at 95฿. It's worth saving the accompanying loaf of bread for lunch. (Pizza from 85฿. Tiramisu 35฿. Open daily 5-11pm.)

ⓖ SIGHTS

Wat Phra That Doi Kongmu, 474m above town, has a panoramic view of the city. Built in 1874, this Shan-influenced temple is Mae Hong Son's most important wat. To get to either wat, head west on Udom Chao Nithet Rd. and turn left at the end. On the right is Wat Phra Non, and the road to the hilltop vista of Wat Phra That Doi Kongmu is the right before the stadium. Nearby **Wat Phra Non** houses a 12m Burmese-style reclining Buddha and the ashes of Mae Hong Son's kings. Get there by turning left at the end of Udom Chao Nithet Rd.

A jogging track circles **Jong Kham Lake.** Feed the fish (fish food 5฿) or visit the lake's south side to see the two famed wats. **Wat Chong Klang** is on the right, with Buddhist glass paintings and wooden dolls brought from Myanmar over 100 years ago. (Open daily 8am-6pm.) Next door, **Wat Chong Khum,** built in 1827, shines with gold-leafed pillars.

Once you're weary of watting, the **Pa Bong Hot Springs** offer a different type of soul-cleansing. The relaxation center, 10km south of town toward Mae Sariang, pipes the spring water into private baths. (Small bath 40฿, large 200฿. Thai massage available. Open daily 9am-7pm.)

ⓝ TREKKING

Mae Hong Son has some of the best trekking in Thailand—several Chiang Mai-based treks descend here. The surrounding hills support villages of Lisu, Lahu, Hmong, and Karen tribes, as well as Shan and Kuo Min Tang (KMT) zones. During low season, putting your own crew together can lower prices, since Mae Hong Son hosts fewer travelers than Chiang Mai and there aren't always organized groups. TAT can provide you with a list of the 28 licensed travel agents in Mae Hong Son. Once you decide on a company, it can never hurt to check their status with the tourist police. For those heading to the sights by themselves, the tourist police still have the best free regional map. More accurate detail is found in the regional map produced by the **Pai Association for Travelers** (available at some restaurants and trekking agencies; 10฿). **Sunflower Tours,** in Sunflower Cafe (see **Food,** above), offers consistently good butterfly- and bird-watching tours as well as treks featuring elephants, bamboo rafts, and visits to hill tribes. Owner La leads most outings and can tailor trips to your interests (1- to 5-day trips 600฿ per person per day; 4-person min.). Treks with **Mae Hong Son Guest House,** 20 Singhanat Bamrung Rd., east of the traffic light, also receive favorable reports. (☎620 105. 3-day trek 1800฿ per person; 4-person min.)

🔁 DAYTRIPS FROM MAE HONG SON

Border politics dominate Mae Hong Son Province. The Burmese Red Karen state is across the border and farther north lie various rebel camps. Trips to Myanmar from here are illegal and dangerous. No other city in Thailand makes it so easy to experience such an array of ethnic cultures and political backgrounds. Renting a motorcycle (150฿), rather than using the fickle or sometimes nonexistent public transportation, provides access to Karen, Lisu, Hmong, and Lahu hill tribe villages, Shan towns, and KMT camps.

NAI SOI (LONG-NECKED KAREN VILLAGE)

Take a songthaew from Mae Hong Son's day market to the Shan town (leaves when full, 30฿); then walk or hail another for the 3km to Nai Soi. Returning can be tricky; a motorbike is your best bet (250฿). For those with their own transportation, the turn-off is at the 199km road marker on the highway to Pai. Turn left at this point, and take the first left 500m down. There is a sign at this second turn-off, but it is obscured. Entrance 250฿. Open daily 6am-6pm.

Travelers in Thailand can't make it as far as Mae Hong Son Province without hearing of these Burmese refugees. The women wear metal rings that crush their rib cages and collar bones (see **The Plight of the Padong,** p. 262). Many find the zoo-like atmosphere disturbing, however, with vendors selling postcards of the women or wood carvings of their long necks.

THAM PLAA AND HIGHWAY 1095 TO PAI

Hop on a Pai-bound bus and signal the driver to stop at the cave. 10฿.

Some of Thailand's most stunning, jagged scenery graces Hwy. 1095 between Mae Hong Son and Pai (111km). About 35km from Mae Hong Son and 20km before the turn-off to **Mae La Na** are two lone peaks. The **Sunnyata Forest Monastery** is nearby. Shan and Hmong villages, a waterfall, mountain panoramas, and the KMT village of **Mae Aw** are situated on a mountaintop right on the Burmese border. You need a motorbike to make it; during the muddy rainy season it's better to have a four-wheel-drive. The Fish Cave—**Tham Plaa**—waits next to the road, 16km north of Mae Hong Son. The Shan villagers who look after the fish never catch them, believing that the spirit of the mountain guards the fish from harm. As a result of their protected status, the fish grow quite large (many more than 80cm long). Recently, a scuba-outfitted Australian camera crew penetrated the pool's depths and discovered a waterfall and an open-air cavern within a waterfall deep below the surface. Local lore has it that Japanese soldiers retreating from Myanmar buried treasure in such caverns. Visitors, however, are relegated to the circuitous nature trail that passes by the aquatic peep holes (Free. Visitor information open daily 8am-4pm.)

The KMT village of **Mae Aw** is on a mountaintop, straddling the Burmese border. You'll need a motorbike to make it. The village entrance is marked by a gate with Chinese script and the words "Ban Rak Thai"—its Thai name. The stunning trip, including valley crossings and mountain panoramas, is best appreciated by taking the turn-off from Hwy. 1095 to Nai Soi (also marked to Pha Sua); follow the road as it veers right at the turn-off 500m farther. Shan and Hmong villages dot the road, as well as **Pha Sua Waterfall,** approximately 27km from Mae Hong Son. Those organized enough to bring lunch can dine in natural splendor at the picnic tables. The return trip can be completed via Tham Plaa; at Mok Chom Pae, take the direct route to the highway. Be careful not to miss this turn-off, as it's unmarked. From there, signs lead the way to Tham Plaa.

SOPPONG

Buses stop in Soppong on their way between Mae Hong Son (2hr., 4 per day 10am-5:30pm, 30฿) and Pai (1½hr., 4 per day 9am-6pm, 30฿). The last bus to Chiang Mai is at 2:30pm (5½hr.).

If you've ever wanted to jump off a bus and frolic through the countryside (to, perhaps, a huge cave and underground river), Soppong's the place to live out your dreams. New Soppong skirts the highway where buses stop; Old Soppong dozes along the road curving from the bus station 500m toward Pai. This road follows the 9km route to the ◪**Tham Lod** (Lod Cave). Prehistoric remains have been found among its stalagmites and stalactites. Visitors must hire a guide at the entrance to take them through the three gigantic underground caverns (100฿ for 1-4 people). The highlight of the final chamber, where the burial remains lie, is the subterranean river crossing. A boatman will take you down the cave's river for another 100฿ per four-person raft. Unfortunately, during the lowest point of the dry season, the water is often only at knee-level and many choose to wade. The best time to visit the cave is about 1½hr. before sunset. That way, the tour will conclude with the aerial display put on by swifts as they return to the cave. Those in search of "bat-trics" may be disappointed, as the bats exit under the veil of darkness. Sunrise provides a clearer view of the swift vortex that forms in the cave before the birds' exit. A 20min. walk around the side of the cave leads to the viewing area. This path can be used to conclude a tour, or to reach the observation point without going through the cave. (Open daily 8am-5pm.)

To get to the cave, catch a motorbike taxi (60฿) or rent your own transportation. **Jungle Guest House** (see below) offers a **jeep** service (seats 5, 350฿ round-trip) and has motorcycles of varying quality (150฿ per day). The repair shop opposite Little Eden also has motorcycles (200฿ per day). There are limited services in Soppong. A **police box** is near the bus stop. The **police station** (☎617 173) is about 2km from the bus station toward Mae Hong Son. Immediately after the police station is **Pang-mapha Hospital** (☎617 154), with limited English. **Soppong Post Office,** between the bus station and Jungle Guest House, is equipped with CATNET Internet access. (☎617 165. Open M-F 8:30am-4:30pm.) There is also **Internet** access at **Soppong River Inn** (2฿ per min., 100฿ per hr.).

Travelers intending only to see Tham Lod may find that the serene environs and attractive accommodations provide an incentive to stay longer. The nearby **coffin caves** can be explored from Soppong—inquire at guest houses for directions to the surrounding caves, and information on obtaining guides (if desired). **Jungle Guest House ❶,** 300m toward Mae Hong Son from the bus stop, has a range of rooms along with a fabulous restaurant. (☎617 099. 10-bed dorms 70฿; rooms 80-100฿; bungalows with bath and hot shower 180-200฿.) The most luxurious lodgings are at **Soppong River Inn ❹.** The intimate abodes overlooking the river are unmatched. One night's sleep on the comfy beds may well be worth two nights' rest elsewhere. (☎617 107. Rooms without bath 350฿; bungalows with bath 400฿; deluxe bungalow with attached open-air bath 700฿.) The posh **Little Eden ❸,** formerly T-Rex Guest House, on the main road between the bus station and the turn-off to old Soppong and the cave, is a good family option with comfy bungalows in a riverside garden with swimming pool. (☎617 054; www.littleeden-guesthouse.com. 250฿ low season, 350฿ high season.) There are two

NORTHERN THAILAND

places in the vicinity of the cave which boast stunning and quiet settings well away from the main road. The overlooked **Lang River Guest House ❶,** to the left before Tham Lod's parking lot, is a backpacker's dream. Many will opt to use the riverside setting to bathe. Friendly owner Chalong mingles with guests at night. (Superb partitioned dorms with mosquito nets 70฿; bungalows with bath 100฿ for 1, 150฿ for 2.) The popular **Cave Lodge ❶,** 500m before Lod Cave, features a roomy restaurant/reading room complete with campfire setting. The staff organizes hiking, caving, and kayaking trips (around 450฿ per day). The old dorms are fanless but bug-netted (60฿). Rooms (120฿) and rustic bungalows (150฿) have separate bath. Check to insure a tour group won't be disturbing the peace that evening. Laundry service is available. The kitchen closes at 8pm.

PAI
☎ **053**

An oasis halfway between Chiang Mai and Mae Hong Son, Pai attracts both artists and trendy pilgrims who draw inspiration from the astoundingly picturesque town and surrounding area. Adding to the city's charm are the best selection of budget accommodation in Northern Thailand and the greatest culinary diversity outside of Chiang Mai. The locals, a harmonious melange of cultures and ethnicities, are particularly friendly. Behind the scenes, however, a clandestine heroin and opium culture has come to the attention of local authorities, who are starting to clamp down strongly on nefarious activities in the area.

▆ TRANSPORTATION

Buses: The **station** is on Chaisongkhram Rd. To **Chiang Mai** (4hr.; 8:30, 10:30am, noon, 2, 4pm; 60฿) and **Mae Hong Son** (4hr.; 8:30, 10:30am, noon, 2, 4pm; 48฿, with A/C 67฿) via **Soppong** (2hr., 35฿). To go to **Tha Ton,** take a Chiang Mai-bound bus to **Mae Malai** (3hr., 55฿), then take a bus to **Fang** (2½hr., every 30min. 6:30am-6pm, 45฿). Some buses continue to Tha Ton; otherwise, yellow *songthaew* make the trip from the main road in Fang (45min., 20฿). To make Tha Ton by evening, it is necessary to take the noon bus (at the latest).

Motorcycle Taxis: At the corner of Chaisongkhram and Rungsiyanon at Ban Pai. Shuttle people around town and the surrounding area. Hot springs 50฿; waterfall 60฿; Tham Lot (2hr., 300฿). Possible to arrange drop-off and pick-up.

Rentals: Many shops along Chaisongkhram Rd. and elsewhere rent **motorcycles.** 150฿ per day. **Aya Service,** 21 Chaisongkhram Rd. (☎699 940). Turn left out the bus station—it's 50m down on the left. Motorcycles with insurance 180฿ per day. Open daily 7:30am-10:30pm.

◼◼ ORIENTATION AND PRACTICAL INFORMATION

Pai is 136km northwest of Chiang Mai and 111km northeast of Mae Hong Son. **Hwy. 1095** cuts through town, but most traffic is channeled away from the town center, skirting the western border formed by **Ketkelang Rd.** The bus station is in the middle of the town's northern border, **Chaisongkhram Rd.,** also home to numerous Internet cafes and motorbike rental shops. As you leave the bus station, the town's main street, **Rungsiyanon Rd.,** full of restaurants and trekking outfitters, lies to your right. The **Pai River,** 400m to the left, forms the town's eastern border.

Currency Exchange: Krung Thai Bank, 90 Rungsiyanon Rd. (☎699 028). Open M-F 8:30am-3:30pm. **24hr. ATM** (Cirrus/MC/PLUS/V).

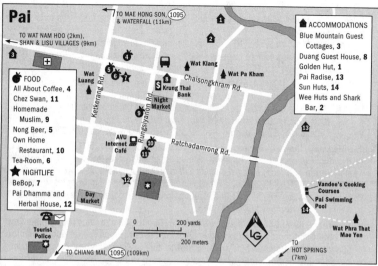

Pai

TO MAE HONG SON, (1095)
& WATERFALL (11km)

TO WAT NAM HOO (2km),
SHAN & LISU VILLAGES (9km)

Wat Klang
Wat Pa Kham
Chaisongkhram Rd.
Wat
Luang
Ketkelang Rd.
Krung Thai Bank
Night Market
Rungsiyanon Rd.
AVU Internet Café
Ratchadamrong Rd.
Day Market
Tourist Police
TO CHIANG MAI, (1095) (109km)

Vandee's Cooking Courses
Pai Swimming Pool
Wat Phra That Mae Yen

TO HOT SPRINGS (7km)

0   200 yards
0   200 meters

FOOD
All About Coffee, **4**
Chez Swan, **11**
Homemade Muslim, **9**
Nong Beer, **5**
Own Home Restaurant, **10**
Tea-Room, **6**

★ **NIGHTLIFE**
BeBop, **7**
Pai Dhamma and Herbal House, **12**

ACCOMMODATIONS
Blue Mountain Guest Cottages, **3**
Duang Guest House, **8**
Golden Hut, **1**
Pai Radise, **13**
Sun Huts, **14**
Wee Huts and Shark Bar, **2**

Markets: The **night market,** which sets up at 3pm on Rungsiyanon Rd. between Chaisongkhram and Ratchadamrong Rd., is a microcosm of market life, with transient food carts and the occasional hill tribe entrepreneur smattered among the regulars. The **day market** on Ketkelang Rd., south of Ratchadamrong Rd., is nothing to email home about—just a bunch of vegetables and plastic toys.

Bookstore: Come Pai, 29 Chaisongkhram Rd., 100m east of the bus station. Books in English, French, and German. Rent 20฿ per day. Large selection of Penguin classics from Austen to Woolf (150฿). Open daily 10am-7pm.

Emergency: ☎191. **Ambulance:** ☎699 031. **Tourist Police (Bangkok):** ☎1155.

Police: 72 Rungsiyanon Rd. (☎699 217), 500m south of the bus station.

Local Tourist Police: On the road to Chiang Mai, after Ketkelang and Rungsiyanon Rd. merge.

Medical Services: Pai Hospital (☎699 031), on Chaisongkhram Rd. 500m west of the bus station. English spoken. **Open 24hr.**

Pharmacy: On Rungsiyanon Rd. between Chez Swan and the police. Open daily 6am-9pm.

Internet Access: Several connections around town. **Avu Internet Cafe,** at the corner of Rungsiyanon Rd. and Ratchadamrong Rd. 1฿ per min. CATNET Internet access (11฿ per hr.) at the post office.

Post Office: 76 Ketkelang Rd. (☎699 208), south of the day market. **International phone.** *Poste Restante.* Open M-F 8:30am-4:30pm, Sa 9am-noon. **Postal code:** 58130.

ACCOMMODATIONS

The number of guest houses in Pai has risen from 15 in 1944 to over 60 today. Prices are similar, but quality varies widely; check rooms before you check in. The easiest way to choose a place to stay is by deciding on your area of preference—next to the soothing Pai river (Golden Hut), in the middle of nightlife (Duang), or in the scenic countryside (Blue Mountain, Sun Hut, Pai Radise).

🔯 **Sun Hut** (☎699 730), in the small town of Mae Yen. Follow the road to the hot springs. Once you cross the 2nd bridge, Sun Hut is on your right. Teak and bamboo huts set in a beautiful garden with pond. The Tarzan Hut constructed in a tree may be your only escape from the 2 dogs and 20 cats. Areas conducive to yoga and meditation. Only 3 of the 14 huts have attached bath. Basic hut with towels, mosquito nets, and fan 100-120฿; average hut 120-150฿; deluxe Jupiter hut with bath 300-400฿. ❶

🔯 **Pai Radise,** 98 Moo 1 Ban Mae Yen (☎098 387 521). Turn left 50m after the 1st bridge on the way to the hot springs. The best-value bungalows in Pai are 200m on the right. Overlooks the Pai Valley rice fields and up into the hills. Rooms are new (renovation completed in Nov. 2001) and exceptionally clean, with large baths and big, comfy beds. Best location, construction, and price combo around. Solid brick and wood lodgings 350฿. ❹

🔯 **Blue Mountain Guest Cottages,** 174 Chaisongkhram Rd. (☎699 282), 1km to the right of the bus station past the hospital. Stellar high season restaurant. With two cats named Ham and Bacon, a dog named Mr. Falang, and an adorable white gibbon monkey named Ooh Ooh who exchanges hugs for fruit, you're sure to make at least one new friend. Live music 10pm-2am. Rustic bungalows with mosquito nets 50-100฿; VIP rooms with bath and fan 150-200฿. ❶

Golden Hut (☎699 024), off Chaisongkhram Rd. Turn left from the bus station, then left again onto a dirt road before the 2nd wat; it's on the left just after Wee Huts. Complex of bungalows and bamboo huts situated next to the Pai River. The best huts are raised to overlook the river. Laundry 20฿ per kg. Rooms and bungalows 100฿, with toilet 120฿, with bath and riverside view 250฿. ❶

Duang Guest House (☎699 101), across the road from the bus station. Well-kept place with a tasty restaurant. Mountain bikes 80฿ per day. Movie showings in attached restaurant. Singles 70฿; doubles 130฿, with bath 300฿; VIP rooms with TV and fridge 400฿. ❶

Wee Huts and Shark Bar & Restaurant, just before Golden Hut. Popular restaurant plays an array of 1960s classics. Standard bug-netted bungalows and chatty staff. Flexible check-out. Bamboo huts 100฿. ❶

🗂 FOOD

Hip cafes are in the center of town. For simple open-air joints, try **Ketkelang Rd.** In the evenings, head to the **night market** on Rungsiyanon Rd. Don't miss the baked goodies at **Homemade Muslim ❶**, at the southern end of the night market. (Delicious coconut cream pie 15฿. Chocolate croissants 10฿. Chicken potato pie 15฿.) Locals also recommend the **noodle shop ❶** at the back left of the day market (*kuay tiaw gai*; noodle soup with chicken 20฿). **Chez Swan ❷**, 13 Rungsiyanon Rd., just south of the Ratchadamrong Rd. intersection, is an authentic French transplant. (Quiche Lorraine 60฿. Creme caramel 35฿. *Patate au gratin dauphinois* 55฿. Open daily 8am-late.) The tastiest of the Ketkelang Rd. joints is the oddly named **Nong Beer ❷**, 39/1 Chaisongkhram Rd., at the somewhat noisy intersection with Ketkelang Rd. (Penang curry pork and rice 30฿. Open daily 7am-10pm.) **All About Coffee ❷**, 100 Chaisongkhram Rd., delivers an early-morning caffeine kick along with breakfast or sandwiches throughout the day. The omelette with tomato, onion, and cheese is the best and biggest of the set breakfast menu (served with homemade bread and coffee 65฿). Look out for the daily specials. (Pai coffee 35฿; international beans 40฿; banana coffee shake 45฿. Yoghurt with fruit salad and muesli 45฿. Open daily 9am-5:30pm.) **Own Home Restaurant ❷**, 9/4 Ratchadamrong Rd., east of the intersection with Rungsiyanon Rd., serves a large variety of vegetarian options. The smoky-flavored aubergine salad (40฿) is particularly tasty. (Fruit salad with muesli 25฿. Open daily 7:30am-11pm; kitchen closes 10pm.)

⊚ SIGHTS

Wat Phra That Mae Yen has sublime views. To get there, head east on Ratchadamrong Rd. and cross the Pai River; the 360 steps to the wat are 1km up. Some may choose to take the easier paved route. Continuing past the Mae Yen River leads to the **hot springs,** 7km from town. Hot enough to fry an egg—well, boil at least—it may be difficult to find a pool to relax in. For a more regal experience, the local resorts (2km before the hot springs) pump the spring water to their grounds. **Natural Hot Spring Bungalows** has individual baths (40฿) or nearby **Thapai Spa Camping** has larger pools for lazing (50฿). It's possible to pitch a tent for free at the hot springs, or for 100฿ at either of the resorts. About 2km before the hot springs (5km from town), there are three **elephant schools.** In the other direction, on the road to Mae Hong Song, is a popular but not spectacular **waterfall,** 11km out of town. To get there, turn left after the army base (5km); it's another 6km from there. The return trip can be completed through Shan and Lisu villages. Returning to the paved road from the waterfall, the dirt road turn-off is 200m on the right. The dirt road will deposit you on the road leading out of town past the hospital. Also on this road, 2km from the hospital, **Wat Nam Hoo** houses **Muang Pai** (Buddha image of Pai). The inexplicable water deposit in the bronze Buddha's cranium is believed to be sacred. Beware of locals offering gifts especially around the waterfall; quite a few foreigners have been ripped off and/or arrested for carrying illegal drugs.

⋀ TREKKING AND RAFTING

Trekking outfitters in Pai are diversifying. Everything from hiking to rafting to elephant rides (300฿ per hr.) is available, so shop around to see what suits you. **Back Trax,** 27 Chaisongkhram Rd., leads groups around the Pai and Soppong areas, giving 15-20% of their proceeds to the villages. Owner Chao, a member of the Lahu tribe, speaks excellent English. (3 days 1500฿. Open daily 8am-8pm.) **Duang Trekking,** at Duang Guest House (see **Accommodations,** p. 268), offers treks that visit Karen, Lisu, and Shan villages along with several waterfalls. (2-day treks 1000฿, with rafting and elephants 1450฿; 3-day treks 1500฿, with rafting 1750฿.)

Bamboo rafting is usually only possible from November to May, since Pai's rivers get rather wild in the rainy season. Whitewater rafting in rubber boats fills the void in the wet season, though by February, the water level again drops too low for white water rafting. **Thai Adventure Rafting** (☎ 699 111), next to Chez Swan (see **Food,** p. 268), and **Northern Green** (☎ 699 385), on Chaisongkhram Rd. next to Aya Service (see **Rentals,** p. 266), have similar adventures down the Khong and Pai rivers. By the time you've finished paddling, you're in Mae Hong Son. (2-day trips stay overnight in established campsitesm, 1800฿. 4-person minimum.)

♫ ENTERTAINMENT

Pai also offers a variety of less strenuous activities. **Vandee's Cooking Courses** at Peter and Vandee's Guest House are widely reported to be some of the best in the country. Head east out of town; it's 500m past the first bridge on the way to the hot springs. (1 day 400฿; 5 days with certificate 1200฿. Prices include recipe book. Start time for lunch 11:30am, dinner 6:30pm.) Next door, plunge into the **Pai swimming pool.** (40฿, children 20฿. Open daily 9am-6pm.) Pai is also the place to pamper your soul—**Pai Dhamma and Herbal House,** on Rungsiyanon Rd. opposite the police, has Thai massage and aromatherapy. Three- to ten-day meditation and massage courses are available, while the "Detox" course is best for those coming off Ko Phangan. (☎ 699 964. Meditation course with detox 1500฿ per day, includes accommodation; 3-day massage course 1000฿ per day. Note that it plans to move in the next year, so check with a tourist agency if it's not on Rungsiyanon Rd.) Across the road, **"Mam"** teaches yoga to those with or without experience. (☎99 544 981. 2½hr. class 250฿.)

The town boogies nightly to blues at the regionally renowned **BeBop**, on Chaisongkhram Rd. between Ketkelang and Rungsiyanon Rd. Show up by 9:30pm to get a seat. (Open daily 6:30pm-12:30am. Music 9-10:30pm.) **Golden Triangle Bar and Restaurant,** at the eastern end of Chaisongkhram Rd., is a more relaxed option. (Open daily 4pm-midnight.) **Ban Klung Pai,** 200m east of the bus station, shows English movies daily at 2:30 and 7:30pm. The "free-spirited" **Tea-Room** next to BeBop also has movies at 7pm, though they request "No Assholes Please." Every kind of tea except Lipton is available, along with a collection of art and photography for sale. The sign on the door says it all: "Open When We're Happy."

THA TON   ☎053

The scenic boat trip down the Kok River to Chiang Rai is reason enough to visit idyllic and sleepy Tha Ton. Although few visitors stay long enough to explore the ethnic villages nearby, they come in droves to stay the night. Arriving from Chiang Mai before noon allows travelers to soak up the scenery over lunch, ascend the surrounding hills, and stroll among life-size Chinese, Hindu, and Buddhist figures at Wat Tha Ton—all before hopping onto a chartered longtailed boat the next morning.

▛ **TRANSPORTATION. Rte. 1089,** which continues across the river to Mae Chan 62km away, is Tha Ton's main road. Mae Salong is 43km away, Chang Rai 92km away, and Chiang Mai 175km away. Most **buses** leave from the north side of the bridge. Those to **Chiang Mai** (4hr., 6 per day 6:25am-2:25pm, 70฿) depart from a lot 100m north of the river. Buses to **Mai Sai** (2½hr., 3pm, 35฿) stop near the police box just beyond the bus lot. For **Chiang Rai,** take a Mai Sai-bound bus to **Mae Chan** (1hr., 20฿) and wait for a connecting bus (45min., 10-15฿). Yellow *songthaew* head to **Fang** (45min., every 10min. 5:30am-3pm, 20฿) and to **Mae Salong** (1½hr., every 30min. 7:30am-4pm, 50฿) from a lot north of the bus station and around the bend. **Longtailed boats** leave from the pier on the river's south bank for **Chiang Rai** (4hr., 12:30pm, 250฿; the boat stops for 20min. in Ruammit). If you're coming from Chiang Mai, it's necessary to take the 6:25 or 8am bus (3-5hr., 200฿) in order to reach Tha Ton in time to catch the longtailed boats to Chiang Rai. Reserve a seat at the **Tha Ton Boat Office** by the pier. (☎459 427. Open daily 9am-3pm.) Chartered private craft (seats 6-8 depending on season, 1600฿ including guide) won't leave after 3pm, as the ride is dangerous in the dark. In the high season it is preferable and possible to put together your own group of 6. This way, the enticing plunge into Kok River and village stops are possible.

▟ **PRACTICAL INFORMATION.** While there are no banks or exchange booths, **Tha Ton Tour** at Chankasem Guest House near the pier might exchange small sums. The nearest **ATM** is in Fang. A **morning market** sets up 200m south of the bridge and leaves a fruit stand behind for the rest of the day. (Open daily 5:30-7:30am.) The closest **hospital** (☎459 036) is in Mae Ai, 7km south. In an emergency, call your guest house or the **Bangkok tourist police** (☎1155) for transportation; ambulances are slower. A **tourist police box** is just before the pier. (Open 8:30am-4:30pm; 24hr. emergency.) A **pharmacy** sits next to the morning market. (Open daily 8am-8pm.) **ABC Amsterdam Restaurant,** north of the bridge next to the bus station, has **overseas calls** (60฿ per min.). **Tha Ton Internet** (1฿ per min.) is across the street from the pier on the south side of the bridge. A

post office sits on the main road opposite the entrance to Wat Tha Ton. (Basic postcard and letter service only. Open M-F 8am-noon and 1-4:30pm.) **Postal code:** 50280.

⚆⚆ ACCOMMODATIONS AND FOOD. Most budget digs lie on the Kok's south side while resorts clog the left side of the river. Affordable **Thip's Travelers House ❶**, just south of the bridge on the main road, is run by the lovable English-speaking Mrs. Thip. (☎459 312. Restaurant open daily 7am-9pm. Laundry. Bicycle rental 80฿ per day. Singles with private cold showers 100฿; doubles 150฿.) **Apple Guest House ❶** has bungalows in two locations. To reach the more affordable ones, head south from the bridge and take the second left; it's on the right 150m down. (☎459 315. Singles 100฿; bungalows 150฿, with hot shower 250฿; triples 200฿.) **Tha Ton Garden Riverside ❸** has fabulous bathrooms with Western toilets and hot showers in a manicured garden along the river. To get there, take the first left after the river; it's past the Tha Ton Chalet. While you're there, try the *tom yam* soup with shrimp for 60฿. (☎459 286. Restaurant open daily 7am-10pm. English menu. Riverside bungalows 200฿, with TV instead of view 300฿. Look for new 150฿ rooms coming soon.) Continue down the road from Tha Ton Garden Riverside to get to **Garden Home ❷**. This huge, shaded property has its own riverside beach. (☎495 325. Basic rooms with fan and cold shower 150฿, with hot water 200฿; quality and price of rooms increase as you move toward the river.)

⚅⚄ SIGHTS AND ACTIVITIES. Wat Tha Ton dominates the hillside above Thip's Travelers House. The temple features life-size representations of figures from Hindu, Buddhist, and Chinese mythology hidden away in manmade caves, as well as fantastic views of the town and countryside. A visit to the two huge Buddhas is 20฿, but exploring the

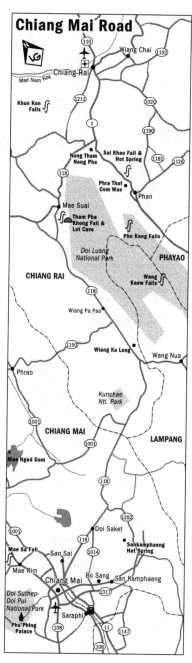

Chiang Mai Road

NORTHERN THAILAND

complex's other scenic areas costs nothing but a climb. The easiest route up the hill begins at the arch across the road from the post office. When you reach the fork in the path marked by the full-fed figure, turn left for the massive golden dragon-headed Buddha, or right for the 12m tall white Buddha.

The **Mae Kok River** originates in the mountains of Myanmar's Shan states, enters Thailand above Tha Ton, and flows 200km to meet the Mekong River in Chiang Saen. **Bamboo rafting** to Chiang Rai (a 3-day excursion) is a quiet, leisurely method of exploring villages along its banks. The Akha town of **Mae Salak** is the biggest you'll pass; it serves as a starting point for journeys south into the Wawi area, home to numerous Lahu, Lisu, Hmong, Akha, Karen, and Yao hamlets. **Phatai** is a Black Lahu village on the north bank. **Jakue** has numerous Lahu products for sale and a Catholic missionary school. **Pha Khang** has picturesque mountains, and **Pha Keau** has steep cliffs. The stop everyone makes is **Ruammit,** 45min. from Chiang Rai, a large Karen village that now resembles a traveling circus complete with elephant rides (400฿ per hr.), photos with boa constrictors (10฿), and endless souvenirs. From there, it's another 20min. to the **Temple Cave. Tha Ton Tour** (☎373 143), before Chankasem Guest House, offers floats and treks to Chiang Rai. (2-day raft and boat trek, 1500฿ per person; 3-day Akha and Lalu village trek and boating 1800฿ per person; elephant rides and longneck village extra. Open daily 10am-8:30pm.) **Thip's Travelers House** (☎459 312) leads bamboo raft trips down the Mae Kok (3-days, 2000฿ with an elephant ride) and is conscious of eco-tourism issues. All prices assume at least four participants. Be sure to understand what any chartered trip entitles you to, and to check the experience of your boatman; the sometimes shallow waters can be difficult to navigate.

CHIANG RAI   ☎ 053

Chiang Rai has always played second fiddle to its southern neighbor, Chiang Mai. The rivalry began when King Mengrai built Chiang Rai in 1262 and used it as his central command post for three decades before switching allegiance to Chiang Mai. Besides offering stunning surrounding vistas and quality guest houses, Chiang Rai also features a night market, which stocks a wider array of tribal handicrafts than the infamous and larger Chiang Mai market, and a hill tribe museum. Those overnighting in Chiang Rai before proceeding to Laos leave feeling they've glimpsed authentic Thai city living without contending with the characteristic tourist traps of other popular destinations. Basking in the poppy glow of the Golden Triangle, the city also serves as an ideal base for one-day exploration or longer treks to villages in the mountains near the Myanmar border.

◰ TRANSPORTATION

Flights: Chiang Rai International Airport (☎798 000), 7km out of town on Hwy. 110. To **Bangkok** (1hr.; 9:40am, 12:45, 3:50, 7:50, 9:50pm; 2645฿) and **Chiang Mai** (25min.; 8:40am, 8pm; 880฿). **Thai Airways,** 870 Phahonyothin Rd. (☎711 179), 1 block south of Teepee Bar. Open M-F 8am-noon and 1-5pm.

Buses: Chiang Rai Bus Station (☎711 224), on Prasopsuk Rd., one block east of intersection with Phahonyothin Rd., next to the night market. To: **Bangkok** (12hr., 4pm, 264฿; 2nd- and 1st-class A/C 8 per day 8am, 4:30-6:45pm, 351฿ and 370฿; VIP 7pm, 700฿; private companies 8am-7:15pm, 452฿); **Chiang Khong** (2½-3hr., every 30min. 7am-5pm, 42-54฿); **Chiang Mai** (3½hr., 6 per day 6:15am-5:30pm, 77฿; A/C 13 per day 7:30am-5pm, 139฿); **Chiang Saen** (1½-2¼hr., every 30min. 6am-6pm, 25฿); **Khon Kaen** (12hr.; 5, 9am; 239฿; 2nd-class A/C 2, 4pm; 335฿; 1st-class A/C 6pm, 430฿) via **Phitsanulok** (6½hr.; 139฿, 2nd-class A/C 195฿, 1st-class A/C 250฿); **Lam-**

Chiang Rai

ACCOMMODATIONS
Baan Bua Guest House, 11
Ben Guest House, 12
Chat House, 3
Chian House, 1
Mae Hong Son Guest House, 2
Pintamom Guest House, 4

FOOD
Cabbages and Condoms, 5
Golden Triangle Restaurant, 6
La Cantina, 9
Nakon Panton, 8

NIGHTLIFE
Cat Bar, 10
Par Club, 13
Sperm Pub, 14
Teepee Hippee Happy Bar, 7

TO PIER (1km) & THAMTUPU (3km)

Winitchaikul Rd.

TO RUAMMIT & THA TON

Wat Doi Thong

Kraisorasit Rd.

Ananmuay Rd.

Ratdamnong Rd.

Wat Ngam Muang

Government Office and Town Hall

Ratyotha Rd.

Utarakit Rd.

Sangkaew Rd.

Wat Phra Kaew

Mae Kok River

Dusit Island

Ngam Muang Rd.

Thanalai Rd.

Wat Ming Muang

Trairat Rd.

TAT

Banphraprakan Rd.

Sanambin Rd.

Seon Motorcycle

Market

Wat Phra Singh

Ruang Nakhon Rd.

Thanon Rd.

Sankhongnoi Rd.

Surkatthit Rd.

Wat Klangwiang

Santirat Rd.

Wang Come Hotel

Pama Boat Rd.

Clock Tower

Rattanakhet Rd.

Singhaklai Rd.

2

Satham Payabam Rd.

Wat Jet Yod

Jet Yod Rd.

Siam Used Books

Thanalai Rd.

Koh Loh Rd.

Thai Military Bank

Phahonyothin Rd.

Thai Always Office

Wisit Wuang Rd.

Wat Sriboonruang

TO & (2km)

Wiang Inn

Night Market

PDA Hill Tribe Museum

Phahonyothin Rd.

Sriboonraung Rd.

San Pannat Rd.

Utarakit Rd.

King Mengrai Monument

Prasopsik Rd.

Sankongchang Rd.

Wat Si Koet

Sigad Rd.

110

TO CHIANG MAI

1

1232

Wat Pranon

0   0
0   0

meters   300
yards   330

N

TO MAE SAI, CHIANG SAEN & (9km)

NORTHERN THAILAND

pang (5hr., every 20min. 5:20am-3pm, 81฿); **Mae Sai** (1½hr., every 15min. 6am-6pm, 25฿); **Mae Sot** (10hr., 7:20am, 200฿; A/C 9:20am, 360฿) via **Tak** (8hr.; 165฿, A/C 297฿); **Nakhon Ratchasima** (12hr., 3:30pm, 262฿; 1st-class A/C 6:15am, 1:15, 5:30pm; 472฿; VIP 7pm, 550฿) via **Phitsanulok** (6½hr.; 139฿, 2nd-class A/C 250฿; 1st-class A/C 292฿); **Nan** (6hr., 9:30am, 95฿); **Pattaya** (16hr., 4 per day; 309฿, A/C 556฿, VIP 649฿); **Phitsanulok** (8hr., A/C every hr. 7:30-10:30am, 214฿) via **Sukhothai** (6½hr., 190฿).

Boats: Leave from the pier (☎ 750 009), on the north bank of the Mae Kok river next to the Mae Fah Luang Bridge, 1km northwest of the city. To **Tha Ton** (4hr., 10:30am, 200฿) via **Ruammit** (45min., 50฿). Charter boats 1500฿ per day; maximum 6 people.

Local Transportation: Songthaew, tuk-tuk, and **samlor** cluster on Utarakit Rd. around the market and in the evening on Phahonyothin Rd. near the night bazaar. Fares in city 10-20฿. Within 10-15km radius, *songthaew* and tuk-tuk should cost under 50฿; trips to airport up to 100฿.

Rentals: Practically every guest house rents motorcycles through **Soon Motorcycle,** 197/2 Trairat Rd. (☎ 714 068), which offers a convenient drop-off/pickup service from guest houses as well as free transport to the bus station. New motorbikes 200฿; secondhand 150฿; 4WD Suzuki Jeep 1000฿, with insurance 1500฿. Reduced rates for longer rentals. Open daily 8am-7pm. **Avis** is at the airport (☎ 793 827).

■★🛈 ORIENTATION AND PRACTICAL INFORMATION

The **Mae Kok River** flows west to east, forming Chiang Rai's northern border. **Singhaklai Rd.,** site of the TAT office and guest houses, skirts the river. The northern part of town lies between Singhaklai and **Banphraprakan Rd.,** 500m south and parallel to it. The most helpful landmark, the **Haw Nariga (clock tower),** stands in the middle of Banphraprakan Rd. forming a chaotic roundabout. **Jet Yod Rd.,** chock-full of bars, leads south from there. One block east, a portion of **Phahonyothin Rd.,** runs parallel to Jet Yod Rd., while the upper half curves around above the bus station.

Tourist Offices: TAT, 448/16 Singhaklai Rd. (☎ 744 674). Receptive and organized office. Offers free maps (with bus schedules), brochures, a list of trekking outfits, and regional info. English spoken. Lenso phone outside. Open daily 8:30am-4:30pm.

Currency Exchange: Thai Military Bank, 897/7-8 Phahonyothin Rd. (☎ 715 657). Open daily 8:30am-9pm. **24hr. ATM** (AmEx/Cirrus/MC/PLUS/V). Thai Military Bank currency exchange booth, on Phahonyothin Rd., next to entrance to night bazaar. Open daily 6am-10pm.

English-Language Bookstores: Siam Used Books, 169/157 Pamavipat Rd., opposite Wang Come Hotel. Large selection of new and used books. Rental 80฿ per book. Open daily 10am-8pm.

Emergency: ☎ 191. **Ambulance:** ☎ 711 366. **Tourist Police (Bangkok):** ☎ 1155.

Police: Chiang Rai Provincial Police Station (☎ 711 444), at the intersection of Rattanakhet Rd. and Singhaklai Rd. 1 block east of the TAT. **Open 24hr.**

Local Tourist Police: ☎ 717 779. Downstairs from the TAT. Will gladly give a "background check" on tour agencies. **Open 24hr.**

Medical Services: Overbrooke Hospital, 444/3 Singhaklai Rd. (☎ 711 366), 250m west of TAT. **24hr. pharmacy.** AmEx/MC/V.

Telephones: Telecommunications Office (☎ 776 738), on Ngam Muang Rd. at the west end of town. CATNET Internet access, fax, overseas calls. Open M-F 8am-8pm, Sa-Su 8:30am-4:30pm. AmEx/MC/V.

Internet Access: Post@Cafe, 869/64-73 Phahonyothin Rd. (☎752 207), one block north of Pamavipat Rd. 20฿ for first hr., 0.34฿ per min. thereafter. Open daily 7:30am-9:30pm. **Chiang Rai Cyber Net,** 869/147 Pamavipat Rd. (☎752 090), between Jet Yod and Phahonyothin Rd. 30฿ per hr., 10min. minimum.

Post Offices: 486/1 Mu 15 Uttarakit Rd. (☎711 421), 200m south of the TAT and 300m north of clock tower. HCD phone booth. *Poste Restante.* Open M-F 8:30am-4:30pm, Sa-Su and holidays 9am-noon. **Postal code:** 57000.

ACCOMMODATIONS

Over 30 guest houses and hotels have opened since a tourist boom hit Chiang Rai, and many boast excellent values. The best ones are outside the city center, making them quiet, spacious, and worth the 20min. walk or 20฿ tuk-tuk to reach them. Call ahead in the high season, otherwise you're likely to have to "settle" and pay more. Guest houses can arrange motorbike rental (150-500฿), and provide luggage storage. Check-out is usually between 11 and 11:30am and all have hot water.

Mae Hong Son Guest House (☎715 367). From the TAT, head east on Singhaklai Rd. and take the 2nd left (at the intersection with Rattanakhet Rd.) onto Santirat Rd. Follow the road to the far end. Friendly manager, Kuan, keeps guests entertained as he works the bar in an intimate garden cafe. All rooms with wooden-framed beds, fans, and mosquito nets (essential here). Laundry 45฿ per kg. Trekking service. Singles 80฿; doubles 100฿; triples 150฿, with bath, furnishings, and western toilet 150-200฿. ●

Chian House, 172 Sriboonraung Rd. (☎/fax 713 388). From the TAT, head east past the Rattanakhet Rd. intersection. Take the next left (onto Koh Loh Rd.), cross bridge, and then follow signs. Owner speaks excellent English. Perks include restaurant with cable TV and salt-water swimming pool. Laundry 25฿ per kg. Internet access and overseas calls. Family-oriented. Singles 60฿; doubles 120-250฿, with A/C 300฿; bungalows 250-300฿/350-450฿. ●

Chat House, 3/2 Sangkaew Rd. (☎711 481), down the soi directly across from Overbrooke Hospital on Trairat Rd. Cheap and quiet with comfortable patio and small garden setting. Laundry and trekking service. Bicycle rental 80฿ per day. Low season bargaining. Popular 3-bed dorms 50฿; singles 70฿; doubles 120฿, with bath 160-180฿, with A/C 250฿; triples 180฿. ●

Ben Guest House, 351/10 Sankhongnoi Rd., Soi 4 (☎716 775). Call ahead for a free pickup, or head west on Banphraprakan Rd. from the clock tower, turn left at the first traffic signal onto Sanambin Rd., right on Sankhongnoi Rd., right again on Soi 4, and walk to the end. Charming teak wood house with veranda and adjacent brick wing. Rooms with bath are better value. Rooms 120฿, with bath 200฿; new wing (with carpet and A/C) 350฿. ❷

Pintamorn Guest House, 509/1 Rattanakhet Rd. (☎714 161). A 10min. walk north on Phahonyothin Rd., then Rattanakhet Rd., from the bus station. Backpacker central. 24hr. kitchen big on Western food (cheeseburger 50฿). Cable TV, pool table, book exchange on the patio. Free luggage storage. Book ahead. Singles 80฿, with bath 150฿; doubles 100฿/180฿. ●

Baan Bua Guest House, 879/2 Jet Yod Rd. (☎718 880). Heading south from the clock tower, the soi is 3 blocks down on the left, after Siam Used Books. Spacious and immaculately clean rooms in surprisingly quiet backstreet location despite its close proximity to bars. All rooms have fan, western toilet, and hot water. Tiled rooms with bath 180฿; larger rooms 200฿; twins 220฿. ❸

🗂 FOOD

Chiang Rai's culinary scene is concentrated in the neighborhood bounded by Jet Yod, Banphraprakan, and Phahonyothin Rd. Menus catering to Western palates cram the entrance to the night bazaar on Phahonyothin Rd. The best food, however, lies in open-air joints unmarked by the Roman alphabet. Guest house kitchens are another alternative; **Chian House** (try the baguette sandwiches) and **Mae Hong Son Guest House** (huge sundaes) are particularly tasty options. The buffet feast in elegant surroundings at 🔲**Wiang Inn ❸**, 893 Phahonyothin Rd., seems too good to be true. (☎711 533. Open M-F noon-2pm. 100฿.)

🔲 **Nakon Pathon** (no English sign), 869/25-26 Phahonyothin Rd., caters almost exclusively to the Thai working crowd. Small English menu. Run by an energetic husband and wife team. Unbeatable *kiaw moo dang* (barbecue pork with rice; 30฿), washed down with Iced Milo (10฿). Noodle soups 30฿. Open daily 6am-3pm. ❷

Cabbages and Condoms, 620/25 Thanalai Rd., east of Pintamorn Guest House. C&C Chiang Rai raises money and awareness for the AIDS campaign. *Tom-yam* 60-70฿. Condoms are free and work better than cabbages. Open daily 11am-midnight. AmEx/MC/V. ❷

Golden Triangle Restaurant, 590 Phahonyothin Rd., diagonally across from the night market. Thai dining with an informative English menu describing the local cuisine. Various curries, rice dishes, and noodles. Delicious *gaeng kiaw wan* (green sweet curry) 45-60฿. Open daily 7am-10pm. ❷

La Cantina, 1025/40 Jet Yod Rd. High quality Italian food in a relaxing atmosphere. 150-200฿ per person. Extensive menu of homemade pasta served with unlimited bread and butter. Pizza 90-180฿. Open daily 8am-10pm. ❸

👁 SIGHTS

According to local lore, the *stupa* of 🔲**Wat Phra Kaew,** originally known as Wat Pa Yier, was struck by lightning in 1434 and revealed an Emerald Buddha; the temple's name changed to "Wat of the Emerald Buddha" as a result. Today, the original sits in Bangkok's Wat Phra Kaew (see p. 113), and a new image, commissioned in China and carved from Canadian jade in 1991, sits in its place. The wat is a must-see for all those who haven't seen the original. (Wat Phra Kaew is at the west end of town on Trairat Rd., opposite Overbrooke Hospital. Open daily dawn-dusk.)

At the west end of town, walking from Trairat Rd. past Chat House on Sang Kaew Rd., rests **Wat Ngam Muang** on top of the hill of the same name. Its *stupa* contains King Mengrai's ashes and relics. In a line east from Wat Ngam Muang is **Keng Mengrai's shrine,** at the point where Phahonyothin Rd. merges with Hwy. 101. Many make the pilgrimage to the site and light incense and candles to pay their respect and draw strength from King Mengrai, their honored founder.

The **PDA Hill Tribe Museum,** 620/25 Thanalai Rd., 300m east of Pintamorn Guest House, isn't nearly as informative as the one in Chiang Mai. The 25min. slide show on the region's different tribes will give you the basics although the background music proves to be distracting. (☎740 088. Open M-F 8:30am-8pm, Sa-Su 10am-8pm; closes 6pm in low season. 50฿. Slideshow 50฿.)

Chiang Rai's city sights are all easily accessed by bicycle, and the trip there may even be more exciting than the sights themselves. The energetic can continue to **Thamtupu,** where Buddha images sit inside cliff caverns, and are also carved on the limestone faces. The dirt road from Thamtupu is in good condition and makes for great, flat mountain bike rides between jagged rocky peaks interspersed with corn and banana plantations. The turn-off to Thamtupu is on the left, 700m after Mae Fah Luang Bridge (pier to Tha Ton), traveling north from Chiang Rai. The cave is a further 1km on a partially sealed road.

🎵 ENTERTAINMENT

Teepee Hippie Happy Bar, 542/4 Phahonyothin Rd., just south of Banphaprakan Rd., an American West decor shop, hosts an occasional acoustic blues band (after 10pm in high season), and offers a vegetarian menu. (Open daily 11am-5pm and 6:30pm-1am.) Head to **Cat Bar,** 1013/1 Jet Yod Rd., for jamming sessions or a game of pool. (☎714 637. Small beer 50฿. Open daily noon-1am.) Next to Cat Bar on Jet Yod Rd., an endless row of bars sit next to each other, with comparable music and atmosphere. The bars on the soi linking Jet Yod Rd.'s northern end with Banphaprakan Rd. at the clock tower dismiss the pretense of karaoke and go straight to go-go. The most popular disco in town is the **Par Club** in the Inn Come Hotel, 172/6 Rajbamrung Rd., accessible by tuk-tuk. (☎717 850. Cover 100-150฿ includes free drink. Open daily 9pm-1am.) Nearby **Sperm Pub**'s disco, in the Ruentip Hotel at the corner of Rajbamrung and Phahonyothin Rd., is more innocent than the name suggests. (☎754 179. No cover. Open daily 8pm-1am.)

🏠 MARKETS

The **day market ❶** is a massive affair encompassing an entire square block, the north-east corner of which nips at the post office on Uttarakit Rd. Lots of vegetables and fresh fruit (pineapple 10฿) are on the north end along Uttarakit Rd. Inside is a winding maze of, well, everything. Bakeries sit next to tailors, next to pharmacies, next to wide selections of plastic combs. The only consistency can be found at the south end, which is full of dead cows, pigs, and fish. **Food vendors ❶** move to the streets surrounding the market at night—go right there for delicious and cheap dining (before 10pm). The streets of the **night market ❶** are closed to all but pedestrian traffic making it more manageable than its southern counterpart. The market contains a massive amount of hill tribe products (including Akha ware) on the soi leading to the bus station off Phahonyothin Rd. Following it leads to a wider variety of tapestries, intricately carved boxes, hand bags, instruments, head dresses, and Hello Kitty lights. A great selection of food (fruit shakes 15฿, papaya salad with seafood 30฿) surrounds a courtyard on your left at the end of the soi. The focal point of the courtyard is the large stage where traditional hill tribe music and Thai dancing occurs. A smaller stage lies on the soi between Phahonyothin Rd. and the bus station. (Nightly performances on both stages 8-10pm.)

🥾 TREKKING

Chiang Rai's bucolic province—full of ethnic hill tribes—offers trekking routes less traveled than those around Chiang Mai. As always, trek prices should include food, transportation, and an informed guide. Typical treks run 3 days/2 nights (2-4 people around 3000฿ per person; 5-7 people around 2500฿ per person; see TAT's pamphlet), but you can do as short as a day or as long as a week. Many companies have access to horses, elephants, rafts, mountain bikes, and plain old hiking boots; mix and match your itinerary and then consider which hill tribes you'd like to visit, as they're vast and varied in the area. Finally, make sure you like your guide, because your life, fun, and money are in his hands. If you're considering a service that's not listed below, check its status with the TAT. Tours to Laos or Myanmar may be illegal, so check that with the TAT, too.

Population and Community Development Association (PDA), 620/26 Thanalai Rd., which funds rural development, family planning, and AIDS education/treatment/ prevention programs among hill tribes, offers treks and one-day tours (see p. 92). If all you crave is to see the world from atop an elephant, the PDA has daytrips to Ruammit (the Karen elephant camp), which stop at a waterfall and some Yao and Akha villages. Company treks are pricier than those run out of many guest houses. PDA also accepts volunteers for many of its health-related projects. Most of the volunteers are selected through the Bangkok office, although occasionally the Chiang Rai office will accept applications directly. Thai language skills are strongly favored. If you're still interested, bring a resume and plan to wait a week. (☎/fax 740 088. 3-day/2-night trek to Lahu and Akha villages, including elephant and longtail boat rides, 3700฿ per person, minimum 2 people. Daytrips to the Golden Triangle 1500฿ per person, minimum 2 people. The more people, the lower the price. Maximum group size is 12.)

If you don't mind paying for your volunteer experience, **Greenway** (www.green-waythailand.org) runs excellent work camps where volunteers spend two weeks helping in a hill tribe community (see p. 91). To volunteer with Greenway, you must complete your applications in your home country.

Ben's Guest House, Chat House, Chian House, and **Mae Hong Son Guest House** all run flexible treks with guides who are registered with the TAT.

MAE SALONG   ☎ 053

Fifty years after the Chinese Nationalists' 93rd Division fled China in the wake of the Communist victory and settled in this mountaintop village, Mae Salong maintains its Chinese identity. Chinese characters adorn doorframes, tea houses feature red-lanterns, and the dialect of China's southern province, Yunnan, is more common than Thai. The steep slopes surrounding Mae Salong, once covered in lush tropical jungle, now lie barren in order to accommodate the year-round harvest of tea. Pockets of natural beauty still exist, making Mae Salong an appealing daytrip and escape from the city bustle. The best time to visit is in February when the cherry blossoms are in bloom.

⌐❷ TRANSPORTATION AND PRACTICAL INFORMATION. *Songthaew* are frequent early in the morning and leave when full; you can pay the full fare (300฿) if the wait is unbearable. To get to **Chiang Rai,** take a light blue *songthaew* to **Ban Pasang** (1hr., 7am-2pm, 50฿), and then flag down a passing bus (1hr., every 30min. 6am-6pm, 20฿). Yellow *songthaew* to **Tha Ton** (1½hr., 7am-2pm, 50฿) leave from the small **day market,** 1km toward Tha Ton from the town center. The market features Akha wares and Chinese herbs. The **main road** through Mae Salong stretches 2.5km and is a continuation of roads from Tha Ton (Rd. #1234) and Ban Pasang (Rd. #1130); the Khumnaipol Resort marks the Tha Ton end, the Mae Salong Villa marks the Ban Pasang end. The town center is near the guest houses and has daytime **food vendors** and a **mosque.** Starting before dawn, locals mingle at the **morning market** off the road to the Mae Salong Resort, on the road that leads directly under Shin Sane Guest House. Opposite Khumnaipol Resort is a **Thai Military Bank.** (☎765 159. Open M-F 8:30am-3:30pm. AmEx/Cirrus/MC/PLUS/V **ATM** open daily 6am-10pm.) The **police** (☎767 7109) have a booth near the Mae Salong Villa. The nearest **hospital** is in Mae Chan. **Golden Dragon Inn** has an **Internet** connection (60฿ per hr.). There are **no international phones.**

⌐◖ ACCOMMODATIONS AND FOOD. The family-style **Akha Mae Salong Guest House ❶,** off the main road near the mosque, has four huge rooms with wood floors and common bath. The owner sells Akha ware, distributes useful

BORDER INTRIGUE The Golden Triangle, opium capital of the world, produces 70% of the world's heroin. In addition, the Golden Triangle's *ya ba*—speed, a methamphetamine often coated in chocolate—has caught on with teenage users as a cheap alternative to opium and heroin. Drug money is the lifeblood of impoverished hill tribes and nearby paramilitary organizations. The drug mystique has resulted in flourishing tour companies, which fill buses with tourists eager to get a whiff of the intrigue. Trekkers with addicted guides are often convinced that opium is an integral part of tribal culture (see **Hooked on Thailand,** p. 21). Although a few traditional medicines of Northern Thailand use opium as a painkiller, frequent opium use today is considered shameful in most communities.

maps (10฿), arranges one-day horse treks (400฿), and speaks English. (☎765 103. Singles and doubles 100฿; triples 150฿.) Next door, **Shin Sane Guest House ❶** has bungalows with obscured view of the valley, and cheaper rooms on the overhead bridge. (Singles 50฿; doubles 100฿; bungalow with western toilet 200-300฿.) **Golden Dragon ❸,** on the main road between the Mae Salong Resort and Akha Guest House, has peaceful rooms with hot showers. (Boasts coffee in a land of tea. Singles 200฿; doubles 300฿.)

Yunnanese **noodle shops** and **vendors** abound (5฿ per serving). Tea shops provide a relaxing ambience; a kettle of Mae Salong tea soothes for 50฿. **Mini ❷,** 300m toward Tha Ton from Golden Dragon Inn, serves *khanom jun naam ngiaw* (Yunnanese noodle soup; 25฿), the town specialty. Ask for vegetarian options. Join the local schoolchildren in karaoke...Well, hum at least. (Lao beer 50฿. Open daily 7am-10:30pm.) Lazy susans abound at **Sakura Restaurant ❸,** a popular Thai/Chinese restaurant for tour groups in Mae Salong Resort. (Translated menu may make you wish it wasn't—braised sea slugs (250-350฿). Also has standard fare: chicken with cashew nuts small 80฿, large 120฿. Open daily 7am-10pm.)

❺ SIGHTS. For an awesome view, follow the road to the Mae Salong Resort and walk up the steps to the **pagoda.** From here, a road continues 4km through mountain scenery and finally curves back into town via the day market. Area hill tribes include **Akha, Lahu,** and **Lisu,** and in smaller numbers, **Hmong** and **Yao.** There aren't many organized trekking groups, although the intrepid can set off alone. Pick up a map at Shin Sane Guest House (10฿), but don't wander too far; in addition to hill tribe villages, pockets of Shan and KMT groups line the Burmese border. Drug trade and clashes have erupted between Khun Sa's Shan United Army and the Wa National Army. Ask in town about the current situation. The walk-weary can inquire about 4hr. **horseback riding treks** at Shin Sane or Akha Mae Salong guest houses (400฿ per person).

Ban Lorcha is more illuminating than a visit to a museum, for those who don't have time and/or resources to overnight in a hill tribe village. The Akha village, with the help of the PDA (see **Chiang Rai,** p. 278), has established the **"Living Museum"** in order for the villagers to benefit from tourism without its exploitative and corruptive powers. An entrance fee of 40฿ includes a guide who will walk you through the village. While the experience is contrived—the blacksmith doubles as the drum player for the welcoming dance—visitors are left for the most part to observe village life without the "zoo-like" experience commonly associated with similar visits (see **Plight of the Padong,** p. 262). Other villages are marked for sustainable tourism which will help alleviate all the attention on Ban Lorcha. Ban Lorcha is on Rte. 1089 between Tha Ton and Mae Chan, 1km toward Tha Ton from the turn-off to Mae Salong. From Mae Salong, take yellow *songthaew* headed to Tha Ton (20min., 15฿).

NORTHERN THAILAND

NARCOTRAFFICKING
The Thai-Burmese Tug-of-War

Technological innovations have facilitated a faster flow of people, ideas, and products around the globe. But criminal organizations, too, are benefiting from this progress, and nowhere more than in the Golden Triangle. Entrepreneurs in the illegal drug trade and its adjunct industry, money laundering, use sophisticated operating procedures, which result in the degeneration of local societies in faraway markets.

Drug supply trends linking the Golden Triangle, the Andean Region, and Afghanistan illustrate that, like cola or cigarettes, drugs are a competitive, market-driven industry in which a high premium is placed on technological advances. The faster a meth tab can be made or shipped or sold, the more money can be made. Just as the Asian financial crisis hit, Burmese producers met the Thai need for an inexpensive quick-fix by flooding the market with *ya ba*, a methamphetamine. The synthetic drug also proved friendlier to suppliers because of its transportability and over-the-counter ingredients (see, p. 332).

Stomping out drug supply has been likened to squeezing a balloon: a bulge just forms somewhere else. Following US efforts to curb cocaine supply from Colombia, Myanmar met US demand for a substitution by increasing its heroin supply. In 1998, Myanmar became the world's largest opium producer. After the Taliban banned opium cultivation in 2001, Myanmar upped production even more. Post-Taliban Afghanistan is now the world's top opium producer.

A disturbing trend is the link between armed guerrilla groups and the drug business. Organizations like the United Wa State Army (UWSA) in Myanmar, once viewed by the international community as an isolated insurgent group that only controlled remote territory, is now, particularly after September 11, 2001, being closely monitored. Groups like UWSA do not depend on legitimate states; instead, they wreak havoc because they maintain political autonomy by funding themselves.

The economic and political ramifications of the new links are worrisome. When risk-reward analyses favor the drug trade, investment funds are diverted into criminal activity. According to the US Drug Enforcement Agency, Chinese investment drives the Golden Triangle's illicit drug trade. That means less legitimate investment in China and more money for Wa armaments, fueling violence and displacement. As rebels (like UWSA) force families into refugee status by spilling over into Thai territory, the families suffer and the old Thai-Burmese tensions flare up.

The situation in the Golden Triangle illustrates the importance of regional perspectives on fighting drug trafficking and its corrosive adjunct activities. The difference of interests between the Thai and Burmese with respect to control of the Wa Army demonstrates this point. Thailand wants to stop the flow of *ya ba* through its borders and halt the refugee spillover caused by the Wa. It therefore wants the drug business shut down. The government of Myanmar, however, is more concerned that the Wa will become an internal security threat, so their tolerance of the drug business appeases the fighters.

Thailand has largely eradicated opium cultivation within its borders. The Royal Projects, particularly in Northern Thailand, pays workers to grow strawberries instead of opium. Fortunately, the ethnic groups that were producing opium were not closely involved with powerful armed insurgencies as in Myanmar. But drug use is again an epidemic in Thailand, and Thailand remains a narcotics transportation hub. In the globalization era, when borders are meant to be fluid, Thailand is fighting to seal its frontiers from drugs and refugees. Thailand knows that drugs will find users. So they, the Burmese, and global forces have to look beyond their own interests to contain the problem.

Derek Glanz was the editor of Let's Go: Spain, Portugal & Morocco 1998. *He is now a freelance journalist who recently began pursuing postgraduate studies in international relations. He has been published in* The Associated Press *and* The Miami Herald *(via AP), and served as a guest TV analyst on Colombia's* TeleCartagena.

MAE SAI ☎053

One of Thailand's main links with Myanmar, Mae Sai is a bustling border town during the day, but turns into a ghost town in the evening when the border shuts down. With an established opium trade and a burgeoning gem trade stemming from a recently discovered sapphire mine in the Shan State, Mae Sai's future as a trade center looked bright—until a full scale three-way battle broke out in February 2001 among the Shan, Thai, and Burmese troops. Three Thai civilians died in the shelling, and the resulting tensions caused the border to close for four months. A similar situation erupted in early 2002, when Burmese officials accused the Thai military of aiding the Shan (see **Thai-Burmese Relations**, p. 24). While the trade of precious stones and antiques from Myanmar and China is no longer what it was, it's hard to tell this from the bustle in the streets. Aside from the border intrigue, spelunkers can find impressive caves and national parks near Mae Sai's center.

⊏ TRANSPORTATION

Buses and Songthaew: Mae Sai Bus Terminal, 4km south of bridge along Phahonyothin Rd. Red *songthaew* head there every 10min. (5฿). To: **Bangkok** (14hr.; 7am, 4, 5:30pm; 481฿); **Chiang Mai** (5hr.; 6, 8, 11am, 1:45, 3:30pm; 95฿, with A/C 133-171฿); **Chiang Rai** (1½hr., every 15min. 6am-6pm, 25฿) via **Ban Pasang** (30min., 15฿), where *songthaew* go to **Mae Salong** (1hr., leave when full 7am-2pm, 50฿); **Nakhon Ratchasima** (14hr.; 5 per day 5:15am-6pm; 281฿, with A/C 590฿); **Pattaya** (14hr., 5 per day 5:15am-6pm, 530฿). South of Thai Farmers Bank, blue *songthaew* go to **Chiang Saen** (1hr., every hr. 7am-2pm, 30฿) via **Sop Ruak** (40min., 20฿).

Local Transportation: Motorcycle taxis and **samlor** smother Mae Sai. Rides within the city 10-30฿. Green *songthaew* go up and down Phahonyothin Rd. (5฿).

Rentals: Thong (☎732 815), on Silamjoi Rd. near Porm Charern Minimart, rents **motorcycles.** 150฿ per day. Passport deposit required. Open daily 8am-5pm.

✴ 🛈 ORIENTATION AND PRACTICAL INFORMATION

Mae Sai is 61km from Chiang Rai, 68km from Mae Salong, and 35km from the Golden Triangle. Hwy. 110 ends at the **border crossing** marked by the new gate. **Phahonyothin Rd.** hosts a dusty carnival of *farang*, Thais, and Burmese who browse, bargain, and beg at the street stalls. **Silamjoi Rd.** jogs along the river, heading west from the Friendship Bridge toward guest houses.

Immigration Office (☎731 008), on Phahonyothin Rd., 2km south of bridge. 10-day visa extension 500฿; 1-month visa extension for 60-day tourist visas. Bring 2 photos and 2 photocopies of passport. Open daily 8:30am-4:30pm. For a cheaper option, see **Border Crossing: Mae Sai/Thachilek,** p. 284. Immigration Office at the **border** (☎733 261). Border open daily 6:30am-6:30pm. Tourists are asked to cross back by 5pm.

Currency Exchange: All along Phahonyothin Rd. **Thai Farmers Bank,** 122/1 Phahonyothin Rd. (☎640 786). Open M-F 8:30am-3:30pm. **24hr. ATM** (Cirrus/MC/V).

Markets: During the day, stalls line Phahonyothin Rd.—check out the base of the bridge for herbs, gems, teak, and flowers. 200m south, level with and opposite the police, is "ruby alley." Food stalls set up at night near the bridge. The market in **Thachilek,** immediately to the right of the bridge, peddles pirated CDs, cheap (in price and quality) cigarettes, and standard regional market fare. The Thai baht is the accepted currency.

Emergency: ☎191. **Ambulance:** ☎731 300 or 731 301. **Tourist Police (Bangkok):** ☎1155.

Police: ☎731 444. On Phahonyothin Rd. 200m south of bridge. Call the local tourist police first.

Local Tourist Police: ☎733 850. In a booth next to the bridge. Open daily 8am-5pm.

Pharmacy: Drugstore, next to and south of police station. Owner speaks excellent English. Open daily 8am-8pm.

Medical Services: Mae Sai Hospital, 101 Mu 10 Pomaharat Rd. (☎751 300 or 751 301), off Phahonyothin Rd. Head 2km south. Turn right into the soi just after the overpass. Hospital is 400m down.

Telephones: Mae Sai Telecommunications Center, next to the post office. Fax. No HCD. CATNET Internet access. Open M-F 8:30am-4:30pm. LENSO phone at the 7-Eleven 200m south of the bridge.

Internet Access: Take the last right before the bridge, look for the sign leading to the 2nd fl. 20฿ per 30min.; 30฿ per hr. Open daily 9am-9pm.

Post Offices: Mae Sai Post and Telegraph Office, 230/40-41 Phahonyothin Rd. (☎731 402), 4km south of the bridge and despite the address, not on the main road. *Poste Restante.* Open M-F 8:30am-4:30pm, Sa-Su 9am-noon. **Postal code:** 57130.

▐ ACCOMMODATIONS

Mae Sai Guest House, 688 Wiengpangkam Rd. (☎732 021), 30 ft. from Myanmar at the far west end of Silamjoi Rd. Idyllic escape with thatch-decorated bungalows, hot water, restaurant, and laundry service. Best value singles and doubles 100฿-150฿; doubles with bath 200-300฿; bungalows overhanging the water 400฿. ❶

King Kobra Guest House, 135/5 Silamjoi Rd. (☎733 055). Owner Joe and his Kobra mate John have travel info and can offer advice on motorcycle treks to Northern Thailand, Myanmar, and China. Restaurant, laundry service, and nightly movies. Singles 120฿, with bath 200฿; doubles 150-250฿; "VIP" room 350฿. ❷

Chad Guest House, 52/1 Soi Wiengpan (☎732 054), off Phahonyothin Rd., 1km south of bridge. Quiet, cheap place run by friendly English-speaking family. Map available for guests. Rooms with shared toilet and shower. Singles 50-100฿; doubles 100-150฿. ❶

Northern Guest House, 402 Timphajom Rd. (☎731 537), between King Kobra and Mae Sai Guest House. Follow Silamjoi Rd. along the river. Lush tropical garden on the riverfront. Rustic wooden huts with fan have most appeal (80฿). Rooms with cold shower 120-150฿; modern units at the edge of the river with hot water and bathtub 250฿, with A/C 350฿. ❷

▐ FOOD

The **night market ❶** along Phahonyothin Rd. has dishes on display, so a quick "point and shoot" will get you what you want. (Open daily 7-10pm.) Pamper your palate at **Jo Jo Coffee House ❷,** 233/1 Phahonyothin Rd., opposite the Thai Farmers Bank. Food tastes even better than it looks on the menu. Use the a la carte option to sample several flavors (small 30฿; medium 40฿; large 50฿). Bitter melon soup with white gourd on rice is 35฿; a banana split is 40฿. (Open daily 6am-5pm.) Going down the soi directly opposite Thai Farmers Bank leads to a series of stands with tables that specialize in phat thai (20฿). Night restaurants are limited, but **Rabieng Kaew Restaurant ❸,** 150m south on Phahonyothin Rd. of the bridge, is a good option. Their minced pork and coconut in chili paste (50฿) is a spicy treat. (Specials 80-150฿; coconut ice cream 20฿. Open daily 9am-10pm.)

Around the Golden Triangle

Road
River

MYANMAR

(109)
(107)

Tha Ton
(1089)

Mae Salong
(1234)

▲ Dol Tung

Ban Lorcha
(PDA Living Museum)
(1089)

Pong Phra
Baet Falls

Den ●

Chiang Rai

Ban Du

TO CHIANG MAI

Huai Doi

Wiang Chai

(211)

(1152)

(1314)

(1130)

Ban Pasang

Mae Chan

(110)

(1209)

(1098)

Pong Noi

(1271)

(173)

Wat Phra That
Dol Tung

Mae Fah
Luang

Huai
Khrai

(1149)

(110)

Ban Akha
Pha-mi

Tham
Luang

Mae Sai

Thachilek

Sai River

MYANMAR

(1290)

(1016)

Chiang
Saen

Sop Ruak

The Golden
Triangle

Mekong River

LAOS

Ban Saew

(1098)

Ban Kaen

(1020)

Ban Chom Phu

(1155)

Pang Hat

(1174)

Ban Sri
Donchai

Chiang
Khong

(1129)

Mekong River

0   10 kilometers
0   10 miles

MYANMAR

NORTHERN THAILAND

DAYTRIPS FROM MAE SAI

Tham Luang National Park (Great Cave) lies 5km south of Mai Sai 2.5km off Hwy. 110. Its caverns burrow 200m into the mountain. Other caverns in the National Park include the very manageable **Buddha Cave** and the 7km-deep **Royal Luang Cave.** (Open daily 6am-6pm.) Postered maps of the area are available at the entrance. The office has lanterns (30฿) for a quick glimpse—any extended exploration requires flashlight and supplies. There are no guides available, but locals, who sometimes wait at the park, could be convinced to join you for a nominal fee. At the southern end of the national park, **Khun Nam Nang Non (Sleeping Lady Lagoon)** is a popular picnic spot with locals. Its undulating rock formations are said to resemble a reclining woman. A *tire* (20฿) can be rented to float on the lagoon. (Open daily 8:30am-4:30pm.) Take a green *songthaew* (10฿) to the turn-off to Khun Nam Nang Non on the west side of Hwy. 110 (approx. 7-8km). Motorcycle taxis often wait here to take visitors the remaining distance. Walking the 3 or 4km is possible. After the three-headed dragon continue straight ahead for Khun Nam Nang Non or take the first right and then next left (about 1km) on paved roads to Tham Luang.

Two more caves are inside **Wat Tham Pla,** 12km south and 3km west of Mae Sai along Hwy. 110. *Samlor* along the highway will take you for 20฿. Fresh water surges through **Tham Plaa (Fish Cave),** also called "Monkey Cave" because of gamboling primates. They're everywhere, so hold on to small children and your belongings. Wear boots and long pants, and feed them at your own risk. The more adventurous can explore **Tham Gu Gaeo,** rumored to ultimately lead to Myanmar. The path to the right of the temple leads to attendants who take visitors to a Buddha village 2km away (50-70฿ per person). Bring a flashlight. You can buy incense and candles and dedicate them to the Buddha for protection from the cave spirits.

 BORDER CROSSING: MAE SAI/THACHILEK 30-day and 60-day visas can be renewed by crossing into Thachilek and returning to Mae Sai on the same day. At the immigration office, 2km south of the bridge, obtain a departure stamp, and make sure you are given an arrival card for your return. Then proceed across the bridge and hand over 250฿ and your passport. The Myanmar border control will stamp your passport and hold onto it until you exit the country. When you re-enter Thailand, you'll be able to stay another 30 or 60 days, depending on your visa. If you do not want a new visa, proceed directly to Thai border control at the Friendship Bridge with two photocopies of your passport (5฿ at stores by bridge). Surrender your passport and your photocopies to the Thai authorities who will stamp the photocopies, which you'll then give along with 250฿ to the Myanmar border control. All stamps are on the copies; when you return to Thailand, you get your unmarked passport back. Myanmar authorities will keep one copy, Thai authorities the other. Either way, when you surrender your passport/photocopies to the Burmese, they will give you a very thin piece of paper—that piece of paper is your passport. Hold on to it if you ever want to see home again. The border is open daily 6:30am-6:30pm. Myanmar is 30min. behind, so its border is open daily 6am-6pm. Thai immigration officials ask that you cross back by 5pm. (See **Myanmar, To Go or Not To Go?**, p. 312.)

The **Royal Villa** at **Doi Tung** lies 32km from Mae Sai, and was the home of the Princess Mother (king's mother) from 1988 until 1994, when she passed away at the age of 94. The palace, constructed of recycled pinewood crates at the request of the Princess Mother, has an exquisite carving of the zodiac in the grand reception hall. The warmth of the beloved king's mother can be seen in the pictures of her gardening in Switzerland, which adorn the walls—her chamber is preserved much as it was. Visitors to the royal palace are asked to dress conservatively. If standards are not appropriate—singlet, shorts, or miniskirt—a denim number, best left in the 80s, is provided. **Mah Fah Luang Gardens** flow down the hill from the Royal Villa. The peaceful setting has a portion in bloom year-round. (Royal Villa: open daily 7am-5pm. 70฿. Mah Fah Luang: open daily 7am-6pm. 50฿. Both 100฿.) To reach Doi Tung, take a green *songthaew* to **Mae Chan** (15฿). At the turn-off from Hwy. 110, purple *songthaew* take visitors for the other half of the trip. There is a stunning backroute to Doi Tung from Mae Sai, which weaves its way along the border. The road, however, is **extremely dangerous.** If you accidentally stray into Myanmar, consider yourself lucky if you only end up with a gun pointed at your head. King Kobra Guest House can provide current information about travel in the area. The route along the highway to Doi Tung is heavily touristed and safe to travel.

CHIANG SAEN ☎ 053

King Saen Phu founded this small town in 1328 as the capital of the Chiang Saen Kingdom. In 1803, Rama I destroyed the city to keep it from the Burmese and the district did not recover until the 1880s, when Rama V kicked out the remaining Burmese and repopulated the city with Thais. Remnants of Chiang Saen's former Lanna glory now border the modern concrete creations. As the gateway to the Golden Triangle, *farang* flock here by the busload, but have yet to disrupt the sedate feel. With no attractive budget accommodations, daytripping to this small town may be the most cost-efficient.

☐ TRANSPORTATION. From the river end of Phahonyothin Rd., **buses** go to: **Bangkok** (12½hr.; 3pm, 283฿; with A/C 4:20pm, 594฿); **Chiang Mai** (6hr., 8:20am, with A/C 150฿); **Chiang Rai** (1½hr., every 30min. 5:15am-5pm, 25฿) via **Mae Chan** (45min., 15฿). The booking office for Bangkok (☎ 650 822) is in an unmarked house set back from the street east of Siam Commercial Bank. Blue **songthaew** go to **Mae Sai** (1hr., every 40min. 7am-5pm, 15฿) via **Sop Ruak** (20min., 10฿) from across the main road. Green *songthaew* to **Chiang Khong** (2hr., 9am-3pm, 50฿) wait on Rimkhong Rd., 150m south of Phahonyothin Rd. Pricey longtailed **charter boats,** leaving from the "T" intersection, head up and down the Mekong from 8:30am to 6pm to **Chiang Khong** (2hr., 1800฿ per boat) and Sop Ruak (40min., 400฿ per boat, 500฿ round-trip, up to 6 people). *Samlor* wait at stands on the river (10-20฿ to guest houses).

■ ⁊ PRACTICAL INFORMATION. Chiang Saen's two main roads form a "T." The top of the "T," **Rimkhong Rd.,** runs north-south along the **Mekong River,** which separates Thailand from Laos to the east. The tail of the "T" is **Phahonyothin Rd.** Route 1016 from Mae Chan bypasses the southwest end of town and continues to Chiang Khong. Following Rimkhong Rd. upstream leads to **Sop Ruak.**

Chang Saen's facilities are scattered along Phahonyothin Rd., all within walking distance. A **24hr. ATM** (Cirrus/MC/PLUS/V) is at **Siam Commercial Bank,** 773 Phahonyothin Rd., which also exchanges currency. (☎ 777 041. Open M-F 8:30am-3:30pm.) The **day market** spills onto Phahonyothin Rd., 75m from the river. Food vendors on the road lead to fish and fruit inside. A **pharmacy,** on Phahonyothin Rd., is at the "T" junction with Rimkhong Rd. (☎ 651 108. Open daily 8am-8pm.) The **police** (☎ 777 111) are opposite the pharmacy. **Chiang Saen Hospital** (☎ 777 017) lies 1km from the river. Walking from the river on Phahonyothin Rd., the **immigration office** is at the first crossroad on the left. (☎ 777 118. Open M-F 8:30am-4:30pm.) At the intersection, there is **Internet access** (30฿ per hr.; open daily 9am-6pm), **motorbike** rental (180฿; open daily 8am-5pm), and **international telephone** calls from vendors with cell phones. The **post office** with CATNET Internet access is 600m from the river on Phahonyothin Rd. (☎777 116. Open M-F 8:30am-4:30pm, Sa-Su 9am-noon.) **Postal code:** 57150.

⌐☐ ACCOMMODATIONS AND FOOD. With the river to your back, walk west on Phahonyothin Rd. and turn right before the post office. Just past a bank 100m down on the right, is **J.S. Guest House ❶**, with cozy and quiet rooms with fans and common bath—Chiang Saen's best deal. Stick to rooms in the house. (☎777 060. Rooms 100฿.) **Gin Guest House ❸**, 1.5km upstream of Rimkhong Rd., is the upmarket choice. Day hikes are pricey (2400฿ for 1-4 people) and include car and driver but not food, rafting, or elephant riding. (☎650 847. Bungalows with fan, bug nets, and hot showers 200฿; big tiled room with sitting room 300฿; family room 400฿.) **Chiang Saen Guest House ❶**, 45 Rimkhong Rd., north of the "T" just before the wat, papers the walls of its restaurant with "green" editorials. The owner, an avid bird-watcher, can point out the many species in the area. (Concrete singles 80฿; doubles 120฿; twins with bath and view of Mekong 150฿; triples 200฿).

In the evenings, the **market ❶** on Phahonyothin Rd. is the best option (phat thai 20฿). Stalls congregate on **Rimkhong Rd.** 300m south of the "T." *Paw pia thawt* (spring rolls) are great. Those without tongues of steel may want to order dishes *mai champ phèt* (not spicy).

◧ SIGHTS. Chiang Saen National Museum is on Phahonyothin Rd., at the entrance to the city across from the post office. Along with a life-size model of a *plaa buek* (giant Mekong catfish), the museum has impressive 15th- to 16th-century Lanna art and a well-done exposé on hill tribe cultures and costumes. (☎777 102. Open W-Su 9am-5pm. 30฿.) Next door, a 13th-century brick *chedi* dominates **Wat Chedi Luang**, the tallest Lanna Thai monument at 58m. **Wat Pasale** is outside the ancient city wall, 800m west of the river. The ornate *chedi* isn't as impressive, but its bucolic location ("Pasale" means "of the teak forest") makes it a pleasant stop. (Open daily 8am-6pm. 30฿.) Following the road along the moat next to Wat Pasale leads to **Wat Chom Kitti**, 2km out of town. The hilltop outlook offers compelling views of Laos and the Mekong, but is outdone by **Wat Phra That Pha-Ngao**, which includes Chiang Saen in the vista 4km southeast of town on the road to Chiang Khong. **Chiang Saen Lake**, a bird-watching site with the largest variety of water fowl in Southeast Asia, is a 7km ride southwest. The turn-off is marked off the route to Chiang Rai.

▣ DAYTRIP FROM CHIANG SAEN: SOP RUAK (GOLDEN TRIANGLE). Sop Ruak may be its official name, but most refer to the confluence of the Sai River and the wider Mekong where Myanmar, Laos, and Thailand meet as **Sam Liam Tongkham (Golden Triangle).**

Songthaew bound for **Mae Sai** (45min., 25฿) and **Chiang Saen** (20min., 15฿) pass through the center of town between 7am and 2pm. Longtail **charter boats** seat up to 6 people and leave from various spots along the river to **Chiang Khong** (2hr., 1500฿) and **Chiang Saen** (50min., 400฿). Golden Triangle boat rides tour the area (300฿ for 30min., 400฿ for 1hr.; boats accommodate 1-6 people). The few guest houses that existed have been bulldozed in anticipation of the boom expected to hit the region, now named the **Golden Quadrangle** after the addition of China, resulting in a lack of budget hotels.

In the middle of town, the **House of Opium** features exhibits on the history and cultivation of opium with pipe displays, information on drug warlords, and a diorama of a drugged-out old man. Dioramas on the **Padong** (longneck villagers) and *plaa buek* (giant catfish) are thrown in for good measure. (☎784 062. Open daily 7am-7pm. 20฿.) Next door, **Siam Commercial Bank** runs a **currency exchange** booth which accepts all traveler's checks and has MC/V cash advances. (☎784 191. Open daily 9am-5pm.) For a view capturing the three countries, head up the five-dragon-headed staircase next to the bank, then follow the road behind **Wat Phra That Doi Pu** up the hill to the viewpoint.

CHIANG KHONG ☎053

Chiang Khong is the archetypal border town. There are no museums, parks, or interesting shops, but several banks line the interminable main street and wait for tourists transitioning between countries and currencies. The premier attractions of Chiang Khong are rest and relaxation. Many guest houses overlook the majestic Mekong and afford alluring views of greener Laos. The engaging surroundings may distract delayed travelers during the wait.

⌐ TRANSPORTATION

Most **buses** leave from the market, 100m southeast of the bridge near the Esso gas station. Buses go to **Chiang Mai** (6hr.; 6am, 121฿; with A/C 8am, 218฿ and 11am, 169฿). The **booking office** for bus tickets to Chiang Mai (☎655 732) is between the bridge and service station. Guest houses also run a **minibus** to Chiang Mai (5hr.; 10:30am, 6pm; 220฿). Buses to **Chiang Rai** leave from the market (3hr., 5am-5pm, 50฿). **Songthaew** to and from **Chiang Saen** (2½hr., 7am-noon, 50฿) gather near Soi 3. A few companies run private buses to **Bangkok.** Ticket offices are scattered along the main road: opposite and toward the pier from Traveler Corner is **Karuhart** (3pm, 490฿); **99** sits at the station 20m before Bamboo Riverside Guest House (7am, 491฿; 4pm, 382฿ and VIP 760฿); **Sombat Tours** is opposite buses to Chiang Mai (☎791 644; 4pm, 491฿). The nicest buses are run by **Siam-first** (4pm; 491฿, VIP 573฿), in the green building opposite Thai Farmers Bank. Check with offices about where buses will depart. Tickets go quickly; buy a seat in the morning to guarantee an afternoon bus. **@Net.com,** in front of Bamboo Riverside Guest house, has **motorbikes** for rent (200฿ per day).

◼◼ ORIENTATION AND PRACTICAL INFORMATION

Chiang Khong is 144km northeast of Chiang Rai and 55km southeast of Chiang Saen. The main drag, **Saiklang Rd.,** runs northwest to southeast, parallel to the Mekong River. Numbered soi run perpendicular to the main road—odd-numbered soi head to the river. **Soi 13** is at the southeast end near the immigration office, bridge, and day market. **Soi 1,** home to the guest houses, is a 25min. walk from the market at the northwestern end of town. Continuing northwest past Soi 1 leads to the **new pier,** then to the turn-off to **Chiang Saen** (Route 1129), and then to the **old pier,** an important landmark for travelers.

Tours: Traveler Corner, 17/3 Ban Wat Kaew T. Wiang (☎655 374), opposite Ann Travel near Soi 2. Run by friendly "Apple." Info, bookings, collect calls (30฿). A good place to meet fellow backpackers. Open daily 8am-9pm.

Immigration Office: ☎791 332. Next to Soi 13. Issues visa extensions for 500฿. Open M-F 8:30am-noon and 1-4:30pm. You'll need to go to a tour agency for Laos visas (see **Border Crossing: Chiang Khong/Houie Xay,** p. 289).

Currency Exchange: Thai Farmers Bank, 20m south of Soi 7. Cirrus/MC/PLUS/V **ATM.** Open M-F 8:30am-3:30pm.

Markets: Every Friday morning the **regional market** spills out onto the main road from the day market up to the immigration office. Pots, pans, and clothing is about as interesting as it gets. Sa evening is the **night market,** where anybody is welcome to deal their wares on the main road around Soi 2.

Emergency: ☎191. **Tourist Police (Bangkok):** ☎1155.

Police: ☎791 426. Next door to the immigration office.

Pharmacy: Boonchai Pharmacy (☎791 013), opposite Soi 7. Open daily 7am-8pm.

Medical Services: Chiang Khong Hospital, 354 Moo 10 (☎791 206), 3km outside of town. Go straight south on Hwy. 1020 toward Chiang Rai. Some English spoken. No credit cards. **Open 24hr.**

Internet: @Net.com (see **Transportation,** above) provides **Internet** access. 40฿ per hr. It's possible to find Internet for 30฿ per hr. at some cafes.

Post Office: ☎791 555. Near Soi 3. **International phone** in the compound and Lenso phone outside. CATNET Internet access. Open M-F 8:30am-4:30pm, Sa-Su 9am-noon. **Postal code:** 57140.

ACCOMMODATIONS

The population of *farang* in Chiang Khong rises and falls sharply with each busload. By 5pm in the high season, the town's best accommodations are at saturation point, so try to call ahead to reserve your preferred digs.

Bamboo Riverside Guest House, 71 Huaviang Rd. (☎791 621), 75m northwest of Soi 1. This fairly new guest house is the best place in town. It's in a peaceful spot along the Mekong River—nothing breaks its serenity except the hordes of *farang* that converge upon it. The guest house also offers a great **restaurant** (see **Food,** below) with Mexican food, fresh baked bread, and a guitar-playing proprietor. Laundry. Dorms 70฿; singles 100฿; bungalows 150฿; doubles with bath 200-250฿. ❶

Ban Tammila (☎/fax 791 234), by Soi 2. Has bungalows with private showers and sells some of the funkiest hammock/tent devices you've ever seen for 1200฿. Restaurant (see **Food,** below). Laundry. Bicycle rental 150฿. Bungalows 200-400฿. ❸

River Guest House (☎791 348). It's the closest place to the bus station; walk toward Chiang Rai from the bridge and turn left at the Esso, then left again onto Soi 15. Once at the river turn right and River Guest House is 50m ahead on the left. For those already—or perhaps still—seeking the isolation of Laos, this is an overlooked gem. Gorgeous bungalows all with private balconies overlooking banana plantation and the Mekong. Bungalows 150฿, with bath 200฿. ❷

Hua Wiang Country Guest House (☎791 134), 150m past Bamboo Riverside Guest House toward the pier. Cheaper, less romantic rooms. Free transport to boat or bus. Laundry. Dorms with 3-5 beds 50฿; singles 60฿; doubles 80฿, with bath 150฿. ❶

FOOD

Noodle-and-rice shops line Saiklang Rd. A morning treat from the **day market ❶,** south of the bridge, is *kanon ton kanon niew* (rice flour balls with coconut filling; 5฿).

Bamboo Riverside Guest House's restaurant (see **Accommodations,** above). Delicious food. Phat thai 30฿; cheese quesadilla 65฿. Open daily 7:30am-noon and 6-9pm. ❷

Ban Tammila's restaurant (see **Accommodations,** above) is a good place for midday fare with an amazing view. Vegetarian menu. Small prices for large portions. Most entrees 25-40฿. Open daily 7am-4pm. ❷

Rimkhong, by the river between Soi 7 and 9. The freedom from *farang* comes at a price. Partially translated menu. Green curry 50฿; warmed spicy sausage salad 50฿. Open daily 7am-11pm. ❷

Teepee, by Soi 2 on Sarklang Rd. Plays Bob Marley by day, holds jam sessions by night, and serves fabulous tofu dishes. Fried tofu with cashews 60฿. Open daily lunchtime until late. ❷

 SIGHTS

KMT Cemetery is 1km out of town on Hwy. 1129 at the top of the big hill on the left. The entrance is on a dirt road not visible from the highway. Although the gate is often locked, the caretaker lets visitors explore during daylight; the barking dogs will alert the caretaker of your presence. Ask at guest houses about bike rides to **Hmong villages,** though they may prove inaccessible in the rainy season (3hr., 3:30pm, 100฿ includes bike and guide). In April and May, **Ban Haadkhrai** hosts the annual giant catfish competition. Lao and Thai boats alternate turns trawling the river in search of the 2.5m, 200kg beasts. Only a few are caught every year. The fishermen must ask permission of the spirits before catching the fish, which have unwittingly moved north from Cambodia to spawn. To get here, head south out of town and take a left at the Esso service station with the police box in front, then walk 1km to Soi 31 and continue to the river. **Wat Haadkhrai** overlooks the pier where the fish are brought ashore. **See Don Chai** is a Lu handweaving village, 14km south of the city. Showrooms are scarce and hours fickle, but poke your head into any house and ask if you can watch for a while. Take a motorcycle or a blue *songthaew* (10฿) south out of town. Alternatively, take a Chiang Mai/Chiang Rai-bound bus and tell the driver where you want to get off.

 BORDER CROSSING: CHIANG KHONG/HOUIE XAY The ferry (20฿) across the Mekong leaves from the old pier and takes less than 15min.; all you need is a visa, available at most guest houses. Alternatively, try Traveler Corner (☎655 374; open daily 8am-9pm) or Ann Tour (☎655 198; open daily 7am-8pm), which both have offices on Saiklang Rd. near Soi 2. Unfortunately, 1-day visas are no longer available. 15-day visas are 1200฿ with a 2-day wait and 900฿ with a 4-day wait. 30-day visas are 1800฿ with a 2-day wait and 1500฿ with a 4-day wait. Going through a guest house instead of a travel agency may raise the price 100฿. To avoid up to 4 days of processing delays, obtain a visa in Bangkok before heading north. Once in Houie Xay, catch a speedboat (6-9hr., 8am-2pm, 1100฿) or a slow boat (2 days, 10:30am, 550฿) to Luang Prabang. If you do the latter, pack food, water, and a good book; the boat will stop intermittently for cargo and stretching before overnighting in Pakbeng. As Lao currency fluctuates constantly, check current exchange rates next to immigration as you enter Laos. Special boats may be organized out of Chiang Khong that make stops along the Mekong for those who want to see more—ask at Traveler Corner for information. It is usually cheaper to cross the river and then buy your tickets—a difference of up to 450฿.

Nan

■ ACCOMMODATIONS

Amazing Guest House, **3**
Doi Phukha Guest House, **5**
Nan Guest House, **7**
PK Guest House, **4**

🍴 FOOD

Rimkaew Restaurant, **1**
Ristorante Da Dario, **2**
Tanaya Kitchen, **6**

NAN

☎ **054**

Hidden amidst the mountains on the outskirts of the Lanna Kingdom, Nan developed a unique culture and history, remaining a semi-autonomous principality until 1931. The distinctive and beautiful architecture of the wats, unlike that of any other region, reflects this. During the 1960s and 1970s, the region's isolation made it a haven for smugglers and the communist rebels of the People's Liberation Army of Thailand (PLAT). Today, Nan's seclusion provokes nothing more threatening than frequent shouts of "I love you" from children unfamiliar with *farang*. Travelers who've been to Nan's mountainous back country, "The Beach of the North," is unlikely to tell you their favorite spot. They'd prefer to keep it to themselves while the mass of tourists falls over one another's heels on the Mae Hong Son loop. Doi Phukha National Park beckons explorers, while the superb museum and mural-bedecked wats provide relaxation, and the isolation itself still lends romance to this renegade town.

▐▊ TRANSPORTATION

Flights: Nan Airport (☎ 771 308), on Worawichai Rd., 4km from town center. **Thai Airways,** 34 Mahaphrom Rd. (☎ 710 377). Open M-F 8am-noon and 1-5pm. Flies to

Bangkok (F 4:30pm, 2195฿) via **Phrae** (865฿). **Air Andaman** at the airport (☎711 222; open 10am-2pm) or booked through Thai Airways flies to **Bangkok** (daily 12:50pm, 2240฿) and **Chiang Mai** (M, W, F, Su 12:30pm; 1025฿).

Buses: The **regional bus station** is on Anonta Worarittidit Rd. To: **Chiang Rai** (blue bus; 5hr., 9am, 90฿); **Phayo** (4hr., 1:30pm, 99฿); **Phitsanulok** (5hr.; 7:45, 9:45, 11:45am, 1:45pm; 146฿) via **Uttaradit** (101฿); **Phrae** (2hr., every 45min. 5am-5pm, 47฿); **Pua** (orange bus; 1½hr., every hr. 6am-6pm, 25฿). Across the street is a booking office (☎710 737) for **Chiang Mai** (6-7hr.; 9 per day 7am-10:30pm; 117฿, 2nd-class A/C 164฿, 1st-class A/C 211฿) via **Lampang** (4hr.; 86฿, 2nd-class A/C 120฿, 1st-class A/C 154฿). Buses to **Bangkok** (☎710 027) depart from a station on Khao Luang Rd., 2 blocks north of Anonta Worarittidit Rd. (10-13hr.; 8 per day 8-9am and 6-7pm; 236฿, 2nd-class A/C 301฿, 1st-class A/C 387฿, VIP 600฿). **Sombat Tours** runs buses at 6:30 and 7:30pm. Book Bangkok buses in the morning to ensure an evening seat on the fastest route.

Rentals: Oversea, 490 Sumon Thewarat Rd. (☎710 258), at Mahawong Rd. **Mountain bikes** 30-50฿ per day; **motorcycles** 150-180฿ per day. Open daily 8am-5:30pm.

◢ ⑦ ORIENTATION AND PRACTICAL INFORMATION

The **Nan River** acts as the town's eastern border. Five blocks west of the river, buses from the north arrive at the station on **Anonta Worarittidit Rd.;** this road runs roughly east-west through the center of town, perpendicular to the Nan River. A block south of Anonta Worarittidit Rd., **Mahawong Rd.** passes the **post office** and goes over the town's bridge; two blocks south, **Suriyaphong Rd.** passes the **police station, City Hall,** and many sights. Intersecting all three of these, **Sumon Thewarat Rd.,** which runs north-south through the town center, is the primary thoroughfare. A useful point of reference, the **Dhevaraj Hotel** rests on this road halfway between its intersections with Anonta Worarittidit and Mahawong Rd. Followed to its far northern end, Sumon Thewarat Rd. leads to **Worawichai Rd.** Parallel to and one block east of Sumon Thewarat Rd. is **Khao Luang Rd.** One block west of Sumon Thewarat lies **Mahayod Rd.,** which runs out the northern end of town via the turn-off to Pua; another block west are **Pha Kong Rd.** and its small nightly food stalls.

Tourist Information: TAT (☎751 029), in the Municipal Office, on Pha Kong Rd. at Suriyaphong Rd. Minimal English spoken. Glossy pictures, free maps, and occasional English pamphlets. Open daily 8:30am-5:30pm.

Currency Exchange: Thai Farmers Bank, 434 Sumon Thewarat Rd. (☎710 162), has a **24hr. ATM** (Cirrus/MC/PLUS/V). Open M-F 8:30am-3:30pm.

Emergency: ☎191. **Tourist Police (Bangkok):** ☎1155.

Police: 52 Suriyaphong Rd. (☎751 681 or 751 033), opposite City Hall.

Pharmacy: 347/5 Sumon Thewarat Rd. (☎710 452), opposite Thai Farmers Bank. Open daily 8am-7pm. Another pharmacy at **Nan Provincial Hospital** (see below).

Medical Services: Nan Provincial Hospital (☎710 138), on Worawichai Rd. at the bend in Sumon Thewarat Rd. 3km north of downtown. Some English. *Songthaew* leave from the Nara department store, 1 block north of Dhevaraj Hotel (5฿). **24hr. emergency care** and pharmacy.

Telephone: Telecommunications Office (☎773 214), Mahayod Rd., 2km outside town 200m past turn-off to Pua. Has international phones, CATNET Internet access, and fax. Open M-F 8am-6pm, Sa-Su 9am-4:30pm.

Internet Access: Easy Internet, 345/8 Sumon Thewarat Rd., opposite and north of Thai Farmers Bank. 20฿ per hr. Open daily 9am-10pm, but these hours are not dependable.

Post Office: GPO, 70 Mahawong Rd. (☎710 176), west of Sumon Thewarat Rd. *Poste Restante.* Open M-F 8:30am-4:30pm, Sa-Su 9am-noon. **Postal Code:** 55000

■ ACCOMMODATIONS

PK Guest House, 33/12 Premphachraj Rd. (☎751 416). Walk north 1.5km on Sumon Thewarat Rd. and make a left after the school; it's down the 2nd soi on the right. New rooms set around a pond and coffee-plantation seedlings. Bicycle and motorbike rental (30฿/150฿). Laundry. Shared bath and Western toilet. Wacky singles in oxcarts 100฿; doubles 150฿; triples 200฿; VIP 250฿. ❶

Nan Guest House, 57/16 Mahaphrom Rd. (☎771 849), a 10min. walk from the bus station. Turn left onto Anonta Worarittidit Rd., then take the 1st right. Follow the signs 2 blocks to the back-street location. Centrally located. Great coffee. Laundry 5-10฿ per piece. Wooden-floored back house 120฿; tiled rooms in main house 130฿. ❷

Amazing Guest House, 25/7 Soi Snow White (☎710 893), 150m past the PK Guest House on the left. Spacious rooms and an intimate environment in the family's teak house. Laundry 40฿ per kg. Massage 150฿ per hr. Singles 100-120฿; doubles 160-200฿; triples 210฿; new private, solid bungalows out back, with bath 200-250฿. Prices drop with longer stays (1 week 10% discount, 1 month 25% discount). ❶

Doi Phukha Guest House (☎751 517), on a marked soi off Sumon Thewarat Rd., 700m north of Anonta Worarittidit Rd., 200m past the first school on the left. Newly reopened after renovations. Large rooms with fan, netted windows, and shared bath. Singles 70฿; doubles 120฿. ❶

■ FOOD

Dining in Nan is an adventure. The region is known for its dog farms (and they're not breeding pets) as well as the famed **Nan River dining** ❶: in an effort to keep cool during Nan's dry and exceptionally hot season (temperatures exceed 40°C), the crazies in Nan sit up to their waists in the Nan River chowing down on tucker from the local food stands at firmly fixed tables. To get to the river dining, turn onto Nokham Rd. from Sumon Thewarat at the wat, one block north of Anonta Worarittidit Rd. The regional specialty, crispy fried dog, will not be obvious to visitors—if you really want to try it, ask in town or head to the outskirts where canines can be bought from farms for 150฿.

Tanaya Kitchen, 75/23-24 Anonta Worarittidit Rd., one block beyond Pha Kong Rd. from the bus station on the right. The friendly owner offers maps, an English menu with separate vegetarian options, delicious red curry for 50฿, and great potato bread for 10฿. Open daily 7am-8:30pm. ❷

Rimkaew Restaurant, on Sumon Thewarat Rd. at the bend 3km from town just before the hospital. Perfectly located at the hot spot for fishing on the Nan River. It serves mostly Thai dishes from a simple English menu for 30-60฿. Open daily 10am-4pm and 7-10pm. ❷

Ristorante Da Dario (☎710 636), next to Amazing Guest House, is a little piece of Italy. Spaghetti pesto Genovese 100฿. Open M-F 10am-2pm and 5-10pm, Sa-Su 5-10pm. Closed Aug. ❸

■ SIGHTS

The **Nan National Museum,** at the Suriyaphong and Pha Kong Rd. intersection, features informative exhibits on Nan's history and Thailand's hill tribes. A revered black elephant tusk is on display. (☎710 561. Open daily 9am-4pm. 30฿.) Nan's ornate, detailed wats are among the most beautiful in northern Thailand. Across the street from the National Museum is **Wat Phra That Chang Kham**, which houses a walking Buddha made of gold. The 400-year-old **Wat Phumin**, on Pha Kong Rd. south of the museum, contains murals depicting the culture of the Lanna people. The distinctive golden *chedi* of **Wat Phra That Chae Haeng** shines 2km beyond the Nan River bridge. Constructed nearly 700 years ago, the wat is the oldest in the region. The zoo to the left of the temple has a **statue** of Sa Jao Wang Tao Kha Kha-ong, the first king of Nan. Southwest of town, **Wat Phra That Khao Noi** offers sweeping views of the valley. The attraction at **Wat Phaya Wat** is the slightly lopsided old pagoda that parallels the bending coconut palm. Go west on Suriyaphong Rd. to Hwy. 101 and turn right after the bridge. Wat Phaya Wat, is on the plain while Wat Phra That Khao Noi is 2km up the road on top of a hill.

Back in town, the **Thai Payap Project** sells hill-tribe **handicrafts** from 15 villages in its showroom on Jettabut Rd. Follow the road directly opposite the Dhevaraj Hotel past the market; it's 400m down on the right. The project also arranges **homestays,** during which travelers may live and work with a family in one of two villages. All proceeds go to community development projects in the area. (☎772 520. Open daily 8:30am-5pm.) The best place to purchase **silver** is direct from the hill tribes (see **Doi Phukha National Park,** below), but, if you can't make the trip, **Chompu Phuka** has a showroom a few kilometers out of town with hill-tribe silverware and fabrics. Follow Suriyaphong Rd. west out of town toward Phayao; the showroom is on the right opposite PT Gas Station. (Open daily 9am-5:30pm.)

▗ MARKETS

A spacious **produce market** sets up on Jettabut Rd. directly opposite the Dhevaraj Hotel. Several counters serve over 20 dishes which you can point at and buy by the bag (10-15฿). Along Anonta Worarittidit Rd. next to the northern bus station is the **day market,** which is big on pineapples and really, really small turtles. The tiny **night market,** on Anonta Worarittidit Rd. outside the 7/11, starts around 6pm. Cheap noodle and rice standards are 20฿. Food gets sketchier around the corner on Pha Kong Rd., but don't miss the fabulous fruit stand at the end of the stalls.

▞ DAYTRIPS FROM NAN

Few travelers get a glimpse of Nan's rugged back country. Nan is now almost entirely safe—some mines remain buried in the most remote areas, but the risks are negligible, especially on roads or trails. Getting lost is actually a greater danger, as English signs are sparse. Try to bring the names of your destination in writing. **Fhu Travel Service**, 453/4 Sumon Thewarat Rd., south of the intersection with Mahawong Rd., leads expeditions around the province. A **trek** with Mr. Fhu is the only way to visit the **Mrabi** (Phi Tong Lueng, "Spirit of the Yellow Leaves"), a tribe found only in the provinces of Nan and Phrae. Year-round **rubber rafting** on the Nan River through **Mae Charim National Park** southeast of Nan is also possible. (☎710 636. Price per person falls as group size increases. 1-day trek to Mrabi territory 1250฿ for 2 persons, 700฿ for 5 or more. 3-day trek 2700฿/1500฿. 1-day rafting 2300฿/1200฿.)

DOI PHUKHA NATIONAL PARK AND ENVIRONS

Take Hwy. 1080 from Nan (past an Esso station on the left) for 60km to Pua. Here, turn right just before the market (you'll have to loop back), then left 100m up the road at the

English sign for the park (Hwy. 1256). The road stretches 47km over a mountain peak and through the park to Ban Bor Kleua. Songthaew, which leave from near Pua's market for Ban Bor Kleua, can drop you at the park office (first songthaew departs between 8 and 10am, others leave infrequently throughout the day, 30฿). Orange buses speed to Pua from the bus station in Nan (1½hr., every hr. 5am-6pm, 20฿). The road to Doi Phukha is steep and windy; check brakes before departing. (Songthaew riders: try to remain oblivious.) Once you're at the park, there's not much to do without private transportation. It's possible to loop your way back from Ban Bor Kleua to Nan taking back routes; pick up the regional map from the TAT.

Dozens of waterfalls and caves dot Doi Phukha National Park, home to Hmong and Mien tribes. (Open daily 6am-6pm. 200฿.) The **park office** (☎ 701 000), 25km up the road from Pua, can sometimes provide **accommodations ❶**; call the National Park Division of the Forestry Service (☎ 02 579 0529), in Bangkok, first to check. (Tent rental 250฿. Camping 30฿; bungalows for two 200฿, for six 1200฿.) A convenient alternative is ▧**Bamboo Huts ❶**, nestled on the ridge of the mountain looking out to Laos. It features basic huts with shared facilities. The turn-off to Bamboo Huts is 1km before the park headquarters; it's a challenging 4km walk to the huts, passing the Thai Lue village that owner William grew up in. The mountain views along this walk are spectacular. Unfortunately, the huts themselves are situated on the mountain such that the views are merely "impressive." The relaxed ambience, good food, and crisp mountain air more than compensate. (Great value treks 1-day 500฿, 2-day 1000฿, 3-day 1500฿. Huts 100฿. 3 meals per day 130฿.)

The most easily accessed point from which to see the prized **Chomphu Phukha tree** *(Bretschneidera sinensis)* is 5km past the park office. Though not the world's only specimen (as locals tend to claim), it is still extremely rare. The slender tree blooms in February, and hordes of Thais come to see its foot-long clusters of red-veined, hibiscus-shaped flowers. Turn left off the highway and north from Ban Bor Kleua; a road leads to **Ban Sapan**, 10km away. After crossing the bridge just before the village, turn right onto a dirt road to reach the **Sapan Waterfall,** off the road to the right, marked by a red Thai sign and a smaller English one. The dry-season flow will probably leave you unimpressed, but it's worthwhile in the wet season.

If you have your own transport, two attractions close to Pua can easily be included in a day visit to the area. **Silaphet Waterfall,** 9km from Pua, is more accurately described as a river cascade. Enjoy a picnic lunch watching tubing Thais bob through the white water. The hill-tribe village of **Phaklang** produces beautiful and inexpensive silverware. Several of the artisans work on site at the display rooms. To get to both places, take the same right before the market in Pua that you would take to get to Doi Phukha National Park. Instead of turning left, however, simply follow the road out of town. The turn-off to Silaphet Waterfall is marked in English from the road; the one to Phaklang is marked only in Thai, but it is on the right, 4km from Pua just before Doi Phukha Resort. It's 3km farther to the showrooms scattered next to a small lake.

LAMPANG ☎ 054

Lampang's history dates back to the 7th-century Dvaravati period, when it played an integral role in the Lanna Kingdom of the "Million Rice Fields." Like other northern cities, it clings to its heritage; unlike other northern cities, it has little to which to cling. Still, while the city may not impress, at least one of its adopted surrounding sights will. Domestic and foreign tourists alike pass up Lampang's overpriced flower-decked horsecarts and concrete-banked Wang River on their way north, but it's their loss, perhaps.

Lampang

⌂ **ACCOMMODATIONS**
9 Mituna, **6**
Riverside Guest House, **3**
Sri Sangar Hotel, **7**
TT & T Guest House, **5**

🍴 **FOOD**
Chom Wang Restaurant, **4**
Riverside Restaurant, **2**
Terrace Riverview
    Restaurant, **1**

▣ TRANSPORTATION

Flights: The **airport** is on Sanambin Rd. 2km from town. **Thai Airways,** 236 Sanambin Rd. (☎ 217 078). Open daily 8:30am-5:30pm. To **Bangkok** (M, Sa 11:15am; 2055฿). **PB Air** at the airport (☎ 226 238; open daily 8am-6pm) flies to Bangkok (Su-F 9:55am, 5:10pm; 2055฿). Departure and insurance tax 105฿.

Trains: Lampang Railroad Station (☎ 318 648 or 217 024), on Prasanmitri Rd. To reach the station, flag down a westbound *songthaew* (10-20฿). Trains to: **Bangkok** (10-12hr.; 6 per day; 3rd-class 146฿, 2nd-class 284฿) via **Phitsanulok** (5hr.; 3rd-class 88฿, 2nd-class 151฿) and **Ayutthaya** (9hr.; 3rd-class 135฿, 2nd-class 261฿); **Chiang Mai** (2hr.; 9 per day; 3rd-class 23฿, 2nd-class 53฿).

Buses: The **bus station** (☎ 227 410) is off Asia 1 Hwy., several kilometers out of town. All prices listed are with A/C. To: **Bangkok** (8hr.; 7:30am-9pm; 193฿, 2nd-class A/C 270฿, 1st-class A/C 347฿, VIP 540฿); **Chiang Mai** (2hr.; every 30min. 2am-9pm; 39฿, 2nd-class A/C 55฿, 1st-class A/C 70฿); **Chiang Rai** (5hr.; every 45min. 5am-5pm; 81฿, 2nd-class A/C 113฿); **Khorat** (10hr.; 9:30, 11:30am, 8pm; 212฿, 2nd-class A/C 297฿, 1st-class A/C 382฿); **Nan** (4hr.; 11 per day 8am-midnight; 86฿, 2nd-class A/C 120฿, 1st-class A/C 154฿); **Sukhothai** (4-5hr.; every hr. 6:30am-4:30pm; 91฿, 2nd-class A/C 127฿, 1st-class A/C 164฿) via **Phitsanulok** (4hr.; 91฿, 2nd-class A/C 153฿, 1st-class A/C 196฿); **Udon Thani** (2, 8, 9-9:45pm; 219฿, 2nd-class A/C 307฿, 1st-class A/C 355฿) via **Loei** (8½hr.; 145฿, 2nd-class A/C 216฿, 1st-class A/C 277฿).

Local Transportation: Blue **songthaew** go anywhere in town (10฿)—flag one down on any major street. Trips to and from the bus and train stations cost 5-10฿ more (for no good reason except that you're a captive customer). **Samlor** usually cost around 50฿. Tours can be arranged from the horse cart stand opposite the police station on Boonyawat Rd.—a unique but expensive way to see the town (15min. 150฿; 30min. 200฿).

✈ 🛈 ORIENTATION AND PRACTICAL INFORMATION

Most roads radiate from the **clock-tower rotary** near the town center. **Boonyawat Rd.** heads east, passing hotels, banks, and shops. In the opposite direction, **Tah Krao Rd.** runs past the **Aswin Market. Suren Rd.**, off Tah Krao Rd., runs to the **train station. Thipchang Rd.**, a commercial avenue parallel to Boonyawat Rd. and the Wang River, lies one block north of the clock tower. The **bus station**, off **Asia 1 Hwy.**, is on **Jantsurin Rd.** 2km from the traffic circle. *Songthaew* from the bus station cut across **Phaholyothin Rd.**, a major commuter road four blocks south of the Wang River, to **Chatchai Rd.**, which terminates at the clock tower.

Tourist Office: ☎218 823. On Boonyawat Rd., just past Praisanee Rd. Go in the gate where the horse carriages line up. Set back 50m from the road. Not to be confused with either of the "tourist info" places by the clock tower. Free tourist brochure which is just as easily obtained from guest houses or the bus station. Open daily 8:30am-4:30pm.

Currency Exchange: Banks line Boonyawat Rd. **Bangkok Bank,** 36-44 Thipchang Rd. (☎228 135). **24hr. ATM** (AmEx/Cirrus/MC/PLUS/V). Open M-F 8:30am-3:30pm.

Markets: Large and lively. **Tesaban Market 1** sets up near City Hall along Rajawong Rd. 1 block toward the clock tower from Praisanee Rd. Dresses, fruit, and underwear in abundance. Watch out for passing motorcycles as you browse. **Aswin Market** is off the traffic circle on Tah Krao Noi Rd. Both are open daily 6am-7pm. **Night food stalls** move in at 7pm and supply cheap food until midnight.

Emergency: ☎191. **Tourist Police (Bangkok):** ☎1155.

Police: ☎221 589. On Boonyawat Rd. opposite City Hall.

Pharmacy: ☎223 869. On the corner of Boonyawat and Praisanee Rd. Open daily 8am-10pm.

Medical Services: Khelang Nakorn-Ram Hospital, 79/12 Phaholyothin Rd. (☎352 432). **Open 24hr.** AmEx/MC/V.

Telephones: Lampang Telecommunication Center, 99 Phaholyothin Rd. (☎221 700), 500m before the hospital heading to the bus station. Overseas calls, CATNET Internet access, and fax. Open daily 7am-8pm. You might also try your luck at the GPO.

Internet Access: CATNET Internet access at the GPO or Lampang Telecommunications Center is the best bet (11฿ per hr.). At night, computer gamers crowd out would be 'net surfers at Lampang Telecommunications.

Post Office: GPO (☎323 497), on Thipchang Rd. Follow Boonyawat Rd. to City Hall and then turn left on Praisanee Rd. *Poste Restante.* **Lenso** telephone. Open M-F 8:30am-4:30pm, Sa-Su 9am-noon. **Postal code:** 52000.

🏠 ACCOMMODATIONS

Riverside Guest House, 286 Talad Gao Rd. (☎227 005). From the clock tower, walk along Boonyawat Rd. with the river on your left, then turn left onto the soi with the sign to the guest house. It's 2 blocks down, where the soi curves. Relaxing veranda over the river. Laundry. Motorbike rental (200฿ per day). Tours of surrounding sights (350฿ each, but 800฿ minimum). Doubles 250฿, riverside 350฿; twins 300฿; suites 600฿. ❸

TT&T Guest House, 55 Pahmai Rd. (☎225 361). A 30min. walk from the clock tower; go east on Boonyawat Rd. until it meets the Khelang bridge on the left. Cross the bridge and take an immediate left; it's 150m on the left. The backpacker's choice. Basic wooden rooms with semi-private bath and fan. Bicycles (40฿) and motorcross bikes (300฿) for rent. Internet (40฿ per hr.). Singles 120฿; doubles 160-200฿. ❷

9 Mituna (Gao Mituna), 285 Boonyawat Rd. (☎222 261), on the 1st block from the clock tower on the right. Clean rooms with hot water and fan. A/C rooms have bathtubs and Western toilets. Singles 143฿, with A/C 286฿; doubles 204฿/306฿. ❷

Sri Sangar Hotel, 215 Boonyawat Rd. (☎217 070), entrance on soi. Standard Thai hotel rooms. Singles 100฿; doubles 200฿. ❶

🍴 FOOD

The Riverside Restaurant, on Thipchang Rd. From the clock tower, walk to the river; it's 250m to the right. Serves up strongly flavored Thai dishes in a cozy benched patio. Pizza on W and Sa-Su. Open daily 10am-midnight; band starts at 7:30pm. ❷

Chom Wang Restaurant, 276 Talad Gao Rd., 50m from Riverside Guest House (no English sign). Delicious Thai favorites on an outdoor deck. Fried chicken in banana leaves 60฿. Open daily 6pm-midnight. ❷

Terrace Riverview Restaurant, 4/1 Wank Kua Rd., along the river by the Wang Koa Bridge. Offers a menu of Thai and Western food (Thai entrees 30-40฿; club sandwich 50฿) that matches the size of its massive verandah. ❷

👁 SIGHTS

Wat Phra Kaew Don Tao, in the northeastern corner of town, housed the Emerald Buddha during the reign of King Anantayot (r. 1436-68). A building to its left holds a golden Buddha. The *wiharn* is open to visitors on Buddhist holidays only. (Wat open daily 6am-6:30pm.) Mentioning **Ban Sao Nak** ("house of many pillars") conjures up a lot of pride for the people of Lampang. After all, it's not every day that the Crown Prince and Princess Consort lunch at your house, which is what happened here in 1977. The owner at that time, Khunying Valai Leelanuj, whose grandfather built the house in 1895, has since passed away, and the house is now open to the public as a museum. The engaging history of the house is as strong as its pillars, but a visit will probably be memorable only to those curious about traditional Lanna architecture. (Open daily 10am-5pm; 30฿ admission includes soft-drink).

Despite the dry name, 🌿**Lampang Medical Plants Conservation Center** (☎350 787) is the coolest place in Lampang. It's best visited by private transport. To get there, ride west on Jamatawee Rd. over the gradual big hill, hang a right on the street across from the 7/11, and turn left on the dirt road just before the bridge; it's 100m down on your left. Set in a luscious garden, this spa/research center has the remedy for whatever ails you—there are over 100 herbal products for sale, designed to do everything from promoting appetite to improving sexual potency. An catalogue in English explains properties of the products. This place is sitting on a gold mine if the "medicinal plant for AIDS immunity" works—but *Let's Go* begs you not to count on it. A practical buy is Porng Karn Yoong Tar Klai Hom (#104), an insect repellent (10-20฿). The physical body cleansing is soothingly indulgent (herbal vapor bath 80฿, herbal bath 150฿, face scrub 50฿, body scrub with herbs 200฿, massage 100฿ per hr., with herbal oil 300฿ per hr.). Fancy organic shampoo is available for earthy types in the vapor rooms and should be enjoyed after the free barefoot health walk around the gardens. (Open daily 8am-8pm.)

HER LEFT FOOT Landmine victims—a common sight in Southeast Asia due to the heavy mining of Cambodia, Laos, and Myanmar—now have the sympathy of the elephant population. In August 1999, on a coffee break from her job as a log-lugger at a Lampang timber camp, a three-ton elephant named Motola stepped on a landmine and blew off her left front foot. The mine was planted during the ongoing guerrilla war between the Karen hill tribe and the Burmese military. After an agonizing three-day trek to safety, Motola arrived at the Hang Chat Elephant Hospital, where doctors immediately pumped her full of elephant-strength painkillers. Thai and international donors contributed over US$125,000 for the three-hour operation to amputate the shredded, infected limb. Within a day she was awake and playful, hand-fed bananas and sugar cane by hospital staff. Vets later fitted Motola with a metal prosthesis.

 DAYTRIPS FROM LAMPANG

THAI ELEPHANT CONSERVATION CENTER

Take a Chiang Mai-bound bus; ask to be let off at the Center (35min., 20฿). The show-ground is 2km farther on foot. ☎ 229 042. Shows daily 10, 11am, and weekends 1:30pm. 80฿.

The Thai Elephant Conservation Center, 28km west of Lampang, is on the highway between Chiang Mai and Lampang, outside the Thung Kwian Forest. Elephants begin training here at age three and continue under one master until they are 61 years old, when they retire from their elephant obligations. The center was established to employ elephants and their mahouts in other pursuits to preserve the species given their decreasing importance in traditional labors such as logging and construction. Shows feature the animals walking in procession, skillfully manuvering teak logs, and wai-ing the crowd. It's amusing to watch these pachyderms with black-and-white vision create modern masterpieces as the mahouts pass them brushes dipped in brightly colored paint. Bundles of sugar cane or bananas are for sale (10฿), while an extra 50฿ buys a 10min. elephant ride. A 30min. ride through the forest costs 400฿. (Rides daily 8am-3:30pm.) The center has a homestay program that lets you stay and work with mahouts. The site is also home to the **Hang Chat Elephant Hospital** (see **Her Left Foot,** above), set up by the Friends of the Asian Elephant. Foundress Soraida Salawala helps treat injured and sick elephants from the region.

   Thung Kwian Market, 5km from the Thai Elephant Conservation Center, is directly off the highway heading toward Lampang. The souvenir facade hides great food options—if you can handle the sight of fried bugs, disemboweled lizards, and cow placentae.

CHAE SON (JAE SORN) NATIONAL PARK AND KEW LOM DAM

To get a songthaew to Chae Son Falls, 70km from Lampang, look for the dirt parking lot 100m down the soi running between Thipchang and Talad Gao Rd., one block toward the GPO from Bangkok Bank (1½hr., 50฿). Returning will be difficult; Let's Go does not recommend hitchhiking, but families visiting on the weekend may offer rides. Waterfall 200฿. Camping permitted 30฿. Tent rental 180฿/250฿ for 2/3 people. 3- to 15-person bungalows for 600-3000฿ (☎ 229 000). Park open daily 6am-6pm. Songthaew to Kew Lom line up on Rob Wiang Rd., behind City Hall. On weekends, you might have to charter one. Dam open daily 6am-6pm.

This award-winning national park boasts modern facilities and **hot springs.** The springs' main draw is not the **bubbling sulfurous pools** reaching 82°C, but rather the luxurious **private baths** (20฿; 5฿ for shower). A less private, but similar, option is to plunge into the **river** where the water from the hot spring merges pleasantly with the river water. **Chae Son Waterfall**, plummeting 150m over six tiers, lies 1km farther up the road. An engineering feat, the concrete staircase leading to the fall's origin is more imposing than the waterfall itself. An easy 3km nature trail along the river links the two sites (fish food 10฿). The **Kew Lom Dam** is a relaxation spot south of Chae Son National Park. Packed during the holidays, the island can be reached by boat (50฿). Make **bungalow** reservations with the Royal Irrigation Department (☎ 02 241 48 06) or Kew Lom Resort (☎ 223 772).

WAT PHRA THAT LAMPANG LUANG

Songthaew to Ko Kha leave from Robwiang Rd., one block west of Praisanee Rd. (20฿). It's a few kilometers farther to the temple—negotiate with a driver. If arriving with private transport from the Thai Elephant Conservation Center, there's no need to backtrack all the way to Lampang; look for signs to the wat and Ko Kha from the highway.

About 18km southwest of Lampang in the town of **Ko Kha** sits Wat Phra That Lampang Luang, one of Northern Thailand's finest displays of religious architecture. Its giant *chedi* and low wooden buildings also hold Lampang's most sacred Buddha. Through the main gate, the central *wiharn* is an open-air Lanna-style structure, supported by 46 laterite columns. Constructed in 1486, the chapel houses two important Buddha images. **Phra Jao Lan Tang,** cast in 1563, is enclosed in a golden *mondop* near the rear of the temple; **Phra Jao Tan Jai** sits behind the *mondop*. Directly behind the *wiharn*, the *chedi* houses relics of the Buddha. **Wiharn Naamtaen,** to the right of the *chedi*, displays murals dating from 1501, while a 700-year-old Buddha image rests inside **Phra Phuttha Wiharn** to the left of the *chedi*. A **Buddha footprint** lies behind **Haw Phra Phutthabat,** a white building constructed in 1149. Only men can enter, whereupon they'll discover a puzzling white sheet before the indistinguishable Buddha footprint. Close the door and a mesmerizing optical illusion results: sunlight reflects off the golden *chedi*, gets inverted by the small slit in the door, and finally reaches the makeshift screen. It appears there like a shimmering and crackly home video complete with upside-down people walking below. (Works best in afternoon light.) Another intriguing mystery: How was Nan Tip Chang able to enter the wat to shoot Tao Maha Yote, thus freeing his people from Burmese rule and establishing himself as king? Ask a believer (any Thai will do) and they'll tell you he crawled through the drain in the back of the wat—an incredible feat even for a small-boned Thai. To find the drain from the bullet hole, walk to the right of the main *chedi* to the back wall. Beyond the back wall of the compound, a prison masquerading as a shrine showcases the temple's most valuable Buddha image, a jade Buddha from the Chiang Saen period (1057-1757). Fortunately, visiting hours are relaxed, allowing worshipers to sit with their caged inmate. In April, during the Thai New Year, the image takes the limelight in a procession through the streets of Lampang.

PHITSANULOK ☎ 055

A staging ground for Ayutthaya's campaigns against the Burmese and the station of the Third Army during Communist uprisings in the Nan hills, Phitsanulok ("Phitlok" or "Philok" to locals) retains its military tradition, hosting the annual Cobra Gold exercises between Thai and American forces. Despite its past martial prowess, Phitsanulok is an unthreatening gateway to Northern Thailand. The busy metropolis welcomes travelers who overnight here while taking in Phra Buddha Chinnarat, one of the world's most famous Buddha images.

🖅 TRANSPORTATION

Flights: Phitsanulok Domestic Airport (☎258 029), on Sanambin Rd. **Thai Airways,** 209/26-28 Srithammatripidok Rd. (☎242 971)—with your back to the TAT it's 50m to the right. Flies to **Bangkok** (daily 6:20am, 1:30, 8:10pm; Th-F, Su 10:05am; M, Sa 12:25pm; 1485฿) and **Lampang** (M, Sa 10am; 955฿). **Air Andaman,** booked through Thai Airways or at the airport, flies to **Chiang Mai** (Tu, Th, Sa 12:30pm; 1185฿). Open M-F 8am-5pm; open at the airport on weekends.

Trains: Phitsanulok Train Station (☎258 005), on Akatossaroth Rd. To **Bangkok** (6-7hr.; 14 per day; 3rd-class 109฿, 2nd-class 159฿) via **Ayutthaya** (5-6hr.; 9 per day; 3rd-class 98฿, 2nd-class 175฿) and **Chiang Mai** (6-8hr.; 7 per day; 3rd-class 105฿, 2nd-class 190฿).

Buses: Bo Ko So Bus Station (☎242 430), on Phitsanulok-Lomsak Rd. east of town. City bus #1 shuttles between the train and bus stations. Buses to: **Bangkok** (6hr.; 25 per day; 121฿, A/C II 169฿, A/C I 218฿); **Chiang Mai** (6-7hr.; 26 per day; 120-140฿, A/C 168-216฿); **Chiang Rai** (6-7hr.; 20 per day; 139-153฿, A/C 195-275฿); **Khon Kaen** (5hr.; 13 per day; 137฿, 2nd-class A/C 192฿, A/C I 247฿); **Mae Sot** (A/C van 5hr., 8 per day 7am-4pm, 125฿); **Nakhon Ratchasima** (6-7hr.; 15 per day; 137-148฿, A/C 192-247฿); **Phrae** (4hr.; 14 per day; 66฿, A/C 92-119฿); **Sukhothai** (1hr.; every 30min. 4:45am-6pm; 23฿, A/C 32฿); **Udon Thani** (7hr.; 9 per day; 122฿, A/C 171-220฿) via **Loei** (4hr.; 79฿, A/C 111-142฿). A/C is not available on all rides to all locations. For major destinations, buses have multiple routes; one route is often up to 1hr. quicker than another.

Local Transportation: City Bus Station, on Akatossaroth Rd., 1 block left of the train station. Buses run daily 5am-9pm. Bus #1 goes to Bo Ko So Bus Station, Wat Yai, and Naresuan University. Bus #4 goes to the airport. Regular buses 5฿, A/C 7฿.

Rentals: Lady Motor, 43/12 Baromtrilokanart Rd., 20m south of Studio 54. Motorcycles 150฿ for 9am-5pm, 200฿ for 24hr. Open M-Sa 8:30am-5:30pm. **Avis** is at Phitsanulok Youth Hostel.

✦ 🛈 ORIENTATION AND PRACTICAL INFORMATION

Phitsanulok lies along the east bank of the **Nan River,** 377km north of Bangkok. **Puttaboocha Rd.** runs parallel to the river. One block east is **Baromtrilokanart Rd.** The main thoroughfare, **Akatossaroth Rd.,** lies two blocks east of the river and also runs parallel to the railroad tracks. **Naresuan Rd.** shoots out west from the **Phitsanulok Train Station** on Akatossaroth Rd., cutting through the busiest part of town, as well as Baromtrilokanart and Puttaboocha Rd. before crossing the river. The famous **Phra Buddha Chinnarat** is at **Wat Yai** at the northern end of Puttaboocha Rd. The **Bo Ko So Bus Station** is 3km east of the wat on the other side of the train tracks.

Tourist Office: TAT, 209/7-8 Surasi Trade Center, Srithammatripidok Rd. (☎/fax 252 742). Helpful staff go out of their way to offer assistance. Info, maps, and timetables for Sukhothai and Phitsanulok. Open daily 8:30am-4:30pm.

Tours: Able Tours and Travel, 55/45 Srithammatripidok Rd. (☎243 851). With your back to TAT, it's 25m to the left. Books domestic and international flights. Open M-F 8am-6pm, Sa 8am-4:30pm.

Currency Exchange: Thai Farmers Bank, 144/1 Baromtrilokanart Rd. (☎241 497), at the clock tower. **24hr. ATM** (Cirrus/MC/PLUS/V). Open M-F 8:30am-3:30pm. Several **banks** are also on Naresuan Rd.

Luggage Storage: At the train station. 10฿ per piece per day. Open daily 7am-11pm.

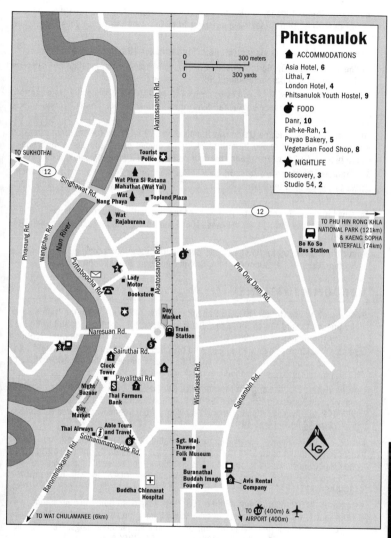

Phitsanulok

▲ ACCOMMODATIONS

Asia Hotel, **6**
Lithai, **7**
London Hotel, **4**
Phitsanulok Youth Hostel, **9**

🍎 FOOD

Danr, **10**
Fah-ke-Rah, **1**
Payao Bakery, **5**
Vegetarian Food Shop, **8**

★ NIGHTLIFE

Discovery, **3**
Studio 54, **2**

TO SUKHOTHAI
12
Singhawat Rd.

Akatossaroth Rd.

Tourist Police ✚

Wat Phra Si Ratana Mahathat (Wat Yai)
Wat Nang Phaya
■ Topland Plaza

Wat Rajaburana

12

TO PHU HIN RONG KHLA NATIONAL PARK (121km) & KAENG SOPHA WATERFALL (74km)

Bo Ko So Bus Station

Pra Ong Dam Rd.

Phraraung Rd.
Wangchan Rd.
Nan River
Puttaboocha Rd.

■ Lady Motor
Bookstore

Akatossaroth Rd.

Day Market

Naresuan Rd.

Train Station

Sairuthai Rd.

Clock Tower

Payalithai Rd.

Night Bazaar
Thai Farmers Bank

Wisukkasat Rd.

Sanambin Rd.

Day Market

Thai Airways
Able Tours and Travel

Srithammatripidok Rd.

Baromtrlokanart Rd.

Sgt. Maj. Thawee Folk Museum

N
LG

Buranathai Buddah Image Foundry

Avis Rental Company

✚ Buddha Chinnarat Hospital

TO WAT CHULAMANEE (6km)

TO 10 (400m) & AIRPORT (400m)

NORTHERN THAILAND

Bookstore: 106-8 Akatossaroth Rd. (☎ 258 862). Asia bookstand with Thai-themed books on travel, language, and religion. Open daily 9am-9pm.

Markets: Day market, north of the train station behind Akatossaroth Rd. One side has the standard collection of inane consumer goods, while the other is devoted to tasty and quick meals. Eventually, the two sides converge into 500m of fruits, vegetables, and meats. **Night bazaar,** on Puttaboocha Rd., 2 blocks south of the bridge. A plethora of great food stalls compensate for overpriced stone carvings. Another **day market** lies at the south end of Puttaboocha Rd., marking the end of the night bazaar.

Shopping: Topland Plaza, at the rotary on the north end of Akatossaroth Rd., is a multi-level department store selling everything from Guy Laroche to gadgetry. Open M-F 9:30am-9pm, Sa-Su 10am-9pm.

Emergency: ☎191. **Ambulance:** ☎1669. **Tourist Police (Bangkok):** ☎1155.

Police: ☎258 777. On Baromtrilokanart Rd. Walking from the train station on Naresuan Rd., turn right onto Baromtrilokanart Rd. It's 20m on the left.

Local Tourist Police: 31/15 Akatossaroth Rd. (☎245 357), from the train station, 200m past back entrance to Wat Yai. Marked as "Tourist Service Center." Some English spoken. **Open 24hr.**

Medical Services: Buddha Chinnarat Hospital (☎219 844), on the southern extension of Akatossaroth Rd. at the turn-off to TAT. (The official street address is on Srithammatripidok Rd.) **24hr. emergency room** and **pharmacy.** 2 more hospitals are nearby.

Telephones: Phitsanulok Telecommunication Center (☎243 116), on Puttaboocha next to the GPO. International phone/fax. CATNET Internet access. Open daily 7am-10pm. AmEx/MC/V.

Internet Access: Speedy Net, 50m west of the river on Naresuan Rd. heading out of town. Open daily 8am-11pm. **Skynet,** 108 Sanambin Rd. Open daily 8am-midnight. Both 30฿ per hr.

Post Office: GPO (☎258 313), on Puttaboocha Rd. 500m north of Naresuan Rd. *Poste Restante.* Open M-F 8:30am-4:30pm, Sa-Su 9am-noon. **Postal code:** 65000.

◤ ACCOMMODATIONS

Phitsanulok Youth Hostel (HI), 38 Sanambin Rd. (☎242 060). From the train station, take bus #4 toward the airport. Cross the train tracks, turn right on Sanambin Rd. and look for the hostel on the left. Clean rooms furnished with Thai antiques. Beautiful grounds include a lush garden with granite benches and a small waterfall. Laundry service. Lenso phone. Open 24hr. Dorms 120฿; elegant singles with bath 200฿; doubles 300฿; triples 450฿. All prices include toast and tea. ❷

London Hotel, 21-22 Soi 1 off Puttaboocha Rd. (☎225 145). From the train station, walk west on Naresuan Rd., take a left on Puttaboocha Rd., and it's 2 blocks down, on the left. Retro downstairs sitting room. Yellow and green rooms with shared toilets. Singles 100฿; doubles 150฿. ❶

Lithai, 73/1-5 Payalithai Rd. (☎219 626). From the train station, walk left and take the second road to the right. 50m down on the left side. High-quality hotel rooms surround vine-draped inner sanctum. Top floor has partitioned rooms with shared bath. Singles 150฿; doubles 180฿; triples 220฿; rooms with bath 200-220฿, with bath and A/C 330-440฿. ❷

Asia Hotel, 176/1 Akatossaroth Rd. (☎258 378). Take a left from the train station, walk 500m, and it will be on your left, or take bus #1 from the city bus station. Noisy location. Laundry 8฿ per piece. Immaculate singles with simple furnishings, Western toilet, and cold shower 200฿, with A/C 300฿; doubles 250฿/350฿. ❸

◤ FOOD

Phitsanulok is known for its open-air restaurants; **Payalithai Road** has the best and cheapest during the day. At night, the food-quake's epicenter is **the night market's northern end** (see **Markets,** p. 301); nearly a solid kilometer of eateries begins at the Naresuan Rd. bridge. All over the city (especially the night market), **flying-vegetable restaurants** ❶ hurl *pak boong fai deng* (flaming morning glory vine) from *wok* to distant plates.

▨ **Fah-Ke-Rah,** 52/6 Pra Ong Dam Rd. Near the mosque, 35m past the train tracks away from town. Muslim restaurant with arguably the best food in Phitsanulok. *Lassi* 20฿. Chicken with yellow rice 25฿. *Roti kaeng* 20฿. Open daily 6am-2pm. ❷

Vegetarian Food Shop, 55/4 Srithammatripidok Rd. With your back to the TAT, walk left 150m rounding the corner. Delicious freshly squeezed orange juice 10฿. Veggie dish of the day with brown or white rice 10฿; 2 choices 15฿. Open daily 6am-2pm. ❶

Payao Bakery, 168 Akatossaroth Rd., opposite and left of train station. Look for cakes in the window. A subdued student hangout with A/C comfort. Brownies (10฿), sundaes, and real food (club sandwich 45฿) too! Open daily 7am-10pm. ❷

Danr, 260/2-3 Sanambin Rd., 300m before airport. No English sign; look for glass windows with overhanging vines and palms. Popular for business lunches. The slightly translated menu offers a mixture of Vietnamese and Thai dishes. Sour lemon-grass soup 50฿. Open daily 10am-10pm. MC/V. ❷

🎥 🎵 SIGHTS AND ENTERTAINMENT

Wat Phra Si Ratana Mahathat (Wat Yai), at the northern end of Puttaboocha Rd., shelters Phitsanulok's jewel. Cast in 1357, the spectacular **Phra Buddha Chinnarat** (Victorious King) is one of the world's most reproduced Buddha images. It can be seen glimmering from afar with an ambiguous smile of contemplation. The wing of the wat that is on the left when you face Phra Buddha Chinnarat has been turned into a museum. (Museum open W-Su 9am-4pm. Wat open daily 7am-6pm. Sporadically enforced 10฿ admission. Sarongs provided free of charge to the bare-legged.)

The **Sgt. Maj. Thawee Folk Museum,** 26/43 Wisutkasat Rd., is doing an incredible job of trying to protect folk culture from being swept away in the sea of globalization. In an attempt to preserve local traditions, displays include items that are no longer in use. Detailed captions in English explain everything from bull-castration techniques to how the snake guillotine catches its prey. (☎212 749. Open Tu-Su 8:30am-4:30pm. Free, but donations accepted and deserved.) Across the street, Dr. Thawee also runs the **Buranathai Buddha Image Foundry,** where you can see handcrafted bronze Buddhas, from figurines to goliaths, in different stages of creation. The house factory also has a gift shop; pick out your own bronzed Buddha. (☎258 715. Open daily 8am-5pm.) **Wat Chulamanee,** built in 1464, is 6km outside the city, best reached by moto-taxi (100฿).

Pubs cluster at the far northern end of **Baromtrilokanart Rd.** About the only thing **Studio 54,** at the Pailyn Hotel, has in common with its infamous New York equivalent is that it hosts the "in" crowd. (Heineken and Carlsberg only, 100฿. Open daily 8am-2am.) For more bar options head to the **Phitsanulok Bazaar** across the bridge on Naresuan Rd. Bars line the quadrangle around **Discovery,** a disco with live bands and the orange-haired rebellious crowd. (Open daily 9pm-1am.)

🏃 DAYTRIP FROM PHITSANULOK: PHU HIN RONG KHLA

The park is best visited during the less-crowded weekdays. To reach the park, take a bus to Nakhon Thai (2hr., every hr. 6:30am-6pm, 28฿) and then grab a songthaew 32km to Phu Hin Rong Khla (1½hr., sporadic, 40฿). Private transportation is needed to see much of the park. To charter a songhaew for the day will cost 1500฿ from Phitsanulok, less from Nakhon Thai. The direct drive from Phitsanulok, starting on Route 12 heading east, takes 2hr. Take Route 12 from Phitsanulok, take a left onto Route 2013 to Nakhon Thai. Turn right onto Route 2331, follow signs to Nakhon Thai or National Park about 70km out on Route 12. Contact the Forestry Department in Bangkok (☎02 579 7223) or Phu Hin Rong Khla Park (☎055 233 527) for more information. Park Headquarters open daily 8am-4pm. Park admission 200฿.

NORTHERN THAILAND

The Thai army and the People's Liberation Army of Thailand (PLAT) clashed around Phitsanulok, on the land that this national park now encompasses. From 1967-1982, PLAT survived in the Phu Hin Rong Khla forests 123km from town near the Lao border. Recruits poured in after the clampdown on student demonstrators in Bangkok in 1976. The government then struck a decisive blow by offering amnesty to all students who joined the movement after 1976. In 1982, the area was declared a national park.

The most visited sight in the park is the **flagpole,** near the old Communist headquarters. A 3.2km **nature walk** leads to the flagpole, where the Thai flag now boldly flies. The flagpole stands on the ridge of the mountain range, offering a panoramic view of the valley below. The nature walk lies 2km from Park Headquarters along a marked and paved road. Pick up a map from Park Headquarters to explore the **waterfalls** and **historical attractions** Phu Hin Rong Khla has to offer.

Phu Hin Rong Khla's Park Headquarters can offer some **accommodations ❶.** (Tent rental 100฿. Camping 30฿; bungalows 600฿.) Those traveling with their own transport will want to explore the many **waterfalls** that lie off Route 12. The best is the three-tiered 40m drop of **Kaeng Sopha Waterfall,** 74km outside of Phitsanulok. The dry-season flow will leave you unsatisfied, but the large valley boulders entwined in trees warrant exploration. The turn-off to Kaeng Sopha Waterfall is 3km beyond the turn-off to Nakhon Thai. It's 2km from the main road to the waterfall. The TAT has a regional map marking the relative positions of waterfalls along Route 12—all turn-offs are well marked, but it's reassuring nonetheless.

SUKHOTHAI ☎055

In 1238, the Thais established the new capital of the Lanna Kingdom near the Yom River and drove the Khmer to the east. Named "Sukhothai," or "Dawn of Happiness," the city marked the birth of the first Thai nation. Sukhothai's period of glory is preserved in its spectacular ruins. It has recently joined Ayutthaya and Kanchanaburi as a sightseeing hot spot—and while Old Sukhothai is fast becoming a laterite theme park, nearby Si Satchanalai, with some of Thailand's most awe-inspiring ruins, remains untrafficked.

▣ TRANSPORTATION

Flights: The **airport** is 26km out of town. **Bangkok Airways** (☎613 075), at the Pailyn Hotel, nestled on the road to the old city, flies to **Bangkok** (daily 12:50pm; Su-M, W, F 4:40pm; 1500฿); **Chiang Mai** (daily 10:40am, 1040฿); **Luang Prabang** (Su, M, W, F 1:10pm; 4300฿). 100฿ departure tax. Shuttle bus to the airport from Sukhothai Travel Service 90฿.

Buses: There is a brand new **bus station** (☎614 529) 3km out of town on Bypass Rd. White, pink, and blue *songthaew* run along Bypass Rd. into town (5฿ before 4pm). Tuk-tuks to town are a self-regulated 30฿. Buses go to: **Bangkok** (7hr.; every hr. 7:50am-11pm; 142฿, 2nd-class A/C 199฿, 1st-class A/C 256฿) via **Ayutthaya** (5hr.); **Chiang Mai** (6hr.; 12 per day 1:20am-5pm; 122฿, A/C 171฿) via **Tak** (1hr.; every hr. 7:30am-6:15pm; 31-43฿); **Chiang Rai** (6-7hr.; 6:40am, 136฿; 9, 11:30am, 190฿); **Nan** (6hr.; A/C 2:30pm, 146฿; 10pm, 104฿); **Phitsanulok** (1hr.; every 30min. 6:20am-8pm; 23฿, A/C 32฿). **Minibuses** to **Mae Sot** (2½hr., 7 per day 8am-4pm, 100฿) leave from a traffic triangle off Charot Withi Thong Rd., 2 blocks north of the main traffic light.

Local Transportation: Tuk-tuks 20-30฿. **Samlor** 10-20฿. At the terminal across the bridge, **trucks** run to the old city (every 20min. 6am-6pm, 10฿). A bus to **Si Satchanalai** runs from the bus station (every 30min. 7am-4:30pm, 30฿).

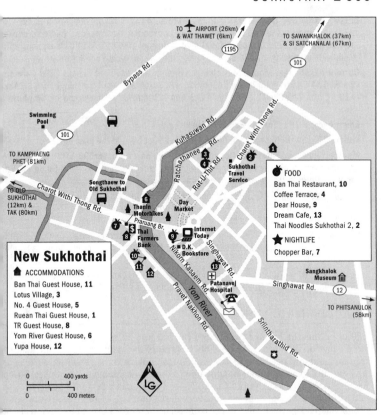

New Sukhothai

🏠 ACCOMMODATIONS

Ban Thai Guest House, **11**
Lotus Village, **3**
No. 4 Guest House, **5**
Ruean Thai Guest House, **1**
TR Guest House, **8**
Yom River Guest House, **6**
Yupa House, **12**

🍎 FOOD

Ban Thai Restaurant, **10**
Coffee Terrace, **4**
Dear House, **9**
Dream Cafe, **13**
Thai Noodles Sukhothai 2, **2**

⭐ NIGHTLIFE

Chopper Bar, **7**

Rentals: Lotus Village and **Ban Thai Guest House** rent **bikes** for 20-50฿ per day. Bikes cost 20-30฿ per day at the Historical Park and 20฿ at Si Satchanalai. **Motorcycles** are for rent at guest houses for 200฿ and at **Thanin Motorbikes,** 112 Charot Withi Thong (☎613 402), 20m past Thai Farmers Bank with 24hr. bell service (150฿ per day; open daily 7am-8pm).

🔼🔢 ORIENTATION AND PRACTICAL INFORMATION

New Sukhothai city, 12km east of the old city (*muang gao*) and 427km north of Bangkok, appears at an L-shaped bend in the Yom River. **Charot Withi Thong Rd.** and **Singhawat Rd.** run a few blocks in from the Yom's eastern bank and converge at Sukhothai's largest intersection near the bend in the "L." From there, Charot Withi Thong Rd. crosses **Praruang Bridge** and continues into the old city, intersecting **Nikorn Kasaem** and **Pravet Nakhon Rd.** along the way. Hwy. 101 bypasses the town at its northern end.

Tourist Offices: The **bus information counter** deals out bus timetables and the same useful tourist brochure as the TAT in Phitsanulok. **Sukhothai Travel Service,** 327/6-7 Charot Withi Thong Rd. (☎613 075), books domestic and international flights. Shuttle to the airport coincides with flights (90฿). Open daily 8am-5pm.

English-Language Bookstore: D.K. Bookstore, 41/2-3 Nikorn Kasaem Rd. (☎612 272), 100m from the bridge, has a shelf of cookbooks, dictionaries, children's books, and an excellent selection of **regional maps.** Michael Map of Sukhothai is a glossy souvenir with interesting insight into the ruins (39฿). Open daily 7am-9pm.

Currency Exchange: Most banks change currency and traveler's checks. **Thai Farmers Bank,** 134 Charot Withi Thong Rd. (☎611 932), at the base of the bridge, has a **24hr. ATM** (Cirrus/MC/Plus/V). Open M-F 8:30am-3:30pm. Other banks are on **Singhawat Rd.**

Emergency: ☎191. **Tourist Police (Bangkok):** ☎1155.

Police: 263 Nikorn Kasaem Rd. (☎613 110), 250m beyond the post office.

Medical Services: Patanavej Hospital, 89/9 Singhawat Rd. (☎621 502), 200m from the intersection of Singhawat and Charot Withi Thong Rd., on the right. Some English spoken. **Open 24hr. Pharmacy** open 24hr. Visa.

Telephones: At the GPO. **International telephone,** fax, and CATNET Internet access upstairs. Open M-F 8:30am-4:30pm, Sa 9am-noon. Lenso telephone at 7-Eleven across the bridge.

Internet: Cafes line Nikorn Kasaem Rd. near the bridge. **Internet Today,** on Charot Withi Thong Rd., 100m into town from the bridge. 1฿ per min., 40฿ per hr. Open daily until midnight.

Post Office: GPO, 241 Nikorn Kasaem Rd. (☎611 645), 1km south of the bridge. *Poste Restante.* Open M-F 8:30am-4:30pm, Sa-Su 9am-noon. **Postal code:** 64000.

♠ ACCOMMODATIONS

Sukhothai has the highest proportion of charming guest houses in the region. From a base in Sukhothai, it's possible to explore the many provincial attractions or branch out into neighboring Tak and Phitsanulok. Several guest houses lie near the centrally located, albeit unappealing, Yom River. Many guest houses fill up during Sukhothai's long tourist season (June-Feb.)—call a few days in advance to guarantee a room. Some guest house owners complain of tuk-tuk drivers who, after being paid by rival guest house owners, lie to tourists at the bus station about certain guest houses being full or dirty. Be firm and check out your intended destination first-hand.

Ban Thai Guest House, 38 Pravet Nakhon Rd. (☎610 163), across the Yom River. Take a left after the bridge at Thai Farmers Bank and walk 300m. Friendly owners. Airy restaurant. Rooms in newly renovated wooden house 120-150฿; concrete rooms or bungalows with bath 200฿. ❶

Lotus Village, 170 Ratchathanee Rd. (☎621 484), 10min. walk from Praruang Bridge. Head away from the old city and take the 1st left; it's on the left after the 4th crossstreet. Rustic singles with mosquito nets in large teak houses over lotus pond. The fact that you can feed the fish through the floorboards may not appeal to everyone. Fortunately, there are other sturdier options. Real coffee and sumptuous homemade jam. Singles 120฿; doubles 240฿, with bath 400-500฿; bungalows 400฿, with A/C 900฿. ❶

Yom River Guest House, on Kuhasuwan Rd., 150m north of Thai Farmers Bank. New place opened by the same couple who runs the Ban Thai Guest House to handle the popularity of their services. From here there is a better view of the river overlooking the wat and day market. Stylish upstairs rooms with shared bath 150฿. Singles and bungalows are under construction. ❷

No. 4 Guest House, 140/4 Soi Klong Maelampan, Charot Withi Thong Rd. (☎610 165). From the bridge, take the 2nd right at the buses to the old city and follow the signs (take a tuk-tuk after dark). Intimate bamboo bungalow village in tranquil field setting. Thai cooking lessons 1500฿ (150฿ per dish). Singles with bath 150฿; doubles 180฿. ❷

Yupa House, 44/10 Pravet Nakhon Rd., Soi Mekapat (☎612 578). Turn-off 25m beyond Ban Thai Guest House. Wonderfully friendly Mr. Chuer and his wife Yupa run this traditional homestay. There's no patio, but top-floor rooms open onto balconies. Cheap laundry service. Dorms 50฿; rooms 100฿, with bath 120฿. ❶

Ruean Thai Guest House, 181/20 Soi Pracharuammit (☎612 444), off Charot Withi Thong Rd., 1km from the bridge away from the old city. Driving enthusiasts will love the room in the back of the truck, and the marble slab with mattress mounted on a car chasis. Beautiful and breezy sitting area. Truck room with nets and fan 100-150฿; rooms 250฿, with hot water 300฿; teak house rooms with A/C 500-600฿. ❶

TR Guest House, 27/5 Pravet Nakhon, behind Thai Farmers Bank. Immaculate tiled rooms with comfy beds, bath, and balcony/drying area in hotel-style accommodation with a location that is not very memorable. Laundry 30฿ per kg. Rooms 150฿, with A/C 300฿; twins 200฿. ❷

◧ FOOD

Daytime food stalls congregate on the side streets west of **Charot Withi Thong Rd.;** at night, the best bet is **Ramkhamhaeng Rd.,** the first cross street on the city side of the river. Try the phat thai here; it's a point of pride for the people of Sukhothai.

▨ Dream Cafe, 96/1 Singhawat Rd., next to Patanavej Hospital. Best restaurant in Sukhothai comes at a price, but it's worth it. The owner, Chaba, will gladly walk you through the extensive menu and explain the subtleties of Thai herbs. Ask her to brew a fruit tea (not on the menu) or take a stamina shot, which improves everything from strength to sexual desire. Roasted eggplant and basil with shrimp 120฿. Open daily 10am-midnight. MC/V. ❸

Thai Noodles Sukhothai 2, 139 Charot Withi Thong Rd. Walk out of the city 1km; it's 300m past the school on the right at the turn-off to Ruean Thai. Look for a restaurant with small ivy-covered fountains. The specialty is *kuaytiaw sukhothai* (noodle soup with pork, green beans, coriander, and chili; 15฿). Phenomenal phat thai 20฿. Top half of Thai menu is noodles, bottom half rice dishes. Open daily 10am-3pm. ❶

Ban Thai Restaurant, 38 Pravet Nakhon Rd., at Ban Thai Guest House. Serves great food on a nice patio. Sweet and sour pork with pineapple, papaya, and mango 60฿. Tofu can be substituted for meat. Milk and fruit shakes 15฿. Open daily 7am-9pm. ❷

Dear House, on Nikorn Kasaem Rd., 50m from the bridge, serves good value American breakfasts (eggs, ham, and toast; 50฿). Thai dishes 25-60฿ on large English menu. Open in the daytime only. ❷

Coffee Terrace, on Rat-u-thit Rd., next to Lotus Village. Pleasant outdoor candlelit dining with elegantly presented food. *Kiao krop* (pork wonton in plum sauce) 65฿. No coffee, despite what the name suggests. Open daily 11am-11pm. ❷

◉ ♫ SIGHTS AND ENTERTAINMENT

Not your typical wat, **Wat Thawet**'s grounds are a three-dimentional maze of brightly colored statues that furnish more than a few morbid illustrations of the punishments awaiting those who disobey Buddhist precepts. Inspired entirely by a single dream of the wat's now-deceased monk, highlights include a woman with a rooster head (the head of the animal she killed) and a man being forced to eat his own intestines. To get there, ride away from town northeast on Charot Withi Thong Rd. Turn left onto Bypass Rd. Go over the bridge, and take the first paved right. The turn-off is 6km down the highway on your right, 700m after the major intersection with another highway. Great fried bananas are sold along the highway for lunch.

The **Sangkhalok Museum** displays hundreds of artifacts detailing the daily lives of people who inhabited the nearby ruins. Ceramic masterpieces from the Kingdom of Lanna, around 700 years old, are also on display. It's 1.5km outside of town. Follow Singhawat Rd. out of the city as it turns into Hwy. 12 (toward Phitsanulok). Turn left at the first major intersection (Hwy. 101); it's 100m on the left. (☎614 333. Open M-F 10am-6pm, Sa-Su 10am-8pm. 250฿, children under 17 50฿.)

The **day market ❶** is defined by the river, Praponbamrung Rd. and Charot Withi Thong Rd. **Food stalls ❶** on Charot Withi Thong Rd. leading up to the bridge have fantastic meals at great prices (20฿). Off the road to the north in front of the wat are a variety of **fruit stalls ❶** (watermelon 10฿). Poking your head in and around the area's **sois** will reveal the usual market produce, meat, and plastic sandals. The produce rolls into the market at all hours of the day due to Sukhothai's crossroad location between north and south; the 2am influx is surprisingly busy as locals bargain for the freshest produce.

A nightspot for *farang* and Thais alike is the **Chopper Bar,** 101 Charot Withi Thong Rd., on your left walking from the river to the old city bus stop. Transsexuality is not the theme; it's incidental but adds flavor. (Folk music 8-10pm. Large Singha 65฿. Open daily 1pm-midnight.)

◪ OLD SUKHOTHAI HISTORICAL PARK

Old Sukhothai Historical Park lies within the triple-layered walls of the ancient city. Outside, fragments of an old wat and *chedi* can be explored, ideally by bicycle, along any of the paths branching out from the park's four main gates. *Songthaew* from Sukhothai will enter through the Old City's East Gate and drop you at the entrance booth before Wat Mahathat. The road from Sukhothai continues to Tak cutting through the western wall of the Old City at its northern end. The **Tourist Information Center,** inconveniently located outside San Luang Gate north of the city, has a model of the environs, and a free brochure. (Open daily 8am-4pm.) It is more time-efficient to buy the better pamphlet from the entrance booth (3฿).

To reach the park, catch a *songthaew* from the lot on the west side of the river, 300m down the road on the right (20min., 6am-6pm, 10฿). Arriving at the park early will help avoid the heat and tour-group mobs, although in the evenings some monuments are stunningly lit. (Park open daily 6am-9pm. 40฿, bike 10฿, motorbike 20฿, car 50฿. Areas outside the North/West/South Gates are an additional 30฿ each.) If you are visiting Si Satchanalai on the same day, it is worth buying the day pass, which includes entrance to all the sites as well as the museum and kilns (150฿).

INSIDE THE OLD CITY WALL. The town centerpiece is **Wat Mahathat.** The main *chedi* is famed for its lotus shape, an architectural feature particular to the Sukhothai period. Also unusual are its several standing Buddha images in the Ceylonese style. Many of the ornate carvings around the wat remain in fantastic condition. Nearby **Wat Sri Sawai,** a south-facing Hindu shrine converted into a Buddhist temple, is the only Sukhothai ruin that doesn't face east. Its centerpiece is a set of three huge *prangs* which shoot out of the temple.

NORTH OF THE OLD CITY WALL. North of **San Luang Gate** is **Wat Phra Phai Luang.** Lying on an island encircled by a moat, the wat has a magnificent Lopburi-style *stupa* and plaster reliefs of the Buddha. There is more room to explore and fewer tourists. The wat is treasured by archaeologists for its traces of pre-Sukhothai period art. **Wat Sri Chum** sits just to the west. Its *mondop* houses the 15m tall "talking" Buddha (see **Legends of King Ramkhamhaeng,** above). The tunnels on your right and left as you enter the temple were escape passages for the King.

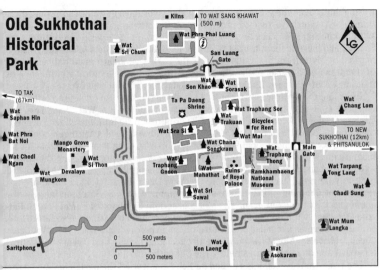

Old Sukhothai Historical Park

Map labels:
TO WAT SANG KHAWAT (500 m)
Kilns
Wat Phra Phai Luang
Wat Sri Chum
San Luang Gate
Wat Son Khao
Wat Sorasak
TO TAK (67km)
Ta Pa Daeng Shrine
Wat Traphang Sor
Wat Chang Lom
Wat Saphan Hin
Wat Trakuan
Bicycles for Rent
Wat Phra Bat Noi
Wat Sra Si
Wat Mai
TO NEW SUKHOTHAI (12km) & PHITSANULOK
Mango Grove Monastery
Wat Chana Songkram
Wat Si Thon
Wat Traphang Thong
Main Gate
Wat Chedi Ngam
Wat Mungkorn
Wat Devalaya
Wat Traphang Ngoen
Wat Mahathat
Ruins of Royal Palace
Ramkhamhaeng National Museum
Wat Tarpang Tong Lang
Wat Sri Sawai
Wat Chadi Sung
Wat Mum Langka
Saritphong
0 500 yards
0 500 meters
Wat Kon Laeng
Wat Asokaram

WEST OF THE OLD CITY WALL. At **Wat Mungkorn,** with its distinctively circular *chedi,* the road splits. To the left lies **Saritphong (Phra Ruang Dam),** an earthen dam 487m long and 4m wide, which today can hold up to 400,000 cubic meters of water. The water was necessary in Sukhothai's glory days to keep the moats full and the gardens green. The road to the right leads back to the main road between Sukhothai and Tak, but not before passing the entrance to **Wat Saphan Hin,** 200m up the hill. The wat contains a towering Buddha in standing position, known as **Phra Attharot.**

EAST OF THE OLD CITY WALL. Ramkhamhaeng National Museum, left of the park's east entrance, houses an eclectic collection testifying to the city's historical and cultural legacy, including a photocopy of the stone on which King Ramkhamhaeng the Great inscribed the first Thai script, considered by some to be his own invention. (Open daily 9am-4pm 30฿.)

▶ DAYTRIP FROM SUKHOTHAI: SI SATCHANALAI

67km north of Sukhothai. Take a public bus from Sukhothai bus station (every 30min. 7am-4:30pm, 30฿). Last bus returns before 5pm, from the main road. Park open daily 8:30am-4:30pm. 40฿. Kilns open daily 8am-4:30pm. 30฿.

LEGENDS OF KING RAMKHAMHAENG

Sukhothai's King Ramkhamhaeng the Great looms large in Thai legend. The Great Father once sucked clean the fishbones of his dinner, tossed them into the river, and watched them turn into the first *pla paruang*—a fish so transparent that its bones are visible through its skin. (The king, who evidently was quite fond of this sort of trick, also lobbed a tamarind seed into a river and created Thailand's first turtle.) To mobilize Sukhothai for war, he gathered the soldiers in front of Wat Sri Chum's massive Buddha image and, in a terrifying supernatural display, compelled the giant image to speak and urge the soldiers to fight bravely. Since those days of yore, a hidden staircase has been discovered that leads to an opening behind the Buddha's mouth.

During the 13th century, Si Satchanalai rivaled Ayutthaya in wealth and sophistication. When Ayutthaya rose to preeminence, Si Satchanalai sank into anonymity. With Sukhothai's success as a tourist attraction, the competition continues. Si Satchanalai has excellent tourist facilities, including the **Visitors Information Center,** marked by signs from the roads entering the park. Headquarters contains a model of the area and a museum detailing the history and architectural significance of the ruins. A brochure in English, photos, and a cryptic map cost 5฿.

Ruins line the southwestern bank of a bend in the Yom River. After a left at the entrance (passing the ticket window), ahead on the right is **Wat Chang Lom,** the city's central wat. According to ancient inscriptions, King Ramkhamhaeng ordered the temple's construction in 1287. Across the road, **Wat Chedi Chet Thaew** combines northern, southern, and local styles. Farther on, **Wat Nang Phaya** is notable for its magnificent stucco reliefs on one wall of the *wiharn.* Upon crossing the bridge into Si Satchanalai from Hwy. 101, you'll see the central complex of the historical park to your right. To the left, where the Yom River loops back on itself, are the remains of **Chaliang,** a pre-established settlement that Si Satchanalai grew to encompass. At the bend in the river 3km east of Si Satchanalai is **Wat Phra Si Rattana Mahathat,** which predates the Sukhothai period. The distinctive square *stupa* actually enshrines a smaller one. A turn-off 500m before the wat leads to **Wat Chom Chuen Archaeology Site Museum,** where 15 excavated human burial remains confirm the existence of communities before the Sukhothai period.

The unearthing of 200 kilns at **Ban Ko Noi,** 5km beyond the park, challenged the conceptions of ancient Siam's isolation and technological simplicity. The city's kilns produced advanced celadons (ceramics known today as *sawankhalok* or *sangkhalok*) for export to countries as far away as the Philippines. The Siam Cement Company has spent 2-3 million baht making a few of these kilns accessible to tourists. Kiln #61 is the first one you reach and has an adjacent museum. Kiln #42 and 123 (together) lie farther up the road and are covered for protection from the elements. Only one ticket is necessary to see both kiln sites.

TAK ☎055

All roads lead to Tak—thankfully, they also lead out. Whether your route is Bangkok-Chiang Mai, Sukhothai-Ayutthaya, or Khorat-Mae Sot, you'll pass through this provincial capital. Despite all of the TAT's attempts to talk it up as a destination in its own right, there's not much to do in town. As direct transportation to trekking destinations farther west becomes more common, more travelers will pass Tak's smiling people and majestic mountain surroundings without bothering to get off the bus.

▐ TRANSPORTATION. The **bus station** (☎511 057), near the intersection of Hwy. 1 and 12, serves: **Bangkok** (7hr.; 17 per day 8:45am-10:30pm; 123฿, 2nd-class A/C 190฿, 1st-class A/C 245฿, VIP 345฿); **Chiang Mai** (4hr.; approx. every hr. 8:30am-7pm; 98฿, A/C 137฿); **Kamphaeng Phet** (1hr., every hr. 6am-7pm, 25฿); **Sukhothai** (1½hr.; every hr. 8:30am-5:30pm; 31฿, A/C 43฿). Orange-and-white **minibuses** venture to **Mae Sot** (1½hr., every 30min. 6:30am-8pm, 44฿).

▐ ORIENTATION AND PRACTICAL INFORMATION. Tak's four main roads run parallel on the east side of the **Mae Ping River,** which flows north to south. Closest to the river is **Kitticarjon Rd.,** then **Chompon Rd.** and its night market food stalls. Next are **Taksin Rd.** and **Mahattai Bamruang Rd.,** lined with hotels. On the town's eastern edge runs **Hwy. 1,** which crosses **Hwy. 12** before going to Chiang Mai.

The **TAT** office, 500m west of the bus station, is a boon to the rare visitor, dishing out regional maps of Tak province including Um Phang as well as timetables. (☎514 341. Open daily 8:30am-4:30pm.) Other services in Tak include: **Bangkok**

Bank, 683 Taksin Rd., near the Sa Nguan Thai Hotel, with a 24hr. AmEx/MC/PLUS/ V **ATM** (open M-F 8:30am-3:30pm); the **GPO,** across an athletic field and to the left from the TAT (☎511 140; open M-F 8:30am-4:30pm, Sa-Su 9am-noon), with **international calls** and CATNET Internet on the second floor (open M-F 8:30am-4:30pm) and a **Lenso** phone outside; **Taksin Hospital** (☎511 025), on Hwy. 1 in the south part of town; a **pharmacy** next to Mae Ping Hotel (☎511 706; open daily 8am-8pm); and the **police station** (☎511 354; **emergency** ☎191; Bangkok tourist police ☎1155), on Mahatthai Bamruang Rd., east of the footbridge over the river. **Postal code:** 63000.

⌐⌐ ACCOMMODATIONS AND FOOD. Sa Nguan Thai Hotel ❷, 6/9 Taksin Rd., one block inland from the night market, is Tak's best value. It's tough to spot— look for the open-air sitting room and second-story wood veranda 20m toward the bridge from Bangkok Bank. (☎511 153. All-wood rooms with baths in the old wing 150฿; doubles in the new wing with TV 220฿, with A/C 300฿; twins 340฿.) Cheap, with squat toilets, the **Mae Ping Hotel ❶,** 231/4-5 Mahatthai Bamruang Rd., is another block inland from Sa Nguan Thai and 150m to the right, on the left side. (☎511 807. Singles 110฿; doubles 140฿, with A/C 200฿.)

Tak doesn't have restaurants. Instead, seek out **noodle shops** near the police station, the **night market** on Chompon Rd., or, best of all, **food stalls** dishing out Tak tasties near the footbridge in the park between Kitticarjon Rd. and Chompon Rd.

◎ SIGHTS. The paved riverside path and popular warped suspension footbridge offer views of the mountains to the west and, near sunset, billows of beautiful clouds. Continuing upstream leads to **Taksin Bridge.** Cutting east at this point, but before the TAT, is the **shrine of King Taksin** (1734-1782). Thais make the pilgrimage to light incense (5฿) and pay their respects to their revered king.

Bhumibol Dam is the eighth-largest in the world. The resulting reservoir is 100 miles long. A 1½hr. bus ride (25฿) from Chompon Rd., near the night market, leads to its base; it's another 3.3km walk up to the dam's crest. There's more than meets the eye—try to finagle a tour of the dam's innards.

Larn Sang National Park is 17km west of Tak on the road to Mae Sot. From where the buses drop you on the highway, it's 3km to headquarters and 5km to the **Visitors Center.** Although *Let's Go* does not recommend it, it's possible to hitch a ride with towel-toting Thais. At **Larn Sang Waterfall,** 150m from the visitors center, clear water cascades down gneiss ledges. Linger on the shady observation deck, or take a plunge. Thai tourists flood the lower falls on weekends, turning it into a makeshift water-park, but leave the upper falls, **Pha Peung** (750m walk) and **Pha Tae** (2.2km), deserted. **Camping ❶** in the park is possible. (Camping with your own tent 30฿, with a small rented one 250฿; bungalows 200-500฿. Park open daily 6am-6pm. 200฿, children 100฿.)

MAE SOT   ☎055

This little city's proximity to Myanmar (7km away) and Karen refugee camps lends a dark side to its multiculturalism: there is widespread exploitation of illegal Burmese immigrants by Thai business owners. All of the winding routes to Mae Sot (also called "Mae Sod") pass through police border checkpoints in an attempt to curtail the influx of the Burmese and Internally Displaced Persons (IDPs). Mae Sot's vibrant day market is a sight to behold, where "Union of Myanmar" currency notes and hill-tribe headdresses mingle with the usual fare of pig heads and mangos. Sitting in one of the many fair-trade coffeehouses, you're just as likely to be surrounded by a group of NGO workers as you are travelers—several programs are based in the region, providing essential health care and education to the refugees and IDPs. While most crash here for a night before heading to trekking adventures in Um Phang, the social situation draws many back to offer their services.

MYANMAR: TO GO OR NOT TO GO? The question of whether or not to go to Myanmar echoes a similar debate that once plagued travelers to South Africa under apartheid. Tourism in Myanmar undoubtedly financially supports one of the world's worst military regimes, but the reality for the people of Myanmar is not nearly so simple. In one of Southeast Asia's poorest countries, the fledgling tourist industry is, for many, the only alternative to state-sponsored slave labor. Increasingly relaxed tourist regulations mean that informed travelers can direct their money to Myanmar's people, not to its repressive government. Many Burmese hope that more travelers will visit their impoverished nation and bring money with them; some also want travelers to witness the political situation and tell others about it. The Burmese government's abuses are not a new story, yet they have only recently come to the attention of the world after the country opened up to foreign investment and tourism in 1989. Many argue that responsible and informed tourism is a far more effective means to change than isolating a military government that then has no incentive to stop its abuse of power. Nonetheless, it is important to note that Burmese citizens have disappeared or been beaten severely for discussing politics with foreigners, no doubt due to an insidious network of government informants. Military intelligence interrogated a family-restaurant owner for 24hr. after he spoke with travelers who tried to visit one of Myanmar's "no-go" areas. For locals' sake, if you decide to travel to Myanmar, **avoid discussion of politics** and educate yourself about how to avoid empowering the military junta. The choice to travel to Myanmar is yours. *Let's Go* only asks that you make it an informed one.

■ TRANSPORTATION

Flights: Mae Sot Airport (☎563 620), 3km west of town. Take a *songthaew* toward the Moei River Market (10฿). Minibus service from the airport daily (80฿). **Thai Airways,** 110 Prasatwithi Rd. (☎531 440), books flights with **Air Andaman.** Open daily 8am-5pm. To **Bangkok** (Su-M, W, F 3pm, Tu, Th, Sa 10am; 2065฿) and **Chiang Mai** (Su-M, W, F 3pm; 1185฿).

Buses: 5 **bus stations** in town. The station (☎532 949) for trips to and from **Bangkok** (10hr.; 10 per day 8-8:30am and 7-9:45pm; fan 172฿, 2nd-class A/C 241฿, 1st-class A/C 310฿, VIP 480฿) is 100m from Asia Rd. Ticket office open daily 9am-5pm. Orange *songthaew* to **Mae Sariang** (6hr., every hr. 6am-noon, 160฿) leave from behind the covered market area south (away from Asia Hwy.) of buses to Bangkok. Orange-and-white minivans to **Tak** (1½hr., every 30min. 6am-5:30pm, 44฿) gather on the east side of the same market. A paved road leading from Intharakhiri Rd., west of the police station, will deposit you at the Mae Sariang *songthaew*. The station (☎532 331) for buses to and from **Chiang Mai** (6½hr.; 6am, 134฿; 8am, A/C 241฿) is 1 block east of the police station. To find *songthaew* to **Um Phang** (5hr., every hr. 7:30am-3:30pm, 100฿), head left with your back to the police station. Take the 1st right, and follow the street past Prasatwithi Rd. and the mosque, then take the next left—you'll see a cluster of blue *songthaew*. White vans to **Phitsanulok** (4hr., 7 per day 7am-3pm, 125฿) via **Sukhothai** (2½hr., 100฿) leave from the station south of the main market. Maps available at guest houses make this information somewhat clearer.

Local Transportation: To go to the **Moei River Market** and the **border,** catch a blue **songthaew** (10฿) opposite Thai Airways on Prasatwithi Rd. Last one returns at 6pm.

Rentals: Guest houses rent **bikes** (30฿). **Motorcycle** rental (☎532 099) is next to Bangkok Bank on Prasatwithi Rd. 160฿ per day. Open daily 8am-5:30pm.

➕ ℹ️ ORIENTATION AND PRACTICAL INFORMATION

Mae Sot is 165km west of Sukhothai. **Intharakhiri Rd.**, with one-way traffic heading east, runs parallel to **Prasatwithi Rd.**, with one-way traffic heading west toward **Moei Market** and the Burmese border. Asia Hwy. bypasses town a few blocks north of these two major roads. The **police station** is on Intharakhiri Rd. in the center of town; guest houses primarily lie on the same road to the west. The **market** sprawls south of Prasatwithi Rd. near the Siam Hotel. Free maps with varying degrees of accuracy are available at guest houses. Among the best are the ones provided by Bai Fern (see **Accommodations**, below) and next door at K.C.B. Snack Shop, which provides a great artist's impression of surrounding sights.

Tours: For your wallet's sake, go to Um Phang yourself to book a trek. To book in Mae Sot, try TAT-approved **Mae Sot Conservation Tours,** 415/17 Tang Kim Chiang Rd. (☎ 544 726), 2 doors toward Prasatwithi Rd. from Pim Hut, which promotes eco-tourism and treks mainly around Mae Sot to avoid the congestion of Um Phang. 3 days/2 nights 5500฿, minimum 3 people. Open daily 8:30am-6pm. To avoid scams, make sure your guide is TAT-approved.

Immigration Office: ☎ 563 003. Next to Friendship Bridge at Moei River. (For visa extension see **Border Crossing: Moei-Myawaddy,** below.) Open daily 6am-6pm.

Currency Exchange: Banks line Prasatwithi Rd. **Thai Farmers Bank,** 84/9 Prasatwithi Rd. (☎ 531 020), has a **24hr.** ATM (Cirrus/MC/PLUS/V). Open M-F 8:30am-3:30pm. It may be possible to buy US dollars from **Bangkok Bank,** east on Prasatwithi Rd.

English-Language Bookstore: DK Hotel, on Intharakhiri Rd., has a small bookstore in the back right corner of the department store on the 1st fl. A collection of English-language Penguin Classics with a bias toward Hardy—or maybe those are just the ones nobody buys. Open daily 8:30am-8pm. A **secondhand bookstore** after the bus station to Chiang Mai, before DK Hotel, offers an eclectic and obscure range of English books. Open daily 10am-4pm.

Markets: The **day market** is south of Prasatwithi Rd. on either side of the Siam Hotel. Remarkably large for small Mae Sot. Crowded sois full of frogs and vegetables bottleneck before opening into large covered areas selling every kind of shirt, from collared to tie dye. The **gem and jade market** on Prasatwithi Rd., opposite Thai Farmers Bank, heats up by noon. The casual buyer will feel intimidated without an eyepiece. The **night market** at the east end of Prasatwithi Rd. is an unimpressive affair where one local entrepreneur offers phat thai in English for 20฿ while blatantly advertising the same in Thai for 15฿. **Moei River market,** at the border 7km west of town, sells Burmese fabrics, foodstuffs, and gems, as well as French skincare products and Sony Playstations. Take a blue *songthaew* from Prasatwithi Rd. opposite Thai Airways (10฿, last return 6pm), or bike past the rice fields for a scenic trip. Open daily 8am-6pm.

Emergency: ☎ 191. **Tourist Police (Bangkok):** ☎ 1155.

Police: ☎ 531 112. At intersection of Tang Kim Chiang and Intharakhiri Rd. **Open 24hr.**

Local Tourist Police: ☎ 533 523. Near Asia Hwy. in the vicinity of the bus station. With your back to the police station, head left, take the first left and follow it to the end; it's on the left. Minimal English. **Open 24hr.**

Medical Services: Pawo Hospital (☎ 544 397 or 533 912), south of town past the market, near the vans to Sukhothai. Private. Some English spoken. **Open 24hr.** MC/V. Has 24hr. pharmacy.

Telephones: Maesot Telecommunications Office, 784 Intharakhiri Rd. (☎ 533 364), 10min. walk west of guest houses. Standard 33฿ for assisted collect call. Lenso phone and CATNET Internet access. Open M-F 8:30am-4:30pm.

IN RECENT NEWS

BONDAGE AT THE BORDER

Visitors to Mae Sot will remain fairly oblivious to the complex topic of border migration, which affects them only at police checkpoints where they have the luxury of showing their passports. The dream of life away from the uncertain future that exists in Burma forces many ethnic Burmese to illegally cross the border into Thailand. The Bangkok lure of the "big city" fed by stories of workers who have returned flush with money convinces jobless Burmese to leave their homes in search of a better life.

The reality is, of course, far from the dream. Many will never make it to Bangkok: arrest or the 7000-10,000฿ broker's fee frequently prevent passage to Thailand. Those that indebt themselves to the broker are often pushed into prostitution to repay the passage costs. And that's only if they get there. In March 2002, thirteen people, including five children, packed beneath roses, suffocated in a truck carrying them to factories outside Bangkok.

With such elaborate measures for people-smuggling, it may seem strange to catch a bus into Mae Sot and see people freely give themselves up at the immigration checkpoint. But this is actually their plan—having earned money in Thailand, they wish to return home. The police arrest them, and cover their room, board, and transportation costs during the wait for deportation. It's easier and cheaper than doing it yourself.

The Thai government continues to address the problem, but there is no easy solution short of a better standard of living for the oppressed ethnic

BORDER CROSSING: MOEI-MYAWADDY A 7km *songthaew* ride away from Mae Sot, this Thai/Myanmar border crossing is a relatively hassle-free way to extend your Thai visa. Show up at the bridge, present your passport to the Thai authorities, walk over the bridge, present your passport to be stamped and US$10 or 500฿, walk back over the bridge and receive your brand-new visa. If you intend to pay in US dollars, bring it with you to Mae Sot, as banks there don't have small bills and authorities are frequently out of change. If you want to see an unrealistic view of Burmese life, daytrips (return by 5pm), usually with a "guide," are permitted; keep in mind that your money will go to a government with an atrocious human rights record (see **Myanmar, To Go or Not To Go?**, p. 312).

Internet: 112/9 Prasatwithi Rd. (☎531 909), 2 doors west of Thai Airways. 20฿ per hr. Open daily 9am-8pm, but Internet access often until midnight.

Post Office: GPO (☎531 277), on Intharakhiri Rd. With back to the police station, head left; it's 150m down the road on the right. *Poste Restante.* Lenso phone. Open M-F 8:30am-4:30pm, Sa-Su 9am-noon. **Postal code:** 63110.

ACCOMMODATIONS

Bai Fern Guest House, 660/2 Intharakhiri Rd. (☎533 343). With your back to the police station, it's 400m to the right. Wonderfully friendly staff. All rooms with fans and shared hot-water bath. Simple singles 100฿; large but noisy upstairs doubles in teak house 150฿. ●

Ban Thai Guest House, 740 Intharakhiri Rd. (☎531 590), 25m farther west from No. 4 Guest House. Set well off the main road, this quiet and spacious new guest house has beautifully appointed rooms with comfy mattress, sitting table, and cushioned seating. All rooms with welcoming shared bath. Dorms 50฿; singles 250฿; doubles 350฿. ●

No. 4 Guest House, 736 Intharakhiri Rd. (☎/fax 544 976; www.geocities.com/no4guesthouse), 200m past Bai Fern, on the right. Bicycle rental for guests 30฿. 11pm curfew. No food service. Futons on hardwood floors with nets and fans in dorm 50฿; singles 80฿; doubles 100฿. ●

DK Hotel, 298/2 Intharakhiri Rd. (☎542 648), 50m east of post office. Multi-story hotel complete with marble floors. Large, impersonal rooms with Western toilet, hot water, and small balcony. Rooms with fan and telephone 250฿, with A/C and TV 450฿. ●

⬛⬛ FOOD AND NIGHTLIFE

Bai Fern Restaurant ❸ serves incredible *farang* fare. The "Bai Fern delight" pizza (ham, veggies, pineapple with bacon- and cheese-stuffed crust; 120) is delicious. Plenty of baked goods as well as fresh bread and espresso. (Open daily 7am-10pm.) The **Crocodile Tear,** on Intharakhiri Rd. before the guest houses, has live music daily from 9pm. The fabulous 2- to 3-man band will let you join their heart-wrenching Dylan covers if you feel inspired. (Singha 60฿. Open daily 5pm-1am.) **Pim Hut ❷,** on Tang Kim Chiang Rd. (near the police station), serves standard Thai and *farang* entrees. (Spring rolls 50฿; fried ice cream 30฿. Open daily 9am-10pm.)

UM PHANG ☎ 055

If Um Phang's vistas from the 1500m high peaks don't take your breath away, the speed of your *songthaew* on the hellish trip from Mae Sot will. Sitting on top is illegal and dangerous, but many travellers do to get a glimpse of the unbelievable view. Tiny Um Phang, whose name is derived from *Umpha,* the document Karen people show for identification, welcomed fewer than 2000 *farang* trekkers last year, compared with the tens of thousands stomping around Chiang Mai. This remote oasis is well known, however, to Thais, who escape on weekends and holidays to see what may be Thailand's most beautiful waterfall—Thee Lor Su.

⬛⬛ TRANSPORTATION AND PRACTICAL

INFORMATION. The main road from Mae Sot forks just before entering Um Phang. **Pravesphywan Rd.,** the left branch, leads into town. **Sukhomwattana Rd.,** to the right (downhill), runs parallel to Pravesphywan Rd. Note that there is not one street sign in Um Phang. The turn-off to the *songthaew* station lies halfway along Pravesphywan Rd., opposite the green-and-cream elementary education building. It's a further 200m uphill on the left. The road with the sign to Ban Pa La Tha at the backside of the wat off Sukhomwattana Rd. leads to the river and several guest houses. *Songthaew* drivers working on commission may deposit travelers on this road. The last *songthaew* to **Mae Sot** leaves between 2 and 3pm depending on demand; the best time to catch *songthaew* is in the morning or between noon and 1pm when trekkers return. Notify *songthaew* drivers at the station that you intend to travel, and they'll pick you up from your guest house (your guide can do this for you).

Burmese population. An amnesty was granted at the end of 2001 for illegal workers to register officially for work permits in Thailand. They were strongly encouraged and motivated to register, with planned crackdowns for 2002. Approximately 580,000 out of the estimated 1-2 million illegals registered. However, the 3250฿ initial registration fee, followed in 6 months with another 1250฿ fee was an obvious deterrent—that's 3-4 months' worth of illegal labor. Those who chose not to register cannot be recognized by the Thai government and thus have no access to health care. Illegal aliens cannot even demand the 136฿ Thai minimum daily wage. Generally, illegal aliens receive 20฿ per day, plus room and board. Only the word of honor of the factory owner holds him to paying the illegal workers. There have been cases in which workers have killed an owner who would not pay.

As a visitor, you will be faced with the vexing question of whether to support services that employ illegal labor. With an estimated 200 factories in Mae Sot capitalizing on illegal and child labor, most of the time you won't have a choice.

Services in town include: **bike rental** from Tu Ka Su Cottages, a 5min. walk farther out of town from Um Phang Hill Resort (☎561 295; 40฿ per day); the **post office** (☎561 127), on the left before the fork as you drive into town, which also has **international telephone** service and CATNET Internet (cash and collect calls only; open M-F 8:30am-noon and 1-4:30pm, Sa 9am-noon); **Internet,** 50m from the end of Pravesphywan Rd. (30฿ per hr., students 20฿ per hr.; open daily 8am-9pm); the **police station** (☎561 001), on Sukhomwattana Rd., 600m into town from the fork; and the **hospital** (☎561 270; **open 24hr.;** some English spoken), opposite and slightly farther uphill from the *songthaew* station. There are **no banks. Postal code:** 63170.

▮▮ ACCOMMODATIONS AND FOOD. There's been an explosion of guest houses here over the past few years. Beware of high-pressure tactics when you arrive, and make it clear that you only want accommodation and will decide on a trek later. More important than where you stay is who your guide will be. Meet him and ensure you like him as your safety and enjoyment will be in his hands. The reputable (amongst international travelers) are Coco and Johnny (best friends) who have 19 years experience between them. Both speak English, Thai, Burmese, and Karen. They are expert guides and have personal relationships with the hill tribes in the area. They work out of Um Phang House.

Um Phang Hill Resort ❶ offers some of the nicest and most expensive accommodations with bungalows by the river (100-500฿). There is also dorm accommodation (50฿). Would-be trekkers, however, may feel ambushed into taking their trekking service. Across the river, **Garden Huts ❸** (☎561 093) has basic bungalows by the river for 200฿ or with full amenities for 300฿. **Um Phang House ❶,** 50m toward the river from Sukhomwattana Rd., shuttles travelers for free between their office and lodgings 1.5km out of town. (☎561 021. Rooms 100฿.) The **Trekker Hill** company ❶ is one of the biggest operations in town, employing many of its own guides. Run by Mr. Jantawong (Mr. T), it has teak and stone shelters with futons, mosquito nets, and toilet paper. The turn-off to Trekker Hill lies down the road from Phudoi Guest House and Campsite, just before Boonchuey Camping on Pravesphywan Rd.; the accommodation is 100m up the hill on the left. (☎561 090. Laundry 5฿ per piece. Small food service available. Semi-private bungalow 100฿ per person.) **Phudoi Guest House and Campsite ❷** is farther into town from Trekker Hill, and caters primarily to Thai visitors. (☎561 049. Rooms with fan, screens, and hot water 150฿.)

Restaurants dot the main street beyond these last two accommodations. Only **Phudoi Restaurant** (not connected to the Phudoi Guest House, above), on the left of Pravesphywan Rd. 100m farther into town from the *songthaew* station turn-off, gets enough customers to keep the chef interested. A small **morning market ❶** sets up next door at the crack of dawn to cater to your breakfast needs. **Tom's Restaurant ❶,** opposite the entrance to the wat on Pravesphywan Rd., serves plates of curries and noodles from the window selection (20฿). For a fresher feed, **Um Phang House ❶** has a small restaurant in town that will whip up simple Thai dishes (chicken with cashew nuts 30฿). Facing the wat, follow the road down the right side to get to Um Phang House and the road headed to the river. Beware: during the low season restaurants close.

▨ TREKS. Two standard treks through well-worn routes operate in the region. Visits are possible year-round to the spectacular **Thee Lor Su,** which plummets over 400m through several deep waterholes. The best viewing is in November after the wet season when individual cascades span 300m across the cliff face. The second trek to **Thee Lor Lay** ("Waterfall over the Cliff") is only worth viewing May-Dec. when the water is flowing. The remoteness of this trek, coupled with the novelty of rafting past the waterfall, make it a popular choice. Treks to Thee Lor Su typically last 3 days/2 nights, while Thee Lor Lay takes 2 days/1 night. Most companies have fixed the price for both treks at 3000฿ per person with a minimum of two people, and include rafting and overnight stay in a hill-tribe village. Elephant riding to relieve weary legs will cost more.

It is possible to view Thee Lor Su without going on a trek in the dry season. The waterfall lies 47km from Um Phang. The first 25km takes 20min. over a paved road to the turn-off to Thee Lor Su Wildlife Sanctuary, just past the Karen village of Doei Lokei. The following 22km take 1½hr. over an extremely rough dirt road inaccessible in the wet season. From the car park, an informative 1.5km **nature trail** leads to the waterfall. You can camp here, but in the high season the grounds resemble a "tent city" as trekking groups clamor for space. (Camping 10฿ per person; tent rental 50฿.)

PHRAE ☎ 054

Most often unnoticed by tourists on their way to Nan or Chiang Rai, Phrae is a quiet, peaceful town, the history and life of which are centered around an old city. Its main tourist attractions—a mini Grand Canyon and Wat Phra Chaw Hae—that lie in the outskirts of town may be not as appealing as other treasures in Northern Thailand. For that exact reason, Phrae is a throwback to a more traditional Thai way of life, virtually untouched by tourism (although this situation may change in the near future as the government conducts feasibility studies to measure the potential of developing tourism in Phrae). Travelers who decide to stay for a night or two will enjoy strolling through the old city outlined by quiet lanes, anchored with wats, and adorned by beautiful teak wood architecture.

⊫ TRANSPORTATION

Flights: Phrae Airport lies 2km from the town center (100฿ taxi ride). As of August 2002, only **Air Andaman,** on the 1st fl. of Nakorn Phrae Tower, operates flights to **Bangkok** (1hr., 11:50am, 1950฿).

Bus: Since Phrae is a gateway town to Nan and Chiang Rai on the route going north, its road transportation is frequent and convenient. The **bus station,** in the northeast corner of Phrae, just east of Yantarkitkosol Rd., runs buses to: **Bangkok** (9hr.; every hr. 8am-5pm; with fan 117฿, A/C 319฿); Nan (2½hr.; every hr. 5am-7pm; with fan 47฿, A/C 85฿); **Chiang Mai** via **Lampang** (4½hr.; 13 per day; with fan 79฿, A/C 149฿); **Chiang Rai** (4hr.; every hr.; with fan 80฿, A/C 150฿); **Phitsanulok** (3hr.; every hr.; with fan 66฿, A/C 119฿).

Train: The nearest **train station** is Den Chai about 25km away and lies on the **Bangkok-Chiang Mai** line. A minibus leaves from a stop on Yantarkitkosol Rd., 400m south of the intersection with Charoen Muang Rd. (45min., leaves when full 9am-6pm, 30฿).

Local Transportation: Bicycles can be rented at Maeyom Palace Hotel (100฿ per day).

◀✷ 🛈 ORIENTATION AND PRACTICAL INFORMATION

Phrae is situated 550km north of Bangkok and 200km southeast of Chiang Mai. There are only two main roads in Phrae: **Yantarkitkosol Rd.** runs north-south, the northern end of which has a part that leads to the bus station; and a road that is split by Yantarkitkosol Rd. into a western piece, **Charoen Muang Rd.,** which reaches the old city, and an eastern part, **Choe Hae Rd.,** which leads to the **hospital** and the airport. The old city is no longer demarcated by walls or forts, but a big rotary identifies the town center. A nighttime food market brings life to **Rob Muang Rd.** in the old city, the first street as you enter the old city from the center of town.

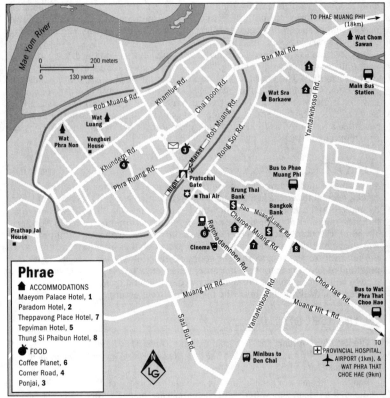

Phrae

♠ ACCOMMODATIONS
Maeyom Palace Hotel, **1**
Paradorn Hotel, **2**
Theppavong Place Hotel, **7**
Tepviman Hotel, **5**
Thung Si Phaibun Hotel, **8**

🍎 FOOD
Coffee Planet, **6**
Corner Road, **4**
Ponjai, **3**

There is no official tourist information office in Phrae. Nuj, one of the few English-speakers in Phrae, runs Tepviman Hotel and will be happy to assist both in-house guests and other travelers. The **Bangkok Bank,** on Charoen Muang Rd., exchanges currency and has an **ATM** (open M-F 8:30am-3:30pm). Several other banks, including **Krung Thai Bank** (just a block west of Bangkok Bank), with ATMs and currency exchange, line the two main roads, Charoen Muang and Yantarkitkosol Rd. A **post office** with telephone service sits next to the central rotary in the old city. (Open M-F 8:30am-4:30pm, Sa-Su 9am-noon.) There's an **international phone** right in front of the post office, which is operated by credit card. Phrae's **pharmacy** is on Rob Muang Rd., just near the entrance to the old city. The **police station** is at the intersection of Rong Sor and Ratchamnoen Rd. Right nearby is **Sathaviriya,** which offers **Internet** access. (15฿ per hr. Open daily 9am-midnight.)

♠ ACCOMMODATIONS

Accommodation options, particularly better-than-decent ones, in Phrae are limited—there may be more banks than hotels in town.

  Tepviman Hotel, 226-228 Charoen Muang Rd. (☎511 003), in the center of town, is the best bet for budget travelers. You won't find any luxuries. The manager, Nuj, speaks excellent English and will provide tons of info. Basic rooms with bath 80-160฿. ❶

Theppavong Place Hotel, 346/2 Charoen Muang Rd. (☎521 985), about 100m from the Yantarkitkosol-Charoen Muang Rd. intersection toward the old city; take a left down an alley. In the midst of a lush garden are 30 clean, cozy rooms with a common satellite TV and homemade food. Rooms with fan 250฿, with A/C 350฿. ❸

Thung Si Phaibun Hotel, 84 Yantarkitkosol Rd. (☎511 011), at the intersection with Charoen Muang Rd. The first budget hotel as you enter town from the bus station. Its rooms are similar to Tepviman's, but some have squat toilets. Rooms with fan 130-180฿. ❷

Maeyom Palace Hotel, 181/6 Yantarkitkosol Rd. (☎521 028), just outside the bus station. The best luxury hotel in Phrae, it has a pool and two restaurants. Bicycle rental 100฿ per day. All rooms with A/C, TV, and telephone. Singles 650฿; doubles 800฿. MC/V. ❺

Paradorn Hotel, 177 Yantarkitkosol Rd. (☎511 059), has over 100 middle-range rooms with its new building across the street. Go out of the bus station, follow Yantarkitkosol Rd. south for 200m. All rooms with TV, telephone, and hot shower. Breakfast included. Singles with fan 270฿, with A/C 350฿; doubles with fan 310฿/430฿. ❸

▐ FOOD

The **night market** ❶ on Rob Muang Rd. is the place locals flock to for dinner. To get a cheap dinner, be prepared to point and use gestures to communicate with street vendors.

▨ **Ponjai,** behind the post office in the old city, serves fun and excellent Kanom Jean-style food (pick your own noodles and soup), as well as good old Thai dishes. Ideal for a relaxing lunch in an open-air, wooden terrace atmosphere. Noodles 10฿; soup 10฿. Open daily 7am-3pm. ❶

Corner Road, a couple blocks west of the rotary in the old city, has a variety of Thai food on an English menu. Dishes range 30-50฿ in this cute and cozy restaurant. Open daily 10am-11pm. ❷

Coffee Planet, on Ratchamnoen Rd. 100m from Rong Sor Rd., offers lattes, espressos, cappuccinos, and the like. Suitable for a morning or a late afternoon cup (25฿). ❶

◉ SIGHTS

PHAE MUANG PHI. About 18km away from town on Hwy. 101, Phae Muang Phi presents strange rock formations and erosions, a miniature version of the Grand Canyon in the western United States. The mystery of its origin and location has made superstitious locals believe that phantoms haunt the area. A path runs through the park for a good 30min. walk, but it gets quite hot at midday. *(A songthaew leaves directly from or near Phae Muang Phi in front of the school on Yantarkitkosol Rd. Open daily 7am-5pm. 30฿.)*

WAT PHRA THAT CHAW HAE. Its 33m high gilded pagoda and Phra Jao Than Jai Buddha image have established this wat to be one of the most important pilgrimage sites in Northern Thailand. Renovations of the area were completed in 2000. *(A songthaew leaves from a stop in front of the provincial hospital roughly every hr. Open daily 7am-5pm. 20฿.)*

WAT LUANG AND WAT PHRA NON. These two wats, situated in the northwest blocks of the old city, are one of the in-town tourist attractions. **Wat Luang** is the oldest temple in Phrae, built in 829, the same year the city was established. Its construction aimed to enshrine the city Buddha image, which originally was covered in gold. A small museum with random antiques, Buddha images, and porcelain objects is next to the wat. **Wat Phra Non,** the building with the beautiful roof, is relatively newer at about 100 years old. It houses an impressive reclining Buddha.

VONGBURI HOUSE AND PRATHAP JAI HOUSE. These houses—the former located in the old city and the latter about 1km from the old city—represent what Phrae is famous for: teak architecture. Both the interior and the exterior of the building are ornately decorated with wood carvings. *(Open daily 8am-5pm. 20฿.)*

WAT CHOM SAWAN. This wat features a fantastic Burmese/Shan-style temple built about 100 years ago. On top of this structural beauty, two holy artifacts make the wat even more special: a 16-sheet ivory book with the teachings of Buddha written in Burmese and a bamboo basket covered in gold.

KAMPHAENG PHET ☎ 055

Just 77km south of Sukhothai, Kamphaeng Phet ("diamond city") attracts daytrippers wishing to complete the set of three World Heritage Sites in Northern Thailand, along with Sukhothai and Si Satchanalai National Parks. The history of this northern town dates back to the Sukhothai period in the 14th century and the Ayutthaya period of the 15th century, when it was a principal northern city strategically located to fight the kingdoms north in Lanna (Chiang Mai) and west in Burma (Myanmar). But its geographical location not only established the city as a military presence, but also as a commercial hub that connected trade from all directions, especially with the benefit of the Ping River running north-south. As a result of its status as a gateway town to Northern Thailand from Bangkok, Kamphaeng Phet continues to thrive. Its combination of religious World Heritage Sites, military past, and developed commercialism, as well as its proximity to three beautiful national parks only draw a trickle of *farang* compared to other popular northern towns, making Kamphaeng Phet all the more alluring.

▐ TRANSPORTATION

The **bus station** is 2km west of Kamphaeng Phet, across the wide bridge. As the halfway point between Chiang Mai and Bangkok, Kampaeng Phet is a transportation hub, and buses heading in both directions stop here as frequently as every hour during the day. To: **Bangkok** (6hr., A/C 212฿); **Chiang Mai** (5hr., A/C 220฿). Buses also run to **Phitsanulok** (43฿). **Songthaew** run to **Sukhothai** (35฿) from the bus station. Upon arrival from other towns, ask to be dropped off on the east side where all the accommodations, restaurants, and sights crowd. Most hotels provide free or cheap transport to the bus station.

▟ ▐ ORIENTATION AND PRACTICAL INFORMATION

Kamphaeng Phet is situated 338km from Bangkok and 337km from Chiang Mai. A large bridge—**Kamphaeng Phet Rd.**—unites the west bank of the **Ping River,** the side on which the bus station is located, and the east bank, where the historical parks, accommodations, and restaurants sit. At the foot of the eastern entrance of the bridge is a rotary that intersects Kamphaeng Phet Rd. and **Tesa Rd.,** which runs south from it into the busiest part of town. Tesa Rd., as well as **Ratchadamnoen Rd.,** which runs parallel to it, are one-way streets that serve as backbones to the whole town. To the north of Kamphaeng Phet Rd. lie the sights of interest: Wat Phra Kaew and Wat Phra That are 5min. from the rotary, and the Ancient Forest Temples Site is a couple of kilometers away.

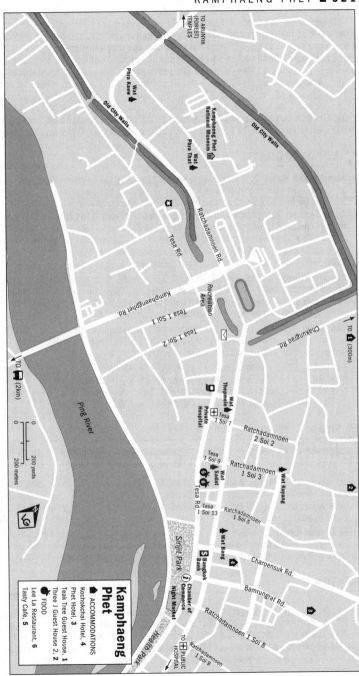

NORTHERN THAILAND

Kamphaeng Phet

➤ ACCOMMODATIONS
Kochokchai Hotel, **4**
Phet Hotel, **3**
Teak Tree Guest House, **1**
Three J Guest House 2, **2**

● FOOD
Lee La Restaurant, **6**
Tasty Cafe, **5**

TO ARUNYIK (FOREST) TEMPLES

Wat Phra Kaew

Old City Walls

Old City Walls

Kamphaeng Phet National Museum

Wat Phra That

Ratchadamnoen Rd.

Tesa Rd.

Kamphaengphet Rd.

Recreation Area

Tesa 1 Soi 1

Tesa 1 Soi 2

Chakungrao Rd.

TO (300m)

Ping River

TO (2km)

0   200 yards
0   200 meters

Wat Thepmolee

Tesa 1 Soi 7

Private Hospital

Tesa 1 Soi 9

Wat Sadat

Tesa Rd.

Tesa 1 Soi 13

Ratchadamnoen 2 Soi 2

Ratchadamnoen 1 Soi 3

Wat Kuyeng

Ratchadamnoen 1 Soi 5

Wat Bang

Bangkok Bank

Charoensuk Rd.

Sirijit Park

Night Market

Chamber of Commerce

Bamrungrat Rd.

Ratchadamnoen 1 Soi 8

Ratchadamnoen 1 Soi 6

TO PUBLIC HOSPITAL

Health Park

Although there is no official tourist office in Kamphaeng Phet, the Chamber of Commerce at the intersection of Tesa and Bamrungrat Rd. provides a free map and answers general questions. Both **ATMs** and **currency exchange** services can be found at **Bangkok Bank** on the southwest corner of Ratchadamnoen and Charoensuk Rd. (Open daily 8:30am-3:30pm.) The **police** are on Tesa Rd., 200m north of the rotary. (**Emergency:** ☎191. Bangkok **tourist police:** ☎1155.) A private **hospital** is on Tesa Rd., just north of Tesa 1 Soi 7, while a public hospital lies on Rachadamnoen Rd. a few hundred meters south of Charoensuk Rd. Also on Tesa Rd., but 200m south of the rotary, is a **post office.** (Open M-F 8:30am-4:30pm, Sa-Su 9am-noon.) There is an **Internet** cafe on Tesa Rd. north of Tesa 1 Soi 7 (15฿ per hr.).

ACCOMMODATIONS

▨ **Three J Guest House 2,** 79 Rachavithi Rd. (☎713 129). Go south on Ratchadamnoen Rd., take a left on Ratchadamnoen 1 Soi 3, go past a big temple on your left, and follow the road for 500m. Brand spanking new—they just opened in March 2002. Three J has 7 cozy wooden bungalows and 3 Flintstone-inspired stone and clay rooms (these 3 rooms scheduled to be finished in December 2002). Other services include: motorbike rental (200฿ per day), car rental (1000฿ per day), bike rental (30฿ per day), email, massage, restaurant, laundry, and free transport to the bus station. Rooms with fan 200฿, with bath 300฿, with bath and A/C 500฿. ❸

Teak Tree Guest House, Chakungrao Rd. Soi 1 (☎01 675 6471). Hang a left on Chakungrao Rd. about 1km from Ratchadamnoen Rd. It's a small yet comfortable guest house with only 3 rooms. Clean shared baths with hot water. Have a pleasant breakfast under the shady mango tree. Singles 150฿; doubles 230฿. ❷

Kochokchai Hotel (☎711 247), a block east of Ratchadamnoen Rd. Decent, though a bit run-down, middle-range hotel in the center of town. Basic rooms with telephone, TV, and private bath. Rooms with fan 290฿, with A/C 330฿. ❸

Phet Hotel, 189 Bumrungrat Rd. (☎712 810), a few hundred meters from Ratchadamnoen Rd. The best luxury hotel in town with a huge lounge area, swimming pool, pub, and restaurant. American breakfast included. Standard singles 550฿, deluxe singles 650฿; standard doubles 650฿, deluxe doubles 700฿. ❺

FOOD

The **night market** ❶ just south of the Chamber of Commerce on Tesa Rd. is a happening place with dozens of food stalls active around dinner time.

Tasty Cafe, between Tesa 9 Soi 1 and Tesa 13 Soi 1 on Tesa Rd. It has no English sign, instead look for the "Food, Ice Cream, Beverage" sign on the window. It may serve tasty dishes, but the portions tend to be small. Nicely air-conditioned. English-language menu available. Fried rice 25-35฿; lychee sundae 35฿. Open daily 11am-midnight. ❷

Lee La Restaurant, 125 Tesa Rd., 2 doors down from Tasty Cafe. Lee La is the place for a nice night out. Classy dark-wood interior, candelit atmosphere, and live music on certain nights. Dishes 50-120฿. Beer 60฿. Open daily 11am-midnight. ❸

SIGHTS

OLD CITY. The northern rectangular section of Kamphaeng Phet, about 1km by 400m, was once surrounded by a fort and a moat, some of which still remains visible. The main attractions of the Old City consist of **Wat Phra Kaew** and **Wat Phra That,** which are situated in a beautifully maintained park. Hundreds of years ago, Wat Phra Kaew was the biggest (and therefore the most important) temple, supposedly housing the Emerald Buddha, now in Bangkok, at one point. Much of the structure has been worn down over the years, but some of the remaining parts like the Buddha images, columns, and the bell-shaped *chedi* still stand impressively. The square faces, joined eyebrows, and almond-shaped eyes of the two sitting and one reclining Buddha images suggest that they are in the U-Thong style of the early Ayutthaya period. Wat Phra That, just southeast of Wat Phra Kaew, is another similarly preserved temple made of laterite and brick. *(Open daily 8am-4pm. 40฿ entrance fee gets you into both the Old City and Arunyik Temples.)*

KAMPHAENG PHET NATIONAL MUSEUM. This museum has an informative display explaining the significance of Buddha images. The museum also outlines the history of Kamphaeng Phet, even as far back as prehistory, and houses a 2.1m Siva bronze statue that is believed to be from the Hindu tradition. *(Next door to Wat Phra Kaew. Open W-Su 9am-noon and 1-5pm. 30฿.)*

ARUNYIK (FOREST) TEMPLES. This beautiful forested area only a couple hundred meters behind Wat Phra Kaew is home to more than a dozen temples built by Sukhothai-era monks. These temples were originally constructed in the relaxing environment of the woods to foster meditative practices for the monks, but today the area has become a peaceful, serene park suitable for a leisurely walk or bike ride. While surveying the area is in itself a worthwhile experience, two temples are of special interest. **Wat Phra Non,** the first big site on your left, was supported by colossal laterite pillars several meters high and a few feet thick, which still stand firmly today. A huge reclining Buddha figure used to lie in the center of the temple, but today only its absence can be felt.

A little north of Wat Phra Non is **Wa Phra Si Iriyabot** with its better-preserved four Buddha images. The square structure in the middle was designed to hold up a roof, which in turn protected the four niches each containing a different postured Buddha: walking, reclining, sitting, and standing. Today, the standing figure is in the best condition of the four. A few hundred meters down the road from the four niches, 68 stucco sculptures of elephants surround the lower base of the temple. The uppermost section of the temple has been completely destroyed, but climbing up there offers a nice view of the area. *(Open daily 8am-4pm. 40฿ entrance fee to Old City also gets you into the Arunyik Temples.)*

SOUTHERN THAILAND

SYMBOL:	❶	❷	❸	❹	❺
ACCOMM.	Under US$3 Under 120฿	US$3-4.50 120-180฿	US$4.50-9 180-360฿	US$9-14 360-560฿	Over US$14 Over 560฿
FOOD	Under US$0.75 Under 30฿	US$0.75-2 30-80฿	US$2-4 80-160฿	US$4-6 160-240฿	Over US$6 Over 240฿

One of the most famous international beach destinations, Southern Thailand is a full-blown vacation mecca. With some of the world's best diving sights, thousands of kilometers of white sand beach, rock climbing, a steady nightlife, and well-developed tourist infrastructure, it's not surprising that millions of tourists visit every year. This steady stream of tourist dollars means that nearly every island and cove is hospitable to visitors, diving and snorkeling tours can be arranged from almost anywhere into the bluest of waters, and English is an unofficial second language. These benefits, combined with the hospitality of the Thai people, cause many travelers who plan on staying a week to stay for months. While the tremendous development provides conveniences, comfort, and adventure, it has also begun to overwhelm both the environment and Thai culture. In mainland towns such as Prachuap Khiri Khan or Surat Thani, away from the beach, night markets and unjaded locals offer glimpses of Southern Thailand beyond the dive shops, *farang*, cyber cafes, and bar scenes. Farther south, mosques gradually replace wats as the ethnic mix turns from Thai to Malay, and the number of tourists dwindles. Those with fantasies of a deserted island won't be too disappointed. For every overcrowded Ko Samui or Phuket, there are islands (off Trang and Satun especially) largely untrodden by 20฿ flip-flops. Still, most travelers today enjoy the middle ground, balancing the extremes of the south, where you can sleep in a hotel one night and a hammock the next, or follow raucous partying with quiet, moonlit swimming. Southern Thailand caters to every taste.

CHUMPHON ☎ 077

For most travelers, Chumphon is a one-night layover en route to the tropical trinity of Ko Tao, Ko Phangan, and Ko Samui. It is also a gateway, both culturally and geographically, to the south. As a transit town, Chumphon holds its own, though it's certainly not a destination in itself. However, with quality accommodations and tourist services, Chumphon is a fine stop for refueling, regrouping, or simply relaxing. The 2km Thung Wua Laen beach makes for a perfectly good daytrip from town.

▛ TRANSPORTATION

Trains: Chumphon Railway Station (☎511 103), at the west end of Krumluang Chumphon Rd. Luggage storage 10฿ per day. To **Bangkok** (regular: 10hr., 7am, 80฿; rapid and express trains: 7-10hr., 1:35-10:30pm, 330-370฿) and **Surat Thani** (3hr., 10 per

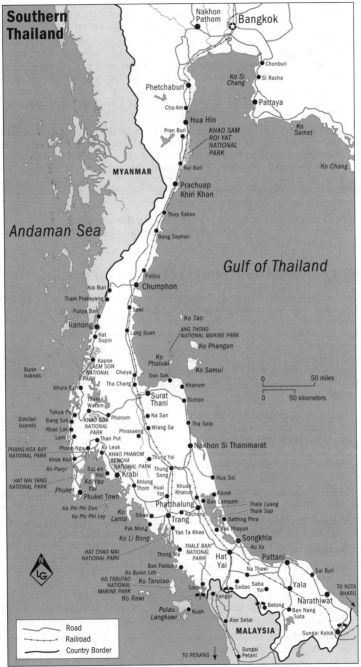

Southern Thailand

Bangkok
Nakhon Pathom
Chonburi
Si Racha
Ko Si Chang
Phetchaburi
Cha-Am
Pattaya
Hua Hin
Pran Buri
Ko Samet
KHAO SAM ROI YAT NATIONAL PARK
Kui Buri
Ko Chang
MYANMAR
Prachuap Khiri Khan
Andaman Sea
Thap Sakae
Bang Saphan
Gulf of Thailand
Pathiu
Kra Buri
Chumphon
Tham Prakayang
Sawi
Ko Tao
Punya Ban
Ranong
Hat Supin
Lang Suan
ANG THONG NATIONAL MARINE PARK
Ko Phangan
Kapoe
LAEM SON NATIONAL PARK
Chaiya
Ko Phaluai
Ko Samui
Surin Islands
Khura Buri
Don Sak
Tham Waram
Tha Chang
Khanom
Takua Pa
Surat Thani
Sichon
Similan Islands
Bang Sak
Phanom
Na San
KHAO SOK NATIONAL PARK
Tha Sala
Khao Lak
Phrasaeng
Wiang Sa
Lam Pi
Than Put
Phang-Nga
Ao Leuk
Nakhon Si Thammarat
PHANG-NGA BAY NATIONAL PARK
KHAO PHANOM BENCHA NATIONAL PARK
Thung Yai
Khok Kloi
Ko Panyi
Susan Hoi
Krabi
Thung Song
Hua Sai
HAT NAI YANG NATIONAL PARK
Ko Yao Yai
Khlong Thom
Huai Yot
Khuan Khanun
Phuket
Phuket Town
Ranot
Ko Phi Phi Don
Ko Lanta
Phatthalung
Ban Lampam
Thale Luang
Ko Phi Phi Ley
Sikao
Kachong
Thale Sap
Pak Mong
Trang
Yan Ta Khao
Sathing Phra
Ko Li Bong
Rak Phayun
HAT CHAO MAI NATIONAL PARK
THALE BAN NATIONAL PARK
Songkhla
Ko Yo
Thung Wa
Hat Yai
Pattani
Ban Pakbara
Na Thawi
Ko Bulon Leh
Sai Buri
KO TARUTAO NATIONAL MARINE PARK
Ko Tarutao
Satun
Sadao
Saba Yoi
Yala
Ko Rawi
Kangar
TO KOTA BHARU
Betong
Narathiwat
Pulau Langkawi
Kuah
Alor Setar
Ban Nang Sata
Sungai Kolok
MALAYSIA
TO PENANG
Sungai Petani

0   50 miles
0   50 kilometers

N

Road
Railroad
Country Border

day, rapid and express 243β). To **Bangkok** via **Hua Hin** (4hr.; regular 49β, rapid and express 293β) and **Phetchaburi** (5hr.; regular 62β, rapid and express 308β).

Buses: Tha Tapoa Rd. Terminal (☎502 725), opposite Tha Tapoa Hotel, runs A/C and non-A/C buses to **Bangkok** (8hr., every hr. 6am-2pm and 10pm, A/C 211β) and **Phuket** (6hr.; 4:30am, 4:30, 10pm; with A/C 196β). Most buses to Bangkok stop in **Hua Hin** (5hr., 126β) and **Phetchaburi** (6hr., 160β). Orange buses leave from across the street, next to Tha Tapao Hotel, for **Hat Yai** via **Surat Thani** (3hr.; every 30-60min. 5:30-11am, 4:30pm; 65β, with A/C 102β). For **Krabi,** take a bus to Chumphon Mueng Mai bus station and change there for a Krabi-bound bus.

Boats: 3 boats leave daily to **Ko Tao. Express boats** (2¼hr., 7:30am, 400β) and **speed-boats** (1¾hr., 7:30am, 400β) leave from piers at **Hat Sai Ree,** 10km outside town. **Midnight boats** ("slow boats") leave at midnight from a different pier (6hr., 200β). Tickets are readily available in Chumphon at tourist agencies and guest houses. Transportation to the pier is free for the faster, morning boats, or 50β for the midnight boats. To visit **Ko Maphraw (Coconut Island),** contact a tourist office 15 days in advance for official tours.

Rentals: Infinity Travel Service (see below) rents **motorcycles** (200β per day) and **cars** (1000β per day). The **Chumphon Cabana Resort** (☎504 442 or 501 633) rents **diving equipment.** Both open daily 9am-8pm.

■■ 🚹 ORIENTATION AND PRACTICAL INFORMATION

Chumphon lies 498km south of Bangkok. The main streets of the town roughly follow a grid system. **Krumluang Chumphon Rd.** runs east from the train station, forming the northern edge of town. The long **Poraminthra Manka Rd.** marks the southern limit; look here for the hospital, post office, and tourist office. The bus station and several travel agencies line **Tha Tapoa Rd.,** running north-south through the western part of the city. Parallel to Tha Tapoa Rd. and one block east is hotel- and eatery-studded **Sala Daeng Rd.** "V"-shaped **Pracha Uthit Rd.** straddles the city center; the day market, *songthaew* to Ko Tao-bound ferries, and Hat Thung Wua Laen are all on this road.

Tourist Office: Tourist Information (☎511 024, ext. 120), next to the post office. Friendly and English-speaking, but most questions can be answered at the more convenient tourist agencies. Commercial tourist agencies sell boat tickets and arrange tours on Tha Tapoa Rd., near the bus station. **Infinity Travel Services,** 68/2 Tha Tapoa Rd. (☎501 937), provides ferry tickets, advance booking for trains and buses, luggage storage, arrangements for scuba diving on Ko Tao, and showers. Open daily 7am-11pm.

Currency Exchange: Bangkok Bank, 111/1-2 Sala Daeng Rd. (☎511 446). **24hr. ATM.** Open M-F 8:30am-3:30pm. Pick up extra cash for later since Ko Tao has no ATMs.

Markets: Day market, on Pracha Uthit Rd. Open daily 5am-5pm. **Night market,** on Krumluang Rd. between Pracha Uthit and Poraminthra Manka Rd. Open daily 6-11pm.

Emergency: ☎191. **Tourist Police (Bangkok):** ☎1155.

Police: ☎511 505. On Sala Daeng Rd., about 50m north of the intersection with Krumluang Rd. Little English spoken. **Open 24hr.**

Medical Services: Virajsilp Hospital (☎503 238), at the south end of Tha Tapoa Rd., a 5min. walk from the bus station. Great service. No credit cards. **Open 24hr.** Also has a **pharmacy.**

Telephones: Several tourist offices and guest houses such as **Infinity Travel** (see above) have **international** phone service.

SPIT OR SWALLOW? Chumphon herbalists consider swallows' nests an all-natural Viagra. Although all nests work, the white ones are most powerful and sell for up to 70,000฿ per kilo. Harvesting nests, permitted for three months per year, is difficult, dangerous work, and people have shot each other over the scraps. After harvesting, the nests are torn into strips, rinsed in cold water for a day, made into a soup, and sold by the bowl. Why do the nests pack such a kick? Perhaps because swallows can stay up (in the air, that is) all day. Most believe, however, that it's a combination of the bird's saliva and the "love nest" itself that provides that special something for your special something.

Internet Access: The **Freshmart** convenience store, at the back of the Suriwong Chumphon Hotel, has a dozen computers in addition to aisles of junk food. 30฿ per hr. (minimum 10฿). Open daily 7am-2am. Internet also available at **Infinity Travel** (see above). 1฿ per min. (minimum 20฿).

Post Office: GPO, 192 Poraminthra Manka Rd. (☎511 041), southeast of town, about 100m past the tourist office. *Poste Restante.* Open M-F 8:30am-4:30pm, Sa 9am-noon. **Postal code:** 86000.

ACCOMMODATIONS

Chumphon has a surprisingly good selection of budget accommodations, and for the price of most guest houses elsewhere, you can upgrade to a hotel. Most hotels and guest houses cluster near the bus station, either on Tha Tapoa Rd., Sala Daeng Rd., or in the alleyways connecting the two.

Sri Chumphon Hotel, 127/22-24 Sala Daeng Rd. (☎570 536). Spacious and comfortable rooms come with luxuries like TVs, private baths, and hot water, all at unheard-of prices. Very clean overall. Absurdly firm pillows. Tea and coffee downstairs. Singles and doubles with fan 250฿, with A/C 350฿. The **Suriwong Chumphon Hotel** next door (☎511 203) has identical rooms at the same prices. ❸

Mayazes Resthouse, 111/35-36 Soi Bangkok Bank, Sala Daeng Rd. (☎504 452 or 01 607 1534; mayazes@hotmail.com). Turn left at the bus station onto Tha Tapoa Rd.; take the 1st right onto an alleyway. Conveniently close to the bus station. Rooms are tidy and cozy. Clean, common baths have hot water. Free water, tea, coffee, and fruit. Ring doorbell after hours. Singles 150-200฿, with A/C 280฿; doubles 250-350฿. ❷

New Chumphon Guest House (☎502 900), 600m from the railway station, off Krumluang Rd., on a side street to the left. One of the cheapest options in town and nicely removed from the hubbub, but still close to the night market. Clean and basic rooms in Thai-style houses with shared baths. Comfortable patio. Breakfast 60-80฿. Annex with more rooms about 100m away. Singles and doubles 120-160฿. ❷

FOOD

For Chumphon's finest victuals, head to the markets. The **main market** ❶ offers the renowned *gluay lep meu* (fingernail bananas) as well as the usual Thai staples. The **night market** ❶ offers phat thai (20฿) and fruits. Find more mouth-watering options at the many cheap, no-name, hole-in-the-wall **restaurants** ❷ on Sala Daeng Rd., some of which have English menus. A **bakery** ❶ on the corner of Sala Daeng and Pracha Uthit Rd. sells great pastries. (Open daily 6am-5pm.) Twenty meters down at the **Tiw Restaurant** ❶, brothers O and Noom serve tasty food late into the night. (Rice and curry dishes 20-40฿. Open daily noon-6am.)

ISLAND LUXURIES: NEED A BOOST? If paradise doesn't satisfy you, ambrosia will. Mouth-watering seafood and phenomenal frozen drinks (virgin or alcoholic) are ubiquitous—it's tough to have a bad meal in Southern Thailand. In fact, it's hard to have a bad day there, too.

Southern Thai food, largely influenced by the Muslim and Malaysian populations, is rich, spicy, hot, and heavy. Fresh tumeric, not the dried powder usually found in classic Thai food, is commonly used to flavor fish and other meats. Curries in the south are also different from those in the northern provinces. Muslim-influenced curries, particularly *massaman*, will seem more Indian than Thai because they are made from roasted, not fresh, herbs and roots.

Kao moek gkai: this chicken dish is served with rice—colored yellow from the tumeric—and flavored with roasted spices and sweet-sour chili sauce.

Roti: not the typical plain flatbread you'll find in other provinces; here, it is a southern specialty that indulges the sweet tooth. It's basically a dense, flaky pancake often stuffed with banana and covered in condensed milk.

Dtom kem gkati bplah doog: the name says it all. Catfish rounds simmered in tumeric and coconut sauce with lemon grass and red shallots.

Kluai buat chi: this dessert, made of bananas cooked in coconut milk and served either hot or cold, tastes like pudding.

Also look out for sun-dried whole squids and freshly caught softshell crabs stir-fried with coconut milk and jasmine leaves. Coconut milk dishes are about as common as the palm trees that produce them. For a snack, you can buy big green pods at a market and munch on its sadaw, a forest seed. Or try them in *pad ped sadtaw*, an intensely spicy shrimp and red curry dish.

◪ DAYTRIPS FROM CHUMPHON

For more extended excursions to explore the caves and other sights in the vicinity of Chumphon, it's best to book a tour with one of the tourist agencies such as Infinity Travel (see p. 326) or guest houses such as New Chumphon Guest House (see above). Two popular destinations are the **Rab Ro Caves** and the **Ka Po Waterfalls**, 30km from Chumphon. Prices vary depending on the number of people, but expect to pay at least 500฿.

HAT THUNG WUA LAEN

In Chumphon, bright yellow songthaew to Hat Thung Wua Laen (sometimes called Cabana Beach) leave from the market along Pracha-Uthit Rd. in front of 7-Eleven and stop at Chumphon Cabana Resort at the south end of the beach (one-way 25฿). You can also take Cabana Beach Resort's shuttle from its office on Tha Tapoa Rd. near the bus station directly to its resort on the beach. Free for Cabana's patrons. Departs around 1 and 6pm, returning at 12:30 and 5:30pm. To return to Chumphon, walk 1km to the main road and take a passing songthaew.

The area's premier beach, Hat Thung Wua Laen, is a 2km long beach that remains pristine, thanks to the lack of foreigners and rules forbidding further development.

Concrete bungalows and restaurants line Mu 8, the road running the length of the beach. At the northern end of the beach, **Seabeach Bungalows ❸**, 42 Mu 8, is covered in bougainvillea. (☎560 115. Doubles with bath 300฿; bungalows with bath and fan 400฿, with A/C 600฿; quads with bath and A/C 600฿.) **Clean Wave Resort ❸**, at the midpoint of the beach, has small, tidy, hotel-like rooms. (☎560 151. Rooms 300฿, with A/C 600฿, with hot water 700฿.) Their excellent **restaurant ❷**

serves Thai food for 60-100฿. **The View Restaurant ❷**, 13/2 Mu 8, has savory seafood plates (50-70฿) served by terminally upbeat young women, and new **bungalows ❹** across the road with amenities like TVs and phones. (☎560 214. Bungalows 400฿, with A/C 600-700฿, with A/C and hot water 800-900฿.)

Divers or those with a bit more time may want to visit two popular islands, **Ko Ngam Yai** and **Ko Ngam Noi**, off the shores of Hat Thung Wua Laen, which are prized for their swallows' nests, coral reefs, and soaring cliffs. They are seldom visited but well worth the trip. Chartering a boat is expensive; it's best to book with an organized tour. Ask at the Chumphon Cabana Resort or at their office in town.

KO TAO   ☎077

One of Southeast Asia's most renowned dive sites, tiny Ko Tao lures an international crowd of scuba neophytes with its cheap certification courses, as well as veterans who relish its clear gulf waters and outstanding reefs. For non-divers, the island offers superb and secluded, sun-baked coves, many of which can be reached only by boat or a long hike. With no airport or luxury hotels and few roads, Ko Tao is underdeveloped compared with its island siblings. Despite its popularity, it remains a laid-back destination for scuba enthusiasts and backpackers alike.

THE VIEW FROM ABOVE

The lowdown: Southeast Asia's biggest dive-training site.
Gateway cities: Chumphon, Ko Phangan, Surat Thani.
Nearby islands: Ko Nang Yuan.
Beaches: Hat Sai Ree, Ao Chalok Ban Kao, Ao Leuk, Ao Tanote, Ao Thian, Laem Taa Toh, Mae Hat.
Highlights: Fantastic snorkeling and scuba diving just about anywhere on the island.

▐ TRANSPORTATION

Boats: Ferries leave Ko Tao from **Mae Hat** to **Chumphon** (slow boat: 5hr., 10am, 200฿; faster boat: 2-3hr.; 10:30, 11am, 3pm; 300-400฿); **Ko Phangan** (slow boat: 3hr., 9:30am, 180฿; faster boat: 1-2hr.; 9:30, 10:30am, 2, 3:30pm; 250-350฿); **Ko Samui** (slow boat: 4hr., 9:30am, 280฿; faster boat: 2-3hr.; 9:30, 10:30am, 2, 3pm; 350-550฿); **Surat Thani** (6½hr.; 10:30am, 500฿; 8hr., 9pm, 400฿). For **Bangkok**, there are ferry/bus combos (9½hr., 11am, 550฿; 15hr., 3pm, 800฿).

Local Transportation: By far the best way to get around the island is to rent a **motorcycle**, available everywhere for 150฿ for 24hr. (passport deposit required). Otherwise, **pickup truck-taxis** go from Mae Hat to anywhere accessible by the island's few paved roads (30-60฿). Slightly expensive **longtail boats** may be hired to reach otherwise inaccessible bays.

◪ ▐ ORIENTATION AND PRACTICAL INFORMATION

Boats arrive at **Mae Hat** (Mother Beach), where most services and travel agencies are located. Facing the island from the pier, a paved road heads left over a small hill to **Hat Sai Ree**, Ko Tao's most popular beach and the heart of the backpacking and scuba scene (3min. by taxi or a 20min. walk). The paved road uphill from the pier eventually bends right, leading to **Ao Chalok Ban Kao**, the main southern beach, and, 500m farther, to **Ao Thian**. A pickup truck-taxi or motorbike ride from Mae Hat to either beach costs about 30-50฿.

Dirt roads branch off the island's only paved road to more beaches, including **Ao Leuk**; **Ao Tanote**, a fantastic snorkeling destination; **Ao Hin Wong**, on the east coast; and **Hat Sai Daeng**, in the island's southeastern corner. These sandy roads can be treacherous for inexperienced motorcycle drivers. With the exception of the

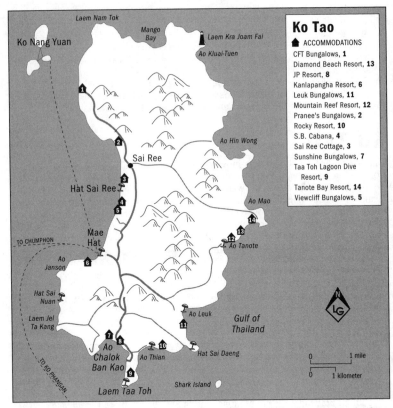

Ko Tao

⬤ ACCOMMODATIONS

CFT Bungalows, **1**
Diamond Beach Resort, **13**
JP Resort, **8**
Kanlapangha Resort, **6**
Leuk Bungalows, **11**
Mountain Reef Resort, **12**
Pranee's Bungalows, **2**
Rocky Resort, **10**
S.B. Cabana, **4**
Sai Ree Cottage, **3**
Sunshine Bungalows, **7**
Taa Toh Lagoon Dive Resort, **9**
Tanote Bay Resort, **14**
Viewcliff Bungalows, **5**

20min. walk from Mae Hat to Hat Sai Ree, the island is difficult to explore by foot during the day; it's almost impossible at night. Taxis go most places but can be hard to flag down in corners of the island. The free *Ko Tao Info* brochure is an excellent guide to the island.

Travel Agencies: Ko Tao has no official tourist office; information and tickets are instead provided by private agencies lining the the pier in Mae Hat and on the main road in Hat Sai Ree. All offer similar services and prices. The omnipotent **Mr. J** (☎ 456 066) claims to provide any type of service, from scoring visa extensions to arranging emergency loans. Find him at any of his three offices/knick-knack shops on the hill just north of the pier, a 5min. walk down the dirt path right off the pier in Mae Hat, before the Buddha View Dive Center in Hat Sai Ree. All open daily 8am-10pm.

Currency Exchange: Krung Thai Bank Booth, on the left off the pier in Mae Hat, has mainland exchange rates. While there are **no ATMs** on the island, an ATM card may be used to withdraw money here at no surcharge (passport required). Generally open daily 9:30am-noon and 1-4pm. Many bungalows and all dive shops accept credit cards.

Markets: Ko Tao lacks street culture. The only *talaat* (market) area on the island is the **Mae Hat pier area.** Buy fruit, postcards, clothes, and snorkel gear here.

Police: ☎ 456 260. A 10min. walk north of the pier on the hill heading toward Hat Sai Ree opposite the school. Some English spoken. **Open 24hr.**

Tourist Police (Bangkok): ☎1155.

Medical Services: There is **no hospital on the island. Nursing stations** are abundant around Ao Chalok, Hat Sai Ree, and Mae Hat, offering basic service for ear and eye irritations, wound dressing, and pregnancy/STD tests. Dive shops recommend the **Chintana Nursing Unit** at the top of the hill to the left, on the road to Hat Sai Ree. Open daily 8am-8pm.

Telephones: Nearly all travel agencies and bungalows offer **international** phone service. About 80฿ per min.

Internet Access: It's impossible to walk two steps without passing an Internet facility in Mae Hat or Hat Sai Ree. Prices don't vary—1฿ per min.

Post Office: There is one privately licensed post office (☎456 122) on Ko Tao, on the main road in Mae Hat. *Poste Restante* (very frequently utilized and reliable). Open daily 8:30am-midnight. **Postal Code:** 84280.

ACCOMMODATIONS AND FOOD

Dive agencies have bungalows that are rented almost exclusively to their clients, but there are plenty of budget places to stay if you're not here to scuba dive. Prices tend to be marginally cheaper elsewhere and the cheapest rooms run 250-300฿. In general, the closer you are to the beach, the more you'll pay. Prices listed reflect high season rates; in the low season, you may be able to knock off 100-150฿. The following accommodations and food options are listed by beach.

MAE HAT. Mae Hat is the food, fuel, and ferry center of Ko Tao. The beach here is unsuitable for swimming, so there's little reason to linger upon arrival; you'll find better beaches and better vibes elsewhere on the island. Should an early morning ferry keep you on Mae Hat, budget accommodations cluster just south of the pier. Just before the Sensi Resort, the dive-oriented **Kanlapangha Resort ❷** has friendly management and cheerfully painted bungalows, complete with swinging hammocks. (☎456 058. Bungalows 150฿ with shared shower, otherwise 250-1000฿, depending on size and proximity to beach.) More bungalows hide north of the pier on the hill between Mae Hat and Hat Sai Ree, a 15min. walk from the pier. Though hardly beautiful, the area is closer to the beaches and dive shops of Hat Sai Ree. Jack-of-all-trades Mr. J owns several sparkling new **bungalows ❸** just behind one of his stores across from the school. (Rooms with private baths and new fixtures 300-400฿.)

Even though Mae Hat may not be the best place to stay, it's one of the better places to eat. The best place to get western-style bread, baguettes, pastries, and sandwiches is the **Swiss Bakery ❷**, just a few steps up from the pier on the right. Try the delicious tuna sandwich for 60฿. (Open daily 6am-6:30pm.) Across the street, **La Matta ❸** not only has authentic Italian pizza and pasta (100-160฿), but authentic Italians making it too. They also serve up fresh salads (40-80฿) and tasty wine for 100฿ per glass. (Open daily noon-10pm.) **Yang's ❷**, next to the Swiss Bakery, has fried noodles with chicken (40฿) and breakfast omelets (30฿), among other cheap Thai eats. (Open daily 6am-10pm.)

HAT SAI REE. Backpackers and divers congregate in the bungalows along this 2km beach, which is Ko Tao's busiest bit of sand. Despite its popularity, the beach is laid-back; candle-lit dinners fade into easy-going nightlife, and by day even the palm trees are too relaxed to stand up straight. However, for better quality swimming, snorkeling, and sand, head elsewhere. To get to the relatively inexpensive **Pranee's Bungalows ❸**, head to the northern end of Hat Sai Ree, a 20min. walk on the sand from the start of the beach. With plywood walls and

IN RECENT NEWS

CRAZY MEDICINE

Thailand has discovered that curbing the demand of one drug does not mean curbing drug demand.

Opium use declined dramatically in Thailand in the mid-90s because social and economic programs reduced both supply and demand. The big push worked—but only for opium. Just at that moment heroin became the world's hip drug. It was abundant, too—produced right in the Golden Triangle. Heroin became a public health nightmare since sharing hypodermic needles sped the spread of HIV/AIDS.

But heroin was only a passing fancy compared to the meteoric rise in the use of methamphetamines. Locally known as "ya ba" (crazy medicine), speed is Thailand's latest drug scourge. The Asian financial crisis only exacerbated the problem. Ya ba became the intoxicant of choice among laborers during the boom years, but its use skyrocketed among disillusioned youth after the collapse.

Ya ba is the perfect narcotic to attract young, new drug users. Heroin prices are generally out of reach for new customers (price fluctuations influence the buying behavior of new users much more than addicts). Speed also fits the pop cultural trend: it's a club drug and a cheap substitute for ecstasy. It produces temporary hyperactivity, euphoria, confidence, alertness, and tremors. Users' heart rate, temperature, breathing and blood pressure increase.

Violent behavior is common, as are anxiety, panic, paranoia, drowsiness, and depression. Effects on the mind

private baths, the accommodations are fairly standard, but the service is friendly, and the clientele relaxed. (☎456 080. Bungalows 350-700฿.) A deservedly popular choice in the center of the beach is the **Sai Ree Cottage ❸,** just past Scuba Junction. Their charming wooden bungalows get points for cleanliness as does the social beachside restaurant, which boasts an extensive menu of inexpensive Thai dishes, milkshakes, and cocktails. (☎456 374 or 01 229 4952. Bungalows 250-600฿, depending on size and proximity to the beach.) Two others to try are the **S. B. Cabana Bungalows ❸** (250-400฿; ☎456 005), before Sai Ree Cottage, which has standard rooms, and, closer to Mae Hat, **Viewcliff Bungalows ❸** (singles 350฿; doubles 600฿).

For culinary offerings, Hat Sai Ree is second-best to Mae Hat. Most bungalows along the beach have good restaurants, ideal for quick between-dive meals and for evening pre-party drinks. The **Lotus Restaurant ❷,** past Sai Ree Cottage at the northern end of the beach, is one of the island's few non-bungalow restaurants specializing in Thai cuisine (dishes 60-100฿). The restaurant has a romantic, quiet ambience and also serves up affordable grilled food. (Open daily 6:30am-midnight.) In the evening, divers put away their gear, and sunbathers slather on aloe vera in preparation for nights passed drinking by the beach. **AC Bar,** at the south end of the beach, draws partiers from all over the island with its theme nights. Stretch out on the beach with your feet in the sand, sipping a cocktail, and enjoy the lazy island night at the **Dry Bar,** smack in the center of the beach. (Happy hour until 10pm. Red Bull & vodka 100฿. Open nightly until late.)

◪ **LAEM NAM TOK.** The paved road continues through Hat Sai Ree town to the northwestern tip of the island, the relatively developed Laem Nam Tok. There are several bungalows along this road, the most scenic of which is the ◪**CFT Bungalow ❶,** at the end of the road. Its huts are set among the large boulders that form the Nam Tok cape and offer spectacular views of Ko Nang Yuan and the sunset. Though there is no beach, it's worth making the trip out here in the late evening. (Bungalows with outdoor showers 100-300฿.) To get there, take a taxi from Mae Hat (40฿) or inquire about boat transport. At the time of update in 2002, CFT Bungalow was closed due to drought; confirm that it has reopened before visiting.

◪ **AO LEUK AND AO TANOTE.** The two major bays on the eastern side of Ko Tao are ideal for solitude seekers and offer fantastic **snorkeling.** They can be accessed by a paved road branching off Ko Tao's main road just south of Mae Hat. It turns into a dirt road and is only recommended for experienced motorbikers because of its steep hills and sandy ditches. **Taxis** to both bays cost 50฿ from Mae Hat. The tiny Ao Leuk has a rocky, less-than-spectacular beach. The only accommodations in the bay are at **Leuk Bungalows ❸.** Scattered about the sprawling grounds are airy, wooden bungalows with porches. (Rooms 250-350฿. Restaurant open daily 7am-10pm.)

About 2km farther north from Ao Leuk along a windy dirt road is **Ao Tanote,** which is more populated and has a better beach than its smaller neighbor. Long-term vacationers recommend meals at **Mountain Reef,** a popular spot in the middle of the bay. On the north end of the beach, there's the slightly upscale **Tanote Bay Dive Resort ❹** with bungalows dotting the hill overlooking the bay. Bungalow No. 29 on the very top of the headland has smashing views of the sea. (☎01 970 4703. Basic bungalows 400฿, with shower and fan 500฿, on the beach 600฿.) **Diamond Beach Resort ❹,** nearby, has cheaper rooms. (☎01 958 3983. Bungalows 400-600฿.)

⛵ AO CHALOK BAN KAO. Chalok Ban Kao Bay is carved out of the island's south end, 3km from Mae Hat (45min. by foot, 50฿ taxi ride). Unfortunately, a dense concentration of bungalows, dive shops, Internet cafes, and restaurants overwhelm the beach, meaning the bay is more convenient than scenic. Solution: head to gorgeous Ao Thian, a 10min. walk away (see below). Most bungalows are affiliated with dive shops, but non-divers seek happy refuge in the new **⛵JP Resort ❸,** smack in the center of the beach. Its cliffside bungalows are squeaky clean with nice views of the bay and private baths. Internet (2฿ per min.) and a relaxed restaurant round out this newcomer. (☎456 099. 300-400฿.) **Sunshine Bungalows ❸** is also conveniently located but features less glamorous plywood bungalows with private baths (250฿). Behind the bungalows toward the island's main road is the **Sunshine Mini Mart,** a well-stocked shop selling anything from mosquito repellent and beach reads to liquor and clothes. (Open daily 8am-11pm.) The mellow, beachside **Reggae Bar,** at the left end of the beach when facing the water, serves drinks for 120-150฿. (Open daily 6:30pm-2am.)

⛵ AO THIAN. An uphill walk south from Ao Chalok leads to a fork in the dirt road. The left path leads downhill to the small but stunning Thian Bay. The bay has an outstanding, white-sand beach (perhaps the island's best), ideal for both swimming and snorkeling (equipment rental including fins 100฿, avail-

may include moodiness and lack of interest in friends, sex, and food. Continued use can cause personality changes, chronic paranoia, increased blood pressure and brain damage.

The Thai Health Ministry estimates that 2.4 million of Thailand's 62 million people use the drug. In 2001, a report by the Thai Narcotics Control Board said that "Never before has any narcotic reached out to all levels of Thai society like methamphetamine does." Most users are ages 15-24, but documented addicts are as young as 5 and as old as 68.

A *ya ba* tab, which can be smoked, injected, or swallowed, can cost as little as a dollar a pill. Tabs have even become a form of currency—Bangkok taxi drivers short on baht have been known to return *ya ba* instead.

And, meth is a supply-sider's dream: there's no fickle crop to deal with; *ya ba* labs can be quickly and easily dismantled; it is cheaply made from available ingredients. It only requires over-the-counter pseudoephedrine (in large supply in India and Indonesia), lithium from batteries, fertilizer, and a few other chemicals. Runners can carry as many as 200,000 tabs in a backpack across the border from Myanmar. An estimated 700 million tablets—more than 10 per person in Thailand—entered Thailand in 2001, mostly crossing the 1300-mile border with Myanmar.

Officials believe *ya ba* use is plateauing. The Thai government is in the midst of a Southeast Asia-wide crackdown on the drug.

Derek Glanz is a freelance journalist and has written and edited extensively for Let's Go.

able on the beach). In addition, small bushes create sanctuaries of shade during the afternoon heat. The only accommodation is ◪**Rocky Resort ❸** on the bay's east end, with simple bungalows, some of which include balconies right over the water. Rocky also doubles as the beach's only restaurant with decent, relatively inexpensive fare. (Bungalows 300-500฿.)

◪ **LAEM TAA TOH.** This lovely cape juts into the gulf, separating Ao Chalok from Ao Thian. To get here, follow the dirt road from Ao Chalok, taking the right path leading uphill at the fork. Besides spectacular views, the cape is home to the **Taa Toh Lagoon Dive Resort ❸,** on Taa Toh Beach halfway around the cape, which has simple bungalows among the weather-beaten boulders rimming the sand. Many guests are divers-in-training at the resort's **scuba school.** (☎377 792; www.taatohdivers.com. Bungalows 300-500฿.) On the way up, stop at the romantic and atmospheric ◪**New Heaven Restaurant ❸,** which has a delicious menu and near-celestial views of Ao Thian. (Excellent Thai dishes 60-120฿; seafood 200฿; drinks 100-120฿. Open daily 6:30pm-midnight.)

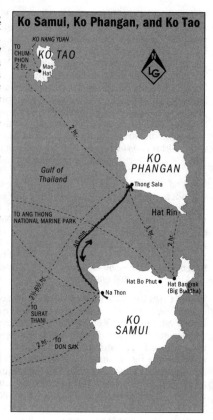
Ko Samui, Ko Phangan, and Ko Tao

ACTIVITIES

Scuba diving is popular year-round in Ko Tao, although late September through December often brings heavy rains and choppy waters. The island also has a unique tide; September to May is high-tide season and better for snorkeling, while May to September is low-tide season and better for basking on the beach. Ko Tao has over 20 dive sites. **Chumphon Pinnacle,** where a granite tower rises 14m above the surface, is a favorite for deep dives. **Southwest Pinnacle** and **Shark Island** are known for gorgeous coral and leopard sharks. **Green Rock** and **Sail Rock** on the way to Ko Phangan are famous for rock "swim-throughs." Closer to Ko Tao, **Hin Wong Pinnacle** and **Ko Nang Yuan** (see **Daytrips from Ko Tao,** below) have coral and fish in shallow waters suitable for snorkeling.

Scuba prices are standardized, so friendliness and professionalism, not price, are the key elements for a good dive shop. Four types of classes are available. Beginners can choose from the four-day open-water certification course (7800฿) or the supervised one-day "discover scuba" dives (1600฿, with the option of additional dives for 800฿). Certified divers can hone their skills with the two-day advanced open-water course (6600฿) or tag along with any dive class on a one-day "fun dive" (one dive 800฿, 700฿ each for 2-5 dives, 600฿ each for 6-9 dives, 500฿ each for 10 or more dives). Bring your own equipment for a 15% discount. Prices include accommodations in affiliated bungalows for the duration of the course. If you choose to stay on your own in non-affiliated lodging, however, prices drop by only 150฿, which means you'll almost certainly lose money during the high season. Snorkelers can also take advantage of the dive scene by tagging along on shallower dives for around 50฿.

There are plenty of dive shops from which to choose. They all have PADI certification, which requires that there be no more than eight people per instructor. The following is an abbreviated list of dive shop operations. The Internet can be a good way to familiarize yourself with the various options, but be sure to talk to the staff and patrons about teaching and equipment before committing. The larger shops have representative offices on Mae Hat.

Asia Divers (☎456 055; www.asiadivers-kohtao.com).

Ban's Diving Resort & Sunshine Divers (☎456 061; www.amazingkohtao.com).

Big Blue Diving Center (☎377 750; www.bigbluediving.com).

Buddha View Dive Resort (☎456 074 or 01 229 4693; www.buddhaview-diving.com).

Scuba Junction (456 164; www.scuba-junction.com).

Taa Toh Lagoon Dive Resort (☎456 192; www.taatohdivers.com).

⚑ DAYTRIP FROM KO TAO: KO NANG YUAN

Ferries depart from Mae Hat catamaran pier (right next to the boat/ferry pier) daily at 10am, 3, and 5pm; return at 8:30am, 1, and 4pm (40฿ round-trip).

About 2km off Ko Tao's northwest coast, lovely Ko Nang Yuan is actually three separate islets connected by a three-pronged stretch of white sand. The beach not only makes a good photo op, but its **snorkeling** is among Ko Tao's best. The steep climb up one of the islets to the **viewpoint** is well worth it. The island is best as a daytrip from Ko Tao, as its only accommodation, **Koh Nangyuan Dive Resort ❺**, is prohibitively expensive. (☎01 299 5212. Rooms 1500-3500฿.) The resort's restaurant also has steep prices (dishes 150-200฿).

KO PHANGAN   ☎077

While Ko Tao draws divers and Ko Samui caters to fat wallets, Ko Phangan remains a backpacker paradise, the island of choice for budget travelers in Southern Thailand. Ko Phangan's beaches range from unspoiled, laid-back beauties like Bottle Beach to the successfully developed, self-contained backpacker universe of Hat Rin Nok. With pirated films playing daily in restaurants and unbeatable drink specials at beachside bars, it's hard not to lose track of time on Ko Phangan, and it's even harder to leave.

THE VIEW FROM ABOVE

The lowdown: Sun-soaked beaches by day, drunken tourist-drenched beaches by night.
Gateway cities: Ko Tao/Chumphon, Ko Samui/Surat Thani.
Nearby islands: Ko Samui, Ko Tao.
Beaches: Hat Khuat (Bottle Beach), Hat Rin Nai, Hat Rin Nok, Thong Sala, Thong Nai Paan Yai, Thong Nai Paan Noi.
Highlights: Hat Rin Nok's wild full moon parties, soothing Bottle Beach, and Than Sadet Historical Park's refreshing waterfalls.

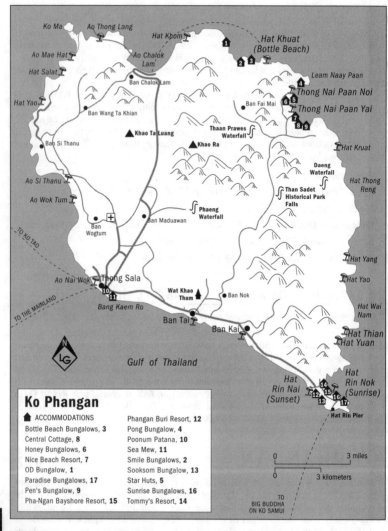

Ko Phangan

🏠 ACCOMMODATIONS

Bottle Beach Bungalows, **3**
Central Cottage, **8**
Honey Bungalows, **6**
Nice Beach Resort, **7**
OD Bungalow, **1**
Paradise Bungalows, **17**
Pen's Bungalow, **9**
Pha-Ngan Bayshore Resort, **15**

Phangan Buri Resort, **12**
Pong Bungalow, **4**
Poonum Patana, **10**
Sea Mew, **11**
Smile Bungalows, **2**
Sooksom Bungalow, **13**
Star Huts, **5**
Sunrise Bungalows, **16**
Tommy's Resort, **14**

SOUTHERN THAILAND

🚢 TRANSPORTATION

Ferries: To get to Ko Phangan, you must go through either Ko Tao/Chumphon or Ko Samui/Surat Thani. From Ko Tao, ferries leave from Mae Hat's southern pier (5 per day 9:30am-2:30pm, 180-350฿). From Ko Samui, boats leave from Big Buddha Pier for **Hat Rin** (100฿) and from Na Thon for **Thong Sala** (9, 11am, 5:30pm; 95฿). You can also head to Ko Phangan directly from Surat Thani via the **Donsak Car Port** (10am, 1, 6pm) or the **town pier** (7:30am, 205฿; 11pm, 400฿). Ferries leaving Ko Phangan depart from Hat Rin and Thong Sala. From the pier at Hat Rin Nai, boats go to: **Ko Samui's Big Buddha Beach** (2hr., 9:30, 11:30am, 2:30pm; 100฿); **Hat Tian** (12:40pm, 50฿); **Than Sadet**

(12:40pm, 80฿); **Thong Nai Paan** (12:40pm, 100฿). From the main pier at Thong Sala, boats go to: **Chumphon** (12:30pm, 650฿); **Ko Samui's Big Buddha Beach** (1hr., noon, 115฿); **Ko Samui's Na Thon** (7am, 12:30, 4pm; 115฿; 10:30am speedboat, 200฿); **Ko Tao** (2hr.; 10, 11:30am, 12:30pm; 180-250฿); **Surat Thani** (night boat 7hr., 10pm, 400฿; express boats via Ko Samui 4hr.; 7, 11am, 12:30, 1pm; 205฿).

Local Transportation: One drawback of Ko Phangan is the cost of getting around the island. **Songthaew** (and their eager drivers) meet ferries at the pier in Thong Sala and run to the island's major beaches. To: **Ban Kai** (20-30฿); **Ban Tai** (20฿); **Chalok Lam** (50฿); **Hat Rin** (50฿); **Hat Yow** (50฿); **Thong Nai Paan** (100฿). In Hat Rin Nai, *songthaew* wait across from the police booth and go to **Thong Sala** (minimum 3 passengers, 50฿). In addition, longtail boats make trips between the major beaches.

Rentals: Motorcycles are available for rent around the pier and on the main street of Thong Sala as well as from several guest houses in Hat Rin Nai (150฿ per day with passport deposit). Though paved, the last 5km of the road to Hat Rin tremendous hills, and enough traffic to result in **serious accidents** each year. Before heading to any remote destination, inquire about the road conditions.

■★ ▐▌ ORIENTATION AND PRACTICAL INFORMATION

Ko Phangan is 100km northeast of Surat Thani and 12km north of Samui. While a few boats depart and dock at the Hat Rin pier, most arrive at the island's unsightly main city and port of call, **Thong Sala,** where many conveniences are located, including ATMs and travel agencies. From the Thong Sala pier, three paved roads cover most of the island; one runs 10km southeast along the coast to the party beaches of **Hat Rin,** which is split into **Hat Rin Nai** to the west and **Hat Rin Nok** to the east. Midway along this paved road, a bumpy dirt road (only for experienced motorbikers) heads to the northeastern beaches of **Thong Nai Paan Yai** and **Thong Nai Paan Noi,** and other dirt trails stretch to more remote coves. A second paved road from Thong Sala (safe for motorbikes) cuts 10km northward through the heart of the island to **Chalok Lam Bay,** a departure point for boats heading to lovely **Hat Khuat.** The third road (alternately paved and dirt) runs a scenic course west along the coast to the less developed bays of **Hat Ao Mae Hat**. More so than other islands, Ko Phangan rewards those who explore the far corners of the island.

Travel Agencies: The serene and helpful **Mr. Kim** (☎377 274), usually hanging around a few meters from the Thong Sala pier on the right, has encyclopedic knowledge of the island. He also books tickets. **Songserm Travel Center** (☎377 096), on the left side of the main road in Thong Sala. Boat and A/C bus packages to: **Bangkok** (450฿); **Krabi** (350฿); **Phuket** (350฿). Open daily 8:30am-5pm.

Currency Exchange: Several exchange booths line the street leading from the main pier in Thong Sala. **Siam Commercial Bank,** 30m from the Thong Sala pier on the left, has a **24hr. ATM.** Bank open M-F 8:30am-3:30pm. In Hat Rin, your best option is the **Siam City Bank** branch on a side street near the middle of Haadrin Rd. Exchange rates here are slightly less favorable than in Thong Sala. Open daily 9:30am-4:30pm.

English-Language Bookstore: Carabou, next to the Siam Commercial Bank, has beach reads and refreshing A/C. Open daily 8:30am-8:30pm.

Markets: Bovy Supermarket (☎377 231), in Thong Sala about 20m from the end of the pier on the right. An eclectic mix of junk food and knick-knacks. Open daily 8:30am-midnight. For fresh fruit and cheap rubber sandals, try the **morning market** farther down. Open daily until evening.

Emergency: ☎191. **Tourist Police (Bangkok):** ☎1155.

Police: Main office (☎377 114), 2km north of Thong Sala on the road to Ao Chalak Lam. English spoken. **Open 24hr.** A small, phone-less **police booth** operates at Hat Rin off Haadrin Rd., opposite the school. Some English spoken. Both **open 24hr.** ⁻ ⁻

Medical Services: Koh Pha-Ngan Hospital (☎377 034), 3km north of Thong Sala. English spoken. No credit cards. **Open 24hr.** In Hat Rin, private **nursing stations** provide basic medical services. For serious medical attention, take a boat to Ko Samui.

Internet Access: There are more Internet terminals per backpacker here than anywhere in the world. True fact. The cheapest access providers dot the road stemming from Thong Sala's main pier (1฿ per min). More expensive providers in Hat Rin (2฿ per min.).

Post Office: GPO (☎377 118), in Thong Sala. From the end of the pier, walk down the main road, take the first right, and follow the road until it ends and turn left; the post office is on the right. *Poste Restante.* In Hat Rin, a private licensed **branch** (☎375 204), on the southern road connecting Hat Rin Nok and Hat Rin Nai, functions as a tourist and telephone office. Open daily 9am-midnight. **Postal code:** 84280.

ACCOMMODATIONS AND FOOD

Most travelers to Ko Phangan head immediately to the southern coast and the beaches of Hat Rin. Those looking for more attractive, secluded beaches should head north to lovely Hat Khuat or mellow Thong Nai Paan Noi. Because transportation is costly and lengthy, chances are your accommodations will define your stay; consider splitting time between Hat Rin and one of the more relaxed bays. Accommodation prices and availability rise and fall with lunar tides. The island fills to maximum capacity in the days surrounding the full moon (see **Sex, Drugs and Lunar Cycles,** p. 339). If you plan to be there for the party, arrive a few days early to score accommodations or be prepared to sleep on the beach. Lunar fluctuations aside, prices jump about 100-200฿ during high season, especially on the Hat Rin beaches. The following accommodations and food options are listed by beach.

THONG SALA. A concrete frying pan, Thong Sala is a lifeline for the island, boasting the cheapest email, most tourist services, and an aggressive barrage of *songthaew* drivers waiting at the pier. Staying here usually denotes an early ferry departure, an inability to find accommodation elsewhere, or a serious inertia problem, but some comfortable rooms lie close to the pier. **Sea Mew ❸,** near the waterfront and to the right heading from the pier, has a great staff. Enjoy the quirky restaurant and the cable TV. Mattresses may be back-straightening, but rooms are clean. (Singles with fan 200-250฿.) Across from the post office, as a last resort, the drab, multi-storied **Poonum Patana ❸** has large, passably clean rooms and tiled private baths. (☎377 089. Singles and doubles 200฿, with A/C 350฿.) The **Corner Kitchen ❷** is on the corner opposite Poonum Patana and serves extensive Thai, European, and Chinese cuisine (35-60฿). Thong Sala's main drag has several decent Western-themed eateries, though all are rather pricey.

HAT RIN NOK (EAST). Introducing Backpacker Land where your every need or fancy can be fulfilled, where the average age is 21, and the average personal savings are approaching zero. Imagine a place where you can watch the latest Hollywood hit as you check email, all the while having your back massaged to pounding techno music and chatting with your new Aussie friend with a mouthful of a 40฿ chicken sandwich. Welcome to Hat Rin Nok. But all joking aside, the place is just serious fun with a beach to boot.

Songthaew from Thong Sala drop off passengers on the main road, just above Hat Rin Nai. From there, it's a 5min. walk to the beach or a 10min. walk to Hat Rin Nok's quieter twin, Hat Rin Nai. The two beaches are connected by several dusty

SEX, DRUGS, AND LUNAR CYCLES Every month on the full moon, backpackers and 20-something tourists from all over Thailand drop what they're doing and hop on the next boat to Ko Phangan to partake in the island's legendary lunar festivities. Originally a modest affair (first hosted by Paradise Bungalows in 1989), the party has mushroomed into a massive all-night beach rave, complete with strobe lights, imported Euro-DJs, and illicit substances galore. More people may mean more fun, but it also means more headaches. Some tips to survive the full moon madness:

Safety: Full moon night is a big night for theft. Keep all your valuables securely locked or in a money belt on your person. Don't leave any important items unlocked in your bungalow or in obvious hiding places such as under your pillow or mattress.

Accommodations: If you want to have a bed in Ko Phangan the night of the full moon, arrive a few days early to secure a spot or even earlier if you want to stay on Hat Rin. Otherwise, stay on either Ko Tao or Ko Samui and take advantage of the special "Full Moon Party boats" that make round-trips to Phangan on the night of the party.

Drugs: Despite stiff penalties imposed by the Thai government, *farang* still flock to Phangan to partake in its thriving drug culture, which crescendos with the full moon. Before taking that joint or tab, be aware that Thai police, both in uniform and undercover, are out in extra numbers on full moon night and won't look kindly on your extravagance. Also, an increasing number of travelers have been reportedly drugged or tranquilized and then robbed. *Let's Go* urges you to be careful.

roads, all of which intersect Haadrin Rd., the area's main artery, which runs parallel to the beach. In this area, you can find most basic services in addition to shops peddling rave gear and hippie paraphernalia.

Accommodations-wise, Hat Rin Nok brims with over-priced and flimsily constructed bungalows along its beachfront road. It's worthwhile to shop around. Your best bet is to start at the northern end of this road where, beyond a gate, is **Pha-Ngan Bayshore Resort ❸**, a well-maintained set of bungalows reaching from the beach to the *songthaew* drop-off. At night, it's quieter than other resorts. (Basic bungalows with fan and shared bath 200฿, with A/C and private bath 500฿.) Toward the center of the beach, things get louder and more crowded, especially at night. **Sunrise Bungalows ❸**, in the middle of the beach, has breezy bamboo cottages with large beds. (☎375 145. Bungalows 250฿, with bath 300฿.) At the opposite end from Pha-Ngan Bayshore is **Paradise Bungalows ❸**, the proud host of the first Full Moon Party in 1989. While the bungalows have balconies and are a bit removed from all the action, they are basic. (☎375 245. Bungalows 200-250฿.) At the beach's northern end (just beyond Pha-Ngan Bayshore), **Tommy's Resort ❷** is an old favorite with some of the cheapest beds on the island, but it's starting to show its age. At night, brace yourself for pulsing techno from the beachside bar. (☎01 926 0515. Bungalows 150฿, with bath 250-600฿, depending on proximity to beach.)

Restaurants, representing at least half a dozen nationalities, line Haadrin Rd. (which connects the southern ends of both Hat Rin beaches) and the small dirt alleys stemming from it. **Mr. Chicken ❷** is something of a landmark and local meeting place. It has chicken sandwiches (40฿) that will make you forget about *phat thai* for a while. Around the corner from Chicken Corner is **Niras Beach Kitchen and Bakery ❷**, which caters to health spa types and sweet tooths. (Excellent chocolate croissant 40฿. Hummus sandwich on homemade bread 50฿. Kitchen open daily 8am-10pm. Bakery open 24hr.) Across the street is **Sao's Kitchen ❷**, which dishes out decent tofu-based vegetarian food to reclining customers under low lights. (☎375 166. Vegetable curries 40฿. Pumpkin soup with coconut milk 40฿. Open daily 8:30am-10:30pm.)

◪ **HAT RIN NAI (WEST).** Though a mere 100m west, Hat Rin Nai is far from its late-night partying neighbor, Hat Rin Nok. The strip of muddy sand at Hat Nai is hardly attractive, but the beach does have its perks—a good selection of bungalows, pretty sunsets, and a location that's close enough to take advantage of Hat Rin Nok's nightlife but distant enough to provide a quiet retreat.

There are a number of basic accommodations, restaurants, and ticket agencies along the ragged main drag heading toward the pier. Beachside budget bungalows lie at the northern end of the beach, a 15min. walk from the Hat Rin Pier and past a rocky outcropping. **Sooksom Bungalow ❷**, just past the rocky outcropping, has simple, wooden huts and a vegetarian-friendly restaurant. (☎375 230. Bungalows 150฿, with bath 300-350฿.) Next door, **Phangan Buri Resort ❸** has concrete bungalows and tiled patios that are more expensive, but cleaner and prettier. (☎375 330. Bungalows 300-800฿.)

◪ **HAT KHUAT (BOTTLE BEACH).** Set against lush hills, this gorgeous and quiet ◪beach lulls those who intend to stay for a few days into spending weeks or months instead. To get there, take a *songthaew* from Thong Sala to **Ao Chalok Lam Bay**, 10km away (20min., 100฿). The bay is the departure point for boats to **Hat Khuat** (9:30am, 3, 6pm; return 8am, 1, 5pm; 50฿.) It's also possible to walk the 4km from Ao Chalok Lam to Bottle Beach.

Once on Bottle Beach, your options are limited to four inexpensive bungalow operations: **Bottle Beach Bungalows 1, 2,** and **3,** and **Smile Bungalows,** all of which are owned by the same family. (You can reach all of them at ☎01 229 4762.) Bottle Beach 1 ❶, in the middle of the beach, is the cheapest, with bath-less bungalows hidden from the beach starting at 100฿. Bottle Beach 3 and **Smile Bungalows ❸** at the far end of the beach have bungalows with private baths and hammocks starting at 250฿. The bungalows at the former sit on the beach but fill up quickly, while the ones at the latter are farther from the beach. All have friendly staff and similar facilities, including restaurants. **OD Bungalow ❶**, situated on a cliff, has great views. (All rooms with squat toilets 100-150฿.)

◪ **THONG NAI PAAN NOI AND THONG NAI PAAN YAI.** With sparkling water and a relaxed atmosphere, these twin beaches offer ample reward for those who endure the hour-long *songthaew* ride from Thong Sala or the boat ride from Hat Rin. *Songthaew* stop first at Thong Nai Paan Noi, the more populated of the two and favored among backpackers. This bay is known for its long stretch of cheap and rustic bungalows. Near the *songthaew* drop-off, the popular **Star Huts ❷** is the largest operator on the beach and teems with long-term guests. (☎299 005. Bungalows 150-200฿, with bath 300-400฿.) Younger backpackers frequent **Honey Bungalows ❸**, which is behind Star Huts away from the beach. The thatched-roof huts propped on concrete blocks aren't as nice, but the atmosphere is friendly and social. (Bungalows 250฿.) At the very north end of the beach, a 15min. walk from the *songthaew* drop-off, **Pong Bungalow ❷** is deservedly popular for its lively bar and its less popular library. (Bungalows 150-180฿, with bath 250-300฿.) Most take their meals at bungalow restaurants, though many recommend **Banglangon Vegetarian Restaurant,** halfway up the beach and known for its pizza.

To the south, Thong Nai Paan Yai is longer, less populated, and has calmer waters more suitable for swimming and snorkeling than Thong Nai Paan Noi. Ask the *songthaew* driver to let you off here or make the pleasant 20min. walk across the small promontory from Thong Nai Paan Noi. At the end of the road to Thong Nai Paan's easternmost point, **Nice Beach Resort ❹** has bright, white-washed rooms with mosquito nets, high ceilings, and private baths. (☎238 542. Bungalows 200-1600฿, depending on season and A/C.) Three bungalow operations cluster toward the middle of the beach. **Central Cottage ❸** provides simple, but comfortable, thatched bungalows and a restaurant. (☎299 059. Bungalows 350-400฿.) **Pen's Bungalow ❸** has clean, white, wooden bungalows with peaceful porches with hammocks. (☎229 004. Bungalows 300฿, 700฿, and 900฿.) Also toward the middle of the beach, **Pingjun Resort ❹** contains charming bungalows on nicely cultivated grounds. (☎299 004. Bungalows 400฿.)

👁 SIGHTS

After full moons and beaches, **waterfalls** are Ko Phangan's major attractions. The most famous stretches of river run through **Than Sadet Historical Park,** a good daytrip from the beach. Kings Rama V, VII, and IX all walked along its bathtub-sized waterfalls and cascades, leaving their initials as seals of inspection. Longtail boats from Hat Rin (50฿) drop off passengers at the mouth of the river. From here, you can make the 2.5km trek to the park by following the parallel road north.

The Sanctuary is a backpacker's spa that comes highly recommended by Ko Phangan's long-term vacationers. It is noted for its seclusion, clean facilities, attentive staff, and free evening meditations. Many are happy to pay 60฿ for a dorm bed and splurge on yoga classes (150฿), oil massages (400฿), and 10-day fasts. The location is only accessible by longtail boat; from Hat Rin; it costs 50฿. (Singles and doubles with bath 200-1000฿.)

🎶 NIGHTLIFE

All of Hat Rin Nok's nightlife essentially takes place right on the beach itself with open-air bars facing the ocean where you can lounge or dance on the beach. During the day, flyers announce special, super-cheap drink specials. **Drop-In Bar** plays consistent Top 40 dance music. The most popular spot these days is the **Cactus Club,** which creates an outdoor ambience with its fleet of oil lamps, and hip, bottle-spinning bartenders. Both offer nightly drink deals or happy hours worth checking out. The Moon party (see **Sex, Drugs and Lunar Cycles,** p. 339) is the stuff of legends. Each month under the full moon, thousands gather on this strip of sand. Bodies gyrate to the latest imported mixes, minds dance to the beat of illicit substances, and stomachs and bladders empty themselves gratefully into the ocean. Even when the moon isn't full, don't come here for a quiet beach. Hat Rin Nok is loud, brash, and proud of it. Besides drinking yourself your silly, you can also indulge in Hat Rin's other popular activities, such as emailing, getting massages, and watching pirated film releases.

KO SAMUI ☎077

Thailand's third largest island has come a long way since its "discovery" by backpackers in the 1970s. Ko Samui ("Coconut Island") is Thailand's biggest exporter of coconuts, the major source of income for its 40,000 occupants. Thousands of travelers, and increasingly more packaged-tour visitors, rush to Ko Samui's beaches, which run the gamut from loud, shop-crammed Chaweng and Hat Lamai to quiet, tropical enclaves like Hat Bo Phut and Hat Choeng Mon. Those looking for a range of entertainment, swimming, and sunbathing options will not be disappointed; those looking for a deserted coconut island most certainly will be.

THE VIEW FROM ABOVE

The lowdown: An island of extremes: from McDonald's to the jungle.
Gateway city: Surat Thani.
Nearby islands: Ko Phangan, Ko Tao.
Beaches: ▨ Chaweng's beach, Ao Thongsai, Ao Yai Noi, Hat Bangrak (Big Buddha Beach), Hat Choeng Mon, Hat Lamai, Hat Mae Nam, Laem Thongson, Na Thon.

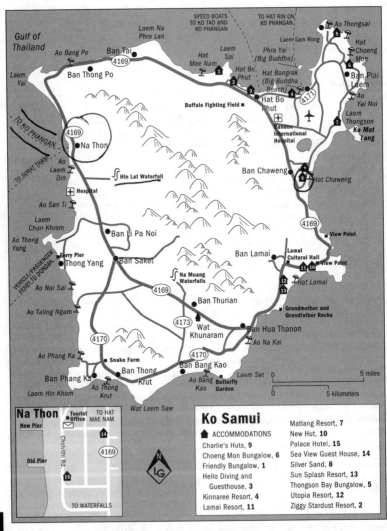

Ko Samui

🏠 ACCOMMODATIONS

Charlie's Huts, **9**
Choeng Mon Bungalow, **6**
Friendly Bungalow, **1**
Hello Diving and
    Guesthouse, **3**
Kinnaree Resort, **4**
Lamai Resort, **11**

Matlang Resort, **7**
New Hut, **10**
Palace Hotel, **15**
Sea View Guest House, **14**
Silver Sand, **8**
Sun Splash Resort, **13**
Thongson Bay Bungalow, **5**
Utopia Resort, **12**
Ziggy Stardust Resort, **2**

📧 TRANSPORTATION

Some short-term travelers arrive on Ko Samui by **plane**, but most come by **boat** via the transportation hub of **Surat Thani** or from neighboring islands.

Flights: Samui Airport is between Hat Chaweng and Big Buddha Beach (Hat Bangrak). **Bangkok Airways**, in Chaweng (☎ 422 2234 or 422 5129, at the airport ☎ 245 6018), flies daily to: **Bangkok** (every hr. 6:30am-7:30pm, 3450฿); **Phuket** (9:50, 10:10am, 3:10pm; 1820฿); **Singapore** (8am, 4690฿). Book tickets at Bangkok Airways or other tourist services on the island.

Trains and buses: Most travel agents can book joint boat/train or boat/bus tickets to the mainland. Prices vary slightly from agent to agent. Tickets to **Bangkok** (16hr.; A/C bus 280฿, sleeper train 700฿) and **Kuala Lumpur, Malaysia** (22hr., A/C bus 800฿).

Boats: There are 3 piers in Ko Samui. The main pier in **Na Thon** is dominated by **Songserm Travel Center,** which runs boats to: **Chumphon** (6½hr., 11am, 745฿); **Ko Tao** (2½hr.; 9, 11am; 345฿); **Krabi** (7hr., 2pm, 250฿); **Surat Thani** (3hr., 2pm, 150฿; night boat 7hr., 9pm, 150฿); Ko Phangan's **Thong Sala** (45min.; 9, 11am, 5pm; 115฿). **Seatran** also sends express boats from Na Thon to **Donsak Pier,** 60km away from **Surat Thani** (2hr. plus 1hr. by bus, 3 per day, 250฿ including bus to Surat Thani). A slow, but cheaper **car ferry** also runs between Na Thon and **Donsak Pier** (5hr., 120฿). The **Raja Car Ferry** runs between a pier 10km south of Na Thon and Donsak Pier. The pier at the **Big Buddha Beach** (Hat Bangrak) has direct service to **Hat Rin** on **Ko Phangan** (2hr.; 10:30am, 1, 4pm; 100฿).

Local Transportation: The cheapest and most convenient way to explore the island is to rent a **motorcycle** (see **Rentals,** below). Clearly labeled **songthaew** congregate near the pier and circle the island frequently 5am-6pm. From Na Thon to: **Hat Bangrak** (Big Buddha Beach; 30฿); **Hat Bo Phut** (20฿); **Hat Chaweng** (40฿); **Hat Lamai** (40฿); **Hat Mae Nam** (20฿). Listed prices are official fares, but actual rates charged tend to be higher. Speedy **motorcycle taxis** also circle the island, providing a faster but more expensive alternative to *songthaew*. From Na Thon to: **Hat Bo Phut** (150฿); **Hat Chaweng** (200฿); **Hat Mae Nam** (100฿). A/C yellow **metered taxis** refuse to use their meters and are the most expensive way to get around, charging 50-100฿ more than *songthaew* and motorcycle taxis.

Rentals: Motorcycles 150฿ per day; **jeeps** 800฿ per day, with insurance 1000-2000฿. Rental places abound all over the island. Officially, there is a 300฿ fine for not wearing a helmet while on a motorcycle, although it's common for motorists to ignore this rule.

✚ 🛈 ORIENTATION AND PRACTICAL INFORMATION

The roughly oval-shaped Ko Samui is encircled by one road **(Rte. 4169),** making getting around fairly easy but somewhat time-consuming since the island is quite large. The island's main transportation hub and service center, **Na Thon,** lies on the west coast. From here, Rte. 4169 runs to **Hat Mae Nam** on the northern coast and cuts down the east coast to **Hat Chaweng,** the island's most celebrated beach, and to **Hat Lamai,** Hat Chaweng's smaller and more budget-oriented sibling. **Route 4171,** enveloping the island's northeastern peninsula, branches off Rte. 4169 just past Hat Mae Nam and reconnects with it in Chaweng. It passes through **Hat Bo Phut** (Fisherman's Village), **Hat Bangrak** (Big Buddha Beach), and the smaller beaches of **Hat Choeng Mon, Ao Thongsai,** and **Ao Yai Noi.** *Songthaew* circulate around Rte. 4169, Hat Chaweng, and Hat Lamai; elsewhere you will have to take a taxi or ride a motorcycle (see **Rentals,** above). In general, Na Thon, Hat Chaweng, and Hat Lamai are the liveliest areas and offer the most services, while Hat Mae Nam, Hat Bo Phut, and Hat Choeng Mon are quiet and more relaxed.

Tourist Office: TAT (☎/fax 420 504 or 420 7202; tatsamui@samart.co.th), on Na Thon Rd. in Na Thon. With your back to the pier, turn left and follow the signs to a cluster of new buildings behind the post office. Helpful, English-speaking staff provides a wide range of maps and brochures on the island and environs. Open daily 8:30am-noon and 1-4:30pm.

Travel Agencies: Hundreds of establishments all over Na Thon, Hat Chaweng, and Hat Lamai sell boat/bus/train ticket combinations and arrange Ang Thon Marine Park tours (from 550฿), fishing trips, and elephant treks. In Na Thon, agencies line Na Thon Rd. near the pier. **Songserm Travel Center** (☎420 157, 236 489, or 236 490), directly

IN RECENT NEWS

WATER, WATER EVERYWHERE, BUT NOT A DROP TO DRINK

After a jaunt in Central and North-eastern Thailand, I was ready to hit the beaches on the Southern kos. But travelers and Thais in Bangkok said there's no water.

"No water?" I said, with shock.

"No. No water."

Southern and East Coast Thailand, particularly the heavily touristed kos, have had a water shortage since the beginning of 2002. While there's plenty of salt water (an ocean-full, actually), the fresh water reserves are dwindling. Because tourism is such a booming industry, all the fresh water resources are allocated to guest houses and hotels. In Ko Samui the drought has been so significant that hotels have had to import water from the mainland; other guest houses have simply closed, unable to afford the substantial costs.

Some guest houses have limited water usage, but most hotels refuse to do so for fear of losing business. In fact, guests at the high-end hotels are largely clueless about the shortage. It is the goal of these island establishments to keep the water flowing as freely as Singha beer.

Unfortunately, at backpacker bungalows, the problem is slightly more apparent. I endured the salty showers on Ko Tao, but farmers and fishermen have suffered much worse. Unable to afford to pump their own water, they are reliant upon the Thai government, who has prioritized the profits of tourism over its local workers and environmentalism.

— *Basil Lee*

opposite the pier in Na Thon, operates most of the ferries (daily 5am-5pm).

Immigration Office: (☎ 421 069), 2km south of Na Thon at the intersection of Rte. 4167 and Rte. 4172. Visa extensions 555฿. Open M-F 8:30am-noon and 1-4:30pm.

Currency Exchange: Dozens of banks offering good rates for currency exchange, credit card advances, and **ATMs** line the main roads of Na Thon, Hat Chaweng, and Hat Lamai. Generally open M-F 8:30am-3:30pm.

Markets: The market on **Thaweerat Pakdee Rd.** in Na Thon has fresh produce. Touristy trinket shops line the streets of most beaches, particularly in Hat Chaweng.

Emergency: ☎ 191. **Tourist Police (Bangkok):** ☎ 1155.

Tourist Police (local): ☎ 421 281. On Na Thon Rd. in Na Thon, 400m south of the pier. English spoken. **Open 24hr.**

Police: ☎ 421 095. On Thaweerat Pakdee Rd. in Na Thon. Other beaches have smaller offices or booths: Hat Chaweng (☎ 422 067), Hat Lamai (☎ 424 068), Hat Mae Nam (☎ 425 070), and Hat Bo Phut (☎ 425 071). **Open 24hr.**

Medical Services: The island has three main hospitals: **Bandon International Hospital** in Hat Bo Phut (☎ 425 382); **Government Hospital** in Na Thon (☎ 421 230); the private **Samui International Hospital** in Hat Chaweng (☎ 422 272). Smaller **nursing stations** can be found in Na Thon, Hat Chaweng, and Hat Lamai. English-speaking staff. Credit cards accepted. **Open 24hr.**

Telephones: GPO, 2nd fl. **International** calls, fax, and cheap Internet. Open daily 7am-10pm. Travel agencies around the island offer pricier international phone service.

Internet Access: Cheapest access at the **Telephone Office** at GPO (30฿ per hr.) Most travel agencies in Hat Chaweng and Hat Lamai provide pricier access (1฿ per min.).

Post Offices: GPO (☎ 421 130), on Na Thon Rd., 50m left of the pier parking lot. *Poste Restante.* Open M-F 8:30am-4:30pm, Sa-Su 9am-noon. Licensed, private **branches** along Rte. 4169. **Postal code:** 84140.

♙♗ ACCOMMODATIONS AND FOOD

Although Ko Samui caters to well-off tourists rather than to backpackers, cheap beds may be found at all of the island's beaches at rates as low as 150฿ for a simple bungalow with shared bath. The following accommodations and food options are listed by beach.

NA THON. Na Thon is Ko Samui's waiting room for visitors killing time until the next ferry. Cheaper communications and souvenirs make it a nice place to spend a rainy afternoon, but unless you have an early ferry to catch or the last *songthaew* has skipped town, there's little reason to spend the night. **Palace Hotel ❹**, 152 Cholvithi Rd., 100m on the right as you exit the pier, has spacious, comfortable rooms with sea views and a very hotel-like feel. (☎421 079. Doubles 400฿, with A/C and TV 550฿; twins 450฿/650฿; triples with A/C 800฿.) **Sea View Guest House ❸**, 67/15 Thaweerat Pakdee Rd., opposite the Shell gas station, has modest-sized rooms with showers and peeling paint. Regrettably, the hotel has no sea view. (☎420 298. Doubles with shower 200-400฿, with bath 300฿, with A/C 400฿.) On the waterfront, food carts sell fruit, meat-on-sticks, noodles, and sandwiches. Popular **Ruangthong Bakery ❷**, opposite the pier, serves breads, pastries, and Thai dishes for 20-100฿. It's a great place to grab a quick meal, cup of coffee, or snack before the ferry ride. (Open daily 6:30am-7pm.)

HAT MAE NAM. With its narrow strip of wet sand, the Mae Nam beach, stretching for 4km along the northern coast of Ko Samui, is probably the island's least spectacular beach. Thanks to its secluded feel (there is no road running along the beach and the way to access it is via dirt paths off Rte. 4169), Mae Nam draws those looking for tranquility and long-termers tired of the hustle and bustle of the island's more popular beaches. Cheap bungalows here are interchangeable; shop around for a resort that suits you. Close to Hat Bo Phut, the popular **Friendly Bungalow ❸** has standard beachside huts with baths and mosquito nets. (☎425 484. Laundry service and rental. 3-night minimum. Small huts 300฿ per day, large huts 400฿.)

HAT BO PHUT. The charming Bo Phut, or Fisherman's Village, offers a pleasant combination of white sand, quiet atmosphere, selection of seafood restaurants, and trendy shops. Though developed, Bo Phut is noticeably less commercial than other areas of island. Its friendly locals and traditional architecture create an ambience that reminds you that you are, indeed, still in Thailand. Bo Phut is spread around one road that branches off Rte. 4169 (Samui's main road) and runs along the coast before reconnecting with Rte. 4169 farther west. The area now has its own hostel, **Hello Diving and Guesthouse ❶**, a few meters from the pier, which boasts cheap dorm beds in a smartly restored wooden house and doubles as a dive shop offering excursions to Ko Tao's dive sites. Those enrolled in their diving classes stay free in the dorms. (☎66 77 427 608; warren@hello-diving.com; www.hello-diving.com. Dorms with fan 100฿, with A/C 150฿.) The old-time favorite **Ziggy Stardust Resort ❹**, farther down the road, has beautiful, spacious rooms with old carved wooden furniture, beds, and clean full baths. The lush garden enveloping the bungalows has a delightful smell. The beachfront bar/restaurant features fabulous homemade yogurt. (☎425 173. Bar/restaurant open daily 7:30am-10pm. Small doubles with fan 400฿; large doubles with fan 800฿, with A/C 1000฿.) For great and affordable Thai food, head to the **No-name Restaurant ❷**, at the end of the road, right as it hooks back to Rte. 4169. (Dishes 35-70฿. Open daily 3-11pm.) Of all the restaurants serving up excellent seafood, try the **Summer Night Restaurant ❸**, in the heart of Bo Phut village on the beach. (Breakfast 80-110฿; seafood 40฿ per 100g; Thai dishes 60-120฿. Open daily 7:30am-11:30pm.) Summer Night also runs a few clean **bungalows** across from the restaurant (300฿, with A/C 600฿).

HAT BANGRAK (BIG BUDDHA BEACH). Big Buddha Beach lies in the north of Samui's northeastern peninsula, along Rte. 4171. Bungalows abound in this lively area, but the rocky, boat-filled beach is not conducive to swimming and the bungalows are small. **Kinnaree Resort ❹**, close to the Big Buddha pier and across from the primary school, is a villa among flower gardens, cooing doves, and beach views. (☎245 111. Motorbike rental. Singles and doubles 400฿, with hot shower and A/C 800฿.)

◪ **NORTHEASTERN PENINSULA: LAEM THONGSON, AO THONGSAI, HAT CHOENG MON, AO YAI NOI.** The northeastern cape wraps around some of the island's best views and most delightfully secluded coves. Beaches are down dirt roads off the mountain highway connecting northern Hat Chaweng to Rte. 4171 and are most easily accessed by motorbikes. Solitude-seekers should follow the signs 2km down to **Thongson Bay Bungalow ❸**, on the tip of the promontory. The beach here, with a view of Ko Phangan, is rocky and scenic but not particularly suitable for swimming. (☎01 891 4640. Bungalows with bath 250-500฿, on the beach 1000฿.)

North of Ao Yai Noi, bordering Ao Thongsai, and 4km north of Hat Chaweng, Hat Choeng Mon's serene beaches are worth visiting, especially if crowds annoy you. **Choeng Mon Bungalow ❸** has modern, well-maintained, concrete bungalows with baths and a quiet, sandy beach. (☎425 372. In high season, singles and doubles 300฿, with A/C and hot water 450-1200฿, with satellite TV 650฿ minimum.)

◪ **HAT CHAWENG.** The biggest and brashest of Ko Samui's beaches, Hat Chaweng roars 5km over the eastern coast. As the sunbathing and party capital of the island, the beach is a loud, happy nation of superb sand, clean waters, cheap booze, and loud music. Even if you don't want to swim, people-watching provides hours of entertainment. Although the Chaweng area teems with luxury hotels, upscale tourist shops, and go-go bars, the quality beach makes it well worth staying. Hat Chaweng's main road, **Chaweng Rd.,** is parallel to the beach and connected to Rte. 4169 via three access roads; most services can be found there.

Budget accommodations in Hat Chaweng are scarce and fill up quickly. By far the best option for those on a budget is **Charlie's Huts ❸**, in the middle of the beach near the turn-off for the lagoon, which caters almost exclusively to backpackers and their ilk. Movies play every evening at 6pm in the attached restaurant. The wooden bungalows have thatched roofs, bamboo walls, and mosquito nets. (☎230 283. Doubles 200฿, with bath and closer to the beach 300฿.) Next door, **Silver Sand ❸** has a few budget bungalows close to the water. The large ones have private baths but are not in particularly good shape. (☎231 202. Bungalows 200-600฿.) Old-timer **Matlang Resort ❸**, 1541 Chaweng Rd., in North Chaweng by the end of the cape, is a quiet hideaway from the main drag. The beach here gets a little too shallow for quality swimming at low tide but is more picturesque than anywhere else on Chaweng. (☎/fax 422 172. Singles and doubles with bath and fan 300-370฿, with A/C 800฿ in high season, 650฿ in low season.) Other accommodations include **Lotus Bungalow**, 60/1 Chaweng Rd., Central Chaweng (☎230 891), and **Suneast Bungalow,** 159 Chaweng Rd., Central Chaweng (☎422 115).

Budget accommodations on Chaweng may be scarce, but budget food is not. Inexpensive food stalls cramming the road by the Green Mango serve pizzas, sandwiches, and Thai favorites to drunken night revelers. **The Deck Restaurant ❸** (☎230 898), before the Green Mango as you approach from Na Thon, has great food (including vegan and vegetarian options), music, and three levels of cushions to enjoy it all on. (3-course breakfast 99฿; 5-course dinner 175฿; Thai dishes 60-80฿; sandwiches 70฿. Open daily 8am-2am.) **La Taverna ❹** on the road on the way to the Green Mango cooks the best Italian food on the beach; feast on good pizzas (120-200฿) and pastas (150฿).

◪ **HAT LAMAI.** Hat Lamai is second to Hat Chaweng in terms of nightlife and beauty, but has a more family-friendly environment, good body surfing, and fewer crowds. Most tourist services can be found in South Lamai on the road running parallel to the beach, while the best budget accommodations are in North Lamai, some distance from the thick of things. **New Hut ❷**, the unofficial backpacker center, is the best and cheapest. Bungalows are clean but small. Cheaper ones are right on the beach and nothing more than a mattress with a triangular straw roof. (☎230 439. Bungalows 150฿, with bath 200-250฿.) Just to the south, **Lamai Resort ❸** has more expensive, sturdier bungalows. (Bungalows with bath 200-450฿.)

Though more centrally located, South Lamai has fewer budget options; most establishments are solidly mid-range. The centrally-located **Utopia Resort ❹** has nice bungalows, a more upscale clientele, and beautifully-groomed gardens. The clean bungalows and rooms have private baths. (Bungalows 500฿, with A/C and hot water 1000฿.) The friendly Italian owners of the **Sun Splash Resort ❹**, next door, keep their rooms in good shape. All bungalows have baths. (☎418 021. Bungalows with fan 400-500฿, with A/C 900-1000฿.)

Most bungalows serve standard meals until 10pm and let more expensive restaurants and pubs along the main drag pick up the slack late at night. Street food abounds. The **Will Wait Bakery,** in the center of Lamai Beach Rd., serves a standard menu of Thai and Western favorites. (Open daily 7:30am-10:30pm.) The **market** at Ban Hua Thanon sells fruit and munchies. (Open daily until sunset.)

👁 SIGHTS

Ko Samui has a few sights and cultural attractions to keep you entertained if you get too sun-burned. Most are located off Rte. 4169; you'll have to take a taxi or walk. Travel agencies also offer 1-day tours of the island for around 1000฿.

▓ WAT KHUNARAM. Rather sensational as far as wats go, this temple, off Rte. 4169 in the island's southeast corner, is known for a **mummified monk** who died in 1973 but somehow evaded decomposition via complex pre-death meditation.

THE BIG BUDDHA IMAGE (PHRA YAI). Ko Samui's most prominent landmark, the golden "Big Buddha" is off Rte. 4171 on Ko Fan Mountain on the island's northeast corner. Overlooking Samui Island from its location near Hat Bangrak (Big Buddha Beach), the 15m statue was built in 1972 as a place for both islanders and *farang* to worship.

SAMUI BUTTERFLY GARDEN. One of Samui's most popular non-beach attractions, the Butterfly Garden maintains over 24 species of southern Thai butterflies in addition to less spectacular (and less popular) species of insects. *(Off Rte. 4170, opposite Central Samui Village. ☎424 020. Open daily 8:30am-5:30pm. 120฿, children 60฿.)*

▐ WATERFALLS. Ko Samui boasts several waterfalls scattered around the interior of the island. Two-tiered **Hin Lat Waterfall,** 3km south of Na Thon, is the most accessible though not the most beautiful. The two **Na Muang Waterfalls,** 11km south of Na Thon, are more impressive. Getting to Namnang requires an exciting hike through the mountainous heart of the island. *(Difficult to reach without a motorbike. Taxis from Na Thon can drop you off at the foot of the waterfalls, and many travel agencies offer waterfall and trekking trips.)*

GRANDMOTHER AND GRANDFATHER ROCKS (HIN TA AND HIN YAI). According to an old Samui legend, an elderly couple was en route to the mainland to procure a wife for their son when a fierce storm pummeled the ship and killed the two seafarers. Their bodies washed ashore, and their respective genitals somehow petrified in the shapes of "Grandfather Rock" and "Grandmother Rock," a set of unusual, and slightly distasteful, natural formations. The rest of their bodies, however, curiously escaped being immortalized in stone. *(On South Lamai Beach.)*

SAMUI SNAKE FARM. This gimmicky complex, on Rte. 4170 in the island's southeast corner, features snakes indigenous to Samui. The snake farmers also offer potentially exciting but absurd events like centipede and scorpion fighting shows. (☎ *423 247. Shows daily 11am and 2pm. Open M-F 8:30am-4pm, Sa-Su 8:30am-noon. 150฿.*)

THE SAMUI AQUARIUM. Thailand's only privately owned aquarium features fish native to the Gulf of Thailand as well as sharks and turtles. The adjacent tiger farm houses several displaced Bengal tigers. (*Off Rte. 4170, south of Lamai Beach near Ban Han and the Butterfly Garden. ☎ 424 017. Open daily 9am-6pm. 250฿.*)

BAN LAMAI CULTURAL CENTER. Located where Rte. 4169 takes a sharp right turn at Kilometer 20, Lamai Cultural Hall's museum holds a small but interesting collection of phonographs, pottery, and weaponry. (*Open daily 6am-6pm. Free.*)

■ NIGHTLIFE

With dozens of pubs and go-go bars, Hat Chaweng is Samui's nightlife capital. The mega-pub **Green Mango** is a massive complex of six bars that draws a raging, young drink-and-dance crowd. The mood picks up at around 11pm and doesn't die until 4am. (Beers 80-100฿. Cocktails 120-150฿. Red Bull & vodka 130฿. Champagnes 800-2000฿. Open daily from 8pm.) The area around the Green Mango overflows with smaller but uninspired bars. The popular **Reggae Pub** attracts an older, more mellow crowd. More like an entertainment center than a "pub," it comes complete with a tacky souvenir shop. Sunday nights attract party-lovers to the drinking contest. To get there, follow the signs to the boxing stadium across the lagoon.

Hat Lamai has fewer nighttime options than Hat Chaweng, but bars and strip joints are popping up by the dozen. **Bauhaus Pub, Bistro and Disco,** south of the go-go bar area, is *the* hot spot for Lamai's young and restless. The Saturday Gin and Vodka party offers half-price cocktails. Foam party takes over on Friday nights. (Most drinks 30-100฿. M-Tu and Th buy-one-get-one-free. Open daily 6pm-2am.)

■ DAYTRIP FROM KO SAMUI: ANG THONG MARINE PARK

*The only way to visit the marine park is on a tour through one of Ko Samui's travel agencies. Songserm (see **Travel Agencies,** p. 343) sends daily boats at 8:30am from Na Thon's pier (550฿ lunch included, return around 5pm). If you have the money, a more worthwhile kayaking option (1800฿) allows you to explore the craggy island inlets.*

Made infamous as the setting for Alex Garland's *The Beach*, Ang Thong Marine National Park is a breathtaking collection of over 40 limestone islands 60km north of Ko Samui. Among the islands are **Ko Mae Ko** (Mother Island), popular for saltwater lake **Thalay Nai** (Lake Crater); **Ko Sam Sao** (Tripod Island), famous for its huge rock arch and fantastic snorkeling; and **Ko Wua Talap** (Sleeping Cow Island), home to the **park office. Ko Lak** and similar limestone formations tower 400m above the water. Dolphins dance in the water around the longtail boats that sail near **Ko Thai Plao.** The waters at **Hat Chan Charat** (Moonlight Beach) are as good for diving as Ko Tao's. Visit the park on your own by arranging transportation with the tour ferry operator. If you end up staying on the island, the park office rents several modest **bungalows** for 1000฿; **camping** is free.

SURAT THANI   ☎077

Most travelers know Surat Thani only as a stopover en route farther south or as a point of departure for Ko Samui and Ko Phangan. The increasing prevalence of joint bus, train, and boat tickets means that only a few stay here for more than a

quick stroll or snack. Overnight visitors, however, are able to indulge in the vibrant and colorful local night market.

TRANSPORTATION

Flights: Airport (☎253 500), 30km outside of town. **Thai Airways,** 3/27-8 Karoonrat Rd. (☎441 137), flies daily to **Bangkok** (noon and 7pm, 2400฿). More destinations accessible from Ko Samui's airport.

Trains: Railway station (☎311 213), in Phun Phin, 13km from Surat Thani. Orange buses run constantly between the local bus terminal (Talaat Kaset 1) in town and the station; catch them anywhere on Talaat Mai Rd. (every 5min., 10฿). Listed fares are for both 3rd- and 2nd-class tickets where they are available; otherwise, they are 3rd-class. Trains to: **Bangkok** (11hr.; 10 per day 10:25am-midnight; 147฿, 508฿); **Butterworth, Malaysia** (11hr., 2:50am, 2nd-class 800฿); **Chumphon** (3hr.; 10 per day 10:25am-midnight; 78฿, 178฿); **Hat Yai** (6hr.; 5 per day 9:20am-1:20am; 120฿, 306฿); **Sungai Kolok** (10hr.; 1:20, 3, 4am; 231฿); **Trang** (5hr.; 6, 8am; 115฿).

Buses: Bus travel in and out of Surat Thani is somewhat complicated. There are 3 bus stations, one for local and provincial travel known as **Talaat Kaset 1;** another one, across the street, for longer routes known as **Talaat Kaset 2;** and a **new station,** just outside of town by the train station, with **Bangkok** buses. Talaat Kaset 1 serves **Chum-**

phon (80฿) and **Surat Thani Province** with frequent buses to the railway station. Talaat Kaset 2 (☎272 341), behind Thai Tani Hotel next to the market, has regular orange buses departing for **Hat Yai** (5hr., 120฿); **Krabi** (4hr., 80฿); **Phang-Nga** (3½hr., 60฿); **Phuket** (5hr., 100฿), as well as other southern destinations (roughly every 30min. 6am-5pm). Tour and travel agencies will try to lure you to **private buses,** which cost 50-100฿ more than public buses but take significantly less time. Private minibuses to: **Hat Yai** (5hr.; every hr. 6:30am-5pm; 150฿, minibus 180฿); **Krabi** (3hr.; every hr. 6:30am-5:30pm; 120฿, minibus 150฿); **Penang, Malaysia** (6hr., every hr. 6am-5pm, minibus 450฿); **Phuket** (3hr.; 8am-5pm; 130฿, minibus 250฿).

Boats: Ferries depart from several points outside of town. **Songserm Travel Center** operates a **daily express boat** that leaves from the pier 8km outside of town to **Ko Phangan** (4hr., 7:30am, 250฿) and **Ko Samui** (3hr.; 7:30, 8am, 2pm; 150฿); ticket includes transportation to the pier. The same company operates a **night boat** which sets off from the Surat Thani pier at 11pm for: **Ko Phangan** (6hr., 200฿); **Ko Samui** (6hr., 150฿); **Ko Tao** (7hr., 400฿). **Samui Tours** offers buses (1hr.; 7 per day 6:15am-4:30pm; 45฿, with A/C 65฿) to the Donsak Car Port, about 60km from Surat Thani, where **Raja Car Ferry** goes to **Ko Phangan** (5hr., 120฿) and **Ko Samui** (2hr., every 2hr. 6am-6pm, 55฿). The new company **Seatran** also leaves from Donsak for **Ko Samui** (ferry 2hr.; 7am, 12:30pm; 250฿; bus service included; the 7am boat continues on to **Ko Phangan**). Buying from an agent will cost an added 50-100฿ surcharge.

Local Transportation: Few tourists stray from the bus-train-ferry station triangle, which is well served by the railway station bus. For beaten-track travel, take a **motorcycle taxi** (20-40฿) or **songthaew** (10฿).

◼🔁 ORIENTATION AND PRACTICAL INFORMATION

Trains arrive at **Phun Phin Railway Station**, 13km from Surat Thani. Phun Phin and Surat Thani are connected by the busy and noisy **Talaat Mai Rd.,** which enters Surat Thani from the southwest and passes the **tourist, police,** and **post offices.** Local buses leave from two separate **markets,** each just a block off Talaat Mai Rd., near the center of town. Ferries depart from the town pier on **Ban Don Rd.,** which runs along the banks of the mighty **Ta Pi River** and from piers outside town. Most budget accommodations, travel agencies, and conveniences are within easy walking distance of the pier and bus station.

Tourist Office: TAT, 5 Talaat Mai Rd. (☎288 817). A 20min. walk on Talaat Mai Rd. from the town center; it's best to jump on an orange local bus heading to the train station. Friendly staff, good info, and **maps.** English spoken. Open daily 8:30am-4:30pm.

Travel Agencies: Agencies touting everything from daytrips to bus and train tickets abound near the pier and on Talaat Mai Rd. between two markets.

Currency Exchange: Surat Thani's exchange rates are better than those on the islands. Banks with **24hr. ATMs** line Na Muang Rd. Usually open M-F 8:30am-3:30pm. **Bangkok Bank,** 195-7 Na Muang Rd. (☎281 298), has a booth in front. Open daily 8:30am-5pm.

Markets: Talaat Kaset 1 and **2,** near the bus stations. The fabulous and popular **night market** sprawls on a single street (Ton Pho Rd.) between Na Muang Rd. and Ban Don Rd. From the bus stations, head toward the river.

Emergency: ☎191. **Tourist Police (Bangkok):** ☎1155.

Police: 188 Na Muang Rd. (☎272 095). Little English spoken. **Open 24hr.**

Hospitals: Surat Thani Provincial Hospital (☎284 700), 1km past TAT on Talaat Mai Rd., on the way to privately-run **Phun Phin Taksin Hospital** (☎273 239). Both have English-speaking staff. Credit cards accepted. **Open 24hr.**

Telephones: Surat Thani Telecommunication Center (☎283 050), on Donnok Rd., 2km from most hotels. Walk down Talaat Mai Rd. toward the TAT from the intersection with Chonkasem Rd. and turn left onto Donnok Rd.; it's 20min. down on the left under the radio tower. **HCD.** Open daily 8am-10pm.

Internet Access: Cheap Internet is available at **Welcome Internet,** by the Muang Tai Hotel on Chonkasem Rd. (20฿ per hr.; open daily 9am-midnight), and at the **ECC,** by the Muang Tai Hotel on Talaat Mai Rd. (25฿ first 15min., 1฿ for each additional min.). Expensive **Internet access** (2฿ per min.) available around the pier area.

Post Offices: GPO (☎272 013), near the corner of Talaat Mai Rd. and Chonkasem Rd. *Poste Restante.* Open M-F 8:30am-4:30pm, Sa-Su 9am-noon. **Postal code:** 84000.

▮ ACCOMMODATIONS

Surat Thani has several good hotels with relatively low prices, though it lacks a quality backpacker option. Most establishments can be found within a few blocks' radius of the pier or around the markets. Ignore touts trying to push you onto a tuk-tuk to take you to your hotel. Unless you're arriving by train or at the new bus station, it's just a short walk.

Muang Tai Hotel, 390-2 Talaat Mai Rd. (☎273 586), at the intersection with Chonkasem Rd. The best option in town, though some rooms capture a lot of street noise from the busy intersection. Rooms are average-sized but come with creature comforts such as tables, cushy chairs, and private baths. Cheerful staff. Singles with fan 240฿, with A/C 360฿; doubles 260฿/390฿; doubles with hot water and A/C 420฿. ❸

Thai Tani Hotel, 442/306-308 Talaat Kaset 2 (☎272 977), off Talaat Mai Rd. between the two markets, right in the thick of things. Reception on 3rd fl. The run-down external façade hides a clean and popular establishment. Rooms include private bath. Singles 240฿, with A/C 320฿; twin beds 260-380฿. ❸

Grand City Hotel, 428/6-10 Na Muang Rd. (☎272 560), at the corner of Chonkasem Rd. Clean rooms with standard amenities in a prime location. Singles and doubles 200฿, with A/C and hot water 350฿; twin beds with fan 250฿, with A/C 500฿. ❸

Mor Or Guest House, 136-8 Ban Don Rd. (☎210 268), across from the pier. Right on the waterfront and cheap, it's a popular spot among backpackers because it's the only place in town to cater to them. However, the rooms are extremely basic and sauna-like with mattresses that induce *rigor mortis.* Common showers and toilets. Internet 2฿ per min. Cafe/restaurant. Singles and doubles 150฿. ❷

Queen Hotel (☎311 831), on the street directly opposite the railway station in Phun Phin, heading away, 100m down. Convenient for early or late trains. Rooms are clean but small and could use a coat of paint. A bevy of tourist services is available in the stairs. Internet 2฿ per min. Singles 200฿; doubles 250-400฿. ❸

▮ FOOD

The **night market** is almost reason enough to spend the night in Surat Thani and is perhaps its most memorable aspect. With a vast variety of vendors offering a tremendous range of snacks, sweets, and meals, the market seems to draw everyone in town. From crunchy bugs to duck eggs to enormous oysters to oil-drenched crepes, this is the place to sample Thai cuisine (try sliced mango with sticky coconut rice). **Talaat Kaset 1** and **Talaat Kaset 2** both have stalls and buffets displaying curries, meats, and vegetables ladled over rice. **Future@Internet ❶,** across from the Thai Tani Hotel, has a very solid and reasonably priced menu of mostly 30฿ items. The *tom yam* (35฿) is particularly good. (Open daily 8am-

9:30pm.) For a variety of Thai dishes and seafood, try the **Ploy Pilim Restaurant ❷**, 100 Chonkasem Rd., 30m behind the post office on the bottom floor of the Tapee Hotel. (Standard dishes 40-60฿; specialties 60฿ and way up. Open daily 7:30am-11pm.) Next door is the **Valaisak Bakery ❶** which has donuts that are mouthwatering when they are fresh. (Open daily 8am-8pm).

🔎 SIGHTS

While the town itself has no true sights, you can visit most of the areas around Surat Thani via *songthaew*. Large **oysters** are bred around the Kadaeh and Ta Tong Rivers. If you're interested in how they're raised and harvested, catch a bus to **Kanchanadit** (15km from Surat Thani) and hire a longtail boat (100-150฿), or contact **Kiang Lay Oyster Farm** (☎ 255 288) for information. For more active distractions, observe primate pedagogy at the **Monkey Training College.** Under the guidance of the affable and popular Somphon, monkeys learn to do tricks like collecting gigantic coconuts and bringing them to their trainer from the river. Local travel agents usually have better deals for larger groups. (☎ 227 351. 1-3 people 300฿, 4-10 people 700฿.) To go on your own, catch a *songthaew* (10฿) on Talaat Mai Rd. on the Phanthip Co. side of the street. Ask to be let off at *Rong Rian Sawn Ling*. Take a motorcycle taxi the rest of the way (20฿) or hike the 2km.

🗒 DAYTRIP FROM SURAT THANI: CHAIYA

The most direct way to get to Chaiya is to take a Chumphon-bound bus from Surat Thani's local market bus station, get off at Suan Mokkha, and catch a north-bound songthaew to Wat Phra That (1½hr. total). From there, it's a 15min. walk to Chaiya town and the Surat songthaew. Another option is to leave from Phang-Nga (see p. 353). Alternatively, you can catch a songthaew from Surat Thani all the way to Chaiya town (1½hr., 25-30฿) and arrange the short transport to the wats from there. The first option is more direct.

If the cultural vacuum of the islands has you yearning for a more historical experience, the town of Chaiya, 40km north of Surat Thani, while lacking splendor, may fulfill your needs. Once a powerful and important city-state in the southern Gulf Coast, Chaiya boasts several temples, museums, and ruins including one of the more revered Buddhist sights in the south. **Wat Phra Borommathat,** known as Wat Phra That, is a 1200-year-old pagoda housing relics and surrounded by 174 Buddha images. Unlike most Thai temples, this one is consecrated to Mahayana Buddhism, the religion of the ancient Sumatran Srivijaya Empire. The elaborate stone *chedi* is considered a masterful example of Srivijaya art. Next door, the small but interesting **National Museum** houses engaging artifacts dating from Chaiya's heyday. (☎ 431 090. Open W-Su 9am-4pm. 30฿.) Situated in a forest along Hwy. 41, **Wat Suan Mokkha Phalaram** (Suan Mok) is more a working monastery than a tourist attraction. Established by one of Thailand's most famous monks, the area contains few modern buildings since it was structured to return Buddhist practice and teaching to a more traditional and serene setting (i.e. the woods), while at the same time incorporating modern influences and design. A daytrip may not bestow enlightenment but will certainly allow a glimpse of the beautiful paths and bizarre collection of modern Buddhist art. As if to combat the indulgent lifestyles of nearby islands, Suan Mok urges restraint in all its attendees, discouraging vices like cigarette smoking and mosquito slapping. Anyone can attend **meditation retreats** (☎ 431 552; 1200฿ covers food, accommodations, and expenses for the 12-day retreat) held by resident monks. Retreats start on the last day of each month and run to the 11th day of the following month. It's not possible or necessary to reserve a spot; you need only show up a few days before the end of the month.

NEAR SURAT THANI: KHAO SOK NATIONAL PARK

Nestled in the mountain ridge separating the eastern and western coasts of peninsular Thailand, splendid Khao Sok National Park is one of the more worthwhile interior escapes in southern Thailand. With travelers heading to the park from both coasts, it is also one of the most popular. A relic of the country's topological past, the 160 million-year-old rain forest (some date it as old as 380 million years) covers roughly 650 sq. km, mostly comprised of jungle-covered foothills and protruding limestone formations. Its unique geography and generous rainfall allow it to sustain a remarkable ecosystem, home to hundreds of wildlife species, including gibbons (commonly seen), bears, elephants, guars, and languars. Tigers and panthers also supposedly live here but are rarely, if ever, spotted, even by park rangers. The park's jewel is doubtless the native flora, which includes dozens of species of orchids and ferns. Most spectacular is the *Bua Phut*, a lotus flower that can grow up to 80cm. The **park headquarters** near the entrance dispenses trail maps and arranges guided hikes to some of the waterfalls and caves. The headquarters also offers a **camping area** (pitch your own) and **bungalows.** Just outside of the park are fun treehouse-style accommodations which are popular among packers. **Art's Riverview Jungle Lodge** or **Bamboo House** are both quality choices. Park admission is 200฿ for three days. For more information on the park's facilities, call ☎ 299 150.

Many Surat Thani travel agencies and private guest houses that cluster near the park's entrance arrange excursions into the park. Otherwise, take a Phuket- or Takuapa-bound orange public bus from Surat Thani's southern market (every 30min. 6am-5pm) and direct the driver to Khao Sok, roughly 60km (1½hr.) away.

PHANG-NGA ☎076

While Phang-Nga Province is rich in natural beauty and cultural attractions, its capital, the small mainland town of Phang-Nga, has not been so blessed. Hot, sticky, and devoid of any worthwhile sights, the city has only two mentionable assets: a friendly population and proximity to some of the most spectacular scenery on the Thai-Malay Peninsula. Understandably, many visit the area around Phang-Nga as a side trip from Phuket (or even Krabi), bypassing Phang-Nga Town altogether. Still, with less tourist traffic and cheaper tour services, Phang-Nga attracts budget travelers who spend a night or two here before heading out to explore the wonders of the bay and province areas.

▐ TRANSPORTATION. The bus station is on **Phetkasem Hwy.** near the center of town. **Buses** run to: **Bangkok** (13hr., 5pm, 357฿; A/C 2, 4:30pm; 441฿); **Hat Yai** (6hr., every hr. 8am-2pm, A/C 220฿); **Ko Samui** (6hr., 9:30 and 11:30am, A/C and ferry 240฿); **Krabi** (1½hr.; every 30min. 7:30am-8pm; 35-40฿, A/C 59฿); **Phuket** (1½hr.; every hr. 9am-9pm; 50฿, A/C 65฿); **Surat Thani** (2½hr., 5 per day 9:30am-5pm, 60฿; A/C 9:30am, 11pm; 130฿); and **Trang** (4½hr., every hr. 7:30am-8:30pm, A/C 139฿). Blue **songthaew** run along the highway from the bus station to points around town (10-15฿) and the pier (20฿). **Motorcycle taxis** cost about 20฿ around town.

▐ PRACTICAL INFORMATION. The unregistered **travel agencies** near the bus station provide most tourist services. These agencies are less professional than those offering tours from Phuket and Krabi but are also about 200-400฿ cheaper (day tours 250-550฿; overnight tours to Phang-Nga Bay 550-750฿). **Sayan Tour,** next to the bus terminal, is one of the more established tour operators. (☎ 430 348. Open daily 6am-8pm.) Other services include: **Thai Farmers Bank,** 126 Phetkasem Hwy., across the street from the bus station, with a **24hr. ATM** (open M-F 8:30am-3:30pm); a **police station,** 193 Borirakbamrung Rd. (☎412 075), 500m to the left of the bus station; **Phang-Nga General Hospital,** 436 Phetkasem Hwy., 2km to the left of the bus station (☎412 034; **open 24hr.;** English spoken; no credit cards); and a **post office** on Phetkasem Hwy. (☎412 171; open M-F 8:30am-4:30pm, Sa-Su 9am-noon) with *Poste Restante* and **international phone** (open daily 8:30am-4:30pm). In an **emergency,** dial ☎ 191; for **Bangkok tourist police** dial ☎1155. **Postal code:** 82000.

⌖⌂ ACCOMMODATIONS AND FOOD. The new kid in town is the centrally located and antiseptically clean **Phang-Nga Guest House ❸** on Phetkasem Hwy., immediately to the right of the bus station near Krug Thai Bank. The spotless new rooms and common baths pass the white glove finger test with flying colors. (☎411 358. Continental breakfast 50฿. Singles with fan 220฿, with A/C 350฿; doubles with fan 250฿, with bath and A/C 400฿.) **Thawisuk Hotel ❷,** 79 Phetkasem Hwy. is in a seemingly ancient building. The hallways aren't great, but the rooms are cozy with the extra bonus of wooden floors. The clean baths have Western toilets. (☎412 100. No A/C. Singles 150฿; doubles 200฿.) A bit farther from town is the **Luk Muang Hotel ❸,** 1/2 Phetkasem Hwy. Exit to the right of the bus station and walk about 10min. past the temple and "Have a Good Trip" sign. Friendly and family-run, the hotel offers comfortable, airy rooms, some with TVs and phones. (☎411 512. Singles 200฿; small doubles 250฿, large doubles 300฿.)

Phang-Nga has several good dining options near the bus station. The best restaurant around, **Duang Seafood ❷,** 122 Phetkasem Hwy., next to Thai Farmers Bank and opposite the night market, serves shrimp fried rice and hot-and-sour seafood soup. (Dishes 50-100฿. Open daily 9am-10:30pm.) **Bismilla ❷,** 247 Phetkasem Hwy., on the same side of the street as the bus station, is a Muslim restaurant with wonderful roti, curries, and Thai soups—especially lemon. (Open daily 7am-11pm.) The **day market ❶,** off Phetkasem Hwy., to the right of the bus station, sells fruit from 4am to 6pm. The **night market ❶** sets up near the post office on Phetkasem Hwy. and along Riverside Rim Kong Rd. (Open daily 4:30pm-midnight.)

▨ DAYTRIPS FROM PHANG-NGA: PHANG-NGA BAY NATIONAL PARK. Travelers don't come to see Phang-Nga Town; they come to see Phang-Nga Province. With its majestic limestone formations and stunning Phang-Nga Bay, the province offers the rugged beauty sorely missing from built-up tourist resorts like Phuket and Krabi. Unfortunately, travelers without a car or boat find the province highly inaccessible. Rather than attempt to go it alone, join one of the day tours or overnight stays offered by many travel agencies (from Phang-Nga 200-500฿; from Phuket 450-650฿).

The real attraction, **▨Phang-Nga Bay National Park** stretches over 400 sq. km, encompassing more than 120 postcard-perfect limestone islands. Though the bay's status as a national park has aided its conservation, responsible ecotourism is critical to prevent damage to the islands. Use the old maxim: see as it is, leave as it was. Most tourists make a beeline to the park's twin jewels, beautiful **Ko Khao Ping Gan** and its satellite, **Ko Tapu,** better known as "James Bond Island"—the 1962 Bond flick, *The Man With The Golden Gun,* was filmed here. While the image of the thin limestone rock that is Ko Tapu (literally, "Nail Island") slicing into the bay is quite striking, be prepared to throw elbows at shell-vendors and tourists to stake a prime photo-taking spot. If it gets too crowded, head to **Ko Khao Ping Gan** where a small pier juts into the bay for more spectacular panoramas. If you have more time, be sure to paddle through the **Tam Lod Grotto,** a sea level, open-ended cave dripping with stalactites. **Ko Khien** displays drawings of boats and animals over 300 years old on the mountain's edge. *Songthaew* run from the Phang-Nga bus station to the pier (15฿), where longtail boats are chartered (600฿ for a few hours). Though more expensive than longtail boat tours, kayaking tours allow more flexibility and time to explore the park.

While larger boats visit from Krabi and Phuket, the most common tours from Phang-Nga are on longtail boats. Most tours include swimming and lunch on the beach. **Sayan Tour** offers half-day (200฿), full-day (500฿), and overnight trips, which include a memorable stay at **Ko Panyi** (extra 250฿). The latter option, whether tacked on after the half-day or full-day tour, is highly recommended (see below). A final option for touring the bay is by kayak. This pricey option (roughly 2000฿) allows you to fully explore the hidden lagoons and wildlife without the deafening buzz of the longtail motor.

NEAR PHANG-NGA

KO PANYI AND THE MUSLIM FISHING VILLAGE. Though technically part of the Phang-Nga Bay National Park, Ko Panyi is worth a separate visit. It is an unexpected highlight of many travelers' Thailand holiday. About 250 years ago, Muslim fishermen from Indonesia settled on the island, constructing homes and businesses on stilts jutting into the water. Almost three centuries later, the Muslim Fishing Village is alive and well, though nowadays it seems to cater more to tourists than to fish. Other than the prominent town **mosque,** there's not much to see in the village (besides a gorgeous sunset and sunrise); the real fascination is ambling down the rickety, suspended streets to watch the town inhabitants—some 200 of them in all—go about their daily chores in the most unusual of settings. Overnight stays are recommended, as the village assumes a different character after daytrippers return to the mainland. It's possible to arrange a room with the locals or book an overnight stay through a travel agency for 500-650฿. Some travelers have complained about the quality of accommodations they received in the village. It's best to book early and make inquiries to avoid receiving a second-rate room.

WAT SUWANNAKUHA. A popular stop for most tourist groups, this pleasant Buddhist temple, known by locals as Wat Tham, consists of several caves, the largest of which measures 40m long and houses an impressive 15m long reclining Buddha. The temple (and its resident monkeys) are best visited late in the afternoon when the tourist buses have returned to Phuket, leaving the temple relatively undisturbed. *(8km outside Phang-Nga, off Phang-Nga Koke Kloy Rd. 10฿.)*

PHUKET ☎076

A tropical playground of international stature, Phuket (FOO-ket) is best compared to other Eden-cum-tourist-meccas. Thailand's biggest island in the Andaman Sea and its most wealthy province, Phuket draws tourists looking for anything but a cultural or solitary experience. Most visitors arrive by plane and are swiftly shepherded into A/C taxis, which deposit them at five-star luxury resorts. Here they frolic and play for a week or two, safely avoiding almost everything having to do with, God forbid, Thailand. Consequently, for the budget traveler, Phuket can be an icky, over-touristed experience. Prices tend to be higher than on other islands and the beaches more crowded. Backpackers relax on beaches like Hat Kamala and Hat Karon by day and revel with randy Romeos cruising the discos in legendary nightlife hub Hat Patong by night. The mantra is simple: give up your dreams of idyllic seclusion for a few nights, soak up a raucous good time with fellow vacationing tourists, and, in your own way, make the most of the "Jewel of the South."

The lowdown: Thailand's biggest and most-touristed island. The Sarasin Bridge connects it to Phang-Nga on the mainland.
Gateway city: Phuket Town.
Nearby island groups: Racha, Similan.
Beaches: Hat Ao Bang Tao, Hat Chalong, Hat Kamala, Hat Karon, Hat Kata, Hat Nai Yang, Hat Patong, Hat Rawai, Hat Surin, Sing Cape, Hat Mai Khao, Friendship Beach.
Highlights: Great snorkeling and diving around Hat Karon and Hat Kata, gorgeous Hat Surin, first-class resorts, legendary nightlife hub Hat Patong, and Phuket Town's Vegetarian Festival (early Oct.).

▐▔ TRANSPORTATION

Because Phuket lacks a public transportation system, getting around is expensive. By far the cheapest and most convenient way to explore the island is by motorcycle. However, it is also the most dangerous, resulting in casualties every month.

Flights: Phuket International Airport, 28km outside of Phuket Town on Rte. 4026. **Taxis** and **tuk-tuks** cruise between the beaches and airport (taxi from airport to Phuket Town 300฿). **Bangkok Airways,** 158/2-3 Yao Warat Rd. (☎225 033; open daily 8am-5pm) and **Thai Airways,** 78/1 Ranong Rd. (☎211 195; open daily 8am-5pm), across from the local bus station, run most domestic and international flights. To: **Bangkok** (every hr. 8am-8pm, 2730฿); **Hat Yai** (12:50am, 1180฿); **Ko Samui** (50min.; daily 11:15am, 4:20pm; 11,870฿; M, W, F, Su 11:10am; 1480฿); **Kuala Lumpur, Malaysia** (daily, 3730฿); **Penang, Malaysia** (Tu, F, Su 12:30pm; 2230฿); **Singapore** (4 per day, 6085฿).

Buses: Intercity bus station (☎211 480), off Phang-Nga Rd. in eastern Phuket Town, behind a shopping plaza. TAT office has a good, free bus schedule. A/C and non-A/C buses to: **Bangkok** (14hr., 19 per day 6am-7pm, 278-755฿); **Hat Yai** (7hr., 12 per day, 150-270฿); **Khao Sok National Park** (7:30, 9am); **Krabi** (4hr., 22 per day, 65-117฿); **Phang-Nga** (2½hr., 5 per day 10:10am-4:30pm, 36฿); **Surat Thani** (5hr., 14 per day, 104-180฿); **Trang** (6hr., 20 per day 6am-6:30pm, 105-189฿).

Boats: Boats to **Ko Phi Phi** depart from Tonsai Bay (9am, 2:30pm, 350-450฿), the deep-sea port on the southeast coast. Tickets are cheaper in Ko Phi Phi—buy your return ticket there. A tuk-tuk to the pier costs 50฿.

Local Transportation: Local bus station on Ranong Rd. in Phuket Town, near the market. Labeled **songthaew** (every 30min. 7am-5pm) to: **Hat Kamala** (25฿); **Hat Karon** (20฿); **Hat Kata** (20฿); **Hat Patong** (15฿); **Hat Rawai** (20฿); **Hat Nai Yang** (30฿); **Hat Surin** (20฿). **Tuk-tuk** to: **Hat Kamala** (250฿); **Hat Kata** (150฿); **Hat Nai Yang** (300฿); **Hat Patong** (15฿); **Hat Rawai** (100฿); **Hat Surin** (250฿). Within Phuket Town, tuk-tuks charge 10-20฿; rates are negotiable to other points on the island and go up after 5pm. **Metered taxis** cost 30฿ for the first 2km and 4฿ for each additional km.

Rentals: Motorcycles (150-200฿ per day) and **jeeps** (600-1000฿ per day) are available for rent all over the island. All vehicles are uninsured, and accident rates for foreigners are alarmingly high. **TAT does not recommend renting a motorcycle.** Helmets are required now for drivers, but amazingly, not even offered to backseat passengers.

✳ ORIENTATION

Getting around Phuket is not particularly complicated, but given the island's size (570 sq. km), traveling takes time. Phuket is connected to the mainland by **Rte. 402,** the island's main north-south artery. Bordered by the Andaman Sea, the west coast is lined with beaches, the province's pride and joy. The northern beaches, especially **Hat Kamala, Hat Surin,** and **Sing Cape** are quieter and prettier, while south of Kamala, party central **Hat Patong** has a sensory overload of tacky bars, cabaret

Phuket

PHANG-NGA

Sarasin Bridge

402

Hat Mai Khao

Phuket International Airport

402

4026

Hat Nai Yang

4031

4027

Khao Phra Taew Royal Wildlife Forest and Preserve

402

4031

▲ Wat Phra Thong

Ko Waeo

Thalang ●

Ton Sai Waterfall

Ko Kata

Ao Bang Tao

4030

402

4027

4025

TO KO YAO YAI →

Heroines Monument ■

Hat Surin
Laem Sing

402

Ao Sapam

Ko Rang Noi

Hat Kamala

Laem Hin Pier ■

Ko Rang Yai

Sapam ●

Ko Maphrao

Kathu ●

402 402

Muang ●

Laem Nga

4029

Hat Patong

Phuket Town ●

Ko Siray

Laem Lajchak

Hat Karon Noi

Fishing Harbor ■ ■ Gypsy Village

Andaman Sea

4022

4021

Tonsai Bay

Hat Karon

Wat Chalong ▲

4023

Ko Taphao Noi

TO KO PHI PHI! (48km) →

Ko Pu
Hat Kata

4028

Ao Chalong

Ko Taphao Yai
Ao Makham

■ Port of Phuket

Hat Kata Noi

Viewpoint ■

Friendship Beach

Ko Lone

■ Marine Biological Research Center

Laem Phanwa

Ko Dok Mai

4024

Hat Nai Han

Viewpoint ■

Hat Rawai

Ko Man

Ko Bon

Laem Promthep

Ko Aew

Ko Mai Thon

Ko Kaeo Yai

↓ TO KO RACHA YAI AND KO RACHA NOI

Ko Hae

0   4 miles
0   4 kilometers

shows, and gimmicky tourist stalls. Farther south are the gentle duo of **Hat Karon** and **Hat Kata,** while a few smaller, less attractive beaches fringe the island's southwestern tip. Phuket's bleak and muddy eastern coast is filled with mangroves, prawn farms, and bobbing boats. On the island's southeast corner, **Phuket Town,** the island's lifeline, offers financial, postal, and telecommunications services in addition to a bevy of good, authentic, budget restaurants. It's not glamorous, but it's a decent base for exploring the rest of the island.

🛂 PRACTICAL INFORMATION

Tourist Office: TAT, 73-75 Phuket Rd. (☎212 213), in Phuket Town, northwest of the clock tower and hidden among furniture stores. Helpful staff provides maps, bus schedules, and accommodation lists. Open daily 8:30am-4:30pm.

Travel Agencies: Tour operators are a dime a dozen in Hat Karon, Hat Kata, Hat Patong, and Phuket Town. Most can arrange tours to Phang-Nga Bay and nearby islands (450-650฿) and bus or ferry transportation to Krabi and Ko Phi Phi. The agency in the **On On Hotel** (see **Accommodations,** below) is reportedly one of the cheapest.

Currency Exchange: In Phuket Town, a slew of banks are on Phang-Nga Rd. in front of the On On Hotel, and several more are one block down on Ratsada Rd. **Thai Farmers Bank,** 14 Phang-Nga Rd. (☎216 928). Open daily 8:30am-5pm. **24hr. ATM.** Currency exchange booths and ATMs abound on the larger beaches, especially Hat Karon, Hat Kata, and Hat Patong.

Medical Services: Phuket has some of Thailand's finest hospitals outside Bangkok. **Bangkok Phuket Hospital,** 21 Hong Yok-H-Thit Rd. (☎254 421), on the northwest side of Phuket Town. **Phuket International Hospital,** 44 Chalerm Prakiat Rd. (☎249 400), on the way to the airport. Credit cards accepted. English spoken. Both **open 24hr.**

Emergency: ☎199. **Ambulance:** ☎1699. **Tourist police (Bangkok):** ☎1155.

Local Tourist Police: 81-83 Satun Rd. (☎225 361), northwest corner of Phuket Town. English spoken. **Open 24hr.** Smaller booths on major beaches.

Police: ☎212 115. Little English spoken. Contact TAT or tourist police first.

Telephones: Phuket Telecommunication Center, 112/2 Phang-Nga Rd. (☎216 861), in the building under the radio tower. **International phone**/fax and Internet. Cheaper than services provided by travel agencies. Open daily 8am-midnight.

Internet Access: Cheapest at the Telecommunications Center (see **Telephones,** above). Purchase of a 100฿ Internet card is required to begin service. 30฿ per hr. Travel agencies and guest houses charge 1-2฿ more per min.

Post Offices: GPO, 12/16 Montri Rd. (☎211 020), on the corner with Talang Rd. *Poste Restante.* Open M-F 8:30am-4:30pm, Sa-Su 9am-noon. **Postal code:** 83000.

PHUKET TOWN ☎076

Lacking the glamor of its beachside siblings, Phuket Town is about as close as you can get to an "authentic" Thai experience on the island. Though tourist dollars have started to trickle in as more *farang* venture here from the island's more alluring beaches, the town still retains its original Sino-Portuguese character. Despite its scant entertainment options, Phuket Town's budget hotels and restaurants make it a popular springboard for exploring the rest of the island.

✴ ORIENTATION

Most of Phuket Town's tourist services and accommodations are concentrated within a small area. The island's **intercity bus terminal** is one block north of the

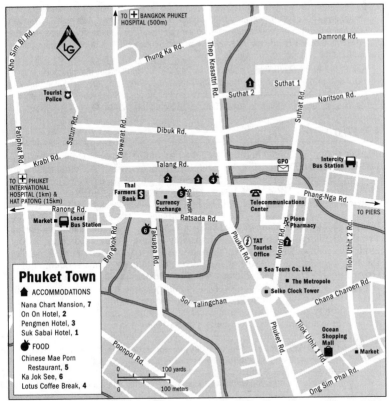

Phuket Town

🏠 ACCOMMODATIONS

Nana Chart Mansion, **7**
On On Hotel, **2**
Pengmen Hotel, **3**
Suk Sabai Hotel, **1**

🍴 FOOD

Chinese Mae Porn
   Restaurant, **5**
Ka Jok See, **6**
Lotus Coffee Break, **4**

main road, **Phang-Nga Rd.**, which runs west from the station to the **On On Hotel** and many banks. Past the **Telecommunications Center** (distinguished by its clock tower), Phang-Nga Rd. intersects **Phuket Rd.**, which runs south past the **TAT** and **Navamindra Memorial Square** to the **Clock Tower Rotary** (not to be confused with the Telecommunication's Center clock tower), a main landmark in the southern part of town. The **local bus/songthaew station** is adjacent to the market on **Ranong Rd.**, on the west side of town.

🏠 ACCOMMODATIONS

Phuket Town has the widest selection of budget accommodations on the island. In the low season, you can sometimes find cheap accommodation on one of Phuket's beaches as guest houses are open to bargaining, but in general, Phuket Town is your best bet.

Pengmen Hotel, 69 Phang-Nga Rd. This Chinese hotel is right in the thick of things. Rents clean, well-maintained rooms with shared bath for an unbelievable 120฿. ❶

Nana Chart Mansion, 41/34 Montri Rd. (☎230 041 or 230 041, ext. 3), opposite the Pearl Hotel. Modern and comfortable rooms come with crisp new sheets and ultra-clean Western toilets. Singles and doubles 250฿, with TV 300฿, with TV, A/C, and hot shower 350-450฿. ❸

On On Hotel, 19 Phang-Nga Rd. (☎211 154 or 225 741), a few houses past the Pengmen Hotel away from the bus station. Architecturally significant and the oldest hotel in town, On On has a devoted backpacker following, drawn by the prices and the hotel's cameo in the Hollywood movie *The Beach*. Internet 25฿ per hr. Singles 120฿, with bath 180฿; doubles with bath 250฿, with A/C 360฿. ❷

Suk Sabai Hotel, 82/9 Thep Kasatri Rd. (☎212 287). From the bus station, follow Phuket Rd. several blocks north until it becomes Thep Kasatri Rd. Turn onto the small alley just before the Ford dealership; the hotel is at the end of the alley. Suk Sabai's main advantage is its quiet location on a side street. Singles 180฿; doubles 250฿. ❸

FOOD

Phuket is famous for its culinary delights, including *tao sor* (Chinese crepes) and *kanohm jin Phuket* (breakfast noodles in spicy curry). The daily **market** on Ranong Rd. sells aisle upon aisle of tropical fruit and seafood. The **night market** is at the junction of Tilok Uthit 1 and Ong Sim Phai Rd. A good *farang* place to grab a Western breakfast or a sandwich is **Lotus Coffee Break ❶**, at the corner of Phang-Nga and Phuket Rd. (Tea 10฿; Thai dishes 25-35฿; shakes 20-25฿; sandwiches 20-30฿. Open daily 7:30am-9:30pm.) The expensive but excellent **Ka Jok See ❹**, 26 Takuapa Rd., is several shops south of the Ratsada Rd. intersection, hidden by plants. The staff treats you like royalty. Thai dishes run 80-380฿. Try the *tom yum* or *goong-sarong* for 150฿ each. (Reservations recommended. Open Tu-Su 6-11pm.) The **Chinese Mae Porn Restaurant ❸**, on Phang-Nga Rd. across from the Pengmen Hotel, is deservedly popular among travelers and Thais alike for its scrumptious dishes and neighborly atmosphere. Portions are on the skimpy side, but taste compensates. (Various seafood dishes or chicken with cashew nuts 60-100฿. Open daily 8:30am-10pm.)

> **!** **BEACH WARNING** Phuket is known for dangerous, sometimes fatal, ocean currents during the rainy season. Exercise caution in the water, especially at high tide. If you're caught in a current, signal distress by waving one arm (wave two arms for serious distress) and try to stay afloat until help arrives.

HAT PATONG

If Bangkok's infamous Patpong ever had a protege, Hat Patong is it. On Phuket's west coast, Hat Patong is the island's nightlife and entertainment center. A tasteless mix of themed bars, strip shows, Thai boxing, and gimmicky souvenir stalls will disappoint—unless you're here to watch sex shows, buy cheap-looking clothes, or blow a budget on a night of overpriced accommodation and drinks. Hat Patong's only redeeming feature is its beach, though these sands seem dirty and crowded when compared to others on the island.

⊞ ORIENTATION. Hat Patong is defined by two roads that run parallel to the 3km of beach. Closest to the water is **Thaweewong Rd.,** crowded with expensive seafood restaurants, outdoor bars, and souvenir stalls. One block east, **Song Roi Pee Rd.** (known as **Rat-U-Thit Rd.** north of the Bangla Rd. intersection) is home to more restaurants and Hat Patong's few budget hotels. Phuket's raciest bars cluster in alleyways off **Bangla Rd.,** which connects Rat-U-Thit and Thaweewong Rd.

⌂ ACCOMMODATIONS AND FOOD. Accommodations in Hat Patong are Phuket's most expensive, although they can be bargained down during the low season. Those who come here to party but don't have a place to stay will have to fork over 200-300฿ for a taxi back to Phuket Town. The cheapest places to stay are on Rat-U-Thit Rd. on the north side of the beach. A sparkling clean new-comer is the **Baan Patong Guesthouse** ❹, 3 Rat-U-Thit Rd., on a small soi about a 5min. walk south of the Bangla Rd. intersection. Its cozy, modern rooms all have large satellite TVs, balconies, and hot showers. (☎344 152. Singles and doubles 400-600฿, with A/C 600-850฿, depending on season.) For clean and simple rooms with both A/C and fan, try **Shamrock Park Inn** ❹, 31 Rat-U-Thit Rd. (☎340 991. Singles high season 500฿, low season 400฿; doubles 600฿/450฿.) Popular with back-packers is the **PS2 Bungalow** ❺, 21 Rat-U-Thit Rd., a 15min. walk north from the Bangla Rd. intersection. The large, squeaky-clean bungalows are decked out with micro-fridges. (☎342 207 or 290 032; www.ps2bungalows.com. Singles and doubles 600-900฿ in high season, 400-600฿ in low season, with A/C and TV 900-1500฿.) The **Chanathip Guest House** ❹, 53/7 Rat-U-Thit Rd., across from Baan Patong Guesthouse, has bright, comfortable rooms with TV, hot water, and fridge. (☎294 088. Singles and doubles 350-800฿, with A/C 600-900฿.)

Like everything else in Hat Patong, food is generally expensive. The **market** ❶ by Chanathip Guest House on Rat-U-Thit Rd. provides the cheapest meals. Nearly every restaurant claims to specialize in European and American food. To minimize the risk of an unpleasant surprise, stick to the basics: pizza, pastas, and sand-wiches. (Avoid "Mexican" food at all costs. You'll thank us later.) **The Pizzeria Hut** ❸, on Song Roi Pee Rd., one block south of the Bangla Rd. intersection, serves brick-oven pizzas (100-200฿) on a shaded outdoor patio. (Open daily 11am-11pm.)

🎵🎭 **ENTERTAINMENT AND NIGHTLIFE.** Night after night, hot-blooded West-ern lads come out in Hat Patong by the thousands, eager to chat up the pretty, young Thai "waitresses" who smile seductively from the bars on every corner. For pre-party boozing, head to **Molly Malone's Irish Pub,** 68 Thaweewong Rd., toward the south side of the beach underneath KFC. If it weren't for the Thai staff, you'd swear you were in Ireland. Guinness and Kilkenny beer on tap, live Irish music, and "tradi-tional pub grub" round out this slick but expensive bar. (Open daily 11am-2am.) Once you're ready to pick up (or be picked up), head to the center of the action on the streets off Bangla and Sawatdirak Rd. Dozens of gay venues with names like "Hot Boys" and "Connect Bar" cluster on Rat-U-Thit Rd., while the renowned **Simon Cabaret**, 8 Sirirat Rd., just south of town, has a hilarious transvestite extravaganza. (☎342 011/5. Nightly 7:30 and 9:30pm. 500-600฿.) Hat Patong's club scene definitely takes a backseat to the more popular go-go bars. **The Banana Disco**, on Thaweewong Rd. two blocks south of the Bangla Rd. intersection, features two wildly popular lev-els: a ground-floor lounge/restaurant (open daily 7pm-2am) and a disco upstairs (open daily 9pm-2am).

HAT KARON AND HAT KATA

Popular with backpackers and package tourists alike, the adjacent beaches of Hat Karon and Hat Kata have the best balance of lively nightlife, plentiful dining options, and sweet sand. Perhaps most importantly, they are blissfully free of the go-go bars that dominate Hat Patong. Though they can get crowded, espe-cially in the area around Hat Kata's Club Med Beach, Hat Karon and Hat Kata are pleasant getaways nonetheless.

🧭 **ORIENTATION.** Hat Karon and Hat Kata are actually three separate beaches. To the north, luxury resorts dot the 3km of Hat Karon. To the south, a hilly, rocky cape separates Hat Karon from Hat Kata. Here, budget restaurants and hotels cluster around **Taina Rd.,** which winds inland from the beachside **Patak Rd.** Hat Kata itself is split into the beaches of **Hat Kata** and **Hat Kata Noi.** While Hat Kata is monopolized by the gargantuan **Club Med**, Hat Kata Noi to the south is the most solitary beach of the three.

■☐ ACCOMMODATIONS AND FOOD. Backpackerland spreads off the beach along Taina Rd. on the cape separating Hat Karon from Hat Kata. One of the best budget hotels is the Scandinavian-themed **▨Little Mermaid Guest House ❹** on Taina Rd. near the highway intersection and opposite the PTT gas station. The four-story multicolored building has rooms with hot water, phones, and optional fridges and TVs (50฿ extra each). Two restaurants, three bars, a pool table, a swimming pool, and Internet access (2฿ per min.) are provided for general use. (☎330 730; fax 330 733; mermaid@phuket.ksc.co.th; www.littlemermaid-phuket.net. Low season: rooms with fan 265฿, with A/C 365฿; bungalows with A/C 850฿. High season: rooms with fan 365฿, with A/C 500฿; bungalows with A/C 590฿. Discounts for long-term stays.) In the same neighborhood but closer to the beach, the small, family-run **Rose Inn ❹**, 114/24 Mu 4 Taina Rd., has simple, clean rooms. The staff speaks little English. (☎330 582; fax 330 591. Singles and doubles 400฿, with A/C 650฿.) Another option is the **Lucky Guest House ❸**, 110/44 Mu 4 Taina Rd., a few meters away from the Rose Inn. It's clean and empty during the off-season. (☎330 572. Singles and doubles with bath 250-450฿.)

Both Hat Karon and Hat Kata have a good selection of inexpensive restaurants on Taipan Rd. **The Kwong Seafood Shop ❷** is a no-frills, no-nonsense place to get a good, fast bite to eat. (Chicken and beef dishes 50-70฿. Seafood dishes 200฿. Open daily 9am-midnight.) At the **Dive Cafe ❸**, 111/25-26 Taina Rd., about one block from the water on the left, divers and beachgoers devour the house specialty, *kai manao* (lemon chicken), for 120฿. (Open daily 9am-11pm.)

▨ ACTIVITIES. For those with the cash, Hat Karon and Hat Kata are perfect for exploring some of the world's best **snorkeling** and **diving** around the Similan and Racha Islands. Head to PADI-certified **Siam Dive n' Sail**, 68/14 Patak Road, Mu 2, behind Club Med near the Jiva Resort. They specialize in live-aboard diving trips, which is all the rage in Phuket now. Four-day trips to Similan and Surin start at 20,000฿ per person, seven-day trips to Myanmar (Burma) start at 57,000฿, and day-trips start at 2000-3100฿ per person. Gear rental costs 700฿ per day. All trips include transportation from your hotel, tanks and weights, and most meals and drinks. (☎330 967; info@siamdivers.com; www.siamdivers.com. Open M-Sa 11am-8pm. MC/V.) **Hat Kata Center**'s bar scene offers rowdy excitement after a long day in the sun, while **Dino Park Mini-Golf** provides more innocent fun. (Golf open daily 10am-midnight. 240฿, children 180฿.)

HAT SURIN, AO BANG TAO, AND HAT NAI YANG

Once known to harbor the most beautiful and undeveloped beaches on Phuket, the island's northwestern shore has exploded with luxury resorts over the past decade. **Hat Surin** is no exception, though there are some cheaper guest houses closer to the highway. Hat Surin was another of the locations featured in the Leonardo DiCaprio flick *The Beach*. Unfortunately, swimming is not recommended due to strong winds and heavy surf. **Tiw-Too Guest House ❹**, 13/11 Srisoonthorn Rd., a 10min. walk from the beach, has exceptionally clean rooms, TVs, refrigerators, and sweet owners—it's easy to feel at home here. (☎270 240. Singles with A/C 400-700฿.) On the southern end of Surin Beach, **Diver's Place** is a beachfront pub with a friendly expat crowd. Diver, who's saved over 90 people over the years, is a good person to ask about the surf. (Beers 60฿.)

If you bring your own food, a towel, and a book, attractive **Ao Bang Tao** makes a decent daytrip, especially between May and July, before the heavy rains hit, but after the crowds have skedaddled. Ao Bang Tao is dominated by two resorts that monopolize access to the water. Squeezed between the two beaches on the road from Surin to Ao Bang Tao, **Bangtao Lagoon Bungalows ❺**, 72/3 Mu 3 T. Cherngtalay, has compact, comfortable huts with a blue patina and marble floors. The bungalows range from standard to deluxe suites. Ask the bus driver from Phuket Town to drop you off here or you may never find it. (☎324 260; fax 324 168; http://phuketbangtaolagoon.com. Standard bungalows 400฿ low season, 680฿ high season; superior bungalows 600฿/1150฿. Extra bed 200฿.)

The National Park of **Hat Nai Yang**, 13km of coconut and rubber trees on the northeastern tip of the island, has kept private developers at bay, although condominium vultures still stalk the park boundaries. In the rainy season, Hat Nai Yang has Phuket's most dangerous riptides. The **Visitors Office** is near the entrance. (☎327 407 or 328 226. Open daily 8:30am-4:30pm.) Its possible to rent **tents ❶** (small sleeps 2-4, 100฿; large sleeps 5-8, 200฿). **Park bungalows ❸** on the beach are popular among Thai vacationers (300-600฿).

HAT KAMALA

Escape to quiet **Hat Kamala** on the way to Hat Surin from Phuket Town (*songthaew* 20฿). There are no luxury hotels and the beaches are decent. To get to the spotless rooms of **Malinee House ❺**, 74/7 Mu 3, follow the beach road from the south end of the beach until it curves inland; the restaurant/guest house is on the right. An Internet cafe is below. (☎324 094 or 271 355. Singles and doubles in high season 650฿, with A/C 950฿; in low season 350/500฿. Cable TV 100฿ extra.)

HAT RAWAI AND AO CHALONG

Squashed into the southeastern tip of Phuket Island, Hat Rawai caters mostly to locals. The beach's narrow strip of sand and muddy water render it quite unappealing; try its more attractive neighbor **Hat Nai Han**. Both slow down during rainy season. At Hat Rawai, **Pornmae Bungalows ❸**, 58/1 Wiset Rd., inside the hair salon opposite the central part of the beach, has simple rooms with fridges. (☎/fax 381 300. Singles and doubles 300-400฿.)

Pleasant Ao Chalong, north of Hat Rawai on the island's southeastern side, is the largest bay on Phuket. Because of its size and shallow, muddy waters, the bay is primarily used for docking. Though the bay makes for mediocre swimming, it's a good place to stay if you want to learn more about the active Andaman Sea yachting culture. A good place to meet other sailors is **Friendship Beach ❺**, 27/1 Soi Mittrapap, about 2km north of Hat Rawai toward Phuket Town on the southern side of the bay, across from the Phuket Shell Museum. Friendly and relaxed, it has bungalows, a restaurant, Sunday jam sessions, a pool table, cable TV, and Internet (1฿ per min.). The kitchen serves good Thai and Western food. (☎381 281; fax 381 424. Spanish omelette 100฿. Bungalows 600฿ high season, 350฿ low season.)

SIMILAN ISLANDS ☎076

While the Southern Thailand backpacker superhighway swallows up other islands, Ko Similan, a national park consisting of nine small islands, remains the untouched virgin beauty of the Andaman Sea. Relative inaccessibility, higher expenses, and the princess's cottage have helped preserve Ko Similan both below and above water. Due to its outstanding 30m underwater visibility and magnificent coral gardens filled with abundant marine life, the Similan Archipelago is considered one of the best deep-water dive sites in the world. Though primarily known for its diving and snorkeling, Ko Similan also has spectacularly fine beaches, majestic rock formations, and fascinating wildlife. If time and budget are relatively far out of mind, Ko Similan is worth the trip (at least November through April, when it's open).

▣ TRANSPORTATION. There are three reasonable ways to access the Similan Islands, either from Ban Thap Lamu pier (3hr., 8am, 2100฿) closest to Phang-Nga Town, by boat from Amphoe Khuru Buri pier (3hr.) farther north, or from Phuket (1½hr., 8am, 700฿). **Met Sine Tours** (☎443 276) at Ban Thap Lamu is the most reliable booking agent. In Phuket, contact Songserm Travel Center (☎076 222 570). Keep in mind that rough seas might result in cancellation or a sickening journey.

▣▣ ORIENTATION AND PRACTICAL INFORMATION. Ko Similan is only open from November to April. The nine islands 60km off the west coast of Phang-Nga are numbered from north to south. The second largest island, **Ko Miang**, is where boats dock and the only island that allows overnighters. It's also the site of the **Visitors Center, Park Headquarters,** and the area's only drinking water. Boat trips between the islands are irregular and cost 250฿ per person. It's best to contact the **Similan National Park Office** (☎411 913) at Thap Lamu pier for any questions regarding transportation and practicalities. There's a 40฿ admission fee to the park, collected at Ko Miang upon arrival. The park is closed from May until November due to rough seas. Services on the Similan Islands are more than limited—they're nonexistent. Think messages in bottles, shells, roots, and sticks.

▣▣ ACCOMMODATIONS AND FOOD. Ko Miang has the only accommodations, a **campground** offering both **tents ❷** (150฿) and **bungalows ❺** (600฿ for four beds). There's a small fee for those who bring their own tent. Elsewhere in the Similan Islands, camping is prohibited, as are campfires. If you're not camping out, it's absolutely necessary to book in advance through the Park Headquarters (see **Practical Information** above). Ko Miang also has the area's only restaurant, a rather over-priced affair so you're better off bringing your own grub.

▣ ACTIVITIES. November through February, sea turtles lay eggs on the beach at **Ko Hu Yong.** To explore the underwater in depth, you'll need to shell out money for a tour. **Khao Lak** on the mainland is the launching point for many of these tours. A typical dive leaves from Phuket and lasts 4 nights and 3 days and includes 10 dives (10,000-20,000฿). If you're not interested in diving, there's superb snorkeling and hiking (with fantastic views) and, well, whatever else one fancies to do in a timeless paradise.

KO PHI PHI DON   ☎075

The secret is out. Beautiful Ko Phi Phi Don—once an untouristed island dotted with swaying palms, shimmering turquoise waters, and isolated spits of sand—is now *the* destination for backpackers in Southern Thailand. Paradoxically, it was the filming of *The Beach*, which depicted secluded beach paradise, on nearby Ko Phi Phi Ley that helped transform the once ignored island into a hub of backpacker activity. Instead of the peace and solace promised by the film, however, travelers will find street after street of restaurants, travel agencies, and guest houses. It's not uncommon to bump into a traveler who, with eyes alight, will refer to Ko Phi Phi Don as "paradise," and the small island's camp-like atmosphere and hedonistic nightlife support the claim. However, pessimists know that utopias are myths and Ko Phi Phi Don may be a more appropriate model for Paradise Lost. The inland is now strewn with garbage; fish-filled fringes of coral are being destroyed; the buzz of longtail boats never ceases. As a result, islanders and the government are currently debating the virtues of shutting down Ko Phi Phi Don for an entire year. Whatever its fate, for now, only Ko Phangan on

the opposite coast can match Ko Phi Phi Don in terms of balancing island entertainment and island ambiance. Yes, the beaches are beautiful, but, to be sure,
none of them is *The Beach*. It's too late for that.

> **NO MORE, WE PROMISE** *Let's Go* promises not to mention *The Beach*
> again in its coverage of Ko Phi Phi Don and Ko Phi Phi Ley to respect the wishes
> of travelers as sick of the reference as we are. Yes, *The Beach* was filmed here.
> Please get over it—we have.

☞ TRANSPORTATION

To get to Ko Phi Phi Don (generally known as Ko Phi Phi), go through either **Ko
Lanta, Krabi,** or **Phuket.** Ferries depart regularly from Ko Phi Phi to the above destinations, except during the low season, when ferry service may be irregular as
rough seas can make travel dangerous. From **Ton Sai Pier,** boats head to: **Ko Lanta**
(2hr.; 11:30am, 2pm; 200฿); **Krabi** (1½hr.; 9am, 1:30pm; 200฿); **Phuket** (1½hr.; 9am,
2:30pm; 250฿). Boats to uninhabited **Ko Phi Phi Ley** depart from the pier and can
also be hired independently from Ao Thon Sai travel agencies. Hire **longtail boats**
for more remote beaches.

◨ ◪ ORIENTATION AND PRACTICAL INFORMATION

Shaped like a lop-sided dumbbell, Ko Phi Phi is small and, without roads, is
devoid of vehicular traffic. It's easy to walk the entire island, save the parts
that consist of high cliffs. The main port of call is pretty **Ao Thon Sai Bay,** nestled
in the narrow part of the island, where travelers come to check email, shop,
eat, make travel plans and party until morning. Only a decade ago, this area
was relatively undeveloped, but today a slapdash network of businesses have
turned Ao Thon Sai Bay into a busy village. On the other side of the island,
beautiful **Ao Lo Dalam** has several bungalows. Smaller, less developed beaches
ring the island's outer peninsulas, the most popular of which is **Hat Yao (Long
Beach),** east of Ao Thon Sai. The more rugged interior affords stellar views of
the bays and surrounding islands.

Travel Agencies: The **TAT** office in Krabi serves Ko Phi Phi (see p. 364). Ao Thon Sai
travel agencies arrange trips to Ko Phi Phi Ley and boat/train/bus combos to Bangkok
and Malaysia. **Maya Tour & Travel** (☎612 403), in Tonsai Bay, is helpful and offers
many tours, including a good snorkeling excursion. From the pier, take a right; it's 20m
on the right.

Currency Exchange: For best rates, get cash before heading to Ko Phi Phi. The **Siam
Commercial Bank** in Ao Thon Sai exchanges cash and gives credit card advances.
Open daily 9:30am-7:30pm. Travel agents have poor rates.

Emergency: ☎191. **Tourist Police (Bangkok):** ☎1155.

Local Tourist Police: Off the pier in Ao Thon Sai. Provides some tourist information.
English spoken. Erratic hours. **Police booth** past the Chao Khao Lodge in Ao Thon Sai.

Medical Services: Pi Pi Hospital (☎622 151), in Ao Thon Sai, to the left of the pier.
Basic medical services. Some English spoken. Open daily 8:30am-noon and 1-4:30pm.

Telephones: Private travel agencies in Ao Thon Sai offer expensive connections. Unless
it's an emergency, wait until you get back onto the mainland.

Internet Access: Plentiful all over Ao Thon Sai. Type fast—it's expensive. 3฿ per min.

ACCOMMODATIONS

Ko Phi Phi's bungalows are plentiful but fluctuate in price and quality between high and low seasons. Generally, the island is more expensive than its neighbors, but rooms are cheaper around the pier and isolated beaches. It pays to explore the outer rims of the island, where fewer mainstream backpackers venture. Accommodations are listed by beach.

AO LO DALAM AND AO THON SAI. The best place for thrifty travelers is Ao Thon Sai's pier area, where loads of fly-by-night travel agencies offer cheap accommodations. It's conveniently located to shops and restaurants, but far from the beach, and the bungalows are poor in quality and value. Don't settle for the closest place to the pier. But if you must, **Chong Khao Lodge ❸**, between the pier and Ao Lo Dalam Bay, is not highly recommended, but it's one of the cheapest places on the island—hence, a backpacker favorite. Plain plywood bungalows have crusty squat toilets and spigots are scattered amidst litter and clucking chickens. The restaurant shows flicks. (Singles 200฿; doubles 300-400฿.) Popular on the island, the slightly upscale **Charlie Beach Resort ❺** has clean bungalows on beachfront property. It has a lively **restaurant ❷** attached. Bungalows in the back are a bit noisier (600-1000฿). Across from Ao Thon Sai, Ao Lo Dalam's handsome crescent-shaped bay is good for swimming and sunbathing.

HAT HIN KOHN AND LAEM HIM. Just southeast of Ao Thon Sai, a path by a rocky hill leads to flat Hat Hin Kohn, a long stretch of sand generously sprinkled with bungalows. The water and sand conditions are decent but far from the island's best. **Andaman Guest House ❺** has rows of new rooms that are plain but fairly clean. (Singles and doubles 500-600฿.) The staff are eager to attract backpackers to the similarly named but more professional **Andaman Resort ❺** at the end of the beach. Clean, white bungalows occupy a quiet spot by the island's sole primary school. (Singles and doubles 850฿.) Heading right from the pier next to the coast takes you along a paved walkway and round a small promontory known as Laem Him (still part of Ao Thon Sai). Past Laem Him is a stretch of quieter beach than Ao Thon Sai, which is completely overrun with longtail boats. Two bungalow operations, inland from the path after the mosque, are great values. **Gypsy 1 ❸**, about 100m from the shore, has clean and basic bungalows with bath at rock-bottom prices by Phi Phi standards, as does **Gypsy 2 ❸**, 50m farther on. (☎01 229 1674. Bungalows 350-600฿ depending on season.)

MA PRAO AND HAT YAO (LONG BEACH). The best option in the area is actually just before Long Beach on a lush promontory called Ma Prao. The aptly named **◧Ma Prao Bungalows ❸** has charming wood and bamboo huts secluded against the hill and only a stone's throw from the water—it's like staying in a jungle treehouse with a tropical pool only meters away. The restaurant has excellent ambiance, music, drink, and food. (☎622 486. Basic bungalows 300฿, with amenities up to 800฿.) Just over the hill, past Ma Prao, is Hat Yao known commonly as Long Beach. It has Ko Phi Phi's best sand and swimming, but staying here can be problematic for latenight partiers. Hat Yao's good mix of budget accommodations complement its pleasant beach conditions. It's possible to walk here from Ao Thon Sai by continuing past Hat Kin Kohn through some rocky jungle, but the 30-45min. walk is a bit tedious. Longtail boats (40฿) from Ao Thon Sai's pier are more convenient. The most wallet-friendly accommodation is the friendly, expat-run **Long Beach Resort ❷**, offering little more than four walls surrounding a bed, but at least it's with a smile. (☎612 217. Singles and doubles 150-350฿.)

🔲 🎵 FOOD AND ENTERTAINMENT

Ko Phi Phi contains an outstanding range of international cuisine as a result of its healthy expat population, many of whom have started businesses on the island. Homesick tourists munch on faux Italian, Mexican, and Swedish fare in restaurants all over the island. The cream of the crop is ▨**Cosmo Resto ❸,** an Italian restaurant with exceptional handmade pasta. Run by an Italian expat, the restaurant is only open for dinner but closes on random days of the week for preparation. When it's open, the tiny, unassuming place is one of Thailand's best restaurants. (No phone. Open for dinner roughly 5 days per week.) The **Lemongrass Restaurant ❷,** off the main drag in Ao Thon Sai, is one of the only places to get good Thai food. (Rice dishes 60฿. Curries 70-80฿. Open daily 9am-11pm.) Ma Prao Bungalows has a charming **restaurant ❷** (see **Accommodations,** above), which serves quality Thai food. There are plenty of pancake stalls, bakeries, and excellent seafood restaurants in Ao Thon Sai. Take your pick.

By night, Ao Thon Sai transforms into a surprising hotbed of nightlife activity. Backpackers wander about, mingling more as alcohol makes the world seem gentler. **Jordan's Irish Bar** denies anything Irish in favor of any music that will make *farang* wave their hands in the air and dance like they just don't care. The self-explanatory **Rolling Stoned Bar** blasts chill music and good times until sunrise. The similarly themed **Reggae Bar** has a large dance floor and a Thai boxing ring featuring nightly matches (starting around 10pm). **Carlito's Bar** on the walkway toward Long Beach has live entertainment. Look for drink specials at all of the above bars.

🐟 WATER SPORTS

Ko Phi Phi's waters are so clear you almost don't need to bother with a mask to check out the marine life. **Bamboo Island** and **Mosquito Island** are famous dive sites. There are many dive shops and tour agents eager—extremely eager—to serve you. Dive courses here generally cost 10,000฿ for a PADI certification course (far more expensive than Ko Tao). **Visa Diving Center** is one of the best. In addition to diving, snorkeling is also outstanding and far cheaper (usually 500฿ for a day trip with lunch and gear included). Longtail boats provide for a more intimate, enjoyable experience than the larger motor boats. **Maya Tour & Travel** (see **Travel Agenices,** p. 305) runs quality half-day and full-day tours.

🔳 DAYTRIP FROM KO PHI PHI: KO PHI PHI LEY

Five years ago, someone filmed a movie on Ko Phi Phi Ley. Struggling to cope with the post-Hollywood tourist demand, the island has become the battleground between corporate filmmakers and environmental groups, which claim that the island's delicate environment has been irreversibly damaged by the planting of coconut palms and beach digging that occurred during filming. Politics aside, the real reason to visit the island is for the natural beauty that made it such a spectacular backdrop in the first place.

Getting to Ko Phi Phi Ley from Ko Phi Phi Don usually involves some sort of organized tour. Plenty of Ao Thon Sai agencies arrange daytrips to the island, but individual longtail boat tours around the island cost less. While the limestone cliffs that practically enclose white-sand Ao Maya make it stunning, the row of longtails and wandering tourists mean that it hardly lives up to expectations created by images from the film. Ao Maya and Ko Phi Phi Ley are really just more stops on any snorkeling or day tour from Ko Phi Phi Don and are nothing to get too excited about. Tours generally include a stop at Ao Maya as well as a look at the prehistoric paintings in the **Viking Cave** at the northeast point on the island.

KRABI
☎ 075

The word is out about Krabi, in particular about the nearby beaches of Hat Rai Lay and Ao Nang. The town of Krabi is little more than a necessary transit point, but it has a mellow vibe all its own, and the emergence of excellent budget accommodations more than redeems overnight stays.

THE VIEW FROM ABOVE

The lowdown: The new budget hotspot.
Gateway cities: Ko Lanta, Phuket Town, Trang.
Nearby islands: Ko Phi Phi Don, Ko Phi Phi Ley.
Beaches: Ao Nang, Ao Lo Dalam, Hat Hin Kohn, Hat Phra Nang, Hat Rai Lay, Hat Yao (Long Beach).
Highlights: Rai Lay's limestone cliffs, Phra Nang's Princess Cave, and beautiful Ko Phi Phi Ley, the filming site of *The Beach*.

⊏ TRANSPORTATION

Buses: The **bus station** (☎ 611 804) is 5km outside town. Red *songthaew* run between the bus station and town (every 15min., 7฿). Buses to: **Bangkok** (12hr., 4 per day 7am-7pm, 486-710฿); **Hat Yai** (5hr., every hr. 9am-3:20pm, 173฿); **Phuket** (5hr., every hr. 9am-5pm, 117฿); **Satun** (5hr., 11am and 1pm, A/C 175฿); **Surat Thani** (4½hr., every hr. 9:30am-1:30pm, 80฿; A/C 3½hr.; 7, 8, 9, 11:40am, 1pm; 120฿); **Trang** (2½hr., every 2hr. 9am-5pm, 90฿). Private travel agents operate **A/C minivans** to various towns in Thailand and Malaysia.

Ferries: Longtail boats leave from **Chao Fah Pier** on Kongka Rd. for **Hat Rai Lay** (30min., 8am-5pm, 70฿). From the same pier, **express boats** go to **Ko Lanta** (2½hr.; 10:30am, 1:30pm; 200฿) and **Ko Phi Phi** (1½hr.; 10:30am, 2:30pm; 200฿). Service is irregular during low season. Tourist offices have up-to-date boat schedules.

Local Transportation: Songthaew waiting opposite the City Hotel by the market go to **Ao Nang** (20฿, 30฿ after 6pm); the **Shell Cemetery** (16-20฿); **Wat Tham Sua** (20฿); and other places near Krabi.

◄◼ ⁊ ORIENTATION AND PRACTICAL INFORMATION

Central Krabi is compact and easily navigable by foot. **Utarakit Rd.,** the city's main street, runs parallel to the **Krabi River** and is home to the post office, telecommunications office, banks, travel agencies, and TAT office. Parallel and one block over, **Maharat Rd.** has shops and cheap eateries. Boats to Hat Rai Lay, Ko Phi Phi, and Ko Lanta leave from **Chao Fah Pier** on **Kongka Rd.,** which branches off Utarakit Rd. and runs along the river.

Tourist Offices: TAT (☎ 612 740), on Utarakit Rd. Good maps. Open daily 8:30am-4:30pm.

Tours: For a small town, Krabi has an obscene number of travel agencies. For boat tickets, go to **PP Family** on Chao Fah Pier (☎ 612 463). The company operates most ferry services from Krabi. Open daily 7:30am-9pm.

Currency Exchange: Several banks line Utarakit Rd including **Bangkok Bank,** at 147 Utarakit. Open M-F 8:30am-3:30pm.

Markets: A large market sets up across from the City Hotel on Sukhon Rd.

Emergency: ☎ 191. **Tourist Police (Bangkok):** ☎ 1155.

Police: ☎ 637 208. 500m past the post office. Little English spoken.

Medical Services: The **Town Hospital** (☎ 611 227), on Utarakit Rd., 2km from town. Some English spoken. No credit cards. **Open 24hr.**

JUST PLANT IT
Community Involvement: Sustainable Development

The Southern Alternative Agriculture Network Committee for Sustainable Agriculture Reform was having a meeting at the village mosque in Krabi. When thirty men had entered the main hall and were seated on the floor in a large U, about ten women quietly filled the space. I was there to follow up on the progress of farms that had adopted four sustainable agriculture techniques: crop diversification (rubber and palm oil plantations have dominated Southern Thai agriculture since the turn of the century, but the products are subject to price fluctuations); organic farming methods; water conservation; and development of value added crops, such as medicinal herbs and rare flowers. As part of my work with the World Computer Exchange, I tagged along with Kumrab Panthong, an Ashoka Fellow who uses technology to set up a rural information network.

"What is sustainable agriculture?" asked the facilitator. "Grow trees," said one man. "I don't know what sustainable agriculture means for today, or tomorrow. Maybe it means something in another three or seven years!" said another man. I learned later that he was referring to the fact that this organization had been visiting and talking about this reform for the past four years. The project had never actually started until the current government finally agreed to provide funding. At the end of the meeting, they asked the villagers to fill out a survey. All of the men, who had been taking notes throughout the meeting (some on their hands), filled them out while the women looked on, penless. "The women have no pens," I noted, implying we should give them some. "Maybe they can't read," replied Kumrab. "We don't want to embarrass them."

That afternoon I tasted a snakefruit, now grown among rubber trees, and fresh sugar milled with a handmade machine powered by a landmower engine, and visited a house where the yard is a lush pharmacopoeia of medicinal plants. As I kept walking, I found myself in what I thought was a virgin jungle. I found shacks in patches cleared of undergrowth, raised to avoid floods, and surrounded by 35m of netting to keep in the chickens. I looked into the trees and noticed a wire, which led into a shack and directly to a TV. At a similar shack, a handmade machine powered by a bicycle pressed rubber into the shape of a doormat. On the way home, I saw a truck snailing along the highway, burdened by hundreds of rubber flaps giving off an overwhelming odor of latex.

Typically set among experimental and demonstration mango orchards, rice fields, and fish farms, the Thai Business In Rural Development (T-BIRD) initiative brings manufacturing businesses such as NIKE to rural areas. Not every factory is a sweatshop. Besides the luxury of being able to stay at home instead of leaving to find work, or *bai ha gin* as the Thais say, meaning "go find eat," in Bangkok, the workers at T-BIRD factories enjoy high employee rights standards plus health and education benefits. Companies are happy with the low turnover rates and strong work ethics of the workers. When you visit the factories, which look like basketball courts with sewing machines, the men and women stop, smile, and say "Hello! Where you come from?"

A better question is: what is sustainable development for Thailand? King Bhumibol's New Theory of Sustainable Development has resulted in Royal Projects scattered around the country. Stop in and look around. There will be people making bamboo products, planting strawberries instead of opium, farming fish, or studying hydroelectric power. They will want to see you. This is the Thai way, to share *Nam Jai* (Heart Water, Kindness).

Brett Renfrew is currently living and working in Bangkok as a teacher, as well as a corporate writer. He also runs a project to import used computers for use in rural schools all over Thailand.

Internet Access: All along Utarakit Rd. in cafes and guest houses (1฿ per min.).

Post Office: 190 Utarakit Rd. (☎611 497), on top of the hill on the left. *Poste Restante.* Open M-F 8:30am-4:30pm, Sa 9am-noon. **Postal code:** 81000.

ACCOMMODATIONS

Krabi has a good selection of budget accommodations, most of which lie one block from the pier along **Utarakit Rd.** Prices below represent high season rates; in the low season rates may be 100-200฿ cheaper.

■ **Chan-Cha-Lay Guest House,** 55 Utarakit Rd. (☎620 952), on the slope uphill. The recently opened guest house is already one of the hippest digs in town, with ultra-clean, bright rooms with showers. Popular restaurant and super friendly staff to boot. The airy blue interior brings the ocean to you. Shared baths. Laundry. Internet. Singles and doubles 200฿; twins 250฿. Reservations recommended. ❸

Grand Tower Hotel, 9 Chaofa Rd. (☎621 456), at the intersection with Utarakit Rd. Multi-storied, it's not your typical guest house, but it's popular with those waiting for the next ferry. Plain, cheap rooms with double mattresses. International phones, Internet, and fax service. Singles and doubles 150฿, with bath 300฿, with A/C 500฿; twins with bath 400฿, with A/C 700฿. ❷

City Hotel, 15/2-3 Sukhon Rd. (☎621 280), between Utarakit and Maharat Rd. in the heart of downtown. Off the main backpacker drag. Spacious, well-furnished rooms, all with cable TV and phone. Singles and doubles with fan 400฿, with A/C 550-650฿. ❹

Siboya Guest House, 69 Utarakit Rd. (☎623 561). Modestly-sized, cheap rooms are cozy with funky, fresh decor. Singles and doubles 120-150฿. ❷

Pan Guest House, 182 Utarakit Rd. (☎612 555), next to the post office. Cheapest place in town—and while it shows, the very basic and plain plywood huts are adequate. A lovely garden surrounds the huts. Singles and doubles 150฿, with bath 300฿. ❷

FOOD

There are two **night markets ❶,** one opposite the City Hotel (until 9pm) and one by the pier. Several *farang*-friendly restaurants and cheap food stalls with everything from Thai food to grilled cheese cluster on **Kongka Rd.,** just north of the pier. For a memorable experience, try **Ruenmai Thai ❷** on Maharat Rd., 2km from town past the hospital (motorcycle taxi 30฿). This huge outdoor restaurant has tables amidst jungle-like vegetation. For 60฿, try the blissful coconut cream prawn soup with *pak mieng* or edible ferns with fish. (Open daily 10am-10pm.) **Kwan Restaurant ❸,** 30 Kongkha Rd., serves reliable and affordable Thai and western meals and shakes. (Open daily 7:30am-5pm, until 9pm in high season.) Hang out with locals at the **Muslim Restaurant ❶,** 110 Praksa-Uthit Rd., a morning meeting spot for *roti* (10฿) and coffee (10฿).

SIGHTS

Krabi's most impressive sight is **Wat Tham Sua,** 8km outside town. A working monastery of monks, nuns, and tourists, the wat is best known for its **Tiger Cave.** Legend has it that a large tiger once lived here, and its footsteps adorn the wat's entrance (donation requested). Outside, stairs by the rear of the monastery lead 30-45min. up the mountain to a pair of **Buddha's footprints.** *Songthaew* (15min., 10฿) from the Sukhon St. market drop you off at an access road 2km from the wat. Otherwise, walk or take a motorcycle taxi (5min., 10฿) to the entrance.

NEAR KRABI

The world-renowned beaches near Krabi are some of Thailand's most popular, so if you're planning on staying at Ao Nang or Hat Rai Lay, it's best to bypass Krabi and head straight for the sand. Locals heartily embrace the arrival of sun- and sand-lovers, mostly for the sake of their wallets. A regional festival in November even celebrates the coming of a prosperous tourist season. Still, a supreme mellowness prevails.

HAT RAI LAY AND HAT PHRA NANG   ☎ 075

With spectacular limestone cliffs dropping onto sand beaches and luminous, turquoise waters, Hat Rai Lay has become a haven for both climbers and beach lovers. It has developed into a climbing mecca, especially for beginners; climbing schools are opening all over the beach. For those who prefer their feet on the ground, Hat Rai Lay also offers hiking trails, a mellow nightlife, and pretty beaches, while Hat Phra Nang's caves provide hours of audacious exploring.

■ ORIENTATION. Hat Rai Lay is actually two beaches, **Hat Rai Lay East** and **Hat Rai Lay West,** which occupy opposite sides of a peninsula that juts out into the sea. The only way to get to Hat Rai Lay is by **longtail boat** docking at Hat Rai Lay East from Ao Nang (50฿) or Krabi (70฿). This side of the peninsula has a few budget accommodations, climbing schools, mangrove trees, and the heart-stopping duo of Hat Rai Lay East and **Hat Phra Nang.** To get to Hat Phra Nang from Hat Rai Lay East, with your back to the boats, turn left and walk to the end of the beach; a dirt path to your right snakes to the limestone cliffs and crystal waters of Hat Phra Nang. Hat Rai Lay West can be reached easily by cutting through Sand Sea Bungalows or Rai Lay Bay Bungalows.

🏠🍴 ACCOMMODATIONS AND FOOD. Finding good deals on Hat Rai Lay can be more difficult than scaling its toughest climb. Prices listed reflect high season (Nov.-May) rates. De-facto segregation keeps backpackers on Hat Rai Lay East. **Ya-Ya Bungalow** (☎ 622 593), the most popular among budget travelers, has the best off-beach location and a lively restaurant. On the northern end of Hat Rai Lay East, **Viewpoint Bungalow ❹** has clean, modern bungalows with enormous windows that put the "view" in Viewpoint and the only Internet access on the beach. (☎ 622 588. Singles with bath 400฿; doubles with bath 500-800฿.) **Diamond Bungalow ❸** has the cheapest accommodations on the island. (Singles and doubles 350฿, with bath 500฿, with fan 700฿, with A/C 900-1200฿.)

Hat Rai Lay West has more upscale accommodations. **Rai Lay Village Resort ❺** charges twice as much as Hat Rai Lay East bungalows for fancy, posh bungalows with nicer baths and landscaping. (☎ 622 578. Bungalows 1200-2500฿.) Out-of-this-world expensive **Dusit Rayavadee Resort ❻** dominates Hat Phra Nang, though there never seems to be anyone staying there. It's much more practical to find cheaper accommodation on Hat Rai Lay East and daytrip it to Hat Phra Nang.

After a hard day of climbing, many travelers flock to **CoCo Restaurant ❷** on the northern part of Hat Rai Lay East for tasty Thai dishes, including chicken wrapped in steamed leaves (60฿). **Cholay Pancakes ❶,** in a booth outside Ya-Ya Bungalow, serves delicious *roti* for 15-30฿. (Open daily 9am-midnight.)

🏔🎭 SIGHTS AND ENTERTAINMENT. The Rai Lay beaches and environs have become the rock climbing capital of Southeast Asia, and several rock climbing schools have popped up to meet the increasing demand. Prices are the same everywhere. **Krabi Rock Climbing,** on Hat Rai Lay East is well-known for its friendly staff. (☎ 676 0642. Half-day course 800฿, 1-day course 1800฿, 3-day course 5000฿.)

Hot Rock Climbing (☎01 677 3727), next to CoCo Restaurant on Hat Rai Lay East, is also popular. Don't let inexperience scare you—tons of others are first-timers too.

Adventures closer to sea level await you on Hat Phra Nang. Extending past the water, dagger-like stalagmites protect **Princess Cave**, which can be explored by land or sea with a flashlight. About halfway down the dirt path to Hat Phra Nang from Hat Rai Lay East, another dirt path leads to a few mountain viewpoints and a lagoon best visited at high tide. Bring sturdy footwear, expendable clothing (especially during the wet season), and companions for the challenging climb to the top. Closer to Hat Rai Lay East beach, a hidden path leads to the popular and appropriately named **Diamond Cave**, whose walls sparkle with the precious stone.

Nights on Hat Rai Lay bring together opposite tourist factions: beach bums and hard-core climbing/hiking/diving types. Everyone achieves equal party status under the moon, relaxing at **Yaya's Bar**, **Last Bar**, or the **beachfront**, where fire dancers sometimes light up the beach to pulsing music.

AO NANG

Ao Nang's accessibility by car gives it a completely different atmosphere from either secluded Rai Lay or Phang Nga. With brightly colored shops and beachfront hotels, it has a very pleasant holiday feel. The bustle dies out past the Phra Nang Inn. From here, you can walk down a dirt road into forested seclusion. Alternatively, rent a bike as an escape and zoom through rice paddies, villages, and the ubiquitous waving kids.

On the road that runs past the beach, there are **moneychangers**, a **minimarket**, restaurants, and **tour offices**. For **police**, dial ☎611 222 (**emergency** ☎191, **Bangkok tourist police** ☎1155). White **songthaew** from Krabi leave from Pattana Rd. opposite the New Hotel (every 15min. or when full, 20฿) to ply the route to Ao Nang and Hat Noppharat Thara.

Sea Canoe Krabi (☎612 740), near Gift's Bungalows, offers half-day (500-800฿) and full-day (800-1200฿) self-paddled trips along the coast as well as rental equipment. A guided trip, including meals, fruit, and water costs 1200-1600฿. Rent **mountain bikes** (30฿ per hr.) at **Ao Nang Adventure Travel and Tour** on the corner before the main shops coming from Krabi. Ask for a map. **Nosy Parker's Elephant Trekking and River Camp** (☎637 464) offers elephant treks (700฿) and half-day tours (1600฿).

Blue Bayou ❸, in the quiet outskirts of town, has kayak rentals (200฿ per 2hr.) and a volleyball court. The **restaurant ❸** serves Thai and Western cuisine. (☎637 148. Single and double bungalows in high season with fan 350-500฿, with A/C 750฿; in low season 200-400/500฿.) If you happen to hit Ao Nang in the low season, fabulous rates abound. One such steal is **For You House ❸**, 245/11-12 Moo 2, which has hotel-style rooms with A/C, minibar, satellite TV, and hot showers. Get off the *songthaew* at Henry's Collection, and walk behind it. (☎637. High season 600฿, low season 300฿.) Other cheap places are in the same soi as For You.

Last Cafe ❷, at the end of Ao Nang Beach, after the road becomes a dirt trail, is only open in the high season. (Muesli with fruit and yogurt 30฿; omelettes 40฿; Thai noodle soup 30฿. Open daily 6:30am-midnight.) The ideally situated **Poda Restaurant ❸**, in Felix Phra Nang Inn, in the circular building, is an alternative to bungalow basics. The green curry soup with shrimp is exceptional. (Open daily 7am-10pm.) **Azzurra Ristorante-Pizzeria ❸** cooks homemade pasta, fresh bread, and focaccia with cheese, tomatoes, and lettuce (80฿). (Open daily 7am-11pm.)

KHLONG THOM

The **Khao Nawe Choochee Lowland Forest** is one of the last remaining forests of its kind in Thailand. Among the 290-plus bird species that nest in the forest is *Pitta gurneyi*, a brightly colored, ground-dwelling bird of which only 150 remain. The **Thung Tieo Nature Trail**, a 2.7km path, eases through some of Thailand's most lush and undisturbed slices of nature. Bring your swimming gear and hop into the natural pool or hot spring for relaxation. To get to the trail, motorbike from Krabi or take a *songthaew* to **Khlong Thom. Mr. Koyou** at the **Krabi Bird Club,** 24 Phetkasem Rd., will haul tourists around in his pickup truck (300฿). Contact him by calling the park's tourist office (☎ 622 124); TAT officials can also track him down. If hiring a motorcycle taxi from Khlong Thom (100฿), arrange return transport.

KO LANTA YAI

Ko Lanta Yai is an up-and-coming island on the ko-hopping backpacker trail. Because the island's industry has yet to be completely shelved in favor of tourism, there's a local flavor here that is lacking on tourist hotspots like Ko Samui. But it's hardly a rugged or particularly undeveloped island, with boats stopping regularly from Krabi at Ko Lanta Yai's **Ban Sala Dan Pier** (2½hr.; 10:30am, 1:30pm; return 8am; 150฿) at the northern tip of the island. Boats also leave from Ko Phi Phi for Ko Lanta (1½hr., 10am-1pm, 150฿). Otherwise, minivans depart year-round from Krabi and connect via ferry to Ko Lanta (2hr.; 11am, 1, 4pm; 150฿). **Ban Sala Dan** is the island's largest town, with plenty of tour operators, a police booth, a post office, Internet cafes, banks, a health center, and other conveniences.

Around the corner from Ban Sala Dan is Ko Lanta Yai's main sandy drag, **Hat Klong Dao,** a 2km beach sprinkled with quality resorts. **Golden Bay Cottages ❺** offers comfortable, spacious accommodations with huge price swings depending on the season. (High season cottages with fan 800฿, with A/C 1500฿; in low season 100฿/ 300-600฿.) Klong Dao has decent corals at its north end. The beach faces directly west making for stellar sunsets. There are eight other beaches on the island, including the beautiful **Nin** and **Kanthiang** beaches for scenery and **Hin** beach for snorkeling. There is excellent diving and snorkeling at the offshore islands. In the interior of Ko Lanta Yai, there are a few outstanding daytrips, most notably the **Tham Mai Ka** caves. You can also see waterfalls and go on elephant treks.

Two hours by boat from Krabi, Ko Lanta is actually closer to Trang. Low season makes the island a ghost town, ideal for those seeking cheap solitude. **Klong Dao Beach** and **Long Beach** are the main beaches in the north; **Kantiang Bay** and **Klong Jak Bay** greet travelers headed south.

TRANG   ☎075

Trang has been riding the highway (Hwy. 4, that is) of prosperity for 30 years. Though the provincial capital itself is hardly worth writing home about, the surrounding areas stockpile 119km worth of national-park beaches and a formidable collection of small islands, all undisturbed by the brazen bandits of large-scale development. Off the usual circuit, Trang is nice for travelers seeking relief from *farang*-heavy traffic and a chance to explore undeveloped areas.

▐ TRANSPORTATION

Flights: Trang Airport (☎ 210 804), on Trang-Palian Rd., 7km south of the city. Take Trang Travel's airport vans (30฿) or a tuk-tuk (50฿) into town. **Thai Airways,** 199/2 Visetkul Rd. (☎ 218 066). Turn right at the clock tower onto Visetkul Rd.; it's several blocks down on the left, just past Soi 5. Open daily 8am-noon and 1-4:30pm. Daily flights to **Bangkok** (9:15pm, additional flights F-Su 6pm; 2575฿).

Trains: Railway station (☎ 218 012), at the west end of Phraram 6 Rd. Fares listed are 2nd-class express. Trains to: **Bangkok** (16hr.; sleeper 2:30, 5:20pm; 970฿) via **Chumphon** (7hr., 571฿) and **Surat Thani** (5hr., 201฿).

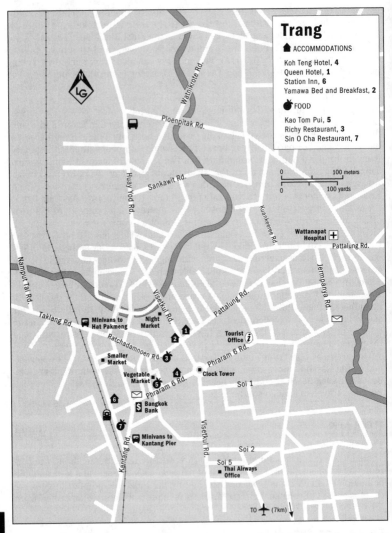

Trang

🏠 ACCOMMODATIONS

Koh Teng Hotel, **4**
Queen Hotel, **1**
Station Inn, **6**
Yamawa Bed and Breakfast, **2**

🍎 FOOD

Kao Tom Pui, **5**
Richy Restaurant, **3**
Sin O Cha Restaurant, **7**

Buses: Bus station (☎215 718), on Huay Yod Rd., north of downtown. Check with TAT for buses that leave from other parts of city. Buses to: **Bangkok** (10hr., 4:30pm, 565฿); **mini-buses** to **Hat Yai** (every 30min. 6am-6pm; 70฿, with A/C 99฿); **Krabi** (2hr., every hr. 7am-6pm, 90฿); **Phang-Nga** (4hr., every hr. 7am-6pm, 139฿); **Phuket** (5hr., every hr. 7am-6pm, 189฿); **Satun** (3hr.; 1:30, 3:30pm; 101฿); **Surat Thani** (3hr., every hr. 9:30am-5pm, 125฿; leaves from train station).

Local Transportation: Tuk-tuks within the city run 15฿. **Taxis** (15฿) and **minivans** (10฿) leave when full from different parts of town (every 20min. 5am-7pm). For vans to **Kantang Pier,** go down Phraram 6 Rd. by the train station, and turn right on Kantang Rd.;

vans line up on the right (15-20฿). Vans to **Hat Tao Mai, Hat Yong Ling,** and **Hat Pakmeng** leave from Tha Klang Rd., also by the train station (every hr. 7am-5pm, 50฿).

✈ 🛈 ORIENTATION AND PRACTICAL INFORMATION

Buses arrive at the **bus station** near the intersection of **Ploenpitak Rd.** and **Huay Yod Rd.,** a 20min. walk north of town or 5min. by motorcycle taxi or tuk-tuk (both 20฿). The **railway station** sits at the west end of **Phraram 6 Rd.,** a large hotel-lined avenue with the **TAT office,** landmark **clock tower,** and most other tourist services, including banks, Internet cafes, and travel agencies. North of Phraram 6 Rd., **Ratchadamnoen Rd.** (which becomes **Pattalung Rd.**) winds roughly parallel to the main day market and connects to Phraram 6 Rd. by Kantang Rd. to the west and Wisekul Rd. to the east by the clock tower.

Tourist Office: TAT (☎/fax 215 580), next to the Trang Hotel on Phraram 6 Rd. Very helpful staff and free maps. Open daily 8am-5pm. Private travel agencies offering organized tours and transport line Phraram 6 Rd.

Currency Exchange: Bangkok Bank, 2 Phraram 6 Rd. (☎218 203), one block from the train station on the right. **24hr. ATM.** Open M-F 8:30am-3:30pm.

Markets: The **Day market** sells mostly produce and is near the train station. One **night market** is outside the Diamond Department Store near the train station; another, bigger one is at the intersection of Visetkul and Phraram 6 Rd.

Emergency: ☎ 191. **Tourist Police (Bangkok): ☎** 1155.

Police: 6 Pattalung Rd. (☎211 311). Some English spoken. **Open 24hr.** There is no local tourist police.

Medical Services: Wattanapat Hospital, 247 Pattalung Rd. (☎218 585), at the intersection with Ploenpitak Rd., northeast of the clock tower. Some English spoken. **Open 24hr.**

Internet Access: All over Phraram 6 Rd. 30฿ per hr.

Post Offices: GPO (☎218 521), at the bend on Jermpanya Rd., which branches north from Phraram 6 Rd. It's a 20min. walk from train station. *Poste Restante.* **International phones.** Open M-F 8:30am-3:30pm. **Branch office** on Phraram 6 Rd., 1 block from train station. Open M-F 8:30am-4:30pm, Sa-Su 9am-noon. **Postal code: 92000.**

🛏 ACCOMMODATIONS

Trang's budget accommodation situation is beginning to brighten as word spreads about the offshore islands and trekking opportunities near the town.

Yamawa Bed and Breakfast, 94 Visetkul Rd. (☎75 216 617; www.trang-yamawa.com), is Trang's first guest house, and an excellent one at that. Ten rooms of varying shapes and sizes are carefully decorated. TVs, reading rooms, a terrace, Internet and massage parlor. Rooftop bar under construction. The staff is very helpful. 200฿ per person; breakfast additional 50฿. Prices may increase. ❸

Koh Teng Hotel, 77-79 Phraram 6 Rd. (☎218 148), 5 blocks from the train station on the left. Koh Teng has recently added ten modern rooms that are reasonably priced and have satellite TV. Request one of these as the older ones don't really cut it. The downstairs restaurant isn't bad. Singles and doubles 180฿. ❸

Queen Hotel, 85-89 Visetkul Rd. (☎218 229; fax 210 415). Standard, clean rooms. Singles 180฿, with A/C 280฿. ❸

Station Inn (☎223 393), 100m left of the train station when exiting. Closest option to the train station. Large doubles are old and passably clean. Rooms with fan 260฿. ❸

SOUTHERN THAILAND

◘ FOOD

Trang's cuisine has a distinct Chinese flavor. Crispy roasted, honey-dipped pork, *paa tong ko* (Chinese doughnuts), and dim sum make delicious breakfasts. The town has two **night markets ❶**, a smaller one next to Diamond Department Store by the train station, and a larger one down Visetkul Rd. from the Phraram 6 Rd. intersection. (Both open daily 6-10pm.) There's also an expansive **day market ❷** by the train station with fresh produce. Nearby, **Sin O Cha ❷** has good service and reasonably priced breakfasts, pastries, and excellent Thai cuisine. **Kao Tom Pui ❸**, 111 Tarad Rd., halfway up Phraram Rd from the train station, on the right, is an open restaurant with excellent Thai fare. (Open daily 5pm-5am.) **Richy ❹**, 126 Rajedmenoen Rd. is a popular and clean place with breakfast, lunch, and dinner, though the portions are laughably small. (☎211 126. Most dishes 60-90฿.)

♫ ENTERTAINMENT

Trang's nightlife doesn't rival that of Phuket or Ko Phi Phi but offers a different kind of fun—the type you'll still remember the next morning. You'll find fierce creatures, not fierce parties. In the morning on Phraram 6 Rd., traders sell colorful **fighting fish.** Makeshift **cock fighting** arenas set up below stilt houses, and **bullfights** are staged once or twice a year (tickets from 100฿). Direct tuk-tuk drivers to Sanam Wuah Chon (10฿) near the bullfight field. The Trang Chamber of Commerce organizes commercial events, like the **Cake Festival** (Aug.) and **Barbecue Festival** (Sept.), which promote Trang's famed dessert and pork.

NEAR TRANG

Trang's surrounding areas offer a bevy of attractions, from caves to natural oceanside Edens, most of them overlooked by travelers making a beeline from Surat Thani to Ko Phi Phi, Phuket, or Malaysia. Expect few travelers in even relatively populated places like **Ko Mook** and **Pakmeng** and only a smattering of locals on isolated **Hat Yong Ling.** Most towns are accessible from Trang by minivans, which depart from various points around town. **Boats** to islands near Pakmeng, such as **Ko Hai** and Ko Mook, leave from **Pakmeng Pier** (100-300฿). Boats to **Ko Sukorn** leave from the pier at Tasae Cape in southern Trang Province.

■ **HAT YONG LING. Hat Yong Ling National Park** has two coves sheltered by wild orchid-covered rocky mountains. Trek through a lush patch of tropical forest and a bat cave to reach one of the best sand-and-sea combos around. Spelunkers should bring flashlights. Along the mountain base, the waves have carved out coves where locals often camp and grill seafood. Minibuses (50฿) leave every hour or when full from the station by the beach. Hat Yong Ling's **National Park Office** also accommodates its distant neighbor **Hat Jao Mai.** (☎210 099. Open M-F 9am-5pm.)

HAT PAKMENG. Busier Hat Pakmeng is the only mainland beach with a significant commercial presence, as evidenced by the numerous seafood stalls and restaurants that serve customers in their beach chairs. This darling beach is long but shallow so not good for swimming, though several picturesque limestone formations dotting the horizon make it pleasant. Minivans (45min., every hr., 50฿) from Trang will take you to the center of the beach or the popular **Pakmeng Resort ❹**, farther south, which has tidy bungalows and private baths. (☎210 321. Singles and doubles 400฿, with A/C 750-800฿.) To return to **Trang**, flag down a white van from the main road (roughly every hr.).

KO MOOK. Easily accessible from Pakmeng Pier, Ko Mook is the most popular choice among European budgeteers, and with four resorts, it's the most developed of the Trang Province islands. There is also a large Muslim community in the area. **Emerald Cave,** so named for its tinted waters, is a spectacular sight. To reach the cliff-surrounded lagoon at the center, visitors must swim. The lovelier and cheaper western side of the island boasts a sweet white-sand beach. Of the island's four resorts, **Had Farung Bungalows ❸** is the least expensive (bungalows 200฿, with bath 300฿), and **Sawatdee Resort ❸** has a highly recommended restaurant (bungalows 300฿). On the west side, similarly-priced **Muk Resort ❸** (☎214 441; bungalows 300฿) and **Muk Garden Resort ❸** (☎211 372; bungalows 300฿) can arrange transportation to the island from their offices in Trang. To get to Ko Mook on your own, take a minivan to **Pakmeng Pier** (1hr., 50฿) and hop on a boat to the island (1hr.; 11am; 400฿, alone 600฿).

KO HAI (KO NGAI). With white-sand beaches and three pricey resorts, teardrop-shaped Ko Hai (sometimes spelled "Ko Ngai") is a true tropical paradise and an excellent dive and snorkeling spot. **Koh Ngai Villa ❹** has the cheapest rooms and arranges transport to and from the island. (☎210 496. Bungalows with fan 400-700฿, depending on season.) More upscale **Koh Ngai Resort ❺** has a diving center. (☎210 317. Bungalows 600-780฿.)

KO KRADAN. Although it's beautifully pristine, Ko Kradan, under the protection of the **Hat Jao Mai National Park,** contains only one high-end resort, which does not do justice to the island. At **Ko Kradan Paradise Beach ❺,** they know you're a hostage, so the food is as expensive as the rooms; bring your own from the mainland. (☎211 391. Bungalows from 600฿.)

HAT YAI ☎074

Crowded and noisy Hat Yai is southern Thailand's transportation, commerce, and prostitution center. Shopping conquers all in this metropolitan arena, since almost everything—pirated Robbie Williams CDs, pet fish, women—is cheaper here than in Singapore or Malaysia. Despite the cosmopolitan veneer, it is a snorkeling hotspot. Travelers drink away their time while trying to fend off aggressive street hawkers valiantly trying to convince them that buying a fluffy purple ostrich on a string is necessary. Travelers would do well to bypass the town, although there are quality accommodations if a stay is essential.

▐ TRANSPORTATION

Flights: Airport (☎251 007), 13km west of Hat Yai. **Thai Airways,** 166/4 Niphat Uthit 2 Rd. (☎233 433). Open M-Sa 8am-5pm, Su 9am-4pm. Flights to: **Bangkok** (1½hr., 6 per day, 2885฿); **Kuala Lampur** (2hr.; F, Su 2:25pm; 9890฿); **Phuket** (45min., 11:15am, 1180฿); **Singapore** (2½hr., 1:10pm, 5760฿).

Trains: Railway station (☎243 705), at the west end of Thamnoon Vithi Rd. Trains to: **Bangkok** (16hr.; 5 per day 2:45-6:10pm; 3rd-class 275฿, sleeper 730-1200฿); **Butterworth, Malaysia** (5½hr., 7:40am, 233฿); **Sungai Kolok** (3½-4½hr.; 4 per day 6:30am-12:15pm; 3rd-class 60฿, 1st-class 159฿); **Surat Thani** (4-5hr., 5 per day, 215฿).

Buses: Bus station (☎232 404), on Ranchanawanit Rd., in the southeast corner of town. Buses also stop at the market on Phetkasem Rd. 10-15min. after scheduled departure time. Tuk-tuk from town to terminal 10฿. Buses to: **Bangkok** (14hr., 9 per day 7am-7pm, 535-830฿); **Chumphon** (9-10hr.; 7:15, 8:15, 9:30, 10:30am, noon; 162-280฿); **Krabi** (5hr., 11am, 173฿); **Padang Besar, Malaysia** (1½hr., every 10min. 5:45am-7:20pm, 26-36฿); **Phuket** (7hr., 13 per day 5:30am-9:30pm, 150-420฿);

Hat Yai

⌂ ACCOMMODATIONS
Cathay Guest House, **5**
King Hotel, **6**
Ladda Guest House, **2**

🍎 FOOD
Shangrila, **4**
T.S. Vegetarian, **1**

★ NIGHTLIFE
Post Laser Disc, **3**

Satun (2hr., every 15min. 5:20am-5:40pm, 36-65฿); **Sungai Kolok** (4hr., 1:30pm, 148฿); **Surat Thani** (5½hr., 10 per day 5:20am-3pm, 103-160฿).

Local Transportation: Tuk-tuks (10฿ inside town; 20฿ outside) and **motorcycle taxis** (20฿) crisscross downtown.

✦ ☎ ORIENTATION AND PRACTICAL INFORMATION

Hat Yai is large, confusing, and difficult to navigate without a map; pick one up from TAT or area hotels. Most travelers arrive at the train station on the west side of town at the intersection of **Rathakarn Rd.** and **Thamnoon Vithi Rd.**, one of the main commercial thoroughfares. Cheap guest houses and tourist services cluster near the train station. Buses enter the city on **Phetkasem Rd.** and drop passengers off in the rather confusing market area north of downtown. Central Hat Yai is organized by a grid system, marked by **Suphasarnrangsan, Prachathipat,** and Thamnoon Vithi Rd., running eastward from the train station; **Niphat Uthit 1, 2,** and **3 Rd.** intersect them from north to south.

Tourist Office: TAT, 1/1 Soi 2, Niphat Uthit 3 Rd. (☎ 243 747). Head south on Niphat Uthit 3 Rd. for 15-20min; it's on the left behind the police station. Enthusiastic staff, timetables, and free maps. Open daily 8:30am-4:30pm.

Tours: Ubiquitous on the Niphat Uthit roads. **Cathay Tour,** 93/1 Niphat Uthit 2 Rd. (☎ 234 535), in same building as the Cathay Guest House. Specializes in transportation to major Thai and Malaysian tourist destinations. Open daily 7am-8pm.

Immigration Office: ☎ 233 760. On Phetkasem Rd., west of the train tracks, next to the police station. Open M-F 8:30am-4:30pm.

Currency Exchange: There are banks on every block. **Bangkok Bank,** 39 Niphat Uthit 2 Rd. (☎ 235 330), near Suphasarnrangsan Rd. Open daily 8:30am-3:30pm.

Markets: Morning market on Niphat Uthit 3 Rd by the clock tower. **Day** and **night markets** between Montri 1 and 2 Rd., off Rathakarn Rd., north of the station. Find your special aquatic friend at the **pet fish market** on Niphat Uthit 1 Rd., south of the fountain.

Emergency: ☎ 191. **Tourist Police (Bangkok):** ☎ 1155.

Local Tourist Police: ☎ 246 733. On Sripoovanart Rd. near its intersection with Niphat Uthit 1 Rd. English spoken. **Open 24hr.**

Pharmacies: Santi Bheasaj, 129/12 Niphat Uthit 3 Rd. (☎ 246 537).

Medical Services: Hat Yai Public Hospital (☎ 230 8001), on Rathakarn Rd. The back of the hospital faces the GPO. English spoken. **Open 24hr.** Also **Songkhla Nakarind Hospital** (☎ 212 070), on Karnchanavanid Rd.

Telephones: Telecommunication Center, 490/1 Phetkasem Rd. (☎ 231 080), east of the rotary. Open daily 8am-midnight.

Internet Access: Plentiful and cheap in the area near the train station. 20฿ per hr.

Post Offices: GPO (☎ 243 013), at the corner of Niphatsongkraw 1 Rd. and Soi 4, 500m north of the rotary. *Poste Restante.* **International phone** upstairs. Open M-F 8:30am-4:30pm, Sa-Su 9am-noon. **Postal code:** 90110.

ACCOMMODATIONS

Many of the cheapest hotels in Hat Yai offer sleazy services, often under the guise of "ancient Thai massage." To avoid such unpleasantries, opt for one of the slightly more expensive but reputable guest houses suggested by TAT or stick to the tried-and-trusted train station area.

Cathay Guest House, 93/1 Niphat Uthit 2 Rd. (☎ 243 815), at the corner with Thamnoon Vithi Rd., a few blocks from the train station. Reminiscent of a university hostel. Backpackers linger over cheap breakfasts. Not the prettiest rooms, but cheap, and the friendly staff offers good tourist services. 4-bed dorms 90฿; singles 160฿; doubles 200฿; triples 250฿. ❶

Kings Hotel, 126/134 Niphat Uthit 1 Rd. (☎ 261 700). With over 75 rooms, this central hotel is remarkably well kept. Rooms come with standard amenities such as TV, A/C, and shower. Good value. Singles 390฿; twins and doubles 490฿; triples 590฿. ❹

Ladda Guest House, 13-15 Thamnoon Vithi Rd. (☎ 220 233), 5min. from train station. Clean baths and a friendly staff make up for the peeling paint. Singles with fan 200฿, with A/C 360฿; twins with fan 240฿. ❶

◪ FOOD

Muslim and Chinese influences are apparent in Hat Yai's dim sum restaurants and *roti* shops. Near Cathay Guest House on Thamnoon Vithi Rd. is **Shangrila ❸**, respected for its dim sum. (Open daily 6am-3pm.) **Food vendors ❶** set up day and night in the Niphat Uthit Rd. area and near the plaza market and cinema on Phetkasem Rd. For local flavor, try *khanom bueng* (crepes with shredded coconut). **T.S. Vegetarian ❶**, 16 Prachathipat Rd., across from Central Department Store, lets you pick three cooked veggies for your rice. (Dishes 20฿. Open daily 7am-8pm.)

♫ ENTERTAINMENT

Your trusty credit card may collapse from expenditure exhaustion on **Phetkasem Rd.** For cheaper, more structured entertainment, check out **Post Laser Disc,** 82-83 Thamnoon Vithi Rd., about two blocks past Niphat Uthit 3 Rd. opposite Indra Hotel. Travelers gather upstairs to watch American movies. There's live music nightly and a daily happy hour 4-9pm with great drink deals. (☎232 027. 30฿ cover charge for a table upstairs. Schedule on sandwich board outside. Open daily 9am-2am.) **Thai Boxing Stadium** hosts matches one or two weekends a month. (Around 180฿. Tuk-tuk to stadium 20-30฿.) **Bullfights** are staged on most weekend days. TAT has schedules and prices. A 35m by 15m reclining Buddha rests in **Wat Hat Yai Nai,** 7km west of Hat Yai. (Open daily 8am-5pm; tuk-tuk to wat 10฿ minimum.)

SONGKHLA   ☎074

With a pleasant mix of museums, restaurants, and guest houses, Songkhla is a rare Southern Thailand town; one that, in terms of interest to the tourist, stands completely on its own, without a nearby beach, island, or national park. As a result of multinational oil companies and academic institutes, it's also conspicuously wealthier and more refined than the average Thai town. Its manicured, wide streets create a suburban appearance and atmosphere. Nearby, Ko Yo contains one of the country's most worthwhile museums. If it's still just a beach you desire, well, Songhkla's got one of those too.

▣ TRANSPORTATION. Songkhla's proximity to Hat Yai (25km away) means that almost all transportation travels via its larger neighbor. **Buses** leave from the main **bus terminal** (☎354 333) on Thanon Ramnwithi Rd. to **Hat Yai** (30min., every 15min., 15฿). In front of Wat Jaeng, **A/C minivans** also depart for Hat Yai (30min., 20฿).

▨ PRACTICAL INFORMATION. The **TAT** in Hat Yai services Songkhla (see p. 377). For **emergencies,** call ☎191 or the **hospital** (☎447 446). You can always contact the **Bangkok tourist police** (☎1155). Banks are common throughout town. For an **Internet** connection, try **Dot Com,** adjacent to the Abritus Guest House. (2฿ per min. Open daily 9am-10pm.) The **post office** is on Thanon Nakhon Nai. (☎311 145. Open M-F 8:30am-3:30pm, Sa 9am-noon.)

▤◪ ACCOMMODATIONS AND FOOD. With its many expats, it's not surprising that Songkhla has a good range of guest houses. ◪**Amsterdam Guest House ❷**, 15/3 Rongmueng Rd., across from the museum, is a civilized European oasis where classical music sets a decidedly refined mood for evening drinks on the patio (or tasty treats in the adjacent Thai restaurant). The seven clean and comfortable rooms are a good value. (☎314 890. Rooms 180-2000฿.) One of the cheapest options in town is **Narai Hotel ❶**, 14 Chai Khao Rd., toward Simila beach by the bottom of Khao Tang Kuan. (☎311 078. Singles 100฿; doubles 150฿.) As the old saying goes, "When in Europe, eat bread." A local favorite, **The Hot Bread Shop ❶**, 33/4 Srisuda Rd., has heavenly baked goods. (☎09 879 4424. Open M-Sa 10am-10pm.)

◙ SIGHTS. Songkhla has a slightly different variety of sights than the typical Thai town menu of wats. **Songkhla National Museum,** on Wichianchom Rd. across from Amsterdam Guest House, is an impressive structure, built in 1878. Originally the mansion of the governor, it now houses a mix of passably interesting artifacts such as pottery, Buddha images, and Chinese panels dating all the way back to the prehistoric era. (Open W-Su 9am-noon and 1-4pm.) At sunset, Songkhla residents gather at **Samila beach** on Ratchamdanorn Rd. It's not suitable for swimming, but it's pleasant for the community feel and stunning sky. The **golden mermaid,** at the beach's heart, is one of Songkhla's most important landmarks.

▣ DAYTRIP FROM SONGKHLA: KO YO. Connected to Songkhla by Thailand's longest bridge, **Ko Yo** is only 20min. from Songkhla but it needs a day to see it all. What may be Thailand's best museum, the **◙Southern Folklore Museum,** can be reached via *songthaew* (10฿) from Jana Rd. The vast museum successfully presents over twenty fascinating threads of Southern culture, from the process of bead-making to a display of phallic coconut-scrapers. Spread over many rooms on a hillside (the exhibit halls themselves are reproductions of traditional Thai architecture), the museum also offers astounding views of the fishing activity—mainly hatcheries for shrimp, crabs, and sea bass—on Songkhla lake. It also includes a shop and cafe. (☎331 184. Open daily 8:30am-5pm. 50฿.) Ko Yo is also famous for its cotton-weaving industry. The Ko Yo **cloth market** is 2km before the museum heading back to Songkhla.

SATUN

☎074

Satun is best known to travelers entering Thailand from Malaysia or passing through Ko Tarutao, the national park off the coast. Since Ko Tarutao is only open from October to May, Satun has little for tourists during the other half of the year. Backpackers sometimes stick around to enjoy Satun's friendly small-town atmosphere, but the town itself has little more than a few open-air bars.

▐ TRANSPORTATION. Non-A/C **orange buses** leave from the school on Satunthanee Rd. for **Hat Yai** (2hr., every hr., 50฿) and from Sulakanukul, Burivanich, or Satunthanee Rd. for **Trang** (3hr., every 30min. 6:30am-5pm, 70฿). For A/C comfort to **Hat Yai,** take a **minivan** from the 7-Eleven on Satunthanee Rd. Also stops across the street from the Wangmai Hotel, in front of the open-air market (2hr., every 30min. or when full 6am-5pm, 150฿). A daily **ferry** service runs from Tamalang Pier to **Pulau Langkawi** (45min.; 9:30am, 1:30, 4pm; 180฿). In high season, **boats** run from Pak Bara Pier, north of Satun, to **Ko Lipe** (departs 10:30am, returns 3pm; round-trip 440฿) and **Ko Tarutao** (departs 10am, returns 3pm; round-trip 300฿).

▣▐ ORIENTATION AND PRACTICAL INFORMATION. At its south end, Satunthanee Rd. forms a "T" intersection with **Samanthapradit Rd.** South on Satunthanee Rd. just before the mosque, **Burivanich Rd.** splits to the right toward the immigration office. (☎711 080. Open M-F 8:30am-4:30pm.) Across the road, the **Thai Military Bank** and **Bangkok Bank** both have **24hr. ATMs** (AmEx/Cirrus/MC/V). The **police** are on the corner of Yarttrasawaddee and Satunthanee Rd. (☎711 025. **Emergency: ☎191. Open 24hr.) Pon Phasaj pharmacy,** 62 Burivanich Rd., is near the police box. (Open M-Sa 7am-9pm.) **Satun Hospital,** 55/1 Hatthakumsuksa Rd., is on the corner of Yarttrasawaddee Rd. (☎732 460. English spoken. **Open 24hr.**) Overseas calls can be made from the **Telecom Office,** 7 Satun Thanee Rd., at the base of the red tower. (Open M-F 8:30am-4:30pm.) Just east of the intersection of Satunthanee and Samanthapradit Rd. is the **post office**. (*Poste Restante*. Open M-F 8:30am-4:30pm. **Postal code:** 91000.) **Satun Travel and Ferry Service,** 45/8-9 Satunthanee Rd., sells tickets and arranges tours. (☎ 711 453. Open daily 8am-5pm.)

⌐◻ ACCOMMODATIONS AND FOOD. For the most central location, the **Satultanee Hotel ❷**, 90 Satunthanee Rd., has spacious, bright rooms with private baths. (Singles with fan 210฿, with A/C 370฿.) Satun's budget accommodation is limited to the **Rain Tong Hotel ❷**, 4 Samanthapradit Rd. From the Satunthanee Rd. intersection, turn onto Samanthapradit Rd. and walk toward the river; it's on the left. The old rooms are plain and clean with private baths and squat toilets. (☎ 711 036. Singles and doubles 140฿.)

Satun's Muslim majority sets the tone for the local cuisine. Several breakfast *roti* places serve patrons throughout the day. Both the extensive **day market ❶** on Satunthanee Rd. and the **night market ❶** on Tammango Uthit Rd. whip up cheap meals. (Duck noodle soup 20฿. Both open daily 5pm-midnight.) For a spicy nirvana, ask locals to point you to **Sri Trang ❷**, 127 Satunthanee Rd., which has served curry and rice dishes for as long as anyone can remember. (Open daily 4-9pm.)

KO TARUTAO NATIONAL MARINE PARK

Once a pirate outpost and then an island prison, Ko Tarutao National Marine Park is an archipelago of 51 spectacular islands in the Andaman Sea. Previously only forest department officials lived on mainland Ko Tarutao, but in the summer of 2002, CBS filmed its fifth season of *Survivor* here, bringing intense publicity to this relatively untouched wilderness. Home to a variety of wildlife, including deer, macaques, and four types of sea turtles, the park is an amazing and delicate ecosystem of coral and tropical jungle that is certain to become a more popular tourist destination.

Ko Tarutao is open from November to May. The park's main island is **Ko Tarutao,** 56km from Langkawi Island, a major point of entry into Malaysia. The largest of the park islands, covering 151 sq. km, Ko Tarutao was a labor camp for political prisoners during the 1940s. The **park office** (☎ 729 002) is at the northern tip of Tarutao on Ao Phante Melaka, near the pier and is only open during peak season. The pier in Pak Bara (☎ 074 783 485) provides tourist information only during peak season. The beaches along the west coast provide the best **campsites ❶** (about 10฿ per night). Bring your own tent. Otherwise, Tarutao provides **park housing ❸** (4-bed rooms 280฿; bungalows with two bedrooms and two baths 400฿; larger cottages with two bedrooms and one bath 600฿). Make reservations in advance with the National Park Division of the **Royal Forest Department** in Bangkok (☎ 02 579 0529) or in Pak Bara (☎ 781 285) before departure.

Ko Tarutao's beaches sprawl on its coral-filled west coast, while farther inland, waterfalls, mountains, caves, and wildlife attract adventurous travelers. From October to January, **sea turtles** paddle ashore to deposit eggs on **Ko Khai** (Egg Island), 15km southwest of Ko Tarutao. A popular way to explore the island is the 2hr. **hiking trail** from Ao Phante Melaka to Ao Talo Wao; it extends south for another 3hr. to Ao Talo U-Dang. For more information on Ko Tarutao, contact **Adang Sea Tour** (☎ 781 268) in Pak Bara.

To get to Ko Tarutao from **Satun,** take a **songthaew** to **La-Ngu,** 60km from Satun (30฿). Here, *songthaew* and **taxis** go to **Pak Bara Pier** (12฿), from which **boats** leave daily for Ko Tarutao (10:30am, 3pm; return 9:30am; round-trip 300฿). Otherwise, charter your own **longtail boat** from the Tarutao pier (from 500฿). From **Hat Yai,** board a **bus** to La-Ngu or go straight to Pak Bara by minivan (2½hr., every 30min. 7am-5pm, 34฿).

NEAR KO TARUTAO: KO BULON LEH

While islands like Ko Tao and Ko Phangan contain pockets of seclusion, tiny Ko Bulon Leh exists entirely inside a pocket, an island free of any modern distraction, but still comfortable enough that days melt seamlessly into each other. It's actually closer to Kuala Lampur than Bangkok, but it doesn't feel like you're close to anything here. For those travelers hoping to seriously unwind, Bulon Leh is a strong choice: you can read hundreds of pages in a sitting, spend hours sifting through shallow waters for shells, or roll over to see a sunrise through your window without a yawn.

☐ TRANSPORTATION. Boats leave from **Pak Bara pier** (the same departure point as Ko Tarutao) (2hr.; depart 2pm, return 9am; 300฿ round-trip). Service between islands is possible at a significant fee (1000฿ for a longtail, more without a group). When the ferries approach Bulon Leh, they moor offshore, forcing you to pay a longtail for the last 5min. of the journey to shore (10-20฿ per person).

◼◪ ORIENTATION AND PRACTICAL INFORMATION. The island can be easily traversed on foot. **Pansand** and **Bulone resorts** are at either ends of the main beach where you are dropped off and **Ban Sulaida** is slightly inland from Bulone Resort. There is one path that begins at Bulone Resort and cuts through the middle of the island—a 10min. walk takes you to the other side of the island where you'll find **Panka Ya** and **Pank Noi,** two bays side-by-side. Take the left along this path for Mango Bay and the smaller, rockier coves on other sides of the island.

The island offers almost no services besides those provided by resorts. Bring enough money to last and forget about checking your email. Bulone Resort has a book exchange and the island policeman regularly plays cards there as well. **Jeb's,** before Bulone Resort, slightly inland, can take care of basic needs, such as fishing line for making a shell mobile.

▮◖ ACCOMMODATIONS AND FOOD. There are now seven bungalow outfits on the island. The best of the bunch is **Bulone Resort ❸,** with basic bungalows effectively spread out along the waterfront and grounds. It also has the island's best **restaurant ❷** (entrees 70-90฿), but the pancakes are especially outstanding. (☎01 897 9084. Bungalows 250-600฿, depending on amenities.) Set on the nicest part of the beach, **Pansand Resort ❺** has gone upscale. While one of the first operators here, it now lacks the Bulon charm, though it has the most comfortable rooms. (☎01 397 0802. Modern bungalows 800-1500฿.) One newcomer, **Ban Sulaida Resort ❷,** right before Bulone Resort by Jeb's, offers four attractive, basic A-frame bungalows (low season 150฿, high season 350฿). A few more operators have cropped up inland, along the path that cuts through the island. They are almost all adequate, but more interesting for their restaurants than their location.

◪ BEACHES. If the handful of other beach-goers on the main beach are crowding your style, head to **Mango Bay,** a peaceful, rocky bay inhabited by *Chao Lay* fishing families—"sea gypsies" who have lived off the sea and in caves on the shore for centuries (see p. 23). Or check out the activity at **Panka Yai Bay** or **Noi Bay,** also rocky bays where fishing boats go about their business. Otherwise, just relax and accept that all man's problems stem from his inability to sit still.

SUNGAI KOLOK   ☎073

Sungai Kolok is a raucous border town through which Malaysians smuggle booze. Most travelers go straight to the train station without staying at the hotels. Ban

SOUTHERN THAILAND

Taba, a small town 5km south of Tak Bai, is the preferred border-crossing point. Ferries from Ban Taba (where border hours are the same) to Malaysia cost 15฿.

TRANSPORTATION. From the **railway station** (☎614 060), on Asia 18 Rd. on the right, trains leave for: **Bangkok** (28hr./21hr.; 11:55am/2:05pm; seats 220-497฿, beds 557-1493฿) via **Chumphon** (12hr./8hr., 150-334฿); **Hat Yai** (3½hr., 82-176฿); **Surat Thani** (8-9hr., 126-279฿). **Thai Airways**, at 53 Soi 1, Charoenkhet Rd. (☎612 132), arranges transport to **Narathiwat Airport** (8am, 140฿), with daily flights to **Bangkok** (3hr., 10:40am, 2950฿) via **Phuket** (1hr., 1155฿). The **bus office**, 95 Vorakamin Rd. (☎612 045), is six blocks from the intersection with Charoenkhet Rd. **Buses** run to **Bangkok** (19hr.; with A/C 8, 11:30am, 12:30pm; 546-1090฿) via **Surat Thani** (9-10hr., 277฿). Buses also run from here to **Phuket** (11hr.; 6, 8am, 5:30pm; 432฿) via **Trang** (7hr., 261฿) and **Krabi** (9hr., 335฿). Private **A/C minivans** (☎614 350) leave from the office opposite the railway station on Asia 18 Rd., one block west from the intersection with Charoenkhet Rd. for **Hat Yai** (4hr., every hr. 6am-5pm, 150฿).

BORDER CROSSING: SUNGAI KOLOK/RANTAU PANJANG
The Thailand/Malaysia border, on Asia 18 Rd. near the Sungai Kolok River, is open daily from 5am to 9pm Thai time (1hr. behind Malaysian time). Thai buses do not cross through to Malaysia, nor do trains on the east coast. Those crossing over into Malaysia can take a share-taxi (RM5 per person; price doubles after dark) or bus #29 (RM2.70, every hr. until 6:15pm) from Rantau Panjang to Kota Bharu. Transportation on both sides of the border is most abundant in the morning. Before you cross, go to Thai Farmers Bank to exchange any leftover baht for Malaysian ringgit. Most banks in Kota Bharu are closed on Fridays.

ORIENTATION AND PRACTICAL INFORMATION. The **border crossing** (see below) is at the end of **Asia 18 Rd.**, a broad avenue running parallel to the train tracks. Heading north, the **Tourist Information Center** (☎612 126), in a building on the right after passport control, has free maps and an English-speaking staff. The **tourist police** are in the same building. (☎612 008. **Bangkok tourist police:** ☎1155. Open 24hr.) **Motorcycle taxis** wait just past the TAT (around town 20฿ or RM2); **bicycle rickshaws** (40-60฿ or RM4-6) may cost less on busier streets. Opposite the train station, **Charoenkhet Rd.** runs perpendicular to Asia 18 Rd., into the heart of Sungai Kolok. The **police station** (☎611 070) is here, opposite the **Narathiwat Immigration Office**, 70 Charoenkhet Rd. (☎611 231; open M-F 8:30am-4:30pm), and **Thai Farmer's Bank**, 1/6 Vorakamin Rd. (☎611 578; **24hr. ATM;** open M-F 8:30am-3:30pm). For **medical services** (☎615 161), you can find doctors at Saitong 6 Rd. For **Internet,** try **CS Internet,** 2-4-6-8 Charoenkhet Rd. (☎615 444. 30฿ per hr.) The **post office** is on On Prachawiwat Rd. (☎611 141. *Poste Restante.* Open M-F 8:30am-4:30pm, Sa-Su 9am-noon.) **Postal code:** 96120.

ACCOMMODATIONS AND FOOD. There is no reason to spend a night in Sungai Kolok unless transportation forces you to. **Savoy Hotel ❷,** 34 Charoenkhet Rd., has a Chinese **restaurant ❷.** Its rooms have fans and bearable baths. Get a room off the street to avoid traffic noise. (☎611 093. Singles with bath 150฿; doubles with bath 170฿. Reception and restaurant both open daily 6am-midnight.)

Sungai Kolok's daily **market ❶** spreads out behind Asia 18 Rd. before the sun gets out of bed. At night, **food vendors ❶** along Shern Maroar Rd. sell local specialties. Those who want to sit while they eat can try the vendors along Vorakamin Rd., starting at the Thai Farmers Bank (fried vegetables on rice 20-25฿). **Siam Restaurant ❸,** 2-4 Shern Maroar Rd., cooks up several extravagantly garnished seafood dishes for 50-150฿. (☎611 360. Open daily 10am-3pm and 5-9pm.)

MALAYSIAN MENUS

If you journey into Malaysia, you'll find that many (if not most) of your food options include fantastic Chinese and Indian restaurants. As delicious as those are, make sure to try the Malay specialties as well. Here are some suggestions:

Char kuey teow: flat rice noodles stir-fried with bean sprouts, seafood, and spicy sauce.

Popia: fresh spring rolls.

Top Hats: crispy bite-size pastries filled with cooked turnips.

Ais Kacang: shaved ice, sweet corn, sweet red beans, *saso,* and syrup.

Chendol: shaved ice with green pea noodles in coconut milk and *pandan* syrup.

Bubur cha cha: sweet coconut milk over ice with chunks of fruit and colorful rice gummies.

Since *satay* is a native Malaysian treat, *satay* street grills (with squid, pork, and chicken) and *satay* dishes are everywhere.

SIDETRIPS

ANGKOR WAT

CAMBODIA PRICE ICONS					
SYMBOL:	❶	❷	❸	❹	❺
ACCOMM.	Under US$3 (12,000R)	US$3-7 (12,000-28,000R)	US$7-12 (28,000-48,000R)	US$12-20 (48,000-80,000R)	Over US$20 (80,000R)
FOOD	Under US$2 (8000R)	US$2-4 (8000-16,000R)	US$4-8 (16,000-32,000R)	US$8-12 (32,000-48,000R)	Over US$12 (48,000R)

With their unrivalled beauty and majesty, the temples of Angkor deserve their reputation as one of the great man-made wonders of the world. Begun in the 9th century, the building process lasted over 600 years, with the last of the temples being built in the later 15th century. The temples are the remains of the mighty Khmer empire that, at its height, extended its reign over most of the Malay peninsula and modern-day Cambodia, Laos, and Vietnam. The name Angkor is believed to be a mispronunciation of the Khmer word *nakhon*, meaning "city." In the 15th century, the Khmer kings abandoned Angkor and moved their capital to the site of modern-day Phnom Penh. Angkor lay in relative obscurity until the diaries of French naturalist Henri Mouhot were published in 1864. Mouhot's description of the beautiful temples sparked international interest, drawing the droves of travelers who now come to see the rising sun break over the temple *stupas* in what the Khmer believe is the gateway between the mortal and celestial worlds.

Cambodia's Khmer civilization (**Kambujadesa** in inscriptions) was the mightiest kingdom in Southeast Asia during this period, drawing tribute from as far away as present-day Thailand, Myanmar, and Malaysia. **Jayavarman II** founded the Angkor state and declared himself **devaraja,** or god-king. After uniting many disparate kingdoms, he established his capital northeast of the Tonle Sap and began constructing the mammoth temple complex of **Angkor** (p. 394). Most scholars attribute Angkor's wealth to booming agriculture and a strong irrigation system, but under various monarchs, Angkor's power waxed and waned. Under **Suryavarman II,** Khmer territory expanded, and construction on Angkor Wat increased, ultimately sapping the country of strength and leaving it vulnerable to Cham invasions in 1177. In 1181, **Jayavarman VII** reunited the kingdom and instituted an ambitious public works program. Following his death, Kambujadesa suffered a slow decline, its territory steadily encroached upon by the Thai and Lao. In 1431, the Thai Ayutthaya Kingdom claimed the capital, Angkor Thom. In 1594, the Thais sacked Angkor.

In the mid-15th century, the capital shifted from Angkor to **Phnom Penh,** a trade hub at the confluence of the Mekong, Tonle Sap, and Bassac Rivers, thereby increasing Cambodia's contact with the outside world. By the 19th century, Cambodia was caught between its territorially ambitious and mutually antagonistic neighbors, Vietnam and Thailand, which each invaded the country several times. Cambodia may well have been swallowed up permanently were it not for French colonists who established a protectorate there in 1863, which came at the price of heavy taxes, onerous *corvée* labor, and neglected education and social welfare.

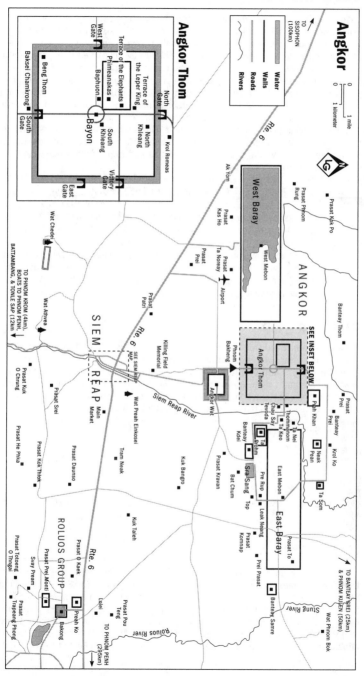

Angkor

TO
SISOPHON
(100km)

Water
Walls
Roads
Rivers

0   1 mile
0   1 kilometer

Rte. 6

West Baray

Prasat Phnom
Rung

■ Prasat Kok Po

Ak Yom

ANGKOR

West Mebon

Prasat
Kas Ho

Prasat
Ta Norey

Prasat
Prei

Banteay Thom

Prasat
Patri

Airport

■ Prasat
Prei

Prasat
Banteay
Prei

Krol Ko

Wat Chedei

Phnom
Bakheng

SEE INSET BELOW

Angkor
Thom

Preah Khan

Neak
Pean

Ta Som

Killing Field
Memorial

SEE SIEM REAP
MAP

Angkor Wat

Chau Say
Tevoda

Thommanon

Ta Nei

Ta Keo

Ta Prohm

East Mebon

Ta Som

SIEM REAP

Siem Reap River

Wat Preah Einkosei

Banteay
Kdei

Sra Srang

Pre Rup

East Baray

Wat Athvea

Prasat Kuk
O Chrung

Main
Market

Tram Neak

Kuk Bangro

Bat Chum

Top

Leak Neang

Prasat To

Prasat Srei

Prasat Daunso

Prasat Kok Thlok

Prasat He Phka

Prasat Kravan

Kuk Taleh

Prasat
Konnap

Prei Prasat

Banteay Samre

TO BANTEAY SREI (25km)
& PHNOM KULEN (50km)

Stung River

Wat Phnom Bok

TO PHNOM KROM (4km),
BOATS TO PHNOM PENH,
BATTAMBANG, & TONLE SAP (12km)

ROLUOS GROUP

Rte. 6

Prasat Totoeng
O Thngai

Svay Pream

Prasat Prei Monti

Prasat
Trapeang Phong

Prasat O Kaek

Bakong

Preah Ko

Lalei

Prasat Pou
Teng

TO PHNOM PENH
(295km)

Roluos River

Angkor Thom

West
Gate

Baksei Chamkrong

Beng Thom

Terrace of
the Leper King

Terrace of the Elephants

Phimeanakas

Baphuon

Bayon

North
Khleang

South
Khleang

North
Gate

South
Gate

Victory
Gate

East
Gate

Krol Romeas

According to Hindu mythology, the gods live on top of five mountains, including central Mt. Meru, surrounded by the cosmic ocean. The structural layout of Angkor is meant to mimic this myth with four smaller towers and one prominent one as well as a surrounding moat. The ancient Khmer also displayed their architectural prowess by devising advanced irrigational techniques that provided enough water to grow and harvest several crops each year in order to support the densely populated empire. Modern Cambodian village architecture takes water into account as well; most structures are built on stilts to prevent flooding or infestation by insects and small animals during the monsoon season.

Angkor Wat is properly named—Angkor has nothing but wats. Most travelers not booked on a tour stay in Siem Reap and go to Angkor during the day. In Siem Reap (see below) you'll find all the amenities and nightlife you need, and even some cultural attractions as well.

BORDER CROSSING: ARANYAPRATHET/POIPET Travelers must obtain visas at the Cambodian embassy in Bangkok (see p. 102). In Aranyaprathet, touts materialize at the train and bus stations to offer trips to Siem Reap. (For travel information on **Aranyaprathet,** see p. 182.) They are helpful in navigating the chaotic bridge and boarding a public pickup for the painful 7-8hr. ride ahead (in cab 350฿, in the back 200฿). Trucks leave from a station 500m past the border on the Cambodian side on the left. Be sure to obtain an exit stamp from Thai immigration (open daily 7:30am-5:30pm) at the bridge. A tuk-tuk from anywhere in town to the bridge costs 60฿.

SIEM REAP ☎ 063

Spurred by improved safety in the region, tourism has taken off in the dusty little city of Siem Reap, which functions chiefly as a gateway to the Angkor temples. Five-star resorts and restaurants line the outskirts of town, and package tour buses are a regular sight. Although Siem Reap may have the highest concentration of moto drivers in the whole country, its secluded waterfalls and isolated temples remain hidden secrets that travelers can explore in peace.

RIEL (R)		
AUS$1 = 2211.30R		1000R = AUS$0.45
CDN$1 = 2577.58R		1000R = CDN$0.39
EUR€1 = 3938.97R		1000R = EUR€0.25
NZ$1 = 1880.71R		1000R = NZ$0.53
US$1 = 4016.90R		1000R = US$0.25
UK£1 = 6216.15R		1000R = UK£0.16
ZAR1 = 382.56R		1000R = ZAR2.61

⎕ TRANSPORTATION

The **airport** is 8km northwest of town off Rte. 6. International departure tax is US$20 and domestic is US$4. Bangkok Airways, 571 Rte. 6 (☎380 191; open daily 8am-4:30pm), flies to **Bangkok** (5 per day, reduced service in low season; US$158). Siem Reap Airlines, in the same office as Bangkok Airways, flies to **Phnom Penh** (3 per day, US$64). Vietnam Airlines, 108 Route 6 (☎063 964 488), flies to: **Danang** (daily, US$166); **Hanoi** (daily, US$226); and **Ho Chi Minh City** (4 per day, US$104). **Minibuses** and pickups go to **Bangkok** (13hr., 7am, US$8) via **Poi Pot** (5-6hr., US$4);

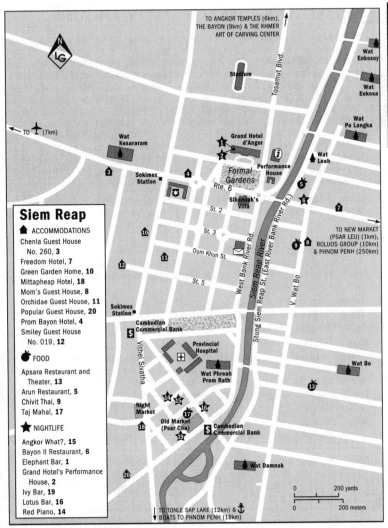

TO ANGKOR TEMPLES (6km),
THE BAYON (9km) & THE KHMER
ART OF CARVING CENTER

Tosamut Blvd.

Wat
Enkosey

Wat
Enkosa

Stadium

Wat
Po Langka

TO ✈ (7km)

Wat
Kesararam

Grand Hotel
d'Angor

Wat
Leah

Sokimex
Station

Formal
Gardens
Rte. 6

Performance
House

St. 2

Sihanouk's
Villa

TO NEW MARKET
(PSAR LEU) (1km),
ROLUOS GROUP (10km)
& PHNOM PENH (250km)

St. 3

West Bank River Rd.

Siem Reap River

East River Bank River Rd.)

V. Wat Bo

Oum Khun St.

St. 5

Sokimex
Station

Cambodian
Commercial Bank

Vithei Sivatha

Stung Siem Reap St. (

Provincial
Hospital

Wat Phreah
Prom Rath

Wat Bo

Night
Market

Old Market
(Psar Cha)

Cambodian
Commercial Bank

Wat Damnak

0   200 yards

0   200 meters

TO TONLE SAP LAKE (12km) & ⚓
BOATS TO PHNOM PENH (18km)

Siem Reap

🏠 **ACCOMMODATIONS**

Chenla Guest House
  No. 260, **3**
Freedom Hotel, **7**
Green Garden Home, **10**
Mittapheap Hotel, **18**
Mom's Guest House, **8**
Orchidae Guest House, **11**
Popular Guest House, **20**
Prom Bayon Hotel, **4**
Smiley Guest House
  No. 019, **12**

🍴 **FOOD**

Apsara Restaurant and
  Theater, **13**
Arun Restaurant, **5**
Chivit Thai, **9**
Taj Mahal, **17**

⭐ **NIGHTLIFE**

Angkor What?, **15**
Bayon II Restaurant, **6**
Elephant Bar, **1**
Grand Hotel's Performance
  House, **2**
Ivy Bar, **19**
Lotus Bar, **16**
Red Piano, **14**

and **Phnom Penh** (7-9hr., 7am, US$8). Inquire at your guest house the night before you leave, and the bus will pick you up. If you are tired of bad roads you can take a **speedboat** to **Battambang** (4hr., 7am, US$12) and **Phnom Penh** (7hr., 7am, US$22). It is advised to leave Siem Reap at 5:45-6am to catch the boat, because it is 18km from Siem Reap to the river and the road is bad.

Any moto driver in town will take you to the **temples** (US$6 per day for the main temples, US$12 per day for Banteay Srei and the far temples, US$4-6 extra to see the waterfalls beyond Banteay Srei). Car and driver can be rented for the day at the tourist office (US$25).

SIDETRIPS

✦ ❷ ORIENTATION AND PRACTICAL INFORMATION

Siem Reap can be navigated by foot, but the heat and unlabeled streets make traveling by moto preferable. **Rte. 6** cuts through the north part of town, running east to the **New Market** and west to the **airport.** Those arriving by boat will follow a road heading north from Tonle Sap. The road forks into **V. Sivatha** on the left and the **West Bank River Road** on the right. V. Sivatha traces the west edge of town, intersecting Rte. 6 in a flurry of guest house signs. North of its intersection with Rte. 6, the West Bank River Road runs past the traffic circle and the Grand Hotel, and on to Angkor, 7km away. Running north-south, the **Siem Reap River** traces the eastern edge of town, with roads lining both banks. The dirt road parallel to the east bank road is **V. Wat Bo,** home to several popular guest houses. The best source of information about Siem Reap is the indispensable and free *Angkor Guide*, available in guest houses, hotels, and restaurants. Inside is a color map of the town and temples complex.

Tourist Office: ☎ 964 371. Opposite the Grand Hotel on the road to Angkor. Not very useful for travelers. Maps of Angkor and Siem Reap. Motorcycle with driver US$6 per day. A/C car with driver US$20-25 per day. Licensed guides US$20 per day. Open M-F 7:30-11am and 2-3pm, Sa 7:30-11am.

Currency Exchange: US dollars and Thai baht are accepted everywhere. **Cambodian Commercial Bank** (☎ 964 392), at the end of the Old Market across from the bridge, exhanges traveler's checks (2% commision). MC/V cash advances. US$5 flat fee, US$200 max. Open daily 9am-4pm.

Markets: New Market (*Psar Leu*), 1km east of town on Rte. 6. The touristy **Old Market** (*Psar Cha*) is at the southern end of the west bank river road.

Police: Foreigner Office (☎ 012 893 297), on the corner of Rte. 6 and V. Sivatha.

Pharmacies: Many located around the town center.

Medical Services: Rustic **Siem Reap Provincial Hospital,** down the side street off V. Sivatha that veers east at Cambodian Commercial Bank; opposite the Apsara Tours branch office. Doctors on call M-F 7-11am and 2-5pm, Sa 6am-noon.

Telephones: Many guest houses offer **international** service (US$2-3 per min). The **post office** also offers international service.

Internet Access: Internet centers are springing up everywhere. A pleasant air-conditioned option is **E Cafe Siem Reap,** 147B Sivatha Blvd., opposite Cambodian Commercial Bank. US$2 per hr. Open daily 7am-9pm.

Post Office: GPO, on the west bank of the Siem Reap River, 500m north of the market. EMS mail service. *Poste Restante.* Open daily 7:30am-5pm.

🏠 ACCOMMODATIONS

Siem Reap is teeming with places to stay, costing from US$2 per night to US$1900 per night. There are new accommodations opening every month, packed with tourists heading to the temples of Angkor. Travelers planning to visit in the high season should make reservations. Guest houses cluster near the **V. Sivatha-Rte. 6 intersection** and on **V. Wat Bo,** south of Rte. 6. Flush toilets are standard. Prices may drop up to 20% in the rainy season.

Smiley Guest House No. 019 (☎ 012 852 955). Coming from Rte. 6 on V. Sivatha, turn left onto the dirt alley opposite 10 Makara High School. Very popular with backpackers; pleasant restaurant and porch. Singles with shared bath US$2-3; doubles with bath US$5-6, with A/C $10. ❶

LANDMINES

Over 25 years of civil war have left Cambodia with many sad legacies, but perhaps the worst are the 6-10 million anti-personnel mines strewn about the countryside. Additionally, there are 500,000 tons of unexploded ordnance (UXO) that the US dropped during the Vietnam War, but which failed to explode. Injuries number between 100 and 300 each month. About half of the injured survive with amputations; one in 236 Cambodians has lost a limb due to a mine explosion. Children are disproportionately at risk, as they frequently mistake UXOs for toys. In 1996, demining groups estimated that at current rates it would take nearly 300 years to clear the fields. Generous international donations have enabled the Cambodia Mine Action Center (CMAC) to carry out demining efforts, but the group is beset with allegations of corruption and misallocation of resources. Improved technology, however, may speed up the project. In December 1997, a Japanese company introduced Mine Eye, a new landmine sensor that is able to differentiate between mines and scrap metal. If contributions continue to increase, CMAC may clear the fields within 10 or 20 years. For now, **when traveling outside touristed centers, never stray from the marked paths.**

Popular Guest House, 33 Boboos St. (☎012 916 165). Head south from the old market along the river; it's on the right 200m after the bus station. Popular by name, popular by nature. Backpackers hang out in the leafy veranda restaurant. Singles with fan and shared bath US$2-4; doubles US$3-7, with A/C US$10. ❶

Chenla Guest House No. 260, 260 Rte. 6 (☎012 835 488), 200m west of the V. Sivatha intersection. Best rooms are in the new building. Some rooms have cable TV and fridge. Singles with shared bath and fan US$3; doubles with private bath US$6, with A/C US$10-15. ❷

Mom's Guest House, 99 V. Wat Bo (☎964 037), 30m south of intersection of Rt. 6. Very clean. Good English spoken. In the old building, rooms are functional; in the new place they're a treat. Singles with shared bath US$3-4; doubles with private bath US$6-10, with A/C US$12. ❷

Orchidae Guest House (☎012 898 178). From Rte. 6, go 500m south on V. Sivatha and take a right before the Sokimex station; it's 30m ahead on the left. Centrally located guest house with clean rooms. Singles US$3, with bath $4; doubles US$4/US$5, with A/C US$12. ❷

Green Garden Home, 051 V. Sivatha (☎012 890 363), about 200m south of the Rte. 6 intersection; look for the blue sign. Lovely rooms with bamboo furniture and relaxing verandas all set in a flower garden. Rooms have bath, hot water, fridge, cable TV, and-fan. Doubles US$10, with A/C US$15-20. Call ahead in high season. ❸

Mittapheap Hotel (☎964 375), on V. Sivatha, a few blocks from the market. With its classy glass exterior and immaculate interior, Mittapheap is a pleasant place to stay. Restaurant. All rooms have A/C, TV, private bath, and refrigerators for US$15. ❹

Freedom Hotel (☎963 476). Rt. 6 on the East Bank of the river near the Central Market. Has all the amenities of a high-range place at mid-range prices. Great restaurant. Large rooms have A/C, satellite TV (HBO), fridge, and private bath for US$15-20. ❹

Prom Bayon Hotel, 546 Rt. 6 (☎963 568). This luxury hotel is a pleasant sanctuary from the dust of the temples and the grime of Siem Reap. Excellent restaurant. Enormous rooms have A/C, large TV, hot water, fridge, and private bath for US$35-40. ❺

FOOD

A small **night market** on V. Sivatha north of the Cambodian Commercial Bank serves noodles for under US$1. A **fruit market** is next door. **Food vendors** also line the road to Angkor and the east bank of the river parallel to the guest house strip. Small restaurants offering meals for a good value are located at the north end of the Old Market.

Arun Restaurant, off the East Bank River Road 50m north of the Rte. 6 intersection on the right. Generous portions of Cambodian and Chinese food. Numerous veggie options. Grilled beef with tofu sauce US$4. Open daily 10am-10pm. ❸

Chivit Thai, 130 V. Wat Bo, near a string of guest houses. Charming, open-air terrace with great phat thai (US$2.50). Open daily 7am-10pm. ❷

Taj Mahal, behind the Old Market. Good Indian food and reasonable prices are two delights too good to be passed up. Entrees US$2-3. ❷

Apsara Restaurant and Theater, on the East Bank of the river, a few blocks from the bridge near Wat Preah Prom Rath. Excellent Khmer Food in a beautiful setting. Entrees US$2-5. ❷

SIEM REAP SIGHTS

A **memorial** to Khmer Rouge atrocities is on the road to Angkor. Take the dirt road turn-off at the "Welcome" sign, 500m past the Grand Hotel. Follow the road to a small wat, next to the ramshackle wooden pavilion that is filled waist-deep with human skulls and bones, serving as a grisly reminder of the Khmer Rouge massacres. For those who can't get enough of Angkor architecture, **Wat Leah,** along the east bank of the river north of Arun Restaurant, has two well-preserved Angkor-period brick sanctuaries behind the modern pagoda. For a chance to watch highly skilled craftsmen create traditional Khmer wood carvings, head to the **Khmer Art of Carving Center.** Look for the sign on the left heading out of town on the road to the temples. (Open daily 7:30am-5pm.) Across the road there is also a small **stone carving workshop.** Small pieces sell for US$10-15.

NIGHTLIFE

Although nightlife in Siem Reap is picking up, it is hampered by the fact that many people get up at dawn to see the temples. The amusingly named **Angkor What?,** a block north of the Old Market on one of V. Sivatha's side streets, and the **Ivy Bar,** at the south end of the Old Market, are both youthful late-night drinking spots. **Lotus Bar,** at the north end of the market, is open **24hr.** For an expensive nightcap, try the **Elephant Bar** in the Grand Hotel d'Angkor, at the north end of the West Bank River Road. The **Grand Hotel's Performance House,** just across the West Bank River Road from the hotel proper, offers a rare chance to see traditional **Khmer dance** and **drama,** but it's quite expensive. (☎963 417. Shows M, W, and Sa. US$22 includes 7pm buffet dinner, 8pm performance.) You can see Khmer dancing for less money at the **Bayon II Restaurant,** on Rd. 6 on the eastern side of the river (nightly performances, US$11). The **Red Piano,** 50m northwest of the old market, is a chic restaurant/bar whose claim to fame is that it was the headquarters of the *Tomb Raider* cast and crew while they filmed at Angkor. Good food beckons everyday travelers to kick back and have a good time after a day of sight-seeing.

TO THE TEMPLES!

If not on a package tour, most travelers stay the night in Siem Reap and hire a **motorcycle** (US$6 per day for the main temples, US$12 per day for the far temples such as Banteay Srei) or **bicycle** (US$5 per day) to see the temples. Rentals can be arranged through guest houses or at the Siem Reap Tourist Office (see p. 390) and require a passport as a deposit. **Cars** with drivers can be hired for US$25 per day from hotels or the tourist office.

Foreigners can buy one-day (US$20), three-day (US$40), or seven-day (US$60) passes from the on-site ticket checkpoint (one passport-sized photo required). Multi-day passes must be used on consecutive days. There is a steep US$80 fine for misusing tickets.

SAFETY CONCERNS AND TEMPLE ETIQUETTE Keep in mind the following concerns and customs while at Angkor:

Mines: The government claims that Angkor has been de-mined, but to be safe, stay on well-trodden paths, especially at more remote temples.

Wildlife: The jungles have poisonous snakes, such as the small bright green *krait*. King cobras, with enough venom to bring down a bull elephant, are rare but not unheard of—avoid dark, isolated chambers within the temples.

Preservation: Don't remove stone fragments from the temples. Government officials search all bags upon departure.

Tickets: Guards check passes at the entrances to most of the temples; it's now virtually impossible to slip in without paying.

THE GRAND CIRCUIT

The following descriptions are arranged in the order that most travelers see the monuments. Beginning at Angkor Wat, the route proceeds clockwise on a roughly rectangular track. During the high season, it may be wise to do the circuit in reverse, since almost everyone starts at the same time and goes the same way.

TOURING TIPS

Angkor's magnificent ruins hold enough secret nooks and crannies for a lifetime of exploration, but with a little planning and prioritizing you can see most of the temple complex in just a few days. Many visitors try to cover as much ground as possible on the first day (including the major sites) and spend their remaining time returning to particularly intriguing monuments or venturing farther afield. Try to get an early start; by 11am temperatures can rise to over 39°C (100°F). Mornings also tend to be drier.

Bring a map of the temple complex, a flashlight, drinking water, and extra film, or buy all these things from vendors outside the temples at inflated prices. A guidebook specifically detailing the history, architecture, and myths of individual temples is recommended. *A Guide to Angkor,* by Dawn Rooney, sold by child vendors at Angkor Wat (US$3-6), has temple plans and is especially useful while navigating the complexities of Tha Prohm, Bayon, and Angkor Wat. If locals come up to you in one of the temples and start to give you information, they will demand US$1 at the end. Don't listen if you don't want to pay.

THE BEST OF ANGKOR

■ **Best carvings:** Angkor Wat and Banteay Srei.
■ **Best spots to sit in quiet bliss:** Banteay Kdei, Prah Khan, East Mebon, and Ta Som.
■ **Best views:** Phnom Bakheng, East Mebon, Pre Rup, and Angkor Wat.
■ **Best "jungle" temples:** Ta Prohm, Ta Som.

ANGKOR WAT. This magnificent 213m tall laterite-and-sandstone complex was constructed during the reign of Suryavarman II (r. 1113-50). The temple faces west, the direction associated with death in Hindu cosmology, leading scholars to believe that it was constructed as a funerary temple. Designed to represent the universe in miniature, its five-tower quincunx—an arrangement that places four of the towers in a square and the fifth in its center—symbolizes the peaks of Mt. Meru used by the Hindu god Vishnu while creating the Universe.

The temple contains 1200 sq. m of sandstone. Incredibly detailed stone carvings line the walls of the first-level gallery and form the largest series of reliefs in the world. Mostly depictions of scenes from Indian epics and Angkor-period warfare, they are best viewed starting on the west side and proceeding counterclockwise around the structure. The first panel depicts the battle of Kuruksetra from the Hindu epic *Mahabharata*. The south wall shows a mighty military procession and a rather gruesome vision of hell. Perhaps the most famous relief in all of Angkor, *The Churning of the Sea of Milk* (see **Churn, Baby, Churn,** p. 395), adorns the eastern face of the gallery. The north depicts Vishnu's victory over Bana the Demon King, a curious-looking hellion on a rhino. The second half of the gallery depicts more universe-saving battles between gods and demons. The north panel of the west gallery depicts the battle of Lanka from the Hindu epic *Ramayana*, in which Rama and his monkey army sought to free Rama's wife Sita from the clutches of the demon Ravana (recognizable by his 10 heads and 20 arms).

On the second level, the Gallery of 1000 Buddhas (of which only a few fragments remain) is on the right, and the Hall of Echoes is on the left. Temple explorers can stand in one corner of the Hall of Echoes, pound their chests like Tarzan, and feel the room thunder in response. The third level has a stunning view of the perfectly symmetrical Angkor Wat complex. Angkor Wat is best seen at sunrise or sunset; arrange with a moto driver the night before, and leave Siem Reap at 5:15-5:30am to catch the sunrise.

ANGKOR THOM. The large temple complex of Angkor Thom (literally "Great City"), constructed by Jayavarman VII (1181-1219), lies 1.5km north of Angkor Wat. Angkor Thom shares Angkor Wat's cosmological layout: a moat symbolizes the oceans, the walls are the land, and the towers represent the peaks of Mt. Meru. The remaining ruins are mainly temples, though it's believed that this vast city once housed many administrative buildings that didn't survive the test of time. Ankor Thom's south entrance passes through a causeway lined with 54 guardian statues of gods and demons. The Angkor Conservancy, however, has replaced many of the original heads to prevent theft. An all-seeing, four-faced, smiling head tops the tower gates.

THE BAYON. Rising in the exact center of Angkor Thom, the Bayon was erected by Jayavarman VII and is dedicated to Buddhism. Its reliefs depict, in addition to the usual epics, scenes of everyday life in Angkorian Cambodia (fishing, chess-playing, hunting, etc.). The Bayon contains two sets of bas-reliefs, which are meant to be viewed clockwise. The lower gallery along the outer wall depicts life in the capital. The south gallery contains perhaps the finest of the Bayon's bas-reliefs, depicting a battle between the Khmers and Chams, while the lower tier of reliefs presents a more peaceful view of Angkorian life. The north gallery, only some of which was completed, contains a depiction of an Angkor circus. The upper gallery contains stories from Hindu epics dotted with faces believed to represent the Bodhisattva Avalokitesvara, who selflessly delayed attaining enlightenment in order to aid humanity.

BAPHUON. A few hundred meters northwest of the Bayon stands the Hindu temple of Baphuon, built by Udayadityavarman II in the late 11th century.

CHURN, BABY, CHURN! An ancient Hindu legend, *The Churning of the Sea of Milk* recalls the problem-solving methods of ancient Hindu gods during the turbulent days when they were busy creating the world. Being new at world-creation, they ran into a small glitch—they lost the elixir of immortality while churning the cosmic sea. It took 1000 years before the gods and demons, in a rare joint effort—aided by Sesha, the sea snake, and Vishnu—recovered the potion. The design of Angkor's temples is based on this ancient legend. The moat represents the ocean, and the gods use Mt. Meru, represented by the tower, as their churning stick. The cosmic serpent, in a rare cameo as the good guy, selflessly offered himself as a rope to enable the gods and demons to twirl the stick and save the Universe.

PHIMEANAKAS. Situated just north of Baphuon, this Hindu monument was erected by three successive kings, Rajendravarman, Jayavarman V, and Udaya-dityavarman I. If the monument is open, the steep climb to the top of the central sanctuary is worth the view that waits at the top. The steep laterite "stairs" are best attempted early in the day before the sun or rain set in. The west staircase has a metal rail that makes climbing slightly easier.

TERRACE OF THE ELEPHANTS. First laid out by Suryavarman I, the Terrace of the Elephants (the Royal Terrace) stretches for 300m from Baphuon to the beginning of the Terrace of the Leper King, past Phimeanakas. The ⬛bas-reliefs of near life-sized elephants seem to emerge like ghosts from the stones. Along the wall near the Terrace of the Leper King is a carving of a five-headed horse.

TERRACE OF THE LEPER KING. Another legacy of Jayavarman VII, the monument lies north of the Terrace of the Elephants. Two galleries of bas-reliefs line the terrace, while mythological creatures and *apsaras* (see **Angkor's Motley Crew**, p. 397) decorate the outer wall. The statue of the Leper King himself is a replica. The National Museum in Phnom Penh houses the original. Some historians believe Jayavarman VII may have suffered from leprosy himself, though others believe that the statue portrays the Hindu god of death, Yama, or Kubera, the god of wealth.

PRAH KHAN. Located northwest of the Bayon outside Angkor Thom, Prah Khan is one of the largest temple complexes and one of the best ways to spend precious exploration time. It was built as a Buddhist temple by Jayavarman VII in memory of his father, and Prah Khan literally means "Sacred Sword." Some archaeologists believe that the two-story building in the northeastern corner of the compound, a location rarely used in Khmer architecture, might once have housed an Asian excalibur, left by Jayavarman VII for his descendants.

NEAK PEAN. This Buddhist temple, east of Prah Khan along the Grand Circuit access road, was also built by Jayavarman VII. Unlike any other Angkor temple, this small and charming temple is made up of five ponds that are now covered in grass. A temple stands in the exact center of what was the large, central pond. Neak Pean is said to represent Lake Anayatapa, a sacred body of water in the Himalayas. The four symmetrical ponds, one at each cardinal point, represent the earth's four rivers. A stone horse, believed to be the sacred steed *Balaha*, drags several marooned sailors toward the island sanctuary in the middle of Neak Pean.

TA SOM. Lying east of Neak Pean along the access road, Ta Som was also built by Jayavarman VII. A small, quiet temple with one sanctuary, it is unrestored and largely in ruins. A four-faced bayon (a monument distinguished by its many sculpted faces) casts its inscrutable smile over visitors as they enter from the west. Continuing to the east gate, the bayon is almost entirely in the clutches of fig tree roots, giving its smile an almost eerie feel.

EAST MEBON. Built in the 10th century by Rajendravarman II in memory of his parents, tranquil East Mebon stands southwest of Ta Som and is accessible only by boat. In the Angkor era, the temple stood in the middle of the large man-made lake *(baray)*. Impressive sculptures of elephants and lions guard each entrance.

PHNOM BAKHENG. Just north and slightly west of Angkor Wat, Phnom Bakheng was built by Yasovarman I in the late 9th century. Travelers struggle up the steep and rocky slope to enjoy a spectacular sunset and view of Angkor Wat. An elephant carriage is available to take the style-conscious and the weary to the top (US$15). Originally, 109 towers, corresponding to the animal zodiac cycle, graced the *phnom*. In January and February, a glorious sunrise directly over Angkor rewards early risers.

WEST BARAY. West of Angkor Thom, this half-filled lake is best seen from Phnom Bakheng. Believed to date from the 11th century, West Baray was built during the reign of Udayadityavarman II. A small, largely destroyed temple, **West Mebon,** stands in the center of the *baray* and is accessible by boat.

TA PROHM. West of Pre Rup and bordering Banteay Kdei, Ta Prohm was built as a Buddhist temple by Jayavarman VII in his mother's memory. This vast, crumbling temple competes with the Bayon and Angkor Wat as the most awe-inspiring of Angkor's treasures and is the most authentic "jungle" temple. Ancient trees have grown into and out of the buildings themselves, creating the visage of a "lost city." Inscriptions reveal that 79,365 people were employed in Ta Prohm's upkeep during its heyday. Early risers can witness its stunning beauty in the morning light.

PRE RUP. Five hundred meters due south of East Mebon lies Pre Rup, a Hindu temple built by Rajendravarman II in the second half of the 10th century to honor Shiva. More impressive than its contemporary East Mebon, this multi-tiered structure affords views of East Baray to the north. Two halls, parallel to the laterite wall as you enter from the east, are believed to have housed pilgrims who journeyed here to worship. The temple is thought to have funerary associations. The vat near the east staircase is thought to have been used at cremations.

BANTEAY KDEI. Banteay Kdei is a Buddhist temple built by Jayavarman VII, southeast of Pre Rup near the Sra Srang Reservoir. A bayon oversees the entrance to this unrestored temple. Lying largely in ruins, Banteay Kdei is more a spot for calm reflection than active exploration.

BANTEAY SREI. Detailed and beautiful Banteay Srei ("Citadel of Women") stands 35km northeast of the main cluster of Angkor temples. Described as the "precious queen" by French archaeologists, Banteay Srei's construction spanned two kingships in the second half of the 10th century. Though smaller in scale than the temples at Angkor, this pinkish temple is home to many exquisite carvings that are based on Indian epics. The south library shows Ravana shaking Mt. Kailusa (east pediment). The north library depicts Indra casting down heavenly rain (east pediment) and Krishna killing his murderous uncle King Kamsa (west pediment). Unfortunately, moto drivers will charge you US$12 for the day to get to Banteay Srei and the other far temples.

ROLUOS GROUP. About 30min. by moto on the incredibly dusty Rte. 6, this collection of three temples represents the very earliest of the Angkor period and is interesting only to die-hard Angkor enthusiasts. Jayavarman II made this capital of Hariharalaya in the 9th century. All three temples were originally consecrated to Hinduism. **Lolei** (north of the other two off Rte. 6), the site of a modern Buddhist wat, has not been preserved very well but boasts a few beau-

ANGKOR'S MOTLEY CREW Several figures and objects make appearances in Angkor's carvings. *Let's Go*'s guide to who's who in Angkor:

Naga: Sanskrit for "snake." These mythical, multi-headed serpents seem to be everywhere at Angkor and often form balustrades. Possibly the most abundant motif in Southeast Asia, *naga* play a marked role in Khmer legends. It is said that the Khmer are descended from the union between a foreigner and a *naga*. According to Hindu myths, the *naga* swallowed the waters of life and were either ruptured by Indra or squeezed by Vishnu's entourage to set the waters free.

Apsara: These celestial beauties, who sprang forth during the *Churning of the Sea of Milk* (See **Churn, Baby, Churn,** p. 395), have become virtually synonymous with Khmer architecture. Their perfect, sensuous beauty was believed to have highly refined powers of seduction, and they are typically depicted facing outward with only their feet in profile. Angkor Wat *apsaras*, widely regarded as the most beautiful (and most well-endowed) nymphs of all the temples, appear individually—unlike the Bayon *apsaras* who appear in groups of three.

Vishnu: An important Hindu deity, Vishnu was widely worshiped during the height of the Angkor period. Married to Lakshmi, he is frequently portrayed with four arms and an ornamental waist sash *(sampot)*. Whenever the earth is threatened by evil, he acts as its savior, assuming an *avatara* (earthly incarnation). He is seen in the bas-reliefs of Angkor Wat both in human form and as a tortoise in the *Churning of the Sea of Milk*.

Ganesha: Parvati created Ganesha, the elephant-headed Hindu god of wisdom, to guard her bath. When Parvati's husband, the powerful god Shiva, tried to gain admittance, Ganesha refused to let him pass. Shiva called upon Vishnu for help, and together they decapitated Ganesha. Rightly furious, Parvati wrought destruction on the world. Since even the mighty Shiva could not handle a women scorned, he resurrected Ganesha and placed upon his body the head of the first being he saw—an elephant.

Garuda: A late addition to Angkor's characters, this half-man, half-bird enemy of the *naga* is Vishnu's preferred means of transport.

Makara: With a face like a Chinese dragon, the body of a crocodile, and a dance costume, this demonic sea monster is often represented on lintel beams with hideous creatures, such as *naga*, coming from his mouth. Lolei, one of the Roluos temples, has a fine representation of the creature.

tiful lintel beams on the four brick towers of the main sanctuary. **Preah Ko** (south of Rte. 6 and north of Bakong), or "Sacred Ox," consists of a central sanctuary with six brick towers. **Bakong,** the largest and most impressive of the Roluos Group is a temple mountain representing Mt. Meru and was once the ancient capital of Hariharalaya.

KBAL SPEAN. About 10km down the road from Banteay Srei, Kbal Spean, "The Head of the Bridge," offers a free and less crowded opportunity to see riverbed *linga*. A *linga* is a symbol of the creative power of nature and is shaped like a male phallus. Water that flows through the channel carved into the side of the *linga* is thought to be blessed. About 15min. up the hill lies the secluded **River of the Thousand Linga.** The stretch of riverbed before the waterfall is carved with *linga* and images of deities. The carvings bless the river's waters as they flow to the temples and fields of Angkor. Its proximity to Banteay Srei makes it practical to combine a visit to the two sites. Moto drivers will try to charge you US$4-6 extra to see Kbal Spean; bargain hard. **Stay on the path marked by red treetrunks, as mines remain a risk.**

PHNOM KULEN. Phnom Kulen looms 50km northeast of Angkor Thom. Due to its distance from Siem Reap, the US$20 entry fee, and the presence of more impressive riverbed carvings at Kbal Spean, the trek to Phnom Kulen is not for the temple-weary. The mountain is one of Cambodia's most sacred sites and on the weekend plays host to hordes of pilgrims. They come to see the **reclining Buddha,** perched on top of a huge boulder on one of the mountain's peaks. The temple sheltering the Buddha has magnificent views over the surrounding mountains, but remember to remove your shoes before climbing the staircase. Ten meters down the hill from the river on the right is a side road leading to a **waterfall,** a popular bathing spot. Vendors set up stalls to cater to picnicking Khmer families on the weekend. The quickest way to get to Phnom Kulen is by **moto** (1½hr. each way, US$20-25 for the whole day). **Be sure you have a reliable guide before venturing off the main road; keep to well trodden paths, as mines remain a risk.**

VIENTIANE   ☎ 21

LAOS PRICE ICONS					
SYMBOL:	❶	❷	❸	❹	❺
ACCOMM.	Under 22,500kip	22,500-37,500kip	37,500-75,000kip	75,000-150,000kip	Over 150,000kip
FOOD	Under 12,500kip	12,500-15,000kip	15,000-30,000kip	30,000-45,000kip	Over 45,000kip

To adventurers from a bygone era, Vientiane conjured up sepia-tinged images of an exotic colonial backwater, where days melted into years and life remained as sluggish as the current of the Mekong. Today, save for a few wine shops, some French expatriates, and baguettes, the "City of Sandalwood" has shed its colonial legacy but has not yet acquired the impersonality of a larger metropolis. For most travelers, this capital's chief appeal is its provincial feel; most linger here a day or two before heading into rural Laos.

Vientiane has earned praise from the US for its cooperation in the "war on drugs" (though Laos remains the world's third-largest producer of opium) and search for American MIAs. As one of the world's 20 least developed nations, Laos receives aid, but the government has trouble distributing and implementing programs to help its people. Up to 80% of employed Laotians are subsistence farmers who benefit little from the country's fledgling capitalist economy.

Buddhist temples, Laos's architectural genius, come in three chief styles. High, pointed, and layered roofs distinguish the **Vientiane style** of architecture found in the capital city. The **Luang Prabang style,** with multi-layered roofs and graceful, sweeping eaves that nearly touch the ground, is similar to that of Northern Thailand. A third temple style, **Xieng Khouang,** was irrevocably lost when American bombers razed Laos during the war. A few temples built in stone or brick with wide and sloping but layerless roofs in the Xieng style remain in Luang Prabang.

⨮ TRANSPORTATION

Flights: Wattay International Airport (☎513 200), on Luang Prabang Rd., 4km from the center of town. Taxi to downtown US$5. **Lao Air Booking Co.,** 43/1 Setthathirat Rd. (☎216 761). Open M-F 1-4:30pm, Sa 8am-noon. AmEx/V. **Lao Aviation,** 2 Pang Kham Rd. (domestic ☎212 057, international ☎212 051). Open M-F 8am-noon and 1-4:30pm, Sa 8-11:30am. MC/V. To: **Bangkok** (1 per day, US$95); **Chiang Mai** (2 per

SIDETRIPS

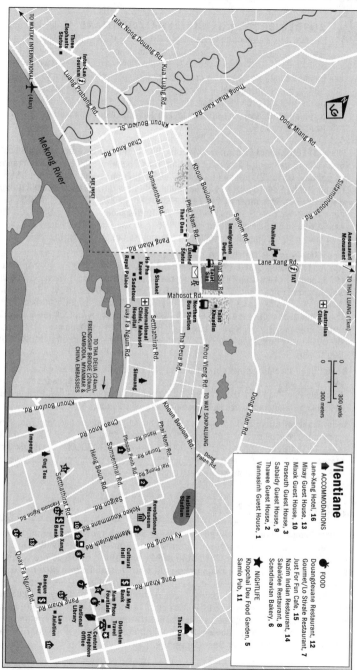

Vientiane

ACCOMMODATIONS
Lane-Xang Hotel, **16**
Mixay Guest House, **13**
Mixok Guest House, **10**
Praseuth Guest House, **3**
Sabaidy Guest House, **9**
Thawee Guest House, **2**
Vannasinh Guest House, **1**

FOOD
Douangdeuane Restaurant, **12**
Gourmet/Lo Stivale Restaurant, **7**
Just For Fun Cafe, **15**
Nazim Indian Restaurant, **14**
Sabaidee Restaurant, **8**
Scandinavian Bakery, **6**

NIGHTLIFE
Khopchai Deu Food Garden, **5**
Samlo Pub, **11**

BORDER CROSSING: NONG KHAI/VIENTIANE 15-day Lao tourist visas are issued on the **Friendship Bridge** for US$30 (3 passport photos required). 30-day visas are available from the Lao embassy in Bangkok (see p. 102) for 1100฿ (3-day processing). Ask Julian at Mut Mee Guest House for the latest info. A tuk-tuk from Nong Khai to the bridge should cost 30-50฿. A bus shuttles people across the bridge for 10฿; once there, expect to pay a 2000kip (10฿) entry tax. On the other side, public buses run the 25km to Vientiane (30฿), or you can take a taxi (150฿). For coverage of **Nong Khai**, see p. 216.

week, US$85); **Hanoi** (1 per day, US$108); **Ho Chi Minh City** (1 per week, US$168); **Houie Xay** (4 per week, US$90); **Luang Nam Tha** (5 per week, US$82); **Luang Prabang** (2 per day, US$112); **Pakse** (1 per day, US$97); **Phonsavanh** (1 per day, US$56); **Phnom Penh** (1 per day, US$140); **Savannakhet** (1 per day, US$80); **Udom Xai** (5 per week, US$72). **Thai Airways,** 27/1 Pang Kham Rd. (☎222 527). Open M-F 8:30am-noon and 1-5pm, Sa 8:30am-noon. AmEx/V. To **Bangkok** (1 per day, US$120). **Vietnam Airlines,** 63 Samsenthai Rd. (☎217 562), in Lao Plaza Hotel. Open M-Sa 8am-noon and 1:30-4:30pm. To **Hanoi** (US$110) and **Ho Chi Minh City** (US$165).

Buses: Northern Bus Terminal (☎216 507), on the corner of Mahosot and Khou Vieng Rd. To: **Friendship Bridge** (#45; 30min., every 20min. 7am-5pm, 1000kip); **Paksan** (#18; 3hr.; 7, 11am, 2pm; 6000kip); **Pakse** (#35; 13hr.; 11am, 1, 3pm; 35,000kip); **Savannakhet** (#36; 8hr.; 7:30, 10am; 25,000kip); **Tha Deua** (#14; 45min., every 20min. 7am-5pm); **Vang Vieng** (#1; 4hr.; 7, 10:30am, 1:30pm; 6000kip). Other buses leave from **Thalat Laeng** (☎413 297), accessible by *tuk-tuk* (3000kip). To: **Luang Prabang** (8hr.; 7, 8:30, 10:30am, 1, 5pm; 50,000kip); **Oudomxay** (15hr.; 6am; 60,000kip); **Phonsavanh** (10hr.; 7:30am; 60,000kip); **Xamnena** (30hr.; 7am; 80,000kip).

Boats: Boat travel to northern towns is possible, but erratic schedules, particularly during the dry season, make buses the preferred means of transport. **Speedboats** go from **Kao Liao Pier,** 3km from the city center, to **Luang Prabang** and **Pak Lay. Private boats** can also be chartered to **Luang Prabang** (10hr.; 10,000kip).

Local Transportation: Taxis congregate at the morning market on Lane Xang Ave. and in front of the Novotel on Luang Prabang Rd. (10,000-15,000kip per hr. or 200,000kip per day). To **Tha Deua** (Buddha Park) 50,000kip. **Tuk-tuk** 6000-8000kip. **Saysouly Guest House** (☎218 383), on Manthatulath Rd. 1 block west of Pang Kham Rd., rents **bicycles** (US$2 per day) and **motorbikes** (US$10 per day).

■ ORIENTATION

The **Nam Phou Fountain,** obscured by trees on Setthathirat Rd. serves as a convenient landmark. Vientiane's three main thoroughfares are **Samsenthai Rd.,** one block north of the fountain; **Setthathirat Rd.,** one block south of the fountain; and **Lane Xang Ave.,** which runs perpendicular to the **Mekong River** until the **Anousavari Monument.** Lane Xang Ave. is home to **Talat Sao** (the morning market), the **GPO,** and most **embassies.** Most restaurants are on **Quay Fa Ngum Rd.,** which is parallel and closest to the Mekong River. **Mahosot Rd.,** parallel to and one block east of Lane Xang Ave., is home to the **Northern Bus Terminal.** Over toward the airport, **Khoun Boulom Rd.** runs inland from Quay Fa Ngum Rd. and loops toward Talat Sao and Lane Xang Ave.

AUS$1 = 4361.50KIP	1000KIP = AUS$0.23
CDN$1 = 5083.93KIP	1000KIP = CDN$0.20
EUR€1 = 7769.10KIP	1000KIP = EUR€0.13
NZ$1 = 3709.45KIP	1000KIP = NZ$0.27
US$1 = 7922.80KIP	1000KIP = US$0.13
UK£1 = 12,260.50KIP	1000KIP = UK£0.08
ZAR1 = 754.55KIP	1000KIP = ZAR1.32

KIP

SIDETRIPS

◪ PRACTICAL INFORMATION

TOURIST AND FINANCIAL SERVICES

Tourist Offices: National Tourism Authority (☎212 251), on Lane Xang Ave. 300m before Anousavari Monument. Flight and bus schedules and travel info. Open M-F 8am-noon and 1-4pm. **Inter-Lao Tourism** (☎214 232), on Luang Prabang Rd. near the Novotel. Open M-F 8am-noon and 1:30-5pm, Sa 8am-noon.

Tours: Diethelm Travel (☎213 833), on Setthathirat Rd. beside the Nam Phou Fountain. Arranges transportation. Open M-F 8am-noon and 1:30-5pm, Sa 8am-noon. **Sadetour** (☎216 314), on Quay Fa Ngum Rd. near the residential palace, is Laos's oldest tour company. Open M-F 8am-6pm, Sa 8am-noon.

Immigration Offices: Immigration Department (☎212 520), on Khoun Boulom Rd. before the Lane Xang Ave. intersection. 15- or 30-day visas can be extended for up to 15 days (US$2 per day). Open M-F 8am-noon and 1-4pm. Other immigration offices are at the airport and next to Mithaphrap bridge (☎812 040).

Embassies: Australia (☎413 610), on the corner of Nehru and Phone Xay Rd., near Anousavari Monument. Open M-Th 9am-noon and 1:30-5pm, F 9am-noon. Serves **UK, Canada,** and **NZ** citizens in emergencies. **Cambodia** (☎314 952), on Tha Deua Rd., 2km outside the city center. One-day visa US$20. Open M-F 7:30-11:30am and 2-5pm. **China** (☎315 103), on War Nak Rd. past Myanmar Embassy. 30-day visa US$50. Open M-F 9-11:30am. **Myanmar** (☎314 910), on Sokpaluang Rd. 500m past Wat Sokpaluang on the left. Tourist visas US$18; 3-day processing. Bring 4 photos. Open M-F 8:30am-noon and 1-4:30pm. **Thailand** (☎214 580), on Phone Keng Rd.; consular office (☎217 154), on Lane Xang Rd., 300m before the Anousavari Monument. 60-day tourist visa 300฿, transit visa 200฿; 2-day processing. Open M-F 8:30am-noon. **US** (☎212 581), on Bartholomie Rd. Open M-F 8am-noon and 1-5pm. **Vietnam,** 60 That Luang Rd. (☎413 400). Tourist visas US$55; 3-day processing. Bring 2 photos. Open M-F 8-10:30am and 2:15-4:15pm.

Currency Exchange: Banque pour le Commerce Extérieur Lao, 1 Pang Kham Rd. (☎213 200). Visa cash advances. Traveler's checks cashed. Open M-F 8am-4pm. **Lao May Bank,** 39 Pang Kham Rd. (☎213 300), and **Lane Xang Bank** (☎213 400), on Setthathirat Rd., provide similar services. Both open M-F 8am-4pm.

American Express: Diethelm Travel (see **Tours,** above) is the Lao representative. Traveler's checks (2% commission) for AmEx cardholders.

EMERGENCY AND COMMUNICATIONS

Police: ☎191. **Fire:** ☎190. **Ambulance:** ☎195.

Pharmacy: Seng Thong Osoth Pharmacy (☎213 732), on the road between the morning market and the Northern Bus Terminal, is one of many. As you move away from the river, it's on the right. Friendly, English-speaking staff. Open daily 8am-5pm.

Medical Services: Australian Embassy Clinic (☎413 603), on Nehru Rd. near the Australian Embassy. Serves Australian, British, Canadian, and New Zealand citizens. Initial consultation US$50. By appointment only. Open M-Th 8:30am-noon and 2-5pm, F 8:30am-noon. **International Clinic, Mahosot Hospital,** Emergency Room (☎214 023), on Mahosot Rd. past Wat Pha Kaew. Not much English spoken. **Open 24hr.**

Telephones: Central Telephone Office (☎214 977), on Setthathirat Rd. Facing Nam Phou Fountain, head 1 block right on Setthathirat Rd.; it's a yellow building on the left. Cash calls only. Fax 500kip per page. Phone cards. Open M-F 8am-4pm, Sa 8am-3:30pm. International phones also at GPO (card calls only).

Internet Access: Planet Online, 205 Setthathirat Rd. (☎218 972), at the corner of Manthatulath Rd., has many terminals and the fastest connections in town. 150kip per min. Open daily 8am-11pm.

Post Office: GPO (☎/fax 217 327), on Khou Vieng Rd. Head away from the river on Lane Xang Rd. and take a right before the morning market. *Poste Restante.*

⚑ ACCOMMODATIONS

▧ **Thawee Guest House,** 64 Ban Ann (☎217 903), 2 blocks northwest of the Cultural Hall. Great guest house with energizing orange walls and wonderfully comfortable rooms; A/C rooms are a nice splurge. Singles with satellite TV and outside bath with hot water US$5; doubles US$10. ❸

Lane-Xang Hotel (☎214 102), on Quay Fa Ngum Rd., near the Royal Palace along the river. An upscale hotel with large rooms and quality service. Doubles with satellite TV, hot water, and A/C US$25. ❺

Praseuth Guest House, 312 Samsenthai Rd. (☎217 932), next to the Cultural Hall. Amicable, family-run business with small but spotless rooms in the heart of the city. Laundry. Rooms US$6-7, with A/C US$7, with bath US$8. ❸

Mixay Guest House, 39 Nokeo Koummane Rd. (☎217 023). From the Nam Phou Fountain, walk 3 blocks down Setthathirat Rd. with the river on your left and turn left onto Nokeo Koummane Rd.; it's on the right near the end. Apart from the giant snakeskin on the lobby wall, Mixay is similar to most guest houses—clean and comfortable. Internet. Doubles with shared bath US$6; with private bath US$7. ❸

Vannasinh Guest House, 051 Phnom Penh Rd. (☎222 020), near the intersection of Samsenthai Rd. with Hanoi Rd. Pretty and in a quiet yet central location. French- and English-speaking staff manage clean, pleasant rooms. Rooms with shared bath US$8; doubles with private bath US$10, with A/C and hot water US$16. ❹

Mixok Guest House (☎251 600), on Setthathirat Rd. 2 blocks west of the Nam Phou Fountain. Small rooms with dorm bunk beds are a good value. Nice balcony looks out onto the street and a temple. All rooms have shared bath. Dorms 15,000kip; singles 30,000kip, with larger bed 36,000kip; doubles 36,000kip; triples 51,000kip. ❶

Sabaidy Guest House, 203 Setthathirat Rd. (☎/fax 213 929). Right by Mixok Guest House. Basic but clean dorms. Communal TV complete with karaoke. Hot water. Dorms 15,000kip; rooms 36,000kip. Bike rental 10,000kip per day. ❶

◪ FOOD

For cheap and delicious Lao food, head to one of the many eateries along the river. Most are open from dawn until late evening and serve a mix of Lao, Thai, and Western style dishes (7000-15,000kip). French bakeries and restaurants cluster near the Nam Phou Fountain.

Scandinavian Bakery, 74/1 Pang Kham Rd. beside Nam Phou Fountain. Expensive but popular. Excellent pastries (5000kip) and lunch options (10,000-18,000kip), CNN, and foreign magazines. Open daily 7am-7pm. ❷

Nazim Indian Restaurant, on Quay Fa Ngum Rd. near the François Nginn intersection. Popular Lao chain with superb food and a great view of the river. Dishes 10,000-18,000kip. Open daily 10am-11pm. ❷

Gourmet/Lo Stivale Restaurant, 44 Setthathirat Rd. Gourmet is a cafe, while Lo Stivale is a classy but expensive restaurant with authentic and utterly delicious food. Comprehensive Western menu (US$4-16 per dish). Panini US$4. Gourmet open daily 7am-8pm; Lo Stivale open daily 10am-10pm. MC/V. ❺

Douangdeuane Restaurant, on François Nginn Rd. off Setthathirat Rd. Delicious vegetarian Lao, Thai, and Vietnamese menus (entrees 8000-16,000kip) and English- and French-speaking staff. Open daily 8am-10pm. ❶

Just for Fun, 15/2 Pang Kham Rd. between the Nam Phou Fountain and Quay Fa Ngum Rd. This quirky eatery specializes in vegetarian food and sells ethnic products and clothing. Most dishes US$1-2. Open M-Sa 9am-9pm. ❶

Sabaidee Restaurant, on the corner of Setthathirat Rd. and Manthatulath St. A pretty courtyard restaurant offering Lao and Western dishes. Breakfast menu. Chicken *laap* 10,000kip. Open daily 7am-10pm. ❶

◎ SIGHTS

Several temples and some of the best-preserved colonial architecture in the city grace tree-lined **Setthathirat Road** and **Quay Fa Ngum Road.** Away from the city center are That Luang, the Anousavari Monument, and the steam baths of Wat Sokpaluang.

THAT LUANG. This 45m gold *stupa* is the Lao national symbol and also one of the most important religious sites in Laos. Four wats once surrounded the lotus-bud-shaped *stupa*, but only the north and south wats remain. Originally built in 1566, it was restored in 1935 by the French colonial regime. Each November, That Luang hosts the **That Luang Festival,** when hundreds of monks gather to accept alms and floral gifts from the faithful. *(On That Luang Rd. 1km inland from city center. Open Tu-Su 8am-noon and 1-4pm. 1000kip donation expected.)*

HO PHRA KEO (HALL OF THE EMERALD BUDDHA). Vientiane's oldest temple has housed Buddhist sculpture and artifacts since 1970. The original temple was built in the mid-16th century by King Setthathirat to house the Emerald Buddha he brought from Chiang Mai. Razed by Thais in 1827, the wat was restored in the 1940s. *(From the Nam Phou Fountain, follow Setthathirat Rd. 100m past the Lane Xang Ave. intersection; the entrance is on the right. Open daily 8am-noon and 1-4pm. 1000kip.)*

WAT SISAKET. Built by King Anou in 1818, the temple houses 7000 Buddha statues and a sanctuary with elaborate murals. *(On the corner of Setthathirat Rd. and Lane Xang Ave. Open daily 8am-noon and 1-4pm. 1000kip.)*

WAT ONG TEU. The largest temple in the capital, Wat Ong Teu has one of the country's most prestigious Buddhist schools and a massive, meditating Buddha. *(At the west end of Setthathirat Rd. at the Chao Anou Rd. intersection.)*

THAT DAM (BLACK STUPA). According to legend, a seven-headed dragon lay under the *stupa* to protect the people of Vientiane from Siamese invaders in 1828. Ever since, the *stupa* has been seen as the city's protector. *(One block north and inland of Samsenthai Rd. on Pang Kham Rd.)*

SIDETRIPS

WAT SOKPALUANG. This wat offers wonderfully refreshing herbal saunas for 6000kip and rigorous 40min. massages for 15,000kip. *(1.5km southeast of the city center. Take a tuk-tuk (5000kip) or walk away from Lane Xang Ave. on Khou Vieng Rd., which runs between the morning market and the post office. The turn-off for the wat is unmarked; it is visible through the trees from the main road. Open daily late morning-8pm.)*

WAT SIMUANG. Built by King Setthathirat in 1566, this wat houses the foundation pillar of Vientiane, which, according to legend, crushed a pregnant woman, Nang Si, as it was lowered. Nang Si is revered as the guardian spirit of the city. *(On Quay Fa Ngum Rd. at the eastern end of town. Open Tu-Sa 8am-8pm.)*

ANOUSAVARI MONUMENT (VICTORY GATE). This bizarre-looking monument, at the inland end of Lane Xang Ave., is akin to a mix between Paris's Arc de Triomphe (the creator's inspiration) and a wedding cake. It was built in 1969 by the government in memory of those who died during the Lao struggle for independence. When builders ran out of concrete, they completed the memorial with US cement earmarked for use in construction of Wattay International Airport. Known to some as the "vertical runway," it has an unparalleled panoramic view of town. *(At the north end of town on Lane Xang Ave. Open daily 8am-5pm. 1000kip.)*

⌂ MARKETS

Talat Sao (the morning market) and **Talat Khuadim** (the evening market) are two of Vientiane's main attractions. Talat Sao is in two green-roofed buildings off Lane Xang Ave. The first sells cheap electric and silver goods; the second sells clothes and wall-hangings. (Open daily 6am-6pm.) Talat Khuadim is the large open-air market behind the Northern Bus Terminal. **Magninom Market,** on Khou Boulom Rd., is piled high with everything a traveler might need. (Open daily 8am-9:30pm.)

▟ ENTERTAINMENT

There is little raucous nightlife in Vientiane—bars and clubs must close by midnight. **Khopchai Deu Food Garden,** next to the Nam Phou Fountain on Setthathirat Rd., has a beautiful courtyard surrounding an aging French colonial building. Its nightly barbecues are one of Vientiane's most popular nighttime hangouts. Khopchai is busy in the afternoons as well. People sit around drinking Lao beer, listening to a looped mix tape of Radiohead, Buena Vista Social Club, and REM. Sit at the outside bar, enjoy a Lao wine cocktail (8000kip), and listen to the live band every Friday and Saturday. (Open M-Sa 9am-11:30pm, Su 5:30-11:30pm.) British **Samlo Pub,** 101 Setthathirat Rd., caters to a tourist/expat crowd. Hang out, shoot pool, or play foosball. (☎222 308. Open daily 11:30am-2pm and 5pm-midnight.)

▐ DAYTRIPS FROM VIENTIANE

THA DEUA

24km from Vientiane. Reachable by bus from the Northern Bus Terminal (#14; 50min.; every 30min. 6am-5pm, 1000kip) or tuk-tuk (45min.; 40,000kip, 1000kip for parking.) Open daily 8am-5pm. 2000kip.

Buddha sculptures are everywhere in this sculpture park built by the same self-described "half-man, half-animal" Lao monk/mystic who designed Sala Kaew Ku following the Communist victory 23 years ago. Both temples have a mix of Hindu and Buddhist themes brought to life in cement sculptures. Fat Buddhas, thin Buddhas, big Buddhas, little Buddhas, Buddha family scenes, and reclining Buddhas all make an appearance.

AO PAKO

50km northeast of Vientiane. Reachable by bus from the Northern Bus Terminal (#19 to Paxxap; get off at Som Sa Mai; 1½hr.; 6:30, 11am, 3pm; 2000kip). Once there, take a motorboat to Lao Pako resort (25min.; 25,000kip per boat.)

A small eco-tourist lodge, **Lao Pako ❶** is popular with Vientiane's expatriates and lies south of Nam Ngum Lake on the Nam Ngum River, 50km from Vientiane. Ausrian owner Mr. Pfabigan organizes treks, river-rafting expeditions, and village visits. The bar/restaurant is popular but expensive; bring your own food and drink if you're staying for a few days. (☎212 981. Dorms 20,000kip; doubles 60,000kip; 2-3 person bungalows 120,000kip.)

NEAR VIENTIANE: NAM NGUM LAKE

Nam Ngum Lake, 90km northeast of Vientiane, is a vast reservoir formed by the damming of Nam Ngum River in the late 1970s. Today, the hydroelectric power plant supplies electricity to much of Laos and parts of Thailand. Nam Ngum's natural setting is spectacular; emerald islets, many of which were prisons and political re-education camps during the 1980s, dot the lake. In the hurry to complete the dam, however, no one thought to harvest the surrounding forest, which was soon submerged. Ingenious Lao loggers have now developed underwater chain saws, and lumberjacks trade in boots for flippers to keep the show going.

Travelers seeking peace and quiet head to **Santipap Island**, the site of a dilapidated but charming **guest house ❷**. An ethereal setting, great swimming, and gorgeous sunsets compensate for the simple lodgings and sporadic electricity (rooms 30,000kip). If it's full, you can sleep in hammocks outside for free. The only **restaurant ❷** on the island, to the left of the guest house, serves fresh fish (10,000-18,000kip). Boats make the trip to the island (15min.; 20,000-40,000kip per boat).

To reach the lake, take a bus from Vientiane's Northern Bus Terminal (see **Transportation,** p. 400) to Ban Thalat. From there, *songthaew* and tuk-tuks run to the lake (10,000-20,000kip), passing the dam complex. To continue farther north of Nam Ngum Lake, head back to Ban Thalat and take a tuk-tuk (30min.; 10,000-20,000kip) to **Phon Hong,** or wait for a full *songthaew* (3000kip). From Phon Hong, a bus goes to **Vang Vieng** (2½hr., 9am, 3000kip), or you can take a full *songthaew*.

PENANG (PULAU PINANG)

MALAYSIA PRICE ICONS					
SYMBOL:	❶	❷	❸	❹	❺
ACCOMM.	Under US$3 (RM12)	US$3-6 (RM12-24)	US$6-10 (RM24-40)	US$10-17 (RM40-68)	Over US$17 (RM68)
FOOD	Under US$1 (RM4)	US$1-2 (RM4-8)	US$2-4 (RM8-16)	US$4-8 (RM16-32)	Over US$8 (RM32)

Those with illusions of a sweet little island are in for a shock. With the second largest economy in Malaysia, Penang is more powerhouse than paradise, as it struggles to balance conscientious productivity with down-to-earth congeniality. The island is home to a number of multinational corporations by the airport, five colleges, and Malaysia's largest Buddhist temple, as well as numerous Malaysian *kampongs* (villages) and *kongsi* (clans) scattered in the rural areas. The dense

SIDETRIPS

jungles contain durian, jackfruit, and nutmeg plantations, and visitors can visit the prestigious Butterfly Farm, new aquarium, botanical garden, and Forestry Museum and Arboretum. Other delights include relaxing by Batu Ferringhi's beaches, temple hopping in Georgetown, and devouring one of Penang's culinary specialties—the minty yet spicy *assam laksa*.

THE VIEW FROM ABOVE

The lowdown: A bustling island off the west coast with a life of its own and the most Chinese in Malaya.
Highlights: Penang cuisine, lush jungles, colorful seasonal festivals, and Malaysia's largest Buddhist temple.

▐▖ TRANSPORTATION

Flights: Bayan Lepas International Airport (☎643 0811), 20km south of Georgetown. Yellow bus #83 (every hr. 6am-10pm) and minibus #32 run between the airport and Pengkalan Weld in Georgetown. **MAS** (☎262 0011) flies to **KL** (45min., every hr., RM109) and **Medan, Indonesia** (45min., 12:55pm, RM253). **Singapore Airlines** (☎226 3201) flies to **Singapore** (1hr., 3 per day, RM295). **Thai Airlines** flies to **Bangkok** (2hr., 8am, RM499).

Trains: The **train station** (☎331 2796; www.ktmb.com.my) is below the ferry landing in Butterworth. Train schedules change bi-annually. To: **Bangkok** (21½hr., 2:20pm, 2nd-class bunks RM88-94.20) via **Hat Yai** (4½hr.; 3rd-class seats RM4, 2nd-class seats RM13); **KL** (10½hr.; 9:55pm; 3rd-class seats RM17, 2nd-class seats RM30, 2nd-class bunks RM37.40-40). Transfer to **KL** for trains to **Johor Bahru** and **Singapore.**

Buses: There are two **bus stations:** one at KOMTAR in Penang and the other below the Butterworth ferry landing. From KOMTAR, **Supercoach** buses run to: **KL** (5hr., 11 per day., RM22); **Kuantan** (8½hr., 10pm, RM35); **Singapore** via **Johor Bahru** (11hr.; 8:15, 9am, 8:30, 9:30, 10pm); RM42); **Taiping** (1hr.; 11am, 1:30, 4, 6pm; RM7.50). **Sri Maju** buses go to **Ipoh** (3hr.; 7:30, 9:30am, 2, 4:30, 7, 9pm; RM11.50). **Kurnia Bistari** buses go to **Cameron Highlands** via **Ipoh** (6hr.; 8am, 2:30pm; RM20), while their minivans go to **Hat Yai** (4hr.; 5, 8:30am, noon, 4pm; RM20). From Butterworth, **Transnasional** buses go to **KL** (5hr., 13 per day, RM20) and **Kota Bharu** (8hr.; 10am, 10, 10:30pm; RM20). **Super Nice** buses also go to **Singapore. Sri Maju** buses go to **Lumut** (3hr., 7 per day, RM10.50). **Mutiara** buses go to **Tanah Merah, Pasir Mas, Kota Bharu, Pasir Puteh,** and **Jerteh. Sri Jengka Ekspres** buses go to **Mentakab, Temerloh, Bandar Pusat,** and **Kuantan** (7½hr.; 8:30, 9, 10pm; RM30-35). **Kurnia Bistari** buses also go to **Cameron Highlands** via **Ipoh** and **Tapah.**

Ferries: A **24hr.** ferry runs between **Georgetown** and **Butterworth** on the mainland (every 20min., after midnight every hr.; RM0.60 to Penang, free to Butterworth).

Taxis: Long-distance taxis (☎333 4459) can be hired in Butterworth. To: **Alor Setar** (RM200); **Cameron Highlands** (RM250); **Hat Yai** (RM220); **Ipoh** (RM120); **KL** (RM250); **Kuala Kedar** (RM200); **Lumut** (RM180); **Padang Besar** (RM150); **Taiping** (RM70).

RINGGIT (RM)		
AUS$1 = RM3.80 (RINGGIT)		RM1 = AUS$0.45
CDN$1 = RM2.44		RM1 = CDN$0.41
EUR€1 = RM3.73		RM1 = EUR€0.27
NZ$1 = RM1.78		RM1 = NZ$0.56
US$1 = RM3.80		RM1 = US$0.26
UK£1 = RM5.88		RM1 = UK£0.17
ZAR1 = RM0.36		RM1 = ZAR2.76

GEORGETOWN ☎ 04

Georgetown is a cultural and culinary mecca, where each street has a blend of ethnic influences. Chulia St. is the main backpacker hangout and buildings here retain the character of Old Penang, but the entire city begs to be explored. On Jl. Masjid Kapitan Keling alone, there are five different religious establishments. Narrow streets and markets pulse with life late into the night, and wandering walks reveal one of Asia's most diverse architectural collections.

▐▀ TRANSPORTATION

Ferries: To **Butterworth** (every 20min.; RM0.60, cars RM7). Express services to **Langkawi** and **Medan, Indonesia** run from the tourist center near the Victoria Memorial Clock Tower. **Langkawi Ferry Services** (☎966 9439) goes to Langkawi (2½hr.; 8am, return 5:30pm; RM35, round-trip RM60) and **Medan, Indonesia** (5hr.; 8am; RM90, round-trip RM160). **Ekspres Bahagia** (☎263 1943) also goes to: **Langkawi** (8, 8:45am; return 2:30, 5:30pm; RM35, round-trip RM60) and **Medan, Indonesia** (8am, return 10am; RM90, round-trip RM160).

Local Transportation: Buses and **Bas Mini** (minibuses) run from the *jeti* (ferry station) and KOMTAR (6am-11pm), making circular routes around the island. Fares vary by distance and bus company; tell the driver your destination to determine exact fare, and always carry loose change. Taxi and *beca* drivers are likely to swindle you, so confirm the price before departing. *Beca* charge more for guided tours of Georgetown but are an ideal way to take in the city's atmosphere. Colorful lines refer to routes. **Yellow** buses go south while **blue** buses go north. Take **red-and-white** bus #1 or 101 to Central Penang, blue bus #93 and transit line #202 to the north shore. However, advertisements often conceal the original colors so bus numbers are most accurate. Both taxi and *beca* are RM20 per hr. and taxis charge 20% more at night. Lh. Chulia to the *jeti* RM5. **Taxis** from the airport are hired through a coupon system. Purchase a coupon at the Teksi counter (Georgetown RM25-30).

Rentals: A valid driver's license with photo is required for all car rentals. **Hawk** has a rental counter in the airport (☎881 3886). Manual from RM150 and auto from RM156.50. **New Bob Car Rental,** at 11 Gottlieb Rd. and at the airport (☎642 1111), has cars from RM170.50. Rental services also provide car delivery.

✦▐ ORIENTATION AND PRACTICAL INFORMATION

Georgetown sits on a peninsula on Penang's east coast. The **ferry terminal** and a local **bus station** are on **Pengkalan Weld Quay**, along Georgetown's southeast coast. Parallel to Pengkalan Weld Quay is **Lh. Pantai (Beach St.),** the financial district, administrative buildings, the **police station,** and the main **post office.** Lh. Pantai runs north to the **Victoria Memorial Clock Tower,** at the intersection with Lebuh Light. Here, **Fort Cornwallis** guards the city while boats leave from the jetty near the **Penang Tourism Centre.** Running northwest from the Penang-Butterworth ferry terminal is **Lh. Chulia.** At the western end of Lh. Chulia, **Jl. Penang** runs north to hotels and south to **KOMTAR,** the cylindrical building that dominates Penang's skyline. At KOMTAR are shopping malls, the **long-distance bus station,** and the **local bus station.** Buses run northwest from KOMTAR to Batu Ferringhi and Teluk Bahang, as well as south toward the **airport.**

Tourist Offices: Penang Tourist Center (☎261 6663), on Pesara King Edward by the clock tower. Maps and info. Open M-Th 8:30am-1pm and 2-4:30pm, Sa 8:30am-1pm. **Penang Tourist Guides Association** (☎261 4461), 3rd fl. of KOMTAR, has an extremely helpful staff. Follow the signs near McDonald's. Open M-Sa 10am-6pm; closed for irregular lunch breaks. Sells *Penang Tourist Newspaper,* which has essential phone numbers and a calendar of events (RM2). **Tourism Malaysia** (Northern Region), 10 Jl. Tun Syed Sheh Barakbah (☎262 0066), near the Penang Tourist Center, provides maps and free copies of the *Langkawi Tourist Newspaper.* Open M-F 8am-4:30pm, Sa 8am-1pm. Closed 1st and 3rd Sa of each month.

Tours and Travel: MSL Travel, Agora Hotel, Jl. Macalister (☎227 2655). Malay and Thai railpasses available with ISIC. Smaller companies along Lh. Pantai and Lh. Chulia offer tours. **Newasia Tours and Travel,** 35-36 Pangkalan Weld (☎261 7933), offers plane tickets, a variety of tours, and minibuses to Thailand. Branch offices at: KOMTAR ground fl. (☎261 5558), off Jl. Ria, and 27 Lh. Chulia (☎264 3930).

Consulates: Indonesia, 467 Jl. Burma (☎227 4686). Open M-F 8:30am-1pm and 2-4:30pm. **Thailand,** 1 Jl. Tuanku Abdul Rahman (☎226 8029). Open M-F 9am-noon and 2-4pm. Visa applications accepted until noon. Two-month tourist visa RM33. Accommodations also help issue visas, but it is advisable to go through a consulate.

Currency Exchange: Several moneychangers on Lh. Chulia and major banks along Lh. Pantai have good rates. **OCBC Bank,** on Lh. Pantai, near Lh. Chulia, has **24hr. ATMs** (PLUS/V). Bank open M-F 9:30am-3:30pm, Sa 9:30-11:30am. **HSBC,** down the road, also has **24hr. ATMS.** There are also banks with ATMs at KOMTAR and on Lh. Pantai.

Emergency: Police: ☎999. **Fire:** ☎994.

Tourist Police: ☎261 5522, ext. 409.

Directory Assistance: ☎103.

International Operator: ☎108.

Pharmacies: A few large pharmacies are on Lh. Pantai. **Ego Pharmacy,** 448 Penang Rd. (☎226 4529), has a wide selection. Open M-Sa 9:30am-7:30pm. The **Guardian Pharmacy** at KOMTAR is open daily until 10pm.

Medical Service: General Hospital (☎229 3333), on Jl. Hospital. English spoken. **24hr. emergency room.** Consultation fee RM2. Performs minor surgery.

Telephones: Telekom office (☎220 9321), on Jl. Downing next to the post office. **HCD/fax. IDD** from any card phone. Open M-F 8:30am-4:30pm.

Internet Access: Many on Lh. Chulia. RM3 per hr. **Eighteen Internet Cafe,** 18 Lh. Cintra, off Lh. Chulia, has speedy connections. Open M-Sa 10:30am-10pm.

Post Office: GPO Penang (☎261 9222), on the corner of Lh. Downing and Pengkalan Weld. Open M-F 8:30am-6pm, Sa 8am-4pm. *Poste Restante.* **Postal code:** 10670 (for post office only).

▛ ACCOMMODATIONS

Budget hotels are on or near Lh. Chulia. Love Lane, named for the Chinese matchmakers who once lived there, intersects the center of Lh. Chulia. Most accommodations book ferry and bus tickets for guests.

Olive Spring Hotel, 302 Lh. Chulia (☎261 4641), above Rainforest Restaurant. Lovely walls awash with Caribbean purples and blues. No skimping on cleanliness here. Lockers available. Laundry. Dorms RM8; singles with fan RM15; doubles RM22-25. ❶

SD Motel, 24 Lh. Muntri (☎264 3743). From Lh. Chulia, take a left off Love Ln. Off the main drag and very quiet. Immaculate rooms. Hot and cold showers. Friendly management. Singles with fan RM15; doubles with fan RM20, with A/C RM28; triples RM28/RM38; 5-person rooms with A/C RM58. ❷

75 Travellers Lodge, 75 Lh. Muhtri (☎262 3378). Popular spot for short stays. In its second year, the guest house is clean but lacks character. Cold and hot showers. Reserve in advance. Thick mattresses. Dorms RM7; singles RM15-18; doubles RM18-22, with bath RM28-32, with A/C RM35-40. ❶

Blue Diamond Hotel, 422 Ln. Chulia (☎261 1089), 1 block before the intersection with Jl. Penang. Beautiful old building with soaring (and echoey) ceilings. Beer garden outside. Movies every night. Email, motorbike rental, and travel booking services. Dorms RM8; singles and doubles RM20-25, with bath RM25-30, with A/C RM45. ❶

Hang Chow Hotel, 511 Lh. Chulia (☎261 0810). From Penang Rd., it's on the 1st block on the right. Clean and spacious rooms with hardwood floors and a sink. Relaxed atmosphere with a cafe downstairs (pizza RM8; beer RM6). Shared toilets only. Doubles with fan RM22, with private shower RM25; quads with A/C RM35-40. ❷

Wan Hai Hotel, 35 Love Ln. (☎261 6853), on the right. Faded, clean rooms with fans and sinks in an old Chinese shop house. Rooftop common area great for sunbathing. Beer RM5. Laundry, motorcycle rental (RM20 per day), bike rental (RM10 per day), and travel booking services. Dorms RM7; singles and doubles RM15-18; triples RM21. ❶

Cathay Hotel, 15 Leith St. (☎262 6271). Traveling buddies and couples enjoy this famous antique colonial with lofty ceilings and white sheets. Check out the antique telephone switchboard and feel like you're walking through a sepia photograph. Doubles with fan RM57.50; standard rooms with A/C RM69; deluxe with A/C RM92. ❹

Hotel Noble, 36 Lg. Pasar (☎261 2372), off Jl. Masjid Kapitan Keling behind Lh. Chulia. Featured in a scene in Michelle Yeoh's film, *The Touch*. Closer to the Indian part of town. Slightly faded rooms all have showers inside but common toilets. Rooms RM18. ❷

🍴 FOOD

The hybrid *nyonya* cuisine reigns supreme in Penang. The best food is found streetside. The **food stall** ❶ on the corner of Lh. Cintra and Lh. Kimberley dishes out exceptional samples of Penang specialties. (Open daily 6pm-1am). General rule of thumb: if it's steaming when you get it, it's sanitary. Another tantalizing favorite is the oxtail soup at a **food stall** ❶ across from Hotel Continental on Penang Rd. Ask locals for their favorite stalls or head to the west end of **Gurney Dr.** overlooking the water (on the outskirts of town on the way to Batu Ferringhi), which is well known for its good *rojak*. Point to the fruits and veggies you want inside, and they'll mix it up for you. The best spring rolls can be found at the **Popia Lazat Enak** ❶ stall with the tweetie bird decoration (on Gurney Dr., RM1.10 each). Hokkien Chinese food dominates **Kg. Malabar,** while Malaysian food stalls line **Lh. Tamil.** Join locals for dinner at the **Pasar Malam (night market).** (Call ☎263 8818 for current location.) Lh. Carnavan, between Lh. Chulia and Lh. Campbell, hosts a bustling **morning market.**

Hameediyah, 164A Lebuh Campbell. Terrific Indian Muslim restaurant with a selection of *Murtabak* curries. Signature Curry Kapitan dish RM3.50. Open daily noon-10pm. ❶

Oriental Seafood Cafe, 62 Jl. MacAlister (☎226 0969), near KOMTAR. Penang's best soft shell crab and baked lobster with cheese. Open daily 5:30pm-midnight. ❸

Rainforest Restaurant, 300 Lh. Chulia. Enveloped by the orange glow from the walls, customers always look happy. Western staples like milkshakes and sandwiches, and homemade health bread with fried eggs (RM3.50). Open M-Sa 8am-midnight. ❶

Green Planet, 63 Lh. Cintra (☎264 1840). Makeshift hut with photos of animals and the Orang Asli people. Scrumptious curry *devil* with lemongrass and turmeric RM12; veggie burger RM7; chicken chop RM15. Open M-Sa noon-3pm and 7pm-midnight. ❸

The Tandoori House, 34-36 Jl. Hutton, 2 blocks north of the intersection with Penang Rd. Georgetown's finest Mughal restaurant. 19 types of *naan* and 11 types of rice. *Tandoori thali* with choice of meat RM14; vegetarian *naurattan qurma* RM11; home-made ice cream *kulfi payalla* RM6. Tax 15%. Open daily 11:30am-3pm and 6:30-10:30pm. ❸

Slippery Señoritas, Lot 83A, The Garage, 2 Jl. Penang. Sangria and Spanish *tapas* are as enticing as the name. Fried calamari RM8; sausages with red wine sauce RM8. ❸

Hard Life Cafe, 363 Lh. Chulia, 400m from Lh. Penang. Pool table and reggae. Beer RM6. Mostly vegetarian dishes (RM5-10). Open late. ❷

👁 SIGHTS

All sights listed except for Wat Chayamang Kalaram, Fort Cornwallis, and the State Art Gallery are near Jl. Masjid Kapitan Keling (formerly Lh. Pitt).

▓ WAT CHAYAMANG KALARAM. The 33m reclining Buddha at this Thai temple is Malaysia's largest, and reputedly the third-largest in the world. Photography is not allowed. *(Accessible by blue bus #93, 94, 102, 202, and minibus #26, 31, and 88. Off the main road to Batu Ferringhi on Lg. Burma. Open daily 8:30am-5:30pm.)* Opposite the temple is **Dhammikarama Burmese Temple,** the only Burmese temple in Malaysia, with intricately carved decorations and a 9m tall Buddha. *(Meditation class and dharma lecture W 8-9:30pm. Open daily 8am-6pm.)*

▓ PENANG MUSEUM AND ART GALLERY. Fantastic displays give a flavor of Penang's history and culture without the dusty aftertaste of many museum exhibits. Sound-byte displays lend deeper insight into the city's heritage. *(On Lh. Farquar, between St. George's Church and the Cathedral of the Assumption. Open Sa-Th 9am-5pm. RM1.)*

▓ KHOO KONGSI TEMPLE. Signs for various *kongsi*, meaning "clan house," are visible throughout the island. This one stands out for its lavish decoration and innumerable ancestral pillars, whose beauty won it the honor as a filming location for the movie *Anna and the King* in 1999. *(On Jl. Masjid Kapitan Kling, near Lh. Acheh. Go through the temple entrance; the meeting hall is on the right, and the temple is down the drive.)* Nearby, on the corner of Lh. Cannon and Lh. American, **Yap Temple** proudly displays intricately hand-carved stone pillars at its entrance. *(Open daily 8am-5pm.)*

FORT CORNWALLIS. A hankering for the imperial past might take you to Fort Cornwallis's cannons and old brickwork at the northeast tip of town. Built by Captain Francis Light as a defense against the French, Kedah, pirates, and Siam in 1786, the fort was the point at which Penang's settlement began. Wander around the old cannons and prisons. *(On Lh. Pantai, beyond the clocktower and tourist center. Open daily 8:30am-7pm. Last admission 6:30pm. RM1.)*

KUAN YIN TENG. Built in 1800, the temple is devoted to the Buddhist Goddess of Mercy. Devotees at Penang's oldest Chinese temple burn joss paper money for prosperity in the afterlife, with prayers for health, wealth, and longevity, in a fog of sandalwood incense. Catch the temple at its liveliest during the feast days for Kuan Yin on the 19th day of the second and sixth lunar months. *(1 block from St. George's. Open daily 9am-6pm.)*

SRI MARIAMMAN TEMPLE. Lord Shiva and his consort Parvati preside over this active Hindu temple, which also shelters the Shrine of the Nine Planets. During the Thaipusam Festival in January or February, the lavish Lord Subramanian statue is paraded from the temple. *(The back of the temple is down Jl. Masjid Kapitan Keling near the intersection with Lh. Chulia. The entrance is one block over on Lh. Queen. Open daily 8am-9pm.)*

ST. GEORGE'S CHURCH. The Anglican church offers Sunday services in English (8:30 and 10:30am) and an interesting contrast with Hindu and Buddhist temples in Penang. (☎ 261 2739. *On Lh. Farquar, next to the Penang Museum.*)

MASJID KAPITAN KELING. A stark contrast to the frenzy of the Kuan Yin Teng. The mosque was founded in 1801 by an Indian-Muslim merchant, "Kapitan Keling." Its floors will cool your feet and its silence will ease your senses. *(Across Lh. Chulia from Sri Mariamman Temple; walk down Jl. Masjid Kapitan Keling. Open daily 9am-5:30pm.)*

APPENDIX

COUNTRY CODES

Australia	61	Malaysia	60
Brunei	673	Myanmar	95
Cambodia	855	New Zealand	64
Canada	1	Philippines	63
Hong Kong	852	Singapore	65
Indonesia	62	South Africa	27
Ireland	353	Thailand	66
Laos	856	UK	44

MEASUREMENTS

1 millimeter (mm) = 0.04 inches (in.)	1 inch = 25mm
1 meter (m) = 1.09 yards (yd.)	1 yard = 0.92m
1 meter (m) = 3.28 feet (ft.)	1 foot = 0.305m
1 kilometer (km) = 0.625 miles (mi.)	1 mile = 1.6km
1 hectare = 2.7 acres	1 acre = 0.37 hectare
1 gram (g) = 0.04 ounces (oz.)	1 ounce = 28.5g
1 kilogram (kg) = 2.2 pounds (lb.)	1 pound = 0.45kg
1 liter = 1.057 U.S. quarts (qt.)	1 US quart = 0.94 liters

LANGUAGE

The Thai language is extremely different from English. Even gifted learners won't be able to pick up more than the barest rudiments of Thai during a short trip, although the rewards of making an effort—however small—to learn local languages are tremendous.

PRONUNCIATION KEY

TONES: Thai (like Lao, Burmese, and Vietnamese) is a tonal language; word meanings are partially determined by intonation and pitch. The five tones in Thai are neutral, low, high, falling, and rising. Neutral tones (unmarked) are spoken in a level voice in the middle of a speaker's vocal range. Low (à) and high (á) tones are spoken in level pitch, and come from the bottom and top of a speaker's range respectively. Falling tones (â) begin high and end low, as in the English pronunciation of "Hey!" Rising tones (ä) begin low and end high, as in the English interrogative "What?"

VOWELS: Vowels are very roughly pronounced as in English, except for the "eu" sound in Thai, which corresponds to the vowel sound in the French "bleu."

CONSONANTS: Consonants are very roughly pronounced as in English.

USEFUL PHRASES

ENGLISH	THAI
1	nèung
2	säwng
3	sähm
4	sèe
5	hâh
6	hòk
7	jèt
8	pàet
9	gâo
10	sìp
20	yêe-sìp
30	sähm-sìp
40	sèe-sìp
50	hâh-sìp
100	róy
1000	pun
Hello	sàwatdee
Goodbye	sawàtdee
Yes / No	chai / mâi chai
Thank you	khàwp khun
Excuse me	khäw tôht
Please repeat	pôod ìk khráng sâi maï
How are you?	ben yahng ngai
Fine/well.	sabai-dee
Help!	chûay dûay!
Fire!	fai mai!
Doctor	mäw
Police	tham ruat
Hospital	rohng paiahban
Toilet	sûam
Where is...?	...yòo têe näi
To the right	khwä meu
To the left	saí meu
Straight ahead	throng bai
How much?	tâo rài
Bus	rót meh
Train	rót fai
Plane	krêuang bin
Car	rót yon
Taxi	rót táek-sëe
Restaurant	ráhn ah-hän
Guest House	bâhn pák
Market	thah làt
Bank	tanahkhan
Post Office	praisanee
Yesterday	mêua wahn née
Today	wan née
Tomorrow	prûng née

LUNAR CALENDAR

Use the chart below to help you figure out the dates of local festivals, which are often based solely on the lunar calendar. Also, if you plan to attend a full moon party, we've listed the optimum arrival date to ensure you get accommodations.

FULL MOON	OPTIMUM ARRIVAL DATE	NEW MOON
December 19, 2002	December 14, 2002	January 2, 2003
January 18, 2003	January 13, 2003	February 1, 2003
February 16, 2003	February 11, 2003	March 3, 2003
March 18, 2003	March 13, 2003	April 1, 2003
April 16, 2003	April 11, 2003	May 1, 2003
May 16, 2003	May 11, 2003	May 31, 2003
June 14, 2003	June 8, 2003	June 29, 2003
July 13, 2003	July 7, 2003	July 29, 2003
August 12, 2003	August 6, 2003	August 27, 2003
September 10, 2003	September 5, 2003	September 26, 2003
October 10, 2003	October 5, 2003	October 25, 2003
November 9, 2003	November 4, 2003	November 23, 2003
December 8, 2003	December 3, 2003	December 23, 2003

CLIMATE

High and low tourist seasons roughly correspond with rainy and dry seasons in Southeast Asia. There is no uniform seasonal pattern for Thailand, except that it is generally very hot. Keep in mind that the monsoon is rarely an impediment for travel in the region. Generally, rainfall peaks from May to September, and from December to March. For a rough conversion of Celsius to Fahrenheit, double the Celsius and add 30. To convert more accurately from °C to °F, multiply by 1.8 and add 32. To convert from °F to °C, subtract 32 and multiply by 0.55.

TEMPERATURE CONVERSIONS

°CELSIUS	-5	0	5	10	15	20	25	30	35	40
°FAHRENHEIT	23	32	41	50	59	68	77	86	95	104

AVERAGE TEMPERATURES

City	January High (F/C)	January Low (F/C)	January Rain (in)	April High (F/C)	April Low (F/C)	April Rain (in)	July High (F/C)	July Low (F/C)	July Rain (in)	October High (F/C)	October Low (F/C)	October Rain (in)
Bangkok	91/33	71/22	0.4	96/36	80/27	2.4	92/33	78/26	5.7	91/33	78/25	7.2
Phuket	90/32	73/23	1.8	93/34	77/25	6.1	88/31	78/25	10.2	88/31	76/24	14.3

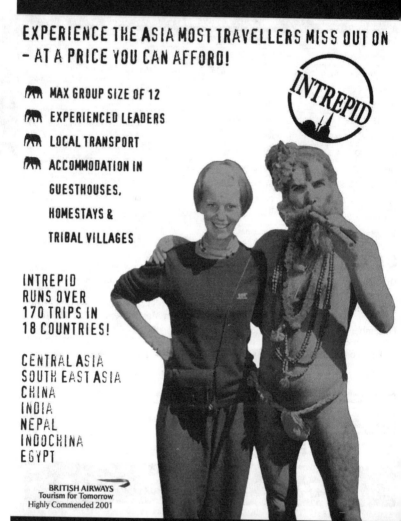

INDEX

H

Q

R

U

WHO WE ARE

A NEW LET'S GO

With a sleeker look and innovative new content, we have revamped the entire series to reflect more than ever the needs and interests of the independent traveler. Here are just some of the improvements you will notice when traveling with the new *Let's Go*.

MORE PRICE OPTIONS

Still the best resource for budget travelers, *Let's Go* recognizes that everyone needs the occassional indulgence. Our "Big Splurges" indicate establishments that are actually worth those extra pennies (pulas, pesos, or pounds), and price-level symbols (❶ ❷ ❸ ❹ ❺) allow you to quickly determine whether an accommodation or restaurant will break the bank. We may have diversified, but we'll never lose our budget focus—"Hidden Deals" reveal the best-kept travel secrets.

BEYOND THE TOURIST EXPERIENCE

Our Alternatives to Tourism chapter offers ideas on immersing yourself in a new community through study, work, or volunteering.

AN INSIDER'S PERSPECTIVE

As always, every item is written and researched by our on-site writers. This year we have highlighted more viewpoints to help you gain an even more thorough understanding of the places you are visiting.

IN RECENT NEWS. *Let's Go* correspondents around the globe report back on current regional issues that may affect you as a traveler.

CONTRIBUTING WRITERS. Respected scholars and former *Let's Go* writers discuss topics on society and culture, going into greater depth than the usual guidebook summary.

THE LOCAL STORY. From the Parisian monk toting a cell phone to the Russian *babushka* confronting capitalism, *Let's Go* shares its revealing conversations with local personalities—a unique glimpse of what matters to real people.

FROM THE ROAD. Always helpful and sometimes downright hilarious, our researchers share useful insights on the typical (and atypical) travel experience.

SLIMMER SIZE

Don't be fooled by our new, smaller size. *Let's Go* is still packed with invaluable travel advice, but now it's easier to carry with a more compact design.

FORTY-THREE YEARS OF WISDOM

For over four decades *Let's Go* has provided the most up-to-date information on the hippest cafes, the most pristine beaches, and the best routes from border to border. It all started in 1960 when a few well-traveled students at Harvard University handed out a 20-page mimeographed pamphlet of their tips on budget travel to passengers on student charter flights to Europe. From humble beginnings, *Let's Go* has grown to cover six continents and *Let's Go: Europe* still reigns as the world's best-selling travel guide. This year we've beefed up our coverage of Latin America with *Let's Go: Costa Rica* and *Let's Go: Chile;* on the other side of the globe, we've added *Let's Go: Thailand* and *Let's Go: Hawaii.* Our new guides bring the total number of titles to 61, each infused with the spirit of adventure that travelers around the world have come to count on.

Book your air, hotel, and transportation all in one place.

Hotel or hostel? Cruise or canoe? Car? Plane? Camel?
Wherever you're going, visit Yahoo! Travel and get total control
over your arrangements. Even choose your seat assignment.
So. One hump or two? travel.yahoo.com

powered by *hp*

YAHOO!
Travel

MAP INDEX

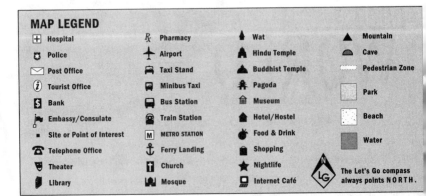

MAP LEGEND

⊞ Hospital	℞ Pharmacy	♣ Wat	▲ Mountain
⊙ Police	✈ Airport	♣ Hindu Temple	◠ Cave
✉ Post Office	🚗 Taxi Stand	▲ Buddhist Temple	⌇ Pedestrian Zone
(i) Tourist Office	🚐 Minibus Taxi	♣ Pagoda	Park
$ Bank	🚌 Bus Station	🏛 Museum	
⚑ Embassy/Consulate	🚆 Train Station	♦ Hotel/Hostel	Beach
▪ Site or Point of Interest	M METRO STATION	🍴 Food & Drink	
☎ Telephone Office	⚓ Ferry Landing	▪ Shopping	Water
🎭 Theater	✝ Church	★ Nightlife	
📖 Library	🕌 Mosque	▢ Internet Café	The Let's Go compass always points NORTH.